INTRODUCTION TO SOCIALIZATION
HUMAN CULTURE TRANSMITTED

Goreu arf, arf dysg

"The best weapon, the weapon of knowledge"

Welsh Proverbial Saying

INTRODUCTION TO SOCIALIZATION
HUMAN CULTURE TRANSMITTED

THOMAS RHYS WILLIAMS

Department of Anthropology, The Ohio State University,
Columbus, Ohio

With a foreword by **Margaret Mead**

With 87 illustrations

THE C. V. MOSBY COMPANY
SAINT LOUIS   1972

 # PREFACE

Many things said in this text rest upon large amounts of complex literature in anthropology, sociology, psychology, biology, medicine, and education. I am solely responsible for the interpretation of the ideas and works of other persons.

The purpose of this text is to make available to students an introductory summary and limited interpretation of some of the major features of the socialization process.

I have written in a manner that will provide for understanding of the socialization process, whether or not students have an expert in the field for a teacher and without regard to their level of study. I have not avoided the unsettled problems in the field, for the study of socialization is a dynamic effort involving diverse views, ways of research, and conflicting assumptions. I have tried to avoid giving the impression that there are easy answers in studying the socialization process. I do not believe that in the scope of a brief work I can give a complete portrayal of all the theoretical ideas and great amounts of factural detail involved in the study of the process of socialization.

I do not intend for this text to serve as a basic reference source for colleagues. Hence, so far as it has been possible, consistent with the highest standards of accuracy and fairness in giving credit for specific ideas, I have not provided exhaustive citations to the research literature in the main body of the text. I do not intend that my discussions of developments in socialization research will serve as definitive statements of the intellectual history of the field.

Too, I do not mean to imply in any way that this text should be considered primarily a work in anthropology. The scope of the study of the socialization process is far too broad to be comprehended from within the confines of only one discipline. I have presented an approach to socialization that includes many of the ways an anthropologist might discuss this process. But not all anthropologists concerned with study of cultural transmission would take the approach used here.

That is as it should be in a field of study just beginning to give sustained attention to the complex problems found in the transmission of human culture.

There have been two major theoretical approaches in modern studies of culture. First, there is the position based in the nineteenth century traditions of naturalism, positivism, and evolution, which depicts culture as an autonomous, superpsychical, and superorganic entity, subject only to its own laws, stages of development, and internal dynamics. Then there is the theoretical position that has its roots in the humanistic traditions of the European Renaissance and the rationalism of the eighteenth century philosophers of the Enlightenment, which depicts culture as the product of human discovery and creativity and therefore fully subject to human control and direction. The outstanding problem in cultural theory today remains the definition of the nature of culture.

This text is not concerned with defining the nature of culture. However, it does use the concept of culture consistently in a broad humanistic and personalistic manner. I see culture in a way that tends to note the role of human intelligence and freedom and the actions of individuals in forming and determining their own cultural destiny as well as the progress of their society. I also see substantial merit in trying to understand the natural origins and the internal logic of an evolving tradition of learned, patterned, transmitted and widely shared behavior. I would suppose that my approach to culture and cultural reality in this text would be similar to the one styled by Julian Huxley* as "evolutionary humanism."

Too, I must say that I am not unmindful of the place and value of the concepts of social system and society in studies of human behavior. I have tried to follow the distinctions between the concepts of culture and social system made by Kroeber and Parsons† without necessarily accepting all of the theoretical definitions used in that work. However, I have assumed that the possibility of understanding the concepts of culture, social system, or society increases in relation to the degree to which the analytic distinctions between them are recognized and followed.

It should be noted that this text is characterized throughout, so far as is possible, by *transcultural*, *transtemporal*, and *holistic* orientations, that is, by specific concerns that general statements about the socialization process are inclusive of all human cultures, through the very long time of the existence of culture, and are based on understandings gained from study of all of culture rather than on some selected parts.

The organization and writing of this text required a selection of published materials. Those finally included appear to be the works students can use in gaining a basic understanding of the socialization process. This text does not generally include citations to socialization publications in the several years immediately preceding its publication. Hence, the latest trends in theory and method are not discussed in detail. However, these ideas and the persons associated with them have been noted where possible to allow students to anticipate future developments in study of the socialization process.

Some recent research will undoubtedly alter the ways in which the socialization process is considered. For instance, Margaret Mead, in *Culture and Commitment* (1970) and elsewhere* has offered a hypothesis that the present generation of young people is participating in a fundamental change in the socialization process—that for the first time, young people know more than their parents, so that children are now informing their elders in ways that parents traditionally have enculturated children. Because Dr. Mead is refining this recent work and since her ideas on the topic are under active consideration by others, her studies in this area have not been considered at length in this text. Similarly, the research of Eliot Chapple, Ray Birdwhistell, Edward T. Hall, Alan Lomax, and others in the area of what may be termed as the "microcultural" level of human communication

---

*Huxley, J. 1957. *New Bottles for New Wine*. New York: Harper and Row.

†Kroeber, A. L., and T. Parsons. 1958. "The Concepts of Culture and Social System," American Sociological Review 23:582-583.

*Mead, M. 1970. *Culture and Commitment; A Study of the Generation Gap*. New York: Natural History Press and Doubleday.

and cultural transmission* likely will lead to significant changes in current theory and method in socialization research. This work is still developing rapidly. Hence, while it has been noted, it has not been discussed in detail. This same procedure of selection has been followed in other instances of major recent advances in socialization research.

This text owes much to the pioneering research of Margaret Mead, especially her many long-term field studies concerned with cultural transmission, learning, human development, and nutrition and her theoretical development of these topics. It has been said that it is difficult to discuss personality theory without reference to the research of Sigmund Freud, Henry Murray, and Gordon Allport. It is similarly difficult to describe our present understanding of the process of socialization without explicitly acknowledging

the great debt owed Margaret Mead for informing us of the possibilities and promise of a scientific understanding of cultural transmission. I have asked Dr. Mead to write a brief foreword to this text to provide some indications of her present thinking concerning the study of the socialization process. Dr. Mead is not responsible for my use and interpretations of her research in this text, or for the text discussions of other socialization research.

During preparation of this work, I was especially aided by the comments of Robert Havighurst, John Honigmann, George Spindler, and Margaret Mead. I am fully responsible, of course, for the ways in which I have finally used and interpreted the suggestions made by each of the persons taking time to carefully read or comment on my work. I appreciate their assistance.

My wife Peggy has provided continuing encouragement and insight in the course of my work. I have learned much about cultural transmission from our sons, Rhys, Ian, and Tom. This work is dedicated to my wife and our sons as a small repayment for their loving patience.

Thomas Rhys Williams

---

*Chapple, E. 1970. *Culture and Biological Man; Explorations in Behavioral Anthropology.* New York: Holt, Rinehart and Winston. Birdwhistell, R. 1970. *Kinesics and Context; Essays on Body Motion Communication.* Philadelphia: University of Pennsylvania Press. Hall, E. T. 1966. *The Hidden Dimension.* New York: Doubleday. Lomax, A. 1968. *Folk Song Style and Culture.* Washington, D. C.: American Association for the Advancement of Science.

 # FOREWORD

by Margaret Mead

Socialization, the process by which human children born potentially human become human, able to function within the societies in which they are born, has been a subject of increasing interest during the last fifty years. Each decade has added new materials, as we began to learn something about child development, something about the kinds of character formation which Freud described, something about the different ways in which children were reared in different cultures, something about learning, and more recently something about the interlocking of instinctive and learned behavior in many animal species and a little about the functioning of the brain. It has been a field that no discipline has been adequate to tackle alone, so anthropologists have relied on the work of psychiatrists and clinical psychologists; sociologists have used the work of anthropologists. Each advance in the field has relied on several different approaches. Of the various approaches it has been said that any one of them left alone long enough might have developed an adequate theory. But in actuality no one of them has been left alone, nor has any of them remained closely enough in touch with what the others have done. The field has steadily become more fragmented.

This textbook is an attempt to bring together within an evolutionary framework evidence from cultural anthropology, experimental psychology, and studies of social behavior within the industrialized world—three areas each of which has developed a rationale of its own. As no one has commanded all three of these fields, no one is in a position to fully introduce this book. It represents an enormous undertaking on the part of the author to start to organize a coherent theory from such diverse materials. I am competent to write only about the anthropological section, and no one of those who have been asked to read and criticize it is competent to judge the whole book. This is inevitable in a new field, a field in which there have been courses long before there were even the beginnings of a text.

The book represents the kind of problem that faces every teacher of university classes in the human sciences, whether that teacher be anthropologist or sociologist or psychologist. In his or her own area, based on experience, he or she can teach from first hand knowledge; for the rest there is dependence upon written reports, films, and tapes, from which the teacher tries to wring a sense of first hand experience. So when Dr. Williams speaks of the Papago and the Dusun among whom he has done field work, they come to life in vivid and concrete detail. For the other fields, he must summarize studies and experiments. But every teacher who has had the same experience should find it congenial to work with these same problems, and, in his or her own turn, contrast what he knows first hand with what is known from the literature, as he as a college teacher struggles, often on some very isolated campus, with articles in some two dozen journals, using half a dozen vocabularies and striking differences in methods and style.

Dr. Williams has also done what I believe every good textbook should do; he has stopped a little short of the present. The book attempts to summarize areas of consensus from which the explorers and innovators of today took off. The student is not presented with the latest controversial results, just hot off the press. At the same time, and this I find most interesting and I believe students will also, the phrasing of the book has been done carefully in the light of what has just been published and may later turn out to be very important.

I have known Tom Williams since 1958. I met him just before his first field trip to Borneo, and we had a long discussion about methods. I have been in close touch with his work ever since. He had entered the field of culture and personality advisedly, after his first field work among the Papago Indians, and finished his graduate work at Syracuse under Douglas Haring, who had worked with Boas and Ruth Benedict and myself at Columbia University. It was through Haring

that Williams became the inheritor of the whole line of thinking which had led Franz Boas to designate the field of the development of the individual in culture as of next importance. In 1922, Boas had said that he realized that the study of diffusion was finished. It had been demonstrated that human cultures could borrow from each other; that each did not have to go through an evolutionary sequence. Now we had to tackle the question of which aspects of human behavior were biologically given and which were due to having been born into one culture rather than another, in a technologically more advanced or technologically simpler culture; on one continent rather than on another. On his first field trip to Borneo Tom Williams took with him this long tradition, which required careful ethnography, i.e., study of the whole culture, and then a study of the way in which children learned that culture. He also brought to his work an interest in the new techniques of adequate photographic documentation, of detailed studies of perception, of careful recording of gesture. He knew the importance of keeping track of his own responses to the field experience. All this he has described elsewhere in his books, *The Dusun; A North Borneo Society*, 1965, *Field Methods in the Study of Culture*, 1967, and *A Borneo Childhood: Enculturation in Dusun Society*, 1969.

I have followed each of these books, and the manuscript which preceded this text, with great interest, and I have learned a great deal thinking about some of the problems the text raises. To me one of the most important contributions is the way in which he has brought some of the very controversial findings of *operant* conditioning into line with much of what we knew about the kind of cultural learning which Boas used to call *automatic* behavior, or cultural behavior that in a sense the child teaches himself. Where so much of the emphasis in the controversy between B. F. Skinner and his critics has turned on manipulation—when looked at from the side of the experimenter—it is refreshing to have a discussion like this, which emphasizes instead what is done by the learning creature. When it was said, some thirty years ago that man is a maze learning animal, the emphasis was on the constructed maze. The pictures that Williams draws here of children who learn without either reward or punishment, who are given the responsibility for learning things themselves, many things which no one bothers to teach them, is congruent with much of our new thinking about education, where the emphasis is shifting from teaching to learning and it is the teacher as well as the pupil who learns.

Dr. Williams came into the field late enough to have the benefit of what had been learned from the cross-disciplinary concept of cybernetics, so that instead of representing the adults as doing something to a more or less ready child, he emphasizes the interrelationships between what the child has already learned on the basis of which the adult takes the next step in response. Nor does he have to waste time on sterile discussion of nature and nurture. Gone are the days, I hope, when students would rebel when I talked in one lecture about innate capacities and individual differences and in the next about the different way in which character is formed in different cultures systematically and how different the results were. Someone was sure to go away muttering: "She can't have it both ways." But, of course, we can. Inborn capacities become capabilities only when

experience makes it possible for them to manifest themselves, and attention to the differences between individuals and between cultures is what makes it possible, in the long run, to identify the similarities also.

Dr. Williams has followed the route that is familiar to anthropologists. He has approached his problem through intensive study of particular cultures, but equipped with many of the ways in which we have learned to look cross-culturally at the whole experience of learning. Initially, like a student well versed in making phonetic transcripts, he learned a particular language; then, informed and transformed by the experience of studying the Tambunan Dusun of Borneo in detail, he has used this experience to work toward a cross-cultural vocabulary at another level.

This text reflects seven years of hard work, combining forays into the extensive and scattered and contradictory literature, with teaching. Each teacher who uses this book will be able to re-enact these same struggles—in his own terms—and students who want to go further will have a platform from which to take off.

NEW YORK, JANUARY 1972

 # CONTENTS

INTRODUCTION

If we could safely transport human embryos to some distant planet or galaxy and mechanically provide all the physical conditions necessary for their "birth" and maturation, the question would arise, "Would the embryos then become human beings as we know them?" The answer is quite clear; unless a way could be found to provide the embryos with culture, they would lack many of the attributes implied by the word *human*.[1] A way would have to be found to transmit the complex whole of knowledge and habits that characteristically are associated with being human.

This text is concerned with the *process of socialization,* which denotes abstract statements of empirical reference concerning the transmission of human culture.[2] The text distinguishes between *socialization,* the process of transmitting human culture, and *enculturation,* the process of transmitting a particular culture.[3] Eskimo infants and children are *enculturated* in Eskimo culture;

all human infants and children are *socialized* in human culture.[4] It is necessary to note this difference to maintain a clear distinction between statements regarding transmission of human culture ("It would appear that, on the whole, adult *Homo sapiens* has rarely taken it for granted that children could or would just naturally learn by spontaneous imitation." [Henry, 1960: 304]) and statements regarding transmission of one culture ("Although there were customs of kindness and tolerance toward children, the society [Nunivak Eskimo] centered in the adult males." [Lantis, 1960: 167]). The confounding of statements regarding socialization and enculturation has led to different uses and definitions of the term *socialization.* Thus Elkin (1960: 4) says:

> We may define socialization as the process by which someone learns the ways of a given society or social group so that he can function within it.

In a review of socialization research, Child (1954: 655) says:

> Socialization is used here as a broad term for the whole process by which an individual born with behavioral potentialities of enormously wide range, is led to develop actual behavior which is confined within a much narrower range —the range of what is customary and acceptable for him according to the standards of his group.

In a text containing a series of essays reviewing research and theory in socialization, Clausen comments accurately that the term *socialization* has a history of varied use. He also says:

> To a large degree, childhood socialization is the social orientation of the child and his enculturation, first within the small social world of family

---

[1] In this text the concept of culture will be used generally as it has been defined by Kroeber and Kluckhohn (1952: 181): "Culture consists of patterns, explicit and implicit, of and for behavior acquired and transmitted by symbols, constituting the distinctive achievement of human groups, including their embodiments in artifacts; the essential core of culture consists of traditional (*i.e.,* historically derived and selected) ideas and especially their attached values; culture systems may, on the one hand, be considered as products of action, and on the other as conditioning elements of further action."

[2] The term *process* refers to a series of interrelated and interdependent events that begin, operate, and conclude with certain defined and recognizable entities or properties.

[3] Mead (1963) has commented on the confounding of the terms *socialization* and *enculturation,* noting that theories arising in such confusion have resulted in general statements about the historical particulars of learning one culture (or *enculturation*) being taken to be statements concerning the process of learning culture (or *socialization*) true of all men. Studies of American, Navaho, Eskimo, and other *enculturation* processes do contribute to an understanding of human *socialization.* But general statements about *human socialization* cannot be taken only from the study of *enculturation* in one society.

[4] I do not mean to imply that Eskimos are not human.

and neighborhood and then in relation to the larger society and culture. (Clausen, 1968: 4.)

Thus Clausen notes a distinction between socialization and enculturation (*cf.* Clausen, 1968: 47), but chooses to use the term *socialization* to refer generally to the transmission and acquisition of one culture, rather than human culture. Aberle (1961: 387) also defines socialization as a process within a particular society when he says:

> In any society or subsystem of a society, socialization consists of those patterns of action, or aspects of action, which inculcate in individuals the skills (including knowledge), motives, and attitudes necessary for the performance of present or anticipated roles.

This text is based on the idea that the systematic study of the socialization process requires concepts and generalizations not limited to the unique history or conditions of one culture, to its particular ethnocentrisms, xenophobias, and special views of the "proper" relations between men or of man's special place in the universe.

It is only because of historic accident that we happen to know a great deal more about the ways some classes of American and Western European children have transmitted to them their local variations of human culture than we do about the transmission of other cultures. The fact that we have a body of literature on the ways European and American cultures are transmitted is very seductive because it leads to the false assumption that Western European and American enculturation processes really represent the prototype of human culture transmission.

The often prevailing tendency to narrowly focus research and theory upon the facts of transmitting particular cultures, rather than on the transmission of human culture, is a transient state. It is very easy to be *culture-bound*, that is, limited to study of one culture, particularly when the tools of research are the written questionnaire, interviews conducted in carefully selected "sample" neighborhoods, a library containing the broad range of journals and texts needed, or the teaching, clinical, or experimental laboratory, readily available and often well supplied with children amenable to being talked to and observed for physical and social reactions. The

problem is that, until recently, many students of the socialization process have not been trained to think about and to conduct their research in *transcultural*, or universally human, terms.

A reading of the history of science makes it clear that it takes no little effort and much reasoned debate to develop a consistent focus of scientific study. Chemists once worried about transmutations of base metals into precious forms. Physics developed partly from very practical concerns with constructing buildings and moving heavy loads. However, chemists and physicists no longer argue among themselves concerning whether they should be concerned with alchemy or with engineering. Scholars concerned with the socialization process have yet to decide whether they will focus their study upon a universally human process or will confine their work to making general statements about that process as it operates within one culture or in several closely related cultures.

It is also important to note that the socialization process is meant to be defined here as comprising the *acquisition* as well as the *transmission* of culture. These two elements of socialization are reciprocals, that is, they conceptually correspond with one another by being equivalent components. In considering the process of socialization it must be remembered that the phrase *cultural transmission* directly implies the process of acquiring culture, while the phrase *acquisition of culture* directly implies the process of cultural transmission. There is no dichotomy, or division into two subordinate and separate parts, denoted in the phrase *socialization process*. In logical analysis the term *dichotomy* refers to the division of a class of events or objects into two subclasses that are contradictory. No such meaning is implied in the definition of the socialization process used in this text.

Furthermore, it should be noted that the term *acquisition* also carries with it the corollary idea of the *consequences* of acquiring culture for the individual. The understanding of the precise ways in which personality traits and patterns leading to individual acts are produced in the socialization process is a very desirable goal in research. However, this text concentrates upon discussing the nature of the process of cultural transmission; it is not primarily concerned with the consequences of the socialization process for individuals.

The study of the consequences of the socialization process for individuals is a thoroughly legitimate area of specialized research. In the field of anthropology this area of research is called *culture-personality studies* or, more recently, *psychological anthropology.* In the field of psychology this area of research is often termed *social psychology* or is sometimes included as part of studies in *child psychology, developmental psychology, motivation,* or *personality.* In sociology this area of research is designated by the name *social psychology* or the term *socialization.* There are a number of textbooks that provide detailed introductions to the study of the consequences of the socialization process.[5] Students and their teachers should not expect this text to be a psychological anthropology, social psychology, or personality development text.

An analogy is useful in trying to make clear the reason for the focus of this text upon the *nature* rather than the consequences of the process of cultural transmission. Suppose that a space pioneer transporting human embryos to a distant planet somehow had lost his wristwatch before returning to earth. Then, imagine one of the embryos, left behind to be mechanically nurtured to adult form but bereft of human culture, picking up the wristwatch from the extraterrestrial ground. Unless this being was equipped with culture for understanding the watch, it would be presented with the puzzle of trying to explain the purposes and origins of the unknown object.

Through the use of modern scientific procedures, which are human cultural inventions, man has come to possess detailed information concerning the objects and events he sees and "picks up" in the natural world. We now have acquired a very great store of descriptive knowledge about "how" natural objects and events occur and are constructed. But so far modern science has not provided very many answers to

the "why" of natural objects and events. For example, it has been demonstrated that ribonucleic acid (RNA) accelerates learning when introduced into the cerebral cortex of some animals; yet we do not know why this occurs. The genetic code contained in deoxyribonucleic acid (DNA) molecules has been described in detail, but we still do not know why DNA operates as it does in hereditary transmission. We know that foreign protein substances introduced into the bodies of many animals produce an outpouring of antibodies that destroy the intruding matter; however, we do not know why the antibodies do not also destroy their host body as the antigen-antibody process occurs.

Similarly, through the use of scientific procedures, we have come to know more about man than ever before. We know from descriptions of how man lives and behaves that much of human behavior is learned, rather than genetically transmitted, and that such learning occurs in a socialization process. We are aware that the socialization process is profoundly important in human affairs; yet we still have to determine why this process came into existence and gained its basic nature and why its origins and nature are related to its consequences for human life and behavior. In some respects, contemporary man is similar to a wristwatch that has come to be possessed of the capacity to pick itself up from the ground and speculate upon its own origins and functions while it marvels at its precise measurement of time, a concept it does not at all comprehend.

There have been a number of scientific approaches to searching out the "why" of the socialization process. One method has been a comparison of careful description and analysis of the details of cultural transmission (enculturation) in specific societies. A second approach has been a concentration upon the description and analysis of the personalities and behavior of individuals who have been socialized. Another approach has been description and analysis of different cultural and social systems, seeking through this procedure to abstract some basic explanations for the socialization process. Each of these efforts has produced a great amount of

<hr>

[5]See Honigmann, 1954, 1967; Goodman, 1967; Wallace, 1970; Barnouw, 1963; Elkin, 1960; and McNeil, 1969.

descriptive material. However, all have been so far unsuccessful in providing insight as to why the socialization process came into existence, why it has a particular nature, and why it affects human individuals in specific ways.

This text will be concerned with examining a number of topics that seem to bear upon a preliminary understanding of the nature, or the structure and functioning, of the socialization process. It will draw upon all the different approaches to study of socialization and will use other relevant data from a wide range of scientific disciplines.

The text begins with four chapters discussing the evolutionary origins and biological bases of the socialization process. Chapter One discusses some of the major details and the main outline of the possible beginnings of the socialization process. Chapter Two describes specific human biological features that appear to serve as organic bridgeheads between human biology and culture in the socialization process. Chapter Three reviews two major models of learning, which are then contrasted to case study data of cultural learning in one native North American Indian society, noting some of the ways human reflective and symbolic processes enter into and are integral to socialization. Chapter Four is a discussion of some of the specific ways that culture and biology may become interrelated in the socialization process.

The next two chapters are concerned with special types of research evidences and assumptions used in study of the socialization process. Chapter Five discusses research data from studies of isolated individuals and twins that can aid in illustrating some of the ways human biology and culture can become interrelated in the socialization process. Chapter Six is concerned with a key hypothesis that has been used often in studies of socialization.

The next four chapters are concerned with the possible relationships between the socialization process and specific cultural patterns and subsystems. Chapter Seven discusses some possible interrelationships between the socialization process and the cultural patterns of kinship and kin groups. Chapter Eight notes some possi-

sible relations between the socialization process and patterns of status-role behavior and class in the cultural subsystem of social relations. Chapter Nine discusses the ways some patterns in the cultural subsystems of technology and ideology may be related to the socialization process. Chapter Ten is concerned with the ways the socialization process may be related to language. The text concludes with a brief epilogue concerning use of knowledge of the socialization process in making public and personal policy. The epilogue is followed by an appendix containing a bibliography of suggested readings on enculturation in 128 societies.

It should be noted that this text uses case studies illustrating features of enculturation in several societies and that all of these discussions have been written in the *ethnographic present*, that is, as if the people being described all live today as they once did, before contact with the modern world. The case studies are written in the ethnographic present only because it is an effective way to present a brief discussion of a specific system of enculturation. It is important to say this at the outset of the text because a great many changes have occurred in most of the previously isolated, nonindustrial societies. These changes were accelerated by the impact of a global war between 1939 and 1945, the rapid dissolution of colonies, and the advent of mass communication and high-speed transportation in all parts of the world. As a consequence of these and other factors, the present generation in most of the cultures described do not follow a great many of the former cultural ways of their parents. Thus it would be a mistake to assume that the cultures described here through use of the literary device of the ethnographic present have remained essentially unchanged. It would also be a mistake to assume that the peoples now learning these variations of human culture have been unaffected personally by events of the past half-century. A great many persons from many of the world's previously isolated, nonindustrial cultures now serve their societies and countries with distinction in a wide variety of highly technical positions. No one reading the case study materials should conclude the text thinking that the peoples referred to in the case study examples are still culturally backward folk surviving at the fringes of Western European and American civilization. Nothing could be further from the truth in this changing world.

It should be noted also that earlier drafts of this work contained a final chapter devoted to a formulation, from the text discussions, of a conceptual model for study of the origin, development, and contemporary nature of the socialization process. However, it became apparent that this summary was considerably broader and much more technical in tone than the remainder of the discussion. Since this text is intended for use as an introduction to study of the socialization process, the draft summary chapter was eliminated. This summary has been published elsewhere (Williams, 1972) in a more technical form, greatly expanded and completely rewritten. Students interested in proceeding to more advanced conceptual levels in their study of the socialization process may find this account useful. Too, teachers of students using this work may find the summary of the structural and functional features of the socialization process to be helpful in making assignments for reading and discussions.

REFERENCES CITED AND SUGGESTED READINGS

Aberle, D. F. 1961. "Culture and Socialization." In F. L. K. Hsu (ed.), *Psychological Anthropology*. Homewood, Ill.: Dorsey, pp. 381-399.

Allport, F. 1967. "A Theory of Enestruence (Event-Structure Theory): Report of Progress," *American Psychologist* 22:1-24.

Barnouw, V. 1963. *Culture and Personality*. Homewood, Ill.: Dorsey.

Brim, O. G., Jr. 1968. "Socialization: Adult Socialization." In D. S. Sills (ed.), *International Encyclopedia of the Social Sciences* 14:555-562. New York: Macmillan and The Free Press.

Burton, R. V. 1968. "Socialization: Psychological Aspects." In D. S. Sills (ed.), *International Encyclopedia of the Social Sciences* 14:534-545. New York: Macmillan and The Free Press.

Child, I. L. 1954. "Socialization." In G. Lindzey (ed.), *Handbook of Social Psychology*, Vol. II. Reading, Mass.: Addison-Wesley, pp. 655-692.

Clausen, J. A. (ed.) 1968. *Socialization and Society*. Boston: Little, Brown.

Elkin, F. 1960. *The Child and Society: The Process of Socialization*, New York: Random House.

Goslin, D. (ed.) 1969. *Handbook of Socialization Theory and Research*. Chicago: Rand McNally.

Goodman, M. E. 1967. *The Individual and Culture*. Homewood, Ill.: Dorsey.

Greenstein, F. I. 1968. "Socialization: Political Socialization." In D. S. Sills (ed.), *International Encyclopedia of the Social Sciences* 14:551-555. New York: Macmillan and The Free Press.

Henry, J. 1960. "A Cross-Cultural Outline of Education," *Current Anthropology* 1:267-305.

Honigmann, J. J. 1954. *Culture and Personality*. New York: Harper.

_____. 1967. *Personality in Culture*. New York: Harper.

Hoppe, R., G. Milton, and E. Simmel (eds.) 1970. *Early Experiences and the Processes of Socialization*. New York: Academic Press.

Kroeber, A. L., and C. Kluckhohn. 1952. *Culture: A Critical Review of Concepts and Definitions*. Papers of the Peabody Museum of American Archaeology and Ethnology, Harvard University, XLVII, Number One.

Lantis, M. 1960. *Eskimo Childhood and Interpersonal Relationships*. Seattle: University of Washington Press.

Linton, R. 1936. *The Study of Man*. New York: Appleton-Century.

Mayer, P. (ed.) 1970. *Socialization; the Approach from Social Anthropology*. London: Tavistock.

McNeil, E. 1969. *Human Socialization*. Belmont, Calif.: Brooks/Cole.

Mead, M. 1963. "Socialization and Enculturation," *Current Anthropology* 4:184-188.

_____. 1971. "Review of P. Mayer (ed.), *Socialization; the Approach from Social Anthropology*," *American Anthropologist* 73:327-328.

Poirier, F. E. (ed.) 1972. *Primate Socialization*. New York: Random House.

Shimahara, N. 1970. "Enculturation—A Reconsideration," *Current Anthropology* 11:143-154.

Spiro, M. E. 1951. "Culture and Personality; The Natural History of a False Dichotomy," *Psychiatry* 14:19-46.

Wallace, A. F. C. 1970. *Culture and Personality*. New York: Random House.

Whiting, J. W. M. 1968. "Socialization: Anthropological Aspects." In D. S. Sills (ed.), *International Encyclopedia of the Social Science* 14:545-551. New York: Macmillan and The Free Press.

Williams, T. R. 1969. *A Borneo Childhood: Enculturation in Dusun Society*. New York: Holt, Rinehart and Winston.

_____. 1972. "The Socialization Process; A Theoretical Perspective." In F. E. Poirier (ed.), *Primate Socialization*. New York: Random House.

ONE  BACKGROUND OF SOCIALIZATION

This chapter is concerned with a brief review of some of the ways the socialization process is based upon and proceeds from the human evolutionary heritage.

■ Postulates for study of socialization

There is abundant scientific evidence to confirm at least two major scientific postulates on which the study of socialization may be based. These postulates are the following.

1. Man's ability for transmitting and acquiring culture derives from his particular kind of anatomy and physiology.
2. Culture is man's natural ecology.

In order to understand these postulates it is necessary to briefly examine the main outline of the facts of human biological evolution and beginnings of culture. The following brief review is intended to provide general data and ideas regarding the ways in which the socialization process has developed from biological bases through natural evolutionary processes and has come to be a significant aspect of being human.

Thinking about human evolution. *Homo sapiens* is the product of a very long biological evolutionary process that began more than a billion years before the present with the extremely complex transition on the earth from inorganic, nonliving substances to organic, living entities. The organisms that evolved through the *Archeozoic* era (Table 1-1) were probably unicellular sea forms. One thing that was true of all of these first living forms, and has remained true of all living forms through evolutionary time, is that living things act in characteristic ways. These typical forms of behavior derive from the kinds of bodies living things possess, whether one is talking about the first fishes

(ostracoderms) of the *Ordovician* period of 500 million years before the present, the giant dinosaurs of the *Triassic* period of 200 million years before the present, or *Homo sapiens*. Man is a living thing and behaves in typical ways that derive from the structure of his body.

Man's body is structurally organized on the basis of characteristics that are the consequence of *cumulative evolutionary adaptations* through an immense span of time; that is, man has inherited the modifications that have taken place in more than a billion years of evolutionary time. Man is an animal with chordate characteristics; however, man does not have all the physical characteristics of all the members of the phylum *Chordata*. Man does not have a skin with placoid scales, as do the sharks and rays, nor does he possess skin with feathers, as is typical of the birds. Man does not possess these characteristics because the particular animal populations from which he has evolved did not adapt to their environments through development of such special structures. And so, the kind of body man has is the product of cumulative evolutionary adaptations in succeeding populations of particular kinds of animals ancestral to man. One major consequence of the concept of cumulative evolutionary adaptations is the avoidance of the "nothing-but" fallacy—"man is nothing but an animal" and therefore has only the attributes of all other animals and can be studied through experimental procedures applied to laboratory animals. This would be false reasoning if applied to any kind of animal. It is very important to realize that, through the evolutionary process of cumulative adaptation, man has come to possess a set of body characteristics not totally shared with any other animal forms.

Table 1-1. Geological time scale of appearance of various forms of life

Life forms	Millions of years since the beginnings of epochs and eras	Epochs, periods	Era
Homo sapiens	1/40*	Recent	Present
Homo erectus	2	Pleistocene	
Homo	12	Pliocene	
Anthropoid apes	25	Miocene	
Primitive apes	35	Oligocene	Cenozoic
Spread of modern mammals	55	Eocene	
Appearance of earliest primates	60	Paleocene	
Rise of mammals and birds	120	Cretaceous	
Spread of primitive mammals	180	Jurassic	Mesozoic
Appearance of primitive mammals	220	Triassic	
Spread of amphibians and insects	285	Permian	
Primitive reptiles, insects, spiders	350	Carboniferous	
Rise of fishes and amphibians	400	Devonian	Paleozoic
First land plants, rise of ostracoderms	450	Silurian	
First primitive fishes, the ostracoderms	500	Ordovician	
No land life in fossil record	600	Cambrian	
Sponges, protozoans, mollusks	925		Proterozoic
Simple one-celled sea forms	1,500		Archeozoic

*NOTE: The dates for appearance of forms of life and duration of epochs have been fixed by the dating techniques of geology and in some instances by radiocarbon analysis. There are disagreements among specialists concerning precise dates for epochs and eras.

Primitive mammals. On the basis of his physical traits, man is classified as a member of the *primate order* of the animal class termed *mammals.* The first primitive animals of the mammal class appear in the fossil record in the *Triassic* period about 200 million years before the present. By the end of the *Mesozoic* era, which lasted approximately from 220 million to 60 million years before the present, primitive mammals had adapted by evolutionary processes (natural selection, mutation, gene recombination, and population isolation) to difficult environmental conditions and had separated into three quite distinct groups: the egg-laying mammals *(Monotremata),* the pouched mammals, *(Marsupialia),* and the placental mammals *(Eutheria).* Primates are placental mammals. The placental mammals first appear in the fossil record in the Cretaceous rocks of Mongolia, some 120 million years before the present.

The fossil record indicates that the placental mammal population of the late part of the Cretaceous period included many widely scattered populations of small, tree-living, insect-eating animals, which when alive probably looked very much like today's tree shrew. These creatures were probably like the contemporary tree shrew in their behavior, that is, they were alert, active, and agile among the high branches of the Cretaceous forests, where they had to come to rely more on their visual sense and less on the ancestral placental mammal evolutionary adaptation to hunting along the ground by the sense of smell. These creatures had to adapt also to grasping for balance among the high tree branches. It is believed that these kinds of animals were possibly ancestral to the primate group.

Changes toward primate structure. The earliest primate populations had the visual, sensory, and grasping equipment of the structure of the primitive mammals. They probably had moveable ears at the top of the head, sensitive tactile vibrissa (hair-like structures) on their long muzzles, a highly developed sense of smell, and generally weak vision. A sense of smell is not as vital as a developed sense of vision in getting food in the trees. Animals living on the ground can easily sniff out food and pick it up with their jaws. In the trees food must be seen to be caught, especially if the diet is insect life. Flying and hopping insects would have to be caught on the jump by use of the forelimbs while the hind limbs were used for grasping, balance, and support on landing. Too, food picked out from under tree bark through use of sharp nails would demand eye and "hand" movements not used in ground hunting of food. Such a sensory adaptation would mean that in time there would be major structural changes in the head and face structure and in brain form. There would be a reduction in size of the external ear and a movement of the ears to the sides of the head, a lessening of dependency on tactile snout vibrissa with their decrease in number and size, a movement of the eyes from the sides of the head to a more frontward location under the dome of the skull, a reduction in the length of the snout as sight hunting replaced smell hunting, and a change in the brain structure as the area devoted to smell diminished in size, while the portion devoted to sight increased. With the need for greater coordination in moving swiftly in arboreal environment, the brain would also increase in size in the area controlling motor skills. These structural changes and the way of life they made possible are reflected today in the modern primates called monkeys.

Thus the first evolutionary adaptations that occurred among the earliest primates were quite similar to those just noted and are the foundation for the three vital aspects of man's structure. (1) The evolutionary development freeing the

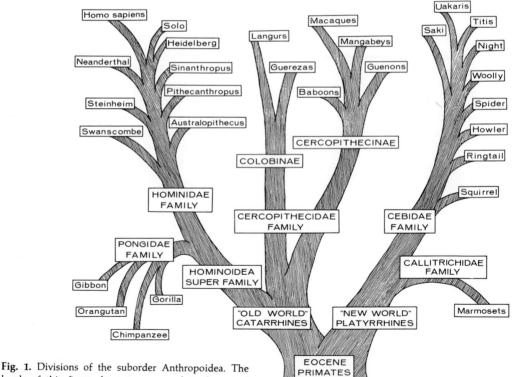

Fig. 1. Divisions of the suborder Anthropoidea. The levels of this figure do not correspond to the actual time of evolution, and the directions of the "branches" have no evolutionary meanings.

forelimbs for the handling of objects in specialized hands in time led to the extremely fine and very complex motor skills needed for tool making and using and made possible a bipedal locomotion on the ground. (2) The increase in dependence on the use of sight brought about the full use of stereoscopic, color vision, which made possible the extension of the "space of recognition" typical of man, that is, it greatly developed the early primate animal's awareness of its environment well beyond its immediate vicinity. Stereoscopic color vision allows a world to be viewed that is increased in area 100 or more times over that perceived by a smell-brained creature. (3) A very early increase in brain size made possible further evolutionary adaptations in intelligence through reason, reflection, and learning.

The apes appear. The fossil record indicates that by the Upper Paleocene period, between 55 and 57 million years before the present, there was in existence a population of ancestral primates, possessed of the first two major evolutionary adaptations, that is, the locomotor adaptation of *grasping* and a *special sensory* adaptation. At the beginning of the Eocene period, about 55 million years before the present, this ancestral primate population was spread over most of the world. By the end of the late Eocene, or the beginning of the early Oligocene period (some 35 million years before the present), because of climate changes of an increasingly more severe nature, the majority of these ancestral primates had become extinct; survivors were restricted to limited areas of Western North America and Northern Europe. It appears that the earth's climate zones became more sharply differentiated in the Eocene and that what are now temperate climate zones became on the average considerably cooler. In the early part of the Oligocene period, perhaps because of increasing cold weather, some primates in Western North America moved into Central and South America. Here, during the late Oligocene and Miocene periods "New World" (*platyrrhine*) primates evolved. It is probable that, at the same time ancestral primates were moving south from Western North America, groups from the same

region migrated across one of the land bridges existing at the Bering Straits area and moved into the regions of Asia, Africa, and Europe. These ancestral primate populations could have given rise to the "Old World" (*catarrhini*) monkeys and apes. It is in the Old World primate populations that the further evolutionary adaptations occurred that made possible the kind of body man now possesses.

The ancestral primate groups that moved into the Old World regions of Asia, Africa, and Europe in the Oligocene period were the inheritors of the first two major structural adaptations, that is, locomotion by grasping and a special sensory reorganization.

The third major adaptation leading to the kind of body man possesses was also a locomotor, or motion, adaptation. This adaptation, termed *brachiation,* involved complex structural changes in the wrist, elbow, shoulder, and chest regions of the body and resulted from the abandoning of motion in the trees by grasping and short hopping to a motion form utilizing the arms, shoulders, and chest for leaping to, grasping, and then swinging to the next tree branch. This adaptation might have originated in a search for food and as a means for protection from harm. Brachiation made it possible for primates to further extend their "space of recognition" by providing for rapid movement over large areas. During the Oligocene period in some parts of Asia and Africa, brachiation became the major means of locomotion of primate populations that were evolving from the Old World (*catarrhini*) forms.

Walking upright. Some time in the early Miocene period, about 20 million or so years ago, a fourth major primate evolutionary adaptation began. This also involved a change in locomotion. This adaptation, called *bipedalism,* involved complex structural changes in the pelvis, leg, and foot bones and muscles, and became the basic adaptation for the appearance of *Homo.* The discovery and approximate dating of fossil bones from a large group of South and East African bipedal hominoids shows that in the early Miocene period a population of primates had moved from an entirely tree-dwelling, brachiating life to at least partial life on the ground.[1] Later members of this form had skulls and brains that were still similar to those now seen in modern apes such as the chimpanzee, but also were possessed of pelvic and leg and foot anatomy similar to that of modern man.

---

[1]The terms *Hominoid, Hominid, Homo,* and *Homo sapiens* have specific definitions in studies of evolution (Hulse, 1971:502).
(a) *Hominoid (Hominoidea)* The super family including the *Hominidae* and *Pongidae:* that is, man and apes.
(b) *Hominid (Hominidae)* The family including all species of *Homo* as well as the *Australopithecines.*
(c) *Homo* The genus to which we belong.
(d) *Homo sapiens* The only living species of the genus *Homo.*

During the Miocene and Pliocene periods the adaptation of *bipedalism* locomotion proceeded until there were many populations of nearly erect primates regularly living on the ground. Bipedalism made possible an even greater extension of the primate "space of recognition" by providing for a form of locomotion that allowed the early ground-living hominoids to move about an area measured in miles rather than in fractions of miles, as among the brachiators, or in yards, as in the instance of the primates who had undergone only the first two adaptations of grasping and special

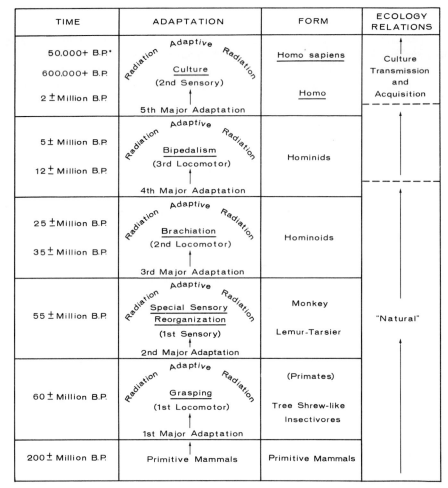

*B.P. means "before the present."

Fig. 2. Major adaptations and population radiations in the primate order.

sensory reorganization. The bipedal hominoids of the late Miocene and Pliocene periods could range about a territory that was expanded a thousandfold over the one covered by their primitive, smell-hunting, pre-primate ancestors. The exponential increase in the primate awareness of the world that came with bipedalism adaptation was one of the factors contributing to the appearance of the fifth major evolutionary adaptation undergone by the primates, that of *culture*.

However, before turning to that final major evolutionary adaptation, it would be useful to review and summarize the discussion to this point. I have postulated that man's nature derives from the kind of body he has, that is, man possesses a set of particular biological characteristics that lead him to behave in typical ways. If modern man is examined carefully he is found to be a structural mosaic of the basic evolutionary adaptive characters of all primates, while at the same time retaining some secondary features that accompanied each major adaptation. The first major adaptation of the primates, that is, the *locomotion adaptation* of *grasping*, shows in man's hands—in his long digits, sensitive tactile pads, and flattened fingernails. The second adaptation, that of a *special sensory reorganization*, shows in man's general head form, brain structure, and vision sense. The third major adaptation, the *second locomotor adaptation* of *brachiation*, is reflected in the bone and muscle structure of man's trunk, shoulders, and arms. The fourth major adaptation and the *third locomotor adaptation* of *bipedalism* is reflected in the bone and

Fig. 3. Possible relationships between change in brain size and cultural development. (Adapted from Brace, C. L., and M. F. A. Montagu. 1965. *Man's Evolution; an Introduction to Physical Anthropology.* New York: Macmillan.

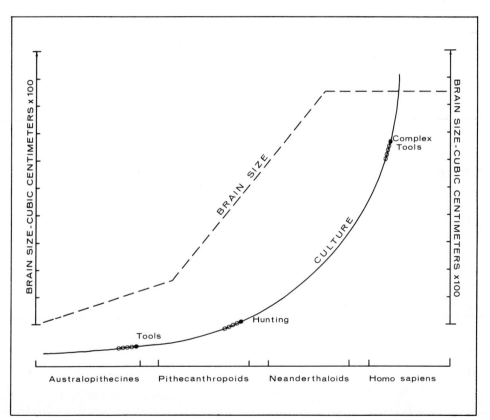

muscle structure of man's pelvis, leg, and foot. The point is that man's body, and hence typical behavior, is shared in *part* with other primates but in *whole* with no other member of the primate order. All primates share the grasping adaptation. The special sensory reorganization adaptation is shared only by the monkeys, apes, and man. The second locomotor adaptation, brachiation, is shared only among the apes.* The bipedal adaptation has been shared only among the members of the *hominid* group. But no modern primate other than *Homo* is possessed of all these physical characteristics.

Tools, bigger brains, and changed behavior. In the time from the beginning to the middle of the Pliocene period, some 12 million to 5 million years before the present, bipedal, small-brained hominid populations were living on the plains and grasslands of East Africa and South Africa. These hominids are termed *Australopithecines*. Because of the bipedal adaptation, Australopithecines had a greatly increased mobility to seek subsistence and eventually turned to use of tools to aid in securing more and greater varieties and surpluses of food. The evidence of tool making and use by an Australopithecine form first designated as *Zinjanthropus* (now termed an *Australopithecus robustus* form), found by L. B. S. Leakey and his wife in 1959 in Tanzania, East Africa, shows that bipedal hominids were using tools at least 600,000 years ago, or in the upper part of the lower Pleistocene period. The Australopithecines probably were mainly vegetarians and used their simple tools to collect different varieties of vegetable foods.

The bipedal hominids of the Pliocene and early Lower Pleistocene periods seem to have been small-headed, small-brained creatures, with cranial capacities of between 500 and 700 cc., in contrast to the modern human average of 1,450 cc., and with a head and face structure generally similar to that of apes of today. But these creatures, at least in their later forms, made and used tools. It had been believed be-

fore the discovery of Zinjanthropus that tools could not be made by bipedal hominids with cranial capacities of less than 750 cc. But the tool evidence associated with Zinjanthropus makes it clear that a brain size of 500 cc. would not limit or preclude tool use by a bipedal hominid. If, as it now seems clear, there is no scientific reason for not assuming that behavioral changes can precede and produce structural changes in evolution, then it could be likely that tool use by small-brained bipedal hominids may have led during the Lower Pleistocene to a significant increase in brain size and changes in the central nervous system, face, head, and hands. And these structural changes in these hominid populations had profound consequences for the further course of the evolution of *Homo*, including making possible a process of acquiring culture.

Talk among tool-using hominids. Since language is such a vital part of socialization in modern man, the important question should be examined concerning whether early Pleistocene bipedal, small-brained, tool-using hominids communicated their experiences and ideas by sounds formed into a language. The question has been answered in several different ways. Montagu believes there were no anatomical reasons to prevent small-brained, bipedal hominids from speaking. Washburn and Avis feel that intelligible speech probably only occurred later in the much larger brained hominids of the Middle Pleistocene period. Broom and Schepers examined impressions made from the inside of Australopithecine skulls to see if these would show any evidences of the brain structure in the parts known to control speech in modern man. They concluded that these bipedal hominids did have the brain centers for articulate speech. However, Vallois, in reviewing available fossil skeletal evidence for speech (jaw, muscle attachment areas, and brain impressions on skull bones), concluded that the anatomical evidence for language in the early bipedal hominids is much too uncertain to draw the conclusions offered by Broom and Schepers.

All the modern apes and most monkeys have highly developed gestures for communication

---

*Some monkeys (*e.g.,* the "spider" monkey) also are brachiators in movement. However, such forms have not fully developed the muscle and bone structure typical of the brachiating apes.

of emotion. The earliest bipedal hominids probably lived in very compact social groups where
they usually were in sight of one another. Too,
they may have depended more on gesture than
speech for communication. Among modern
baboons much communication is by gesture and
has no sound component. The presence of particular scalp and ear muscle attachment points
in the fossil bipedal hominids, which usually
are associated in modern apes with specific
movements of the scalp and ears to convey what
human observers term *emotion*, and their great
atrophy in *Homo sapiens*, would seem also to
point to the small role of articulate speech in
the bipedal hominid forms such as the Australopithecines. Human language also appears
dependent on a large brain. *Homo sapiens* afflicted with microcephaly (an abnormally small
brain and head) have greatly limited linguistic
abilities.

It would seem reasonable to conclude that
communication of ideas by speech probably
came after the significant increase in size of the
brain in the evolutionary changes between the
Middle Pliocene populations of bipedal hominids and the Middle Pleistocene forms of *Homo*.
However, this does not mean that an interchange
of complex, symbolic information by means of
sign, gesture, posture, or gait expression could
not have taken place among the early tool-using
bipedal hominids undergoing the major adaptation of culture. Such acts would leave no records.
A great amount of information and learning is
passed between individuals, both among modern
humans and in many animal groups, by non-
symbolic, unverbalized, inarticulate forms that
leave no artifacts or marks. As the senior female
red deer leads the young of a herd or adult
chimpanzees lead young chimpanzees through
the experiences of a variety of patterned behaviors that are specific to a given natural environment and characteristic of a particular animal, so too the adults of a modern human group
can and do lead their children through similar
patterned behaviors, specific to a cultural ecology, but also characteristic of human cultural
life, without use of linguistic communication.

A transmission of ideas by such *inarticulate*

Conjectural drawing of Australopithecus. (Based on a
drawing by Jay Matternes. In Howell, F. C. (ed.) 1965.
Early Man. New York: Time-Life. Especially prepared
for this text by Priscilla Piros.)

experience probably was a vital part of primate behavior for a very long time before the occurrence of the bipedal adaptation and likely is the base for a still speechless, yet clearly symbolic interaction exchange that occurs regularly among modern monkeys and apes, as well as in some social mammals such as wolves. The question of whether the tool-making, small-brained bipedal hominids of the Late Miocene and Early Pliocene times had intelligible speech communication is very important in the study of socialization because a key part of the contemporary definition of culture is the presence of an active transmission process from one generation to the next of a system of learned behavior that is patterned, or regular, in its form and that is shared widely within a social group. Since language plays a key role in the process by which acquired behavior is transmitted generationally, then these data and conclusions are important for understanding the nature of socialization.

The concept of transmitting culture from one generation to the next has implied to scholars the use of speech which is intelligible to its users and hearers, as in the case of *Homo sapiens.* But, if tool-using, small-brained bipedal hominids of the early Pleistocene can be shown to have transmitted learned, shared, and patterned behavior forms by either "inarticulate experience" or some form of speechless "symbolic interaction," it would be necessary to conclude that the culture concept, and research on socialization, must be broadened to account for transmission and acquisition of culture by other means than language. It probably is not at all correct, as Clark (1961: 28) has argued: "Until hominids had developed words as symbols, the possibility of transmitting, and so accumulating, culture hardly existed."

Homo appears. In the early to middle part of the Middle Pleistocene period, about 375,000 to 230,000 years before the present, tool-using, bipedal hominid populations apparently were dispersed widely over Africa, in the parts of Asia south and east of the Himalaya Mountains, and in the continental offshore islands such as Java and Sumatra. During the Middle Pleistocene period another population of bipedal hominids

appeared regularly in Asia, using complex tools to hunt big game. The Asian populations included the earliest forms of *Homo* and ranged from North China to Java. They are termed *Pithecanthropians.*[2] They were much bigger brained (an average 871 cc. cranial capacity) than the *Australopithecines* of the Lower Pleistocene period (an average of about 576 cc. cranial capacity).

Pithecanthropians made complex stone tools that they could have used to shape other tools, such as wood spears. *Pithecanthropian* remains have been found in association with the bones of elephants, rhinoceros, bison, water buffalo, horses, camels, wild boar, sabre-tooth tigers, cave bears, leopards, and a giant form of hyena, as well as deer, antelope, roebuck, and sheep. The major portion of their diet seemed to have been deer. But these very early forms of *Homo* quite obviously regularly killed large, much

[2]The *Pithecanthropians* are now usually classed in the genus *Homo* with a single species, *erectus,* and three subspecies, *erectus, pekinensis,* and *soloensis.* The *Neanderthals* are also classed in the genus *Homo;* there is some question concerning the number of species and subspecies of this form. The remains of more than one hundred of these fossil forms are usually classed as (1) *early Neanderthals,* and (2) *later ("classic") Neanderthals.* The early *Neanderthals* are associated with the third (Riss-Würm) interglacial period of the European early Upper Pleistocene epoch, some 100,000 years before the present, and are represented by such specimens as *Ehringsdorf, Krapina, Mount Carmel,* and *Galilee.* The later *Neanderthals* are associated with the fourth glacial (Würm I) period of the European Upper Pleistocene epoch, between 100,000 and 50,000 years before the present, and are represented by such specimens as *Gibraltar, Le Moustier, Monte Circeo, Neanderthal,* and *La Quina.* The status of the *Australopithecines* is not yet clear; unquestionably these forms are members of the family *Hominidae.* Whether they are all to be classed as members of a separate subfamily *Australopithecinae,* genus *Australopithecus,* and therefore quite distinct from the subfamily *Homininae,* genus *Homo,* remains open. Leakey claims that a fossil he has termed *Homo habilis,* which he found at the site of *Zinjanthropus* fossil, is a form of man probably directly ancestral to *Homo sapiens.* Other scholars believe this form is similar to the Asian *Pithecanthropians.* The present tendency of specialists in human evolutionary studies is to class *Homo habilis* as being in the evolutionary sequence of the *Australopithecines* until more evidence is available. The present uncertain scientific status of the classification of the family *Hominidae* is reflected in the following classification based on discussion at an international conference in 1962 (I) *Australopithecus* [(1) *A. zinjanthropus boisei;* (2) *A. africanus;* (3) *A. robustus,* and others)]; (II) *Homo habilis;* (III) *Homo erectus* [(1) *Homo erectus erectus* (includes *Pithecanthropus*); (2) *H. erectus sinanthropus* (includes *Sinanthropus pekinensis*); (3) uncertain (*Atlanthropus, Chellan 3* from *Olduvai,* etc.)]; (IV) *Homo sapiens* [(1) *H. sapiens steinheimensis;* (2) *H. sapiens neanderthalensis*] (See Campbell, B. 1963. "Quantitative Taxonomy and Human Evolution." In S. Washburn [ed.], *Classification and Human Evolution.* New York: Viking Fund Publications in Anthropology). See also Campbell, 1966.

more powerful and agile animals. Yet, equipped with only their crude tools of stone and probably wood shaped with stone tools, the *Pithecanthropians* successfully faced a very dangerous natural world. Their success appears to have derived from the fact that they seem to have possessed the greatest advantage in the natural order of their time—the ability to regularly reflect on past and present acts and to benefit, or learn, from these acts in anticipating the future. The possession of a greater degree of *reflection,* or capacity to anticipate future events on the basis of past or immediate experience, not only enabled the *Pithecanthropians* to survive but appears to have set them off distinctly from the earlier bipedal and tool-using, small-brained hominids such as the *Australopithecines.*

The evidence found at the living sites of the *Pithecanthropians* makes clear that, because of their limited tools, this form of *Homo* must have hunted large and dangerous animals through use of a social system of some complexity and by

use of some form of communication and transmission of reflective products, either by speech or by inarticulate experience, or perhaps some combination of both. Immense courage alone could not have led these early *Homo* forms to the regular, successful conquest of larger, stronger, and more agile animals. Some type of social cooperation in driving, herding, and trapping large and dangerous animals must have been regularly used by this early form of *Homo.*

We know that in the late Middle Pleistocene epoch a more structurally advanced form of *Homo,* called *Neanderthal,* used primitive pit traps to kill groups of large carnivores. We also know that both the *Neanderthals* and the *Pithecanthropians* used fire regularly. From the evidences in living sites it has been inferred that fire probably was used by these two kinds of early man as a

Reconstruction of a Swanscombe *(Homo sapiens)* hunting scene. (From a painting by Maurice Wilson. Courtesy British Museum, Natural History.)

tool to make wood weapons, to transform the energy in raw food into a more easily digested cooked form, to heat and light living shelters, and perhaps to frighten away dangerous animals. Too, in the form of torches, fire could have been used as a tool to herd and drive animals into an area where they could be attacked and killed.

Tools and thinking. The regular making and use of tools of special kinds, persisting over long periods, would seem to imply reflection. But the reuse of stone tools would show an even greater capacity for reflection, since reuse involves consideration of effort and time involved in the manufacture of a tool and the meaning of its subsequent discard after use on one or two occasions. Available evidence indicates that *Pithecanthropians* and *Neanderthals* regularly used the same stone tools repeatedly over long periods of time. This reuse of tools indicates a greater degree (not kind) of reflectivity on the part of these forms of *Homo*. When compared to the *Australopithecines*, who appear to have abandoned their tools after limited use, the *Pithecanthropians* and *Neanderthals* reused tools regularly. However, disposal of the dead by the *Pithecanthropians* shows no marked change from the acts of the *Australopithecines*. The ways in which the bones of the *Pithecanthropians* and the *Australopithecines* occur in archaeological sites indicate there was no practice of burial or even the rudiments of ceremonial interment of the dead. In both instances, bones of these forms were scattered about in the same ways as other animal bones.

However, by the time of the appearance of the *Neanderthals*, in the Middle Pleistocene epoch, the concept of ritual interment of the dead had been introduced into the life of man. The *Neanderthals* sometimes used mineral pigments to stain the bodies of their dead and buried them in graves with tools and other objects. It can be inferred from such evidence that the *Homo* forms that generally follow the *Pithecanthropians* in the evolutionary record had developed the capacity for reflection to an even greater degree than had earlier forms.

A screen of culture. While the *Pithecanthropians* appear to have been advanced in their capacity for reflective behavior, especially when compared to the *Australopithecines*, they still failed to make the transition to the even greater degree of reflection clearly exhibited by the *Neanderthals* of a later era. Reflection is a vital prerequisite to the appearance of culture. If one key aspect of culture is the act of transmission of learned, shared, and patterned behavior, then regular reflection, as the ability to anticipate future consequences on the basis of past and present experiences, would seem also to be one of the conditions for culture. The capacity to view and to hope that knowledge and experience would be useful and meaningful to another generation, or even to the dead, as in the instance of the *Neanderthals*, must be present in order for transmission of learned, shared, and patterned behavior acts to take place in a process of socialization.

The capacity for heightened reflection exhibited by the *Neanderthals* of the late part of the Middle Pleistocene apparently continued to expand significantly through the upper portion of that geological epoch. Substantial evidence for the expansion of reflection is found in the increased inventory of the artifact products of these forms of *Homo*. And with regular use of artifacts, the Upper Pleistocene *Neanderthals* brought about a gradual change in their general relations with their natural environment.

The ecology, or the system of mutual relations between an organism and its environment, of *Homo* in the Lower Pleistocene period was a natural one. Early man was born into and lived in a world over which he had no really effective control. In the Lower Pleistocene, populations of *Homo* responded to events in their natural world and only rarely could shape or alter the conditions that adversely affected them. But with the gradual changes in head shape, brain size, and central nervous system function that would have followed from the early attempts to control the natural world through tool use, there came to be an increase of the potential, or ability, within *Homo* populations to more often anticipate natural events before they occurred, or recurred, and to prepare in some ways to deal with conditions that so directly and often violently affected early man. For example, early man was probably the victim of large carnivores that were naturally equipped to outrun, outclimb, outswim, and "outbite" him. Until the advent of a regular use of the capacity for reflection, joined with the making and use of tools, early man had no really effective means of defending himself from attack by prowling carnivores. The invention of the spear, perhaps at first a long branch broken to a point, then later sharpened to a point with a crudely chipped stone adze or knife, gave early man some means of at least delaying or sometimes turning aside the initial onslaught of large carnivores. While the spear would not protect its user, it could allow other members of the group to escape. Recent field observations of Asian tigers hunting game in the open grasslands of India indicate that a solitary Bengal tiger often will not try a second chance to kill a deer or bullock if it misses on the initial rush, apparently because when lacking the vital element of surprise, the tiger cannot cripple its prey by breaking the neck or back in one attack and so hold the animal stationary for further attacks to kill.

East African baboons today protect their troops in a fashion that may be similar to one employed by the small-brained bipedal hominids of the Pliocene period. The larger males of a baboon troop will attempt to turn aside the charges of a predator by lunging boldly at the animal to allow the female and younger members of a group time to flee to the safety of nearby trees. Early man of the Middle Pleistocene period may have considerably improved on this maneuver by adding, through use of reflection on the situation, the throwing of objects such as stones and the making of a sharpened stick to thrust out at, and so to further deflect, the charge of carnivores.

The Dutch zoologist Adriaan Kortlandt has recently observed and filmed the behavior of chimpanzees living on the open African grassland plains of northwest Guinea. When confronted with a stuffed, full-sized leopard animated by a mechanism that caused the head and tail to move, a group of about thirty chimpanzees made an organized attack on the dummy, with enormous yelling and hooting. Kortlandt reports that the chimpanzees threw everything they could pick up with accuracy and that several chimpanzees broke branches off nearby trees, stripped off leaves and twigs and attacked the leopard dummy with great vigor, remaining upright and vigorously swinging their tree branch "clubs" at the intruder.

So the conditions probably were set among the upright hominids and early men in a similar fashion for the further reflection and the tool improvement that could have followed—the cutting of longer and stronger shafts for spears, shaping and hafting or attaching of stone or bone points to inflict pain and hurt on the attacking predators, and perhaps even the idea of the spear thrower. Such improvements on the basic invention of the spear came very slowly in time, for it is not until very late in the Upper Pleistocene epoch that there are stone artifacts even made in a fashion that would clearly indicate they were once hafted onto spear shafts.

As these innovations were occurring, slowly and probably at very great cost in the lives of early men, a "screen of culture" was being built between man and the physical environment in which he lived. At first, and for a very long time, the screen was quite widely meshed; a wooden spear with a tip sharpened by a stone knife and hardened to a point in a fire is not more than a very slight improvement on throwing stones at predators. It is likely that few *Pithecanthropian* or *Neanderthal* "spear bearers" survived many encounters with prowling bears and tigers. What was important was that each invention improved the chances of survival for the population being defended.

Early man likely also improved his chances of survival through application of concentrated heat to otherwise nonedible foods. Many plants, such as tapioca, are inedible by man in an uncooked form. The cooking of animal carcasses undoubtedly made the digestion and absorption of meat easier, since heat energy applied to meat makes the protein more easily digestible by man.

More than stone and bone. It is important to note that the evidence for the evolution of culture as man's natural ecology continues to be limited, since the tools used were likely made of very perishable plant materials such as wood or fiber. Contemporary hunting and gathering peoples have much of their technology in perishable artifacts; only their durable cultural objects such as stone, bone, or carbon from fires could possibly survive long periods of time. Durable artifacts are the only products of reflection that could be expected to have survived over the hundreds of thousands of years since the Middle Pleistocene period. It is helpful also in discussing the evolution of culture as man's natural ecology to point out that the men of the Upper Pleistocene epoch quite probably had an extensive amount of culture that was transmitted to and acquired by infant and young members of these societies. Contemporary isolated native societies, such as those of the Arctic, New Guinea, or Borneo, posses a large and usually complex body of culture that is rarely manifested in their tools.

Breaking out from the limits. By the middle of the Upper Pleistocene epoch, through invention of culture, man had forever altered the relationships between himself and the physical world. The transition was a complex and lengthy one. There were hundreds of thousands of years in the Pleistocene when thousands of *Homo* individuals and hundreds of *Homo* groups lived and died largely as their bipedal, small-brained hominid forebears. But eventually the behavior changes brought about by reflection, invention, and more reflection led to the creation of a system of behavior that could be acquired and shared within a group and then transmitted to the next generation. In this way man transcended the basic physical limitations imposed on other animals in a natural environment. Some, if not all, of each new generation of *Homo* could at least come to know, through cultural transmission, how to avoid the deadly mistakes of the preceding generations in dealing with natural events, whether these were the attack of a cave bear, a flood, or savannah grass fire.

▪ Evolution and socialization

The facts of human evolution and the appearance of culture are directly relevant to our

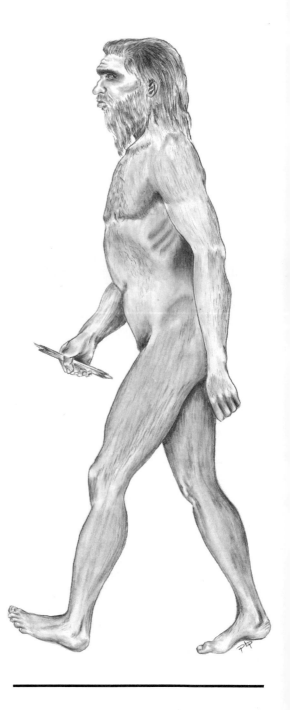

Conjectural drawing of early form of *Homo sapiens.* (Especially prepared for this text by Priscilla Piros.)

understanding of the socialization process. These data indicate that there was a time in the past when essentially human populations lived out their lives as did other animal forms. Then, as reflection underwent evolutionary development, possibly because of tool using, the human animal came to live more and more in a cultural as well as a natural environment. As the products of reflection began to be transmitted regularly to and acquired by succeeding generations, probably first through inarticulate experience, then through use of language, the process of acquiring culture as man's natural ecology had its beginnings. There is no way at present to say exactly when the socialization process began and no certainty as to what constitutes the evidence to be used. However, it seems reasonable to say that by the time of the *Pithecanthropians,* and most certainly by the time of the *Neanderthals,* learning by their offspring of patterned and widely shared products of adult reflection and of experience must have been a regular feature of human life. It can be said "These animals have a culture and are teaching their young to act in cultural ways and so there has come into being a process of socialization."

Most studies of socialization have paid little attention to this question. Research on the transmission and acquisition of culture usually begins with the fact of the existence of socialization in its contemporary form. This has resulted in continuing inattention to a whole series of basic questions. Why did the socialization process arise in the course of evolutionary development? Has the process of socialization persisted unchanged for the past hundred thousand years, or are there still significant evolutionary events at work in this process? What are these events and how are they related to evolutionary processes of natural selection, mutation, gene recombination, and population isolation? What specific features of the socialization process are crucial to its appearance and continued existence, and why? Answers to these and similar questions are needed to illuminate and place in perspective some of the dilemmas of current socialization research. One of the points these data of

evolution and socialization suggest is that it is time that relevant data from evolutionary biology be incorporated into research on socialization. Chapter Two discusses a range of evolutionary products involved in socialization that have been given little or no attention in basic research.

What does all of this mean for the study of socialization? Among other things, it suggests that scholars concerned with socialization might well undertake systematic naturalistic field observations of those primates closest to man in structure and behavior (chimpanzee, gorilla, orangutan, gibbon) to learn of some of the foreshadowings and precursors of the socialization process that might help illuminate and broaden understanding of the questions just noted. Goodall's pioneering field studies of chimpanzees, the basic field work on baboon behavior by Washburn and his students, Schaller's field study of the mountain gorilla, Carpenter's field studies, and the studies of other scholars on other primate behavior provide basic insights into some of the possible beginnings of socialization that have been generally ignored by students of the socialization process. It is important to remember that modern nonhuman primates do not represent the ways of early humans. Studies of nonhuman primates are useful only for gaining clues and ideas concerning some of the behavioral evolutionary processes that might have been at work some 10 million or more years ago among the hominids. Too, more detailed attention must be given to the data and conclusions of modern prehistory research, for these materials surely contain evidences that can be pieced together to help understand the evolutionary nature of the process of human transmission of culture. This is not to suggest that students of socialization should focus their concern upon the artifacts that demonstrate sequences and phases of particular cultures; rather, it must be possible to determine from the data of the evolution of human culture in the last half-million years some of the ways the process of socialization may have operated, changed, remained stable, and so on. Most specialists concerned with socialization know little of such data and have not yet begun to broaden their perspective of that process as a long-term and quite human adaptation to the natural world.

Finally, these data of evolution and the beginnings of socialization suggest that there is a need for a reasoned insistence that socialization be studied as a universally human process. These data of human evolution and the beginnings of socialization make quite clear the fact that the process of cultural transmission is a phenomenon of the human species.

▪ Conclusions

The discussion in this chapter has been concerned with a brief review of some ideas and data that can be of assistance in understanding the process of socialization. If it follows that man's typical behavior derives from the kind of body he has, it should also follow that a careful description and analysis of the nature of human socialization would include statements concerning the ways human biology, especially in its evolutionary perspective, is related to culture, a significant human invention, in a socialization process. The most vital questions in socialization research may well be those concerned with the specific ways human biology and culture become interrelated and operate in a process of socialization.

▪ Summary

This chapter has been concerned with setting forth some of the major details and the main outlines of the evolutionary beginnings of the socialization process. The discussion began with some postulates and ideas necessary for thinking about socialization in an evolutionary perspective. Details were then offered concerning the major primate evolutionary adaptations preceding and leading to the appearance of the adaptation of culture. The discussion then turned to an examination of data concerning the development of culture as a human adaptation, with suggestions concerning some possible ways the socialization process began to function in the transmission to succeeding generations of the reflective products and experiences of early men. The chapter concluded with a series of comments regarding evolution and socialization.

REFERENCES CITED AND SUGGESTED READINGS

Bordes, F. 1968. *The Old Stone Age.* New York: McGraw-Hill.

Brace, C. L., and M. F. A. Montagu. 1965. *Man's Evolution; An Introduction to Physical Anthropology.* New York: Macmillan.

Brace, C. L., H. Nelson, and N. Korn. 1971. *Atlas of Fossil Man.* New York: Holt, Rinehart and Winston.

Broom, R., and G. W. H. Schepers. 1946. *The South African Fossil Ape-Men: The Australopithecinae.* Pretoria: Transvaal Museum Memoir, Number 2.

Campbell, B. 1966. *Human Evolution.* Chicago: Aldine.

Carpenter, C. R. 1964. *Naturalistic Behavior of Non-human Primates.* University Park: Pennsylvania State University Press.

Clark, G. 1961. *World Prehistory; an Outline.* Cambridge: Cambridge University Press.

Darling, F. F. 1937. *A Herd of Red Deer, A Study in Animal Behavior.* London: Oxford University Press.

DeVore, I. (ed.) 1965. *Primate Behavior: Field Studies of Monkeys and Apes.* New York: Holt, Rinehart and Winston.

Garn, S. M. (ed.) 1964. *Culture and the Direction of Human Evolution.* Detroit: Wayne State University Press.

Goodall, J. V. L. 1964. "Tool-Using and Aimed Throwing in a Community of Free-Living Chimpanzees," *Nature* 201:1264-1266.

Hallowell, A. I. 1961. "The Protocultural Foundations of Human Adaptation." In S. L. Washburn (ed.), *Social Life of Early Man.* Chicago: Aldine, pp. 236-255.

Hulse, F. 1971. *The Human Species.* New York: Random.

Kraus, B. S. 1964. *The Basis of Human Evolution.* New York: Harper and Row.

LaBarre, W. 1954. *The Human Animal.* Chicago: University of Chicago Press.

Lancaster, J. B. 1968. "On the Evolution of Tool-Using Behavior," *American Anthropologist* 70:56-66.

LeGros Clark, W. E. 1960. *The Antecedents of Man.* Chicago: Quadrangle Books.

Mayr, E. 1958. "Behavior and Systematics." In A. Roe and G. G. Simpson (eds.), *Behavior and Evolution.* New Haven: Yale University Press, pp. 341-362.

Mead, M. 1958. "Cultural Determinants of Behavior." In A. Roe and G. G. Simpson (eds.), *Behavior and Evolution.* New Haven: Yale University Press, pp. 480-503.

Montagu, M. F. A. 1960. *An Introduction to Physical Anthropology,* ed. 3. Springfield, Ill.: Charles C Thomas.

Schaller, G. B. 1963. *The Mountain Gorilla: Ecology and Behavior.* Chicago: University of Chicago Press.

Sebeok, T. A. (ed.) 1968. *Animal Communication: Techniques of Study and Results of Research.* Bloomington: University of Indiana Press.

Spiro, M. E. 1954. "Human Nature in Its Psychological Dimensions," *American Anthropologist* 56:19-30.

Spuhler, J. N. (ed.) 1959. *The Evolution of Man's Capacity for Culture.* Detroit: Wayne State University.

Vallois, H. V. 1961. "The Social Life of Early Man: The Evidence of Skeletons." In S. L. Washburn (ed.), *Social Life of Early Man.* Chicago: Aldine, pp. 214-235.

Washburn, S. L. 1950. "The Analysis of Primate Evolution with Particular Reference to the Origin of Man," *Cold Spring Harbor Symposia on Quantitative Biology* 15:67-76.

Washburn, S. L., and V. Avis. 1958. "Evolution of Human Behavior." In A. Roe and G. G. Simpson (eds.), *Behavior and Evolution.* New Haven: Yale University Press, pp. 421-436.

Washburn, S. L., and I. DeVore. 1961. "Social Behavior of Baboons and Early Man." In S. L. Washburn (ed.), *Social Life of Early Man.* Chicago: Aldine, pp. 91-105.

Washburn, S. L., and P. C. Jay (eds.) 1968. *Perspectives on Human Evolution.* New York: Holt, Rinehart and Winston.

TWO   ORGANIC BRIDGEHEADS TO SOCIALIZATION

This chapter discusses the kinds of biological equipment a newborn human possesses that may provide organic bridgeheads, or specific links, between biology and culture in the socialization process. The point of the discussion is that it is possible now to make a preliminary identification of some specific aspects of human biology, all evolutionary products, which clearly seem to be involved in the process of socialization.

The organic bridgeheads to socialization comprise four very complexly interrelated classes of phenomena: (1) *species-characteristic behavior*, (2) *reflexes*, (3) *drives*, and (4) *capacities*.

■ Species-characteristic behavior

Instincts. In the period before 1920 students of human behavior, particularly psychologists and sociologists, formulated theories that rested upon the concept of instinct. This term was borrowed from biological studies of animal behavior. It was vaguely defined and at its best was an explanation *obscurum per obscurius*, that is, the term *instinct* explained an unknown phenomenon through use of a still more unknown phenomenon. Before 1920 instinct was supposedly at the base of most human action. However, as the descriptive accounts of human behavior in a great variety of cultural settings began to accumulate, it became apparent that there was a fallacy in attributing highly variable cultural phenomena to a constant biological factor such as instinct.

By the middle 1920's the term *instinct* had been demonstrated to be a less than useful basis for theories of human behavior. However, the term tended to remain in the vocabulary of social and behavioral scientists until about World War II, when it ceased to be used generally as an explanation for any form of human behavior.[1] The term *instinct* remains in everyday use as a popular way of dealing with puzzling and frustrating facets of human behavior and because some students of human behavior continue to employ the term in their explanations of human actions. However, the facts concerning instincts are such that no phenomenon of this nature has been demonstrated in humans.

Another explanation. In the past 35 years biologists doing systematic research on animal learning and behavior, a field study now termed *ethology*, have devoted a considerable effort to the definition and identification of the physical and chemical basis of such phenomena.[2] At the end of the first 20 years of such study, ethologists generally defined an instinct as the *complex unlearned activity characteristic of a species of animals* and proposed four criteria for evaluation of any behavior of an animal as instinctive. (1) Is there a definite physiological basis for the supposedly instinctive action of the animal? (2) Is the supposedly instinctive action universal in the species of animals? (3) Does the physiologically based, universally functioning biological entity clearly determine the behavior in question? (4) Is such

[1] For a discussion of the use of the instinct concept in psychology after World War II, see Nissen, 1953.

[2] *Ethology*, the study of animal behavior and learning, should not be confused with *ethnology*, the comparative study of human cultures. A discussion of the field of ethology is found in Hinde (1963), Klopfer and Hailman (1967), and Eibl-Eibesfeldt (1970).

behavior at all modifiable through experience? By the middle of the present decade, it had become increasingly clear to ethologists that the consistent application of these criteria for evaluating and establishing animal instincts had demonstrated that the concept of instinct was no longer scientifically useful. Students of animal behavior and learning have now generally abandoned the use of the idea of instinct and have substituted the broader concept of *species-characteristic behavior.*

In the course of studies seeking to establish instincts, ethologists found that nearly every form of behavior in all animals studied was capable of being modified through experience and learning. Today species-characteristic behavior is defined as including all those forms of action by an animal that are assumed to have physical/ chemical basis, are "characteristic" of a species, are subject to some modification, but only through long and repeated exposure to specific experiences.

And in man. A newborn human does not seem to possess any species-characteristic behavior forms comparable to the nest-building activity of the South African weaver bird or the honey dance of bees. Weaver birds clearly illustrate a species-characteristic behavior form; they usually construct nests of twigs with a foundation of coarse hair strands. In one study, an experimental adult pair of weaver birds and their descendants were isolated completely from others of the species for six generations. During five generations the birds were not supplied with nest-building materials normally used by their wild ancestors. The sixth isolated generation of birds was provided with the normal nest-building materials, mixed with a variety of other materials. The isolated weaver birds promptly proceeded to select the "proper" material and build their nests in the pattern typical of their wild ancestors. Thus a complex, typical, unlearned form of activity persisted in these creatures while they were isolated over six generations and then "reappeared" once again. Similarly, bees isolated from other bees over many generations continue to collect honey and store it in the typical ways of wild bees and even to perform a complex "dance," which is believed by specialists in bee studies to show the general direction and amount of honey available.

Human infants do not seem to overtly exhibit similar forms of complex unlearned activity. This does not mean that species-characteristic behavior forms are not present in *Homo sapiens.* On the contrary, there is a variety of particular activities exhibited by newborn infants that could be termed as species-characteristic behavior forms. However, most are so diffuse in form and in the past have been considered so unimportant to the survival and the learning of the human infant they they have either been overlooked or have been classified as *reflexes* (see the following section). For example, human infants are born possessed of typical, complex, unlearned tendencies toward gross random movements, including wiggling of the torso, waving of the arms, leg kicking, and noise making of a "babbling" type. These motor patterns cannot be identified as being tied or related directly to any particular environmental or physiological stimulus and seem modifiable only by long and continued exposure to learning situations. These complex, unlearned movements appear to serve as a basis for the maturation of later, specific motor activities, which become shaped and directed through the cultural transmission processes, often through inarticulate learning (see Chapter One). These movements seem to serve as the foundation for the whole range and style of the postures, gestures, gaits, and modes of locomotion typical of adults in a particular culture.*

There also seems to be a broad range of other possible species-characteristic behavior forms in the human infant: (1) *free soiling,* (2) *organic repression of smell,* (3) *organic emphasis of sight,* (4) *organic emphasis of hearing,* (5) *absolute nutritional dependence,* and (6) *infantilization.* There also may be other species-characteristic behavior forms that do not appear until the later periods of infancy and childhood, for example, *nonseasonal*

---

*This text treats socialization as a transactional, doubly contingent process. Thus the question of the "point in time" at which this process terminates is of some importance. The theoretical position used here is that socialization process terminates when significant transactions between parents (or their surrogates) and their children, in terms of cultural transmission, cease, for all practical purposes.

sexuality.[3] The "later appearing" species-characteristic behavior forms are usually expressed at the time and in particular levels of biological maturation. Thus a human male's nonseasonal (regular and continuous) sexual interest in the female begins at about age 11 or 12 and may continue through adult life until old age.

There have also been suggestions that other species-characteristic behavior forms may exist in *Homo sapiens.* Thus, in discussing the incest tabu, Cohen (1964) has said that there is a significant factor in man's biological makeup that disposes him to establish incest tabus at least at the core (parents and their children) of the nuclear family. Cohen believes this is an innate need for a minimal degree of privacy, or a need for freedom from extreme emotional and physical stimulation, especially from other people. The evidences cited by Cohen for such behavior do seem to support a conclusion that he may be describing a species-characteristic behavior form.

In a series of profoundly brilliant texts, Claude Lévi-Strauss has proposed that there is an inescapable pattern underlying human intellectual operations which, somewhat like the "program" of the high-speed computer, directs the work, actions, and shape of most of everything thought, perceived, or undertaken by man. Lévi-Strauss postulates that this pattern probably works like the least common denominator of human thought. If such a pattern does in fact exist, it could be termed a human species-characteristic behavior.

Following the suggestions of Sigmund Freud, Bettelheim and Rapaport, among others, also have suggested that all men are born with certain "apparatuses for relating to reality." These scholars feel that individual personality will fail to develop if these "apparatuses" do not receive adequate development in infancy. This could also be an example of a species-characteristic behavior form. Whether the accounts of Cohen, Lévi-Strauss, Bettelheim, and Rapaport are accurate or not, there are some indications of other examples of what may be species-characteristic behavior in man. The nature of some of the possible dimensions of species-characteristic

behavior in man is discussed in the following paragraphs.

FREE SOILING. The species-specific behavior form of free soiling involves the disposal of body wastes. Waste disposal is as important for animals as food getting. This process is particularly critical in nesting animals, such as birds, where the vulnerable young are kept in a very limited space. Several species-characteristic behavior forms are used in different bird groups to rid the nest of infant waste and prevent free soiling. Infants of some birds of prey eject waste over the nest edge using specially developed muscles. In most perching songbirds fecal matter is encased in sacks of a gelatinous material secreted by the intestine. Parent birds dispose of the sacks after their elimination by the young in the nest. Nestlings of some bird species cannot defecate until a parent taps the cloaca with its beak. These species-characteristic behavior forms cease when the infant birds leave their nest. This form of behavior appears to be a naturally selective, evolutionary adaptive mechanism designed to prevent contagion from nest soiling.

Primates are usually born singly and carried regularly on the mother's body. Hence there is little danger of infection from other young in a confined space. Primate nests, when built, are abandoned as soon as they become fouled with wastes. This evolutionary adaptation in primates has eliminated the problem of nest contagion among infants of this group. Yet this adaptation raises the problem of the primate infant freely soiling the mother with urine and fecal matter. Female gorillas pay regular and very specific attention to grooming and cleaning of the area about the anus of their infants after defecation and are themselves groomed by another gorilla after being soiled by an infant. It is necessary for human adults to undertake quite explicit and repeated steps over a period of several years to make the infant surrender his *free soiling* physiological autonomy and eventually accept cultural controls. In doing so the infant has to come to learn to recognize the meaning of accumulating bowel and bladder pressures and to understand that, despite these body pressure signals, evacuation cannot take place when needed physiologi-

---

[3]LaBarre (1954) has presented a detailed account of these aspects of human biology in an innovative discussion.

cally but rather when specific adults require such release in particular places and at specific times. Thus a purely physiological, probably species-characteristic behavior form of *free soiling* is gradually transformed in a series of culturally structured events into a cultural process. It is in this way that organic bridgeheads to socialization are begun.

REPRESSION OF SMELL. Systematic studies of the human infant's sense of smell have concluded that there is little or no discrimination of odor by the newborn and that infant responses to odors are highly variable. While these experiments have often been confounded by imposition on the infant of the investigator's own culturally structured concepts about smells (pleasant, unpleasant, and so on), research does support the general conclusion that the human infant appears to have a repressed, or limited, sense of smell.

Smell usually depends upon close physical contact and the moisture content of the air. Odors from the thing giving off a smell are very quickly diluted beyond any possibility of perception. High-flying birds of prey such as eagles have had to come to depend upon their sense of vision in hunting over large land areas. Carrion-feeding birds such as the condors and vultures, which should have an acutely developed sense of smell to find their food sources, instead have had to come to depend on vision because of the extreme dilution of odors with distance and moisture content of the air. Hawks and owls, hunting much closer to the land surface, also have been forced to rely on vision rather than a smell sense to locate food.

The human repression of smell is not an ancestral animal trait. Reptiles have a highly developed sense of smell, more so than either their bird or mammal descendants. It is likely that long-term adaptation to life in the air and high trees led in time to recession and repression of the sense of smell among both birds and primates. The repression of smell in the evolving primates was part of the general change in this population from proximity sensory functions (smell, touch, tactile vibrissa) as part of the extensions of the space of recognition so crucial to the transition to culture as man's natural ecology. As a con-

sequence of this evolutionary heritage, *Homo sapiens* is born with a possible species-characteristic form of an organic repression of smell.

EMPHASIS OF SIGHT. The development of stereoscopic color vision as the consequence of the first primate locomotor adaptation of grasping and the second primate adaptation of special sensory organization has meant that for at least the past 55 to 60 million years primates have possessed the ability to see clearly the world in which they live. A dependence by an animal upon the sense of smell as a primary means of dealing with its environment restricts it to very limited amounts of space. Environmental contact through smell depends upon natural energy units consisting of chemical molecules arranged in a particular pattern to comprise a substance. A molecule is the minimal energy unit of any chemical compound and is governed in its actions and relations with other molecules by certain invariable physical laws. A chemical molecule cannot, for example, move at the speed of light. As noted, the speed of diffusion of any odor is limited by the physical properties of the molecules in a particular combination.

However, the vision sense is based upon a very different natural energy unit. Sight depends on quantum units of light, which move at the absolute velocity of all physical forms in the universe. The eye of *Homo sapiens* has been demonstrated to respond to only one quantum unit of light. Since a quantum unit of energy is basic in the universe, this means the eye of *Homo sapiens* is nearly perfectly adapted to its physical environment.

The human infant quickly exhibits a high level of visual acuity, sensitivity, and coordination, although born with an incompletely developed optic nerve and with ciliary muscles not mature enough to permit complete accommodation (adjustment of the thickness of the lens) to bring light to full focus on the retinal structures. In the first few days of life an infant becomes quite sensitive to changes in intensity of visual stimuli. By the fifteenth to the twentieth day after birth, most infants discriminate quickly among colors and can follow objects. A few hours after birth most infants show rudimentary coordination and

"Nellie," a Cheyenne Indian baby (circa 1886). (Courtesy American Museum of Natural History.)

convergence of the eyes and easily fix an object and probably perceive depth of a field. At 8 weeks most infants have such visual responses well organized in their visual explorations of their environment. These visual responses of the infant are among the earliest complex behavior patterns to become organized and functional in the infant's adaptation to his cultural environment.

Well before the time a baby has gained motor control over the trunk and limbs, it is skilled and able to visually explore and command its world of reality. Long before the human infant can actually physically manipulate reality, it is "sizing it up" visually and is well prepared to apprehend and thus comprehend meaningful visual messages carried across long distances in an instant of time by the medium of quantum units of light. Thus emphasis of sight may be said to serve as an organic bridgehead in the process of socialization.

EMPHASIS OF HEARING. The organic emphasis of hearing in *Homo sapiens* also appears to be a species-characteristic form. The sense of hearing in primates is not as efficient as in many mam-

mals that depend on sound comprehension for survival. Bats and dogs seem to possess a much greater and more refined ability to discriminate and to locate sounds well beyond the hearing range of any primate. Because of the placement of their ears, most primates have only a limited sound sensing, or an idea of the direction of sounds. This is so because sound waves strike primate ears in an off-center manner, usually reaching one ear before the other. This "stereo-auditory" sense is not particularly efficient in man, since the distance of a sound-producing source cannot be efficiently discriminated unless the sense of sight is brought into making distance judgments on the basis of learned comparisons of volume and other clues, especially cultural ones.

However, the physical properties of sound in air are such that this general sensory mode was retained through millions of years of primate evolution in the high forests at perhaps the same level of functioning as in the ground dwelling preprimates and was not affected by the demands of tree life, as was the sense of smell.

While hearing bestowed no particular naturally selective advantages on the evolving primates, it was not a disadvantage to life in the high forests. Hence, among the hominoids of the Miocene period, the ancestral primate hearing sense was intact and still functioning. When the evolution of *Homo* had proceeded to the point where the products of reflection and learning could be transmitted to succeeding generations through the use of articulate communication in the form of language, the sense of hearing again came to play a vital part in human biology.

Newborn human infants have a low level of hearing acuity in the first few days after birth, more as a consequence of mucus in the middle ear than lack of maturation of the auditory structures. Soon, however, the infant responds quickly and strongly to different intensities and durations of sounds. Human newborns do not seem to respond well to pitch differences. Pitch discrimination appears to develop to a generally high level after the first few months of life.

Generally, a newborn infant is well prepared biologically to hear and discriminate among the sounds of the world into which he is born. Thus hearing may serve also as an organic bridgehead to socialization.

ABSOLUTE NUTRITIONAL DEPENDENCE. It is an obvious fact that a human infant is completely dependent upon others for its care and feeding. In Chapter Five we will see how this fact has come to be the basis for the myth of *feral* (wild animal-like) children. The feral child myth recognizes more than a common sense observation that infants die unless nurtured by others. It clearly notes the evolutionary organic roots of mammalian and primate society. In the course of the evolution of these kinds of animals, there has been a broad trend toward *meta organisms,* or societies, where many individual animals comprise increasingly larger units for their mutual satisfaction of basic needs and for survival, so that the individual animal, apart from the social grouping, often is unable to survive.

A basic mammal evolutionary adaptation is a nutritional one, as is illustrated today by the surviving primitive egg-laying mammals. The platypus and echidna (spiny anteater) suckle their young born through laying eggs. Another major adaptation of the mammals was that of the marsupial. Marsupial young are born alive in an extremely immature state and for an extended time must live in a pouch on the mother's belly. This provides warmth and some measure of protection for the quasi-fetal young, while they nurse on nipples contained within the pouch.

A further major evolutionary adaptation of the mammals was the endoparasitic placenta; the fetus remains in the mother's body until mature for birth, while taking nutriments directly from the bloodstream, rather than from a nipple on the outside of the body—where the fetus is ectoparasitic.

The special evolutionary adaptation of combining the primitive mammalian adaptation of suckling the newborn by means of external teats and of the placental mammal adaptation of endoparasitic development, which provides for some safety in the bony shelter of the pelvic basin, is the foundation for the absolute nutritional dependence of the primate infant on a parent.

This is because in the course of primate evolutionary changes, newborn infants tended to become smaller, much more helpless, and very much more physically immature. Today among the modern primates, nutritional dependency needs become increasingly greater from lemur to man, with the suckling period increasing from several days to a few weeks to 1 or 2 years. Table 2-1 summarizes data pertaining to the tendency within the modern primate order to greater nutritional dependency by infants.

Thus the human infant is born with a nutritional dependency upon its parents that is long-lasting and important for its subsequent development. This possible species-characteristic behavior is important in socialization, for it has been proposed that it is in the time and the conditions of prolonged nutritional dependency that a number of critical events occur (see Chapter Six) that may be necessary for development of an essential "humanity." However, this species-characteristic form alone cannot be responsible for humanizing the infant.

INFANTILIZATION. The term *infantilization* refers

Table 2-1. The trend toward nutritional dependency in the primate order

Primate form	Pregnancy period	Period of absolute nutritional dependency on mother or mother-surrogate	Suckling period	Social independence	Primate form
Man	266 days	One year or more	1-2 years	6-8 years	Man
Apes	Chimpanzee, 235 days Gibbon, 290 days	3-6 months	2-3 months	12-18 months	Apes
Monkeys	Rhesus, 166 days Marmoset, 150 days	1-3 weeks	2-4 weeks	2-4 months	Monkeys
Lemurs	111 to 145 days	1-3 days	2 days to 2 weeks	2-3 weeks	Lemurs

to a broad tendency in the evolution of primates that seems to have as its consequence the fact that *Homo sapiens* appears to be a "fetalized ape" in his adult form. The modern adult apes such as the gorilla have massive, overhanging brow ridges and heavy, forward jutting jaws. These physical characteristics are not present in new-born great apes. It seems clear from the physical evidences now available that the early progen-itors of *Homo sapiens* were possessed of similar supraorbital brow ridges and projecting heavy jaws in the adult forms. When the evolutionary evidences for *Homo* are considered together, it is clear that the more "modern," that is, the more *gracile,* in structure man has become, the more he has come as an adult to resemble the infant ape. It seems that as his hands became more useful in grasping, throwing, tearing, and lifting and as his brain became more vital in behavior than use of heavy jaw and tooth structure in defense and food getting, evolving man reversed the trend in primate evolution of moving from *gracile* (light) to *rugged* (heavy) physical characters. Thus *Homo sapiens* adults have the smooth, round heads of the ape infant and do not possess the supraorbital (brow) ridges or prognathous (jutting) jaws so typical of contemporary apes. *Homo sapiens* also has late closing skull sutures and relative body hairlessness, both fetal ape characteristics.

The adaptive advantages of infantilization for *Homo sapiens* are significant for understanding socialization. The smallness of the human face is related directly to the size of the brain case. *Homo sapiens* adults have a more massive brain than any other primate adult. The adult gibbon has an average brain case capacity of 97 cc., the chimpanzee, 400 cc., the orangutan, 416 cc., and the gorilla, 519 cc. In contrast, modern human adults have an average brain case capacity of 1,450 cc. These gross differences in brain size are related to the fact that *Homo sapiens* infants persist for a long period after their birth in a fetal stage of active brain growth, which is typical of monkeys and apes. In the rhesus monkey and the gibbon the most active period of brain growth is before the time of birth, when about 70 per-cent of the adult brain size is reached. After birth, gibbon and monkey brains grow at the

same rate as the rest of the bodies of these animals. The gorilla and chimpanzee have a brief period of rapid brain growth just after birth, so that 70 percent of adult brain size is reached in the first year of life. A *Homo sapiens* infant has only 22 percent of its adult-sized brain at birth. Despite a rapid increase in brain size in the first and second years of life, 70 percent of the adult-sized brain is not gained until the first quarter of the third year, and 80 percent of the adult-sized brain is not reached until near the end of the fourth year of life. So *Homo sapiens* continues for three years in a growth activity that is typically fetal in monkeys. Thus human babies have a delayed brain growth dur-ing the very long period of their nutritional dependency on adults.

Bloom's analysis of studies of human learning and physical development (1964) has provided some indications of the probable importance of infantilization of the brain in man with respect to demonstrated adult "intelligence." Bloom has concluded that, in terms of "intelligence" mea-sured at age 17 (by any one of several standard-ized tests), at least 20 percent is developed by age 1, 50 percent by age 4, 80 percent by age 8, and 92 percent by age 13.

While there is obvious difficulty in developing and then administering "intelligence" tests to monkeys and apes, the maturation of intelli-gence in these animals appears to follow the general pattern of body maturity common to these forms. Thus the "wild" rhesus monkey, which has an intrauterine period of 166 days, an infant period of 1.5 years, a juvenile period of about 6.5 years, and an adult period of about 20 years, appears to develop at least 80 percent of its mature intelligence in its very early years. A "wild" chimpanzee, which is intrauterine for 235 days, infantile for 3 years, juvenile for 8 years, and adult for approximately 30 years, also appears to develop at least 80 percent of its mature intelligence in its very early years. So it seems clear that monkey and ape intelligence develops rapidly and early and that these pri-mates are probably functioning at nearly the full level of adult "intelligence" capacity by the beginning of their juvenile growth period.

The vital fact in the process of human infantilization is that there is a general "biological slowing" of infant growth so that the human brain, and human learning, which generally depends upon the size of the brain, develop together during the long period of nutritional dependency on parents.[4]

It can be said that infantilization of the human newborn is also a vital organic bridgehead to socialization, because of this *neotenous* evolutionary feature (*neoteny* means "remaining ever young"), mature humans do not act generally with reference only to their species-characteristic behavior forms, for these have mostly been supplanted in *Homo sapiens* by culture learned in a process of socialization. Through a long-term physical dependence on others of his species the human baby comes to accept through cultural learning those ways most other animals have fixed in their genetic structure. Animal adaptations in evolution ordinarily become gene traits. But the human adaptation to the natural world is culture, which is not fixed in the human gene pool and which therefore must be learned by the child using a biological base of a special kind, comprised in part, at least, of species-characteristic forms that make it necessary for human infants to learn to become human beings.[5]

In conclusion of this brief discussion of this particular species-characteristic trait of the newborn, it should be noted that it is very difficult at this point in research in socialization to say with any certainty whether one particular species-characteristic behavior is more important than others. While infantilization is vital as an organic bridgehead to socialization because it provides for the very long time involved in the process of learning culture, it is not possible now to say that this form is the most crucial of all human species-characteristic behavior forms.

Summary of human species-characteristic behavior forms. In the preceding pages a brief account has been given of seven possible species characteristic forms: (1) random movement, (2) free soiling, (3) organic repression of smell, (4) organic emphasis of sight, (5) organic emphasis of hearing, (6) absolute nutritional dependence, and (7) infantilization. A suggestion was made that there are other possible species-characteristic forms in man that have had little systematic study in relation to their place in the process of socialization. The point of this discussion has been to provide an awareness that there are physical-chemical based forms of activity that are typical of humans and that apparently are not generally subject to modification, except through very long, repeated exposure to learning experiences. The seven species-characteristic behavior forms discussed here have been listed in the order in which they appear subject to whatever modification is possible; random movement appears the most modifiable through long-term learning experiences, while the species-characteristic form of infantilization seems least modifiable through experience. It is important, however, to remember that all seven forms appear to be very little affected by learning when compared with other classes (reflexes, drives, capacities) of biological structures possessed by the newborn human. In the pages to follow, the other three classes, which are increasingly more modifiable through experience, are discussed in some detail.

■ Reflexes

Taxes. The second major class of biological equipment possessed by the newborn human infant that appears to serve as an organic bridgehead to socialization is termed *reflexes*. All or-

---

[4]It is important not to draw the conclusion from this discussion that higher intelligence in individual *Homo sapiens* is related only to a larger brain size. It is reasonably clear now that "normal" *sapiens* cranial capacity ranges from a lower limit of about 900 cc. to an upward limit of 2,000 cc., with an average of 1,400 cc. for all *Homo sapiens*. Anatole France, the celebrated novelist, had a brain size of slightly over 900 cc. "Idiots" may have brain sizes of 1,600 to 1,800 cc. Thus it can be said that, within a broad human range, neither cranial capacity, brain size, nor number of convolutions has anything to do with intelligence or functional capacity (Montagu, 1960).

[5]*Infantilization* and *absolute nutritional dependency* are both features of the general biological principle of *neoteny*. They have been discussed separately since they are special aspects of the biological heritage of a newborn human which can serve, uniquely in each instance, as organic bridgeheads in socialization. It also would be possible to discuss absolute nutritional dependency as a feature of infantilization. But the delayed growth of the brain and a corresponding delay in the development of general "intelligence" clearly seem to be different orders of phenomena and so warrant separate discussion from the fact of the human infant's complete nutritional dependency on its parents.

ganisms are born with "stimulus-bound" behavior forms, that is, because of a particular genetic evolutionary heritage, members of a species will behave in *stereotyped* ways in response to particular stimuli in their environment. The simplest forms of adaptation by an animal to its environment are termed *taxes*. An example of a *taxis* would be an instance in which an organism orients itself in such a way so that it can maintain equal stimulation of two bilaterally symmetrical sensory receptors, or an instance in which an organism alternates right and left movements to equalize stimulation at successive intervals through time. Another illustration would be the instance of a response of an organism to the stimulus of bright light; if the light source is moved laterally, the organism will change its orientation because one eye is receiving more light than the other. If one eye is blocked or removed and the organism is subjected to such a stimulus, it will move in a circle as it seeks to equalize the light stimulus. Such an effort to orientation to a specific stimulus in the environment, continuously made and specifically guided by an external stimulus, is called a *taxis*.

In many instances a *taxis* is part of a whole complex of *taxes*. It is very difficult to separate the specific adaptive mechanisms involved at this level of an organism's behavior. For example, fish usually are oriented in water with the ventral (belly) surface downward, an orientation that depends on both gravitational and light *taxes*. If light comes into a tank of fish from the side rather than from the surface of the water, certain species of fish will orient themselves in a heads-up or heads-down angle to the surface. If the effects of gravity are removed when the labyrinth of the inner ear is destroyed by surgery, some species of fish will orient themselves ventral side up if the light comes from below them. So precise analysis of taxes becomes difficult when there are factors that naturally interfere with a basic orientation of an animal with respect to stimuli in its environment. Too, not all taxes occur in nature in uncomplicated forms. Even the simplest organisms, such as protozoa, show great individual variability in their behavior and are not completely stereotyped in their acts. This is because all organisms are responsive to several features of their environment, including

Fig. 4. Schematic diagram of phylogenetic scale relationships in adaptive activity. (Adapted from Dethier, V. G., and E. Stellar. 1961. *Animal Behavior: Its Evolutionary and Neurological Basis.* Englewood Cliffs, N. J.: Prentice-Hall, Inc.)

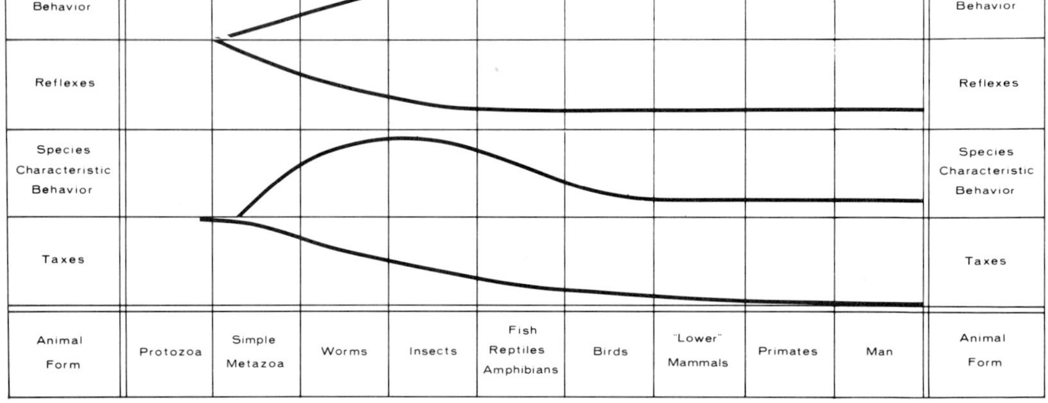

Animal Form	Protozoa	Simple Metazoa	Worms	Insects	Fish Reptiles Amphibians	Birds	"Lower" Mammals	Primates	Man	Animal Form
Reflection										Reflection
Learned Behavior										Learned Behavior
Reflexes										Reflexes
Species Characteristic Behavior										Species Characteristic Behavior
Taxes										Taxes
Animal Form	Protozoa	Simple Metazoa	Worms	Insects	Fish Reptiles Amphibians	Birds	"Lower" Mammals	Primates	Man	Animal Form

as well their own internal states, and so are usually making several different responses to varying stimuli at the same time.

Taxes appear to be almost nonexistent in man. The higher in the *phylogenetic,* or evolutionary, scale, the more modes of behavioral adaptation are found in organisms, so there is less stereotyped behavior in orientations to stimuli. Protozoa, simple metazoa, worms, insects, fish, amphibians, reptiles, birds, and "lower" mammals (such as the platypus and echidna) show a decreasing amount of *taxes* in the way in which they are listed here. "Higher" mammals, including all primates and especially man, exhibit little *taxes* behavior. Fig. 4 illustrates this fact in a simple schematic diagram and also notes some possible relationships between taxes and reflexes.

The nature of reflexes. *Reflexes* are similar to *taxes,* for they are relatively fixed or stereotyped responses to stimuli derived from genetically based nervous system structures and their functionings. In many animals it is very difficult to make a distinction between *taxes* and *reflexes.* The general distinction used by students of animal behavior is that *taxes* usually involve an orientation of the whole body of an animal to a stimulus, which then involves the organism in a number of specific responses. Reflexes may involve all of an animal's body in response to a stimulus, but usually they involve only part of an animal's body, such as constriction of the pupil in response to bright light, or a flexing of a limb to a pain stimulus. Reflexes appear also to have greater variability and modifiability than taxes, especially in higher vertebrate animals, particularly primates.

There are two general classes of reflexes: (1) the *tonic reflexes* are slow, long-lasting responses to stimuli involved in such body processes as maintaining equilibrium, posture, and muscular tone, and (2) *phasic reflexes* are rapid, short-term responses to stimuli such as the one seen in the flexing of a limb under a painful stimulus. Reflexes are integrated at different levels and in complex ways in the nervous systems of the higher animals.

While it is possible theoretically to make an analysis of some of these complex reflex processes in terms of more simple reflex processes, it is now clear that, in the course of evolutionary change, particularly in the primate order, reflexes have tended to become subject to the modifying and mediating influence of higher neural mechanisms such as the brain cortex. Reflexes in man can apparently be altered in their stereotyped forms through learning of culture (see Chapter Four).

Kinds of human reflexes. The human infant is born possessed of a wide range of reflexes: (1) *superficial reflexes* (such as mucous membrane or skin reflexes), (2) *deep reflexes* (such as biceps, knee), and (3) *visceral reflexes* (such as heartbeat, salivary glands, radial muscles of the iris). A partial listing of these reflexes is summarized in the outline below.

SOME HUMAN REFLEXES

I Superficial reflexes
   A. Mucous membrane reflexes
       1. Corneal (eye blink)
       2. Nasal (sneeze)
       3. Pharyngeal (gag)
       4. Uvular
       5. Palatal
   B. Skin reflexes
       1. Interscapular
       2. Upper abdominal
       3. Lower abdominal
       4. Cremasteric
       5. Gluteal
       6. Plantar
       7. Anal

II Deep reflexes
   A. Maxillary
   B. Biceps
   C. Triceps
   D. Periosteoradial
   E. Periosteoulna
   F. Wrist
   G. Patellar
   H. Achilles tendon

III Visceral reflexes
   A. Pupillary reflexes
       1. Pupillary
       2. Consensual
       3. Accommodation
       4. Ciliospinal
   B. Oculocardiac reflex
   C. Carotid sinus reflex
   D. Bulbocavernosus reflex
   E. Bladder and rectal reflexes
   F. Mass (Riddech) reflex

SOME HUMAN REFLEXES—cont'd
III Visceral reflexes—cont'd

    G. Salivary
    H. Smooth muscle of bronchi
    I. Glands of respiratory passage
    J. Smooth muscles in walls of alimentary tract
    K. Glands of alimentary tract
    L. Liver
    M. Sphincters of alimentary tract
    N. Uterine muscle
    O. Pilomotor muscles
    P. Smooth muscle of skin blood vessels
    Q. Smooth muscle of blood vessels of abdominal viscera
    R. Smooth muscle of blood vessels of salivary gland and external genitalia
    S. Sweat glands

Human reflexes functioning. Most reflexes in man are based in or are directly mediated through the spinal cord. The spinal cord integrates reflex behavior that occurs in the trunk and limbs and conducts nervous impulses concerning reflex activity to and from the brain. The basic spinal neural mechanism for integrating reflexes is termed the *reflex arc*.

The spinal cord is connected, through special nerve systems branching off from it, with the *autonomic nervous system,* which innervates the viscera, blood vessels, and other smooth muscles of the body. The autonomic system is divided into two major parts: (1) a *sympathetic nervous system* branch, lying along the middle region of the spinal cord and sending out a diffuse network of nerve fibers to the organs it innervates, and (2) the *parasympathetic nervous system* branch, which arises from the most posterior regions of the spinal cord and the brain and goes directly to the specific organs it innervates. In general, the sympathetic branch of the autonomic nervous system functions in reflexes that expend body energy (increased blood pressure, heartbeat rate, pupil dilation). The parasympathetic branch of the autonomic nervous system is generally reparative in its functions, for it is related to sleep, digestion, and so on.

In adult humans, if the influence of the brain on spinal reflex arcs is undamaged, the complex nature of reflexes increases greatly. This is because there is a nervous conduction to and from the brain by means of bundles of nerve fibers, which are located on the peripheral parts of the spinal cord. In the course of vertebrate evolution the basic structure of the spinal cord has undergone very little change. But as the forebrain area enlarged in primate evolution the ascending nerve bundles on the peripheral areas of the spinal cord extended into the forward area of the brain itself (thalamus), while the nerve bundles descending from the brain came to originate in the highest portion of the brain (cortex). Too, these nerve tracts became more compact, while also becoming more separate, and this has permitted greater refinement and segregation of reflex arc functions. More importantly, these evolutionary changes mean that in man most reflex behavior is integrated and sorted out at several different levels of the central nervous system, including the brain. A reflex may be directly modified, or inhibited, by the higher brain centers on the basis of other data reaching it from other body parts (see Chapter Four). Thus learned behavior or a complex of learned attitudes resulting in an emotional or cognitive interpretation of the reflex experience can delay, modify, or block a reflex action.

Reflexes can be modified. Reflex responses mediated through and interpreted by the brain, as is the case with nearly all human reflexes, become very complex neurosensory phenomena that considerably expand and enhance the behavioral potentials of the human being. Most importantly, however, these properties of human biological structure and function mean that the newborn human has the potential to learn to modify reflexes, which does not appear possible in other animals. The human infant will live on a reflex arc basis; its heart will beat, it will breathe, and it will digest and eliminate its food and wastes on a fairly automatic basis, without effort or special concern on its part. But the human infant, providing there is no central nervous system damage, has an opportunity to learn to culturally modify at least some of its reflexes in a quite significant manner. The fact is, of course, that many cultures do not systematically attempt to modify, repress, or inhibit most reflexes by enculturation. Persons in many cultures, including American culture, even deny that such changes are possible. But there is now substantial evidence that most *Homo sapiens* reflexes are capable of modification through learning. Chapter Four discusses this point in some detail.

▪ Drives

A third major class of biological equipment possessed by the newborn human infant, which can serve as an organic bridgehead to socialization, is known variously by the terms, *drive, need, impulse, tension, urge,* and *appetite.* In the broadest sense all these terms refer to a complex of biological states of an organism and the stimuli leading or motivating it to a given behavior. Although there are some conceptual differences between these several designations, the term *drive* will be used here for the sake of brevity in discussion. Drives are usually seen by psychologists as representing a dynamic force behind the motivations to action of the human being. Drives have been used as explanations and as answers to such questions as "To what is apparent spontaneity of human behavior due?" and "Why in the absence of learning and fatigue does a man's response to a constant stimulus change from time to time?"[6]

A theoretical model. Scholars in biology and psychology have developed a general theoretical model, which has several major variations, to answer such questions. This general theoretical model notes that all changes in an organism's activity not clearly attributable to species-characteristic behavior or to reflexes result from some kinds of changes in the quantity and distribution of *physical, chemical,* or *electrical* energy, which is created within the organism and is then "discharged," "blocked," "released," "stored," or "deflected," as the supposed energy motivates the organism to specific action. It is still not clear, despite more than a century of intensive research and discussion on the matter, whether in fact such "energy" really exists and whether there is any scientific rationale for drive (urge, need, etc.), explanations of behavior being based upon physiological processes that have yet to be empirically

Tambunan Dusun (Sensuron) girls seated in two typically adult female postures (back and right) during a game of "jacks." (T. R. Williams, 1959.)

demonstrated. However, many recent studies of human motivation still assume that there has to be some kind of energy "back of," "behind," or "underlying" spontaneous behavior (behavior not tied to or elicited by any visible stimulus) by the human organism. Most often now, it is assumed that such "energy" arises from a very complex physical-chemical interplay among reflexes and between the reflexes and other genetically transmitted body states, such as species-characteristic behavior forms. Yet there remains a serious question whether motives to human action ultimately are reducible to a finite sequence and specific types of organic structure (such as a nervous system) discharging some kind of "energy" that makes a human being "want" to act in certain ways.

A critique of the model. Hinde, in reaching this conclusion, has reviewed the influential

[6]For some comment on the concept of motivation, see Hunt, 1960; Jones, 1963; Maslow, 1954; Peters, 1958; R. White, 1959; and Arnold, 1968.

variations of the energy model of motivation advanced by Freud, McDougall, Lorenz, and Tinbergen. Hinde (1960) notes that the major problem with all of these variations of the energy model of motivation lies in the fact that, while theorists have talked about motivation as if it arose from some physical structures located within the organism, they usually derived descriptions of all such energy from the overt activities of the animal. Thus, in observing an animal acting in spontaneous ways, the theorists have in effect said, "All that activity, especially when it is not tied to any stimulus in the organism's environment, must mean that there is a store of body energy which is causing the organism to act in these ways." This teleological (being directed toward a specific end) type of reasoning is useful in describing visible changes in an animal's behavior but is not very useful in scientifically describing and analyzing the interplay of diverse factors that occur in man's constantly active central nervous system, where factors such as nonspecific stimuli derived from the brainstem, reticular system, and hormones are now known

Caring for baby—Hidatsa Indian women making a boat, North Dakota (circa 1895). (Courtesy American Museum of Natural History.)

to lead to changes in specific patterns of human behavior. Whether or not human behavior theorists formulate new conceptual models that dispense with concepts of inner energy states leading man to goal-directed actions to reduce physical tensions caused by energy accumulation, it is quite clear that the newborn human possesses a class of biological equipment that is involved in the process of socialization and that is clearly different conceptually from species-characteristic behavior and reflexes.

Inner states and later states. In the newborn human, the biological equipment said to be related to drives appears to be primarily "vegetative" in nature, that is, related to preservation of the human individual through metabolic maintenance. This necessitates the acquisition of oxygen, water, carbohydrates, amino acids, and other essential metabolic elements required by the human body. It also requires maintenance of a constant ionic composition of the blood, relatively constant temperature levels, the elimination of wastes and toxic by-products, and so on. Human metabolic maintenance also requires concentrated periods of sleep, rest, and wakefulness alternated in specific sequences to allow recovery from activities. These requirements are especially crucial for the newborn and have been considered by many scholars of human behavior as the bases of all other drives, needs, wants, tensions, and so on that are developed or acquired later in human life (for example, the need for intimacy or for prestige).

Bell's review (1965) of literature in developmental psychology shows that, while basic research in this area is attempting to identify the neurological and physical-chemical correlates of human behavior and continues to be wide-ranging and searching, it still tends to ignore the specific fact that there is a very limited amount of description and analysis of the precise ways that drives originate and function in the newborn human. The most extensive descriptions now available of the ways drives arise and function in the newborn human are to be found in psychoanalytic and psychiatric literature. Since these descriptions are quite often impressionistic, they have not been accepted widely as meeting the standards of objective, quantified data expected in contemporary psychology.

A view of infant inner life. Until recently, however, many psychologists and psychoanalytic scholars have portrayed human infants in a similar manner as far as drives are concerned: the newborn human infant was pictured by classic psychoanalysis and orthodox learning psychology as an undifferentiated passive recipient of stimulation calling into play its various drives. Bettelheim (1967) has pointed out that he believes this view of human infancy arose from a myth created by scholars concerning the infant's "golden age," when it is assumed to not exist psychologically and responds only through its various drives. We have, according to Bettelheim, imposed our wishful adult views onto the inner life of the infant, to make it passive and receptive, sheltered from all the stresses of later life. Thus, Spitz (1946) pictured the human infant's condition as *anaclitic,* that is, characterized by such extreme dependence that a point is reached where all "psychological" functioning in the newborn is qualified or suppressed by the presence and operation of drives, particularly the hunger drive.

A change of view. There has been a recent withdrawal from this position as extreme. Bettelheim, among others, has noted that the newborn human is clearly an active, competent being in constant reciprocal interaction with its environment. Psychological studies of early development in humans make it clear that there is adequate empirical evidence to support such a shift in general theory. The shift still leaves the reader interested in the phenomena of the socialization process with the choice between one of several energy models as the basis of drives and with very little accurate notion of how drives, when they can be specifically noted, are used to transform a human organism into a human being in the course of socialization.

The rubber band analogy. The general energy model for the explanation of drives leaves much to be explained, particularly in the classic psychoanalytical view, which says the "hunger drive" is supposed to become operative about 18 to 36 hours after birth, when the blood sugar level of the infant drops markedly and then takes pre-

cedence over and is more vital than other body processes by creating a "tension" that can be reduced only by specific acts of the mother or a mother-surrogate (such as a wet nurse). A rubber band analogy is often implied in such tension reduction explanations of infant behavior. When a new rubber band is stretched to near its breaking point there is a rearrangement of the molecules within the structure because of heat and pressure. If the tension on the rubber band is released and the structure is allowed to return to its normal shape, there will be a slight change in the original structure resulting from the permanent changes in molecular arrangement created in the initial stretching process. Each time the rubber band is stretched again a further molecular rearrangement occurs until the structure begins to assume a new shape.

Thus some psychoanalytic scholars have said that, when the internal tension created by lowering of the glycogen level, which leads the infant to many kinds of random behavior such as sucking and head turning, is finally reduced by a feeding act by the mother or mother-surrogate, there is a basic change in the hunger drive because of the specific ways in which the tension was reduced by the mother or her substitute. These scholars also say that each reduction of this tension leads to yet more modification of the hunger drive, until finally the drive is "socialized" and the infant begins to assume management of the drive himself.

Contrary evidences. Recent experimental psychology studies of satiation and hunger drive reduction in human and other mammal infants (rats, cats, puppies, monkeys) tend to show that the rubber band analogy, which presumes the hunger drive to be derived from a lowering of the glycogen level, is much too simple. Newborn animals whose stomachs were loaded with food well before any hunger tension could have possibly appeared demonstrated the same overt behavior (suckling, gross body part movements) as newborn animals of the same species deprived of food. Studies of newborn human infants also indicate that babies sucked as much when satiated and experimentally aroused as when they were deprived of food but equally aroused experimentally. Thus it can be concluded that the descriptions of what has been taken to be hunger drive behavior in newborn humans are confounded by a lack of specific knowledge concerning the ways a baby is aroused or stimulated by other factors, internal and external to its being. It may well be that a great deal of basic revision in thinking will have to be done concerning the role of drives in socialization, similar to the effort that occurred in the instance of the concept of instinct and its replacement by the concept of species-characteristic behavior. If the overt behavior forms that are said to specifically and clearly indicate drives can be exhibited in the absence of the drives, then other explanations for such behavior must be used. This does not necessarily mean that drives do not exist and that the concept of drive is not a useful way to begin thought on this class of biological equipment in the newborn human. It does mean that at present it is exceedingly difficult to say that a specific

Caring for baby—South Africa (circa 1930). (Courtesy American Museum of Natural History.)

drive, dealt with in a particular way by adults, leads to specific behavior in the human infant. And it then becomes even more difficult to explain specific kinds of human behavior in later life as being drive-based and drive-derived.

■ Capacities

Possible and actual capacity. A fourth major class of biological equipment possessed by the newborn human infant, which can serve as an organic bridgehead to socialization, has been termed variously as *capacity* and *potential.* In the broadest sense, these terms refer to the fact that the human infant is born possessed of gene patterns that can come into play at particular stages of growth and development only when elicited through specific combinations of physical and cultural circumstances. Each human infant possesses the possibility of body growth and maturation of action. Whether the infant actually grows and acts, and the ways he grows and acts, depend upon the fact of his survival and the ways he is cared for and learns as he does mature. His strength, speed afoot, balance, body flexibility,

coordination, dexterity, learning, and so on depend first on the presence of specific gene material and second on whether these potentials are brought into play through their being developed and expressed in particular cultural, social, and physical circumstances.

An example of a distinction. An example of the distinction being made here between the *possible* as opposed to the *actual* capacities of human individuals is to be found in the fact that many peoples living on the island fringes of Asia (Japan, Taiwan, Philippines, Borneo, Celebes, Java, Sumatra) traditionally have had a subsistence diet comprised largely of white, polished rice. Too, whatever their other physical characteristics (skin color, hair form), these peoples are short, ranging on the average from 5 feet, 1 inch to 5 feet, 2 inches in stature. Explanations for this average short stature have ranged from a lack of minerals in soils to the fact that these peoples all belong to the Mongoloid race or *clinal population.* However, none of the explanations is sufficient to explain the short stature among island Asia peoples. Soils vary considerably in their mineral content from Japan to Java. Members of the Mongoloid clinal population living on the Asian mainland vary greatly with respect to their stature.

One factor that the people of island Asia share in common is their diet of white, husked rice. Europeans and Americans forced for long periods as prisoners of war to subsist entirely on white, husked rice developed the diseases of pellagra, black tongue, hyperkeratosis, staggers, and edema. These diseases are generally not found among the peoples of island Asia eating a diet mainly of white, husked rice. Experimental animals raised on a white, husked rice diet are much smaller than other animals of the same genetic strain raised on diets normal for such animals. A white, husked rice diet introduces a basic amino acid deficiency; there is enough protein in such rice to sustain life, but not enough to encourage or allow full growth and action potentials. The peoples living on the island fringes of Asia have become genetically adapted to the white, husked rice amino acid deficiency and so now do not usually suffer the diseases that afflict other humans who eat such a diet. This adaptation by island Asian peoples has resulted in an average short stature.

The tropical island peoples of the Pacific who live to the east of island Asia and are generally believed to be the descendants of the white, husked rice-eating peoples are, on the average, much taller. This is because they have developed a diet rich in animal proteins and most vitamins, including such foods as fish, pig, yams, taro, and coconuts.

Thus the peoples of island Asia have the *potential* for larger size, both in stature and weight, but have not actually *realized* such potential because of their basic subsistence diet of white, husked rice. Marked changes in social and cultural patterns following World War II have altered this diet form as a part of life in this geographic area and likely will result in significant changes in the average stature of some island Asian (Japan, Taiwan, Philippines) peoples. This stature change has proceeded most rapidly in post World War II Japan among the children born since 1950.

It follows from this example that statements concerning human capacities have little real meaning unless they include an exact specification of the physical, cultural, and social contexts in which a capacity manifests itself. Twin studies, which are discussed in Chapter Five, are vital to understanding human capacities because they allow some specifications of the ways physical, social, and cultural factors can affect the actual potentials as opposed to possible potentials of human individuals.

Research on capacities. The literature on human capacities is fragmented and often unclear. Research on the nature of human capacities has been concentrated in the three areas of (1) motor functions (strength, speed, coordination), (2) cognitive functions (concepts of mass, weight, number, logical thought), and (3) learning. For the most part, data of human capacity have been derived in these three areas of research by the methods of *factor analysis* and *psychological tests.*

The newborn human appears to come equipped with a very wide range of possible development in each of the three areas of capacity that have been studied. However, psychologists using developmental examinations in early infancy usually report near zero correlations between these tests and later expressions of motor, cognitive, and learning capacities. On the other hand, some physicians have reported correlation values near .50 between tests in infancy after 6 months of age and later development of these kinds of capacities. These differences may arise from the smaller groups studied by psychologists, from the fact that psychologists really have been studying motor functions rather than capacities, and because psychologists lack basic training in neurology and so miss many clues in infancy related to later development of capacities. Whatever the reasons for these differences in prediction of later capacity development from tests and observations made in early infancy, it seems clear that the newborn human does exhibit some broad indications of later capacities. As the infant matures and depending upon the physical, social, and cultural circumstances in which he matures, these general kinds of capacities do become more amenable to observation and testing. After about age 4 children seem to exhibit in broad outline their adult motor, cognitive, and learning capacities.

The capacity for learning. The learning capacity has been the most investigated of all human capacities. There is now general agreement among psychologists that social and cultural experiences play a central role in development of human learning. Two general studies (Hunt, 1961; Cattell, 1963) of the human capacities for cognition and learning make it clear that the human infant is born possessed of genes that fix very broad limits for the possible development of the learning capacity and also that humans are not genetically equipped in any way that ensures that such potential will be realized automatically. Hunt has also presented evidence against the assumption that there is a genetically predetermined learning capacity development, that is, against the idea that the capacity to learn unfolds automatically as body and nervous system structures mature. Hunt therefore believes that *what* and *how* infants and children learn at particular times in their physical maturation

become crucial to understanding the future development of their learning capacity.

However, studies of human capacities have usually been confined to Western European cultures. Some studies, using what are assumed to be "culture-fair" (or "culture-free") methods, have been made of psychomotor, cognitive, and learning capacities in a few non-Western cultures or on small groups of individuals from non-Western cultures. Despite the fact that psychometric methodologists have assumed that a culture-fair test can be developed, the observations of Sarason and Gladwin (1958:142) still hold, that is, at present no tests exist to transculturally measure human capacities. It is reasonable to say that, while several capacities are part of the biological equipment of the newborn human, little is known concerning the human range of capacities, as compared to specific knowledge of the capacities found expressed in Western European and American culture.

A random distribution. There is no present evidence of any basic neurophysiological structural or functional difference between human populations with respect to any capacities. There is ample evidence for the fact of individual variations within the broad range of the basic structure and functions of human neurophysiology. And the evidences note that such variations are randomly distributed in the entire human population. The neurosurgeon has no problems in performing his special surgical techniques in different human populations, whether they are American, Dobuan (a Melanesian island people), Ituri (a Congo forest pygmy people), or Tiwi (an Australian aborigine people). However, the neurosurgeon knows and expects that individual Americans, Dobuans, Ituri, or Tiwi may well have slight differences of the structural and functional aspects of neurophysiology.

A similar randomness of variation within a very broad range appears to apply equally to human capacities. Thus far, no scientific study has provided convincing proofs for fundamental variations (the presence in some, the absence in others) among human populations in motor, cognitive, and learning capacities. However, there is a substantial body of folk culture "truths" in the United States, with counterparts in most other cultures about the world, that impute to other populations a different, and usually much smaller capacity for motor, cognitive, or learning activities.

■ Conclusions

There is a basic paradox in the fact that, although human culture can easily be demonstrated to persist beyond the life-span of any one person, without the human individual there is no identifiable place, or *locus*, in nature for this phenomenon. Pareto (1935), in a theory of "challenge-and-response," White (1959), in a theory of "culturology," and Kroeber (1952), in a theory of the "superorganic," have sought to transcend this paradox through treating the concepts of culture and society as being generally unrelated to the acts or concerns of individuals. These theories are *reifications* and *anthropomorphizations* of the logical abstraction of culture, that is, this concept is treated as though it is possessed of the powers of living beings, with human-like abilities to feel, think, move, and so on.

It seems clear that the fundamental place of culture in the natural world is in the *cultural* behavior of the individual. If this is so, then the key scientific questions become, "How does an individual human being acquire behavior forms which are cultural?" "Are these forms transmitted through the germ plasm of the human population?" "If cultural behavior forms are not transmitted genetically, then how does an individual acquire them?"

These are among some of the principal questions in the area of the study of the nature of the socialization process. In Chapter Five evidence is examined which clearly indicates that human cultural behavior forms are acquired in a socialization process and do not automatically appear in the human individual, as would be expected if these forms were genetically transmitted as species-characteristic behavior forms. This chapter has been concerned with assisting in gaining an understanding that there are specific features of human biology which serve as the points of transition between human biology and cultural behavior. The answer to the question, "If cultural behavior forms are not transmitted geneti-

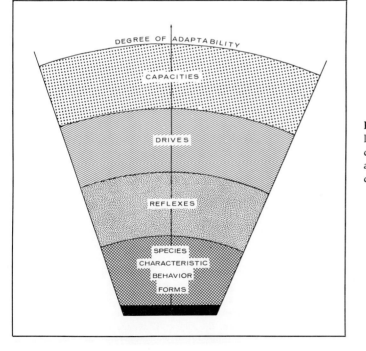

Fig. 5. Relationship between increasing levels of behavior organization and the degree of adaptability in species-characteristic behavior forms, reflexes, drives and capacities.

cally, then how does an individual acquire them?" must begin with specification of those aspects of human biology such as species-characteristic behavior, reflexes, drives, and capacities, that are amenable to modification through experience in a socialization process and therefore can serve as the organic bridgeheads between the phenomena of human biology and culture.

Thus it is clear that any discussion of the cultural transmission process must proceed from a basis of knowledge concerning the several types of organic bridgeheads to socialization. It is likely that, despite our present limited knowledge of these links between culture and biology, significant advances in specific understanding of the ways they are interrelated will come through basic research on the manner these organic bridgeheads are modified, accentuated, and perhaps limited in a socialization process.

▪ Summary

A human infant is born possessed of at least four interrelated classes of biological equipment that can serve as organic bridgeheads in socialization: (1) *species-characteristic behavior,* (2) *reflexes,* (3) *drives,* and (4) *capacities.* The preceding pages have described these organic bridgeheads and have noted some of the conceptual differences and problems involved in discussions of these phenomena. It should be remembered that each of these classes is interrelated with the others in very complex ways, most of which are not yet understood or even fully identified, and that each is an evolutionary product. The point of this chapter has been that culture, man's natural ecology, begins to affect the activities of the human organism through the specific biological features (species-characteristic behavior, reflexes, drives, capacities) possessed by the human infant. Most important is the fact that each of these aspects of human biology is, in varying degree, amenable to modification through cultural experience.

REFERENCES CITED AND SUGGESTED READINGS

Arnold, W. (ed.) 1968. *Nebraska Symposium on Motivation.* Lincoln: University of Nebraska Press.

Aronoff, J. 1967. *Psychological Needs and Cultural Systems.* Princeton, N. J.: Van Nostrand.

Bell, R. Q. 1965. "Developmental Psychology." In P. R. Farnsworth and others (eds.), *Annual Review of Psychology,* Vol. 16. Palo Alto, Calif.: Annual Reviews, Inc., pp. 1-38.

Bettelheim. B. 1967. *The Empty Fortress.* New York: Free Press.

Bindra, D. 1959. *Motivation: A Systematic Reinterpretation.* New York: Ronald.

Bloom, B. 1964. *Stability and Change in Human Characteristics.* New York: Wiley.

Boas, F. 1911. *Changes in Bodily Form of Descendants of Immigrants.* Washington, D. C.: Government Printing Office.

————. 1940. *Race, Language and Culture.* New York: Macmillan.

Cattell, R. B. 1960. "The Multiple Abstract Variance Analysis Equations and Solutions: For Nature-Nurture Research on Continuous Variables," Psychological Review 67:353-372.

————. 1963. "Theory of Fluid and Crystallized Intelligence: A Critical Experiment," Journal of Educational Psychology 54:1-22.

Chusid, J. G., and J. J. McDonald. 1964. *Correlative Neuroanatomy and Functional Neurology,* ed. 12, Los Altos: Lange.

Cofer, C. N., and M. H. Appley. 1964. *Motivation: Theory and Research.* New York: Wiley.

Cohen, Y. A. 1964. *The Transition from Childhood to Adolescence.* Chicago: Aldine.

Dethier, V. G., and E. Stellar. 1961. *Animal Behavior.* Englewood Cliffs, N. J.: Prentice-Hall.

Douglas, R. 1967. "The Hippocampus and Behavior," Psychological Bulletin 67:416-442.

DuBois, P. H. 1960. "Individual Differences." In P. R. Farnsworth and others (eds.), *Annual Review of Psychology,* Vol. 11. Palo Alto, Calif.: Annual Reviews, Inc., pp. 225-254.

Eibl-Eibesfeldt, I. 1970. *Ethology: The Biology of Behavior.* New York: Holt, Rinehart and Winston.

Ferguson, G. A. 1965. "Human Abilities." In P. R. Farnsworth and others (eds.), *Annual Review of Psychology,* Vol. 16. Palo Alto, Calif.: Annual Reviews, Inc., pp. 39-62.

Frank, L. K. 1938. "Cultural Control and Physiological Autonomy," American Journal of Orthopsychiatry 8:622-626.

Fraenkel, G., and D. Gunn. 1961. *The Orientation of Animals.* New York; Dover.

Freud, S. 1933. *New Introductory Lectures on Psychoanalysis.* New York: Norton.

————. 1940. *An Outline of Psychoanalysis.* London: Hogarth.

Frisch, K. von. 1953. *The Dancing Bees.* London: Methuen.

Gellhorn, E. 1967. *Principles of Autonomic-Somatic Integrations.* Minneapolis: University of Minnesota Press.

Guttman, R., and L. Guttman. 1963. "Cross-Cultural Stability of an Intercorrelation Pattern of Abilities:

A Possible Test for Biological Basis," Human Biology 35:53-60.

Hall, J. F. 1961. *Psychology of Motivation*. Philadelphia: Lippincott.

Hersher, L., J. B. Richmond, and A. U. Moore. 1963. "Modifiability of the Critical Period for the Development of Maternal Behavior in Sheep and Goats," Behaviour 20:311-320.

Hinde, R. A. 1955. "The Modifiability of Instinctive Behaviour," Advancement of Science 12:19-24.

_____1960. "Energy Models of Motivation," Models and Analogues in Biology, No. XIV, pp. 199-213.

_____. 1963. "Some Recent Trends in Ethology." In S. Koch (ed.), *Psychology: A Study of Science*, Vol. II. New York: McGraw-Hill, pp. 561-610.

Hinde, R. A., and N. Tinbergen. 1958. "The Comparative Study of Species-Specific Behavior." In A. Roe and G. G. Simpson (eds.), *Behavior and Evolution*. New Haven: Yale University Press, pp. 251-268.

Hunt, J. McV. 1960. "Experience and the Development of Motivation: Some Reinterpretations," Child Development 31:489-504.

_____. 1961. *Intelligence and Experience*. New York: Ronald.

Jones, M. R. (ed.), 1963. *Nebraska Symposium on Motivation*. Lincoln: University of Nebraska.

Klopfer, P. H., and J. R. Hailman. 1967. *An Introduction to Animal Behavior: Ethology's First Century*. Englewood Cliffs, N. J.: Prentice-Hall.

Kroeber, A. L. 1952. "The Superorganic." In A. L. Kroeber (ed.), *The Nature of Culture*. Chicago: University of Chicago Press, pp. 22-51.

LaBarre, W. 1954. *The Human Animal*. Chicago: University of Chicago Press.

Lévi-Strauss, C. 1949. *Les Structures élémentaires de la parenté*. Paris: Presses Universitaires de France.

_____. 1956. *Tristes Tropiques*. Paris: Librairie Plon. (*A World on the Wane*. London: Hutchinson, 1961.)

_____. 1958. *Anthropologie Structurale*. Paris: Librairie Plon. (*Structural Anthropology*. New York: Basic Books, 1963.)

_____. 1962a. *LaPensée Sauvage*. Paris: Librairie Plon. (*The Savage Mind*. Chicago: University of Chicago Press, 1966.)

_____. 1962b. *Le Totémisme Aujourd'hui*. Paris: Presses Universitaires de France. (*Totemism*. Boston: Beacon, 1963.)

Lorenz, K. 1952. *King Solomon's Ring*. New York: Crowell.

_____. 1965. *Evolution and the Modification of Behavior*. Chicago: University of Chicago Press.

Maddi, S. 1968. *Personality Theories*. Homewood, Ill.: Dorsey.

Maier, N. R. F., and T. C. Schneirla. 1935. *Principles of Animal Psychology*. New York: McGraw-Hill.

Marler, P., and W. Hamilton. 1966. *Mechanisms of Animal Behavior*. New York: Wiley.

Maslow, A. 1954. *Motivation and Personality*. New York: Harper and Row.

_____. 1962. *Toward a Psychology of Being*. Princeton, N. J.: Van Nostrand.

McClelland, D., E. Atkinson, R. Clark, and E. Lowell. 1953. *The Achievement Motive*. New York: Appleton-Century-Crofts.

McDougall, W. 1923. *An Outline of Psychology*. New York: Methuen.

Mead, M. 1942. "Anthropological Data on the Problem of Instinct." In *Psychosomatic Medicine*, Vol. 4. Baltimore: The Williams & Wilkins Co., pp. 396-397.

Montagu, M. F. A. 1960. *An Introduction to Physical Anthropology*, ed. 3. Springfield, Ill.: Charles C Thomas.

Nissen, H. W. 1953. "Instinct as Seen by a Psychologist," Psychological Review 60:291-294.

Pareto, V. 1935. *General Treatise on Sociology (The Mind and Society)*. New York: Harcourt.

Peters, R. S. 1958. *The Concept of Motivation*. London: Routledge and Paul.

Rapaport, D. 1958. "The Theory of Ego Autonomy: A Generalization," Bulletin of the Meninger Clinic 22:13-35.

Sarason, S. B., and T. Gladwin. 1958. "Psychological and Cultural Problems in Mental Subnormality: A Review of Research," Genetic Psychology Monographs 57:3-290.

Scott, J. P. 1958. *Animal Behavior*. Chicago: University of Chicago Press.

Spitz, R. 1946. "Anaclitic Depression," Psychoanalytic Study of the Child 2:313-342.

Stellar, E. 1954. "The Physiology of Motivation," Psychological Review 61:5-22.

Stone, C. P. (ed.) 1951. *Comparative Psychology*, Englewood Cliffs, N. J.: Prentice-Hall.

Stevenson, H. W., E. H. Hess, and H. L. Rheingold. 1967. *Early Behavior: Comparative and Developmental Approaches*. New York: Wiley.

Thorpe, W. H. 1956. *Learning and Instinct in Animals*. Cambridge: Harvard University Press. (See also Methuen, 1956.)

Thorpe, W. H., and O. L. Zangwill (eds.) 1961. *Current Problems in Animal Behavior*. Cambridge: Cambridge University Press.

Tinbergen, N. 1951. *The Study of Instinct*. Oxford: Oxford University Press.

White, L. 1959. *The Evolution of Culture*. New York: McGraw-Hill.

White, R. W. 1959. "Motivation Reconsidered: The Concept of Competence," Psychological Review 66:297-333.

Young, P. T. 1961. *Motivation and Emotion*. New York: Wiley.

THREE  MODELS OF LEARNING AND THE PROCESS OF SOCIALIZATION

This chapter provides a brief review of two major theoretical models of learning used in socialization studies: (1) *Thorndike-Hull behaviorism* and (2) *Freudian personal character processes*.[1] These models of learning are contrasted with case study data of the process of enculturation among the Papago, a native North American Indian society. It becomes apparent from this comparison of the theoretical models of learning with data of enculturation in a non-Western culture that perhaps too little attention has been given in formulation of learning models to the role of symbolic and reflective learning in socialization. Honigmann (1954: 430-431) proposed this when he noted that formal learning theory, with its emphasis on reward and punishment, helps us to understand how some patterns of cultural behavior become established but is not adequate to explain all patterning of personal character, and that attention must be devoted not only to *what* is transmitted in the learning process but also to *how* that transmission takes place. Hallowell (1953: 610) also makes a similar observation when he points out that the learning process has been conceptualized too simply in the past since we now know that to say that the individual acquires culture through learning in a socialization process is only a confession of ignorance as to what this process actually involves.

Thorndike-Hull behaviorism

The most elaborate and precisely formalized model of learning used in studies of human behavior is found in the efforts of Hull to integrate the "conditioned response" learning formulations of Pavlov with the concept of "learning through reinforcement" from the studies of Thorndike. This model of learning consists of a set of generalizations derived largely from observations of behavior of infrahuman organisms (rats, cats, monkeys) subjected to experimental conditions.[2] This model is usually termed *behavioristic,* since it is based on data obtained from measurements of the visible behavior of organisms and is not generally concerned with certain sense events (such as thinking, feeling, and desiring) occurring within an organism.

Behaviorists postulate that all action by any organism, including man, is an effort to satisfy physiological needs. Furthermore, a corollary of

---

[1] The concept of learning has been defined by Hilgard (1956: 3) as the process by which an activity originates or is changed through reacting to an encountered situation, provided that the characteristics of the change in activity cannot be explained on the basis of native response tendencies, maturation, or temporary states of the organism (*e.g.,* fatigue, drugs, etc.).

[2] As the literature of learning research will demonstrate (Hilgard, 1956; Deese, 1952; Spence, 1951a, 1951b; McGeoch and Irion, 1952; Estes and others, 1954; Mowrer, 1954), there are a number of learning theories. These are generally classed as: (1) *stimulus-response reinforcement theories,* as in the work of Pavlov (1927, 1928), Thorndike (1911, 1932, 1933, 1935), or Hull (1942, 1943, 1950, 1951, 1952); (2) *stimulus-response contiguity theories,* as set forth by Guthrie (1935, 1952); (3) *dual theories of learning,* as represented by the works of Skinner (1938, 1953) and Mowrer (1950); (4) *cognitive, "sign," or holistic learning theory,* as represented in the works of Tolman (1932, 1951), Stern (1938), G. W. Allport (1937), Angyal (1941), and Leeper (1951); (5) *classic gestalt theory,* as in the works of Wertheimer (1923, 1925), Koffka (1924), and Köhler (1925); (6) *field learning theory,* as found in the works of Lewin (1935, 1936) and his students; and (7) *functional learning theory,* as represented in the works of Woodworth (1918, 1929). The present discussion is concerned with details of the stimulus-response reinforcement model of learning since it has greatly influenced research in studies of socialization.

this postulate proposes that physiological needs are the source of all other needs of an organism, including any social or cultural needs. In whatever form it is used, behaviorism holds the concept of learning of central importance in understanding the activity of an organism. Learning is conceived by behaviorists as a process whereby drives are met, or supplemented, by adaptive action, which enables an organism to act relevantly to its physiological requirements.[3]

Thorndike and learning concepts. Fundamental for an understanding of the behavioristic learning model are two concepts first formulated from experimental studies by E. L. Thorndike and later revised and elaborated by Clark Hull. These are the concepts of (1) *trial and error* and (2) *reward and punishment.* Thorndike noted in his observations of the behavior of cats, chickens, and monkeys that, in the course of numerous encounters with its environment, an organism will tend to show increasing modification of behavior and an increase in skill of movement, as a consequence of an apparent elimination of "wrong moves" and a consolidation of "correct moves." Thorndike concluded from his experimental studies that the general trend of behavior in all animals is to more efficient satisfaction of innate needs. To account for later experimental evidences, which indicated that *rewards* (such as food or water) or *punishments* (such as electric shock or other noxious stimulation) administered to an organism had a specific effect on behavior directly preceding the administration of rewards or punishments, Thorndike formulated the *principle of reinforcement,* or as it is currently designated, the *law of effect.*[4] This principle asserted that the response of an organism to a stimulus is automatically strengthened if it is followed by a reward. Conversely, the response of an organism to a stimulus is automatically extinguished if followed by punishment. To Thorndike, the administration of rewards and punishments to an organism, as it went about seeking to reduce its physiological needs, was a satisfactory means

of explaining the behavior of all organisms, including man.

Hull and learning concepts. Thorndike's concepts of learning were subjected to a number of revisions and extensions from 1925 to 1945. The most widely used revision is Hull's formulation of the postulates of *stimulus-response reinforcement* learning.[5] Hull's theory of learning evolved from his efforts to synthesize Thorndike's conception of the law of effect and Pavlov's postulates of conditioned learning. Pavlov and Thorndike both had formulated their initial conceptions of learning by the early 1900's. Although these were similar in several ways, they differed profoundly in one respect. Pavlov's "conditioned reflexes" were preparatory movements (salivation) by an organism directed at particular goals (eating). Such movements were not held by Pavlov to be *instrumental* in attaining a goal. In contrast, Thorndike's law of effect attempted to explain *goal-directed* or *instrumental behavior.* Thorndike's experimental subjects had to undertake movements to enable them to attain food by escape from confinement. Thorndike assumed that rewarded movements (escape for attainment of food) became a lasting part of the sensory-motor systems of an animal because of physiological satisfactions achieved as a consequence of movements to a goal.

Hull formulated a theory of learning that combined Thorndike's principle of instrumental learning with Pavlov's neurophysiologically based concept of conditioned learning. To accomplish this end, Hull assumed that in all organisms, including man, there exists an innate sensory-motor network of such a nature that any stimulus (such as food) that would begin agitation in the sense organs would be transmitted automatically as an electrical-chemical impulse via the nervous system to the muscles, thus bringing about motor activity leading to direct movement of an animal toward the source of stimulus. When a second stimulus occurred with the first (for example, a ringing bell and food) the second

---

[3]Asch (1952: 12-13) has given a concise review of behavioristic premises.
[4]For a discussion and a detailed critique of the law of effect, see Postman (1947) and Meehl (1950).

[5]For detailed evaluations and reference to the range of Hull's research, see Spence (1952), Koch (1954), and Hilgard (1956). For critiques of Hull's ideas, see Leeper (1944, 1952), Skinner (1950), and Seward (1954).

stimulus could, if presented often enough, set off motor patterns derived from lasting and remaining traces of the first stimulus, although the first stimulus was absent. Hull further assumed that, once an organism regularly responded to the second stimulus, the reintroduction of the first stimulus could be said to act as a *reinforcement* of the *conditioned* (or second) stimulus. Thus Hull's model of learning rests on conditions established by the research of Thorndike and Pavlov attempting to explain the manner by which organisms acquired habitual ways of behavior.

However, to provide further explanation of instrumental uses of acquired habits in the behavior of organisms, Hull turned to the concept of *need,* which he later elaborated to the more inclusive concept of *drive.* Hull identified conditions of need as identical with the basic somatic processes of hunger, thirst, sleep, and so on. He noted that unsatisfied needs in an organism set up internal stimulations that had to be removed through motor activity. Thus *a state of need* was viewed by Hull as a condition of somatic tension, or disequilibrium, that ultimately had to be reduced through motor activity for survival of the organism. In his experimental research, Hull attempted to demonstrate that the specific effect of internal tension caused by somatic need was to motivate, or "drive," the organism to random trial and error efforts. When the organism behaved in such a way as to reduce or eliminate a need driving it to action, the relationship between the stimulus situation (somatic needs) and the response actions (trial and error behavior) was supposed by Hull to be automatically strengthened and subsequently retained as a basic pattern of behavior. Hull further held that, in other situations of a similar nature at a later time, an organism would respond to its somatic needs in a form consistent with initial reductions of the drive to behavior, particularly if on subsequent occasions the need was reduced in a more useful manner. Hull believed that through the duplication of sequences of primary reinforcement an organism would learn to reduce its drives by behaving in habitual ways.

According to Hull, then, learning is the association and reinforcement of any number of

stimulus-response connections stemming from the reduction of basic body needs. Thus Hull's revision of Thorndike's ideas, through the joining of Pavlov's concept of the conditioned reflex with the construct of need, or drive, reduction led to a model of learning based on the assumption that the sources of energy for learning in all organisms are found in and derived from somatic or body needs. Under the laws of this model, primary body tensions are designated as having the capacity to impel an organism to behavior. All modification of behavior, or learning, is derived from and is a function of innate needs.

The concept of secondary drives. In the course of his formulations of a stimulus-response reinforcement learning model, Hull gave attention to the question of "secondary drives," that is, drives that develop as a consequence of positive reinforcement of stimuli arising from the environment of the organism. In earlier formulations of his postulates of learning, Hull utilized the concept of drive to refer to either external or internal sources of stimulation of basic body processes.

In later statements Hull offered more precise, though brief, comments concerning drives derived from stimuli external to the organism. At the same time he considered the possibilities of reinforcement for such "secondary" drives. The revised concept of secondary drives may be illustrated by the example of "fear" as a secondary drive. The primary or innate somatic drive is an avoidance response to pain, which produces the basic drive stimulus. Neutral stimuli associated with the drive to avoid pain give rise to fear responses, similar in form to the responses of the organism to pain. The consequences of the associated, or learned, responses subsequently produce a drive stimulus that serves as a "secondary drive." Thus an otherwise neutral stimulus may, under given conditions, become a secondary drive for an organism, if such stimuli are associated with diminution of a primary drive response.

The concept of acquired drives. The general postulates of the Thorndike-Hull learning model have been used as a basis for several efforts to systematically analyze human social and cultural behavior. Perhaps the most influential generalization of the Thorndike-Hull learning model to studies of human behavior is found in the work of Miller and Dollard. Proceeding generally from Hull's synthesis of the learning formulations of Thorndike and Pavlov, and specifically from Hull's concept of secondary drives, Miller and Dollard advanced the concept of *acquired drives* as an explanation for motivations to instrumental behavior that develop as a direct consequence of positive reinforcements of stimuli derived from the social and cultural environments of the human organism.

In seeking to apply the concept of secondary drive to human behavior, Miller and Dollard began by modifying Hull's earlier drive-reduction assumption to a form that has been termed *drive-stimulus reduction learning.* According to this theory, drives arising as a consequence of behavior through which an organism seeks to reduce the effects of stimulation are held to be identical to basic or innate drives that impel attempts to escape injurious stimuli. Thus the theoretical basis for learning was expanded by Miller and Dollard to incorporate all sources of stimulation from the human social and cultural environment. In attempting to generalize the concept of *acquired drives* to human social and cultural learning and behavior, Miller and Dollard proposed a hierarchy of drives, commencing with Hull's primary, or innate, drives, then proceeding to a series of *learnable drives* (such as fear, gregariousness, social conformity, prestige seeking, desire for money, and imitativeness) and then subsequently to *higher mental processes.* Choosing *imitation* as an example for their detailed study of the nature of acquired drives, Miller and Dollard note that imitative behavior is essential to survival of any society through production of joint, or group, action and in maintaining social conformity and discipline.

Influence of Thorndike-Hull learning concepts. The principles of learning that form the body of Thorndike-Hull behaviorism, and the Miller-Dollard extension of this model, have now been widely diffused to all areas of scholarship concerned with scientific studies of human behavior. The impact of this conception of learn-

ing on the social sciences has been profound. The basic formulations of the Thorndike-Hull model of learning were widely accepted by anthropologists and sociologists because these ideas offered a basis for a denial of the prevailing doctrine of instinct.

■ **Freudian personal character processes**

A number of attempts have been made to extract a theory of learning from the writings of Sigmund Freud.[6] This has not been an easy task, for the human problems Freud dealt with were not those that most concerned behavioristic learning theorists. However, the consensus of those who have attempted to find a general learning theory in Freud's work appears to be that, while the propositions of classic psychoanalysis are complex and so diffusely stated that it is difficult to subject them to empirical test, learning concepts and a form of learning theory exist in the totality of Freud's works. Perhaps the most formidable difficulty in dealing with Freudian learning concepts lies in the changes by Freud in his statements of theory over half a century.

Despite these problems in analysis of Freudian learning theory, there are several major parallels between Freudian theory and learning formulations by behavioristic theorists. There are three psychoanalytic principles similar in form to Thorndike-Hull behavioristic learning concepts: (1) the *pleasure principle,* (2) the *reality principle,* and (3) the *principle of repetition-compulsion.*

Freud's statements concerning the seeking by humans of pleasurable experiences and avoiding painful stimuli appear to correspond to the Thorndike-Hull formulations of the *law of effect.* The common ground between these ideas is the assumption of genetically transmitted need states leading to somatic disequilibrium with a consequent requirement of lowering of such tensions

---

[6]For detailed discussion of Freud's views and their uses in studies of human behavior, see Anna Freud (1936), Hall (1954), Hall and Lindzey (1957), and Munroe (1955). No attempt is made here to deal with the writings of those scholars called by Hall and Lindzey (1957: 143) "major revisionists" in psychoanalytic theory. Freud's statements concerning learning are far more elaborate than any offered by writers seeking to modify his ideas.

for survival of the organism.[7] There is little doubt that these particular conceptions of Freud and Thorndike-Hull behaviorists are derived from the same assumption concerning man's innate drives to reduce pain and increase pleasure.

As formulated by Freud, the *reality principle* holds that, rather than seeking immediate pleasure, humans will try to identify and eliminate, through a series of random moves, those stimuli that potentially bring pain. This concept is similar to the *trial and error* learning formulations of the Thorndike-Hull behavioristic learning theory. Too, the Freudian conception of *repetition-compulsion* corresponds to Thorndike-Hull behavioristic learning formulations concerning acts that do not "extinguish" under repeated negative reinforcement, that is, acts once learned that are unusually resistant to extinction by adverse stimuli.

In addition to these parallels, other topics in Freud's writings bearing on learning have been explored by learning theorists. These have been derived from Freud's concerns with the origin, development, and operation of individual personality. In the instances of the specific Freudian studies of *anxiety, aggression, repression, forgetting,* and *recall,* the interests of learning theorists in Freudian ideas have centered on those aspects of personality clearly within behavioristic conceptions of innate need or drive states.

However, learning theorists have generally ignored those aspects of Freud's work pertaining to personality development and functioning that cannot be related directly to behavioristic assumptions or experimentally based conceptions of the nature and operation of basic drives. For the most part, Thorndike-Hull behavioristic learning theory has been concerned primarily with synchronic aspects of behavior, that is, with those *present* behavior forms and their properties whose nature could be circumscribed precisely in a limited time, under experimental conditions. The synchronic orientation of Thorndike-Hull behavioristic learning research resulted in in-

attention to the broad areas of Freudian ideas. Freud's writings give substantial evidence of his concern with the historical, or diachronic, continuities in individual personality and contain two learning concepts that appear central to his general theory of human behavior. These concepts are *identification* and *introjection.*

In an early work Freud (1910) refers to his theory of personality as "a dynamic conception which reduces mental life to the interplay of reciprocally urging and checking forces." Terming these forces *cathexes,* Freud used the concept in subsequent writings as denoting the investment of a charge of psychic energy in objects external to the organism *(object cathexes)* or in the self *(ego cathexes).* He held that at birth the human organism was possessed of only a primitive psychological structure, operated by a limited amount of psychic energy generated by inherited body needs and seen in individual behavior as *instincts* seeking gratification. Freud supposed that initially all individual psychic energy is dissipated in random, gross motor activity. Later, as the human organism matured biologically, physical, social, and cultural environmental circumstances caused the primitive psychological structure to undergo a series of specific modifications through transformation of the basic psychic energy into purely psychological processes such as perception, memory, ideas, and feeling. Thus as the human organism, with specific inherited body need states, comes into more direct and continuous contact with objects and events in its surroundings and begins to be aware of itself, it begins to transform body need energy into instinctual, or psychological, energy, by means of which it is able to deal, through time, with objects or events by *cathecting* (or perceiving and retaining) their qualities in the form of memories, ideas, and feelings. As the human organism becomes more mature and experiences added contacts with various parts of its environment, greater amounts of body energy flow into and make up complex and intimately interrelated perceptual, mnemonic and ideation systems, which then form the basic personality structure.

Cathexes, identification, and incorporation. Freud's earliest and best known statements con-

---

[7]For Freud, instincts seeking gratifications lead to states of body tension that must be lowered. In the Thorndike-Hull model, drives arising from innate states lead to consummatory responses by the organism.

cerning the genesis, development, and functioning of personality stated that permanent traits of character, however complex their appearance, were simply perpetuations of inherited basic body needs. Later, as he modified his theory of personality, Freud set forth the notion that individual personal character is developed equally from inherited body needs and cathexes, as the mechanisms through which specific social and cultural forms and their symbols are *incorporated* into the organism. He believed that through incorporation specific *identifications* are made with parental and other authority figures and their symbols.

Freud conceived *identification* as the general transformation of a cathexis for the perception (or memory) of an object or event into a cathexis for a perception of the self. *Incorporation* similarly represents a general change in cathexis from a psychological content with an outer referent to a psychological content with a self, or inner referent. Thus, through cathexes, the world of the objective and external becomes transformed into properties of the individual self.

Freud published several accounts of the structuring of individual personal character through the transformation of body need energy into psychological processes, and the operation of these processes through the mechanisms of identification and incorporation. His final formulations of personality theory identified the primary divisions, or portions, of personal character by the designations of the *id, ego,* and *superego.* For Freud, the mechanisms of identification and incorporation were of particular importance in the inception, development, and operation of the superego. Freud believed the superego was the last and the most vital of the provinces of personality to be formed. While identification and incorporation were also said to be operative in the origin and operation of the id and ego, Freud believed these processes to be the basic means by which the superego is developed and maintained through the life span of its individual.

Freud postulated that the superego originates in early childhood through substitution of identifications with parents for earlier, conflicting feelings of hate and love created by parental denials of satisfaction of the child's basic body needs. Thus the superego is formed from both early and subsequent cathexes of parents and parental behavior. Such cathexes, once incorporated into the existing character structure and forming the superego, become the prototypes for the child's subsequent social relationships with other persons, especially those in positions of authority and those representing the moral and ethical codes of a society. Freud noted that the formation and operation of the superego, by means of cathexes and their transformations, particularly are related to the special qualities of parents and their surrogates as punishing and rewarding agents. These introjected parental qualities serve, said Freud, as the basis for the two major divisions of the functioning superego, the conscience and the ego-ideal. Punishing qualities of parents and their surrogates become cathected into that aspect of superego Freud terms the *conscience,* while rewarding qualities are cathected into that aspect of the superego called the *ego-ideal.* Freud held the ego-ideal to be the mechanism that sets standards of personal ethical conduct, as these standards were directly incorporated from the parents and their surrogates. Conscience was viewed by Freud as a mechanism acting in the role of a personal censor or judge, setting specific punishments for the self for violation of ego-ideal standards.

Freud felt that most rewarding and punishing identifications which were incorporated into the self, in the formation and subsequent operation of the superego, were primarily in the form of direct parental commands, threats, accusations, or specific exhortations and encouragements. He noted, however, that the severity, or strength, of superego is determined not by the severity of parental treatment of the child but by the strength of the cathexes for parents and parent-surrogates that are subsequently transformed into cathexes for the child's self. Thus the innate reservoir of body energy for cathectic processes is seen by Freud as being of more fundamental importance than actual parental behavior in the socialization process. In general, Freud felt that parents follow their own superego dictates in rearing children. Thus the child's superego is not, according to

Freud's ideas, a direct consequence of parental behavior, but rather is a precipitate, first of the child's cathectic energies, and then of the parental superego structure. According to Freud, the superego of each member of a human generation represents the accumulated influences of the social behavior of past generations on the present social behavior of the individual as these influences are mediated by the biologically inherited energies available for the processes of cathecting social and cultural objects or events.

In review, Freud held that a child learns the social and cultural traditions of his group by cathectic processes of identification with parents and their surrogates and the incorporation of such identifications into the character structure, and particularly the *superego*. Parents and their surrogates, as agents of a social and cultural tradition, use specific rewards and punishments to lead children to acceptance of the demands of the society. As a consequence of such rewards and punishments, and through the processes of identification and incorporation, the superego aspect of character takes on the roles of external authority, forcing conformity of the self to group social traditions.

Influence of Freudian learning concepts. Freudian concepts of character formation and operation have had great influence on research in the social sciences. For instance, Kluckhohn (1944a: 590) in reviewing this influence has noted that American anthropology has seemed to find only in Freud's ideas the basis for a workable cultural psychology. Hallowell disagrees with Kluckhohn's opinions of the fundamental importance of Freud's propositions in anthropological research, particularly as it has been concerned with learning. In reviewing the uses of learning models and concepts used in anthropology, Hallowell (1954: 214-215) concluded that Thorndike-Hull behavioristic theory has furnished the major model for research. However, social science publications, particularly the literature of socialization and enculturation studies, tend to show that the Freudian model of learning has been used in the social sciences nearly as widely as the Thorndike-Hull behavioristic model.

■ Models of learning and understanding Papago enculturation

Attempts to employ the Thorndike-Hull or Freudian learning models have been largely unsuccessful in fully and adequately describing the ways children are encultured in different societies. One reason for this is the fact that children seem to "learn" culture in a variety of ways not generally accounted for in either the Thorndike-Hull behavioristic or Freudian personal character models of learning. The discussion that follows is a brief case study of the main features of enculturation among the Papago, a native North American Indian society. It is intended to emphasize the ways human symbolic and reflective capacities enter into and are an integral part of the socialization process. This discussion is not intended to deny the utility of the Thorndike-Hull and Freudian learning models in studies of cultural learning. It is intended to extend understanding of events in the socialization process.

The Papago now number about 15,000 persons. About 12,000 Papago live on three federal reservations in the vicinity of Tucson, Arizona. Most Papago occupy a 2.75 million acre reservation centered about 80 miles west of Tucson. This reservation is located in traditional Papago lands. The area is in a physiographic zone known as the *Sonoran Desert,* which is characterized by less than 5 inches of rain each year and daily temperatures that for 7 months of the year may rise over 100° F.

Most Papago on the reservations live by cattle ranching and farming; irrigation is provided by modern wells. Some 2,000 Papago work away from the reservations as laborers and technicians for large agricultural, mining, or industrial firms in or near Phoenix and Tucson. Before the Europeans arrived, Papago lived by hunting desert animals, gathering desert plants, and growing agricultural products such as beans and corn on farms irrigated by floodwaters coursing through the desert after heavy seasonal rains. The Papago were greatly feared by their neighbors about the fringes of the Sonoran Desert.

Before 1880, Europeans had only sporadic contacts with the main population of the Papago. Papagos remained generally unaffected by Euro-

Papago family (circa 1893). (Courtesy American Museum of Natural History.)

pean culture for nearly 200 years after the first Spanish missions were founded near and to the south of their desert homeland. This was because of the harsh desert environment, the warlike reputation of Papago, and their tendency to avoid regular contacts with strangers.

However, the Papago are a hospitable people, with a broad sense of humor. Papago are highly adaptable in unusual situations. The Papago have a continuous cultural heritage, which may reach back at least 10,000 years before the present. In that time they have met the challenges of a hostile environment and their contacts with alien cultures.

Papago tribal council chairman, Enos Francisco (left) and son. (T. R. Williams, 1953.)

Focal values in Papago enculturation. On the basis of studies of Papago culture, five functionally related focal values appear to impart characteristic uniqueness to Papago enculturation.[8] These are: (1) *children who cannot talk cannot understand;* (2) *children who cannot understand cannot be expected to exhibit appropriate social .behavior;* (3) *children will learn appropriate social behavior when* *ready and capable of doing so;* (4) *adult social behavior is the sole standard of conduct;* and (5) *children are desirable because they increase the status of parents as adults.* These five focal values are seen regularly in Papago life. They are significant in understanding Papago enculturation because of their direct relationship to choices of actual or potential action on the part of adults in elicitation of desired social behavior in the maturing child.

These focal values have been abstracted from two reciprocally related sets of behavioral data. The first data set is crucial in use of the concept of value in studies of enculturation. These data consist of statements by Papago concerning the worthwhileness of personal conduct and of cultural goals. Such statements of value, secured

---

[8]DuBois (1955) uses the concept of *focal value* as a means of denoting a second-level abstraction of value from observed social behavior. At the first, or *specific value,* level of abstraction are found statements of judgments of worthwhileness of behavior. Second, or *focal value,* level abstractions are statements synthesizing a series of first level values. In turn, third-level, or *basic postulate,* statements reflect abstractions from a series of focal value statements organized around third-level judgments of worthwhileness of behavior. For further discussion of these concepts, see Chapter Nine.

Papago boys, second grade, Sells, Arizona School. (T. R. Williams, 1953.)

by means of interviews and use of various tests, reveal many desirable and potential cultural goals, principles of Papago conceptualization and ideal order among possible behavior forms. However, they do not put Papago informants to the test of actual behavior, where they become responsible for making specific choices between ideal and actual cultural means and ends and where all the consequences of the making of a choice would be publicly visible.

The second set of data from which these five Papago focal values have been abstracted are termed *behavior kinds,* that is, ethnographic records of well-identified Papago adults behaving repeatedly in ways that can be counted and classified. Behavior kind data are comprised of descriptive accounts of people interacting socially in regular ways and of the objects they make and use in shaping their environment. Such behavioral data are assumed to reflect culturally standardized preferences, or judgments, concerning worthwhileness of particular behavior forms, as mediated through individual perceptions of social goals, ends, and so on. The five focal values listed here have been abstracted through the process of systematically relating the first set of data (ideas expressed by Papago adults about worthwhileness of behavior) to the second set of data (behavior kinds).

An added dimension of Papago value, which was not usually immediately available, was gained in following disparities noted to exist between the first and second sets of data. Thus some Papago statements of worthwhileness, on observation of behavior, were found to be justifications of the informant's actual course of action, which ran counter to prevailing judgments of worthwhileness made by most members of the society. On the other hand, some forms of behavior, assumed to be expressions of judgments about worthwhileness of action, were found to be false. This dimension of worthwhileness provided data concerning *behavior kinds* not judged appropriate by the community, yet of sufficient merit to be known, used, and transmitted by some adults seeking publicly to gain approval for their behavior, or to discredit the conduct of others when their own social actions appear to be beyond limits of worthwhile conduct.

The focal values presented here are useful in two ways in considering the question of how Papago children learn desired forms of behavior. In the first instance, the focal values comprise the essence of a Papago learning theory, with special reference to Papago ideas concerning the ways desired forms of behavior are best transmitted to children. In the second instance, the focal values provide for a form of analysis that allows, through use of concepts derived from behavioristic and psychoanalytic models of learning currently employed in socialization research (such as "reward and punishment"), examination of both data of Papago enculturation and the formal learning concepts and models.

The first two focal values appear to be guides in most enculturation activities by Papago adults from a child's birth through the fifth to seventh year. The third focal value is applied by adults generally in enculturation activities between the fifth to seventh through the twelfth to fourteenth year. After the fourteenth year a child is expected to conform to adult standards of social behavior.

Children are desired and welcomed in Papago society as important additions to the maintenance and functioning of the cultural system.

However, such valuation seems to be without consideration of any intrinsic, or innate, worth of a child as a person. There appears to be no general merit attached to childhood behavior independent of its specific approximation to adult behavior. The pronounced and pervasive worth of Papago adult behavior appears to imbue all Papago judgments concerning learning by children with a tone that has been mistaken by observers for "permissiveness." Papago adults, on initial observation, appear to have exaggerated respect for the behavior of their children. However, describing Papago enculturation behavior as permissive is misleading, since such a classification is based on a category of experience peculiar to European and American life. The idea of permissiveness assumes the intrinsic merit of a child as a basis for parental indulgence of behavior. Imposition on Papago behavior of this European and American cultural theme (see Chapter Nine), with its Western assumption concerning the basic nature of man, can lead to misinterpretation of the nature of Papago enculturation. Papago adults view enculturation with reference to five focal values whose sum is to give to parents and other adults a specific concern that a child eventually becomes an adult whose behavior conforms to adult standards. The specific course of a child's progress to an adult stage is generally of very little significance to most Papago adults, since it is assumed that children will in time behave as adults do.

In the initial period of a child's life, from birth through five to seven years, adults give little specific attention to the beginnings of child behavior that approximate adult behavior. Younger children are simply not expected to behave in ways that are adult. Thus, under the first focal value, Papago adults make no public observance of events in the initial period of a child's life. There are no ceremonies for physical maturation, such as first steps, the initial haircut, loss of teeth, and so on. Similarly, little public concern is exhibited by adults at the presence or absence of any type of first actions or social achievements by a child. This lack of concern is reflected also in the general absence of specific age-grading terms (such as "young baby"

Papago girls, second grade, Sells, Arizona School. (T. R. Williams, 1953.)

or "little child") for children in the first five to seven years of life and in special ritual actions by Papago adults that specifically align the child with his kin and the supernatural. A ceremony of formal social acceptance is thought unnecessary, since a child unable to talk and understand is believed by Papago adults not to comprehend the complex reciprocal rights and duties of Papago kinship. Alignment of a child with the supernatural is viewed by the Papago as necessary only for protection of adults. A child derives his protection from supernatural forces directly from his relationships with parents and ritual specialists, and only incidentally from the fact of participation in any special rituals. Children are present at most adult gatherings, including those of considerable religious or political significance. But unless a child is in grave danger

of physical harm, few efforts are made by adults to prevent behavior by children that disrupts or interferes with adult proceedings.

The first two focal values are also directly operative in enculturation of particular physiological systems (hunger, thirst, sexual, bowel, bladder) in the first five to seven years of a child's life. However, Papago children are cared for with little general reference to adult management of such physiological systems. Infants and young children are usually fed on demand. Unless a mother is pregnant, weaning is of incidental concern. No adult foods or ways of eating are forbidden to children. Bowel and bladder processes tend to be treated with few general concerns for control or signs of physiological autonomy. Little significance is attached to matters of personal cleanliness or grooming by children. Sexual behavior in young children is generally ignored. No attempts are made to lead young children to be independent of adults or peers in any behavior. For children under 5 to 7 years of age, physical independence, in terms of personal care of physiological systems, is a matter of very little concern to Papago adults.

This general enculturation process continues in the period from the fifth to seventh through the twelfth to fourteenth years. Among themselves, however, adults begin in this time to use the third focal value in commenting on behavior by a child not approximating adult standards. Few comments are made directly to children regarding failure or success in uses of adult behavior forms. Most Papago children, by their eighth to ninth year, have begun to exhibit knowledge and some uses of acceptable adult Papago behavior. In this age period, children assume some regular household duties. Although sporadic efforts toward such an assumption are made by children as young as 3 and 4 years, by the tenth year both boys and girls are making some contributions toward family economic activities. Such duties are not usually assigned; most children take up chores without seeking adult direction. No ritual observances are offered by adults in recognition of an older child's assumption of some adult tasks or to signal his uses of adult behavior forms in systems of control and appropriate releases of sex, aggression, dependence, cleanliness, modesty, and so on.

The age period of 14 to 16 years and on through the end of the teens is marked for a Papago by a very gradual display of increasingly more responsible adult tasks and the granting by adults of adult privileges. Papago adults say, "When a child does an adult's work, he is an adult." However, public recognition of increasing responsibility by children is minimal, with open note of attempts at more complex adult tasks being avoided by adults. A primary adult privilege, social seniority, is accorded to older children as they assume a proportionately larger share of responsible adult tasks and successfully approximate adult behavior standards in their activities. The privileges of seniority enable an older child, when addressed by adults, to speak as an adult on matters judged to be of concern to adults. While seniority is related directly to age in later life and particularly after the birth of a first child to a young married couple, among adolescents and young adults the privilege of being referred to as an adult by adults is related directly to greater assumption of adult responsibility and exhibition of expected forms of behavior.

■ Discussion of Papago enculturation

In application of the Thorndike-Hull and Freudian models to human learning, the concept of *reward* has come to denote two broad categories of behavior by adults with reference to children: (1) *material rewards* and (2) *verbal rewards*. Material reward has been given the meaning of a tangible remuneration as an incentive for repetition of approved forms of behavior by a child. Verbal reward generally denotes use of speech forms by adults to elicit desired behavior or to approve and encourage repetition of approved behavior. Following the concepts of the Thorndike-Hull model, Miller and Dollard noted that sometimes there is an intrinsic reward factor for a child in the circumstances of particular social situations. Thus unlimited freedom of social action at particular times may be viewed as a rewarding event. Extending the concepts of the Freudian model of learning, Ruesch and Kees have also suggested that action language, or movements used by adults to convey to children codifications of concepts, specific words, numbers, or objects, can serve also as statements of reward. Thus a child can ascertain approval of his behavior by adults through the nonverbal messages of approval conveyed in culturally standardized body postures, gaits, gestures, or movements.

The concept of punishment has similarly come to be extrapolated from the Thorndike-Hull and Freudian learning models to include several categories of behavior: (1) *physical punishment*, (2) *verbal punishment*, (3) *intrinsic situational punishment*, and (4) *action language punishment*. Physical punishment includes both blows and physical isolation. Verbal punishment includes all uses of speech sounds intended by adults to convey disapproval of behavior by the child. Thus verbal punishment may include punishment by direct disapproval of behavior, threats of physical punishment, punishment by direct denial of nurture of affiliation, punishment by threat, suggestion, or implications of denial of material recompense or special social privileges, punishment by threat of social isolation, punishment by ridicule or shame, punishment by fear, and punishment by verbal frustration (that is, to confuse issues by volume of words or use of meanings unknown to the child). Punishment through intrinsic situational factors is a category that has rarely been used in studies of learning in socialization. However, when children are confronted regularly with aspects of social situations that denote disapproval of some behavior forms, such confrontations imply chastisement for being a child. Thus, fulfillment of particular social roles may, for a child, involve a form of punishment for being a child. As a category of punishment, action language has come to include all of the threatening, menacing, abusive, and ominous gestures, body postures, or demeanors by the adults of a society with reference to child behavior.

Papago rewards and punishments. An analysis of Papago enculturation through use of the standard concepts of reward and punishment provides the following data. Papago adults very rarely give children tangible remunerations as incentives for repetition of desired behavior. Use of speech forms to elicit approved behavior is infrequent among the Papago. Praise is generally absent in the Papago enculturation process. Permission to behave is seldom given as approval for exhibition of action. Parents and parent-surrogates almost never strike or physically threaten children. Striking, slapping, pushing, or touching a child violates an adult pattern of a supernatural sanction for control of social behavior. Adults say that a mysterious illness and eventual death will befall any individual who touches another Papago in anger. Physical

activities are seldom restricted for children as a disapproval for behavior. It is uncommon for Papago children to be isolated for behavior. In the instance of one major restriction of action imposed on children, the limitations are those holding also for adults. Certain locations are known sources of physical danger at particular seasons. Thus in the summer season of heavy rains and flash floods, children and adults avoid the many drywash stream beds crisscrossing Papago country. Locations likely to contain harmful animals such as snakes and mountain lions are known and avoided by adults and children alike.

Verbal disapproval of behavior is uncommon among the Papago. Direct adult prohibitions or orders to children for social action are not heard often. Threats of physical violence, by blow or isolation, are uncommon. Disapproval of a child through denial by adults of their nurture or affection is rare. Direction revocation of social privilege or suggestion of denial of approval is uncommon. Threats of social isolation are rare. There is a paucity of disapproval of children by means of verbal frustration. Ridicule is used very sparsely, and then only in the sporadic instance of nonapproved behavior by an older child (14 years old or older) noticed by the general community. When an older child interrupts the conversation of adults or directly questions adult behavior or meanings, he may be rebuked by means of a teasing commentary, generally addressed to the onlookers, which draws an analogy between the behavior of a coyote and the child: "It is known that coyotes run about sticking long noses into the business of other people."

Techniques of producing in children a consciousness of personal shortcoming, impropriety of behavior, or personal disgrace are very seldom used by the Papago. Reproaches for child behavior that shame or lead to a sense of personal denigration are scarce. Disapproval through use of fearful personalized supernaturals is sporadic and generally confined to recounting adult fears in myth, legend, and folk stories. The fears expressed by adults are usually apprehensions common to most Papago and center upon particular events, objects, and animals. The darkness of late night,

Teenage Papago girls, Gu Achi, Arizona (T. R. Williams, 1956.)

blood from particular wild animals, the breath of dogs or wild animals, the screech of an owl, the night cry of the eagle or hawk, and glances at the full moon or at the midday sun are events that dismay all Papago. The sense of terror that may sometimes be imparted through stories regularly told to groups of children by adults is diffused to the entire gathering, rather than focused on the real or anticipated misdeeds of one child. Children are rarely purposely terrified or deliberately alarmed for a particular behavior.

In contrast, less frequently used theoretical categories of learning appear to provide for more detailed understanding of learning in Papago enculturation. The method of imparting states of emotion or meaning by culturally standardized action language is used by Papago adults to convey covert notice of child behavior. Thus, while adults take no open note of the behavior of younger children, they do appear to exhibit action language preferences for the behavior of older children and adolescents. Among themselves, adults are often amused at failures of younger children to succeed in tasks deemed a necessary part of Papago life. A clumsy use of eating utensils, awkward handling of work tools, or inappropriate performance of tasks may evoke humor that for the most part appears unnoticed by the younger child. However, by the ninth to eleventh years, most children have clearly noticed the action language forms of approval for completion of a difficult task, or for making repeated attempts to undertake work beyond their physical capacities or knowledge. The primary action language form seems to be a series of body postures used by adults to convey pride in the older child's efforts at approximation of adult standards of behavior. These postures are illustrated in the ways in which older children and adolescents will exaggerate action language postures of approval by adults for completion of difficult tasks. Boys mastering for the first time the difficult technique of staying aboard a bucking horse sometimes verbalize action language rewards by fathers and other male kin by saying, "I ride like a man," while simultaneously striking poses similar to those used by adult onlookers to impart approval through action language.

Papago action language forms of disapproval appear much more subtle than those used in expressing approval for exhibition of desired behavior. Action language disapproval is expressed by body postures that convey some note of particular behavior forms of older children and adolescents. Adults may move, stand, or sit in any one of a series of Papago culturally conventionalized positions of inattention while observing or listening to older children. Such adult body positions generally denote adult personal detachment and imply to older children and adolescents a nonapproval of their actions.

Some circumstances of social action that denote approval or disapproval of child behavior are also used by Papago adults as enculturating techniques. Most societies publicly laud appropriate social behavior exhibited by persons holding key social positions. The forms of commendation vary from awarding of a medal for bravery to general public approval as a "good person." This process also may be self-administered, that is, a person holding or anticipating a key social assignment commends himself by performing in a manner he knows is expected and approved by the community. For Papago children, approvals for expected behavior appear mostly self-administered. In behaving as if they occupied adult status, Papago children gain acceptance as they mature for their right to be assigned to the adult social positions.

Many situations of social action involving Papago adults and children possess intrinsic commendation factors through the implied desirability of adult status. Other intrinsic situational approvals are occasionally derived from adult social positions being ascribed to children because of reputations of their kin or the nature of economic, political, or religious behavior powers wielded by a child's parents or relatives. However, the most persistent Papago intrinsic situational rewards are found in the nearly unlimited freedom of social action permitted to children of all ages. Such freedom of action appears to permit a long-term repetition, or rehearsal, of approved adult behavior with a minimum of adult interference in a child's attempts at adult behavior forms. Most younger children, when not actually attempting adult tasks, spend much of their time playing at adult ways appropriate for adults of their sex. Approval of exhibition of behavior approximating that of adults appears self-administered when children play alone, as is common among four- to six-year-olds. In play groups that are common to ages 7 to 12 years, children assume a variety of adult roles, thereby creating situations of social action that in part duplicate intrinsic situational commendations for exhibition of desired adult behavior forms.

Many circumstances of Papago social behavior in which children participate regularly appear to imply disapproval of any behavior other than adult behavior. Papago adults make a variety of judgments of worthwhileness regarding forms of social deference. Among the Papago such deference is given to all seniors in age, usually regardless of the senior's sex, social or economic rank, or degree of kinship. A well-behaved younger person generally is humble, unobtrusive, and reserved in speech and action with a person senior by many years. These same personal characteristics usually mark the social relation-

Teenage Papago boys, Santa Rosa School, Gu Achi, Arizona. (T. R. Williams, 1956.)

ships of younger persons with those only a few years their senior. The pattern of deference permits the senior person to expect constant attention to his wishes in most situations. This pattern is rarely questioned by juniors. In addition, the powers and privileges of seniority are based on a belief which holds that a senior must consider fairly the interests and desires of his juniors. Seniors rarely impose hardships on juniors. Public ridicule and gossip are directed at the adult who abuses his seniority powers and privileges. However, in application of the pattern of deference to children, particularly younger children, adults follow the several focal values imparting structure to Papago enculturation. As a

consequence, the reciprocal obligations of a senior to a junior become greatly diluted, or are entirely absent, in social situations involving adults and younger children.

Adults generally do not expect deference from children and, although some deference is a part of the regular behavior of most children by 5 to 7 years of age, adults usually ignore exhibition of such forms. Young children are not supposed to command the reciprocal fairness exhibited by adult seniors to their adult juniors. Thus, in social interaction with adults, children are constantly confronted with reminders of their inability to be or act like adults. Although children do laud themselves for exhibition of adult behavior forms when alone or in their play groups, with adults there is no escape from the fact of being clearly excluded from the adult seniority behavior pattern. Most older children and adolescents are aware of their specific omission from deference reciprocity, for while they behave in accordance with expected forms of the seniority pattern, Papago adults clearly do not impart the usual adult meanings to such forms. This is most noticeable in situations in which children have fulfilled most or all expectations in deference to seniors, only to be totally ignored by adults.

As older children begin to regularly and successfully assume adult tasks and to behave in expected ways in most social situations, adults will accord them the reciprocal notice of adult senior-junior patterns of behavior. While being humble and unobtrusive, the older child is given to know, generally through action language, that he is accepted in the adult deference pattern. A Papago child may also be confronted with implied disapproval through judgments of his seniors concerning the valuations to be accorded

members of low rank household or kin lines, political factions, or religious behavior grouping. Papago adults are often concerned with some matters that involve open, long-term community discussion of behavior forms indulged in by members of such groups.

■ Conclusions

A comparison of these data of Papago enculturation with major models of learning commonly utilized in socialization studies leads to the conclusion that analysis of Papago enculturation through means of more commonly employed learning concepts of reward and punishment gives evidence that these concepts yield little information in answer to the question of *how* Papago children learn expected behavior. Conversely, analysis of data of Papago enculturation through concepts of learning much less frequently employed in studies of human learning of culture appears more productive of preliminary general statements with reference to the question of *how* Papago children learn to behave in acceptable ways.

Papago house constructed in traditional style, Gu Achi, Arizona. (T. R. Williams, 1953.)

It has been noted that both the Thorndike-Hull and Freudian models of learning place primary emphasis on, and proceed from, premises that assume the fundamental role of drives in all human learning and action. Hence concepts formulated under the assumptions of these models tend to stress the necessity of reduction of human learning to physiological bases and properties. It is important also to note that attempts to extend principles of these models to human learning have proceeded to a very different level of analysis, through acknowledging the existence of a basic human capacity for learning through *symbolic* and *reflective* processes. The discussions and research of Mowrer, G. W. Allport, Murray, Sears, Verplanck, and F. W. Allport, among many others, in extending to human learning the ideas of the Thorndike-Hull learning model, are quite similar to the discussions of Sullivan, Fromm, Horney, Kardiner, and Erikson, among others, in seeking to apply Freudian concepts to human learning. Generally, these writers have acknowledged human reflective and symbolic processes to be as fundamental in human learning as the somatic processes accentuated by Thorndike, Hull, and Freud.

Somatic, reflective, and symbolic processes in socialization. The distinction between somatic processes, variously called *drives, tensions, urges,* or *needs* (see Chapter Two), and *reflective* and *symbolic* processes is one that has not yet been given a satisfactory definition in contemporary behavioral science studies. However, there can be no doubt that drives as physiological processes and the human capacities for reflection and symbolism are all fundamentally biochemical in nature.

Reflectivity, as the capacity regularly to go beyond observed properties of particular objects or events, to draw, on the basis of past or present experiences, added inferences about unobserved properties of such objects or events, seems to be a distinctive human capacity. Such a capacity involves an attention to symbolic reproductions of past experiences that allows consideration of alternative possibilities of immediate and future behavior to enter into a consideration of present conduct. The *Homo sapiens* reflective capacity is dependent for effective operation on acquisition of human language. Unlike drives that are elicited through physical and chemical changes within the body, the human reflective capacity does not seem to become operative, except at a quite minimal level, unless the individual has the opportunity to acquire the uses of the language employed by members of a culture.

Human reflection appears to be related to no human capacities other than speech, in a manner that will allow for it to be stimulated through particular uses of other capacities developed independently of reflection. Studies of experimental isolation of adults and in situations of so-called brain washing and studies of deculturation (see Chapter Five) demonstrate that the capacity for reflection is not characterized by a tendency to return to a low level of operation once initiated. Thus, while sensory disturbances are created by extreme physical isolation, extreme social isolation in itself may not impair or alter the adult capacity to reflect. The level of operation of the reflective capacity is dependent on cultural forms of behavior available to the individual in an enculturation process as he matures and behaves in his society. The capacity for reflection tends to be characterized by a concern with future and nonsensory events rather than immediate and sensory-based behavior. Hence, where drives usually must be reduced in brief periods, the capacity for reflection may operate at sustained levels over long periods with apparently little effect on the nature of the survival of the human organism. The human capacity for reflection appears *polyphasic,* that is, capable of several operations at one time.

The defining of essential differences between human drives, reflectivity, and symboling will continue as basic research is conducted on the nature of each and as studies proceed on mutual influences between drives and the reflective and symboling capacities. Research such as that conducted by Miller and others, as cited in the next chapter, gives substantive evidence that human reflection may possibly alter basic human physiological processes. Such "operant conditioning" research may lead to increased understanding

Desert scene near Gu Achi, Arizona. (T. R. Williams, 1953.)

of the nature of drives and reflection and symboling in human learning of culture.

Phylogenetic reductionism. Confusion between drives and the capacities for reflection and symboling has resulted in a regular and widespread use of an assumption about learning in the socialization process. The assumption may be termed *phylogenetic reductionism.* Hull (1945: 56) set forth explicitly the nature of the phylogenetic reductionistic assumption when he assumed that all behavior of the individuals of a given species and that of all species of mammals, including man, occurs according to the same set of primary (biological) laws. Hilgard (1956: 461), in a review of learning theory, has commented on this assumption by noting that, while such a position is more often implied than asserted, it is strange that the opposite point of view is not more often

made explicit; that is, at the human level there have emerged capacities for retaining, reorganizing, and foreseeing experiences that are not approached by other animals, including other primates. Phylogenetic reductionistic reasoning can lead to the fallacy of "nothing but . . .," that is, "man is nothing but an animal." Julian Huxley and G. G. Simpson, among others, have discussed the effects of the use of this assumption by students of human evolution and behavior. Simpson (1950) has observed that, while it is important to realize that man is an animal, it is even more important to realize that the essence of man's nature lies precisely in those characteristics not shared with any other animal. Peters (1958) has noted that such a conclusion seems rather obvious. However, it is a fact that with some exceptions, such as brief discussions by

Papago family, Gu Achi, Arizona. (T. R. Williams, 1954.)

Bateson, DuBois, and some others, very little attention has been given in terms of ethnographic research data to the nature and consequences of learning theories adopted and used in attempts to differentiate between the different levels and kinds of learning involved in socialization.

Data offered here with regard to Papago enculturation suggest the conclusion that at least two major models of learning used in many socialization studies do not provide entirely adequate theory for analysis of human learning. These data of Papago enculturation also suggest the difficulties for the observer of actually applying, in some field research settings, the specific ideas of the Thorndike-Hull and Freudian learning models. Papago adults do not seem to be really concerned with enculturating their children. It is very difficult for an observer from another culture to discern much that would fit the usual definitions of "learning" by Papago children. One reason for this problem of observation and description of how Papago children learn Papago culture is that the traditional Thorndike-Hull and Freudian models of learning stress the somatic basis, or the drive level, of learning, while Papago enculturation is primarily concerned with the use of reflective and symbolic capacities of children in the learning of culture.

In concluding this chapter it should be noted that the study of the human learning process is a field of very specialized study. Clausen (1968), Honigmann (1967), and others have noted that a valid and general learning theory is essential for any adequate theory of socialization and for any effective design for socialization research. However, currently available learning models are much too sparse for grasping the full richness and great complexity of what really occurs in the socialization process.

■ **Summary**

This chapter first reviewed some details of two major models of learning used in socialization studies. Then case study data of the process of enculturation among the Papago, a North American Indian society, were presented to note the roles of reflective and symbolic learning in the socialization process. The chapter concluded with comment concerning ways human reflective and symbolic capacities may be involved in learning culture.

REFERENCES CITED AND SUGGESTED READINGS

Allport, F. H. 1955. *Theories of Perception and the Concept of Structure.* New York: Wiley and Sons, Inc.

Allport, G. W. 1937. *Personality: A Psychological Interpretation.* New York: Holt.

Angyal, A. 1941. *Foundations for a Science of Personality.* New York: The Commonwealth Fund.

Asch, S. E. 1952. *Social Psychology.* Englewood Cliffs, N. J.: Prentice-Hall, Inc.

Bateson, G. 1942. "Social Planning and the Concept of Deutero-Learning." In Bryson, L., and L. Finkelstein (eds.), *Science, Philosophy and Religion,* Conference on Science, Philosophy and Religion, New York. Garden City, Long Island: Country Life Press, pp. 81-97.

Castetter, E. F., and R. Underhill. 1935. "The Ethnobiology of the Papago Indians." *University of New Mexico Bulletin,* Ethnobiological Studies in the American Southwest, No. 2, Biological Series, Vol. IV, No. 3. Albuquerque: University of New Mexico Press.

Clausen, J. A. (ed.) 1968. *Socialization and Society.* Boston: Little, Brown.

Deese, J. E. 1952. *The Psychology of Learning.* New York: McGraw-Hill.

Dollard, J., and others. 1939. *Frustration and Aggression.* New Haven, Conn.: Yale University Press.

DuBois, C. 1944. *The People of Alor.* Minneapolis: The University of Minnesota Press.

———. 1949. "Attitudes toward Food and Hunger in Alor." In D. G. Haring (ed.), *Personal Character and Cultural Milieu.* Syracuse: Syracuse University Press, pp. 196-204.

———. 1955. "The Dominant Value Profile of American Culture," American Anthropologist **57**:1232-1239.

Erikson, E. H. 1950. *Childhood and Society.* New York: Norton.

Estes, W. K., and others. 1954. *Modern Learning Theory.* New York: Appleton-Century-Crofts.

Freud, A. 1936. *The Ego and Mechanisms of Defense* (translation, 1937). London: Hogarth Press.

Freud, S. 1905. "Three Contributions to the Theory of Sex." In *The Basic Writings of Sigmund Freud,* pp. 553-629. New York: Random House, 1938.

———. 1908. "Character and Anal Erotism." In *Collected Papers,* Vol. II, pp. 45-50. London: Hogarth Press, 1924.

———. 1910. "Psychogenic Visual Disturbance According to Psycho-Analytical Conceptions." In *Collected Papers,* Vol. II, pp. 105-112. London: Hogarth Press, 1924.

———. 1911. "Formulations Regarding the Two Principles in Mental Functioning." In *Collected Papers,* Vol. IV, pp. 13-21. London: Hogarth Press, 1925.

———. 1912. "Types of Neurotic Nosogenesis." In *Collected Papers,* Vol. II, pp. 113-121. London: Hogarth Press, 1924.

———. 1913. "Totem and Taboo." In *The Basic Writings of Sigmund Freud,* pp. 807-930. New York: Random House, 1938.

———. 1914. "On Narcissism: An Introduction." In *Collected Papers,* Vol. IV, pp. 30-59, London: Hogarth Press, 1925.

———. 1920a. *A General Introduction to Psychoanalysis.* New York: Boni and Liveright.

———. 1920b. *Beyond the Pleasure Principle* (translation). New York: Liveright.

———. 1921. *Group Psychology and the Analysis of the Ego* (translation). New York: Liveright, 1922.

———. 1923a. *The Ego and the Id* (translation). London: Hogarth Press, 1927.

———. 1923b. "The Libido Theory." In *Collected Papers,* Vol. V, pp. 255-268. London: Hogarth Press, 1924.

———. 1925. "Negation." In *Collected Papers,* Vol. V, pp. 181-185. London: Hogarth Press, 1950.

———. 1926. *The Problem of Anxiety* (translation). New York: Norton, 1936.

———. 1930. *Civilization and Its Discontents.* Hogarth Press: London.

———. 1933. *New Introductory Lectures on Psychoanalysis.* New York: Norton.

———. 1938. *The Basic Writings of Sigmund Freud* (translation). New York: Modern Library.

———. 1939. *Moses and Monotheism.* New York: A. A. Knopf.

———. 1940. *An Outline of Psychoanalysis.* New York: Norton, 1949.

Fromm, E. 1941. *Escape from Freedom.* New York: Farrar and Rinehart.

Goodman, M. E. 1967. *The Individual and Culture.* Homewood, Ill.: Dorsey.

Guthrie, E. R. 1935. *The Psychology of Learning.* New York: Harper.

_____. 1952. *The Psychology of Learning* (revised). New York: Harper.

Hall, C. S. 1954. *A Primer of Freudian Psychology.* Cleveland, Ohio: World Publishing Co.

Hall, C. S., and G. Lindzey. 1957. "Freud's Psychoanalytic Theory of Personality." In C. S. Hall and G. Lindzey (eds.), *Theories of Personality.* New York; Wiley, pp. 32-55.

Hallowell, A. I. 1950. "Personality Structure and the Evolution of Man," *American Anthropologist* 52:159-173.

_____. 1953. "Culture, Personality and Society." In A. L. Kroeber (ed.), *Anthropology Today.* Chicago: University of Chicago Press, pp. 597-620.

_____. 1954. "Psychology and Anthropology." In J. Gillin (ed.), *For a Science of Social Man.* New York: Macmillan, pp. 160-226.

Hilgard, E. R., L. S. Kubie, and E. Pumpian-Mindlin. 1952. *Psychoanalysis as Science.* Stanford, Calif.: Stanford University Press.

Hilgard, E. R. 1956. *Theories of Learning,* ed. 2. New York: Appleton-Century-Crofts.

Honigmann, J. J. 1954. *Culture and Personality.* New York: Harper.

_____. 1967. *Personality in Culture.* New York: Harper.

Horney, K. 1939. *New Ways in Psychoanalysis.* New York: Norton.

Hull, C. L. 1929. "A Functional Interpretation of the Conditioned Reflex," *Psychological Review* 36:498-511.

_____. 1930. "Simple Trial-and-Error Learning: A Study in Psychological Theory," *Psychological Review* 37:241-256.

_____. 1932. "The Goal Gradient Hypothesis and Maze Learning," *Psychological Review* 39:25-43.

_____. 1934. "Learning: II. The Factor of the Conditioned Reflex." In C. Murchison (ed.), *Handbook of General Experimental Psychology.* Worcester, Massachusetts: Clark University Press, pp. 382-455.

_____. 1939. "The Problem of Stimulus Equivalence in Behavior Theory," *Psychological Review* 46:9-30.

_____. 1942. "Conditioning: Outline of a Systematic Theory of Learning." *The Psychology of Learning, Chapter 2, National Society for the Study of Education 41st Yearbook,* Part II, pp. 61-95.

_____. 1943. *Principles of Behavior.* New York: Appleton-Century-Crofts.

_____. 1945. "The Place of Innate Individual and Species Differences in a Natural-Science Theory of Behavior," *Psychological Review* 52:55-60.

_____. 1950. "Behavior Postulates and Corollaries—1949," *Psychological Review* 57:173-180.

_____. 1951. *Essentials of Behavior.* New Haven, Conn.: Yale University Press.

_____. 1952. *A Behavior System: An Introduction to Behavior Theory Concerning the Individual Organism.* New Haven, Conn.: Yale University Press.

Huxley, J. 1941. *Man Stands Alone.* New York: Harper.

_____. 1957. *New Bottles for New Wine.* New York: Harper.

Joseph, A., R. B. Spicer, and J. Chesky. 1949. *The Desert People.* Chicago: University of Chicago Press.

Kardiner, A. 1939. *The Individual and His Society.* New York: Columbia University Press.

_____. 1945. *Psychological Frontiers of Society.* New York: Columbia University Press.

Kluckhohn, C. 1944. "The Influence of Psychiatry on Anthropology in America during the Past 100 Years." In J. K. Hall, G. Zilboorg, and H. A. Bunker (eds.), *One Hundred Years of American Psychiatry.* New York: Columbia University Press, pp. 589-617.

Koch, S. 1954. "Clark L. Hull." In W. K. Estes and others (eds.), *Modern Learning Theory.* New York: Appleton-Century-Crofts, pp. 1-176.

Koffka, K. 1924. *The Growth of the Mind* (translated by R. M. Ogden), London: Kegan Paul, Trench, Trubaer & Co., Ltd.

Köhler, W. 1925. *The Mentality of Apes* (translated by E. Winter). New York: Harcourt, Brace.

Leeper, R. W. 1944. "Dr. Hull's Principles of Behavior," Journal of Genetic Psychology 65:3-52.

_____. 1951. "Cognitive Processes." In S. S. Stevens (ed.), *Handbook of Experimental Psychology.* New York: Wiley, pp. 730-757.

_____. 1952. "Review—Essentials of Behavior by Clark L. Hull," American Journal of Psychology 65:478-491.

LeVine, R. 1963. "Behaviorism in Psychological Anthropology." In J. M. Wepman and R. W. Heine (eds.), *Concepts of Personality.* Chicago: Aldine, pp. 361-384.

Lewin, K. 1935. *A Dynamic Theory of Personality* (translated by D. K. Adams and K. E. Zener). New York: McGraw-Hill.

_____. 1936. *Principles of Topological Psychology* (translated by F. Heider and G. M. Heider). New York: McGraw-Hill.

Lindesmith, A. R., and A. L. Strauss. 1949. *Social Psychology.* New York: Dryden Press.

_____. 1950. "A Critique of Culture-Personality Writings," American Sociological Review 15:587-600.

McGeoch, J. A., and A. L. Irion. 1952. *The Psychology of Human Learning.* New York: Longmans.

Meehl, P. E. 1950. "On the Circularity of the Law of Effect," Psychology Bulletin 47:52-75.

Miller, N. E. 1941. "The Frustration-Aggression Hypothesis," Psychological Review 48:337-342.

_____. 1944. "Experimental Studies of Conflict." In J. McV. Hunt (ed.), *Personality and the Behavior Disorders*. New York: Ronald Press, pp. 431-465.

_____. 1948. "Studies of Fear as an Acquirable Drive (Fear as Motivation and Fear Reduction as Reinforcement in the Learning of New Responses)," Journal of Experimental Psychology 38:89-101.

_____. 1951a. "Learnable Drives and Rewards." In S. S. Stevens (ed.), *Handbook of Experimental Psychology*. New York: Wiley, pp. 435-472.

_____. 1951b. "Comments on Multiple-Process Conceptions of Learning," Psychological Review 58:375-381.

Miller, N. E., and J. Dollard. 1941. *Social Learning and Imitation*. New Haven, Conn.: Yale University Press.

Mowrer, O. H. 1950. *Learning Theory and Personality Dynamics*. New York: Ronald Press.

_____. 1954. "Learning Theory: Historical Review and Re-Interpretation," Harvard Educational Review 24:37-58.

Mowrer, O. H., and C. Kluckhohn. 1944. "Dynamic Theory of Personality." In J. McV. Hunt (ed.), *Personality and the Behavior Disorders*. New York: Ronald Press, pp. 69-135.

Munroe, R. L. 1955. *Schools of Psychoanalytic Thought*. New York: Dryden.

Murray, H. A. 1951. "Toward a Classification of Interactions." In T. Parsons and E. Shils (eds.), *Toward a General Theory of Action*. Cambridge, Mass.: Harvard University Press, pp. 434-464.

Pavlov, I. P. 1927. *Conditioned Reflexes*. London: Oxford University Press.

_____. 1928. *Lectures on Conditioned Reflexes* (translated by W. H. Gantt). New York: International.

Peters, R. S. 1958. *The Concept of Motivation*. London: Routledge & Paul.

Postman, L. 1947. "The History and Present Status of the Law of Effect," Psychology Bulletin 44:489-563.

Ruesch, J., and W. Kees. 1956. *Nonverbal Communication: Notes on the Visual Perception of Human Relations*. Berkeley: University of California Press.

Sears, R. R. 1944. "Experimental Analysis of Psychoanalytic Phenomena." In J. McV. Hunt, (ed.), *Personality and the Behavior Disorders*. New York: Ronald Press, pp. 306-332.

_____. 1951. "Social Behavior and Personality Development." In T. Parsons and E. Shils (eds.), *Toward a General Theory of Action*. Cambridge, Mass.: Harvard University Press, pp. 465-478.

Sears, R. R., E. E. Maccoby, and H. Levin. 1957. *Patterns of Child Rearing*. Evanston, Ill.: Row, Peterson.

Seward, J. P. 1954. "Hull's System of Behavior: An Evaluation," Psychological Review 61:145-159.

Simpson, G. G. 1950. *The Meaning of Evolution*. New Haven, Conn.: Yale University Press.

Skinner, B. F. 1938. *The Behavior of Organisms: An Experimental Analysis*. New York: Appleton-Century-Crofts.

_____. 1950. "Are Theories of Learning Necessary?" Psychological Review 55:193-216.

_____. 1953. *Science and Human Behavior*. New York: Macmillan.

Spence, K. W. 1948. "The Postulates and Methods of Behaviorism." Psychological Review 55:67-78.

_____. 1951a. "Theoretical Interpretations of Learning." In S. S. Stevens (ed.), *Handbook of Experimental Psychology*. New York: Wiley, pp. 690-729.

_____. 1951b. "Theoretical Interpretations of Learning." In C. P. Stone (ed.), *Comparative Psychology*, ed. 3. Englewood Cliffs, N. J.: Prentice-Hall, Inc., pp. 239-291.

_____. 1952. "Clark Leonard Hull: 1884-1952," American Journal of Psychology 65:639-646.

Spicer, E. H. 1941. "The Papago Indians," *The Kiva, Arizona Archaeological and Historical Society* 6:21-24. Tucson: Arizona State Museum.

Stern, W. 1938. *General Psychology from the Personalistic Standpoint*. New York: Macmillan.

Sullivan, H. S. 1947. *Conceptions of Modern Psychiatry*. Washington, D. C.: The William Alanson White Psychiatric Foundation.

Thorndike, E. L. 1911. *Animal Intelligence*. New York: Macmillan.

_____. 1932. *The Fundamentals of Learning*. New York: Columbia University Teachers College.

_____. 1935. *The Psychology of Wants, Interests and Attitudes*. New York: Appleton-Century-Crofts.

Thorndike, E. L. and others. 1933. "An Experimental Study of Rewards," Teachers College Contributions to Education, Number 580.

Tolman, E. C. 1932. *Purposive Behavior in Animals and Men*. New York: Appleton-Century-Crofts.

_____. 1951. *Collected Papers in Psychology*. Berkeley: University of California Press.

Underhill, R. 1934. "Notes on Easter Devils at Kawori'k on the Papago Reservation," American Anthropologist 36:515-516.

_____. 1936. "The Autobiography of a Papago Woman, Chona" (Memoirs), American Anthropological Association 46:3.

_____. 1938a. "A Papago Calendar Record," Anthropological Bulletin Series, Vol. 2, Number 5. Albuquerque: University of New Mexico Press.

_____. 1938b. *Singing for Power: The Song Magic of the Papago Indians of Southern Arizona*. Berkeley: University of California Press.

_____. 1939. "Social Organization of the Papago Indians," Columbia University Contributions to Anthropology, Vol. 30. New York: Columbia University Press.

_____. 1940. "The Papago Indians of Arizona and Their Relatives the Pima," Sherman Pamphlets, No. 3. Lawrence, Kansas: Publications of the Branch of Education, Bureau of Indian Affairs, Department of the Interior.

_____. 1946. *Papago Indian Religion.* New York: Columbia University Press.

Verplanck, W. S. 1955. "Since Learned Behavior Is Innate and Vice Versa, What Now?" Psychological Review **62**:139-144.

Wertheimer, M. 1923. "Untersuchungen zur Lehre von der Gestalt, II." Translated and condensed as "Laws of Organization in Perceptual Forms." In W. D. Ellis (ed.), *A Source Book of Gestalt Psychology.* New York: Harcourt, Brace, 1938.

_____. 1925. "Uber Schlussprozesse im Produktiven Denken." Translated and condensed as "The Syllogism and Productive Thinking." In W. D. Ellis (ed.), *A Source Book of Gestalt Psychology.* New York: Harcourt, Brace, 1938.

Whiting, J. W. M. 1941. *Becoming a Kwoma.* New Haven, Conn.: Yale University Press.

Whiting, J. W. M., and I. L. Child. 1953. *Child Training and Personality.* New Haven, Conn.: Yale University Press.

Williams, T. R. 1958. "The Structure of the Socialization Process in Papago Indian Society," Social Forces **36**:251-256.

Woodworth, R. S. 1918. *Dynamic Psychology.* New York: Columbia University Press.

_____. 1929. *Psychology* (revised edition). New York: Holt, Rinehart and Winston.

FOUR — OPERANT CONDITIONING AND SOCIALIZATION

This chapter begins by discussing ethnographic reports of some of the ways culture and human biology appear to become interrelated in the socialization process. Then a brief account is given of the concept of *operant conditioning* and the ways this special learning research procedure has been used to experimentally study various kinds of interrelationships between behavior and body functions. The chapter concludes with a discussion of some implications for socialization studies to be drawn from ethnographic data and experimental studies of operant conditioning. This chapter is concerned with providing a preliminary understanding of some of the ways in which the socialization process makes it possible for individual humans to learn to modify body features such as *drives* and *reflexes*.

▪ Culture and human biology

Ethnographic reports of voluntary control of reflexes. The practitioners of the Indian religious discipline of *yoga* regularly engage in a series of body exercises that demand voluntary control over a number of body reflexes. These reflexes are generally believed by most Europeans and Americans to be beyond any kind of voluntary control. In the exercise of *diaphragm raising,* the yoga practitioner stands nearly erect, his knees a little bent, his upper torso leaning slightly forward. He tries to force all the air from his lungs, then pulls his rib cage up sharply in a simulated inhalation, causing an extremely deep depression of the abdomen, which results in a sharp raising of the entire diaphragm muscle.

In the yoga practice of *voluntary vomiting,* the individual drinks a half dozen or so full containers of water, bends sharply forward, places his hands on his knees, and exhales deeply. Then the abdominal muscles are sharply contracted upward and backward and quickly relaxed. These sharp upward contractions and downward relaxations are repeated at a rate of six to ten each minute, until the water in the stomach is vomited forth. A skilled yogi can very quickly cleanse his stomach in this manner.

Another method of stomach cleansing used in yoga exercises is to swallow a thick piece of heavy cloth, about two to four inches wide and some twenty feet in length. After all the cloth is in the stomach, except for the end clasped firmly between the teeth, the practitioner engages in the two techniques of diaphragm raising and sharp abdominal contraction-relaxation, but with special attention to voluntary use of the *rectus abdominis* muscles. First the diaphragm is sharply raised. Then the part of the abdomen above the pubic arch is voluntarily pulled downward and forward to expose beneath the surface of the skin the long, flat rectus abdominis muscles, extending vertically on either side of the abdomen. These two muscles are manipulated by the yogi through rapid contraction and relaxation, first on the right side and so on, in a rolling, rhythmic sequence.[1] After about 20 to 30 minutes of such rolling manipulation of the *rectus abdominis* muscles, the diaphragm is relaxed and the cloth is pulled from the stomach.

[1] The patterned muscle twitchings interpreted by the Apache Indians as predictions of future events and by the Navaho Indians in religious divination are quite similar to yoga muscle control patterns (see Henry, 1949; Wyman, 1936).

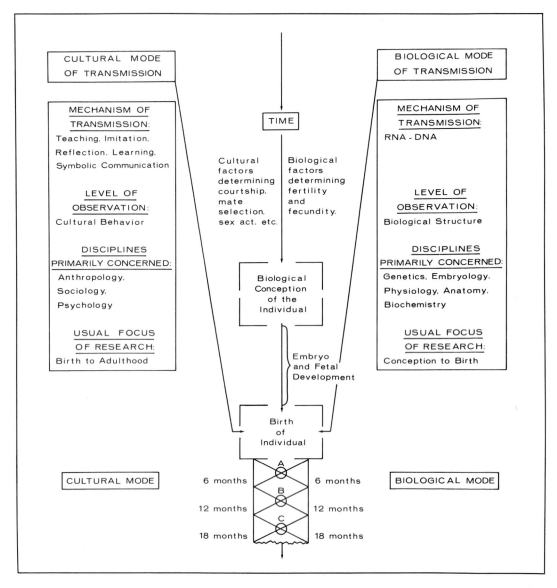

Fig. 6. Biological and cultural modes of transmission in the socialization process. (After Davis, K. 1949. *Human Society.* New York: The Macmillan Co.)

These techniques are also used in yoga exercises to voluntarily cleanse the colon of fecal impurities. When the *rectus abdominis* muscles have been isolated, a partial vacuum is created in the lower colon, enabling the yoga practitioner to draw up water into the rectum after voluntarily opening the anal sphincters. A similar technique is used to voluntarily clean the bladder of urine impurities, except that a tube of lead or silver is inserted to open the urethral sphincters, which apparently are beyond voluntary control for yoga practitioners. By undertaking the isolated, voluntary manipulation of the *rectus abdominis* muscles, the yogi can draw up substantial amounts of water into his bladder, retain it for long periods, and finally discharge it to "cleanse" himself of bladder "impurities."

Voluntary control of the anal sphincters is regularly practiced in yoga. When this technique is combined with the technique of diaphragm raising, through relaxing the sphincters with each inhalation and contracting them with each exhalation, gases are forced from the lower colon and fresh air is taken in from outside the body.

Yoga practitioners also voluntarily roll their tongues backward and upward to cover the posterior cavities leading into the pharynx at the base of the skull. This exercise sometimes but not always requires severance of the vertical membrane at the base of the tongue.

There are also reports that yoga practitioners voluntarily open and close the pyloric valve of the stomach to allow large amounts of water to pass through the alimentary canal. The reports of this exercise do not at present seem as reliable as observations of other yoga practices. Physiological studies of the autonomic functions in yoga practitioners have shown a lower rate of respiration, an increase in skin resistance, and no consistent changes in heart rate or blood pressure during their exercises. Electroencephalograms have shown marked change during their exercises and meditation on yoga practices.[2]

Voluntary control of pain reflexes. Voluntary control of pain reflexes is widely known and practiced in human cultures. Among the accounts of voluntary control of pain reflexes are the acts of young male Cheyenne Indians during a religious ritual, the Sun Dance. Cheyenne boys were taught by adults to believe that self-torture was a special way to achieve the state of psychological oblivion necessary for access to the supernatural visions sent by the creator to those mastering public displays of pain. One principal technique of self-torture practiced by the Cheyenne during the Sun Dance was to drive small wooden skewers under the skin of the upper back or chest and then to attach the skewers to leather thongs. The skewers were inserted by a Cheyenne *shaman*,

a specialist in ritual actions. Then the young man would be tied up to the top of a high pole to hang suspended by the thongs attached to the skewers inserted under his skin. Here he remained for long periods without displays of pain.

Another example of voluntary control of pain reflexes is to be found in behavior during the initiation rituals for membership in the *Onayanakia* order of the Zuni Indian "Great Fire Fraternity." At the beginning of this century Stevenson (1904: 495) noted that participants in the *Onayanakia* initiations regularly walked and stamped in the glowing coals of large fires, then scooped up great handfuls of hot coals to literally

Cheyenne Sun Dance initiates (circa 1890). (Courtesy American Museum of Natural History.)

[2]See Wenger, Bagchi, and Anand, 1961; Anand, China, and Singh, 1961; Wenger and Bagchi, 1961.

Sun Dance ritual (circa 1892), Piegan Reservation, Alberta, Canada. (Courtesy American Museum of Natural History.)

bathe themselves in red hot embers. Stevenson also described participants placing burning coals in their mouths, holding hot embers in their hands, and engaging in a prolonged rubbing of live coals on the backs of each other and the initiates, all without seeming to show pain responses of any type.

Still another illustration of voluntary control of pain reflexes is to be found in reports of ritual firewalking from the central Pacific islands such as Raiatea and Fiji and from the western Pacific islands such as New Britain. In the act of firewalking an individual makes his way across a surface of irregularly shaped rocks that have been heated to an incandescent glow by burning hardwood logs placed beneath the rock surface. The fire pit is usually 8 to 10 yards square, but often is smaller. Before the act begins, the surface of the hot rocks is swept clear of burning embers and hot wood cinders. A ritual specialist then conducts a series of prayers, songs, and dances, with the onlookers participating. Then, those participating in the walk move slowly and deliberately across the glowing bed of rock to the opposite side of the fire pit.

Participants in the fire initiation and the firewalk do not seem to respond to the intense heat of the coals or rocks by manifesting pain. Some reports have suggested that the fire initiation participants and firewalkers are in hypnotic states induced by ritual specialists, or have smeared their hands, feet, legs, or bodies with some special ointment that protects them from burns. Other reports have suggested that firewalkers and fire initiation participants have heavily calloused hands and feet from regularly walking barefoot or from hard manual labor and therefore feel no heat, and that the palms and soles of the firewalker's and fire initiate's feet produce a coating of sweat that cools and protects the skin. An analysis of the ethnographic literature concerning these rituals leads to the conclusion that participants are controlling pain responses in voluntary ways not practiced in American or European cultures. Trained observers have been

Preparation of fire pit, Fiji (1970). (Courtesy Hiram Walker, Inc.)

Fiji fire walk ritual (1970). (Courtesy Hiram Walker, Inc.)

unable to note clearly any trance, hypnotic, or disassociative states on the part of participants in these events. No ointments or lotions have been observed in use before or during the ritual acts. Until recently most participants have walked barefooted regularly or have worked hard at hand labor, but few were observed to have had palms or soles calloused so thickly as to block out the pain responses from the hot cinder and rock surface.[3]

The ritual acts of firewalking and fire initiation are closely associated with a pattern of religious belief in the places where they have occurred. These patterns are quite similar in meaning to that also used by the young Cheyenne males in their vision quest through suppression of self-inflicted pain. The participants in the firewalk and fire initiation rituals are enculturated to believe that an inability to feel pain or to display hurt in special situations that ordinarily would cause great pain and harm places men in closer relationships to the powerful supernatural forces controlling their destiny. It is believed that the act of voluntary control of ordinary pain responses makes humans less ordinary and therefore closer to the nonhuman world of powerful beings and forces.

Systematic observations of yoga exercises and of pain reflex suppression make it clear that these activities are learned and are within the physical capability of most adult humans. The fact that the muscles and reflexes involved are not "normally" used or controlled voluntarily in American or European cultures does not mean Indian yoga practitioners, Cheyenne and Zuni Indians, Polynesians, and Melanesians have special or extra human biological features. It means simply that it is well within the range of human behavior to learn to exercise firm, voluntary control over the diaphragm, several muscles of the ventral wall of the abdomen, certain smooth muscles of the stomach and alimentary tract, the anal sphincters, certain tongue muscles, and particular pain reflexes. It clearly is possible for humans to learn to regularly control and use some *superficial* re-

flexes (pharyngeal, uvular, palatal, upper abdominal, lower abdominal, anal) and some *visceral* reflexes (bladder, rectal, and smooth muscles of the walls of the alimentary tract). Yoga novices have been observed learning such voluntary control over these superficial and visceral reflexes. The ways of teaching the novice by the yoga master have been carefully observed and recorded in detail. Thus the response is negative to the question of whether these practices of reflex control and use are specific to a local human population and are extrabiological, that is, are special structural features peculiar to only one group of humans. Many human reflexes are apparently within the range of voluntary control and use. The fact that a local group does not choose to learn voluntary control of reflexes should not be taken to mean that reflective and symbolic control and use of some or even all human reflexes is beyond possibility for man.

Ethnographic reports of voluntary control of drives. In Chapter Two the concept of *drive* was noted as referring essentially to a complex of biological states of an organism and the stimuli motivating it to a given behavior. It was noted also that many scholars making studies of drives have assumed that some type of body energy lies "back of" spontaneous behavior in organisms and that descriptions of *drives* are based most efficiently on the overt activities of an organism. The principal sources of body energy underlying basic drives are said to be derived from activities of an organism directed toward acquisition of metabolic ingredients essential for survival and action. Some essential drives in man have been said to be directed toward (1) acquisition of oxygen, (2) acquisition of water, (3) acquisition of carbohydrates, (4) acquisition of amino acids, (5) acquisition of vitamins and minerals, (6) maintaining a constant ionic composition of blood, (7) elimination of body wastes, and (8) concentrated periods of sleep and rest.

Many substances required by humans for metabolism may be stored in the body for future use. But an average daily intake of metabolic requirements, discharge of wastes, and sleep still seem essential to maintain body functioning and homeostasis, or physiological balance. Any

---

[3]For a detailed eyewitness account of personal participation in "firewalking" by an American surgeon, see Feigen, 1969.

deficiency in these average metabolic requirements may not be fatal to the individual or population unless prolonged. A prolonged deficiency in acquiring energy producing foodstuffs, in discharge of wastes, in sleep, and so on leads to progressive loss of body weight and muscle strength, emaciation, and a general inability to carry on usual activities.

A study of the ethnographic reports of the varied ways the world's peoples seek to meet their common human metabolic requirements leads to two conclusions: (1) that human metabolic requirements can be met in very diverse ways, and (2) where some of the metabolic requirements of a human population cannot be supplied, special patterns of cultural behavior will function in such a way as to compensate for metabolic needs in the form of voluntary decrease or restriction of individual action.[4]

Diverse ways of meeting human metabolic requirements. The quite different ways humans meet their specific metabolic requirements can be illustrated best by some examples taken from the ethnographic literature concerning the ways hunger and thirst are treated by some of the world's peoples.

The *Vedda* of Ceylon regularly ate at least five different kinds of quite rotted wood, often garnished with honey, bark, leaves, or varieties of fruits. Among some South American *Guiana* tribes, when their cassava root bread is scarce, greenheart tree seeds are prepared with rotted wood in a bread substitute. There are reports of native peoples eating small pebbles after a meal. The peasant peoples of *Styria*, in southeast Austria, are reported to have taken from 2 to 5 grains of arsenious acid each day with their food as a "seasoning" to avoid disease.

Among the tribes of the Amazon River basin the practice of eating clay is known and tolerated. Schoolboys in Morocco have been reported regularly to eat potter's earth to promote learning in school. Clay eating is an expected feature of the behavior of pregnant women in some northern Borneo cultures. Children and adults in rural

Mississippi are reported to have eaten clay and certain soils.

Many humans learn to tolerate and to prefer very putrefied materials to meet the hunger drive. Thus, the Dusun of Northern Borneo place meat from a variety of animals, including house rats, in sealed bamboo tubes, allow the meats to spoil to liquefaction in the heat of the sun, and then consume it with rice. The sauce used on rice dishes by Vietnamese peoples is prepared from putrefied materials.

Humans obtain their metabolic requirements from nearly every possible source of food. The Indians of South America eat monkeys (sometimes with the hair still on the body), frogs, iguanas, grubs, bees, the larvae of any insect, and head lice. The *Shoshone* Indians of Utah were reported to have eaten over one hundred kinds of seeds, roots, and nuts. The *Dusun* of Northern Borneo eat snake, gibbon, anteater, mice, rat, and a great many different kinds of insects. While cannibalism is based on a great variety of cultural meanings, among some tribal groups in South America, Melanesia, and Africa *food cannibalism* was common. Human flesh was sold and eaten in "butcher shops" in aboriginal markets in New Britain. Among the tribal peoples in parts of Africa, in countrysides plentiful with wild game, human flesh was a part of the diet.

Because of the limitations of a harsh environment or because of specific cultural choice, some human groups have subsisted on diets restricted almost entirely to animal products. The Polar Eskimo live primarily by consuming meat and fish, rarely eating vegetable products. In contrast, the *Bemba* of Africa live almost entirely on one type of grain and some vegetables and rarely eat meat.

The kinds of liquids taken by humans in meeting their metabolic requirements are very greatly varied. Humans slake their thirst with water and animal products, both milk and blood, and with a broad range of vegetable products such as fruit juices, juices from plant stalks and leaves, and cocoa, coffee, and tea. Fermented animal and vegetable products are used regularly to reduce thirst—for example, *Kumiss,* a fermented mare's milk used among Asian pastoral nomads; beers

---

[4]This second conclusion was first stated in this form by Gillin (1944).

made from wheat, rice, and maize; wines and ciders from fruits; the saps of certain plants such as palm tree toddy; and sugar cane juice and *maguey* juice in pre-European Mexico. Too, the juice products of certain plants, such as *kava*, were drunk in Polynesia. Fermented honey, or *mead*, was widely used in early Northern European cultures. Distillation of the juices from certain grains, sugar cane, grapes, or potatoes, a recent invention, has produced liquors, rums, cognacs, vodkas, and tequilas. Thus humans can and do meet their specific metabolic requirement for the intake of fluids by a great many different means.

Cultural patterns and voluntary meeting of metabolic requirements. In man, the hunger drive occurs periodically. However, the periodicity of this drive is highly patterned by cultural learning. All cultures have a practice of taking food at least once in 24 hours. Within this 24-hour period there is very great variability in meeting the hunger drive. Americans usually take three meals in 24 hours, with standard intervals of 4 to 5 hours between the first and second meals and 5 to 6 hours between the second and third meals. In pre-World War II Europe, four meals each 24 hours was a standard procedure in the German and English cultures, while five and six meals were eaten in parts of Scandinavia. Among the *Bemba* of East Africa it was usual to eat a single meal at varying times each day. The *Dusun* of Northern Borneo eat two meals each day, early each morning and at dusk.

A concentration on a single meal, or two meals, or six meals in 24 hours requires that children be enculturated in such a manner as to voluntarily "feel hungry" at the appropriate times. In cultures that eat many meals each day, the enculturation process must focus on children having the hunger drive specifically elicited at regular intervals. In general, in these societies, children are fed generously at the specific times of meals, but vigorously denied access to any foods between these times. In contrast, in societies that eat a single meal each day, such as the Bemba, children are enculturated with respect to a voluntary control of the hunger drive by being permitted light snacks throughout the day. Only as children ap-

proach adolescence or in times of food shortages are they required to give up the snacks and to concentrate on eating only one meal.

Because they have to face regular periods of short food supplies, many societies have developed patterns of fasting for most adult members, which make a virtue of the necessity of long periods of hunger. No culture has developed a pattern of fasting for everyone for periods as long as a month or 6 weeks. The longest, non-fatal individual human fasts recorded have varied between 50 and 60 days. Fasting, as a specific cultural pattern for voluntarily delaying or displacing the hunger drive, rarely lasts longer than 3 days. In some cultures, such as the *Papago* Indians of Arizona, the usual adult pattern of brief fasting at times of short supplies of food was also practiced in a purification ritual of warriors returning after battle. If a warrior had taken an enemy life in battle, he usually fasted for a period of 16 full days, taking only water in which a handful of corn had been allowed to soak.

Humans have used many substances that in moderate amounts diminish sensibility, relieve pain, and produce lassitude, stupor, or sleep to aid in seeking to delay voluntarily the meeting of metabolic requirements. The Indian porters of the South American Andean region are accustomed to the chewing of coca leaves instead of eating when walking over the mountains with heavy burdens. The cocaine in the coca leaves tends to inhibit hunger and fatigue. This practice also eliminates the need for adding food supplies to the burdens carried.

Other substances that inhibit hunger or thirst, such as *parica* and *peyote*, have been eaten in culturally patterned forms to delay or to restrict individual action that would require metabolic output at times of famine or a severely restricted food supply. The peoples of Northern Borneo chew *betel*, a preparation from the nut of the *arecca* palm and other substances, in efforts to voluntarily control hunger and thirst. Tobacco, coffee, and tea also have been widely used in many societies to delay and reduce the hunger and thirst drives. The native peoples of Gabon, West Africa, chew the yellowish root of a plant (*Tabernanthe iboga*) to offset hunger. Taken in large doses, *iboga* causes excitement, confusion, and a drunken-like state.[5]

Some peoples afflicted with chronic, long-term food shortages have developed and used cultural patterns to voluntarily reduce their regular total daily caloric intake well below the levels ordinarily said to be necessary for human survival and for attainment of maximum longevity. For example, the *Bemba* of Africa live in an area with barren soils and uncertain seasonal rainfall and where the animals and people are subject to regular attacks of severe diseases. The Bemba face a constant struggle to simply maintain themselves. They grow a crop of finger millet and have no cattle, because of the presence of the tsetse fly. Millet is grown on an 8- to 13-acre field cleared of low trees and shrubs by a hand axe and prepared with a simple hoe. A meal for a Bemba consists of millet porridge eaten in heavy, quickly cooked lumps and "eased" down by a relish of a vegetable and, on very rare occasions, of meat or fish. In the Bemba language the word *nbwali* stands for the millet porridge. This word recurs repeatedly in proverbs, folktales, puns, jokes, folksongs, and riddles and is a one-word surrogate for many ordinary daily affairs. In this respect, *nbwali* is somewhat comparable to the word *bread* in English, as in the expressions, "Give us this day our daily bread," "Earning our bread and butter" and so on. A Bemba will say, "How can a man refuse to help his mother's brother who has given him *nbwali* all these years?"

In Bemba ritual and ceremonial, *nbwali* stands for *life* and *health*. The term figures in this way in important tribal political actions, in female initiation, in marriage ceremonies, and in kinship relations and is abstained from by those who feel possessed by evil spirits. Thus the Bemba concentration on a single food runs as a theme throughout their culture.

It is a rare time when Bemba produce enough of a millet crop for the entire year. The last three months of the year are termed by Bemba as the *hunger months*. When millet becomes scarce the whole community life slows in pace and is affected. Adults reduce their meals and millet beer is no longer brewed. Children eat only one small meal late each day and are allowed none of the frequent snacks they have been given in the other months of the year. Most Bemba experience times of severe hunger, when they must go 2 or 3 days without eating. Then the people stay in their huts, where they take large amounts of water and inhale snuff to reduce their hunger.

Systematic samples of individual Bemba diets show that the number of calories eaten each day has averaged 1,706 per adult male, compared to an average of 3,000 calories for individual male Americans and Europeans. The average individual adult male daily caloric intake in one typical year was from a low of no calories through 286 calories to a high of 3,164 calories. The Bemba live consistently at a subsistence intake of calories well below that felt to be adequate for human health, "normal activity," and attainment of an ordinary life span.[6]

When a Bemba village or family obtains an unexpected supply of meat, it is an occasion for suspension of the ordinary rules and courtesies of eating; everyone gorges until all the meat has been eaten. Bemba life at such times has been described as characterized by intense excitement, with adults and children singing and dancing in spontaneous ways not seen in ordinary Bemba activities, as if they have had temporarily lifted from them the oppression of the fears of their constant hunger.

Thus, facing such a chronic shortage of food, the Bemba have developed a whole set of culturally patterned behaviors, beliefs, and values that serve to focus attention on voluntary control of hunger.

Cultural structuring of other features of human biology. In addition to reflexes and drives, there are some other aspects of human biology that appear to be subjected to cultural shaping in their forms of individual voluntary control,

---

[5]For an extensive review of the ways humans use plant products to allay hunger and fatigue and to induce trance behavior, see Schultes, 1969.

[6]Tolley (1948) has concluded the average daily caloric intake cannot fall below 2,000 if a population is to survive.

release, and use. For example, the consistency of human feces appears to vary among cultures, even in instances in which diets are similar. Mead has reported that the degree of constipation or looseness of the bowels is subject to specific cultural structuring among the Iatmul of New Guinea and among the Manus of the Admiralty Islands.[7] The Itamul spend a great deal of time teaching their children not to step in human or animal feces, but otherwise follow a quite relaxed enculturation process with regard to sexual prudery or rigid training of schedules of feeding, weaning, independence, or aggression. Mead notes that, from her observations, the Itamul have loose and frequent stools. The Manus people, living as the Itamul do on sago, fish, and yams, spend a great deal of time training children to be sexually prudish and are quite rigid in their schedules of enculturation for feeding, weaning, independence, and aggression. Mead notes that, from her observations, Manus adults have hard, formed stools and defecate only once each day in the early morning at a fixed time and place.

Mead concludes from these data that the degree of constipation or looseness of feces is subject to cultural standardization in an enculturation process. She reaches this conclusion on the basis of research reports of intensive American and European studies of selected individual cases in which chronic constipation apparently has no physiological basis but rather has come about as a symbolic expression of a psychological mood that is being displayed in a general somatic alteration such as severe constipation. She concludes that it is possible for such a general somatic alteration to be taught to every person born into a culture, as in the case of the Iatmul or Manus, where once begun the process may be irreversible for the individuals involved.

Too, circumstances that produce individual nausea and vomiting are highly structured culturally. In fact, in some cultures vomiting is an extremely feared behavior and the ordinary reaction of extreme disgust is defecation. Mead reports that the Arapesh of New Guinea pattern eating in such a way that throughout the enculturation process strong ties are stressed between the eaters and what remains after they have eaten, while the social relations between parents and child, husband and wife, elders and youth are conceived specifically in terms of which person is responsible for feeding the other person. Thus vomiting is considered as an extreme negation of proper social relations between persons. In this cultural setting, the Arapesh view defecation as the "proper" and "acceptable" reaction to extremely upsetting or nauseous situations.

A heavy flow of saliva is not always associated with food, as it is in American and European cultures. Fijian men report that they experience a very heavy flow of saliva at the sight of a beautiful woman.[8]

A distinguished psychologist, Cannon, has noted that an individual can become convinced that he is the victim of witchcraft to the point where he experiences such severe disturbances of body functioning that he dies.[9] Many irregularities in circulatory and respiratory functions have been said to be the results of cultural beliefs concerning magic. Thus the idea of "magical fright," which is known widely in Middle American cultures, is said to be the cause of severe irregularities in pulse functions.[10].

Other vascular responses also seem structured by cultural patterning. Thus blushing, a peripheral vascular response, tends among most Europeans and Americans to be essentially a facial response. There are ethnographic reports that, when extremely discomforted socially or caught up in a situation that is culturally defined as "embarassing," many of the world's peoples do not blush on the face. Rather, the peripheral vascular system response is exhibited on other body parts such as the surface of the chest, the upper arms, or the thighs.

Fatigue is another aspect of human biology that is highly culturally structured. The definitions of and responses to fatigue are quite culturally variable.[11]

---

[7]See Mead, 1956: 610.

[8]See Quain, 1948: 322.
[9]See Cannon, 1942.
[10]See Gillin, 1948 and 1951.
[11]For some examples of cultural patterning of fatigue, see Mead, 1946: 676; and Benedict, 1946: 180-181, 230, 257, 268.

The ways a people gesture, walk, stand, sit, and move in specific social situations also vary greatly among cultures. Among the Jalisco of Mexico the height of a child, object, or animal is indicated with the edge of the palm to the ground, not with the palm parallel to the ground, as among Americans. The Semang of Malaya thrust their head sharply forward for "yes" and cast their eyes down for "no." The Dayak of Borneo raise their eyebrows to say "yes" and contract them to say "no." Maroi say "yes" by tilting the eyes upward, while Sicilians say "no" in the same manner. Navaho Indians point out objects with pursed lips. Copper Eskimo welcome strangers by sharp blows to the head and shoulders, and Polynesian males greet each other by embracing closely and rubbing each other's backs. Weeping is generally a feminine trait in American culture, while it is appropriate male behavior among the Kiowa Indians of North America. Japanese approve behavior and show deference to superiors by hissing, and the Basuto of Africa applaud through hissing, but in the United States hissing is a rude social response. Spitting on one another among the Masai of Africa is a symbol of great personal affection. American Plains Indian ritual specialists regularly spit on their patients to show that they have great hope for a cure. Americans stand in the presence of a superior, Fijians sit down in the same circumstances. There are distinctive differences in walking gaits between the Dusun of the Northern Borneo mountain interior and the Bajau, a coastal people of Northern Borneo. Experienced observers often can detect Dusun from Bajau by watching their gait, even though Bajau and Dusun are dressed in the same style. Movies made in India are nearly incomprehensible to Europeans and Americans, who lack an essential understanding of the basic meanings of the subtle kinesthesia uses in Hindu culture.[12]

Mead has observed the enculturation of motor patterns among Balinese children. She finds that, compared to American children, Balinese children spend much more time in other stages of motor development. Balinese babies greatly pro-

long the "frog squatting" sequence in learning to walk. Balinese children are taught to emphasize the outward rotation and extension of the little finger sides of their hands, rather than the inward rotation and closure of the thumb and forefinger sides of the hands, as is typical in American enculturation of children. Balinese children are also enculturated to have a type of "meandering" body posture, in which some limbs or parts are relaxed and flexible while other parts are at the

Fijian girl (circa 1921). (Courtesy American Museum of Natural History.)

---

[12]For more extensive discussion of this point, see LaBarre, 1947; Kluckhohn, 1954.

same time flexed or tensed. These children also are taught to move smoothly from a posture of complete relaxation to one of great tension. In contrast, American children are enculturated to sit or stand with all body parts in the same degree of tension-relaxation and to move from one extreme (relaxation) to the other (tension) through well-defined body sequences.[13]

It has also been noted that certain aspects of human reproductive physiology are very culturally structured, particularly where cultures contain patterns of ceremonial continence, celibacy, and activities that increase or decrease male and female fertility.[14]

Cultural concepts of number, time, and sequence also are imposed on particular features of human biology. Mead notes the frequent relationship between the sacred or magical number of a culture and the day on which a baby's umbilical cord "falls off." In Bali, where the mother is in a special state of ritual isolation for 3 days, the cord tends to fall off in 3 days. Among the Iatmul of New Guinea, where 5 is the magical number, the cord tends to fall off in 5 days. This frequent relationship seems to hold also for the Dusun of Northern Borneo, but in a somewhat more variable manner.

There also is a cultural structuring of biology in different societies with regard to the time involved in the healing of body wounds. In the New Guinea and Indonesian regions, where there is a hot, tropical climate, the problem is to close the wound for proper healing. Mead points out that among the Itamul, a New Guinea people, wounds close slowly, even with medical attention. The Itamul manifest very little concern with most wounds. However, Mead notes that in Bali, where there is a great fear of any injury to the surface perfection of the body, wounds heal very rapidly. Balinese insist on keeping the smallest cuts open for several days with continuous application of wet dressings to avoid the tendency of a wound to heal and then to fester under the scab. Balinese wounds apparently tend to heal more rapidly even when dressings are not used.

[13]See Mead and MacGregor, 1951.
[14]See Ford and Beach, 1951; Coon, 1950.

In the United States most wounds, even those surgically induced, are supposed to take from 7 to 14 days to heal. In fact, wounds do tend to heal within this period. In contrast, the Dusun of Northern Borneo, living in a hot, tropical rain forest climate, believe wounds should be healed by the last "lucky day" before the end of an 8-day period. If wounds appear ready to heal over by the last "unlucky day" in the week after a wound is received, Dusun may open the cut to keep it from an unlucky closing. Dusun will use strong poultices in wounds to keep them open for a lucky day healing.

Conclusions: culture and biology. In the preceding pages a brief review has been given of some of the ways human culture and biology are known to be interrelated. It has been suggested that humans can use capacities, such as those for reflection and symbolism, to voluntarily shape common human features of biology such as reflexes and drives. Some examples of voluntary control were given for other features of human biology whose present status as reflexes, drives, species-characteristic behavior forms, or capacities is yet unclear.

The discussion so far in this chapter has proposed that there are some specific relationships between various features of human biology such as reflexes and drives and particular cultural features. The theory of socialization upon which these suggestions have been based has not been discussed. A brief and condensed statement of this theory should help clarify some of the problems and questions that have been raised in this discussion.

What has been said to this point is derived from the following theoretical paradigm. (1) *The preoccupations of the adults in a society, which are cultural preoccupations, may result through time in a child also becoming preoccupied, as a function of a child's various responses to adult pressure to conform and his own physiological functions and reflective and symbolic capacities. (2) This derived preoccupation of the child in turn helps shape adult attitudes and values toward their own preoccupations.* Therefore the form of the socialization process in any particular culture represents a historically developed working process between a local

cultural tradition (which provides for the preoccupations of adults) and the maturing child.[15]

Some brief specific examples of this *transactional* or doubly contingent paradigm of socialization might be helpful. In the Arapesh culture
of the Admiralty Islands parental preoccupation
with the intake of food eventually results in a
child's preoccupation with food intake, which is
a function of the Arapesh child's response to
parental pressures and his own physiological
functions. As the Arapesh child demonstrates a
derivative preoccupation with intake of food,
he in turn shapes his parent's cultural preoccupation with the intake of food. The further and
later training given to the Arapesh child in bowel
and bladder sphincter control depends on the
prior training given them in regard to eating,
on the child's responses to that previous training, and on the parent's responses to those
responses by the child. But Arapesh children's
sphincter training also is dependent upon cultural
behavior forms that are standard for stages of
life not yet reached by a child. A parent's training of the Arapesh child with regard to sphincter
control reflects not only the prior training of
food intake, but also the cultural belief that
dying old people must attempt to control their
body functions and still drag themselves to the
edge of the village to defecate. Thus the Arapesh
child has his biology culturally shaped and
directed through responses to him by his parents, through his parent's responses to his responses, and further through his parents applying
consistently to him in their evaluation of his
responses to their concerns cultural definitions
appropriate for behavior at stages of life not yet
reached by the child. This theoretical paradigm
is illustrated in its major outlines in Fig. 7.

In this theoretical model, culture is viewed
not as a set of *external* and *outside* events to which
the individual is subjected without protection or
recourse, but as one of two primary facts in the
development of the individual (the other primary
fact is human biology), which results in his having, as an adult, a biological structure, a kind of

Looking Elk, Sioux ritual specialist. (Courtesy American
Museum of Natural History.)

biological functioning and a set of behavioral
attributes very different from individuals who
have been enculturated in another tradition.

In this theory, immersion in a culture through
regular social contacts with other individuals
who have been immersed in a similar way develops in the growing human organism a great
number of specific biological and behavioral
tendencies and abilities that become increasingly
more irreversible. The total functioning of an
adult individual is fully dependent upon the interrelationships between such biological-behavioral
tendencies and the presence of individuals of
both sexes and different ages.

Thus a Samoan individual is enculturated
from his birth to sit on the floor. As an adult
he sits cross-legged for hours without fatigue.
At the same time he learns to sit on the floor
he also is learning a whole group of cultural behavior forms and values directly related to this
sitting position. He must learn that it is rude to
talk while standing up. He must learn that, before
he uses either or both hands in accepting a cup,

---

[15]This summary of theory in socialization follows that first
presented by Mead (1956: 610).

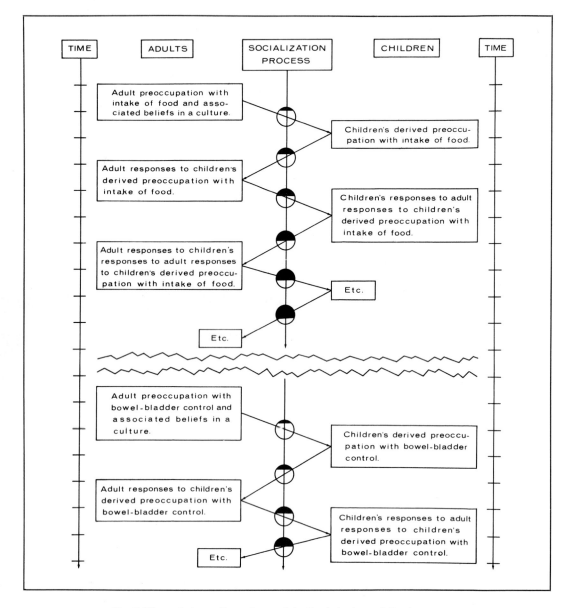

Fig. 7. Theoretical paradigm of mutual feedback in the socialization process.

he must pay attention to the relative distances at which his fellows on his right and left are seated. He must learn that his back is considered outside the formal circle of social intercourse as he sits on the floor, so he can wipe food from his hands on his back, or on the back of his head, or on the housepost on which he leans, but that he must never wipe food on his front to avoid giving grave social offense. A Samoan must learn that the person who stands up when another person is seated is one of higher social rank. He must learn that he must bow low if he passes before a seated person of equal or higher rank. All of these complex behavioral patterns are in turn directly related to a whole system of social status-role behavior. If we ask an adult Samoan to sit on a chair at a social occasion, we ask much more of him than merely sitting in a different position. In revising his basic posture orientation, from floor to chair, the Samoan is disturbing the whole of his usual personal perceptions in social relations. He becomes truly disoriented, for he is asked to "feel" and perceive in ways that a previous lifetime of experience has not prepared him for. And a Samoan's disorientation in this situation will be quite different from that experienced by members of another culture to whom sitting has quite different cultural significance.

Although an adult Samoan may learn to deal with Americans or Europeans, he will react essentially in terms of being Samoan, that is, by "feeling" about and "perceiving" the social situation with the integrated sum of both his being (his biology) and his beliefs and values (his culture). An adult Samoan may learn to adapt to a new culture, but he will do so by confronting the new culture situation in terms of his "Samoan-ness," which has been developed in him from a complex, life-long interplay between his individual biology and his Samoan culture. As an adult he will not and in fact cannot fully discard his Samoan-ness when confronting a new culture. He will attack the problems involved in culture contact by use of his essential Samoan-ness. Because of this, adult Samoans regularly facing a situation of culture contact will display very many regularities and uniformities in their responses to the new culture.

When phrases such as *voluntary control, voluntary meeting, voluntarily,* and so on were used earlier in this chapter, they were not meant in the everyday sense of conscious, willful, or deliberate. Rather they were used in the conceptual sense that it is through the complex and reciprocal interplay of human biology and culture over the long time of socialization that an individual comes as an adult to be possessed of an *ability* that has been developed uniquely out of the socialization process. This ability (and not a capacity) might be defined as the way an adult individual in any culture can, through time, *generate* out of the complexly interrelated bio-

Adult preoccupations become the preoccupations of children; Chippewa Indian mother and daughter (circa 1910). (Courtesy American Museum of Natural History.)

logical and cultural materials available to him, specific ways of altering, shaping, or directing both the internal and physiological and the external and social events directly affecting him.[16]

Fig. 8 presents a diagrammatic scheme of the way in which biology and culture, having become interrelated through a socialization process, produce a human ability to voluntarily shape, control, or direct specific features of biology. (Fig. 8 is an enlarged presentation of the bottom portion of Fig. 6.) It represents the way in which human culture and biology mutually and reciprocally interact through time in a socialization process to produce the ability of adults to voluntarily deal

[16]For some discussions of this ability, see Goodman, 1967; Allport, 1955; Maslow, 1954.

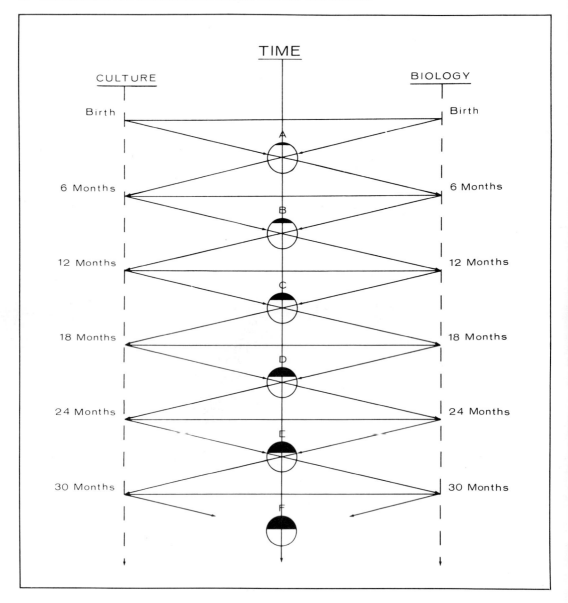

Fig. 8. The emergence of human abilities through the interplay of culture and biology in the socialization process.

with basic aspects of their biology, such as reflexes and drives. In Fig. 8 the open circle, *A*, at the point of intersection of the arrows from *culture to biology* and *biology to culture*, represents the place at which a specific human ability, contained at birth *neither* in human genetic materials nor in culture, can appear in the human process of socialization. At *B*, after some 6 months of life, the open circle has some shading, representing the beginnings of a particular ability as the consequence of the reciprocal interplay between culture and biology in the socialization process. If a culture or cultures emphasizes a particular ability, the circles at each successive intersect between culture and biology will become more shaded *(C to F)*.

This conceptual way of considering a human ability developing from the mutual and reciprocal feedback between biology and culture in a socialization process underlies the discussion in the earlier part of this chapter. It is important to remember that this chapter has focused on only one of the several abilities humans can develop in a socialization process—the ability to voluntarily control specific features of their biology. Man has the potential for developing many different kinds of abilities through the socialization process. For example, in addition to the ability for voluntary control of features of his biology, *Homo sapiens* can develop abilities to be highly creative intellectually and artistically, to become culturally innovative, to be penetrating and efficiently perceptive in social relations, to be highly independent of the other persons in a society, to be and remain nonaggressive, and so on.

Whether or not individuals in a society possess any of these particular abilities appears to depend upon whether the long-term conditions of reciprocal interplay between culture and biology are maintained throughout a particular enculturation process. Too, whether certain abilities are developed depend upon the priorities set within a culture for the stimulation of and provision for some abilities as compared to others. For example, it seems that in American culture we have chosen to give a relatively low priority to development of an ability to voluntarily control most features of biology, in favor of emphasis on abilities that are ranked more highly, such as intellectual creativity in technological and managerial behavior. Many Americans are, in this theoretical sense, enculturated in such a manner as to ensure the development of some kinds of abilities rather than some others. But then, so are yoga practitioners, Cheyenne Sun Dancers, Polynesian firewalkers, and so on.

It is vital to remember, in considering how a people come to have voluntary control over some features of their biology, that *voluntary* should not connote a yoga novice standing with his eyes tightly closed while trying very hard to make his exercises in diaphragm raising successful; rather, we should recall that yoga novices are Indians and have been raised to adulthood in a specific Hindu cultural context in which year upon year of mutual, reciprocal feedback between culture and human biology constantly prepares a man to become a yoga if he so chooses, by developing consistently over a long time a set of circumstances that favor appearance of the ability to voluntarily control certain features of human biology. Thus, wherever voluntary control of features of biology occurs, it does so because the enculturation process in a society provides for the conditions for an ability to do so.

The theoretical distinction between a human capacity (see Chapter Two) and a human ability essentially lies in the fact that a *capacity* appears to be a genetically transmitted "organic bridgehead" already possessed by humans at birth, while *abilities* appear to be developed out of the mutual feedback process between culture and biology through the long period of socialization. Human capacities seem related to human abilities in very complex ways, which at present are understood only vaguely. It appears that, if the basic human capacities for reflection and for symboling are impaired, deficient, or incapable of being expressed because of disease or accident, then there will be no real emergence from the socialization process of an ability for voluntary control over features of biology. However, if these capacities are not impaired in any way and if the socialization process as expressed in the enculturation practices of a particular society provides for the emergence of the ability for voluntary control of features of biology, then humans in that situation will be able, through use of their reflective and symboling capacities, to learn such voluntary controls of biology as may be specified in a culture.

This theoretical point is important in the development of the discussion in this chapter because it is quite apparent now that there may be a great range of possible human abilities, which when used in conjunction with human capacities can lead to new dimensions of human experience, including significant voluntary control of human biological features.

■ Experiments in operant conditioning

In the past three decades experimental psychologists have developed a method of learning research that has been termed *operant conditioning.* The basic studies of operant conditioning were undertaken by Skinner.[17] In considering some of the problems of the Thorndike-Hull behavioristic learning model, Skinner noted that the *law of effect* (which specifies that the response of an organism to a stimulus is automatically strengthened if it is followed by a *reward* and automatically extinguished if followed by a *punishment*) involves a simple time relationship between a response and a consequence. Skinner called the time relationship between response and consequence *operant.*

Skinner boxes. In his efforts to study the time relationship factor in learning, Skinner developed an experimental soundproof box containing a lever that could be depressed by an experimental subject. The depression of the lever by the subject, whether accidental or purposeful, delivered a reward in the form of food. If an experimental subject such as a rat or a pigeon is placed in the Skinner-type apparatus, initially it will not seek out the lever and depress it. However, when through accidental contact the experimental subject depresses the lever, it will receive a reward, usually food. Each time the subject engages again in the lever-pressing response it may receive a reward again. As the repeated lever-depressing responses are administered by the experimental subject to itself without the interference or influence of the experimenter, it receives further rewards and so it conditions itself "operantly."

Measures of behavior. The typical scientific measure of behavior made in such an apparatus is the rate of lever pressing, that is, the number of times in a given period that the subject depresses the lever to receive a reward. Automatic response-recording devices have been attached to the experimental box so that a continuous graph

recording of the number and rate of lever depressions can be made, even in the absence of the experimenter. The recording device moves a pen across paper at a constant speed. Each time the experimental subject depresses the lever the recording pen moves higher on the paper; if no responses are made by the subject, the pen traces a horizontal line. As the subject makes increasingly more responses more quickly, the pen line will ascend on the paper in a way that shows the experimenter, by the steepness of the ascending line, not only how many times the lever was depressed but also how rapidly the lever was depressed.

Schedules of reinforcement. In training animals in this type of an experimental device, Skinner and other psychologists have used different "schedules of reinforcement," that is, they have varied the number of times an animal was rewarded for pressing the box lever. A schedule of reinforcement asks the question, "What happens if rather than rewarding the subject every time it presses the lever, it is reinforced (rewarded) for only some of its responses?"

Experimental psychologists now use four main types of *schedules of reinforcement* to seek answers to this question: (1) *fixed ratio schedules,* (2) *variable ratio schedules,* (3) *fixed interval schedules,* and (4) *variable interval schedules.* A fixed ratio schedule of reinforcement involves a response (lever pressing) being reinforced (rewarded) after a fixed number of unrewarded responses counted from the last rewarded response. A variable ratio schedule of reinforcement is similar to the fixed ratio schedule, except that reinforcements are scheduled randomly and arbitrarily. A fixed interval schedule of reinforcement involves the reward of the first response which occurs after a specific length of time, measured from the last rewarded response. Variable interval schedules of reinforcement are similar to the fixed interval schedules except that reinforcements are scheduled for random and arbitrary intervals of time.

Partial reinforcement effect. By varying the ways experimental animals are rewarded for lever pressing, Skinner and other psychologists have discovered that animals rewarded only part of

---

[17]See Skinner, 1938.

the time appear to have built up a greater operant strength, that is, were more resistant to loss of the rewarded behavior (lever pressing) than were the animals rewarded every time they pressed the lever. This result has been called the *partial reinforcement effect* (PRE). Skinner has made no attempt to explain why partial reinforcement schedules affect experimental subjects so they appear more resistant to loss of the rewarded behavior than animals continually rewarded. He simply has reported these data and left interpretations of this phenomenon to others. Skinner's essential concern in his research has been in choosing what he considers the only two reliable and basic measures of behavior—(1) the rate of responding and (2) the number of responses made by a subject after all rewards available to it have stopped.

However, Skinner's refusal to try to explain the PRE phenomenon in learning has led many others to try to explain it. One reason for a wide and very lively interest in this particular fact of operant learning is that, outside the psychological laboratory, in the human world, most rewards seem to be provided by adults to the maturing child in an intermittent manner, very much like the noncontinuous schedules of reinforcement used in operant experimental studies. Thus adult responses to children seldom are precisely consistent in form each time they occur and may not always involve the same "reward." The PRE formulation seems to be an adequate explanation for humans learning culture. However, this is a conception of human learning that sees children acquiring cultural and social behavior because adults do something to or for them. The discussion of Papago Indian enculturation in Chapter Two makes it clear, however, that in some human societies rewards and punishments for behavior are administered much more by the child to himself than by adults. The socialization process is vastly more complex than the PRE. Trying to apply the PRE concept as a satisfactory explanation for how and why humans become socialized is to misunderstand the nature of culture and of human biology and their interrelationships.

However, a very large number of human operant learning studies have been conducted in the past 20 years. Many of these studies have used infants and young children as experimental subjects.[18] Other studies of human operant learning have been conducted to discover whether the physiological functioning of humans can be permanently influenced or altered.

Human operant conditioning. Studies of operant responses of infants and children are of two kinds: (1) activities involving bar pressing, knob pulling, window pressing, and box opening and (2) activities involving thumb-sucking, verbal and vocal behavior, stuttering, and smiling.[18] Operant research involving the first type of activities typically use devices developed from Skinner's experimental apparatuses. Thus in laboratory studies with infants, Rheingold, Stanley, and Cooley employed an "experimental crib" similar to the one illustrated in Fig. 9, *I*.[19] Research projects on preschool and school-age children have used operant devices similar to the ones developed by Bijou (Fig. 9, *II*), or the one developed by Gewirtz and Baer (Fig. 9, *III*).[20]

In the studies using experimental cribs, infant subjects are seated in a special chair, so that they are partially reclining. They face a screen on which brightly colored, moving images are projected for an instant if they reach out with either hand and merely touch a ball mounted atop an upright lever and placed within their reach. The ball lever may be made into the antenna of an oscillator circuit serving as a sensitive relay to automatically show the number of operant responses of the infant over a given period.

In studies using lever-pressing type devices, preschool and school-age children have been given the opportunity to use a lever as they choose to do so, with rewards such as a movie or music being presented to the child as long as he keeps the lever either depressed or lifted, depending on the act to be rewarded in experimental situations. In a somewhat more complex type of study of operant conditioning, preschool and school-age children sit before a device with two holes in its top surface and an opening at

[18]For a review of such research, see Bijou and Baer, 1966.
[19]See Rheingold, Stanley, and Cooley, 1962.
[20]See Bijou, 1957; Gewirtz and Baer, 1958.

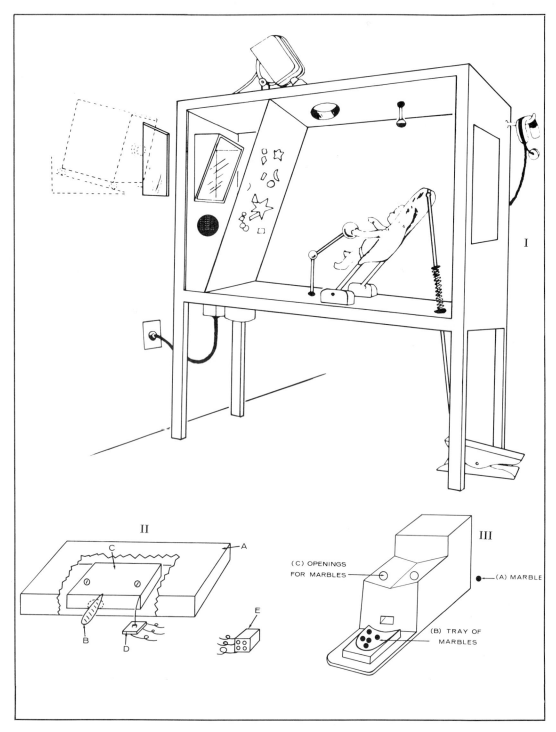

Fig. 9. I, Experimental crib used in operant studies of infants. **II,** Operant conditioning device used in studies of preschool children. *A,* Cover box; *B,* handle of lever; *C,* modified sponge mop assembly; *D,* switch for recording electrical contact; *E,* recording device. **III,** Operant conditioning device used in studies of school-age children.

the base in the front. When the child takes marbles from the tray under the opening in the base and drops them through the two openings in the top of the device, he trips a series of internal switches that record the response and control the dispensing of the reward (food, music, pictures, and so on).

In studies of operant conditioning of thumb-sucking behavior, rewards presented to preschool and school-age children were withdrawn when they sucked on their thumbs. Children were exposed to long sessions of sound movie cartoons. At the times they sucked their thumbs the movies were shut off. When the children took their thumbs from their mouths, the movies continued. The rate and time response of the children in this situation were "judged" by observers screened behind one-way glass. The judges each depressed a recording device when the child sucked his thumb and held it as long as thumb-sucking continued.[21] This procedure of operant conditioning, which both punished thumb-sucking and rewarded thumb removal, is said to have yielded increasingly greater depression of thumb-sucking rates and times after three experimental sessions spaced a few days apart. However, there seem to be no reports of a permanent loss of thumb-sucking behavior through such operant conditioning procedures.

The verbal and vocal behavior responses of infants have been studied, using modifications of the operant conditioning techniques just described. These studies involved observing and recording the discrete sounds of infants, ignoring coughs, whistles, squeaks, and noisy breathing snorts. Little note was taken during the studies of the phonetic characteristics of infant sounds. In one study the observation time used was a set of three 3-minute periods, three times a day for 2 days. This served as a "baseline" for study. Then, during the first 2 days of the research an experimenter stood motionless over the crib of the infant being observed, while an associate stood away from the crib, out of the infant's sight, recording vocalizations by the baby. In the second 2 days of the study, vocalizations

were rewarded by a smile of the observer standing over the crib, by use of the sounds *tsk, tsk, tsk,* and by a light touch administered to the baby's abdomen. In a final 2 days of the study the same procedures used in the first 2 days were repeated. This particular study reported that during 2 days of rewarding of vocalizations by the observer the rate of the baby's vocalizations nearly doubled that recorded in the study "baseline" rate. Furthermore, the study reported the rate of vocalization by the infants studied dropped back during the last 2-day period to almost the baseline rate. This particular operant conditioning experiment was repeated with some minor changes in procedures and the results reported were similar to those of the first study.[22]

More complex studies of operant conditioning of vocalization and verbal behavior have been undertaken with older children in the past decade. These studies sought in various ways to "shape" or to "control" the use of children's speech through operant procedures, that is, rewarding successively closer approximations to the desired response until the subjects learned to verbalize the precise way desired by the experimenters.[23] One of the experimental devices used in these studies is illustrated in Fig. 9, *III.*

Studies of stuttering in children have concluded that it is possible to "weaken" or lessen hesitant speech patterns by means of operant conditioning procedures. In one study, children wearing earphones in an isolated setting were presented a 6,000 cycle tone at an intensity of 105 decibels.[24] To provide for an ongoing operant level of speech during the experiment, children read aloud from materials considered by the experimenters to be easy and interesting for their particular age levels. If a child exhibited any hesitation, stoppage, repetition, or prolongation in his speech as he read, the experimenters judged it to be stuttering behavior. Children were operantly conditioned through use of *avoidance* and *escape* schedules. In avoidance conditioning the 105-decibel tone was continuously

[21]See Baer, 1962a.

[22]See Rheingold, Gewirtz, and Ross, 1959.
[23]See Lovaas, 1961; Baer, 1962b.
[24]See Flanagan, Goldiamond, and Azrin, 1958.

present and a 5-second termination was dependent or contingent upon the child's stuttering. In the escape conditioning a 1-second blast of the 105-decibel tone was presented through the child's earphones following each stuttering response. The results of the research showed that the presentation of the tone as a consequence of stuttering weakened the stuttering speech pattern and that halting the tone when the child stuttered strengthened or led to an increase in stuttering speech.

Efforts have been made to operantly condition smiling behavior in infants. In one study, 4-month-old infants were observed through eight separate 5-minute intervals during which the experimenter stood motionless over a baby's crib, holding her expressionless face about 15 inches from the infant's face.[25] The rate of each infant's smiling was noted during these eight sessions. Then in operant conditioning sessions that consisted of from ten to twelve 5-minute sessions the experimenter rewarded smiling by the infant by smiling in return and also by cuddling the baby. The rate of smiling was counted during these periods. During a later set of observations comprising fifteen 15-minute periods the experimenter, using the same research procedure as in the first set of observations (standing over the crib with an expressionless face), counted the number of smiling responses by the infant subjects. The study concluded that the rate of smiling during the *conditioning period* (when the experimenter smiled back and cuddled the infant) was considerably higher than the rate during the *operant period* (the first time the experimenter stood motionless over the infant and counted smiling responses). The rate of smiling in the *extinction period* (the second time the experimenter stood motionless over the infant and counted smiling responses) was lower than during either the operant (the first) or the conditioning (the second) period.

Contributions of respondent conditioning studies. Studies seeking to determine whether the behavior of humans can voluntarily influence their physiological functioning have been derived

directly from earlier research on the nature of respondent conditioning situations and their physiological correlates. The term *respondent* was used by Skinner at the time he was defining the concept of operant conditioning. A respondent is an unlearned reaction to a specific stimulus, an unconditioned response to an unconditioned stimulus. The contraction of the pupil of the eye in bright light and the galvanic skin reaction to electric shock are examples of respondents. Pavlov's experiments (see Chapter Three) were concerned with respondent conditioning. In contrast, *operants* were said by Skinner to be responses by an organism that occur but that are not elicited by any known stimuli. Hence *respondents* and *operants* are the conceptual opposites of one another.

As early as 1879 Pavlov had reported changes in heart and blood system functioning related to his conditioning of dogs. He noted that, as dogs were trained to salivate at the presentation of stimuli such as tones and lights rather than at the taste or sight of food, the conditioning process also produced some physiological changes in the dogs.

These observations led other persons to investigate the psychophysiological relationships involved in and accompanying respondent conditioning situations. A great many respondent conditioning studies have been conducted in the past half-century, producing a very large body of knowledge and contributing substantially to learning research methodology.

Physiological changes and operant conditioning. After 1950 interest grew in seeking out physiological changes that might accompany or follow from the operant conditioning process. In part, this interest stemmed from the growth of new experimental devices, which made possible a more carefully controlled situation for observing and measuring such changes. Because of the newness of the ideas involved and the long tradition of respondent research, operant conditioning studies of physiological changes tended at first to concentrate on transient, or short-lived, respiratory and cardiovascular responses to operant experimentation with laboratory animals. Then operant conditioning studies

---

[25]See Brackbill, 1958.

began to focus on more durable, or longer lasting, physiological changes involving the endocrine system, the gastrointestinal system, and infectious disease processes in laboratory animals. Quite recent studies of operant conditioning of physiological states have concentrated on seeking durable physiological changes in the cardiovascular system and in brain functions in laboratory animals.[26]

Research on operant conditioning of physiological states in laboratory animals has led to various results. For example, when rats were confined on a small perch and had to move their heads to lift a panel to avoid a bright light being flashed directly into their eyes, their respiration rate increased greatly during the conditioning periods and decreased to normal during the extinction periods.[27] When cats were subjected to intermittent punishment by blasts of air and electric shock during feeding and had to press levers or lift lids to avoid the punishments, they exhibited elevations in blood pressure and a decline in a blood plasma substance termed *pepsinogen* during the conditioning periods and returned to normal physiological functioning in the extinction periods.[28]

In another set of experiments rats had electrodes implanted in different areas of their brains, so that when they pressed a lever they administered a low-voltage discharge to a part of the brain. This research showed that the self-administered electrical stimulations during a conditioning period produced significant changes in rat heart rates when the electrodes were placed in particular parts of the brain (for example, the hypothalamic region). The research also found that, when electrodes were implanted in another part of the rat brain (septal area), the heart rate was significantly decreased during the conditioning period.[29]

Similar research has demonstrated that there are changes in brain wave patterns in operant

situations. For example, monkeys were prepared for research by surgical implantation of electrodes deep into their brains. During experimental periods they were restrained in special chairs; the electrodes were attached to special brain wave recording instruments. Then the monkeys were subjected to several different operant conditioning procedures, including lever pressing to obtain sugar pellets or to avoid a mild electric shock punishment. Through the course of the conditioning periods marked changes were noted in brain wave activity patterns of the monkeys. In the extinction periods of research these changes were no longer noted.[30]

More durable physiological change as the consequence of operant conditioning has been reported from a number of experimental studies. In one study, rats were operantly trained to lick fluid from the end of a tube in order to avoid electric shocks to their feet. Each lick postponed the shock for 15 seconds. Rats could avoid all shocks by licking the tube each 15 seconds. These animals were subjected to this procedure in alternating 1-hour periods (one of conditioning, one of rest), 24 hours a day for 20 days. In this time the subjects consumed twice their normal intake of fluids and almost doubled their body weights. These rats did not lose weight or body fluids in the period of extinction.[31]

A broad range of hormonal changes have also been reported in operant conditioning of rhesus monkeys. There were marked and permanent alterations in thyroid, gonadal, and adrenal hormones produced by a continuous stress administered to the monkeys over a 72-hour period by means of a special conditioning technique. Some of the hormonal processes that changed did not return to their normal values for nearly 3 weeks after the extinction period of research.

In a series of recent experiments, Miller and his associates at Rockefeller University have further refined procedures and a theory for research on operant conditioning of basic physiological states.[32] Miller is interested in demon-

[26]Brady has provided a review and discussion of much of this research (1966). See also Reynolds, 1968.
[27]See Eldridge, 1954.
[28]See Shapiro and Horn, 1955.
[29]See Malmo, 1961; Perez-Cruet, Tolliver, Dunn, Marvin, and Brady, 1963.

[30]See Hearst, Beer, Sheatz, and Galambos, 1960.
[31]See Williams and Teitelbaum, 1956.
[32]See Miller, 1969.

strating that the learning which occurs in classic (respondent) conditioning and that which occurs in operant conditioning are not two different kinds of learning, but rather are manifestations of the same phenomenon expressed under different conditions. His experiments are discussed in the following paragraphs as examples of operant conditioning of physiology and without comment on the proposal (demonstrated by his research) that there is but one kind of learning with different facets; that topic is beyond the scope of an introductory work on socialization.

In one research project Miller and an as-

sociate spent one 45-minute operant conditioning session each day for 40 days experimenting on the salivation of dogs. Dogs in one group were rewarded with water when they showed a burst of salivation, so they would be operantly conditioned to increase their salivation. Dogs in a second group were rewarded whenever there was a long interval between their spontaneous bursts of salivation, so they would be operantly conditioned to decrease salivation. The results of the research strongly suggested that both groups of dogs were operantly conditioned to salivate.

Miller noted that the group of dogs rewarded for increases in salivation seemed to be more aroused and active during the experiment. Concerned that all the experiment had done was to change the level of skeletal and muscle activity

Adult preoccupations become the preoccupations of children; Tambunan Dusun (Sensuron) female ritual specialists entering into trance state on behalf of child at right. (T. R. Williams, 1959.)

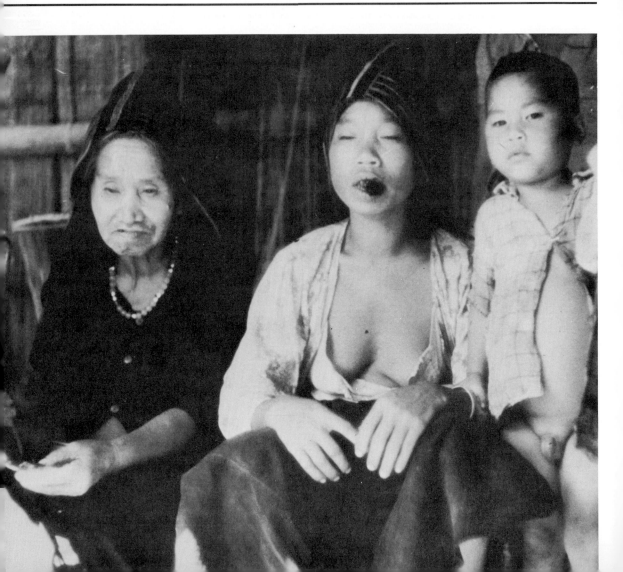

of the dogs, which in turn affected their salivation (and therefore ruled out evidences of operant conditioning), Miller tried a second experiment on salivation operant conditioning. In this experiment he began by paralyzing the dogs with curare to make certain that skeletal movements did not affect the salivation process. This experiment was abandoned when it was found that the use of the curare drug resulted in continuous and large amounts of salivation in all the dogs used and caused such a thick saliva that instruments were fouled beyond any possibility of recording.

Miller and his associates then turned to a study of operant conditioning of the heartbeat rate in rats that had been paralyzed with curare. Two groups of experimental rats were rewarded with direct electrical stimulation of certain areas of their brains as they showed changes, whether an increase or a decrease, in the heartbeat rates in an operant conditioning situation. The rats rewarded in this fashion showed increases and decreases in their heart rates, but the amount of change in heart rate was still so small that Miller developed another, similar experiment in heart rate change to see if he could "shape" the operant changes. In the shaping process, he immediately rewarded the first, very small change in paralyzed rat heart rates that occurred in the desired direction (either an increased rate or a decreased rate), then required progressively larger changes in heart rate for further rewards. In this experiment Miller and his associates quickly produced significant operant conditioning changes.

Miller then turned to the questions of whether these operantly conditioned rats could bring their responses under control and whether these operantly conditioned responses in the form of increased and decreased heart rates were "remembered." These two questions were of interest to Miller because they involved two of the more important characteristics of operant learning. Discrimination learning and memory have been felt not to be typical of respondent, or classic, conditioned learning.

Miller experimented with the rats in a procedure similar to the one used in his previous research to see whether or not they could learn to give a great response in heart rate changes when a flashing light and a tone were associated with the reward. This experiment demonstrated that in fact the rats did learn to clearly discriminate between rewards accompanied by a light and tone and rewards not accompanied by these stimuli.

Miller and his associates then took rats that had been put through one operant conditioning session and returned them to their cages for 3 months. Then these rats were curarized again and returned to the operant conditioning situation. Miller notes that these rats showed a good, reliable memory of their initial and brief training.

Miller also sought to demonstrate that the paralyzed rats could be operantly conditioned to avoid, or to escape from, a mild shock delivered shortly after a shock signal had been given to the rat. During the first 10 seconds after the shock signal the paralyzed rats could turn off the mild shock by making the "correct" (increased or decreased) change in its heart rate by a required amount. If the rats did not make a correct response in the 10-second period after the shock

Rat paralyzed by curare, artifically respirated by a face mask, and rewarded by direct electrical stimulation of the brain for learning changes in heart rate. (From laboratory of Neal E. Miller, Rockefeller University, 1971.)

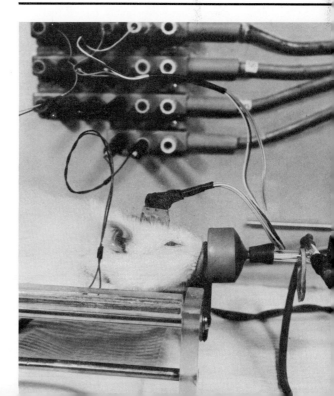

Apparatus for rewarding free-moving rat for changes in heart rate. (From laboratory of Neal E. Miller, Rockefeller University, 1971.)

signal, they were given a continuous shock of electric current until they made the correct response, which then turned off both the shock and the shock signal. Each of the rats in this experiment showed considerable operant learning when escape and avoidance were used as rewards in the conditioning process.

Next, Miller turned to experiments in operant conditioning of the heart rate of rats in a noncurarized, or "normal" state. In his first experiments he had sought to rule out by use of curare the possibility that his subjects were somehow learning the performance of skeletal and muscle responses that were indirectly causing the changes in heart rates being recorded. As he repeated his basic experiments he found that rats not paralyzed by curare showed the same basic changes in heart rates under operant conditioning but did not

show any skeletal or muscle changes that could be related to such heart rate changes. In fact, Miller found that while greater changes in heart rate were being learned by the rats, there were increasingly smaller amounts of respiratory and muscle activities.

Miller then turned to testing the precise specificity of physiological change possible in operant conditioning. First, using curarized rats, he demonstrated that operant conditioning of intestinal contractions is possible in these mammals. In another experiment he determined that the rate of urine formation by the kidney could be changed in curarized rats rewarded by direct electrical stimulation of the brain. In a further experiment Miller and his associates demonstrated that the stomach walls of curarized rats can be operantly conditioned to contract and expand and that altered vasomotor responses affecting the amount of blood in the stomach mucosa, or wall, were amenable to operant conditioning. Miller then turned to research on peripheral vasomotor responses in operant conditioning. He found that curarized rats rewarded by electrical stimulation of the brain could be operantly conditioned to show quite specific and significant changes in the amount of blood in the vessels of their extremities (tails, ears). Miller also demonstrated that changes in systolic blood pressure of curarized rats could be operantly conditioned.

Encouraged by their success in operant conditioning of so many different and specific visceral functions, Miller and his associates turned to experiments on the operant conditioning of brain wave changes. First, cats were equipped with electrodes attached to their brain surfaces. The electrodes picked up the cumulative effects of electrical activity over a considerable area of the brain and a permanent record, called an *electroencephalogram,* was made during the research. When the cats were aroused and active the electroencephalogram showed fast, low-voltage electrical activity. When the cats were quiet, drowsy, or sleeping, the electroencephalogram showed slow, high-voltage activity. The cats were rewarded in the operant conditioning process with direct electrical stimulation of a specific area of the brain (medial forebrain bundle). This stimulation for reward produced a slight average lowering of voltage recorded on the electroencephalogram record. One group of cats was rewarded for showing an increased rate of fast, high-voltage brain electrical activity, and another group was rewarded for showing an increased rate of slow, low-voltage activity. Both groups appeared to become operantly conditioned to changes of rates of brain wave activity. Since the cats were able to move about during the research, it was not clear whether the changes in rates of brain waves might not be in some way related to their freedom of movement. In order to rule out the consequences of muscle tension, movement, and posture on brain wave changes, curarized rats were subjected by Miller to operant conditioning and were found to exhibit a rate of brain wave changes similar to that found in the freely moving cats.

In one other experiment, Miller and his associates sought to determine whether animals could be operantly conditioned to maintain their

Professor Neal E. Miller with equipment for rewarding free-moving rat for changes in heart rate. (From laboratory of Neal E. Miller, Rockefeller University, 1971.)

total physiological balance, or homeostasis. Rats were injected with a hormone (ADH) that was antidiuretic, that is, which prevented loss of body fluids, if they chose one arm of a T shaped maze. If they chose the other arm of the maze they were injected with an isotonic saline solution. The ADH hormone permitted water to be reabsorbed in the kidney so that a smaller volume of more concentrated urine was formed. Thus, for normal rats loaded in advance of the experiment with water, the ADH injection interfered seriously with excess water excretion required for homeostasis, while the isotonic saline solution allowed the excess water to be excreted. The rats in the experiment learned to select the side of the T maze that assured them of an injection of saline so that their glandular response could restore their physiological balance. Miller concluded from this, and from two similar control experiments, that rats would in fact learn in an operant manner to make those specific glandular and visceral responses that would restore a physiological balance.

A number of persons have sought recently to duplicate Miller's results in operant conditioning of specific features of physiology through research on human subjects. In an experiment conducted at the Harvard Medical School, Shapiro, Tursky, Gershon, and Stern developed automatic instruments that yielded a continuous measure of a human subject's systolic blood pressure on each successive heartbeat.[33] This device was then used in operant conditioning of systolic blood pressure in twenty "normal male" subjects between 21 and 27 years of age. The subjects were given twenty-five trials, with each trial being 25 seconds long. The beginning of each trial was indicated by a blue light. Ten subjects were rewarded for increasing their systolic pressure, while ten were rewarded for decreasing their systolic pressure. The reward used was a brief flash of red light and a short tone of moderate intensity. The results of this study tend to confirm the fact that a specific feature of human physiology, such as systolic blood pressure, can be operantly conditioned. Similar human operant conditioning re-

search has been undertaken by Engle of the National Institute of Child Health and Human Development on heart rate and rhythms, by Kamiya of the Langley Porter Institute on brain waves, and by Lang of the University of Wisconsin on human heart rates.

In a series of experiments on the physiological effects of "transcendental meditation," a Hindu form of concentrating the reflective process on body functions, Wallace of the University of California at Los Angeles noted the oxygen consumption, heart rate, skin resistance, and electroencephalographic measurements of subjects before, during, and after their state of meditation. He says that there were "significant changes" in all of these physiological measures during the time of meditation for each of fifteen subjects. During meditation, oxygen consumption and heart rates decreased markedly, skin resistance increased, and the electroencephalogram showed specific changes in certain brain wave frequencies. Wallace believes these changes were all consequences of the meditation process.[34]

It should be pointed out that Miller and others have warned that, in addition to the question of whether operant conditioning effects will be durable in humans, there is the serious question in human studies of whether the changes recorded really represent true operant learning of physiological responses or the unconscious learning of those muscular and skeletal responses that can produce physiological changes. Miller feels that the experimenters working with operant conditioning of physiological functions are developing the scientific controls and procedures to be able to answer these questions. He believes that the cumulative results of this research tend to demonstrate that the autonomic nervous system is quite probably within the scope of change, and voluntary control, through operant conditioning techniques. He also believes that this research shows that there is no validity to the hypothesis that there are two very different, separate mechanisms of learning involving different parts of the nervous system and that cannot be influenced by one another.

---

[33]See Shapiro, Tursky, Gershon, and Stern, 1969.

[34]See Wallace, 1970.

One area of research that recently has been opened by these studies of operant conditioning of physiological states and by recent advances in research in genetics and biochemistry is the field of behavioral genetics. For instance, mice have been operantly conditioned to be aggressive toward mice that have not been trained to fight. The untrained mice, when placed in a "no-escape" situation with "aggressive" mice, cowed in a corner and responded with such high adrenal output changes that their hearts and kidneys were damaged to the point that they died shortly after the experiments. The "aggressive" mice responded to the confrontations with untrained mice through an initial high level of adrenal output, but their previous operant conditioning to aggression behavior appears to have allowed for a return of the adrenal output to a near normal state. Analysis of the brain cells of the two groups of mice revealed distinctly different quantities of RNA. The mice trained in aggression behavior had one pattern of brain cell RNA, while the untrained mice had another pattern of RNA.[35] RNA (ribonucleic acid) and DNA (deoxyribonucleic acid) are two types of nucleic acids. Nucleic acids have been identified as the basic stuff of all hereditary materials. Depending upon the organism, either DNA or RNA can carry a genetic code. Thus significant changes in the RNA patterns in operantly conditioned organisms, including humans, may give clues to the ways naturally selective, or evolutionary, changes can take place in populations of animals subject to common experiences, including socialization.

Furthermore, it has been suggested that nucleic acids of nerve cells, and particularly nerve cell proteins, contain learned information. This idea is based on the fact that the growth of a nerve cell and its connections depends upon the long-term responses it makes to repeated stimulation. Since all cell growth basically involves the synthesis of nucleic acids and proteins, it may be that different kinds of stimulation that produce cell growth would lead to the formulation of different nucleic acids and proteins. Thus different

kinds of stimulation should be reflected in differing patterns of nerve cell nucleic acids and proteins.

In a novel experiment to test these ideas, Hydén and Egyházi investigated the way learning and memory are linked to so-called "messenger" RNA (mRNA); mRNA is the cell physiology process by means of which proteins are specified, or identified.[36]

In this operant conditioning experiment, rats were required to reach into a cylinder to obtain a reward of food. Each rat was allowed twenty-five extractions of food to show a "handedness" (or "pawness") preference. When a rat used the right paw in twenty-three of the twenty-five extractions, it was labelled "right-handed" and was then forced to use the opposite paw to extract the food reward. This was accomplished by moving the wall of the Skinner box type experimental apparatus so that the rats could not use their right paws to obtain the food reward. During the 4 days of the experiment, each rat made between 400 and 500 attempts to extract the food reward. After the 4-day experimental period, the nerve cell bodies from the right and left sides of the rat brain cerebral cortexes were removed from the area known to control handedness and analyzed for mRNA content. Nerve cells from the right side of the cortex were designated "learning" cells, while those from the left side of the cortex were termed "control" cells. The experimenters knew that if the forced transfer to left-handed food getting had led to any change in the mRNA contents of cortex cells, it would appear on the right (learning) side area of the brain. The analysis of mRNA content of the cortex cells showed a significantly higher amount of mRNA in each of the right (learning) side nerve cells. To demonstrate that the increase in mRNA had in fact taken place in the right side cortex cells during the transfer of handedness in the experiment, Hydén and Egyházi examined right-handed rats of the same genetic strain not subjected to the operant condition process and found no significant difference between the amount of mRNA in the right and left cerebral

---

[35]See Stock, 1969.

[36]See Hydén and Egyházi, 1964.

cortex cells. Thus these results provide some support for the hypothesis that the learning process results in an increased production of nucleic acids and proteins in the nerve cells directly involved. These results must be interpreted and understood, however, in the context of other operant conditioning experiments concerning the effects of certain drugs, such as *actinomycin D* and *puromycin,* on the nerve cell production of mRNA in learning. These experiments tend to show that the roles of nucleic acids and proteins in learning are time-dependent processes, that is, are linked directly to the amount of operant conditioning given to an animal. This area of research promises to provide fresh and exciting insights into the fundamental biological bases of learning and learned behavior.

Conclusions: operant conditioning studies. The concept of operant conditioning and the research evidences that have been derived in support of it provide a vital departure from models of learning in which various "external" influences automatically produce behavioral responses by an organism. There now is a systematic way to consider that organisms can learn through directing their own responses to many different stimuli, whether these arise within the body or in the outside environment. Operant conditioning research has made it possible to shift the emphasis in theories of behavior away from inexactly defined motivational states (such as "drive") to explanations focusing upon specific, observable, physiological processes. In other words, the procedures of operant conditioning research are precise enough to allow a clear determination of whether a behavior form really is caused by something that has been observed and can be specified. Research on operant conditioning has greatly clarified the specific relations between behavior and biology.

The application of operant research procedures to normal human behavior is severely limited by ethical and moral considerations, which are quite proper and should continue. It is unlikely that any investigator will try to curarize a human infant or adult to fully control skeletal and muscle influences on operant conditioning of specific physiological processes. Thus, whether operant research procedures lead to long-lasting changes in humans and really are the consequence of operant learning still remains an open question. It is possible that research on human volunteers who are afflicted with diseases of a fatal or very severely limiting nature can provide some additional evidences concerning the application of operant conditioning techniques to man. Thus patients suffering from fatally high blood pressure or severe spastic colitis, asthma, cardiac arrhythmias (irregular heartbeat), insomnia, or epilepsy may be helped greatly through attempts at therapeutic alleviation of their conditions by operant conditioning methods. In turn, such therapeutic alleviation and change may possibly provide research data for answers to the questions of the durability and specific nature of operant learning in man.

▪ Conclusions

The first part of this chapter noted that there are ethnographic reports suggesting a variety of specific relationships between culture and human biology. Until recently these data have generally been relegated to the status of scholarly curios. Ethnographic accounts as diverse and esoteric as yoga exercises, Cheyenne pole swinging, Zuni fire initiations, Polynesian firewalking, food practices of South American Indians, Borneo peoples, and African natives, varying conditions of constipation, diarrhea, and nausea among New Guinea peoples, magical fright in Meso-America, blushing and fatigue patterns, different ways of walking, standing, and sitting, different culturally styled gestures, and the different ways number, sequence, and time concepts seem to be related to features of human biology in different cultures all seemed to have little place in a scientific understanding of human behavior.

However, the development of theory in socialization and emergence of operant conditioning methods in psychology have lifted such ethnographic reports from the file of curious human customs and have placed them in the forefront of research seeking to understand the specific ways human culture and biology became interrelated in a process of socialization.

SUMMARY OF OPERANT CONDITIONING OF
SPECIFIC PHYSIOLOGICAL PROCESSES IN
ANIMALS AND HUMANS

I. Animal subjects
  A. Respiratory rate
  B. Blood pressure levels
  C. Endocrine
  D. Gastrointestinal
  E. Infectious diseases
  F. Brain wave
  G. Body weight
  H. Salivation
  I. Heart rate
  J. Intestinal contractions
  K. Mucosa blood supply
  L. Peripheral vascular responses
  M. Homeostasis

II. Human subjects
  A. Systolic blood pressure
  B. Heart rate
  C. Brain waves

For example, anthropologists have long been able to reach into their ethnographic store of esoteric customs to bring forth numerous citations to the many different ways humans flush and blush in different circumstances. These facts of custom meant little until the development of precise experimental procedures in the operant conditioning of peripheral vascular responses, that is, until it was demonstrated by Miller and his associates that at least one kind of mammal could learn on its own to control and adjust the flow of blood to its extremity surfaces, with more or less blood flowing to the tip of a tail or to the right rather than the left ear. Too, the customs of humans in meeting starvation conditions, in defecation, and so on were only mildly interesting events until the demonstration in operant conditioning research of the specific ways some mammals can direct and control contractions of the intestine and stomach, as well as the amount of blood flow to the stomach wall.

Now, using these different kinds of data it is possible to begin thinking and talking more clearly about what has been termed in this chapter as the mutual, reciprocal feedback process between culture and human biology. Studies of operant conditioning not only indicate *how* particular physiological processes might be controlled by an organism on its own volition or through its own choices, but as well may indicate *how* immersion in a culture develops in the human organism a great number of biological/behavioral abilities that in time become firmer and more irreversible. In brief, the studies of operant conditioning, and particularly the operant conditioning of specific physiological processes, possibly can indicate how humans actually acquire culture and use it as the base for their behavior.

Another contribution that operant conditioning research may make to a more precise understanding of socialization is by providing a broader theoretical base for study of that process. In the preceding chapter an effort was made to show that too little attention had been given in formulations of the major models of learning to the ways human capacities, such as reflection and symboling, were directly involved in the process of socialization. The case data from Papago enculturation was presented to provide an illustration of the ways a culture can come to focus its enculturation process on capacities such as reflection and symboling. An attempt was made to demonstrate that Papago adults rarely have used or depended primarily upon their "doing something" (overtly rewarding or punishing) to children as they matured. Rather, Papago have placed the general burdens of the enculturation process onto their children, who must interpret, define, and choose for themselves the behavior that might be rewarded or punished by adults if the adults were in fact active in administration of such rewards and punishments.

In the sense of the traditional learning models, Papago enculturation seems so diaphanous in its texture as to be nonexistent. That is, if you set out to describe Papago enculturation using the Thorndike-Hull behavioristic model, for example, you could find very little actual "classic conditioning" of children by adults. However, the concept and results of operant conditioning research make it clear that Papago children can contribute greatly to enculturating themselves in the context of Papago culture. In fact, operant conditioning research suggests the following theoretical model of Papago enculturation: Papago children generally become enculturated by regularly selecting out for themselves the features of their behavior which, if they were adults, they would reward. Then, after engaging in such behavior, Papago children administer rewards to themselves for behaving in a manner which, if they were Papago adults and if adults provided rewards, they would reward to show their approval. Too, Papago children become enculturated through regularly selecting out for themselves features of their behavior which, if they were adults, they would punish. Then, after such behavior, Papago children administer punishments to themselves for behavior in a way which, if they were Papago adults and if adults provided punishments, they would punish to show their disapproval. In the course of administering to themselves the rewards and punishments Papago adults know but generally avoid using, Papago children can be said to be operantly conditioning themselves to their culture.

The key features of such self-administered rewards and punishments in Papago enculturation would seem to be the genetically transmitted capacities for reflection and symboling. Papago children, in common with most children, are born with capacities to go beyond the observed properties of a specific object or social event, to draw conclusions on the basis of their past experiences concerning unobserved properties of objects or events, and also to symbolically reproduce these conclusions and project them into the future so they can consider alternative possibilities of immediate and future behavior before they act. In this way, and through these capacities, they can come to administer to themselves rewards and punishments for their behavior that are consistent with cultural standards and values they are not actively taught but must observe and about which they must draw proper conclusions. Once these conclusions are drawn, Papago children must then symbolically project them into a future time when they will be adults to determine which of the many alternative courses of action they would, if they were adults, approve of and provide rewards for children like themselves.

It is clear that these genetically transmitted capacities and their specific uses in this type of learning of culture are not confined to Papago children. They have been noted in use in enculturation in most other cultures. For example, DuBois, in observing the ways Alorese children learn adult views that food is valuable, important, and in uncertain supply, used the concepts of "absorptive learning" and "psychic osmosis" to note that these Indonesian children learn for themselves proper attitudes toward food from observing, reflecting upon, and symbolically reproducing for themselves the cultural values of adults about food and hunger.[37] Gardner has described a similar enculturation process among the Paliyans of South India. Paliyan children seem to be subjected to only a minimum of adult direction as they learn their culture. In fact, Paliyan enculturation closely resembles Papago enculturation in making children essentially responsible for their learning of culture.[38] An examination of the records of enculturation processes described by trained observers leads to the hypothesis that considerably more of human culture is transmitted to children through an operant conditioning like self-enculturation use of the capacities for reflection and symboling than through use of overt parental rewards and punishments for behavior of children. The Papago style of allowing children to almost fully enculturate themselves is an unusual one among the world's cultures. But then, so is the enculturation style proposed under the formulations of traditional behavioristic models of learning unusual among the cultures of the world. In fact, there is no example to be cited of such a culture. Apparently there are no historic or contemporary records of any cultures that have developed enculturation processes in which children regularly and constantly are subjected by parents to specific rewards and punishments for all their behavior. The general style of enculturation, from the present record, appears to be somewhat about a midpoint between the two hypothetical extremes of (1) enculturation by full and constantly active parental administration of rewards and punishments and (2) full self-enculturation.

---

[37]See DuBois, 1941.
[38]See Gardner, 1966.

The record of the enculturation process in contemporary American society, for instance, seems to show a combination of uses of some quite specific forms of rewards and punishments for certain kinds of behavior (especially sexual, anal, aggression, and dependence learning) with a substantial amount of reliance of children enculturating themselves in broad areas of the culture (such as technology, political values, and social organization). Thus Americans tend to assign to their children the responsibility for learning by themselves many substantive features of American culture. American adults are then very surprised when they discover that self-enculturation may result in serious misunderstanding of and rapid changes in culture.* When the adults of a culture allow children to reward or to punish themselves for behaving in ways which, if they were adults, they would reward or punish, they run the great risk of having their children seriously misperceive the style, flavor, intents, and latent meanings of a culture. Adults in some cultures, such as the Kaoka speakers of Guadalcanal, use comment at specific points in a child's enculturation just to ensure that he does not misperceive the intent of values of behavior held important in adult life.[39]

Teleological reasoning in studies of socialization. It is important not to conclude from the discussion and examples in this chapter that humans are born with an innate impetus to move through the socialization process toward the specific goal of acquiring and using culture. Human infants are born into an ongoing cultural system. They are equipped with some biological features that they can use in a long-term process of learning culture. But whether or not human infants learn culture depends upon a large number of complex, nonbiological factors over which a baby has no effective control. In order to learn culture, infants must be born with certain biological features unimpaired, must live and grow, and must be in a situation of regular communica-

tive contact with adults (see Chapter Five). Human infants will not learn culture because they are born possessed of some biological features such as reflexes, drives, and capacities that can be used to learn culture; there is no demonstrable "grand design" or larger plan for socialization. The kind of reasoning which explains events in terms of their contribution to goals or ends of a larger plan is termed *teleological.* The concept of socialization is in a limited sense teleological because it looks forward to the goal of humans acquiring culture. The concept is teleological in another limited sense, since it also looks back to the beginnings of the process of transmitting and acquiring culture.

But the whole idea of teleological explanation has inherent in it a basic logical problem. On the one hand, teleological explanation involves a demonstration that it is a fundamental part of what is explained to have specific goals which themselves contribute to the success of a larger whole or design. Thus the physiological working of the kidney would be explained teleologically by saying that the regular removal of tissue wastes contributes to homeostasis and therefore to the continuation of the life of the organism. What is being explained (the workings of the kidneys) is teleologically accounted for when it is said to have specific consequences for a larger complex (homeostasis) and system (life).

On the other hand, teleological explanations can be put easily in a reverse fashion, that is, the thing to be explained (the workings of the kidney) is understood because it has the consequences it has for a larger complex (homeostasis) or system (life). In this kind of a reversed teleological explanation, the end brought about (the workings of the kidneys) is viewed as "designed" by "something" or "someone" as part of a plan to ensure the success of the larger complex or system.

An understanding of these two kinds of teleological explanation, termed by Spencer in 1879 as "legitimate" and "illegitimate," might be found in two examples.[40] First we ask the question, "How do we explain the form of marriage among

---

*Mead has suggested that the American enculturation process now also involves children informing their parents about vital elements of American culture and thereby reversing the traditional form of the enculturation process (see Mead, 1970).

[39]See Hogbin, 1965: 33-34.

[40]See Spencer, 1879.

the Dusun of Borneo?" Then we apply the two types of teleological explanations to seek our answer. The first kind of teleological explanation, which Spencer calls "legitimate," would note that the form of marriage among the Dusun is to be explained by observing that it produces the integration and cohesion of larger and unrelated social groups. This form of explanation looks forward to a goal or purpose for the form of Dusun marriage. The second kind of teleological explanation, which Spencer terms "illegitimate," would ask an opposite question about the form of Dusun marriage, that is, "Why does marriage among the Dusun take this particular form?" This question presupposes that Dusun marriage is part of an original and larger design, or plan, for human marriage and looks back to that plan to understand the form that Dusun marriage has taken.

This chapter and text seek to discuss on an introductory level several aspects of the socialization process. The discussion is not concerned primarily with explaining the consequences of the socialization process for individual learning and behavior. There has been no attempt to account teleologically for the socialization process by saying that it has specific consequences for a larger complex (the learning of individual behavior) or larger system (culture or biology). It was suggested in the first chapter that the process of socialization arose in the course of the long-term, reciprocal, mutual feedback between human biology and behavior. The socialization process is to be accounted for as an emergent evolutionary fact of both man's body and his natural ecology, or culture, and is best explained in these terms. There is no scientific evidence that the socialization process is the consequence of and exists because of some grand design or plan. The socialization process apparently arose as a natural, random, chance occurrence in the long time of man's physical evolution and his adaptation to culture as his natural ecology. The socialization process clearly did not arise solely from human biology, or only from culture, and is not to be explained finally in terms of its intended or actual consequences for either human biology or culture.

Circular reasoning in studies of socialization. Finally, it should be noted that there has been no attempt in this chapter or in this text to explain some of the ways the mutual, reciprocal feedback process between human biology and culture functions through use of a circular reasoning or logic. An example of circular reasoning would be to say, "B causes C to behave in ways 1, 2 and 3; therefore C causes B to behave in ways 1, 2, and 3." This chapter has attempted to set forth some data and to explain a few of the ways that human biology and culture may become interrelated through a socialization process. It can appear on a casual reading that what has been said is circular in form. The intention here has been only to give some brief indications that the biological and cultural modes of transmission in the socialization process become, through time, complexly interrelated through a doubly contingent and reciprocal feedback from one mode into the other. It has been suggested also that, in the course of this long-term feedback process, abilities are developed that are not present in the biology or behavior of a newborn child. The biological precursors, that is, signs or indications, of such abilities are part of the genetic heritage of all humans. But the development of abilities depends upon the specific conditions and history of the local culture into which a human child is born and especially upon the conditions, through a long period of time, in which the mutual interplay between biology and culture takes place. There was no intention to say that B (biology) causes C (culture) to develop in ways X, Y, and Z and that therefore C (culture) causes B (biology) to develop in ways X, Y, and Z. And there was no intention to claim that human abilities arising in the course of the socialization process causes biology to influence culture, which in turn causes culture to influence biology.

■ **Summary**

This chapter has been concerned with discussing some of the ways culture and human biology become interrelated in the socialization process. It began with some ethnographic examples of the various ways humans culturally structure reflexes and drives, metabolic requirements, and some other features of their biology. That portion of the chapter concluded with a brief summary of the socialization theory used in the chapter and text. The second part of the chapter was concerned with a brief account of the concept of learning through operant conditioning and of the ways this research method has been used to alter various types of physiological processes and behavior in laboratory animals and in human subjects. It was noted that data and conclusions of operant conditioning research provided some innovative ways to understand ethnographic accounts of humans learning in a socialization process to control reflexes, drives, and other features of human biology. The chapter ended with a discussion of some of the ways that conclusions from operant conditioning studies, when joined with the kinds of ethnographic data discussed in the first part of the chapter, may provide for a broader theoretical base for the concept of socialization.

REFERENCES CITED AND SUGGESTED READINGS

Anand, B., G. China, and B. Singh. 1961. "Some Aspects of Electroencephalographic Studies in Yogis," Electroencephalography and Clinical Neurophysiology 13:452-456.

Allport, G. 1955. Becoming. New Haven, Conn.: Yale University Press.

Baer, D. 1962a. "Laboratory Control of Thumbsucking by Withdrawal and Re-presentation of Positive Reinforcement," Journal of Experimental Analysis of Behavior 5:525-528.

_____. 1962b. "A Technique of Social Reinforcement for the Study of Child Behavior: Behavior Avoiding Reinforcement Withdrawal," Child Development 33:847-858.

Benedict, R. 1946. The Chrysanthemum and the Sword. Boston: Houghton-Mifflin.

Bijou, S. 1957. "Methodology for an Experimental Analysis of Child Behavior," Psychological Reports 3:243-250.

Bijou, S., and D. Baer. 1966. "Operant Methods in Child Behavior and Development." In W. K. Honig (ed.), Operant Behavior: Areas of Research and Application. New York: Appleton-Century-Crofts, pp. 718-789.

Brackbill, Y. 1958. "Extinction of the Smiling Response in Infants as a Function of Reinforcement Schedule," Child Development 29:115-124.

Brady, J. 1966. "Operant Methodology and the Experimental Production of Altered Physiological States." In W. Honig (ed.), Operant Behavior: Areas of Research and Application. New York: Appleton-Century-Crofts, pp. 609-633.

Cannon, W. 1942. "Voodoo Death," American Anthropologist 44:169-181.

Cooper, J. R., et al. 1970. Biochemical Basis of Neuropharmacology. New York: Oxford Press.

Coon, C. 1950. "Human Races in Relation to Environment and Culture with Special Reference to the Influence of Culture on Genetic Changes in Human Population," Cold Spring Harbor Symposia on Quantitative Biology 15:247-258.

Corning, W., and S. Ratner. 1967. The Chemistry of Learning. New York: Plenum Press.

DuBois, C. 1941. "Attitudes Toward Food and Hunger in Alor." In L. Spier, A. Hallowell, and S. Newman (eds.), Language, Culture and Personality: Essays in Memory of Edward Sapir. Menasha, Wisconsin: Sapir Memorial Fund, pp. 272-281.

Eldridge, L. 1954. "Respiration Rate Change and Its Relation to Avoidance Behavior," Doctoral Dissertation, Columbia University.

Feigen, G. 1969. "Bucky Fuller and the Firewalk," Saturday Review, July 12, 1969, pp. 22-23.

Flanagan, B., I. Goldiamond, and N. Azrin. 1958. "Operant Stuttering: The Control of Stuttering Behavior Through Response-Contingent Consequence," Journal of Experimental Analysis of Behavior 1:173-177.

Ford, C., and F. Beach. 1951. Patterns of Sexual Behavior. New York: Harper.

Gardner, P. 1966. "Symmetric Respect and Memorate Knowledge: The Structure and Ecology of Individualistic Culture," Southwestern Journal of Anthropology 22:389-415.

Gewirtz, J., and D. Baer. 1958. "Deprivation and Satiation of Social Reinforcers as Drive Conditioners," Journal of Abnormal and Social Psychology 57:165-172.

Gillin, J. 1944. "Custom and Range of Human Response," Character and Personality 13:101-134.

_____. 1948. "Magical Fright," Psychiatry 11:387-400.

_____. 1951. The Culture of Security in San Carlos. New Orleans: Middle American Research Institute.

Goodman, M. 1967. The Individual and Culture. Homewood, Ill.: Dorsey.

Hearst, E., B. Beer, G. Sheatz, and R. Galambos. 1960. "Some Electrophysiological Correlates of Conditioning in the Monkey," EEG and Clinical Neurophysiology Journal 12:137-152.

Henry, J. 1949. "Anthropology and Psychosomatics," Psychosomatic Medicine 11:216.

Hogbin, I. 1965. A Guadalcanal Society: The Koaka Speakers. New York: Holt, Rinehart and Winston.

Hydén, H., and E. Egyházi. 1964. "Changes in RNA Content and Base Composition in Cortical Neurons of Rats in a Learning Experiment Involving Transfer of Handedness," Proceedings of the National Academy of Sciences, U.S.A. 52:1030-1035.

Kluckhohn, C. 1954. "Culture and Behavior." In G. Lindzey (ed.), *Handbook of Social Psychology*, Vol. II. Cambridge, Mass.: Addison-Wesley, pp. 921-976.

LaBarre, W. 1947. "The Cultural Basis of Emotions and Gestures," Journal of Personality 16:49-68.

Lovaas, O. 1961. "Interaction Between Verbal and Nonverbal Behavior," Child Development 32:329-336.

Malmo, R. 1961. "Slowing of Heart Rate After Septal Self-Stimulation in Rats," Science 133:1128-1130.

Maslow, A. 1954. *Motivation and Personality*. New York: Harper and Row.

Mead, M. 1946. "Research on Primitive Children." In L. Carmichael (ed.), *Manual of Child Psychology*. New York: Wiley, pp. 667-706.

——————. 1956. "The Concept of Culture and the Psychosomatic Approach." In D. G. Haring (ed.), *Personal Character and the Cultural Milieu*. Syracuse, N. Y.: Syracuse University Press, pp. 594-622.

——————. 1970. *Culture and Commitment; a Study of the Generation Gap*. New York: Natural History Press and Doubleday.

Mead, M., and F. MacGregor. 1951. *Growth and Culture*. New York: G. P. Putnam's Sons.

Miller, N. 1969. "Learning of Visceral and Glandular Responses," Science 163:434-445.

Needham, A. E. 1964. "Biological Considerations of Wound Healing." In W. Montagna and R. E. Billingham (eds.), *Advances in Biology of Skin*, Vol. 5. Oxford: Pergamon, pp. 1-29.

Perez-Cruet, J., G. Tolliver, G. Dunn, S. Marvin, and J. Brady. 1963. "Concurrent Measurement of Heart Rate and Instrumental Avoidance Behavior in the Rhesus Monkey," Journal of Experimental Analysis of Behavior 6:61-64.

Quain, B. 1948. *Fijian Village*. Chicago: University of Chicago Press.

Reynolds, G. 1968. *A Primer of Operant Conditioning*. Glenview, Ill.: Scott, Foresman.

Rheingold, H., J. Gewirtz, and H. Ross. 1959. "Social Conditioning of Vocalizations in the Infant,"

Journal of Comparative and Physiological Psychology 52:68-73.

Rheingold, H., W. Stanley, and J. Cooley. 1962. "A Crib for the Study of Exploratory Behavior in Infants," Science 136:1054-1055.

Schultes, R. 1969. "Hallucinogens of Plant Origin," Science 163:245-254.

Shapiro, A., and P. Horn. 1955. "Blood Pressure, Plasma Pepsinogen and Behavior in Cats Subjected to Experimental Production of Anxiety," Journal of Nervous and Mental Disease 122:222-231.

Shapiro, D., B. Tursky, E. Gershon, and M. Stern. 1969. "Effects of Feedback and Reinforcement on the Control of Human Systolic Blood Pressure," Science 163:588-590.

Skinner, B. 1938. *The Behavior of Organisms*. New York: Appleton-Century-Crofts.

Spencer, H. 1879. *The Data of Ethics*. New York: A. L. Burt.

Stevenson, M. C. 1904. *The Zuni Indians*. Washington, D. C.: 23d Annual Report of the Bureau of American Ethnology.

Stock, R. 1969. "The Mouse Stage of the New Biology," New York Times Magazine, December 21, 1969, pp. 8ff.

Tolley, H. 1948. "Populations and Food Supply," Chronica Botanica 11:217-224.

Wallace, R. 1970. "Physiological Effects of Transcendental Meditation," Science 167:1751-1754.

Wenger, M., and B. Bagchi. 1961. "Studies of Autonomic Functions in Practitioners of Yoga in India," Behavioral Science 6:312-323.

Wenger, M., B. Bagchi, and B. Anand. 1961. "Experiments in India on 'Voluntary Control' of the Heart and Pulse," Circulation 24:1319-1325.

Williams, D., and P. Teitelbaum. 1956. "Control of Drinking Behavior by Means of an Operant Conditioning Technique," Science 124:1294-1296.

Wyman, L. 1936. "Navaho Diagnosticians," American Anthropologist 38:236-246.

Zborowski, M. 1952. "Cultural Components in Responses to Pain," Journal of Social Issues 8:16-30.

FIVE A SOCIALIZATION RESEARCH STRATEGY
STUDIES OF ISOLATED CHILDREN AND TWINS

This chapter discusses two types of evidence now available that can aid in illustrating the ways human biology and culture become interrelated in socialization. The first kind of evidence comes from studies of children isolated for long periods from the usual enculturation process in their society. The second kind of evidence comes from studies of twins who share the same or nearly the same genetic heritage and who are enculturated separately in the same society. The first kind of study illustrates the point that, if a newborn child has its basic drives met even at the most minimal levels, it will mature biologically, although fitfully, and perhaps well below its potential growth pattern. However, there will be no accompanying development of cultural and social behavior forms, for these must be acquired in the context of regular communicative contact with other persons. The study of twins helps us see more clearly that, while individuals sharing a common genetic heritage can be very much alike biologically, they also may behave quite differently, depending on the enculturation processes they are exposed to as they grow up.

■ **Isolated children**

Types of studies. A significant amount of evidence demonstrating the fundamental ways in which species-characteristic behavior forms, reflexes, drives, and capacities may serve as organic bridgeheads to socialization is to be found in the literature of studies of isolated infants and children. This literature is quite large and is fragmented into loosely related topics. Sociologists have tended to concern themselves with studies of socially isolated and culturally deprived infants and children. Psychologists have tended to concern themselves with studies of twins separated from one another at or near birth and raised in different physical,

social, and cultural environments. Some psychologists concerned with clear definitions and evidence in support of a "critical incidents" hypothesis (see Chapter Six) have worked with experimentally isolated laboratory animals (monkeys, rats) to study the long-term effects of imprinting and the deprivation of maternal care and social contact. Physicians and psychiatrists have tended to be concerned with studies of severely emotionally disturbed (autistic) children and children isolated socially and culturally because of immobilizing biological limitations (blindness, brain damage at birth, and so on).

To make these accounts easier to understand, this widely scattered literature has been categorized in this chapter under general headings. It is important to recall that the entire discussion is concerned with the vital question, "What happens to the infant or child raised in conditions of extreme physical or social isolation, with a minimum of stimulation to cultural learning?" It is also important to remember that the instances of isolated infants and children demonstrate in a unique manner the role of socialization in the development and expression of what we ordinarily take to be "human *(Homo sapiens)* nature" and human "personality." The scientific studies of isolated infants and children tend to strongly support the statement that most of the behavior we feel to be somehow "normal" in *Homo sapiens* does not in fact occur outside of a process of socialization.

Feral children: an apocryphal tale. Studies of isolated human infants and children must labor under a very heavy burden of folk tales concerning children who are supposed to have been raised by animals. All of us are familiar with the tale of Romulus and Remus, legendary founders of Rome, who were said in the ancient Roman folk tales to have been suckled and cared for by a wolf mother. Many of us have read, or have had read to us, stories such as Kipling's *Mowgli*, the boy supposedly raised from infancy by wolves and friend of Bagbeera, the black panther. A recent American television series for children depicted a young boy being raised with tigers.

Unfortunately, such folk myths have also become established in the general literature concerned with studies of isolated infants and children. Stories such as those of Victor, "the Wild Boy of Aveyron," the "Hessian Wolf Boy," Amala and Kamala, the so-called "Wolf Girls of Midnapore" and Parasram, the "Wolf Boy of Agra" have tended to provide support, more often from the fact of the great length of time the tale has been in print (Victor was found near Aveyron in 1799) than from any credible scientific proof for folk-culture myths, that human infants and children can be and are raised by animal parents.[1]

The basis of myth. Bettelheim has examined this literature and has concluded that such tales arise from the fearful delusions in parents created by the presence of severely emotionally disturbed, or *autistic*, children in human society. Bettelheim believes that the feral infant and child myths also reflect a very human desire to want to believe that a benign nature looks after lost or abandoned autistic children. When isolated autistic children have come to general attention it appears, says Bettelheim, that we are unwilling to admit that such creatures could have any human past. We need desperately to believe, Bettelheim points out, that only the most incredible accidental circumstances could reduce a child to such a "subhuman" state.

Bettelheim concludes that the more recent cases of so-called *feral* children (Amala and Kamala; Parasram) appear to him to be instances of *autistic* children, that is, children who have been abandoned emotionally by parents and so pushed beyond their capacity to cope with reality. Too, Bettelheim notes that some cases of reputed

feral children could also be instances of feeble-mindedness (a limited genetic capacity for learning) or of brain damage at birth, which makes possible the animal-like behavior typically recounted in stories of feral individuals. Reported feral behavior includes profound withdrawal from contacts with other people, desire for sameness, mutism, an inability to laugh, and very disorderly personal appearance, including matted hair and dirty skin. The descriptions by Kanner and Bettelheim of the behavior and appearance of autistic children lends general support to the conviction of Bettelheim that most accounts of feral infants and children have been descriptions of recently abandoned *autistic* individuals.

It could be concluded from the examination of organic bridgeheads to socialization that human infants deserted by adults before they can shift for themselves will die for lack of physical care. There is no scientific evidence available to demonstrate that any animal adult, including all of the adult primates, could care adequately for a human infant, especially in terms of meeting demands of species-characteristic behavior, reflexes, and drives, to enable them simply to survive the time of their utter dependency.

Autistic children. Prior to about 1940 infants and children with severe emotional and behavioral impairments were believed to be brain-damaged or to be feebleminded. After this date some physicians, clinical psychologists, and psychiatrists began to recognize that some infants and children with severe disturbances in behavior showed little or no neurophysiological deficiencies. Some persons began to recognize that such children, with apparently "normal" physical equipment for their ages, were typified by quite similar ways of acting. A central feature of these actions was an extreme disturbance of contacts with other persons to the point where the child seemed totally unaware of his environment. Bettelheim's case history descriptions (1967) of "Laurie," "Marcia," "Joey," "Ken," and "Mitchell" vividly portray the very different and seemingly inexplicable behavior of the infant and child afflicted with autism. Bettelheim and Kanner have demonstrated that autism is a functional disturbance, that is, an acquired or learned disturbance, which is reversible in many instances

---

[1] See Itard, 1932; Silberstein and Irwin, 1962; Rauber, 1888; Singh and Zingg, 1942; Gesell, 1940; Ogburn, 1959. It should be noted that Victor was not reported to have been raised by animals.

if treated early and over a very long period in special settings.

The roots of autism. It appears, say Bettelheim and Kanner, that autism has its roots in a child's being born into a cultural environment in which it is deserted emotionally and cared for in ways that emotionally traumatize it to the point where it can be said that a parent, or in some instances both parents, actually do not wish the child to live. Thus the cultural basis of autism appears to rest on the fact that some infants are utterly unacceptable to a parent. Bettelheim says that autism stems from a realization by the infant that nothing can be done about a world that sometimes offers some unwanted satisfactions and that is very frustrating in even those few satisfactions allowed. In time, with repeated frustrations and because he cannot obliterate himself as his parents expect and wish him to do, the infant begins to withdraw from all contacts with others and becomes apparently incapable of being stimulated to engage in behavior dealing with any other human beings.

MARCIA. Whatever the reasons for origins of autism (Bettelheim's theory is not the only possibility), close observation for very long periods of the victims of infantile autism has dramatically demonstrated the role that the socialization plays in the process of taking on, through learning, most of those attributes we ordinarily associate with being human. Autistic children are so "unhuman" in their actions that state institutions have refused them care. Marcia (Bettelheim, 1967), at 3 years of age, had stopped looking at the world and at people by regularly stuffing her fingers in her eyes. Sometimes she sat for hours, tapping her chin with her fingers while staring fixedly and without sign of comprehension at movement about her. At the age of 10 she sat for hours in a yoga-like position, either motionless or excitedly rocking up and down. She would say "no," but never "yes," and would echo only a few words in a whisper. Marcia had to be dressed; the act of dressing required infinite patience in waiting for her to finally whisper her private language utterance of "fas...EN," her plea to be helped. Marcia was obsessed that people meant to devour her and had confused the phrase "we eat her" with the word "weather" and so was compulsively concerned with a watch on the daily movement of weather. Bettelheim also says that she refused food to keep herself from being devoured, as she had to devour the food.

JOEY. Joey functioned as a machine, a mechanical boy, run by imaginary machines created by him and beyond his control. His body movements were those of a complex machine. Bettelheim notes that it often took a conscious act of will to make himself perceive Joey as a child. When Joey was "at rest" he remained as motionless as a machine. Joey carried a series of tubes, small motors, and so on about with him, which he believed served as sources of power for his machine body. When he started up from his motionless machine existence, he would come "alive" in a machine fashion, with noises of a berserk nature. Wherever Joey went he laid down an imaginary wire to an imaginary power source, and insulated himself with a wire to a piece of furniture. He could eat, sleep, play, defecate, read, or move only with his power "plugged in" because it ran his body. Bettelheim (1967) says that Joey's pantomime was so skilled and his concentration so contagious that those who watched him seemed to suspend their own existence and become observers of another reality.

Thus studies of autistic children demonstrate the ways in which a lack of socialization or deficient socialization may produce disorganization of behavior in an otherwise physically capable and healthy child.

Cases of extreme social and cultural isolation. Feurbach's account in 1832 of the isolation of a boy named Kaspar Hauser posed quite precisely, for the first time, the question of "What happens to the person who is raised in extreme social and cultural isolation?"[2] This instance of isolation now appears to be one of a lost or abandoned older autistic child who somehow managed to survive. When found, Kaspar was bereft of many responses and actions usually associated with a boy of his age. Since the accu-

---

[2]For a discussion of Feurbach's account of Kaspar Houser, see Wagler, 1928. Again, the point is that cases of "feral" children appear to be those involving abandoned autistic children, made more so by being left alone. This resulted in the adults discovering such a child having a need to explain the child's survival and condition.

racy of the reports by Feurbach is in general question, it was not until reports by Davis of the case of Anna and by Mason and Davis of the case of Isabelle that reliable descriptions of extreme instances of social and cultural isolation became available.

ANNA. Anna was an illegitimate child whose grandfather so disapproved of her mother's behavior that he forced the baby to be confined in an upstairs room, where the infant was provided only the physical care needed to keep her alive. Anna was infrequently moved from one position to another, and her clothing and bedding were rarely changed. Apparently she had no friendly instruction and minimal social contact. Anna was found and taken out of the room when she was 6 years old. She could not walk or talk and showed no behavior that could be called "intelligent." She was emaciated and badly nourished, apathetic, expressionless, and apparently indifferent to everything about her. She made no movements on her own behalf to feed, dress, or care for herself. Davis (1949) has noted in describing Anna's case that her condition shows how little her purely biological resources, when acting alone, could contribute to making her a complete person.

At the age of 10½ years Anna died from hemorrhagic jaundice. But she had made considerable progress in learning social and cultural behavior in the four years after she was discovered. She had learned to follow verbal directions, could identify a few colors, build with play blocks, and respond to "attractive" and "unattractive" pictures. She cuddled and played with a doll. She had learned to talk in phrases. She could clearly repeat words and tried regularly to carry on a conversation. She learned to regularly wash her hands before and after eating and to care for her teeth by brushing. She tried to help in care of other children in the county home setting where she was being cared for by untrained persons. She learned to walk well and to run without falling. While she was easily excitable, Anna was reported to have a pleasant disposition. In all, at the time of her death, Anna's social behavior was estimated to be that of a child of 2½ to 3 years of age. A fully complete interpretation of Anna's development was made impossible by her death. It is probable that Anna was somewhat deficient, or feebleminded, from the outset. But it is quite clear that Anna made extraordinary progress in her social and culture learnings in a very short period, so any hypothesis that she was a fully feebleminded child is ruled out. This case illustrates the point that communicative contact is one of the elements making up the very essence of the socialization process.

ISABELLE. The other well-documented case of extreme social and cultural isolation is that of Isabelle, who was found at 6 years of age in circumstances very much like those in which Anna was discovered (Davis, 1949). Isabelle was an illegitimate child and was kept in seclusion because of her illegitimacy. Her mother was a deaf mute. Isabelle and her mother spent most of their time together in a darkened room. She communicated with her mother by means of gestures and did not develop her speech beyond a few croaking sounds. She was suffering badly from rickets because of her diet and lack of sunlight. When found, her actions seemed to show "fear" and "hostility." At first, after being taken from her isolation, observers were unsure that Isabelle could hear. It was concluded that her behavioral development was approximately that of a 19-month-old child. The first medical specialist to work with Isabelle pronounced her to be feebleminded. But the trained persons in charge of her care set her about a carefully designed program learning to speak and act. At first Isabelle showed little response, but over the next months she began to exhibit more skills in her use of language and in her behavior. Then she went rapidly through each of the "stages" of social and cultural learning said to be typical of children in American society. In less than 3 months after speaking her first words she was putting sentences together. Ten months later she could identify words and sentences printed on cards and pages. She could write legibly, add to ten, and retell a story in the general sequence in which it had been told. In another 7 months she had an estimated vocabulary of between 1,400 and 2,000 words and was capable of asking and answering complex questions.

So, beginning at age 6 with an apparent level of social and cultural learning of between 1 and 2 years, Isabelle reached a social and cultural level typical of an American 6-year-old in a 2-year period. Another way to state this would be to say that in 2 years Isabelle learned the social and cultural skills ordinarily believed to take 6 years for American children to learn. Isabelle eventually entered a public school, where she took part in school activities without special provisions for her. By the time she was 14 years old she was in the sixth grade, where her teachers rated her as a competent and well-adjusted student. Isabelle is reported to have completed high school with better than average grades, to have married, and to have her own "normal" family.

Comparisons and contrasts. Isabelle's case is different from Anna's in several important respects. Although both girls were judged to have a very low "intellectual" level to begin with, and both reached a considerably higher level of social and cultural skills than when first brought from their situations of isolation, Isabelle telescoped into 2 years the same kinds of learning Anna took 4½ years to acquire or did not acquire at all prior to her death. This suggests that Isabelle had a greater learning capacity to begin with and that Anna probably was somewhat deficient in such a capacity. However, it should be recalled that Isabelle had prolonged and very expert training, while Anna did not. Davis says that if Anna had started her speech patterns earlier, after being brought from her isolation, she might have progressed more than she did.

What is important is that there would appear from these instances of extreme isolation to be a process of accelerated recovery in which the isolated child goes through what have been said to be the usual stages of human socialization at a more rapid pace than is the instance in "normal" development of cultural learning. No one knows at present at what age a person can recover from extreme social and cultural isolation and still fully acquire culture. Davis estimates it could be as old as 15 years or as young as 10

years. Whatever the case may be, it is quite obvious that the human propensity for acquiring culture is very durable and quite "tough" in the adverse circumstances of extreme isolation.

Degrees of isolation: biological, social, cultural. The cases of Anna and Isabelle illustrate the extreme in cultural isolation. However, there are a number of other, less extreme, forms of isolation that are also important in understanding socialization. Generally these are of two types—(1) *immobilizing isolation* and (2) *nonimmobilizing isolation.* For the most part, immobilizing isolation is the result of children being biologically incapable of participating in the socialization process. These children include all those born with deficient capacities for learning and cognition, those born with brain damage, deafness, dumbness, or blindness, or those suffering from diseases that seriously cripple the central nervous system.

BEING IMMOBILIZED. There are many degrees of immobilizing isolation, ranging from the child with cerebral palsy to children afflicted by rheumatic fever. In most instances such children regularly miss participating in some significant aspects of the socialization process. Thus a mentally deficient or brain-damaged American child cannot hope to compete in society for high-status positions that are earned through success in the competitions in athletic skills, in crafts, and in schools, colleges, and universities. A child not severely immobilized sometimes can learn successfully to participate in the ongoing life of his society through substitution of one or another of his psychomotor, cognitive, or learning capacities that remain unimpaired by his illness. We are all familiar with or have read reliable accounts of individuals who have been born with severe limb handicaps and have subsequently learned to drive an automobile, type, use a pencil, and so on.

Even persons born with severely immobilizing defects can learn to overcome them if other capacities remain unimpaired and are of high potential. The account of Helen Keller's recovery from her nearly total cultural isolation because of her blindness and deafness is a dramatic example of the ways other capacities, in this instance the use of the sense of touch, can sometimes break down the barriers of immobilizing isolation. The cases of autistic children also indicate that even the most severe emotional isolation, which is nearly fully immobilizing, sometimes can be overcome with patient and long-term efforts to engage the child in caring about himself and others.

NOT BEING IMMOBILIZED. Nonimmobilizing isolation from the socialization process is of three types—(1) social, (2) locational, and (3) cultural. These kinds of isolation are characterized by the fact that an infant is born with unimpaired or undamaged species-characteristic behavior forms, reflexes, drives, and capacities, but because of some particular feature of his local culture he is still unable to participate fully in the process of enculturation.

SOCIAL ISOLATION. The better known examples of social isolation are those in which there are culturally ascribed "defects" of race, class, caste, clique, clan, club, or religion, so a child finds it very difficult to gain access to full participation in the enculturation process of his society.

Social isolation can range from the almost inconsequential because it can be easily overcome, as in the instances of children who attend sessions for private instruction after completion of their public school day, to being of major consequence, as in the instances of children unable to obtain any except minimal public schooling because of their race, economic or social class, or religion.

In a large and heterogenous society, such as the modern American society, there are many diverse factors of social isolation in operation. Each person has been isolated to some degree from some aspects of all possible cultural learning. The factors of social isolation with the greatest effect on the American infant and child, such as race, social and economic class, and religion, may bar him from lifelong, effective participation in his society by causing him to be regularly isolated from the practical knowledge, details, and basic ideas widely shared in the life of his society.

There are also some factors of social isolation that derive from biological bases but are not immobilizing. Such factors are generally physical disfigurements that limit certain kinds of social action and learning. These factors, which vary greatly from culture to culture, include facial and body warts, moles, scars, large birthmarks, harelips, gross overweight and underweight, dwarfness, giantism, and grotesque misshapeness ("hunchback," missing or deformed limbs, and so on). Individuals afflicted with such limited disfigurements often find themselves blocked off from learning and participating in many activities in their culture. Thus it is rare to see an American corporation executive, public official, or professor with such nonimmobolizing but biologically based defects.

LOCATIONAL ISOLATION. Factors of locational isolation are found to some degree in all large societies. Individuals are born and often live in only one region of the geographic territories occupied by their society. If a society is large and spreads across great land areas, regional isolation may play an important part in the enculturation process of the society. This is especially so where there is a limited technology, which does not include high-speed transportation, television, and radio, all of which tend to break down barriers of locational isolation. In most of the larger societies of the world there are some significant differences in the enculturation process because of locational isolation.

This has been true until this past decade in the United States. Accents, folk culture content (in some regions a "sack" is a "poke," while in others it is a "bag") and even styles of posture, gesture, and gait are still recognizable and often are used as bases for permitting social access to facilities and ideas.

Locational isolation also includes housing and neighborhood features. Growing up in a particular section of a city or county may result in a whole range of isolating factors coming into play, including an individual's access to recreation, housing, education, transportation, and communication. The street address of a child is vital to his enculturation, for when he goes to a neighborhood school he may be limited by traditions that impose upon him a special pattern of access to his society's broad range of cultural behavior.

ISOLATED FROM A CULTURE. Cultural isolation includes all those factors related to an individual being unable to gain access to the widely shared patterns of learned behavior transmitted in his society from one generation to the next. These factors include linguistic, customary behavior and value judgment forms of action and belief. There are individuals in American society unable to participate in many patterns of American culture because they do not speak English, or speak and comprehend the language badly. There are more than a quarter million American Indians living in the territory of the United States. Probably half of these individuals do not speak English as a "first" language. Many speak so little English as to be incapable of carrying on a simple conversation. There are millions of foreign-born residents of the United States, a large number of whom speak very little English. Typically the children of these persons, both American Indian and immigrant, are handicapped in their access to the dominant cultural patterns of American culture. Language is a formidable isolation factor, especially when coupled with other factors of locational and social isolation.

Many individuals have been isolated from widely shared cultural patterns in their societies because of their having learned particular beliefs or ways of action that are especially provincial or parochial in form and meaning. In the United States, for example, success in certain occupations such as banking, medicine, dentistry, law, and the military is often limited or enhanced by the fact of whether a person has a particular set of values. Thus it is difficult to reach and to retain an executive position with a working man's values. The attitudes and judgments expected by boards of directors in large corporations are not usually learned by sons of laborers. In some instances the American system of free public education has made it possible for the son of a laborer to learn to express and even to comprehend the values of other occupational groups, providing, of course, other significant factors of isolation were not operating in the individual's life career. The factor of cultural isolation in socialization can affect large segments of a society organized by castes or classes based on specialized education and occupations.

Individuals in extreme situational isolation; reversing the socialization process. There are other instances of isolation that are extreme in nature and that may be as inescapable as are the various factors of immobilizing and non-immobilizing isolation. For adults, and even children, these situations can lead to a reversal of the socialization process. The first evidences of this fact came from experimental studies of human isolation through the use of drugs or mechanical devices that obstruct or muffle senses. However, these experimental situations are not so totally overwhelming as when there remains no hope of escape and relief.

NAZI DEATH CAMPS AND REVERSAL OF ENCULTURATION. Bettelheim worked with autistic children in Germany from 1932 until 1934. Then he was imprisoned in a Nazi concentration camp until 1938. In these years, as a trained observer of human behavior, he sought to defend himself psychologically from the constant danger and inescapability of the camp by trying to study clinically the reactions of his fellow prisoners. Bettelheim witnessed in many of his fellows a continuous deculturation process, or a constant wearing away of those learned attributes of self and of many forms of cultural behavior that had characterized the German prisoners before their arrest. Bettelheim's observations are mostly confirmed by Cohen's (1953) study of concentration camp behavior. In the camps the first response of many prisoners to their danger was to pay the minutest attention to every sign of harm, to each guard, to the prisoner foreman, to each noise in the distance, and to each abrupt or large-scale movement. Finally, after long-term stress caused by such concerns, prisoners either "converted" themselves from their Judaic religion to a synthetic faith and action or moved on to a form of psychological adaptation that involved paying less attention to mortal danger and more to self-preservation actions such as trying to find "safe" or less difficult job assignments, making friends to share a confidence with, and finding a better place to sleep.

CONVERTS TO DEATH. Those prisoners who responded to the constant danger by professing a synthetic religion became increasingly more focused on extreme dangers in the camp to the exclusion of every other matter, so that all actions by everyone, prisoners as well as guards, became destructive in design and intent. Bettelheim (1967: 77) notes that for these prisoners nothing existed except the unrelieved prospect of death. Psychologically, these prisoners responded to external dangers with defenses that caused continuing debilitation of their acquired selves to the point of an autistic-like withdrawal from all contacts with life and reality.

Converts to life. In contrast, the prisoners who moved on from initial perception of a mortal danger to concerns with self-preservation adapted psychologically by hopeful thinking and daydreaming and by plotting revenge and making elaborate plans to this particular end. There apparently was considerably less debilitation of self resources for such prisoners. Through these insignificant (in terms of "normal" situations) actions, many of these prisoners survived psychologically and were not subject to deculturation. Bettelheim is of the opinion that these persons saved their lives and selves in an extreme situation by taking a hand in their own fate, through forcing their attention toward something besides the never-ending threat of death.

Prisoners of war and reversal of enculturation. An extensive study of Americans captured and imprisoned by the North Koreans and Chinese in the Korean War confirms Bettelheim's conclusions about extreme situational isolation potentially producing a reversal of the socialization process. Although this study set out to identify ". . . those attributes, those traits or skills which are required by soldiers to aid them in resisting the enemy if captured," (U. S. Senate, 1956: 79), it produced quite valuable knowledge regarding the ways the socialization process may be reversed. A total of 3,323 repatriated American prisoners was separated into two groups: (1) those who resisted the enemy while prisoners and (2) those who "participated" (or "collaborated") in enemy activities while prisoners. Based on the interviews conducted by armed services personnel, about 500 individuals of the second

group were recommended for courtmartial, dishonorable discharge, or other forms of less than honorable separation from the armed forces. A civilian psychologist working under contract to the army later made a study of these individuals and of a sample of other non-collaborating soldier prisoners of similar rank, race, length of service, length of captivity, and places of imprisonment. Using the personnel dossiers of all the prisoner soldiers in the study, the psychologist obtained more than 300 items of "personal information" and developed 27 "rating scales" to judge the reported prison camp actions of each prisoner in terms of his civilian and military background.

A study of collaboration. The study tended to show that 70 percent of all the Americans held as prisoners during the Korean War (whether courtmartial proceedings had been used or not after release) had made at least one contribution to the enemy's propaganda effort. The main effort with the prisoners by the Korean and Chinese captors was to seek to have the soldiers "accept communism as a social and economic system above and beyond their prior beliefs and concepts" (U. S. Senate, 1956: 89). The most common method used in seeking this change in values among the American prisoners was a simple lecture approach rather than widespread brutality and torture, use of drugs or sex, and so forth. Some lectures were conducted for their captors by American prisoners. As a consequence of these lectures, 39 percent of all prisoners signed enemy propaganda petitions, 22 percent made propaganda recordings, 11 percent wrote propaganda articles, 5 percent wrote petitions, 5 percent circulated petitions among their fellows, and 16 percent had full-time propaganda jobs (U. S. Senate, 1956: 88). At least 10 percent of the prisoners were regular informers for their captors.

Brainwashing and brainwashing. The vital point of this study is that the techniques usually associated by the public with the so-called brainwashing process—in which an individual is isolated from all normal associations and his usual environment, is deprived of food, water, and sleep, and is subjected to gross physical brutality while kept in solitary confinement except when undergoing long periods of indoctrination and interrogation—were not generally used on the American prisoners who participated in the enemy war effort.

Even more important for studies of human response to extreme isolation and consequent possible reversal of the socialization process was the fact that the research psychologist, after careful study using standard psychological methods, could find little significant difference between those who resisted most efforts at value change and those who participated in their captors' efforts. He noted that there were no significant differences between these two groups with respect to age, education, civilian occupation, marital status, or the region of the country from which they came or in which they were born. There was some slight difference in the two groups in terms of their general intelligence levels. The soldiers who were the most active collaborators were somewhat less intelligent, as measured by army tests administered at the time of enlistment or induction.

OTHER FACTORS. Thus the factor of cooperation with or resistance to their captors by American soldiers appeared to have been based on some other aspect of their experience. The psychologist directing the study concluded that whether a man collaborated with his captors or not depended largely upon his response to the captors' promises of immediate material rewards (more blankets, a warmer hut, new clothes) rather than the purely ideological inducements offered by the guards and interrogators. Offers of special treatment and privileges in the severe living conditions of the Korean prisoner of war camps, especially during the harsh winters, seems to have been the key to the prisoner's behavior. It appears that the offers of material rewards for cooperation were real and were usually fulfilled for those soldiers willing to pay the price of cooperation.

Thus 70 percent of the American prisoners were induced by their captors to abandon some basic American values to maintain other values. Studies of American values indicate that the American conception of "material well-being," which was used as a lure to collaboration by Korean and Chinese captors, is a very old, widely shared, and deeply felt American value.

Analysis of American values suggests that the focal value (see Chapter Nine) of material well-being is vital in American culture, since it appears directly linked to a basic American premise, that of believing man is the master of the universe. Americans hold this premise in most life situations. This value notes that a high standard of living is an inherent and natural "right" to be demanded by everyone and that success in attaining material goods (a new car, house, suit) carries a moral sanction; it is believed not only to be "right" to seek out comfort, but to be a moral virtue of a high order. Americans have relatively little tolerance for pain, brutality, or threat of death since these all interrupt access to success in gaining material well-being. Americans are usually repelled by contact with poverty and misery and try to seek an immediate release from such situations. It appears that the captors of the American soldiers were well aware of the intensity and long history of the focal value of material well-being in American life and used it deliberately to their advantage in seeking collaboration from prisoners.

VALUES IN DECULTURATION. So, when the experience of American prisoners of the North Koreans and Chinese is compared with the experience of the Nazi concentration camp prisoners, there emerges a clear indication that not only can humans in extreme situations suffer from a deculturation process but that this process consists at least partly of a striving to adjust new and peculiar circumstances to be congruent with values ordinarily learned in a process of socialization.

Extreme isolation—conclusions. Studies of individuals in situations of extreme isolation tend to support the general conclusions noted earlier in this chapter concerning the complex ways the biological and the cultural transmission processes become interrelated in the life career of individuals undergoing a process of enculturation. The cases of autistic children and Anna and Isabelle show the vital place of communicative contact in socialization. Studies of extreme situational isolation demonstrate that it is possible to desocialize individuals as well as to socialize them, or at least to bring about a refocusing of acquired basic values in such a way that a focal value, or even a basic premise of a culture, comes to take precedence in the fight to live and to escape from extreme isolation.

It also should be noted that while there have not yet been any extensive studies of the topic, there now is substantive evidence from eyewitness testimony, autobiographies, and personal diaries that illegal imprisonment in a penal institution or a "mental hospital," as a strategy of personal and political harassment and constraint, can also be an extreme situation of isolation and may lead to reversal of the socialization process. In fact, some nations of the modern world employ the authority of the practice of psychiatry to use mental hospitals as political prisons for ideological dissenters. Persons illegally held in such situations for long periods seem to suffer from the same effects as the prisoners in Nazi, Korean, and Chinese camps, especially if they are held captive among genuinely ill individuals. There are strong indications that the process of growing old also may involve a reversal of the socialization process. In Anderson's study (1969) aged Americans appeared to be systematically deculturated as preparation for their status as aged persons.

These data all seem to indicate that the socialization process could be as well studied from observing and analyzing the effects of extreme situations. Most studies of socialization concentrate now upon developmental, or ontogenetic, factors. It may be as useful to learn about the ways extreme situations may break apart the links forged between biology and culture in a socialization process.

▪ Twin studies

Additional scientific evidence demonstrating the ways in which human biology and culture become related in socialization is to be found in the literature of studies of twins.

Identical and fraternal twins. There are two types of twins: *monozygotic* ("one egg" or "identical") and *dizygotic* ("two egg" or "fraternal") twins. Monozygotic twins are derived from the same fertilized egg because of an accident of development in the course of initial cell division after conception; monozygotic twins have iden-

tical genetic materials. Dizygotic twins are derived from an almost simultaneous impregnation by sperm of two eggs; dizygotic twins do not have identical genetic materials, since the sperm and the ova that joined in the two instances of fertilization have different assortments of gene stuff.

Monozygotic twins are always of the same sex and have the same features of skin, hair and eye pigmentation, and blood group type. Monozygotic twins are also alike in many other physical-chemical factor compositions, including those of their saliva and urine, and they manifest similar patterns of brain electrical activity. It is usually possible to determine from such similarities whether twins are monozygotic or dizygotic. The physical-chemical (saliva, urine) similarities of monozygotic twins may remain even in the cases of such twins separated shortly after birth and raised in very different home environments.

Twin studies and their limits. It would seem that careful study of twins, especially monozygotic twins, would provide detailed information concerning the ways different cultural environments, both between cultures and within the same culture, will affect the same gene materials as children mature. It would appear that studies of monozygotic twins separated at birth and then raised in very different circumstances could provide answers to the special questions concerning the ways the biological and cultural modes of transmission in socialization are interrelated and function together. Unfortunately, this has not been the case, for a significant amount of twin research over the past half-century has demonstrated that even monozygotic twins show consistent individual differences, although they were raised in the same family setting.

TWINS T AND C. Gesell and Thompson studied monozygotic twins "T" and "C" for a period of 14 years after their birth. The method of "co-twin control" was employed in this study; twin T would be given early special training in such actions as block building, manual coordination, and so on, while twin C was left untrained. At first, twin T excelled in such skills, but twin C was just as skilled when she reached the same level of physical development. This study demonstrated clearly that there were a number of persistent differences between T and C. T was quicker, while C was more careful. T used straight lines and angles while drawing, while C consistently drew curved lines. T gave quicker attention, but C was more alert. T learned a bit more quickly, but C was more adept in a social situation. It can be concluded from this study that even monozygotic twins reared together will show basic differences in their learning and behavior.

MABEL AND MARY. Newman's description of "Mabel" and "Mary" makes the conclusion easy to accept that monozygotic twins reared in quite different settings are very different because of their different home environments, unless these data are contrasted with the work of Gesell and Thompson. Mabel and Mary were separated shortly after their birth. Mabel lived in a country home and grew up working at strenuous farm chores. She completed the eighth grade in a rural school. Mary grew up in a city of medium size. She completed high school in city schools. She became a music teacher after her graduation. Mabel and Mary both lived in fairly well-to-do homes. At 29 years of age Mabel and Mary were studied and found to be at least 17 points different on the Stanford-Binet intelligence test. Mary was judged to be high-average and Mabel was judged to be low-average in intelligence. Mabel was phlegmatic and slow in her social responses. Mary was very excitable. Mabel was very masculine in appearance and had a masculine walk and a large, 138-pound, hard-muscled frame. Mary was quite feminine, with a 110-pound, soft-muscled body. Mabel and Mary seemed quite unlike the identical twins they were, in nearly every aspect, except for a general "family" resemblance.

Thus this case would seem to demonstrate the striking way in which different cultural environments produce very different individuals even though they share the same gene stuff. But this conclusion is not as firm or valid as that of the study of twins T and C.

This problem is complicated because studies comparing monozygotic and dizygotic twins reared in different and similar environments have tended to ignore the crucial facts that twins separated (usually by adoption) are not often randomly placed in their new homes and that the home environments of separated monozygotic twins sometimes could be more alike than the environments of separated dizygotic twins.

RECENT EFFORTS IN TWIN STUDIES. Recently there has been an effort by psychologists to account for such problems in use of the twin study method in investigations of the interrelations between the biological and cultural modes of transmission in socialization. Cattell has argued that the style of twin research similar to that used by Newman, Koch, and others should be modified to another kind of methodological approach, which he terms "multiple abstract variance analysis." This method, which is statistical in form and content, involves study of variations in the four factors of (1) differences in the environments between families with twins, (2) differences of heredity between families with twins, (3) differences of environments for individuals within the same family, and especially for twins, and (4) differences of heredity between siblings in the same family, including twins. Cattell claims this approach avoids the often artificial and limited nature of the twin study method by seeking to determine the relative importance and specific relations between the biological and cultural modes of transmission in socialization.

Twin studies and socialization. Vandenberg has reviewed the contributions of the twin research method to the study of socialization and concludes, with Burt, Hebb and Melzack, that, while the twin study method has contributed greatly to understanding the broad outlines of the nature of the interactions of the biological and cultural modes of transmission in socialization, the method has limitations for future research. However, twin studies have been a basic source of data for trying to understand the general ways human biology and culture are interrelated and function together to produce a socialized human being.

■ Conclusions

Data from studies of isolated and autistic children and twin studies demonstrate the fact that, without regular communicative contact with parents and other agents of socialization, the process of transmitting and acquiring culture is modified or altered in significant ways. Such studies provide evidences that, without a socialization process, there is little that can be recognized in the everyday sense of the term *human being.*

A newborn human takes on the ideas, habits, thoughts, emotions, preoccupations, and so on of the generations that have preceded him in his culture. These ways, many of which are quite specific to a local society, are not transmitted to him through his genes. The infant must learn to walk, sit, talk, love, hate, fear, hope, and so on by participating in a process of enculturation. If he is denied access to or cannot fully participate in the enculturation process and fails to take on, through communicative contacts, instruction, imitation, and reflection the ways necessary to behave as a human being, he will be severely limited in his ability to make full use of possibly unique combinations of his gene material.

Data of the consequences of extreme situational isolation, while far from complete, tend to show that the socialization process is capable of being reversed, even after a long period of time. There is no evidence that the same is true of the expression of gene materials; once eye color, stature, nose shape, hair form, and so on are expressed in the course of maturation, they do not seem reversible or capable of being altered except in some cases of quite drastic experimental radiation and surgical procedures. The fact that the socialization process is so plastic in its form is important for understanding the nature of that process.

Although limited by certain research problems, twin studies show promise as a general method to see the ways biology and culture may become interrelated in the socialization process. These studies highlight the complex nature of these relationships and make it clear that neither "nature" (biology) nor "nurture" (culture) is more important as an aspect of socialization. On the contrary, twin studies assist us in seeing the fallacy of the nature vs. nurture (or heredity vs. environment) arguments of the past.

■ **Summary**

This chapter has discussed studies of isolated and autistic children and of twins in an effort to provide some understanding of the way in which human biology and culture may become related in the socialization process. The chapter also included an account of the ways in which socialization might be "reversed" or significantly altered in situations of extreme isolation.

REFERENCES CITED AND SUGGESTED READINGS

Anderson, B. G. 1969. "The Process of Deculturation; Its Dynamics Among The Aged." Paper read before the 1969 Annual Meetings, American Anthropological Association, New Orleans, La., November, 1969.

Barber, B. 1957. *Social Stratification. A Comparative Analysis of Structure and Process.* New York: Harcourt.

Bendix, R., and S. M. Lipset. 1953. *Class, Status and Power.* New York: Free Press.

Bettelheim, B. 1943. "Individual and Mass Behavior in Extreme Situations," Journal of Abnormal and Social Psychology **38**:417-452.

————. 1959. "Feral Children and Autistic Children," American Journal of Sociology **64**:455-467.

————. 1960. *The Informed Heart: Autonomy in a Mass Age.* New York: Free Press.

————. 1967. *The Empty Fortress.* New York: Free Press.

Bronfenbrenner, U. 1958. "Socialization and Social Class through Time and Space." In E. E. Maccoby, T. M. Newcomb, and E. L. Hartley (eds.), *Readings in Social Psychology,* ed. 3. New York: Holt, pp. 400-425.

Burt, C. 1963. "Is Intelligence Distributed Normally?" British Journal of Statistical Psychology **16**:175-190.

Cattell, R. B. 1960. "The Multiple Abstract Variance Analysis Equations and Solutions for Nature-Nurture Research on Continuous Variables," Psychological Review **67**:353-372.

Cohen, E. A. 1953. *Human Behavior in the Concentration Camp.* (Translated by M. H. Braaksma.) New York: Norton.

Davis, K. 1940. "Extreme Social Isolation of a Child," American Journal of Sociology **45**:554-565.

————. 1947. "Final Note on a Case of Extreme Isolation," American Journal of Sociology **52**:432-437.

————. 1949. *Human Society.* New York: Macmillan.

Fuller, J., and W. Thompson. 1960. *Behavior Genetics.* New York: Wiley.

Gesell, A. 1940. *Wolf Child and Human Child.* London: Methuen.

Gesell, A., and H. Thompson. 1929. "Learning and Growth in Identical Infant Twins: An Experimental Study by the Method of Co-Twin Control," Genetic Psychology Monograph **6**:1-124.

Goffman, E. 1961. *Asylums: Essays on the Social Situation of Mental Patients and Other Inmates.* Garden City, N. Y.: Doubleday.

Hebb, D. O. 1949. *The Organization of Behavior.* New York: Wiley.

Hirsch, J. (ed.) 1967. *Behavior—Genetic Analysis.* New York: McGraw-Hill.

Hrdlička, A. 1931. *Children Who Run on All Fours.* New York: McGraw-Hill.

Husen, T. 1960. "Abilities of Twins," Scandinavian Journal of Psychology 1:125-135.

Hsu, F. L. K. 1963. *Clan, Caste and Club.* Princeton, N. J.: D. Van Nostrand.

Itard, J. M. G. 1932. *The Wild Boy of Aveyron.* New York: Appleton-Century-Crofts.

Johnson, R. C. 1963. "Similarity in I.Q. of Separated Identical Twins as Related to Length of Time Spent in Same Environment," Child Development 34: 745-749.

Juel-Nielsen, N., and B. Harvald. 1958. "The Electro-encephalogram in Uniovular Twins Brought Up Apart," Acta Genetica 8:57-64.

Kanner, L. 1943. "Autistic Disturbances of Affective Contact," Nervous Child 2:217-250.

————. 1944. "Early Infantile Autism," Journal of Pediatrics 25:211-217.

————. 1949. "Problems of Nosology and Psychodynamics of Early Infantile Autism," American Journal of Orthopsychiatry 19:416-426.

Kanner, L. (ed.) 1948. *Child Psychiatry.* Springfield, Ill.: Charles C Thomas.

Keller, H. 1911. *The Story of My Life.* New York: Grosset and Dunlap.

Koch, H. L. 1966. *Twins and Twin Relations.* Chicago: University of Chicago Press.

Lilly, J. C. 1956. "Effects of Physical Restraint and Reduction of Ordinary Levels of Physical Stimuli on Intact Healthy Persons," New York: Group for the Advancement of Psychiatry, *Symposium Number Two,* pp. 13-20.

Mason, M. K. 1942. "Learning to Speak after Six and One-half Years of Silence," Journal of Speech Disorders 7:295-304.

Melzack, R. 1964. "Early Experience: A Neuropsychological Approach to Heredity-Environment Interaction." In G. Newton (ed.), *Early Experience and Behavior.* Springfield, Ill.: Charles C Thomas.

Newman, H. H., F. N. Freeman, and K. J. Holzinger. 1937. *Twins: A Study of Heredity and Environment.* Chicago: University of Chicago Press.

Newman, H. H. 1940. *Multiple Human Births.* New York: Doubleday.

Ogburn, W. F. 1959. "The Wolf Boy of Agra," American Journal of Sociology 64:449-454.

Rauber, A. 1888. *Homo Sapiens Ferus, oder die Zustaende der Verwilderten.* Leipzig: J. Brehse.

Schein, E. 1956. "The Chinese Indoctrination Program for Prisoners of War; A Study of Attempted Brainwashing," Psychology 19:149-172.

————. 1957. "Methods of Forceful Indoctrination: Observations and Interviews," New York: Group for the Advancement of Psychiatry, *Symposium Number Four,* pp. 253-284.

Shields, J. 1962. *Monozygotic Twins.* London: Oxford University Press.

Silberstein, R. M., and H. Irwin. 1962. "Jean-Marc-Gaspart Itard and the Savage of Aveyron: An Unsolved Problem in Child Psychiatry," Journal of the American Academy of Child Psychiatry 1:314-322.

Singh, J. A. L., and R. M. Zingg. 1942. *Wolf Children and Feral Man.* New York: Harper.

Svalastoga, K. 1964. "Social Differentiation." In R. E. L. Faris (ed.), *Handbook of Modern Sociology.* Chicago: Rand McNally, pp. 530-575.

Szasz, T. 1970. *Ideology and Insanity: Essays on the Psychiatric Dehumanization of Man.* Garden City, N. Y.: Doubleday.

United States Senate. 1956. Communist Interrogation, Indoctrination and Exploitation of American Military and Civilian Prisoners. Hearings before the Permanent Subcommittee on Investigations of the Committee of Government Operations, U. S. Senate, June 19, 20, 26, 27, 1956. Washington, D. C.: U. S. Government Printing Office.

Vandenberg, S. G. 1966. "Contributions of Twin Research to Psychology," Psychological Bulletin 63:327-352.

Wagler, L. 1928. *Die Bilanz einer hundertjaehrigen Hauserforschung.* Nuremberg.

Williams, R. 1960. *American Society,* ed. 2. New York: Knopf.

Wright, L. 1961. "A Study of Special Abilities in Identical Twins," Journal of Genetic Psychology 99:245-251.

SIX   THE CRITICAL PERIODS HYPOTHESIS

This chapter discusses an influential hypothesis often unstated or implied in socialization studies.

▪ Origin and nature of the hypothesis

Beginning in the middle 1920's several individuals observed phenomena which suggested the idea that there are vitally important points, periods, or stages in the behavioral development of organisms. These seemed to be times when an animal was most receptive to specific stimulation from its environment. The studies of Von Senden on the behavior of congenitally blind persons after corrective eye surgery led him to the conclusion that visual space and shape perception in man depends on specific experiences that must occur early in life for normal vision to be present. At the same time, Piaget was conducting his pioneering studies of language and reasoning development in infants and young children. Piaget also concluded that there is a time of quite limited duration when an infant or child must be exposed to certain learning experiences if specific actions are to become a regular part of his adult behavior. Somewhat later, Lorenz reached a similar conclusion from his observations of animal behavior. He noted there are antecedent, or earlier, experiences that must occur very early in the life of an animal if it is to successfully perform later in more complex ways.

Spitz also reached the same conclusion after observing the behavior of orphaned and abandoned infants and children raised by hospital staff members.[1] He suggested that human infants have a special stage of increased efficiency for the learning of specific cultural responses, before which such responses cannot be acquired and after which the chances of learning them are markedly reduced. During this time Gesell also formulated a theoretical model of child development in which the interplay and reciprocal influence of two opposite and supposedly biologically inherited tendencies to behavioral integration and differentiation were said to occur at critical times of limited duration.[*]

A critical periods statement. In essence, these individuals all were formulating a hypothesis that can be briefly summarized as follows.

> There are critical periods, or stages, in the development of animals, including man, during which the individual is most receptive to learning from particular kinds of experiences. These periods are of very limited duration. If an experience is to become a regular part of an individual's later behavior it has to be acquired during the critical period when the individual is most ready to learn from that kind of experience. Earlier or later exposure to such experience will produce little or no effect on the individual's later actions.

Research efforts. This hypothesis produced very great interest among those conducting socialization research since it promised, once particular processes and behavior forms were identified and their critical periods specified, an understanding of the acquisition of culture and of personality development and a possible solution to a whole range of difficult social problems such as delinquency, alcoholism, divorce, and so on.

In the time after World War II a variety of efforts were made to provide experimental evidences to support the critical periods hypothesis. Research efforts centered upon studies of (1) sensory processes, (2) imprinting, and (3) the social and sexual behavior of experimental animals. The results of these studies have often been

---

[1]For a review of similar studies after the time of Spitz's research, see Yarrow, 1961.

[*]Gesell's model provides for a number of critical periods during maturation, with some occurring in late childhood and adolescence.

generalized to man and then used in research on the socialization process, either as hypotheses for research or as unstated assumptions concerning the nature of man and the phenomena of socialization.

CRITICAL PERIODS IN SENSORY PROCESSES. A number of studies of sensory deprivation have been made to test the critical periods hypothesis. Some typical examples were reported by Riesen in 1961 at a conference on the critical periods hypothesis. In one test of the effects of early vision deprivation on later ability to perceive movements, four groups of cats were exposed to four different sets of conditions: (1) a normal laboratory environment, (2) 1 hour each day of diffuse light, (3) a normal laboratory environment, with all movements restricted by a special harness, and (4) 1 hour each day of free moving light. The cats in the second and fourth groups were raised from birth to 8 weeks of age in total darkness and were then placed in the conditions noted above. After the experimental period all the cats were tested for their abilities to choose visually between a rotating and a stationary X, placed on two doors that had to be pushed to obtain a food reward. The cats of the second and third groups could not discriminate between the rotating and stationary X's, while the cats of the first and fourth (or control) groups did so without apparent difficulty.

In a second study using the same conditions of experimentation, cats were subjected to three tasks of visual discrimination learning: (1) discrimination of light and dark, (2) discrimination of horizontal and vertical stripes, and (3) discrimination of a black, a stationary, and a bouncing dot. No differences were found among the four groups in discrimination of light and dark and only slight differences between the control (first and fourth) and other (second and third) groups with regard to discrimination between horizontal and vertical stripes. However, there was a marked difference between the cats of the first and fourth groups and those of the second and third groups with respect to discrimination of movement. The control (first and fourth) groups learned the discrimination of movement after 450 and before 900 trials, while the other

groups (second and third) still had not learned to discriminate movement after 2,000 trials.

In another study, cats exposed to 5 months of darkness, after 5 months of normal rearing, performed normally in movement discrimination. It was concluded from this study that the critical period for visual perception with regard to later movement discrimination is during the first 5 months of life for cats. It also was concluded from another study with cats that animals raised without a background of visual experience, that is, raised in total darkness, tend not to exhibit fear responses when finally exposed to unfamiliar objects, as do cats raised in normal laboratory conditions. Some other studies noted also that cat eye coordination is highly dependent on early visual experience.

These studies, and others similar to them, seem to indicate that at least in some animals there are specific times, of very limited duration, in which certain sensory experiences must occur if the animal is to behave "normally" as an adult. However, it has also become obvious from these studies that there are differences of a rather marked kind in critical periods of sensory learning in different kinds of animals. The fact that cats appear to have to be subjected to movement discrimination experiences in the first 5 months of life does not seem applicable to members of other animal groups such as fish, birds, and amphibians, and cannot even be generally extended as a principle to other kinds of mammals such as rats or monkeys.

IMPRINTING. A century ago, in the course of observing the behavior of young animals, Spalding noted that infant birds, ducklings, goslings, and chicks seemed to follow their parents as soon as they were hatched. He also noted that these young animals would as easily follow many other kinds of substitute parents; chicks would follow an adult duck or human as well as a hen. Spalding also pointed out that after a young bird had followed a substitute parent for a time it usually would not then follow its own parent.

Spalding's observations provided the basis for an intensive effort to understand the nature of *imprinting,* as the tendency to follow parents or substitute parents has recently been termed.

Thorpe has summarized the results of research since Spalding's time concerning the imprinting process in this manner: (1) imprinting is a process of social attachment that seems to be confined to a specific period of limited duration and often to a particular set of environmental circumstances; (2) once a following attachment is formed it tends to be extremely strong and often irreversible; (3) imprinting is often completed prior to the development of other behavior patterns with which imprinted behavior will finally be linked; and (4) the imprinting process is characteristic of an entire species, rather than being an individual activity.

Hess has further refined these observations through noting that, (1) an animal can become attached to a "parent object" even though it may not be the biological parent or a member of the same species; attachments to physical objects can be made as easily as to other animals, and (2) even after long separation from the "imprinted object" an imprinted animal will continue to demonstrate following behavior toward that object.

The critical period for imprinting in some animals is very early and brief. For example, chicks have been shown to have a maximum receptivity to imprinting 16 hours after hatching and cannot usually be imprinted after 32 hours or later after hatching. However, in many other animals the period during which imprinting occurs is delayed significantly if the animal is deprived of visual experiences after birth. Too, the following response is "lost" at a much earlier age in socially reared chicks and ducks than in isolated animals. Isolated chicks have shown a very wide variation in their initial responses to an imprinting object, ranging from "flight," "fear," and "apathy" to "aggression."

IMPRINTING IN MAN. Many studies have been undertaken of the possibilities of an imprinting process in man. These studies have been inconclusive regarding existence of any type of imprinting process in humans. It seems that critical periods for imprinting experience become less fixed and involve much more complex phenomena as the phylogenetic scale is ascended. Too, attempts to experimentally demonstrate

critical periods phenomena in human infants have confounded biological and cultural factors, such as one study of the smiling response in infants stimulated at feeding by the presentation of smiling human adult portraits. It was concluded from this study that the human smiling response is a function of the age at which a smiling adult face (or portrait) is first presented to the infant, thus indicating existence of a critical period for imprinting human smiling. However, studies of enculturation provide evidence that casts doubt on the validity of such generalizations concerning the existence in man of a critical period for a smiling response. Despite arguments by some ethologists to the contrary, there seems to be no natural and universally human "language" of emotional gesture, including smiling, greeting, grief, and so on. The meanings attached to such behavior forms are highly culturally structured.

CRITICAL PERIODS IN DEVELOPMENT OF SOCIAL AND SEXUAL BEHAVIOR. It was noted in Chapter One that man and other primates share many structural characteristics. This is especially so in the instance of the primates of the *hominoidea* group, which includes chimpanzees, gorillas, orangutans, gibbons, and modern man. Man and the chimpanzee are particularly alike in body anatomy, blood serum proteins, chromosome number and form, and dentition. They also share a great many behavioral characteristics, including the ability to learn to make and use tools. Man shares considerably fewer structural and behavioral features with lemurs, lorises, tarsiers, marmosets, macaques, and baboons. The fewest features of structure and behavior among all the primates are shared between man and lemurs.

However, because of the availability and size of monkeys, particularly those of the genus *Macaca*, species *mulatta* (the "Rhesus" monkey), experimental studies seeking to understand critical periods in human social and sexual behavior have often been based on this particular kind of primate. Since monkeys share fewer characteristics of structure and behavior with man than is the case for some other primates (*e.g.*, members of *hominoidea*), there are fundamental questions concerning the conclusions drawn from such studies. Comparative experimental studies may not reveal as much as has been expected or hoped, for the basic logical fault in use of monkeys in experimental studies of human critical periods learning is that more than 30 million years of separate evolutionary development is involved in monkey and human social and sexual behavior.

ISOLATED AND MOTHERLESS MONKEYS. Many studies have been made of monkeys reared in laboratories and subjected to various kinds of experimental tests. Mason raised six monkeys in conditions of "social restriction" and then compared them at 2½ years of age with a group of six monkeys born and raised in a wild, or free-ranging, environment. Mason found the restricted monkeys to be more aggressive socially and to seldom engage in grooming behavior, a regular feature of free-ranging monkey behavior. The socially restricted monkeys were said to possess sexual responses that were "inefficient," "unintegrated," and "disorganized" in comparison to the "normal" sexual responses of the free-ranging group. Socially restricted male monkeys seemed unable to mate when given a choice of females. The free-ranging animals made mating choices quickly. In situations in which a choice was possible between engaging in social or isolated activities, the socially restricted monkeys seemed indifferent to each other and to prefer isolation.

In other observations of groups of socially restricted and free-ranging monkeys, Mason noted that when exposed to unfamiliar environments, socially restricted monkeys exhibited crouching, self-clasping, and rocking behavior, while free-ranging monkeys explored widely as well as played normally in the same situation. It was concluded from these studies that the first year of life in monkeys is a "true critical period" for development of their basic social and sexual responses.

To demonstrate the validity of this hypothesis, Mason studied twelve 1-year-old "normal" laboratory monkeys, placing six of them in a setting of individual isolation, and housing the other six together in pairs. The paired monkeys demonstrated less self-clasping, thumb sucking, and grasping behavior and cooperated more easily in learning tasks demanding social

action. When the two groups were placed together at 2½ years of age, the isolated monkeys remained more apart from social play than any of the paired monkeys, but otherwise behaved as would be expected. Mason concluded that these data also provided evidence that the first year of life is a crucial period in the monkey's experience.

In other studies of critical periods of social and sexual development, Harlow placed infant monkeys (1) with wire "surrogate mothers" that were "hard," "cold," and "unresponsive" and (2) with terry cloth and foam rubber "surrogate mothers" that were "soft," "warm," and "unresponsive." Later, when these two groups of young monkeys were exposed to stressful stimuli in the form of a colorful and noisy toy drummer, the wire-reared monkeys were fearful, disorganized, and withdrawn, while the foam rubber–reared monkeys were generally organized, composed, and even curious.

Harlow also investigated the hypothesis that learning is better before love than after love, using wire and terry cloth surrogate mother-reared monkeys in a variety of novel experiments. Monkeys raised with the cloth mother surrogates appeared not to suffer any impairment of their ability to perform a variety of tasks, nor harm to their normal growth, in comparison to mother-reared monkeys. Both wire and cloth surrogate-reared monkeys were less responsive than mother-reared monkeys in some sexual and social behavior forms: surrogate-reared monkeys played less, were less curious, and more frequently engaged in self-clasping, rocking behavior.

On the basis of these and many other experiments with surrogate-reared monkeys Harlow concluded that monkeys raised apart from their mothers found it very difficult as adults to develop and engage in usual monkey social and sexual companionship with their "normal" mother-reared counterparts. Harlow also concluded that the development of affection between a mother and infant monkey was a necessary antecedent, or condition, for a later normal development of affection between young monkeys; surrogate-reared monkeys seemed unable to relate affectionally to other monkeys. Harlow feels that critical periods exist in monkey social and sexual development with a number of crucial antecedent experiences necessary before later normal social and sexual behavior can develop.

Conclusions from critical periods experiments. Studies of sensory development and imprinting have clearly demonstrated the existence of some critical periods for learning in cats, fishes, ducks, chickens, rats, and mice. There are antecedent experiences and functions that must occur early in the maturation of these animals if they are to later perform more complex behaviors. It is apparent, however, that there are significant differences between these species and other kinds of animals with regard to existence and functioning of critical periods in behavior. The studies of sensory functions and imprinting and studies of monkey and human infants suggest that, if they exist, critical periods become much less fixed and much more diffuse as significant natural boundaries (such as phyla, class, order, family, and so on) are passed, where differences between animals become less of degree and more of kind. To date, studies of the application of the critical periods hypothesis to man has produced no scientifically acceptable evidences that such periods exist which are specifically antecedent to consequent adult human behavior forms. This does not at all mean that earlier learning in man is not the basis of later learning; it means simply that the critical periods hypothesis has not yet been demonstrated in man.

■ **The psychoanalytic critical periods hypothesis**

It would be inappropriate in a discussion of the critical periods hypothesis not to briefly consider similar ideas developed in psychoanalytic studies with regard to the existence of critical periods in human development and the relations between these periods and their consequences for later behavior.

During the 1920's and 1930's a body of psychoanalytic theory was developed which predicted that infants and children would modify their behavior because of rewards and punishments received from adults in five "primary" learning areas: (1) oral, (2) anal, (3) sexual, (4) dependency, and (5) aggression. Oral learning clues are said to be received by a child especially in the ways he is fed and weaned. Anal clues are said to come to the child especially in the ways he is made to control his anal sphincter. Sexual clues are said to come from activities by adults that especially draw a child's attention to his genitals. Dependence clues are said to come to a child from stimulation by adults to be dependent on them. Aggression clues are said to come from stimulation by adults to act in aggressive ways.

A set of research hypotheses was developed by psychoanalysts regarding these five learning areas. These can be summarized as follows.

1. Early permissiveness or indulgence by adults in any one of the five primary learning areas will accentuate and heighten the capacity of that area to evoke satisfaction in later life.

2. Early restrictions or frustration in any one of the five primary learning areas will accentuate, heighten, or evoke conflict, guilt, shame, incapacity, and frustration in later life.

Thus, recent psychoanalytic theory has predicted that there were specific critical periods (feeding, weaning, toilet training, and so on) which took place in development and which then were directly related to particular adult forms of behavior. It must be noted that recent psychoanalytic theory has not predicted that a single event was a cause of a later specific adult behavior. Rather, it has been felt by some psychoanalytic theorists that a series of similar, or related, events, focused in a period of time upon and about one of the primary learning areas (oral, anal, sexual, and so on) could directly lead to particular kinds of later adult behavior.

Consequences and critiques. This theory and the hypotheses derived from it stimulated much research in the fields of anthropology, psychology, sociology, education, and social work. However, in the later 1940's and during the 1950's several series of critiques were published concerning the psychoanalytic variation of the critical periods hypothesis (Orlansky,

1949; Lindesmith and Strauss, 1950; Sewell, 1952). All of these critiques noted that no firm research evidence had been offered demonstrating that in fact such critical periods in infancy invariably were related to any particular later human behavior. The authors of the critiques did not deny that in general the early experiences of a child are related to later patterns of behavior. However, they challenged the scientific validity and accuracy of a kind of psychoanalytic theory which proposed that some special critical periods in infancy and childhood are causally related to particular kinds of adult behavior. Although there is substantial doubt at present concerning this particular psychoanalytic variation of the critical periods hypothesis, research and discussion of this theory have drawn attention to the socialization process and stimulated a greater concern for improving observational methods and the design of research seeking to demonstrate specific cause and effect sequences in human behavior.

■ Isolated and autistic children and the concept of critical periods

The critical periods hypothesis involves a major problem as a useful statement for understanding socialization when considered in the context of reports of isolated children. If the accounts of Anna and Isabelle (see Chapter Five) are credible, there may be no really critical periods in development of most of those skills and acts that traditionally have been said to be requisites for being human.

Both Anna and Isabelle were prevented from having the kinds of experiences, at the times other children in American culture tend to undergo them, which would have served as the basis for a later acquisition of more complex cultural ways. The descriptions of both children make it clear that, when found, they both were without most of those cultural and social responses that ordinarily would be present in American children of the same age. Yet Anna, with only routine custodial care by persons untrained for teaching "retarded" or "slow-learning" children, quickly acquired and began to regularly display attributes and skills that have been thought to be difficult

or impossible to display unless specific earlier, or antecedent, experiences were present and undergone by a child. The evidences of Isabelle's transition in 2 years from an estimated cultural and social level of less than a 2-year-old American child to that of a 6-year-old American child, while under the care of professionally trained and quite sympathetic persons, raises this question even more dramatically concerning the application of a critical periods hypothesis to humans. If there are critical periods in human acquisition of culture, of limited duration and during which certain experiences must occur if such experience is to be a regular part of an individual's later cultural behavior, then they must be of the order of very many years in length or the experiences which "must" take place are so generalized or so very diffuse in nature (such as at least being exposed to regular physical contact with at least one other human, even though that person is deficient in many, or most, "normal" social and cultural learnings) that the general assumptions of the critical periods hypothesis are not applicable in their original form to humans and the socialization process. The evidence of Isabelle's having a routine later schooling and marrying also indicates that if critical periods do exist in socialization, then much later exposure to the "usual" experience of culture not only can produce marked and quite dramatic effects on the course of acquisition of culture, but as well erase, or completely overlay, many of the apparent emotional traumas and stresses of extreme early isolation.

Too, the case histories of children who have "recovered" from their long-term states of autism with skilled and patient special care and then have gone on to leading socially and culturally "normal" adult lives also make it apparent that the critical periods hypothesis, as it has been formulated, probably is only broadly applicable to the socialization process. Formerly autistic children have been reported as adults to have earned doctoral degrees, to be teaching college courses in several academic disciplines, to be working in demanding business occupations, and to have married and regularly assumed the routines of raising their own children "normally."[2,3] If such reports are highly probable, and there are no reasons to believe they are not, then it is likely that socialization does not operate primarily through specific events occurring in finite periods early in a child's life.

Some future directions of research. It is quite possible, of course, that other procedures of research, especially in the growing areas of human psychobiology, brain chemistry, and operant conditioning (see Chapter Four), may provide dramatic new evidences of some specific interrelations between biology and culture that must occur at precise times in physical maturation for a child to begin acquiring culture. The various experiments on animals with strychnine-like chemicals and with some antibiotics have tended to demonstrate, at least in rats, mice, and goldfish, that there may be natural chemical substances which enhance or prevent certain kinds of learning. Strychnine-like compounds have been used experimentally to "raise" the levels of learning in so-called "less intelligent" animals to the performance levels of "bright" animals of the same species. When these data are considered in the context of the evidences cited so far in this discussion, including those of autistic and isolated children, it is clear that acquisition of culture involves extremely complex interrelationships between biology and culture that obviously have to be "time-bound," that is, take place in some identifiable span of time. Continued research on humans possibly will begin to provide some indications of specifically when and how socialization is related to events or times in infants' and children's physical maturation.

■ **Summary**

This discussion has been concerned with an examination of a key hypothesis that often has been unstated or is implied in socialization research. First the origins and the general nature of the critical periods hypothesis were briefly examined. Then brief consideration was given to research on sensory processes, imprinting, and the development of social and sexual behavior, which is said to support the critical periods hypothesis. Comments on some of the methodological and theoretical problems of applying conclusions from this research to man were noted before a short discussion of a major variation of the critical periods hypothesis used by psychoanalytic scholars in their studies of socialization. Comments also were made on the application to man of the psychoanalytic critical events version of the critical periods hypothesis. The chapter closed with a series of observations regarding the meaning of the critical periods hypothesis when contrasted to data derived from studies of isolated and autistic children.

REFERENCES CITED AND SUGGESTED READINGS

Bettelheim, B. 1967. *The Empty Fortress.* New York: Free Press.

Erikson, E. H. 1939. "Observations of Sioux Education," Journal of Psychology 7:101-156.

_____. 1943. "Observations on the Yurok: Childhood and World Image," University of California Publications in American Archaeology and Ethnology 35, No. 10.

_____. 1950. *Childhood and Society.* New York: Norton.

_____. 1956. "Growth and Crises of the Healthy Personality." In C. Kluckhohn and H. A. Murray (eds.), *Personality in Nature, Society and Culture.* New York: Knopf, pp. 185-225.

Fromm, E. 1943. "Sex and Character," Psychiatry 6:21-31.

_____. 1949. "Psychoanalytic Characterology and Its Application to the Understanding of Culture." In S. S. Sargent and M. W. Smith (eds.), *Culture and Personality.* New York: Viking Fund.

_____. 1956. "Individual and Social Origins of Neurosis." In C. Kluckhohn and H. A. Murray (eds.), *Personality in Nature, Society and Culture.* New York: Knopf, pp. 515-521.

---

[2]I am not concerned here with the origins of infantile or childhood autism. I recognize that Bettelheim (1967) in fact has developed a variation of the critical periods hypothesis as the basis of his theory of autism. I am concerned only with the fact that autistic children, who were clearly very disturbed for long periods during which they ordinarily would have been exposed to usual cultural and social learnings, have later "recovered" to the point where they can function normally in everyday life and can compete intellectually in demanding statuses. Thus it is obviously possible to "recover" from long-term and severe emotional isolation to the point of later learning the cultural forms and meanings needed to function successfully as adults.

[3]Margaret Mead (personal communication, January, 1972) has suggested that the *quality* and *intensity* of learning and behavior allowed by parent surrogates or caretakers may be vital in the process of accelerated recovery by isolated or autistic children.

Gesell, A. 1954. "The Ontogenesis of Infant Behavior." In L. Carmichael (ed.), *Manual of Child Psychology,* ed. 2. New York: Wiley, pp. 335-373.

Goodall, J. M. 1962. "Nest Building Behavior in the Free Ranging Chimpanzee," Annals, New York Academy of Science **102**:455-467.

_____. 1963. "Feeding Behavior of Wild Chimpanzees," Symposium, Zoological Society of London **10**:39-48.

_____. 1964. "Tool-Using and Aimed Throwing in a Community of Free-Living Chimpanzees," Nature **201**:1264-1266.

_____. 1965. "Chimpanzees of the Gombe Stream Reserve." In I. DeVore (ed.), *Primate Behavior: Field Studies of Monkeys and Apes.* New York: Holt, Rinehart and Winston, pp. 425-473.

Goldman-Eisler, F. 1956. "Breast Feeding and Character Formation." In C. Kluckhohn and H. A. Murray (eds.), *Personality in Nature, Society and Culture.* New York: Knopf, pp. 146-184.

Gray, P. H. 1958. "Theory and Evidence of Imprinting in Human Infants," Journal of Psychology **46**:155-166.

Guiton, P. 1958. "The Effect of Isolation on the Following Response of Brown Leghorn Chicks," Proceedings of the Royal Physiological Society, Edinburgh **27**:9-14

Harlow, H. 1958. "The Nature of Love," American Psychologist **13**:673-685.

_____. 1959a. "Affectional Response in the Infant Monkey," Science **130**:421-432.

_____. 1959b. "Basic Social Capacity of Primates." In J. N. Spuhler (ed.), *The Evolution of Man's Capacity for Culture.* Detroit: Wayne State University Press.

_____. 1961. "Social and Sexual Behavior." In "Critical Periods of Development: Report on a Conference," Social Science Research Council, Items **15**:16-17.

Harlow, H., and M. K. Harlow. 1962. "Social Deprivation in Monkeys," Scientific American **207**:136-146.

_____. 1965a. "An Analysis of Love," Listener **73**:255-257.

_____. 1965b. "Romulus and Rhesus," Listener **73**:215-217.

Harlow, H., M. K. Harlow, and S. J. Suomi. 1971. "From Thought to Therapy: Lessons from a Primate Laboratory," American Scientist **59**:538-549.

Hess, E. H. 1957. "Effects of Meprobamate on Imprinting in Water Fowl," Annals, New York Academy of Science **67**:724-733.

_____. 1959. "Two Conditions Limiting Critical Age for Imprinting," Journal of Comparative and Physiological Psychology **52**:515-518.

_____. 1961. "Imprinting." In "Critical Periods of Development: Report on a Conference," Social Science Research Council, Items **15**:14-15.

Inhelder, B., and J. Piaget. 1958. *The Growth of Logical Thinking from Childhood to Adolescence.* New York: Basic Books.

Kagan, J. 1964. "American Longitudinal Research on Psychological Development," Child Development **35**:1-32.

Krech, D. 1968. "Scientist Says Control of Intelligence is Possible," New York Times, April 3, 1968, p. 32c.

LaBarre, W. 1947. "The Cultural Basis of Emotions and Gestures," Journal of Personality **16**:49-68.

Lancaster, J. 1968. "On the Evolution of Tool Using Behavior," American Anthropologist **70**:56-66.

Lindesmith, A. R., and A. L. Strauss. 1950. "A Critique of Culture-Personality Writings," American Sociological Review **15**:587-600.

Lorenz, K. 1952. *King Solomon's Ring: New Light on Animal Ways.* New York: Crowell.

_____. 1965. *Evolution and Modification of Behavior.* Chicago: University of Chicago Press.

Marler, P., and W. Hamilton. 1966. *Mechanisms of Animal Behavior.* New York: Wiley.

Mason, W. A. 1961. "Social and Sexual Behavior." In "Critical Periods of Development: Report on a Conference," Social Science Research Council, Items **15**:15-17.

McGaugh, J. L. 1968. "Drug to be Used as Learning Aid," New York Times, May 4, 1968, p. 79.

Moltz, H. 1960. "Imprinting: Empirical Basis and Theoretical Significance," Psychological Bulletin **57**:291-314.

_____. 1963. "Imprinting: An Epigenetic Approach," Psychological Review **70**:123-138.

Moltz, H., and L. J. Stettner. 1961. "Some Parameters of Imprinting Effectiveness," Journal of Comparative Psychology **54**:279-283.

Orlansky, H. 1949. "Infant Care and Personality," Psychological Bulletin **46**:1-48.

Piaget, J. 1926. *The Language and Thought of the Child.* London: Kegan Paul, Trench, Trubner.

_____. 1932. *The Moral Judgment of the Child.* London: Kegan Paul, Trench, Trubner.

_____. 1955. *The Construction of Reality in the Child.* New York: Basic Books.

_____. 1965. *The Child's Conception of Space.* New York: Humanities.

_____. 1969. *The Child's Conception of Number.* London: Routledge and K. Paul.

Riesen, A. H. 1961. "Sensory Processes." In "Critical Periods of Development: Report on a Conference," Social Science Research Council, Items **15**:13-14.

Spalding, D. A. 1873. "Instinct, with Original Observations on Young Animals," British Journal of Animal Behavior **2**:2-11.

Salk, L. 1962. "Mothers' Heartbeat as an Imprinting Stimulus," Transactions of the New York Academy of Sciences **24**:753-763.

Scott, J. P. 1962. "Critical Periods in Behavioral Development," Science **138**:949-958.

—————. 1963. "The Process of Primary Socialization in Canine and Human Infants," Monograph of the Society for Research in Child Development **28**:1-47.

Sewell, W. H. 1952. "Infant Training and the Personality of the Child," American Journal of Sociology **58**:150-159.

Spitz, R. 1946. "Anaclitic Depression," Psychoanalytic Study of the Child **2**:313-342.

Thorpe, W. 1963. *Learning and Instinct in Animals.* London: Methuen.

von Senden, M. 1960. *Space and Sight: The Perception of Space and Shape in the Congenitally Blind Before and After Operation,* Translated by Peter Heath. New York: Free Press.

Weidmann, U. 1956. "Some Experiments of the Following and the Flocking Reactions of Mallard Ducklings," British Journal of Animal Behavior **4**:78-79.

Yarrow, L. J. 1961. "Maternal Deprivation; Toward an Empirical and Conceptual Re-Evaluation," Psychological Bulletin **58**:459-490.

SEVEN  KINSHIP, KIN GROUPS, AND SOCIALIZATION

This chapter examines various ways in which the socialization process may be related to some major forms of human behavior. The chapter begins with a brief review of ways of thinking systematically about culture. The discussion continues with some ethnographic examples of relationships between kinship, kin groups, and socialization. It concludes with observations concerning the study of kinship, kin groups, and socialization.

■ Subsystems and patterns of culture

Human culture can be thought of as containing at least four *subsystems:* (1) *the subsystem of social relations,* (2) *the subsystem of language,* (3) *the subsystem of technology,* and (4) *the subsystem of ideology.*[1] A large number of whole categories of culture, or *patterns,* make up each subsystem of culture. The following outline lists many of the patterns that can be grouped under the different cultural subsystem headings.[2]

SUBSYSTEMS AND PATTERNS OF CULTURE*

Social relations
1. Kinship
2. Kin groups
3. Community
4. Territory
5. State
6. Government

Social relations—cont'd
7. Law
8. Justice
9. Daily routine
10. Recreation
11. Entertainment
12. Status-role
13. Class
14. War
15. Health
16. Sickness
17. Death
18. Sex
19. Reproduction
20. Infancy
21. Childhood
22. Adolescence
23. Adulthood
24. Old age

Language
1. Speech
2. Vocabulary
3. Grammar
4. Phonology
5. Semantics
6. Style
7. Signs

Technology
1. Food quest
2. Animal husbandry
3. Agriculture
4. Food processing
5. Clothing
6. Adornment
7. Shelter
8. Processing of materials
9. Construction
10. Equipment
11. Energy
12. Machines
13. Tools
14. Property
15. Exchange
16. Marketing
17. Finance
18. Labor
19. Transportation

---

[1]It is important to understand that some cultural anthropologists would include one or two fewer, or several more, subsystems of culture and perhaps would use somewhat different labels for the different subsystems. (See Bock, 1969:352-355.)

[2]For one example of a listing of the major patterns of culture used by cultural anthropologists in their studies, see Murdock and others, 1969.

*There may be more or fewer patterns in a particular subsystem than noted here. Some patterns could be included in other subsystems, depending on the nature of the cultural theory used. The concept of *pattern* is a generalization by the observer about what people regularly do or should do. For discussion of pattern, see Kluckhohn, 1949, and Herskovits, 1960.

SUBSYSTEMS AND PATTERNS OF CULTURE—CONT'D

Ideology

1. Arts
2. Religious belief
3. Ecclesiastical belief
4. Numbers
5. Measures
6. Ideas about nature
7. Ideas about man
8. Ideas about society
9. Ideas about culture

It is important to understand that every pattern, in each subsystem of culture, contains within it specific kinds of learned, shared, and transmitted behavior that is regular in form. Patterns of culture are comprised of culture trait complexes. Trait complexes are clusters of similar traits in a culture. Culture traits are the minimally significant units of culture that can be isolated by direct observation. Fig. 10 illustrates these conceptual levels and arrangements of the theoretical parts of culture.

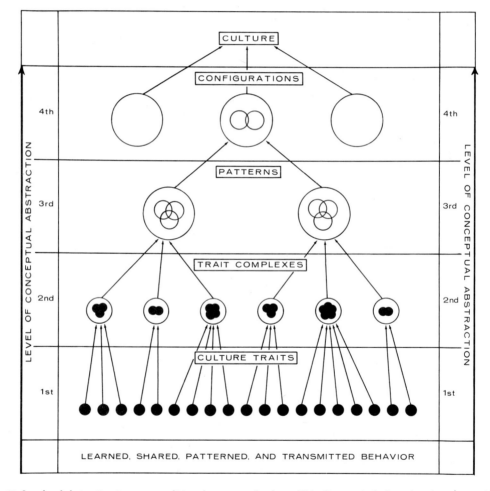

Fig. 10. Levels of abstraction in conceptualizing the nature of culture. This diagram includes a fourth conceptual level, *configuration*, between the abstractions of *patterns* and *culture*, since it appears there is a need for some way to group patterns of similar form, meaning, or function. However, this level of abstraction is not generally utilized in the discussion, other diagrams, and analyses of this text. The conceptual and theoretical modes of analyses used here are not unique ones; such analyses are widely used in modern scientific and cultural anthropological studies.

A conceptual model of culture using these ideas might be represented as in Fig. 11. The four subsystems of culture are shown, with the major patterns making up each subsystem noted as circles linked to one another by straight lines. The lines are meant to indicate a long-lasting relationship of interdependence between each of the patterns in a subsystem. These lines are drawn also to show long-lasting links of interdependence between patterns in one subsystem and patterns in the other subsystems in culture. This is intended to convey the idea that culture is a highly integrated *whole* of many interrelated parts, each dependent on the other.

There is not space in an introductory socialization text to examine and illustrate all the ways each pattern in the four subsystems of culture are related specifically to socialization. However, the patterns discussed in the chapters to follow, such as kinship, kin groups, status-role, and classes, have been chosen for discussion since they have been described and analyzed more

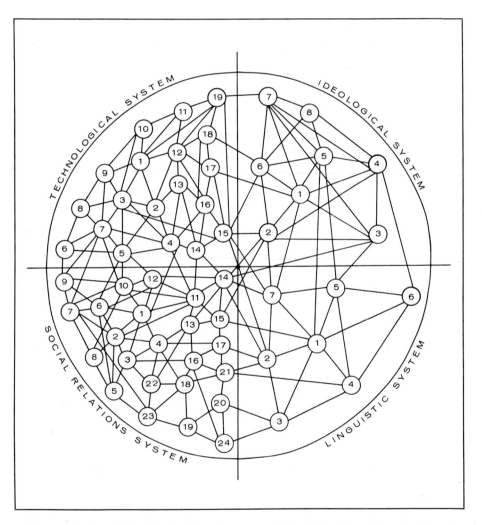

Fig. 11. Relations of interdependence of patterns in subsystems of culture. Note: the number of patterns in each subsystem of culture does not correspond to the number of patterns listed on pp. 125-126; this diagram is intended only as an ideal conceptual model.

clearly than many other patterns. A full understanding of socialization will probably require careful study of the ways each pattern, in each subsystem of culture, is related to the process of socialization. Such understanding may be attained in the years ahead, depending upon the scope of research efforts in the field of socialization and developments in socialization theory and research methods.

■ Kinship

In the past century, anthropologists and sociologists have used the word *kinship* to refer to several different kinds of relationships between human individuals. Sometimes the term has been used to indicate a biological relation between persons. The term has also been used to refer to particular kinds of social behavior between individuals. In other instances, kinship has meant the kinds of special language terms used by some individuals in their social relations with each other.

In fact, the cultural pattern of kinship contains all three of these features of behavior. One feature is based on the fact of human life that every living person is part of a biological network. Persons who have contributed genes to other persons are biological kinsmen. Humans have developed quite complex and often very elaborate conceptions of how far and in what ways the biological network of kinsmen extends from any one individual. Hence, biological kinsmen have been categorized into many different kinds of persons and have been given special names when they belong to each kind. Kinship terminology in a society serves as a basic guide for individuals to the different categories of the biological network of kinsmen.

Too, humans have developed a great many expectations for social behavior by persons in the different categories of kin called and addressed by special names. The form of expected behavior for persons occupying special kin categories also serves as a guide to the biological network of kinsmen. An individual's special social behavior toward persons he recognizes as his biological kin may indicate his continuing affirmation of his place in a biological kin network.

A way of understanding kinship. When an-

thropologists study these three different trait complexes in the pattern of kinship, they use diagrams for ease in portraying the very complex social relations that different societies have evolved; on these diagrams a triangle usually represents a male and a circle indicates a female. One straight line between two persons indicates a recognized biological, or *consanguineal,* relationship, while two short parallel lines between male and female symbols indicates a marriage, or *affinal,* relationship. The *generation* of individuals is indicated on kinship diagrams by placing all children below, and connecting them with vertical lines to their parents. To avoid confusion, kinship diagrams always begin description at one point. The point is that of one person, termed *Ego.* The symbol for a male or female Ego is usually shaded on a diagram. The other persons related to Ego are usually labelled by abbreviations for English language kinship terms. Thus, Ego's father and mother are labelled in a kinship diagram as *Fa* and *Mo.* Ego's brothers are *Br* and his sisters are *Si.* An X drawn through a symbol indicates a person is deceased. A lower case *x* beneath a male or female symbol indicates a special kind of cousin relationship, termed a *cross-cousin* relationship. A // symbol beneath a male or female symbol on a kinship diagram indicates a *parallel cousin* relationship. Ego's *MoSi's* and *FaBr's* children are his (or her) *parallel cousins,* while Ego's *FaSi's* and *MoBr's* children are his (or her) *cross-cousins.* Fig. 12 illustrates these symbols and lists some of the many abbreviations used in studies of kinship.

It takes some practice to read kinship diagrams, but use of these symbols and abbreviations makes possible the collection and study of the special kinship terms used in a society and aids in formulating descriptions of how a people conceive of the ways they should behave with and toward individuals called by such terms.[3] Fig. 13 is a typical kinship diagram.

---

[3]For an introductory account of such uses in anthropology, see Schusky, 1965. For a more advanced discussion, see Bohannan, 1963. For a description of American kinship, see Schneider, D. M. 1968. *American Kinship.* Englewood Cliffs, N. J.: Prentice-Hall, Inc.

SYMBOLS

△	Male		⊠	Deceased Male
○	Female		⊗	Deceased Female
▲	Male Ego		△̷	Cross Cousin (male or female)
●	Female Ego		○̷	Parallel Cousin (male or female)
=	Affinal Tie		—	Consanguineal Tie

ABBREVIATIONS

SINGLE

Father	- Fa		Wife	- Wi
Mother	- Mo		Husband	- Hu
Brother	- Br		Sibling	- Sb
Sister	- Si		Child	- Ch
Son	- So		Nephew	- Ne
Daughter	- Da		Niece	- Ni
Spouse	- Sp		Inlaw	- La

DOUBLE

Father's Father	- FaFa	Father's Brother	- FaBr
Father's Mother	- FaMo	Father's Sister	- FaSi
Mother's Father	- MoFa	Mother's Brother	- MoBr
Mother's Mother	- MoMo	Mother's Sister	- MoSi

TRIPLE

Father's Brother's Son	- FaBrSo	Wife's Brother's Son	- WiBrSo
Father's Sister's Daughter	- FaSiDa	Sister's Daughter's Son	- SiDaSo
Mother's Brother's Son	- MoBrSo	Brother's Son's Daughter	- BrSoDa
Mother's Brother's Daughter	- MoBrDa	Son's Son's Son	- SoSoSo

Fig. 12. Some symbols and abbreviations of kinship studies. It should be noted that social anthropologists in the United Kingdom and elsewhere favor use of *Z* for sister and *S* for son.

Kinship systems. Comparisons of the patterns of kinship for a great many of the world's societies shows that there are at least six basic kinds of kinship systems. The principle of classification used in defining these six systems depends upon the ways Ego addresses his cousins. Thus, in the *Eskimo* type kinship system, all cousins are equated with each other and are differentiated from Ego's siblings, or brothers and sisters. In the *Iroquois* system, sibling terms usually are extended to parallel cousins and there are separate kin terms for cross-cousins. In the *Hawaiian* system, sibling terms are used to address all cousins. In the *Crow* kinship system, *FaSiSo* is called by Ego by the term for *Fa, FaSiDa* is

called by Ego by the term used for *FaSi,* while *MoBrSo* is called by Ego by the term for *So* and *MoBrDa* is called by Ego by the term for *Da.* All parallel cousins are called by the terms used for siblings. In the *Omaha* system, *FaSiSo* is called by Ego by the term used for nephew, while *FaSiDa* is called by Ego by the term used for niece. *MoBrSo* is called by Ego by the term for *MoBr,* and *MoBrDa* is called by the term used for *Mo.* All parallel cousins are called by the terms used for siblings. In the *Sudanese* system each cousin is called by a distinct term and is separated terminologically from siblings.

The questions of whether a Crow Indian really believes that *FaSiSo* is his *Fa* and that *MoBrSo*

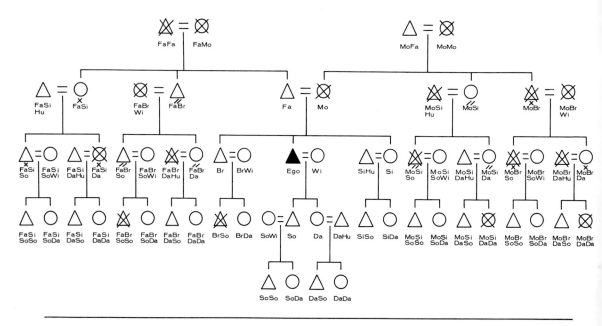

Fig. 13. A kinship diagram. The symbols for parallel-cousin (//) and cross-cousin (×) have been entered under the symbols for kin in the first ascending generation to aid students in tracing out these particular cousin relationships. It is important to recall that cousins, whether parallel or cross, are always found in the same generation as Ego and not in ascending or descending generations from Ego.

is actually his own *So,* or whether an Omaha Indian thinks his *MoBrSo* is really his *MoBr* or his *MoBrDa* is actually his *Mo,* have caused extended discussion, comment, and argument in anthropology. There have been two points of view on the matter. One view, first set forth by Lewis Henry Morgan, a nineteenth-century American student of kinship, was that kinship terms are indications of the ways a people actually have organized and see their society. A second view, which tends to prevail today, is one offered first by A. R. Radcliffe-Brown, a twentieth-century English student of kinship. He noted that kinship terms are "signposts" for interpersonal conduct, telling a people of their reciprocal social rights, duties, privileges, and obligations. Thus, a Crow Indian boy does not believe *FaSiSo* is his biological *Fa.* Rather, in the act of calling this particular cousin, who likely is the same age, by the term for *Fa,* Ego sets up a life-

long series of culturally important expectations in his social relations with that cousin, while the cousin addressed as *Fa* must reciprocate toward his *"So"* through a whole series of culturally important behavior forms. Similarly, an Omaha Indian boy does not believe *MoBrDa* is his biological *Mo.* But in calling her *Mo,* the Omaha boy sets in action a lifelong series of culturally important social relationships between himself and this particular female cousin, which she will reciprocate to keep a balance in her social relationships with her *"So."* This also is true in societies that use the kin term for *Mo* to address all of *MoSi* and *FaSi.* Hawaiians use this type of terminology (technically, "generational kinship terminology") but do not believe they have many biological mothers.[4] However, they do learn as they grow up that it is culturally very important to act toward all *MoSi* and all *FaSi* as one ideally

---

[4]In addition to the six major cousin term classifications, kinship terms also have been classified by the ways members of the *parental generation* are addressed. Thus, when a people call *Mo* by one term and *FaSi* and *MoSi* by another term, the system is termed *lineal.* The American kin system is a lineal one. In the *generational* system *Mo, FaSi,* and *MoSi* are all called by the same term. In the *bifurcate merging* system *MoSi* is called by the term for *Mo* but *FaSi* has another term. In the *bifurcate collateral* system each woman in the parental generation is addressed by a special kin term.

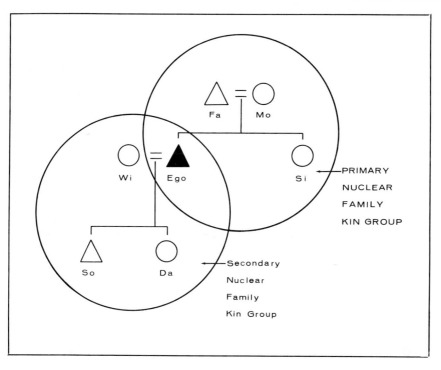

Fig. 14. Primary and secondary nuclear family kin groups. The term "nuclear" family is an analytical concept and does not require any particular Ego to start in describing a genealogical system.

acts toward and with *Mo;* however, *Mo* is still treated specially by Hawaiians.

■ Kin groups

In studies of kinship and kin behavior, anthropologists and sociologists have noted that there are a number of human groups in which the social relationships between persons making up the groups are marked by a regular use of kinship terms and recognition of kinship ties. These groups have been labelled *kin groups.* There are two basic types of *kin groups:* (1) *family kin groups* and (2) *consanguineal kin groups.* One difference between these types of kin groups is that all family kin groups contain *affines,* or relatives by marriage, but consanguineal kin groups contain no affines. Another difference is that all family kin groups have at least one social relationship that includes shared sexual behavior. Consanguineal kin groups exclude relationships of shared sexual behavior. Too, individuals may be excluded from consanguineal kin groups be-

cause of their place of residence, occupation, or adherence to special religious beliefs. Family kin groups rarely exclude persons for such reasons.

Family kin groups. The fundamental family kin group can be called the *nuclear* family. Sometimes this kin group also has been termed a *biological family,* an *elementary family,* or a *conjugal-natal family.* This kin group is marked by a set of basic social relationships, based upon the two different criteria of sex and descent. In the nuclear family an adult man and woman have entered into "marriage," a public recognition that a man and a woman have been granted special kinship rights to each other and can directly share sexual activities with each other but not with any of the children that may be born to them. In addition, in the nuclear family kin groups there are special social relationships based on descent between a mother and her son, and between a mother and her daughter. There are also the same special social relationships of descent between a father and his son and between a father and his daughter. There also are special social relationships based on descent in a nuclear family kin group between brothers, between sisters, and between brothers and sisters. These eight special relationships, based on sex and descent, characterize nuclear families in all human societies.[5]

Every person not orphaned at birth and who marries is a member of two nuclear family kin groups. First, he (or she) is a member of the *primary nuclear family kin group,* into which he is born. Then, when he marries, he founds with his wife and becomes a member of a *secondary nuclear family kin group.* Fig. 14 illustrates the way human primary and secondary nuclear family kin groups are formed. Sometimes the primary nuclear family kin group is termed the *family of orientation,* to note that it is in this social unit that enculturation begins. The secondary nuclear family kin group also has been called the *family of procreation,* to note that it is in this social unit, founded upon directly shared sexual relations between Ego and his *Wi* (or Ego and her *Hu*), that Ego produces children and begins their enculturation. All primary nuclear family kin groups dissolve upon the deaths of members.

The nuclear family kin group has several major functions in many societies. Besides providing a locus, or setting, for direct, shared sexual activity between two adults and for the production of children, this kin group also may serve as a basic unit for economic activities as well as for the transmission and acquisition of culture. The ways different societies regularly undertake these functions vary greatly.

The nuclear family is the sole form of the family kin group in about a quarter of all human societies. In somewhat more than half of all human societies the nuclear family kin group is part of two types of larger kin groupings. These groups are usually called (1) *extended family kin groups* and (2) *polygamous family kin groups.*

EXTENDED FAMILY KIN GROUPS. This type of kin group is created when two or more nuclear family kin groups are linked together through either a special form of parent-child or brother-sister kin relationship. In the formation of extended family kin groups, common residence and a variety of shared economic and social activities usually occur. In a *virilocal* (or *patrilocal*) type of extended family kin group, boys continue to live after their marriage in or near to the dwelling of their father, adding the nuclear family grouping of their wives and children to their father's nuclear family kin grouping. The sisters of these brothers go to live with or near to their husband's nuclear family kin grouping. An *uxorilocal* (or *matrilocal*) type extended family is created when girls remain in or near to the nuclear family of their mother after marriage, adding the nuclear family grouping of their husbands and children to that kin group, while their brothers, after marriage, go to live in or near to the nuclear families of their wives. A few societies have emphasized close, nonsexual relationships between brothers and sisters by creating a *matrilateral* type of extended family kin grouping. This kind of extended family kin group consists of a woman, her brother, and her offspring. The woman's husband is treated as an outsider in family affairs. The husband, wife, and children reside together but do not interact socially as a nuclear family group. For example, among the *Dobu* of Melanesia, children cannot eat the food grown in their father's fields, inherit or use his personal property, or really enjoy his trust and confidence; Dobuans believe their husbands and fathers to be hostile to them and a magical enemy. Children eat food provided by their *MoBr,* inherit and use *MoBr* personal property, and believe him to be their protector and guardian. Thus, while there is a "nuclear family" kin group in Dobu, it is only a *household,* that is, a residence unit. The "real" Dobuan family is the *susu,* or matrilaterally extended family kin group.

There are some other varieties of extended family kin groups. In some societies a husband

---

[5]A recent development of method for classifying kinship terms, called *componential analysis,* has been used to broaden the understanding of reciprocal social relations among kinsmen. This method has also turned up one society, the Kalmuck Mongols, who apparently do not see kin terms as "signposts" to reciprocal social behavior, but rather see them as indicating a whole field of relatives for Ego, so that the way Ego terms these relatives has little to do with his behavior toward them or with the behavior of relatives toward him. (See Goodenough, 1967.)

takes his wife to live with or very near his male matrilineal kinsmen, that is, his *MoBr's*. This creates kin grouping that can be called an *avunculocal* extended family. Too, some instances have been reported in which a married couple do not live regularly with one another, but remain members of their own nuclear families, with any children residing with the mother. This type of extended family kin grouping could be called *duolocal*.

It is important to know and understand that anthropologists use the terms *virilocal, uxorilocal, matrilateral, avunculocal,* and *duolocal* to refer specifically to rules of marriage residence and to note patterns of descent. These concepts have been used here to define different types of extended family kin groups in order to explain and

make clear the several ways the nuclear family kin group can be extended to other forms.

POLYGAMOUS FAMILY KIN GROUPS. Nuclear family kin groups can also be extended through marriage relationships. This kind of extension occurs in two forms: (1) the *polygynous family kin group* and (2) the *polyandrous family kin group*. A polygynous family kin group is formed when a man marries two or more wives and becomes husband and father in several nuclear family kin groups. A polyandrous family kin group is formed when a woman marries two or more husbands and is a wife and mother in several nuclear family kin groups. Fig. 15 illustrates these marriage extensions of the nuclear family kin group.

Polygynous family groups are not uncommon in human society, especially where there is a

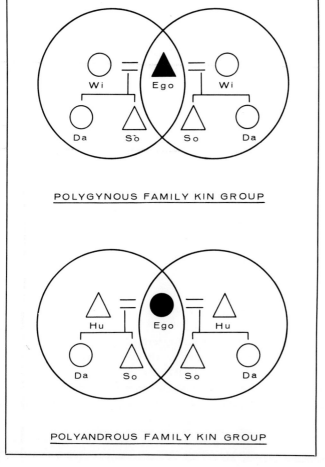

POLYGYNOUS FAMILY KIN GROUP

POLYANDROUS FAMILY KIN GROUP

Fig. 15. Polygamous family kin groups.

great economic demand for women to become co-workers of a first wife. In many societies practicing polygyny, co-wives are sisters. This is termed as sororal polygyny. There are less than ten societies known to have practiced polyandry. Polyandrous extended family kin groups are commonly based on the fact of co-husbands being brothers, a practice technically called *fraternal polyandry*.

Consanguineal kin groups. As noted previously, there are kin groups that differ from family kin groups because they contain no relatives by marriage, or affines, permit no shared sexual relationships, and may practice various forms of social exclusion. Anthropologists divide such groups, which are termed *consanguineal kin groups*, into two main types, *unilineal* and *bilateral*. About one-third of human societies have bilateral consanguineal kin groups. The remaining two-thirds have unilineal consanguineal kin groups.[6] Both types of consanguineal kin groups depend upon a recognition of a particular kind of *descent* between parents and children.

In a bilateral type of consanguineal kin group children are said to be equally related to and descended from their father and mother and the ancestors of their father and mother. This creates a large group of kinsmen, designated by anthropologists as the *kindred*. A kindred includes persons from both father's and mother's families who may be present at important ceremonial and ritual occasions such as births, deaths, religious events, severe illness, and so on. Members of a bilateral kindred visit and entertain one another and support each other in time of economic and personal need. Ego's kindred theoretically includes every person to whom he can trace a kin relationship because of their common descent from a specific male or female ancestor. However, in most bilateral societies, kindreds are limited to that group of relatives in Ego's *Mo's* and *Fa's* families who have an actual and abiding interest in him as a kinsman. This smaller group of bilateral kin has been termed a *ramage*. A ramage is centered upon a particular Ego and

shifts in its composition from one Ego to the next.

In a unilineal consanguineal kin group, Ego is related to one line of male or female relatives. If the relationship of descent is traced only through males, the unilineal kin group is termed *patrilineal*. In a patrilineal type unilineal kin group, children of both sexes belong to the kin group of their father, which in turn is the kin group of his *Fa*, his *FaFa*, his *FaFaFa*, and so on, as far as descent can be remembered or has been recorded. In a *matrilineal* type of unilineal kin group, children of both sexes belong to the kin group of their mother, which is the kin group of her *Mo*, her *MoMo*, her *MoMoMo*, and so on. In societies organized on this principle, a unilineal consanguineal kin group is usually a *corporate* unit, that is, it has the possibility of holding and assigning property. In some unilineal societies individuals have legal and political status only if they are members of such corporate groups.

There are, in turn, several kinds of patrilineal and matrilineal unilineal consanguineal kin groups. The most elementary is known as the *lineage*. Lineages are unilineal consanguineal kin groups descended from a named and known ancestor who actually lived only five or six generations before Ego. Lineages are either *patrilineages* (if the founder was a male) or *matrilineages* (if the founder was a female). The lineages of a society may be subdivided into several smaller units. Thus, among the *Nuer* of the Nilotic Sudan, each major or maximal patrilineage of the society is divided into two *secondary lineages*, which in turn are divided into four *tertiary lineages*, which themselves are divided into eight *minimal lineages*. Fig. 16 illustrates the Nuer conception of their lineage divisions.[7] In some societies, it is possible for boys to join the lineage of their fathers, while their sisters join the lineages of their mothers. This procedure is termed *parallel descent*. In some other societies the choice of lineage is left to Ego. He may join the lineage of either parent. This procedure is known to anthropologists as *multilineal descent*.

---

[6]These figures are from Table 17-1 in Schneider and Gough, 1961: 663.

[7]For a description of Nuer lineage organization, see Evans-Pritchard, 1940 and 1951.

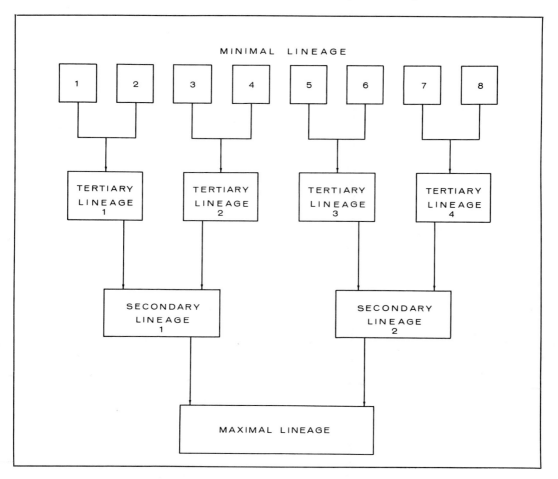

Fig. 16. Nuer lineage organization. (See Evans-Pritchard, E. E. 1940. *The Nuer.* Oxford: Clarendon Press; and Evans-Pritchard, E. E. 1951. *Kinship and Marriage Among the Nuer.* London: Oxford University Press.)

When a society considerably enlarges membership in a lineage group by including all persons who claim descent from a mythical founding ancestor, the group is termed a *clan*. Thus, a clan is a lineage with a membership considerably expanded through use of the fiction of common descent from a remote ancestor. Members of clans often claim the founding ancestor to have been a real person and believe that they and other members of the clan behave the way they do because they are the descendents of the clan ancestor. Founding ancestors of clans are sometimes said to be animals, or the offspring of a marriage between an animal and human parent. Thus, among the Dahomeans of West Africa, one clan founder was believed to have been the son of a father who was a peanut magically transformed into a man, who then married a woman. Other Dahomean clan founders are believed to be the offspring of marriages between a woman and a pig, a woman and a toad, a woman and a dog, and a woman and a horse.[8] Clans do not always have clearly recognizable lineages within them, just as lineages exist in many societies without being organized into clan groups. It is also possible for a society to have both patrilineal and matrilineal clan groups.

[8]See Herskovits, 1933: 24-27.

If a society has at least four clan groups and follows a principle of formal social reciprocity between the groups, it may organize the clans into units that cooperate with one another legally and economically, in regulation of marriage and sometimes in warfare. The formal social linking in a society of two or more clans into one large kin group, which is recognized as different from another grouping of two or more clans, creates a unilineal kin group termed a *moiety*. The Iroquois Indians possessed moieties. However, if a society possesses many clans and informally practices reciprocity between them, the unilineal kin groupings that result are termed as *phratries*.

The Hopi Indians of Arizona have a very large number of matrilineal clans, which are organized into twelve phratries. The Aztec of prehistoric Mexico had twenty clans organized into four phratries. Phratries are not common forms of unilineal kin groups because they perform few meaningful social functions, as do clans and moieties. Clans and moiety kin groups function to regulate marriage, provide personal assistance and protection, give legal and political assistance, and provide economic, religious, and ceremonial help to members. Fig. 17 illustrates the ways lineages, clans, and moieties can ideally be related in various societies.

Fig. 17. Theoretical relationships of lineage, clan, phratry, and moiety.

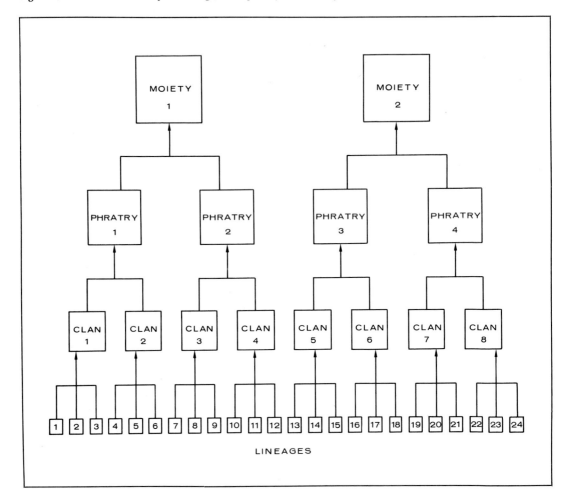

■ Ethnographic examples of relationships
between kinship, kin groups,
and socialization

Kinship and kin groups are important for
understanding socialization because, as children
learn their various social positions, they develop
major patterns of social behavior that become
part of their lifelong models for relations with
others in their society. While this is not the only
model for social and cultural behavior children
learn, it seems to be vital to their access to
other aspects of culture.

An attempt will be made in the following
pages to briefly summarize ethnographic data
concerning the ways kinship, kin groups, and
socialization are interrelated in two societies,
the Arunta of Australia and the Ashanti of West
Africa.

**Arunta kinship, kin groups, and encultura-
tion.** Europeans began to settle the Australian
continent in 1788. It has been estimated that at
that time there were perhaps 300,000 Australian
natives, divided into some five hundred tribal
groups widely scattered over all of the Australian continent. At the beginning of the nineteenth century the native population of the
central desert of Australia, an area of some
200,000 square miles, was estimated at 18,000
persons, organized into between twenty-five and
fifty different tribes. The largest central Australian desert tribe is known as the *Arunta* (also
known as the *Aranda*).[9]

In 1896 the Arunta numbered about 2,000
persons. Arunta technology was quite limited.
Crude stone and wooden tools and weapons
were used in hunting, gathering and preparing
food, in protection, and in war. The Arunta did
not use the bow and arrow, an important tool
among many of the world's isolated and nomadic
peoples. The Arunta made no pottery or baskets,
used no cooking utensils, and wore no clothing.
Each Arunta nuclear family was almost a self-
contained economic unit. A typical permanent

Arunta encampment usually consisted of a
father and mother and their children. This social
unit lived in shelters of interlaced sticks made
into low, domed structures thatched with grasses.
Nuclear families moved regularly, as they hunted
through the local dry desert territory for kangaroo, wallaby, emu, and smaller birds and animals. Family members also gathered seeds, roots,
edible fungus, bird and reptile eggs, the pupae
of moths, caterpillars, beetles, flies, ants, and
rodents. In their temporary hunting camps,
nuclear families built a low stick and grass wall
to shelter themselves from the sun and wind.

Arunta nuclear families feel themselves to be
a part of a larger unit of related nuclear families.
Anthropologists have named these loose col-
lections of nuclear families *local groups*. Arunta
local groups are *exogamous* and *virilocal*. The
local group of a male Ego would contain his
Fa and *FaFa*, his *Br*, and, through the time of
his life, his *So*, *SoSo*, and all the *Br* and unmarried *Si* of these men. A male Ego's married *Si*
and their children live in the local groups of
their husbands. Ego's local group also contains
wives, brought into the local group from other
local groups.

The Arunta practice a system of marriage
exhange in which a male marries his *MoMo-
BrDaDa*, a "second cross-cousin," while his *Si*
marries the *Br* of his wife. Thus, Ego's *Wi* comes
from a local group that contains his *MoMoBr*
patrilineal relatives, a local group different from
the one in which his *Fa* had chosen a *Wi*. In
this way, the Arunta use kinship to bind together from four to eight local groups. Such
kin ties were vital to the stability of Arunta
social life, since they had no formal political
or governmental organization to regulate daily
life.

Among the Arunta the term *Wi* refers to all
females of the kin category ("second cross-
cousins") from which Ego would select a *Wi*.
Ego's grandparents address him and he addresses
them by use of the same kin term. The children
of Ego's *Br* are called by one term, while the
children of Ego's *Si* are called by a different kin
term. Ego's *FaBr* is addressed by the same term
as *Fa*, while *MoBr* is addressed by a special kin
term. Ego's *Mo* and *MoSi* are addressed by the

[9]For readings on Arunta culture and society, see the discussions and references in Basedow, 1925; Berndt and Berndt,
1964; Davidson, 1926; Elkin, 1933 and 1954; Elkin and Berndt,
1950; Mathews, 1907 and 1908; Pink, 1936; Radcliffe-Brown,
1930; Róheim, 1925 and 1933; Spencer, 1928; Spencer and
Gillen, 1927 and 1938; Service, 1963: 3-26; Murdock, 1934:
20-47.

Temporary Australian native camp, Northwestern South Australia (circa 1920). (Courtesy American Museum of Natural History.)

same term, while *FaSi* is addressed through use of a separate kin term. Arunta also distinguish between parallel cousins (*MoSi* and *FaBr's* children) and cross-cousins (*FaSi* and *MoBr's* children). Ego also addresses the children of his *Br* and *Si* in a parallel and cross fashion, that is, the children of *Si* and *Br* are addressed through use of the same term used for Ego's *Da* or *So*.

An Arunta infant spends most of his time with his mother. She carries him as she goes about her search for food and as she walks from one camp to another. When she kneels, digging for roots or grubs, he lies in a curved wooden food-carrying dish. Sometimes he is carried in a net-bag slung from his mother's forehead over and down her back. As he grows older, he sits astride her shoulders, clutching her hair. An Arunta in-fant learns very early that the women his mother calls "sister" will also care for him, even nurse him. He also learns that his *FaMo* or *MoMo* may concentrate her affection on him and serve him as a mother as well. He learns too that there are many men besides his biological father whom he will call father. He learns that these men will address him as "son" and will act toward him in the same way as his father does when he cares for him, protects him, or disciplines him. In some Australian aborigine local groups, a child learns that certain men older than his own father will sometimes assume a formal responsibility greater than his biological father for his enculturation. Among the Arunta, a baby's *FaFa* and *FaFaBr* have a large share of formal responsibility for his en-culturation. In some special instances, *MoMoBr* also will take on duties of enculturation as well as the biological father.

An Arunta child learns the content of kin-ship terms as he interacts daily with specific people. He is informed repeatedly by adults who individuals are and how he should act toward them and expect them to behave toward him. He may be told by an adult, "This person is your sister, you call her [kin term] and you must look after her. When you get older you must give her some of the meat you catch and she will give you vegetable foods. You are not to say her name, but when she gets married, her husband will give you gifts and if her husband treats her badly you must take her part." On another occasion he may be told about a little girl walking by him, "She is your mother-in-law. You mustn't look at her face to face, or speak to her, but later when she is married you will send her gifts of meat, and if she bears a daughter, she may give her to you for a wife."

Arunta children often rehearse kin behavior in play situations. For instance, children play at being husbands and wives, making separate windbreaks and fires and pretending to cook food. Sometimes they also play at adultery, with a boy running away with the "wife" of another boy. Adults generally indulge this play, which often confuses actual kin categories. But, when children who really will address each other as *MoLa* and *SoLa* (mother-in-law and son-in-law) try to play such games together, they quickly are separated with sharp rebukes.

Thus, children must learn early that some persons in particular kinship categories have to be dealt with in ways that are very restrained and circumspect, that other individuals must be completely avoided, and that, while some others cannot be spoken to, some individuals can be the subjects of broad, joking speech. Children must learn also that there are persons with whom they can interact socially in complete freedom and that there are others with whom all social interaction must be marked by a very high degree of mutual cooperative actions in both ordinary and ritual events.

For instance, a male must learn to avoid his *MoLa*, to not ever speak her name, and to avoid speaking to her except through intermediaries or by use of a special language, if no one is available to relay his immediate concerns. A female must learn to turn away quickly and

Arunta woman and daughter (date unknown). (Courtesy American Museum of Natural History.)

face the opposite direction when she sees or is told her *SoLa* is approaching her. She must learn the special restrictions on the way she handles meat given to her by her *SoLa*. But she also comes to know that if she is in trouble she can expect aid from her *SoLa*, particularly if anyone abuses or threatens her in his hearing. A *SoLa* is expected to be implacable in seeking revenge from those inflicting injury or death on his *MoLa*.

Boys also must learn that a similar, although not as severely restrictive, avoidance relationship is expected between the persons addressed as *FaLa*, *WiBr*, *SiHu*, and *WiMoBr*. Girls also must learn such general avoidance patterns for the persons they address as *HuBr*, *SiHu*, or *HuMoSi*.

Arunta children soon learn to know which categories of kin they can be open with in their speech and action. For instance, a man's *FaSi* (who is addressed as *Fa* in some Australian native societies) regularly is available to a boy for advice and counsel as he grows up. A boy comes to know that he is expected to be emotionally close to and frank with his sisters and that he is their champion, protector, and if need arises, disciplinarian. If a brother overhears a sister being scolded by her husband, he may take up his spears and threaten her and all of her sisters, actual and classificatory (classificatory kin terms are those which class certain relatives under one term), including the sister actually involved. Brothers learn that they are responsible for the general good behavior of anyone they call sister. Sisters come to expect that they must be circumspect in argument and disagreement

when their brothers, actual or classificatory, are nearby. Sisters must learn to avoid engaging in sexual acts in sight of their brothers. Brothers are supposed to speak in whispers when near sisters, and both avoid speaking each other's personal name.

Arunta children learn that persons who share the same names comprise a special kin status category and must behave toward and with each other with regard to their special bond. Such persons are expected to be close friends and to aid each other in economic and personal affairs. Too, they come to learn the special kin status terms and role behavior forms for individuals who undergo initiation rituals together (see Chapter Eight), who have been born at the same time, or for all those persons who have shared with them some extraordinary event, such as a victory in a fight. In all, an Arunta child must learn more than ten categories of such kinship terms and associated ways of behavior.

An Arunta child also learns a very complex series of special hand signs, which indicate all the different kinship terms and roles he must know for ordinary and special social behavior. These signs are unitary, that is, each one stands for a separate and distinct kinship term and its associated ideal role forms. These signs are part of a much larger hand sign vocabulary used by Arunta to communicate complex information across a distance. Arunta children regularly practice these signs and try them on each other as they play.

Arunta kin groups include unilineal descent groups, clans, and moieties. An Arunta child must learn the ways these groups are formed and influence his daily life if he is to function successfully as an adult. The Arunta unilineal descent group is based on patrilineal descent. Children are affiliated with the named group to which their father belongs and, in the case of boys, are formally initiated into it at puberty in a series of complex ceremonies. Children learn that their father's patrilineal group holds and controls use of land in its own name. They learn that, with permission, other friendly patrilineal descent groups can enter the land claimed by their father's descent group and can hunt or gather foods within

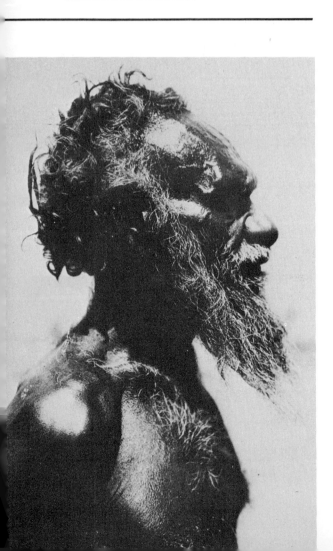

Arunta male (date unknown). (Courtesy American Museum of Natural History.)

its limits. They also learn that other patrilineal descent groups must always avoid the special locations where sacred objects are stored. These sites are the "totem centers," that is, the resting places of the spirits of the human ancestors of the patrilineal descent group to which their father belongs. Children are told that when a woman who has married a man in their descent group becomes pregnant it is because she was impregnated by a totem spirit of her husband's patrilineal descent group. Thus, Arunta children learn to know their "father" as a "social father" but not as their progenitor, since they learn they have been created by the totem spirits of the descent group. Arunta children come to understand that they are forever bound to the land of their father's descent group because they are themselves totem spirit children. If an Arunta child thinks of "home," it is always in terms of the special totem spirit locations of his father's patrilineal descent group and not with reference to the location of his nuclear family's permanent camp. Thus, the Arunta term "home" has an essential religious and magical component, for it refers to the resting places of a patrilineal descent group's ancestor spirits.

Arunta boys receive two names. One name is sacred and secret, associated with the totem spirits who have fathered him, and known only to the old man who made their personal totem symbol, or *churinga,* which is used at a boy's initiation into his father's patrilineal descent group. A secret name is never made known to women and uninitiated children and is used only on important ritual occasions celebrated by the men of the descent group. All children also receive a personal name, which may not refer in any way to the patrilineal descent group to which they belong. Arunta also use nicknames and special age, sex, and achievement terms in speaking to other persons.

Arunta girls must learn that, although they are members of their father's descent group, because they too are totem children, they also must move out of the totem lands at their marriage to join the patrilineal descent group of their husbands. But girls come to know, too, that their primary spiritual and emotional ties are expected to always remain with the descent group of their father. While they have to leave their totem lands, they do not give up their spiritual heritage by their absence.

Arunta children must also learn that all administrative powers in the lands of their descent group are held by the oldest men of their father's patrilineal descent group. They come to know that the most important of these older males is the *inkata,* or totem leader, who conducts all the sacred rituals of the descent group. They learn that the *inkata* can magically communicate with the totem symbols, whether these are represented in the forms of animals or plants. They also come to know that an *inkata* is responsible for the care of the personal *churinga* of each person born into the descent group. Arunta children learn that their *churinga* is stored in one of the sacred totem places and is taken out and used in important rituals such as the *mbanbiuma,* or totem increase ritual, which is held each year at the time when the animal or plant totem representative of a father's descent group produces fruit or seed or bears its young. Uninitiated boys, girls, and women are barred from

Arunta spearman (date unknown). (Courtesy American Museum of Natural History.)

the secret ritual activities in which the *inkata* magically seeks to increase the numbers of totem plants or animals, and symbolically eats a portion of a totem animal or plant and then finally passes the totem animal or plant to all the initiated boys and men of the descent group, so they may also make a symbolic communion

Arunta woman and daughter (date unknown). (Courtesy American Museum of Natural History.)

with the totem spirit. Children take part in the public portion of the *mbanbiuma* ceremony, when everyone belonging to their father's patrilineal descent group feasts on the totem animal or plant. In this way women, girls, uninitiated boys, and special guests from other patrilineal descent groups can also share in the magical protection of the totem spirits of a descent group.

Among the Arunta, clans are formed by alliances among those patrilineal kin groups which claim their common descent from mythical ancestors, or totem spirits. Arunta clans are patrilineal and exogamous, that is, children automatically belong to their father's clan and must marry persons not members of the same clan. Thus, the Arunta clan does not consist of individuals able to trace their actual kinship across the boundaries of the several patrilineal descent groups making up this consanguineal kin group. Rather, individuals are members because they belong to particular patrilineal descent groups who have linked themselves together since they claim a totem or ancestor in common.

The patrilineal descent groups that comprise Arunta clans usually live in the same area or adjacent areas. Arunta believe all forms of life share certain attributes and feel that these derive from a mythical past, or *alchera* ("dream time"), when the self-created hero ancestor, *numbakulla,* made all the various totems and natural geographic features and deposited them about the Arunta territory, after imbuing them with spirits from his own body. Thus, Arunta clans are based on more than a recognition of inclusion of persons who share a common area, or totem; their heritage has derived from *numbakulla's* mythical spirit many vital attributes that are palpable, observable, and sacred since these qualities all come from the *alchera* time. This special relationship is symbolized for members in the displays of special, sacred clan decorative art patterns and particular clan myths, songs, and stories. Too, there are Arunta linguistic terms, as well as special dialects, used by clan members to show their special qualities of relationship. This is particularly so in use of "secret" clan names and the dialect used only in special, secret rituals.

Since the clans are exogamous, every Arunta child's parents must belong to different clan groups. Hence, within the primary nuclear family there are two special and different clan dialects known and used by mothers and fathers. As an Arunta child grows up he first learns the clan dialect of his mother, despite the fact that he is to be a member of his father's clan. Then, as he grows older, he comes to learn and use the dialect of his father's clan. The clan dialects used in a local area are similar enough for a general mutual understanding between members of different clans, yet different enough to ensure the distinctive nature of each clan. Thus, Arunta children must forge a personal as well as a social identification in the context of learning two distinctive dialects. But this is not an unusual situation in Arunta daily social life, which continually places individuals in situations of having to seek a delicate balance between social sameness and differences and social unity and separation in nearly every facet of the kinship and kin group activity.

An Arunta child learns to know that there is one nonalterable entity in his life, that of his totem spirit. Arunta children learn that their spirit returns after their death to the totem center to await reentry into another human body. Thus, the many tugs and pulls created by having to cope with and balance out clan dialects and other opposing features of kinship and kin group life are counterweighed by the specific knowledge for the child that, whatever occurs, he is part of all that has or will exist spiritually and magically in Arunta life.

Arunta clans meet on sacred occasions to make complete the myths of the dream time, or *alchera.* Members of one clan cannot own or cannot formally know a complete myth from the *alchera* times. Even though Arunta children, with parents from different clans, learn and can often repeat all the parts of myths not "officially owned" by their father's clan, elders of the clans must meet formally in order to bring together the parts of ritual stories necessary to increase their totems. Arunta children and most women are barred from all totemic rituals to protect them from the very powerful forces basic to human existence that are abroad at the times of the ceremonies.

Clans are summoned to ritual meetings through use of special message sticks, feathered strings, or miniature copies of sacred objects. Arunta children play at making and sending clan message forms.

Clans maintain an effective internal discipline of members through the threat and practice of sorcery and magic. Every clan has a sorcerer skilled in the magical arts of defending clan members against harm by other clan sorcerers and believed capable of turning harmful magic against outsiders. All clan sorcerers are also suspected of being capable of using harmful magic for personal reasons or from sheer whimsy. Thus, few clan members willingly seek to offend the sorcerer and usually follow his wishes.

Arunta discipline for children involves few severe restrictions, beyond those associated with totemic centers and activities, rare physical punishment, and a considerable amount of direct, continuing verbal instruction by specific adults in the primary nuclear family and patrilineal descent group. After puberty, when both boys and girls have undergone a series of initiation rituals, there is a shift in authority and instruction in enculturation from the nuclear family and patrilineal descent group to the clan. Then the clan sorcerer becomes a visible and threatening figure of severe discipline for unusual behavior. Too, after a child's puberty rituals, all adult members of the clan ideally are entitled to intervene in the initiated child's behavior when they view it as inappropriate. Before initiation, clan members rarely interfere with the rights of adults in the nuclear family and patrilineal descent group to instruct, discipline, or reward a child. After initiation, it becomes the responsibility of all adult clan members to ensure proper conduct.

Arunta regularly distinguish all persons by their membership in one or the other of the two large groups made up of Ego's *Fa's* relatives and Ego's *Mo's* relatives. This is so even if a person is actually not a relative but a member of a clan linked to his father's or his mother's clan. These two inclusive groups comprise the Arunta moiety system. Arunta moieties are named social units and have totems, special linguistic uses, rituals, and taboos generally similar to those of clans. The moieties are exogamous, that is, a person must marry into the opposite moiety. Among the Arunta, moieties also are patrilineal. Thus, Arunta children automatically become members of their father's moiety. Arunta moieties divide persons on a "horizontal scale," that is, without regard to their age, sex, or knowledge, and with reference only to whether individuals are members of the group of Fa's or Mo's relatives.

Arunta also separate persons socially on the basis of a "vertical scale," that is, with reference

Australian native child and female (date unknown). (Courtesy American Museum of Natural History.)

to adjacent generations. Thus, Ego's generation is differentiated from Fa's generation and So's generation but not from Fa's Fa or So's So generation. These two organizing principles of horizontal (or moiety) separation and of vertical (or adjacent) generation separation have been combined by the Arunta in the southern part of the central Australian desert into a social system that has been technically termed a *four-class system*. This means that an Arunta child must learn that there are four distinct kin groupings, in addition to his nuclear family, patrilineal descent group, and clan, which are important in daily life. These four groups of persons, consisting of the two moieties and the two generational groups, are important to a child because they define the locations of possible marriage partners and set the very important rules of etiquette for respect and avoidance between persons in adjacent generations. As noted earlier, an Arunta man ordinarily selects a wife from the group of his MoMoBrDaDa. In the Arunta four-class system only one of the four classes includes marriageable persons such as MoMoBrDaDa. That same class also includes some persons, such as first cross-cousins, who cannot marry Ego. However, Arunta in the northern part of the central Australian desert have created eight rather than four named classes of kin by the fact of regularly separating first cross-cousins from second cross-cousins. Thus, the eight classes of the northern Arunta are derived from the two moieties and two adjacent generations and from distinguishing between first and second cross-cousins in each of the two moieties. The complex cognitive map of different social groups must be learned by the Arunta child, for without it the kinship terms and ways of behaving associated with them would be confusing. Children learn to depend first and regularly upon kin terms used in the nuclear family and descent groups and only later come to use the terms that need to be employed in dealing with clan, moiety, and marriage class relatives.

Ashanti kinship, kin groups, and enculturation. When Europeans came to the west coast of Africa in the late sixteenth century, they found many small native chiefdoms, each with its own capital town and political organization. By the

Ngatatjara rock painting, Puntutjarpa rock shelter, Northern Warburton Range, Western Australia (date unknown). (Courtesy American Museum of Natural History.)

late seventeenth century the economic and military pressures of the Europeans had caused a series of wars, during which some of the independent native kingdoms had allied themselves into states. One of these states was formed in the geographic area that later became the British colony of the Gold Coast, now the independent nation of Ghana. The African people who allied to form this powerful state through the eighteenth and nineteenth centuries belonged to tribes called *Ashanti*.[10] The native Ashanti state lasted until conquered by British forces in two bitter wars fought in 1873-1874 and 1900-1901.

Originally, the Ashanti may have been sedentary farmers on the grasslands of the Western Sudan. But, under constant pressure from raids by nomadic Moslem peoples, small Ashanti groups began to migrate westward, finally settling in the tropical forests near the West African coast. The Ashanti forest villages were very small and isolated from one another until the arrival of the Europeans. The total Ashanti population is now estimated to be more than 800,000 persons.

The Ashanti forest lands are very fertile, hot, and somewhat mountainous. Heavy rains fall from April to November and are followed by a very dry season. The Ashanti have been afflicted with a wide variety of serious tropical diseases, including malaria, typhoid, typhus, cholera, leprosy, elephantiasis, sleeping sickness, intestinal parasites, and skin diseases.

[10]For readings on Ashanti culture and society, see the discussions and references in Busia, 1951 and 1954; Fortes, 1949b and 1950; Hoebel, 1954; Matson, 1953; Rattray, 1923, 1927, and 1929; Service, 1963: 366-386.

Ashanti technology includes hand-modeled pottery and wood carvings, made by specialists. Iron is worked with a bellows and charcoal fire by experts adept at making axe and hoe blades, hammer heads, nails, knife blades, and spear points, as well as finely detailed chains, containers, bells, and a variety of ornaments. Before their contact with Europeans, Ashanti made bark cloth for clothing. In the late seventeenth century Ashanti men learned to make small looms and to weave cotton fabrics with complex designs. Intricate designs are stamped onto cloth worn as clothing.

Ashanti live in scattered villages and small towns in houses of wooden sticks and daubed-on mud wall construction, with roofs of grass or leaf thatching. Houses of wealthier Ashanti are usually arranged in compounds, that is, connecting buildings that face inward onto a central courtyard. Less affluent Ashanti live in small rectangular dwellings. Most Ashanti houses have a wide veranda along the length of one side of the structure. Houses of both the poor and the rich often have painted and carved designs on the exterior walls and roof support posts.

Except for the craft specialists, Ashanti gain their living by farming crops of manoic, yams and plaintains, millet, beans, peanuts, and onions, and through raising fruit and oil palm trees. Oil palm products are used in a wide variety of cooking and domestic activities and are made by Ashanti into liquor. Because of the fertile land and climate, some vegetable crops are harvested twice a year. Fields are prepared by burning off the weed or forest cover and then are cultivated with an iron hoe blade. Fields are located outside villages and towns, so that Ashanti often must travel some distance to their farms.

Most Ashanti live in dwelling groups, or *fie.* A *fie* ideally consists of persons connected by matrilineal kinship and incorporated by ties of affinity. By Ashanti law and custom, the *fie* is the place where a person's matrilineage is located. If possible, women return to their childhood *fie* to bear their children. A child becomes a citizen in an Ashanti chiefdom because he is born in his *MoMo fie.* However, the dwelling group is not necessarily a place where fathers, mothers, and their children live together. In a stable Ashanti community, about half the people live in matrilineal *fie* under female heads, and only about one-third of all married women live with their husbands, with the remainder living with matrilineal kin. In the evenings in an Ashanti village, many children are to be seen carrying prepared foods from the houses in which they reside with their mothers, to the houses where their fathers are residing. Ashanti children may sleep in their *Mo's fie* but often will eat their meals in their *Fa's fie.* It is considered contemptible for a man to live in his wife's house, and normal for him to live in the house of his mother or one of his sisters.

Thus, the Ashanti dwelling group does not have a common food supply and does not share incomes for mutual support of members. Aid given within the *fie* occurs because members are matrilineal kin and not because they reside in the *fie.* A dwelling group usually contains three or more generations, consisting of a mother, her children, and her mother. Both men or women can be the head of a *fie,* depending on whether they are senior in age or generation to other members of the group. *Fie* heads usually own the house in which the group lives.

Although the *fie* centers upon one woman and her children and the children of her daughters, men living in the *fie* actually become heads of such groups about twice as often as women. Such a position for a man means simply that, because of the menstrual taboo on women, he must publicly represent the *fie* in the place of the senior female member of the group. Every Ashanti aspires to have *Mo* settled in her own *fie,* since concepts of personal dignity are closely related to one's *Mo* being head of such a group or to residing in one's *Mo's fie.* Ideally, a man is supposed to set up his own dwelling group at marriage, and to have his wife and children live with him. But the economic problems involved in building a house are usually too great for most young Ashanti men. So, they continue to live on after marriage in the *fie* of their *Mo* or *Si,* while their wives and young children stay in the *fie* of the wife. In addition, the ties of matrilineal kinship for both the young husband and wife are as strong as those imposed initially by marriage and parenthood. While the cultural ideal is for the young Ashanti man to set up a *fie* and to have his wife and children with him, the traditions of the matrilineage exert strong tugs to another way of behaving.

There is no more basic social tie for the Ashanti than between a mother and her children. This tie is considered the ultimate and minimally irreducible element of all Ashanti social life. Children rarely question their mother's position of privilege, deference, or rank in the *fie*. When the senior female of a *fie* dies, her children may separate and establish independent dwelling groups of their own. More often than not, however, the *fie* is maintained by the sisters, daughters, or granddaughters of the deceased woman, while her sons try to move out to set up their *fie*.

A woman must try to reconcile her duties to her *Hu* with her strong attachment to her *Mo* and *MoMo*, to her *Si*, and to her *MoMoSi*. A man has to reconcile his duties to his *Wi* with his strong attachment to his *Mo* and *MoMo*, to *MoSi*, and to his own *Si*. Ashanti men and women also have to try to balance out their relations to their own children and the children of their own *Si* and *Br*.

An Ashanti man is the legal guardian of his *SiCh* rights, for they are his legal heirs. If a man's *Si* dies, his *Wi* cannot expect him to exclude his *SiCh* from the *fie*. Ashanti say that men use cross-cousin marriage (that is, men marry their *FaSiDa's* and *MoBrDa's*) as a way to unite their love of their own children with their loyalty to and responsibility for their *Si* children. However, less than 10 percent of Ashanti women actually marry their cross-cousins. Ashanti seek to balance the social stresses that occur in the matching of ties of maternal kinship and parenthood by saying that a father is responsible for the care, support, and guidance of his children until they are adolescents, when they become the primary responsibility of their *MoBr*. A man and his *WiBr* will try not to share the same *fie* to avoid the conflicts of loyalty that will arise in enculturation. Ashanti children must learn to handle the stresses generated by their form of social organization.

Ashanti kinship terminology is of the Crow type, that is, *FaSiSo* is called by the term used for *Fa*, while *FaSiDa* is called by the term used

for *FaSi*. *MoBrSo* is called *So* and *MoBrDa* is called *Da*, while all parallel cousins are called by the terms used for siblings.[11] Ashanti address all women of their *Mo's* generation as *Mo*. All the men of *Mo* generation are called *MoBr*, while all men and women of *MoMo* generation and all the children in Ego's grandchildren's generation are called by the same term. Ashanti women address all members of their children's generation as *child*, while men address all members of their children's generation as *SiCh*. Too, any male member of Ego's *Fa's* lineage may be addressed as *Fa*, while any female member of *Fa's* lineage may be called *female father*.

The regular care of Ashanti infants is the general responsibility of their mothers. This often is formally shared with *MoMo*, in order that daily farming and other economic tasks may be carried out. This practice may cause some problems between a young mother and her own *Mo*, since it is not uncommon for *MoMo* to argue strongly that she has the final say in raising an infant because a baby belongs more to the matrilineage (or *abusua*) than to its parents. This argument is usually overcome by a baby's *Mo* when she notes that a moral and spiritual bond exists between a *Mo* and her child that is much stronger than the one between *MoMo* and her grandchildren. Ashanti mothers traditionally make all personal efforts to ensure their children's welfare. Ashanti mothers are symbols for protection and support of their children. Children grow up expecting to fully obey and defer to their *Mo*. Ashanti believe disrespect to one's *Mo* is a grave religious offense, since *Mo* represents all female ancestors. Ashanti children learn very early that an offended *Mo* will not punish or publicly ridicule her children. But they also learn to fear the dangers of the special form of witchcraft *(bayi)* that only a *Mo* can loose upon children regularly unmindful of her wishes and commands. Children learn that *MoSi* are to be treated and responded to as their own *Mo* would be, for Ashanti consider it disgraceful conduct to differentiate

---

[11]There is a possibility of classifying Ashanti cousin terminology as *descriptive* rather than as *Crow*. A descriptive system uses terms for cousins that are derived from other "elementary" kin terms (*Fa, Mo, Br, Si,* etc.). See Murdock, 1967: 66.

between *Mo* and her *Si* in any public way. Ashanti children expect that their unruly behavior will be dealt with by their *MoBr* as *Mo's* disciplinary representative. While children may show temper toward a *MoBr*, they also learn very quickly that he speaks for and with the authority of his sister.

The relationships between an Ashanti father and his children are marked by the fact that he is recognized as the sole contributor of two basic aspects of each child's personality, which are called *sunsum* and *kra*. A child's *sunsum* dies with him, but his *kra* returns to the Ashanti creator god. A father is believed to directly transmit his own personality to each of his children. When a father's *sunsum* is alienated through magic or witchcraft Ashanti believe a child's personality will be affected, too. Thus, it is not uncommon for fathers to want to be ritually treated along with their ailing children. The bond between an Ashanti *Fa* and his *So* is particularly close and affectionate because it is felt they share the same personality more fully than do *Fa* and *Da*. Until a child's puberty, fathers are held formally responsible for the behavior of their children, and especially their sons. Because they share the same *sunsum*, fathers are legally liable in Ashanti law for the behavior of their sons. Mothers are held accountable for the immoral acts of their daughters because of the "blood" (or matrilineage) ties between them. Thus, while a girl inherits her personality from her *Fa*, she is directly accountable to her *Mo*, who in turn is legally liable for her daughter's actions.

Initially, and for a time immediately after a child's birth, the relations between Ashanti fathers and children are based solely on the fact of biological paternity. But when a man finally chooses a personal name for each of his children, he passes on, in addition to his *sunsum* and *kra*, a pride in the traditions of his own ancestors. The right of naming provides the Ashanti *Fa* with further opportunity to bind his children to his own consanguineal kin group.

Despite their personal liability for their sons' acts, Ashanti fathers have no legal authority over children. A *Fa* cannot require his children to live in his *fie*, nor can he claim their custody if he divorces his *Wi*. It is believed a duty of fathers to feed, clothe, and train their children, whether they reside in their *Mo's fie* or not. Ashanti *Fa's* are supposed to help all their children get started in their adult lives, by providing economic aid, advice, and directions.

Ashanti *Fa's* are said to be exacting in requiring their children's obedience, deference, and respect. Fathers do not hesitate to physically punish children when they misbehave. The Ashanti say that the ties of love and respect for a *Fa's* contributions to their *sunsum* and *kra* make children willing to submit to a more severe discipline than they would receive from their *Mo* or members of their *Mo's* kin group. Children cannot inherit their *Fa's* property. However, a *Fa* can make small bequests to children during his lifetime. Ashanti believe that to insult or deprecate a father is a grave wrong against his ancestors, as well as the creator, which will bring them continuing bad luck. Ashanti believe that no father can love his *SiCh* as much as his own *Ch*. In organized warfare an Ashanti *Fa* prefers his sons to accompany him into battle, rather than to have his *SiSo* by his side.

An Ashanti child learns, however, that his mother's oldest living brother within the matrilineal kin group, traced from his *MoMoMo*, is the male of the parent generation with sole legal authority over him. A *MoBr* will not discipline a child unless he is requested to do so by his *Si.* A *MoBr* can and does command obedience to his wishes. Ashanti *MoBr* have had the power to pawn their *SiSo* to secure a loan for his own use; a young boy could be put to work for other persons, as security against default on a loan to his *MoBr*. A *MoBr* can demand financial help from *SiSo*, as he also can generously provide for his *SiSo's* welfare. It is expected that a *SiSo* will repay the help provided by *MoBr* by treating his own *SiSo* generously as they grow up, or through assistance to other matrilineal kin in need. The prime aspect of this relationship is the fact the *SiSo* is the legal heir of *MoBr*. The importance of this is seen in the fact that a man's own *Ch* will address his *SiSo* as *father* to show respect to him as their potential legal guardian should *MoBr* die. Too, a man can address his *MoBrWi* as *wife* because he will inherit her as a wife if his *MoBr* should die. However, no other social relationship of the Ashanti child is so ambivalent as the one with *MoBr*. The ideal is that *MoBr* and *SiSo* are like *Fa* and *So*. The reality, which involves the problems of inheritance and of the legal authority of *MoBr*, is that such relations are very stressful for children, despite the fact that *MoBr* and *SiCh* often live in the same dwelling group.

Ashanti children learn to pay great respect and deference to the parents of both their *Fa* and *Mo*, since grandparents ideally embody the essence of Ashanti ways. Because of her position as the link between children and their matrilineage, *MoMo* has great influence on the enculturation of an Ashanti child. She takes pride in her grandchildren's conformity to Ashanti ideal ways, cares for them regularly during infancy, and provides them with lavish displays of affection. Grandparents rarely punish their grandchildren for minor disobedience. They will ask a child's *Mo* or *Fa* to administer discipline to children for serious misbehavior, since grandparents, and especially *MoMo*, are supposed to maintain harmony in the dwelling group. Children learn from all their grandparents the traditional Ashanti knowledge and folklore, such as proverbs, tales, myths, and songs. Too, grandparents regularly recount to children the histories and fortunes of their particular kin group and ancestors. If Ashanti children have living great grandparents they regard them with near religious awe, for these old persons form a human link to the long dead ancestors. Children learn that the kin term for grandparent *(nana)* is used by an Ashanti as the title of greatest respect when addressing or referring to his chief or king and that chiefs, priests, and political leaders use the reciprocal term *(nana)* in addressing their followers. Thus, the relationships between grandparents and grandchildren are the formal models of behavior throughout the Ashanti political, religious, and legal institutions.

Too, Ashanti children learn to be respectful to their *FaSi*, as a symbol of their *Fa*. A *FaSi* may scold her *BrCh* for their misbehavior, since she represents to children all of the claims, privileges, and authority of their *Fa*'s matrilineage. Since under the ideal Ashanti practice of cross-cousin marriage, *FaSi* is a potential *MoLa*, and formally is charged under Ashanti law with looking after the ways her *Br* treats the property her *Ch* will inherit, children do not often seek out *FaSi* for help or affection. *FaSi* may act for her *Br* at the time of the ritual naming of his *Ch*.

Ashanti children must also learn to regularly defer to and be respectful of older *Br* and *Si*. An older sibling is able to physically and verbally punish a younger *Br* or *Si* for misbehavior and is responsible to their parents for assistance to a younger sibling in trouble or in need of help. These privileges and responsibilities are especially those of the firstborn *Ch*, who is said by Ashanti to be the "head" of the *Ch* group. Parents continually stress the need for sibling unity and presenting a common front against misfortune or personal attack. The only real informality permitted in Ashanti social relationships occurs between siblings. *Br* and *Si* may joke and tease and be somewhat immodest in dress in the presence of one another. These forms of behavior are considered unthinkable with other persons. Children learn that *Br* and *Si* trust and confide in each other on all vital matters and that as adults they will continue to do so, to the exclusion of their own *Hu* and *Wi*. Siblings will entrust highly personal confidences to each other that they would not share with their parents, wives, or children. Ashanti children are taught that siblings are supposed to unite in the face of opposition from spouses or children.

Ashanti children learn to understand messages sent and repeated by adults across long distances by use of "talking drums." Cedar wood and elephant ear membrane drums are used in sets to imitate, through drum beats, the tones of Ashanti words. The Ashanti language, like many African languages, is tonal, that is, a large amount of meaning for most words is demonstrated in the sounding of the word. Drums are used by Ashanti to closely reproduce the tones of words and punctuation in *set holophrases*, that is, very complex ideas are expressed in stylized beats that are so well known that all who hear the "language" can quickly and precisely understand the messages sent on the drums. Children learn early to read these messages, which usually summon political leaders to meetings, give public notice of the death of important persons, and discuss vital events such as impending war, widespread disease, and so on. Some special drums are used only to broadcast traditional proverbs that stress loyalty, duty, hard work, and other ideal personal virtues. Drummers, with the minstrels who sing traditional songs at rituals and on special occasions, transmit a substantial amount of culture to children as they mature in Ashanti society.

The Ashanti believe children are physically a composite of the "blood" (mogya) of their Mo and the "spirit" (ntoro) of their Fa. The link between each Ashanti generation is believed to be provided by Mo's blood. Every child is a member by birth in his Mo's "blood group," (or abusua). Too, every child is a member also of his Fa's "spirit group," or ntoro.

The Ashanti abusua is a matrilineal kin group consisting of all the persons of both sexes who trace their descent through the female line to a named, real, common female ancestor and who lived some ten to twelve generations before Ego's Mo generation. The abusua group is much more important in a child's social life than the ntoro, or patrilineal kin group, for it is the social unit where the most important Ashanti economic, political, and religious activities occur. Matrilineal descent determines the right to own and use land, inheritance of most other property, political succession, social rank, many statuses, and formal titles. However, every Ashanti matrilineage has a male head, chosen from among all the males of the kin group. The head (abusua panin) is formally responsible for the welfare of all lineage members and is expected to settle disputes between them. Too, he is supposed to lead in organizing its rituals, ceremonies, and economic and political activities. He oversees the marriages, remarriages, and divorces of lineage women, makes offerings to the female ancestors, cares for ancestor shrines, deals with the lineage gods, and holds in trust the sacred symbols of the lineage. The male Ashanti matrilineage head also represents the entire lineage at the councils of the heads of all the matrilineages in a village, town, or district.

One of the important functions of a man acting as a lineage head is to be a combined symbolic MoBr and Fa to all its children. If an Ashanti child wishes special, formal permission to engage in out-of-ordinary ways, he seeks out his MoBr, and also the head of the segment of his lineage (or yafunu) in his dwelling group (if this is a man other than his MoBr), then goes to the matrilineage head to request the permission he needs. As a child proceeds from the generally constrained and formalized contact with his MoBr and the yafunu head to the head of his lineage, he experiences a marked change of attitude. Matrilineage heads look upon children in the kin group as their own children and so are much less formal and more openly affectionate, even-handed, and considerate of a child's feelings than MoBr and the yafunu head need to be with children asking special favors or aid.

A lineage head chooses a senior woman of the kin group to assist him in watching over women's morals, to supervise girls' initiation ceremonies, to make peace in lineage quarrels, to be the genealogical expert for the group, and to serve as a symbolic Mo for the entire lineage. In this role she is the living symbol of the fact that lineage members all share "one blood," or mogya.

Ashanti matrilineages have a segmentary structure. The segments, called "children of one womb," or yafunu, generally consist of the descendents of a common ancestress not more than four or five generations antecedent to the persons making up a segment. Most often a yafunu consists of matrilineal kin whose female parents and grandparents grew up in a single dwelling group, or fie, as a group of siblings. The kinship terms of reference and address that are used in the yafunu are those applied to all members of the maximal matrilineage. The members of a yafunu may all be part of one fie, or dwelling group, or may live in adjacent fie. The number of segments in one Ashanti matrilineage varies from generation to generation, for the yafunu tend to disappear as the founding female ancestors die.

An established and old Ashanti village is divided into a number of "wards" (brono), each one of which is occupied by the male and female members of one matrilineage. Neighborhoods within the brono consist of groupings of the several segments, or yafunu, of the maximal matrilineage. The numbers of matrilineages in a village vary, but usually at least half the population belongs to two or three lineages, while the remainder are members of "stump lineages," that is, matrilineal kin groups brought into the community by migrants, refugees displaced by wars, or occupational specialists such as weavers, smiths, and woodcarvers.

A maximal lineage is regarded by Ashanti as a local branch of one of the seven or eight widespread matrilineal clans, or *mmusuaban*. The lineages of one clan are regarded as the matrilineal descendants of a single, remote ancestress, for whom a mythological birth and magical life is claimed and in whose name special rituals are observed and certain shrines and religious symbols are maintained. Ashanti usually do not know the names of their clan ancestresses, but still may behave toward each other in daily affairs as if they were members of the same matrilineage. The matrilineal clans have a vital function in Ashanti social life, for they are the social units that ensure that every Ashanti individual belongs to a kin group that is named and known both in location and in Ashanti history. In the recent past, clans may have had special totem animals and special totem rituals.

A child's membership by birth in his *Fa*'s patrilineal kin group, or *ntoro*, involves him with persons said to share the same *sunsum*, or personality. Ashanti view an individual's personality as the "child" of his *Fa*'s *ntoro* kin group. The number of Ashanti *ntoro* varies from area to area. Ashanti say there are from seven to twelve such patrilineal kin groups. Each *ntoro*, and hence each member of such a group, is believed by Ashanti to be under the protection of a particular god, or *abosom*. The god of a *ntoro* is said to share the *sunsum* and *kra* (personality and life force) of the creator god (or *Onyankopon*) as Ashanti children share the *sunsum* and *kra* of their *Fa*. Thus, Ashanti children learn early that their *sunsum* and *kra*, derived from their *Fa*, is a heritage from the *abosom* of their *Fa*'s patrilineal kin group, given to it by the god of all Ashanti.

Each *ntoro* has a special name, which indicates the dominant personality type to be expected from its members. Some names of Ashanti *ntoro* are, in translation, "the tough," "the human," "the liberal," "the fanatic," "the audacious," and "the fastidious." Thus, a child is born with his personality not only fully shaped and inherited from his *Fa*, but as well firmly fixed for his lifetime by the character stereotypes ascribed to all members of a *ntoro*. Too, each *ntoro* group uses special surnames, so its members can be distinguished easily by their characteristic name.

Each patrilineal kin group has some special taboos to observe. Thus, the *ntoro* called *Bosommuru* ("the distinguished") cannot eat or harm an ox, python, or dog. These animals are totems, said to have given special services to the *ntoro* god or founding ancestors. Each *ntoro* has a "sacred day" on which it ritually purifies its members. The *ntoro* gods are associated specially with rivers, lakes, and the sea. A sacred day ceremony usually involves "washing the spirit" of the *ntoro* in a purification ritual to cleanse the *susum* and *kra* of all the members of this kin group. Ashanti children witness and are present at these special ritual activities. At these times, they learn the sacred lore of the *ntoro*, such as the special form of greeting used between members of the group to enable them to fully identify one another. An Ashanti child's principal contacts with most members of his *Fa*'s *ntoro* are at the times of the sacred day ceremonies.

Ashanti children must also learn to comprehend the ways their society is formally stratified into large groups of persons. In addition to kinship terms and kin groupings, Ashanti order their social life through identifying certain ideal and expected behavior forms with occupational and ritual specialties (smith, weaver, woodcarver, priests), ranks (kings, chiefs, nobles, commoners, slaves), income (wealthy, poor, destitute), mobility (geographic changes of residence because of politics, war, famine, disease), and education (apprenticed to an occupational or ritual specialist). Ashanti children must learn about these categories of persons and the social ways associated with them, for everyday conversation and life are permeated by reference and action with respect to whether or not particular individuals have such socially meaningful characteristics. Ashanti society is open, that is, it is possible for the children and grandchildren of slaves, or of unredeemed pawns (that is, children of a man placed in forced labor by his *MoBr* as security on a loan) to attain positions of social and economic power and great political influence. An Ashanti chief swears a sacred oath on taking office which includes a formal declaration that he will never reproach subjects for being the descendants of slaves or pawns, thus ensuring lower ranked and poor children the opportunity to regain or to gain new social positions of greater prestige and influence.

■ Conclusions

This chapter has been concerned with a discussion of what children learn in social situations that involve conceptions and definitions of kinship and kin groups and the ways these cultural patterns are interrelated with the socialization process. Case study data from Arunta and Ashanti cultures have been presented to illustrate the fact that there are very great variations in the patterns of kinship and kin groups, so that children growing up in some societies learn specific ideas about these particular patterns of culture markedly different from those learned by children in other societies. Some principal differences in Arunta and Ashanti kinship and kin groups are summarized in Table 7-1.

However, it is important to note that, despite such differences, the enculturation process in Arunta and Ashanti cultures has some fundamental similarities. Thus, it can be said with regard to these two cultures that both utilize

Table 7-1. Some contrasts between Arunta and Ashanti patterns of kinship and kin groups

	Arunta kinship and kin groups*	Ashanti kinship and kin groups*
Family organization	Independent polygynous families with sororal polygyny permitted; co-wives live in the same quarters	Small, extended polygynous families with sororal polygyny permitted but not frequent; co-wives live in separate quarters
Social group focus	Local groups (exogamous, patrilocal)	Dwelling groups (exogamous, avunculocal with virilocal and duolocal alternatives)
Cousin terms	Iroquois cousin terminology	Crow cousin terminology (possibly descriptive type)
Cousin marriage	Nonlateral cousin marriage; preferred with *MoMoBrDaDa* or *FaMoBrSoDa*	Duolateral cousin marriage; matrilateral cross-cousin marriage preferred
Property exchange at marriage	Dowry or transfer of property from bride's kinsmen to kinsmen of the groom	Bride-price or transfer of property from groom's kinsmen to kinsmen of the bride
Community organization	Clan communities; each community consists of a single exogamous clan	Agamous communities; community has no localized clan or marked tendency to exogamy or endogamy
Kin groups	Patrilineages are a major consanguineal kin group	Matrilineages are a major consanguineal kin group; segmentary matrilineages have social functions
Kin groups	Clans; exogamous kin groups formed of patrilineal descent groups whose members live in one community	Clans; exogamous kin groups whose core membership lives in more than one community
Kin groups	Moieties formed of two maximal patrilineages	Patrilineages are present and perform special ritual and social functions
Settlement pattern	Fully migratory bands	Compact and relatively permanent settlements in villages or towns
Social stratification	No stratification by occupation, income, education, social classes, or social mobility	Social stratification by occupation, rank, income, and education; recognized social classes with mobility possible in and between classes
Status-role terms	Family, in-law, generational, lineage, clan, and moiety status terms	Family, in-law, generational, lineage, clan, and nonfamily (chief, lord, commoner, etc.) status terms

*See also Murdock, 1967: 13, 27, 66-69, 94-97, and Service, 1963: 747-762.

their patterns of kinship to provide for a very large number of parent surrogates, or alternates, so that culture is transmitted to and acquired by children effectively and well. In both cultures there is wide opportunity for infants and children to learn from and observe many people acting in the ways that must be known for successful adult behavior. This broad diffusion of the responsibility for the cultural transmission process through use of the patterns of kinship and kin groups means that in both Arunta and Ashanti cultures, widely shared concepts, ideas, and ways of acting are elaborated upon and regularly emphasized by many individuals other than a child's biological parents.

Too, in both Arunta and Ashanti cultures the competing demands on children by different kin groups are balanced in the enculturation process through use of concepts such as totem and life spirits and supernatural forces. In these cultures, competing kin groups subject infants and children to contrary pressures for social sameness and difference and for social unity and separation. These competing kin group demands can be quite intense, for example, when an Ashanti boy must choose to obey the commands of his *Fa* or his *MoBr*, or when an Arunta girl must be loyal to her *Fa's* descent group as well as to the local group in which she resides with her *Hu.*

Such competing and highly personal demands are met in both Arunta and Ashanti cultures through appeals to nonhuman beings, spirits, and forces. For instance, Arunta seek a balance in such competing kin group demands through myths of the *alchera,* or dream times, when there were no clan or moiety divisions in Arunta society and all Arunta were believed to have belonged to one small local group. Arunta also use the concept of totem spirit descent from one powerful creator god to balance competing kin group demands. Thus, Arunta children learn that, although they are regularly subjected to conflicting demands by kin groups with different concerns, such pressures are only incidental to the basic fact of all Arunta being part of one group. As in the case of Arunta children, Ashanti children also learn to meet the demands upon them by different kin groups through reference to a common, mythical past, totem spirits, and a common descent. In both Arunta and Ashanti cultures children learn to understand that such pressures are immediate and situational, and what really matters is the fact of being "Arunta" or "Ashanti" and living as a member of the Arunta and Ashanti societies.

Finally, both the Arunta and Ashanti enculturation processes essentially depend upon the various special social roles played by the parents of *Mo* and *Fa* in the transmission of the ideal history and beliefs of these cultures. It is primarily from grandparents that Arunta and Ashanti children learn the ways these cultures came into being, have met past challenges and tests in the human and natural worlds, and the reasons used to justify special social forms or acts. In both cultures, grandparents also provide children with their basic understanding of the ways the many parts of culture are supposed to be interrelated. This aspect of the cultural transmission process in Arunta and Ashanti cultures provides for children's basic understanding of the *ethos* and *eidos,* or the overall cultural form and style of Arunta and Ashanti life. In other words, it is from grandparents that Arunta and Ashanti children have their enculturation in those dominant ways of thought and behavior which constitute the "flavor" and the "coherence" of Arunta and Ashanti cultures.

These three features of enculturation (use of the configuration of kinship to provide a large number of parent surrogates in cultural transmission; balancing of competing kin group demands through use of concepts of common descent, totem, life spirits, and forces; grandparents providing the principal portrayal of cultural history and cultural *ethos* and *eidos*), which are common to Arunta and Ashanti cultures, also seem to be found in the process of cultural transmission in many other societies.

For example, the Appendix of this text provides a bibliography of enculturation in 128 societies. A careful study of data of enculturation in these societies indicates that the three features of enculturation noted in common between Arunta and Ashanti cultures also appear to be present in 99 (or approximately 77 percent) of 128 cultures. Table 7-2 notes the names of the cultures

Table 7-2. 128-culture sample for three features of enculturation*

New world cultures (39)		Pacific cultures (31)	Old world cultures (58)		
North America (26)	Central and South America (13)	Australia, Indonesia, Borneo, New Guinea, Pacific Islands (31)	Eurasia (15)	Europe and Circum-Mediterranean (11)	Africa (Sub-Saharan) (32)
3 features present (23)	3 features present (9)	3 features present (28)	3 features present (9)	3 features present (5)	3 features present (25)
Apache	Camayura	Alor	Ainu	Arab	Ashanti
Arapaho	Jivaro	Arapesh	Andamanese	Lapp	Azande
Cheyenne	Kaingang	Arunta	Baiga	Riffians	Baganda
Comanche	Sherente	Bali	Chenchu	R'wala	Basuto
Eskimo	Siriono	Chamorro	Deoli		Bemba
Flathead	Tenetehara	Dobuans	Lakher		Bena
Hopi	Wapisiana	Dusun	Lepcha	One or more	Bushmen
Hupa	Witoto	Fijians	Palaung	features	Chagga
Kaska	Yagua	Ifaulk	Yakut	absent or	Chewa
Klamath		Ifugao	Yukaghir	data unclear	Dahomean
Kutenai	One or more	Ilocos		(6)	Gusii
Kwakiutl	features	Kwoma		English	Kikuyu
Navaho	absent or	Lesu	One or more	French	Lamba
Omaha	data unclear	Malaitans	features	German	Masai
Paiute	(4)	Malekula	absent or	Israeli	Ngoni
Papago	Abipon	Manus	data unclear	Russian	Nuer
Sanpoil	Ona	Maori	(6)	Zadruga	Nyakyusa
Slave	San Pedro	Marquesans	Balahi		Pygmies
Taos	Warrau	Murngin	Chinese		Swazi
Teton		Ontong-Javanese	Japanese		Tallensi
Dakota		Pukapukans	Koryak		Tanala
Wichita		Samoans	Okinawan		Tiv
Winnebago		Tikopia	Rājpūts		Tswana
Zuni		Trobriands			Yoruba
		Trukese			Zulu
One or more		Ulithians			
features		Wogeo			One or more
absent or		Yungar			features
data unclear					absent or
(3)		One or more			data unclear
American		features			(7)
Mexican		absent or			Bapedi
Puerto Rican		data unclear			Kongo
		(3)			Pondo
		Javanese			Thonga
		Kiwai			Tonga
		Nauru			Turkana
					Venda

*The time of the "ethnographic present" is about 1948-1950. Inclusion of Japanese and Chinese data is on the basis of reports of traditional, nonindustrial life. References for cultures listed here may be found in the Appendix. It should be noted that many of these cultures have alternative names (*e.g.*, the *Bemba* also are termed the *Awemba*, *Babemba*, and *Wabemba*). See Textor (1967), Appendix One, for an alphabetical listing of culture names and their alternatives. See also Murdock, 1958.

in which these three features of enculturation seem to be present. In 29 of the 128 societies, one or more of these three features of enculturation are missing, or ethnographic data are so unclear that it is very difficult to be certain concerning the presence or absence of such features of cultural transmission.

There are six societies (American, English, French, German, Israeli, Russian) of the 128 cultures in the Appendix in which all three features of enculturation seem absent. These societies also have contrasting kinship and kin group forms. All of these six societies are industrialized and urbanized. Each one of the 99 societies listed in Table 7-2 with the three features of enculturation have in common the fact that they have possessed a nonindustrial economy and were organized in nonurban forms of social living.

These data suggest that the three features of enculturation found in 99 cultures of a 128-culture sample may illustrate the possible interdependence of patterns in the cultural subsystems of social relations, technology, and ideology. Another way to state this would be to say that, as industrialization and urbanization occur and belief and values associated with industrialization and urbanization are introduced into and spread through a culture, (1) the number of parent surrogates is progressively reduced, (2) kin group demands are increasingly replaced by demands made on individuals by technological institutions ("the firm," "the company," "the guild," "the craft," "the union") with the consequences that traditional social balancing mechanisms (conceptions of totem, life spirits, and forces) no longer are effective, and (3) grandparents come to be unable to serve as guides for children to the *ethos* and *eidos* of a culture. In fact, descriptions of the enculturation process in contemporary industrialized and urbanized cultures (see Appendix) make it apparent that there are very few parent surrogates in enculturation, that competing kin group concerns are actually minimal or entirely absent, and that schools and other social, political, and economic institutions have largely taken over the special roles of grandparents in transmitting culture history and cultural *ethos/eidos* conceptions. Urie Bronfenbrenner's studies of American and Russian childhood and enculturation make it especially clear that at least two of the world's most industrialized and urbanized societies have turned significantly away from use of the three features of enculturation that appear in many of the world's cultures.

The conclusions about the three features of enculturation must be qualified by both methodological and theoretical exceptions. In the course of comparing transcultural data of enculturation, it is necessary to account for what has been termed by Naroll (1961-1964), Driver (1968), and others as "Galton's Problem," that is, to take

extreme care that the cultures chosen for a comparative sample really have been independent of one another, with no history of borrowing of culture or use of the same language. Too, scientific logic suggests care in making statements which imply or state that all the patterns of a culture are equally involved in determining the state, or condition, of either the whole culture or any of its subsystems. Simply to assert that two or more parts of a culture are functionally interdependent begs the questions of whether or not they actually are so linked. Such assertation also ignores the very important theoretical problem of whether all cultural patterns are equally independent, that is, whether each one has an equal capability of survival when separated from the other parts.

The statements made here about the presence or absence of three features of enculturation in 128 cultures are drawn from a study sample in which several cultures have historical relationships through diffusion and language. This fact biases the conclusions noted above. It similarly would bias any conclusions about socialization where there were demonstrable relationships of diffusion and language between the cultures of a sample. The statements concerning the three features of enculturation do not include consideration of whether each feature is functionally equivalent or differentially weighted. This may bias the conclusions offered here and in any other transculturally based study of socialization.

Whether or not the hypothesis in the example concerning the effects on the socialization process of the transition from nonindustrial, nonurban life to industrial, urban living is of any worth and will be borne out by further study of the ethnographic literature and in field studies, the point of the illustration is that in the process of socialization the patterns of kinship and kin groups must be treated as functionally linked, or interdependent, with other and different patterns of not only the social relations subsystem, but other cultural subsystems.

Contextual analysis of cultural data. One of the most fundamental theoretical insights of modern cultural anthropology has been that all cultures are complexly interrelated wholes. Cultural anthropologists have learned to understand that, when they study a culture such as the Dusun of Borneo, the pattern of Dusun mothers holding their babies and the pattern of disposal of a baby's umbilical cord may be linked to the pattern of Dusun songs, the pattern of designs woven by Dusun into baskets, and the pattern of Dusun house door carvings. The anthropologist expects that all of these cultural patterns, which occur as part of different subsystems of Dusun culture, when viewed in their special relation of interdependence through historic time, can offer profound insights in the analysis of the patterns of culture widely shared in Dusun society. In other words, cultural anthropologists have come to see that no aspect of a culture, whether Dusun, Arunta, or Ashanti, stands alone and unrelated to the other aspects of culture.

An understanding of the importance of a *contextual analysis* of culture is not gained by the cultural anthropologist through reading descriptions of culture, although ethnographic readings are an important part of preparation for research. A cultural anthropologist learns finally about the ways different aspects of culture are interrelated by being totally immersed in an alien culture for a long period.

Cultural anthropologists must live in alien cultures as human beings, where they become intensely aware of new social environments as they make consistent efforts to interact regularly with their fellows on terms they comprehend and in their language. In the process of totally experiencing another and very different culture, the anthropologist comes to be able to illustrate that cultures are wholes, made of complexly interdependent parts, each of which can be finally understood only in its relations to other parts of a culture.

The sensitivity to the *contextual* (or *holistic*) nature of culture gained by cultural anthropologists through long-term field studies produces a unique theoretical outlook. This outlook deeply affects modern anthropological writings and is the background against which much of cultural analysis is conducted and judged by contemporary cultural anthropologists.

One of the principal problems in socialization research has been that general conclusions about that process and about its consequences have tended not only to be limited to one culture, or a group of closely related cultures, but as well to not specify the ways the aspect of culture being studied is set in a *contextual whole*. For example, studies of "political socialization," or the transmission to children of political beliefs and behavior, generally have not attended to the contextual nature of culture. There are few studies of the learning of political beliefs and behavior that look to the functional interdependence of this one pattern (government) of the social relations subsystem with other patterns in that same subsystem and in other cultural subsystems. When reference is made in such studies to other cultural patterns, imprecise terms and unclear concepts such as "family" often are used, without recognition that these terms are essentially meaningless when lacking their transculturally valid modifiers (such as "nuclear," "extended," "polygamous," and so on).

There have been some descriptions and analyses of cultural transmission in which the functional relationships between the patterns of kinship and kin groups and other patterns of culture have been specified and illustrated. An exemplar of such studies is one by Mead concerning the ways that the patterns of kinship and kin groups are related to the cultural transmission process in Arapesh society. Too, while not approaching the published detail of the Mead study, some other studies, such as the Whiting and co-workers' "six cultures" research, have set the enculturation process in the context of whole cultures and generally have specified the ways kinship and kin groups are related to that process.[12]

Statistical analysis of cultural data. Statistical procedures have been employed frequently in socialization research to systematically seek to reduce the tangle of human phenomena and to try to demonstrate relations of functional interdependence between socialization and various

---

[12]See LeVine and LeVine, 1966; Minturn and Hitchcock, 1966; Romney and Romney, 1966; Fischer and Fischer, 1966; Nydegger and Nydegger, 1966; and Maretzki and Maretzki, 1966. See also Whiting, Child, and others, 1966: chapter 2.

aspects, parts, and patterns of culture.[13] The model for most such research is an innovative study by Whiting and Child (1953). This study proceeded in a series of five steps. First, the authors abstracted from the ethnographic literature of 75 generally nonliterate, nonindustrial, and nonurban societies specific data of infant care and of some later patterns of adult behavior. Then the authors constructed a set of ratings for the severity of care of infants in these 75 societies with respect to enculturation of feeding, excretory, aggression, dependency, and sexual behavior. They also constructed a set of ratings, noting the presence or absence of particular adult patterns of behavior in each of the samples studied. The statistical procedure known as the *correlational method* was used to determine if there were any links of functional interdependence between specific patterns in infancy and later patterns of adult behavior. Finally, on the basis of these statistical procedures, Whiting and Child drew some general conclusions concerning the ways some specific patterns in human child care appeared causally related to later adult patterns of behavior.[14]

Whiting and Child's correlational procedures have been used by others to try to show relations of functional interdependence between specific patterns in infant and child care and adult patterns of behavior, including, among other behavior, crime, art styles, cognition, subsistence, puberty rituals, games and folk tales, supernaturalism, drinking, punishment, sex and menstrual taboos.[15]

This approach of trying to statistically demonstrate some functional interrelations between specific features of socialization and patterns of culture has also been used by Textor in a

computer compilation and analysis of data from a sample of 400 largely nonliterate, nonindustrial, and nonurban cultures. Textor's study is based on the abstraction of a large number of dichotomous, or contrasting, features of culture (for example, cultures in which wife-lending or wife exchange is present; cultures in which wife-lending or wife exchange is unimportant or absent), which were then put through a computer in a series of four "runs" to contrast each dichotomous feature against all other such features. This produced almost 20,000 different correlations, which were then "printed out" by the computer in the form of 480 tables showing statistical measures of the strength ("phi coefficient"), significance ("chi square" and "Fisher Exact Test") and the probability ("P value") of the correlations between particular dichotomous features.

Approximately 116 (or 24%) of the 480 tables in Textor's study seem concerned specifically with relationships of functional interdependence between dichotomous features of socialization. Each one of the 116 tables indicates the specific number of cultures in the sample of 400 for which Textor found ethnographic data concerning particular features of socialization either unclear or unreported. In the 116 tables the number of societies for which socialization data are unclear or unreported average approximately 336 (or 84%) of the 400-culture sample.

Textor notes that he used the concept of "pattern," from cultural anthropology, as the basis of his computer program design. This program design, which Textor terms, "Pattern Search and Table Translation Technique," rests upon his definition of *pattern* as a "concatenation of co-occurrences" among the dichotomous attributes he considered important in the research. For Textor, the concept of pattern is a statement contrasting isolable classes of specific data of one culture or between cultures. Textor notes that he believes that his research employs an holistic, or contextual, rather than an "atomistic" approach to seeking relations of functional interdependence between features of culture and adult behavior.

However, Textor's definition and use of the

[13] A bibliography listing more than 300 such studies can be found in O'Leary, 1969.
[14] For the general conclusions of Whiting and Child, see their 1953 text.
[15] See Bacon, Child, and Barry, 1963 (crime); Barry, 1957 (art styles); Fischer, 1961 (cognition); Barry, Child, and Bacon, 1959 (subsistence); Brown, 1963; Cohen, 1964; Whiting, Kluckhohn, and Anthony, 1958 (puberty rituals); Roberts, Arth, and Bush, 1959; Roberts and Sutton-Smith, 1962 and 1966; Roberts, Sutton-Smith, and Kendon, 1963 (games and folk tales); Spiro and D'Andrade, 1958 (supernaturalism); Bacon, Barry, and Child, 1965 (drinking); Triandis and Lambert, 1961 (punishment); Stephens, 1962 (sexual anxiety); and Stephens, 1967 (menstrual taboos).

concept of pattern and of contextual analysis seems different from the one developed and used in many studies of culture and behavior. The conceptual scheme for the study of culture outlined briefly at the beginning of this chapter has been developed from a theory quite different from the one used by Textor and some others employing statistical procedures in study of cultural phenomena. At the turn of this century anthropologists of the "historical" theory school, and principally Boas, developed the idea that the minimum theoretically significant unit of culture isolated by directed observation is a *trait*. Boas noted that traits in a culture can be grouped at a higher level of abstraction into a conceptual unit, which he termed a *trait complex*. These traits, he noted, were alike in most respects. In elaborating on these ideas, Wissler later developed the concept of *universal culture pattern*, which he defined as a group of closely related culture trait complexes typical of a culture. Later, too, Kroeber elaborated on the concept of pattern as defined by Wissler. At the same time Wissler was developing his ideas, Sapir was formulating the concept that all cultural behavior is *symbolic*, that is, based on *meanings* for behavior *forms* that are widely shared, communicated, and transmitted generationally in a society, and that the cultural meanings for behavior forms in a society appear to an observer not as truly objective entities but rather as conceptually abstracted summaries, or *configurations*, of cultural ideas and behavior patterns.

In developing these concepts *(trait, trait complex, pattern, meaning, form, configuration)*, Benedict proposed that it is in the specific ways the patterns of a culture are interrelated that give form and meaning to the whole culture. Benedict also pointed out that cultures differ not only because their culture traits or trait complexes or patterns are different, but because they are oriented as wholes, that is, as entire cultures, in quite different directions and toward very different goals and purposes, due to the ways the patterns of a culture are interrelated with one another.

Somewhat later, Linton refined all of these concepts by adding the concept of function from the theoretical works of Malinowski and Radcliffe-Brown. Linton noted that the *form* of every cultural trait, trait complex, pattern, or configuration results from the sum and arrangement of its component features in ways that are learned, shared, and transmitted from one generation to the next in a society. Linton also defined the *meanings* and *functions* of cultural traits, trait complexes, patterns, and configurations as the dynamic and regularly observed qualities of cultural reality in a society.

Later, Kluckhohn extended and further refined these conceptions in a series of basic theoretical studies that sought to precisely state not only the terms but as well the levels of conceptual abstraction involved in their use. Kluckhohn's definitions of these conceptual ideas are implicit in a general definition of culture by Kroeber and Kluckhohn, now widely used in theoretical and analytic studies in cultural anthropology.

The theoretical efforts of Wissler, Sapir, and others appear to have been based on the assumption that cultural data specified by the higher level of abstraction concepts of pattern and configuration contain within them the sum total of the cultural data specified in the lower level, or in less general concepts, such as trait and trait complex. Thus, when cultural traits sharing common forms, meanings, or functions are identified by an observer, they have a conceptual integrity as a unit, or whole entity, of that culture. That whole entity, or culture trait complex, when arranged by the observer with other trait complexes sharing common forms, meanings, or functions, also has a conceptual integrity of its own as a whole entity of culture. In turn, that whole entity, or culture pattern, when arranged with other patterns sharing common forms, meanings, or functions, has an integrity as a whole entity of culture. And, in turn, that entity, or culture configuration, when arranged with other configurations sharing common forms, meanings, or functions, makes up a whole entity of a culture.

It is important to understand that under this theory each whole entity of culture, at each level of conceptual abstraction, presumes the integrity of all of the entities that have been arranged together to comprise it. Thus, the concept of culture pattern, at the third (or fourth) level of abstraction from cultural behavior, carries within it the implicit assumption that the conceptual integrity of the culture traits and trait complexes have remained intact.

Any type of statistical treatment of cultural data inevitably violates the assumed integrity of such concepts through the practice of abstracting specific aspects of culture and then treating them as being capable of being analyzed alone, without reference to other aspects of culture. Statistical analysis of cultural data usually gives little attention to the different levels of conceptual abstraction involved and often treats data of culture traits as comparable to data of patterns and configurations. Statistical analysis of cultural data usually tends to hold constant the important theoretical variables of common or dissimilar form, or meaning or functions. Statistical treatment of cultural data also involves the procedural error of holding cultural phenomena to be strictly equivalent and capable of manipulation as if they truly represented dynamically equivalent natural entities.[16]

The nineteenth century physical science theories from which modern statistical procedures have been derived are based on the assumption that nature is dynamically equivalent in all of its parts, that is, each part or aspect of any natural phenomenon corresponds conceptually to all other parts or aspects of the same phenomenon, wherever it is found—for example, the study of carbon atoms in physical chemistry. Under the doctrine of the dynamic uniformity, or equivalence of nature, a chemist would assume that all carbon atoms are exactly the same, whether in the laboratory or the far reaches of the universe. This nineteenth century assumption is reflected clearly in the "laws of thermodynamics."

Studies of cultural phenomena began in the mid-nineteenth century by treating all aspects of human behavior as dynamically equivalent. However, by the end of that century it had become apparent that this assumption was not applicable to study of culture. The development of a major part of cultural theory since early

in the present century has been markedly away from the conception of dynamic equivalence. The efforts to use statistical procedures in analysis of interrelationships in culture usually ignore these aspects of cultural theory.

This does not mean that all statistical treatment of cultural data is in basic error or should be avoided. Indeed, there are very many problems in the study of culture that involve measurable incidence and intensity, that is, where counting, weighing, and scaling are useful and important techniques. For instance, Fortes clearly has demonstrated how certain aspects of the Ashanti pattern of kinship (for example, marital residence patterns) become evident only through use of a statistical description. The study of the data of archaeology, or cultural data from a time long past, often fruitfully employs statistical methods. Physical anthropological studies also employ modern statistical procedures to great advantage. But Fortes, in common with Kluckhohn and others, notes that a singular dependence upon purely statistical procedures, with their inherent lack of accounting for contextual nature of cultural phenomena, are not likely to contribute to the main, unresolved problems in the study of culture.[17]

Thus, the dependence on statistical techniques in research seeking to demonstrate relations of interdependence between the socialization process and various patterns of culture has led to a situation where the total context, internal dynamics, textural qualities, and regular articulation of cultural parts are being bypassed for the sake of an apparent, but theoretically misleading, ease in formulating, "testing," and "confirming" hypotheses of interdependence.

This identification and brief discussion of three features of enculturation that appear to be common to 99 of a sample of 128 societies involves a conceptual abstraction process that seeks, in so far as is possible using whole ethnographic accounts, to pay attention to the total context, internal dynamics, textural qualities, and regular internal articulation of cultural parts

---

[16]For further discussion of these points, see Kluckhohn, 1954: 958-960; Bateson, 1947: 651; and Williams, 1959.

[17]See Fortes, 1949b: 59; Kluckhohn, 1954: 959.

(traits, trait complexes, and so on) of each culture studied. The end-product of this kind of conceptual abstraction process is only a limited and restricted descriptive account of the gross appearance of one possible phenomenon in the study of relations between the socialization process and the patterns of human kinship and kin groups. The contextual abstraction process employed to gain this description begins by rejecting nineteenth century physical science models and methods, and nineteenth century assumptions concerning culture, and proceeds with the cultural theory formulated by Boas, Wissler, Sapir, and many others, uses personal sensitivities to the contextual nature of culture gained from long-term field work in alien social and cultural settings, and comes to full focus through an understanding that no real scientific gains are likely to be made in analysis of the relationships between the socialization process and patterns and configurations of culture until a new mathematics for cultural study has been developed and successfully applied. Recently some limited uses have been made of matrix algebra and topological mathematics, the mathematics of nonlinear partial differential and integrodifferential equations and of Markov process analysis in serious efforts to develop a mathematics that can account for the known nature of cultural data and accommodate a general theory of culture widely used in modern anthropology.

But, uses of these mathematical techniques so far have been largely unsuccessful, for much the same reasons that statistical analysis has been unsuccessful in efforts to demonstrate relations of interdependence between the socialization process and various patterns of culture. For the present, and until a mathematics is developed and available for study of cultural phenomena that accounts fully for their contextual integrity, dynamic interrelatedness, and so on, it may be preferable to use a contextual abstraction process to produce general descriptive statements, to the giving of an appearance of scientific certainty through use of statistical devices such as "P values," "phi coefficients," "chi-square," and "Fisher Exact Tests." The late Norbert Wiener, a widely respected mathematician, has pointed out that scientists do not have the right to give the impression of a mathematical analysis of complex and difficult-to-understand situations and events, unless they use a language they can fully understand and correctly apply. Short of this, Wiener noted, a purely descriptive account of the gross, or whole, appearance of a phenomenon is more scientific.[18]

■ Summary

This chapter has been concerned with a discussion of some of the possible interrelationships between socialization and the patterns of kinship and kin groups. The chapter began with a brief summary of some ways of thinking about culture and the topics of kinship and kin groups. Then, case study data from ethnographic accounts of Arunta and Ashanti societies were presented to illustrate some of the differences and similarities in the ideas and ways of behaving children may learn concerning the patterns of kinship and kin groups. The chapter concluded with comment on some of the problems and present challenges in study of the relationships between patterns of kinship, kin groups, and the socialization process.

---

[18]See Wiener, 1950: 26.

REFERENCES CITED AND SUGGESTED READINGS

Bacon, M., I. Child, and H. Barry III. 1963. "A Cross Cultural Study of Correlates of Crime," *Journal of Abnormal and Social Psychology* **66**:291-300.

Bacon, M., H. Barry III, and I. Child. 1965. "A Cross Cultural Study of Drinking: II. Relations to Other Features of Culture," *Quarterly Journal of Studies on Alcohol, Supplement* **3**:29-48.

Barry, H. III. 1957. "Relationships Between Child Training and the Pictorial Arts," *Journal of Abnormal and Social Psychology* **54**:380-383.

Barry, H. III, I. Child, and M. Bacon. 1959. "Relation of Child Training to Subsistence Economy," *American Anthropologist* **61**:51-63.

Basedow, H. 1925. *The Australian Aboriginal.* Adelaide: Preece.

Bateson, G. 1944. "Cultural Determinants of Personality." In J. McV. Hunt (ed.), *Personality and the Behavior Disorders,* Vol. II. New York: Ronald Press, pp. 714-735.

_____. 1947. "Sex and Culture," *Annals of the New York Academy of Sciences* **47**:647-660.

Benedict, R. 1932. "Configurations of Culture in North America," *American Anthropologist* **34**:1-27.

_____. 1934. *Patterns of Culture.* Boston: Houghton-Mifflin.

_____. 1946. *The Chrysantheumum and the Sword.* Boston: Houghton-Mifflin.

Berndt, R., and C. Berndt. 1964. *The World of the First Australians.* Chicago: University of Chicago Press.

Boas, F. 1911. *The Mind of Primitive Man.* New York: Macmillan.

_____. 1927. *Primitive Art.* Oslo: H. Aschehoug.

_____. 1930. *The Religion of the Kwakiutl Indians.* New York: Columbia University Contributions to Anthropology, Number 10 (2 vols.).

_____. 1932. *Anthropology and Modern Life.* New York: Norton.

_____. 1940. *Race Language and Culture.* New York: Macmillan.

Bock, P. 1969. *Modern Cultural Anthropology: An Introduction.* New York: Knopf.

Bohannan, P. 1963. *Social Anthropology.* New York: Holt, Rinehart and Winston.

Bronfenbrenner, U. 1970. *Two Worlds of Childhood: U. S. and U. S. S. R.* New York: Basic Books.

Brown, J. 1963. "A Cross-Cultural Study of Female Initiation Rites," *American Anthropologist* **65**:837-853.

Busia, K. 1951. *The Position of the Chief in the Modern Political System of Ashanti.* London: Oxford University Press.

_____. 1955. "The Ashanti." In C. D. Forde (ed.), *African Worlds.* London: Oxford University Press, pp. 190-209.

Cohen, Y. 1961. *Social Structure and Personality; A Casebook.* New York: Holt, Rinehart and Winston.

_____. 1964. *The Transition from Childhood to Adolescence.* Chicago: Aldine.

_____. 1968. "Macroethnology: Large Scale Comparative Studies." In J. A. Clifton (ed.), *Introduction to Cultural Anthropology: Essays in the Scope and Methods of the Science of Man.* Boston: Houghton-Mifflin, pp. 402-448.

Davidson, D. 1926. "The Basis of Social Organization in Australia," *American Anthropologist* **28**:529-548.

Driver, H., and R. Chaney. 1968. "A Sixth Solution to the Galton Problem," *American Anthropological Association, Bulletins* **1**:35-36

Elkin, A. 1933. "Studies in Australian Totemism," *Monographs,* Number Two (*Oceania* 3, Numbers Three and Four; 4, Numbers One and Two).

_____. 1954. *The Australian Aborigines: How to Understand Them,* ed. 2. Sydney: Angus and Robertson.

Elkin, A. R., and C. Berndt. 1950. *Art in Arnhem Land.* Chicago: University of Chicago Press.

Evans-Pritchard, E. 1940. *The Nuer.* London: Oxford University Press.

_____. 1951. *Kinship and Marriage Among the Nuer.* London: Oxford University Press.

Fischer, J. 1961. "Art Styles as Cultural Cognitive Maps," *American Anthropologist* **63**:79-93.

Fischer, J., and A. Fischer. 1966. *The New Englanders of Orchard Town, U.S.A.* New York: Wiley (Volume V, Six Cultures, Studies of Child Rearing Series).

Fortes, M. 1945. *The Dynamics of Clanship Among the Tallensi.* London: Oxford University Press.

_____. 1949a. *The Web of Kinship Among the Tallensi.* London: Oxford University Press.

_____. 1949b. "Time and Social Structure: An Ashanti Case Study." In M. Fortes (ed.), *Social Structure.* London: Oxford University Press, pp. 54-84.

_____. 1950. "Kinship and Marriage Among the Ashanti." In A. R. Radcliffe-Brown and D. Forde (eds.), *African Systems of Kinship and Marriage.* London: Oxford University Press, pp. 252-284.

Galton, F. 1889. "Comment on a Paper by Edward B. Tylor: On a Method of Investigating the Development of Institutions; Applied to the Laws of Marriage and Descent," *Journal of the Royal Anthropological Institute* **18**:245-272.

Geertz, H. 1961. *The Javanese Family; A Study of Kinship and Socialization.* New York: Free Press.

Goodenough, W. 1955. "A Problem in Malayo-Polynesian Social Organization," *American Anthropologist* **57**:71-83.

_____. 1967. "Componential Analysis," *Science* **156**:1203-1209.

Herskovits, M. 1933. *An Outline of Dahomean Religious Belief.* Memoir 41, The American Anthropological Association.

_____. 1960. *Cultural Anthropology.* New York: Knopf. (An abridged version of *Man and His Works.*)

Hill, R., and R. König. 1970. *Families in East and West; Socialization Process and Kinship Ties.* The Hague: Mouton.

Hoebel, E. 1954. "The Ashanti; Constitutional Monarchy and the Triumph of Public Law." In E. A. Hoebel (ed.), *The Law of Primitive Man.* Cambridge: Harvard University Press, pp. 211-254.

_____. 1966. *Anthropology; The Study of Man.* New York: McGraw-Hill.

Homans, G. 1950. *The Human Group.* New York: Harcourt-Brace.

_____. 1961. *Social Behavior; Its Elementary Forms.* New York: Harcourt-Brace.

Hyman, H. 1969. *Political Socialization: A Study in the Psychology of Political Behavior,* New York: Free Press.

Kluckhohn, C. 1936. "Some Aspects of Contemporary Theory in Cultural Anthropology." Unpublished doctoral dissertation, Harvard University Press.

_____. 1941. "Patterning as Exemplified in Navaho Culture." In L. Spier, A. I. Hallowell, and S. Newman (eds.), *Language, Culture and Personality; Essays in Memory of Edward Sapir.* Menasha, Wisconsin: Sapir Memorial Publication Fund, pp. 109-130.

_____. 1949. *Mirror for Man.* New York: Whittlesey House.

_____. 1951. "Values and Value Orientations in the Theory of Action." In T. Parsons and E. Shils (eds.), *Toward A General Theory of Action.* Cambridge: Harvard University Press, pp. 388-433.

_____. 1954. "Culture and Behavior." In G. Lindzey (ed.), *Handbook of Social Psychology.* Cambridge: Addison-Wesley, pp. 921-976.

Kroeber, A. 1948. *Anthropology.* New York: Harcourt-Brace.

Kroeber, A., and C. Kluckhohn. 1951. *Culture: A Critical Review of Concepts and Definitions.* Cambridge: Harvard University, Peabody Museum Papers, Volume 47, Number One.

LeVine, R., and B. LeVine. 1966. *Nyansongo: A Gusii Community in Kenya.* New York: Wiley (Volume II, Six Cultures, Studies of Child Rearing Series).

Lienhardt, G. 1966. *Social Anthropology.* London: Oxford.

Linton, R. 1936. *The Study of Man.* New York: Appleton-Century-Crofts.

_____. 1945. *The Cultural Background of Personality.* New York: Appleton-Century-Crofts.

Maretzki, T., and H. Maretzki. 1966. *Taira; An Okinawan Village.* New York: Wiley (Volume VII, Six Cultures, Studies of Child Rearing Series).

Mathews, R. 1907. "Notes on the Aranda Tribe," *Journal and Proceedings of the Royal Society of New South Wales 41.*

_____. 1908. "Marriage and Descent in the Aranda Tribe, Central Australia," *American Anthropologist* **10:**88-102.

Matson, J. N. 1953. "Testate Succession in Ashanti," *Africa* **23:**224-232.

Mead, M. 1934. *Kinship in the Admiralty Islands.* New York: Anthropological Papers, American Museum of Natural History, vol. 34, part 2.

_____. 1935. *Sex and Temperament in Three Primitive Societies.* New York: Morrow.

_____. 1937. *Cooperation and Competition Among Primitive Peoples.* New York: McGraw-Hill.

_____. 1938-1949. "The Mountain Arapesh," I-V, *Anthropological Papers of the American Museum of Natural History* **36:**145-349; **37:**317-451; **40:**163-419; **31:**289-390.

_____. 1949. *Male and Female: A Study of the Sexes in a Changing World.* New York: Morrow.

Minturn, L., and J. Hitchcock. 1966. *The Rājpūts of Khalapur, India.* New York: Wiley (Volume III, Six Cultures, Studies of Child Rearing Series).

Murdock, G. 1934. *Our Primitive Contemporaries.* New York: Macmillan.

_____. 1949. *Social Structure.* New York: Macmillan.

_____. 1958. *Outline of World Cultures.* New Haven: HRAF Press.

_____. 1967. *Ethnographic Atlas.* Pittsburgh: University of Pittsburgh Press.

Murdock, G., and others. 1969. *Outline of Cultural Materials,* ed. 4. New Haven: HRAF Press.

Naroll, R. 1961. "Two Solutions to Galton's Problem," *Philosophy of Science* **28:**15-39.

_____. 1964. "On Ethnic Unit Classification," *Current Anthropology* **5:**283-291.

_____. 1968. "Some Thoughts on Comparative Method in Anthropology." In H. Blalock and A. Blalock (eds.), *Methodology in Social Research.* New York: McGraw-Hill, pp. 236-277.

Naroll, R., and R. D'Andrade. 1963. "Two Further Solutions to Galton's Problem." *American Anthropologist* **65:**1053-1067.

Needham, R. 1962. *Structure and Sentiment: A Test Case in Social Anthropology.* Chicago: University of Chicago Press.

Nydegger, W., and C. Nydegger. 1966. *Tarong: An Ilocos Barrio in the Philippines.* New York: Wiley (Volume VI, Six Cultures, Studies of Child Rearing Series).

O'Leary, T. 1969. "A Preliminary Bibliography of Cross-Cultural Studies," *Behavior Science Notes* **4:**95-115.

Parsons, T., R. Bales, and J. Olds. 1955. *Family, Socialization and Interaction Process.* Glencoe, Ill.: Free Press.

Pink, O. 1936. "The Landowners in the Northern Divisions of the Aranda Tribe," *Oceania* **6:**275-305.

Radcliffe-Brown, A. 1930. "The Social Organization of Australian Tribes," *Oceania* **1:**34-63.

Rattray, R. 1923. *Ashanti.* Oxford: Clarendon Press.

_____. 1927. *Religion and Art in Ashanti.* London: Oxford University Press.

_____. 1929. *Ashanti Law and Constitution.* London: Oxford University Press.

Roberts, J., M. Arth, and R. Bush. 1959. "Games in Culture," *American Anthropologist* **61:**597-605.

Roberts, J., and B. Sutton-Smith. 1962. "Child Training and Game Involvement," *Ethnology* **1:**166-185.

_____. 1966. "Cross-Cultural Correlates of Games of Chance," *Behavior Science Notes* **1:**131-144.

Roberts, J., B. Sutton-Smith, and A. Kendon. 1963. "Strategy in Games and Folk Tales," *Journal of Social Psychology* **61:**185-199.

Roheim, G. 1925. *Australian Totemism.* London: G. Allen and Unwin.

_____. 1933. "Women and their Life in Central Australia," *Journal of the Royal Anthropological Institute* **63:**241-250.

Romney, K., and R. Romney. 1966. *The Mixtecans of Juxtlahuaca, Mexico.* New York: Wiley (Volume IV, Six Cultures, Studies of Child Rearing Series).

Sapir, E. 1924. "Culture, Genuine and Spurious," *American Journal of Sociology* **29:**401-429.

_____. 1927. "The Unconscious Patterning of Behavior in Society." In E. S. Drumner (ed.), *The Unconscious.* New York: Knopf, pp. 114-142.

_____. 1949. "Selected Writings of Edward Sapir." In D. G. Mandelbaum (ed.), *Language, Culture and*

Personality. Berkeley: University of California Press.

Schneider, D., and K. Gough (eds.) 1961. *Matrilineal Kinship.* Berkeley: University of California Press.

Schusky, E. 1965. *Manual for Kinship Analysis.* New York: Holt, Rinehart and Winston.

Service, E. 1963. *Profiles in Ethnology.* New York: Harper and Row.

Spencer, B. 1928. *Wanderings in Wild Australia.* London: Macmillan.

Spencer, B., and F. Gillen. 1927. *The Arunta: A Study of a Stone Age People.* London: Macmillan (2 vols.).

_____. 1938. *The Native Tribes of Central Australia.* London: Macmillan (2 vols.).

Spiro, M., and R. D'Andrade. 1958. "A Cross-Cultural Study of Some Supernatural Beliefs," *American Anthropologist* **60**:456-466.

Stephens, W. 1962. *The Oedipus Complex: Cross-Cultural Evidence.* New York: Free Press.

_____. 1967. "A Cross-Cultural Study of Menstrual Taboos." In C. Ford (ed.), *Cross-Cultural Approaches.* New Haven, HRAF Press, pp. 67-94.

Strehlow, T. G. H. 1947. *Aranda Traditions.* Melbourne: Melbourne University Press.

Textor, R. 1967. *A Cross-Cultural Summary.* New Haven: Human Relations Area Files.

Thurnwald, R. 1916. *Banaro Society.* Memoir 3, Number Four, The American Anthropological Association.

Triandis, L., and W. Lambert. 1961. "Sources of Frustration and Targets of Aggression: A Cross-Cultural Study," *Journal of Abnormal and Social Psychology* **62**:640-648.

Whiting, J., and I. Child. 1953. *Child Training and Personality.* New Haven: Yale University Press.

Whiting, J., I. Child, and W. Lambert. 1966. *Field Guide for a Study of Socialization.* New York: Wiley (Volume I, Six Cultures, Studies of Child Rearing Series).

Whiting, J., R. Kluckhohn, and A. Anthony. 1958. "The Function of Male Initiation Ceremonies at Puberty." In E. Maccoby, T. Newcombe, and E. Hartley (eds.), *Readings in Social Psychology.* New York: Holt, Rinehart and Winston, pp. 359-370.

Wiener, N. 1950. "Some Maxims for Biologists and Psychologists," *Dialectica* **4**:22-27.

Williams, T. 1959 "A Critique of Some Assumptions of Social Survey Research," *The Public Opinion Quarterly* **23**:55-62.

_____. 1969. *A Borneo Childhood: Enculturation in a Dusun Society.* New York: Holt, Rinehart and Winston.

Wissler, C. 1923. *Man and Culture.* New York: Crowell

_____. 1926. *The Relation of Nature to Man in Aboriginal North America.* New York: Oxford University Press.

EIGHT STATUS-ROLE, CLASS, AND SOCIALIZATION

This chapter is concerned with the ways the cultural patterns of status-role and class are related to the socialization process. The discussion begins with an examination of the concept of status-role and an account of transitions in status-role that may be required of children as they mature in a culture. The second part of the chapter briefly examines the concept of social class and notes some studies of relations between class and the socialization process. The chapter concludes with comment concerning the part played by these patterns in the socialization process.

■ Status-role and socialization

The culture of each human society possesses patterns that contain details of work to be undertaken for survival of the society, clear definitions of the ways jobs or tasks are to be performed, and the usual practices of recruitment of individuals to such tasks. Malinowski noted that these patterns, which he termed a "cultural charter," are sometimes explicitly stated in a culture's rituals, informal law, myths, folk tales, songs, jokes, riddles, proverbs, puns, and ideology. However, some features of a cultural charter must be determined from statements about behavior made by persons recruited to perform specific tasks. And some features of a cultural charter can be determined only through direct observation of the behavior of individuals performing specific tasks.

Conceptions of status-role. In an influential 1936 work, Linton defined *status* as a "polar position" in a pattern of reciprocal social behavior. He also noted that a polar position consisted of a collection of social rights and duties.

Linton termed the precise ways rights and duties are put into effect as "roles." Linton illustrated these definitions by pointing out that persons occupying similar polar social positions would tend to behave in similar ways.

For example, at times of ritual feasting and celebration among the Dusun of Northern Borneo, it is usual for men to sit scattered about the interior central area of a house. On the other hand, women walk about or stand as they serve food and drink or while busy preparing food. Later, when gong music begins or singing commences, women enter the main feasting area and walk freely among the men during dancing and song harmony. However, it is not until quite near the end of a feast that women are supposed to be seated among the men.

Dusun culture also prescribes that, on meeting, younger men address older and unrelated women as "aunt," while older women must reciprocate through addressing younger, non-related males as "nephew." Similarly, younger women are supposed to address unrelated, older males as "uncle," while older men must respond to such greetings through use of the term "niece."

In addition to these social statuses and their associated roles, which are based on criteria of sex and age, Dusun must learn and use at least eleven other status-role classifications. Fig. 18 notes the thirteen different status-role classes that could be involved in the instance of the social situation when a middle-aged Dusun male meets a young Dusun woman walking along a village path. Based on their estimate of the situation, each individual would have to choose appropriate ways of behaving toward the other person. In most instances, except for sex and age, the many

Nampaya, Hopi pottery maker (date unknown). (Courtesy American Museum of Natural History.)

statuses held by each adult in the Dusun cultural system can be freely entered, filled, and left. However, the roles associated with each Dusun status can be performed only in a face-to-face situation, after decisions by an individual based on an estimate of the polar social positions potentially occupied by another person. Thus, a young Dusun women meeting her mother's older brother on a village path should have full knowledge of all of the polar positions that could be occupied by the older man in the Dusun social system (see Fig. 18). Hence, she could quickly choose to show the appropriate role behavior toward the older man, without the risk of major personal offense. In the Dusun cultural

charter, *age, sex,* and *kinship* status-roles tend to dominate personal relationships. Thus, on meeting an older man a young Dusun woman ordinarily would not behave in roles usual for her *service* status as a "rice field laborer," or in role ways reflecting her *expressive, proprietary, recreational,* or other statuses. However, at certain times, such as during a special ritual observance to protect the entire community from epidemic disease, a face-to-face meeting between a young Dusun woman and her mother's older brother might be dominated by her ritual status as a *female ritual specialist* capable of conducting the special magical acts involved in the village ceremony. An older Dusun man, with the primary

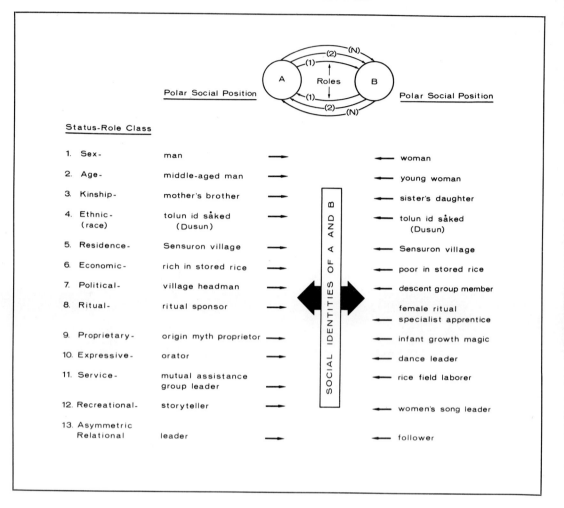

Fig. 18. Some Dusun status-role definitions. (After Linton's conceptions of role-status, 1936; see also Goodenough, 1965.)

responsibility for organizing and economically sponsoring a ritual, would probably behave toward a younger woman in a socially deferential manner, since as a ritual specialist the younger woman has a supernatural "power," that is, she is believed to be in contact with the most fearful and omnipotent forces and beings of the universe.

The thirteen status-role classes listed in Fig. 18, which follow Linton's concepts of status-role, appear to be universal in human culture, that is, to occur in the charters of all human societies. There also may be some other status-role classes. Substantial variations occur between societies in the total numbers of subclasses in particular status-roles.

For instance, in 1959 and in 1960 the Dusun cultural charter in the interior mountain village of Sensuron specified a total of approximately 43 subclasses within one (the service status) of the thirteen classes of status-role.

Table 8-1 notes these Dusun service status differentiations. In contrast, in July, 1970, there were more than 400 different service status differentiations listed in the Yellow Pages of the telephone book for the city of Columbus, Ohio. Some examples are listed in Table 8-2. Thus, in

Zuni woman carrying water (circa 1920). (Courtesy American Museum of Natural History.)

No complete accounts exist for all the status differentiations in any cultural charter, or of the many roles attached to each of the statuses within the major status classes. It may be possible that, while there are approximately thirteen status classes in the human cultural charter and a great many differentiations within each status class, the numbers of human roles can encompass all of the discrete ways humans behave in social situations. Thus, the great number of roles asso-

<hr>

[1]For some contrasts between Sensuron Dusun and American kinship status-role differentiations, see Williams, 1962, and Schneider, 1968.

Australian native hunter (date unknown). (Courtesy American Museum of Natural History.)

terms of service status differentiations, the village of Sensuron, with a population of 947 persons, contrasts markedly with the city of Columbus, with a 1970 census population of 539,677 persons. Such status differentiation contrasts between an isolated Dusun community and an American city also seems to extend to other differentiations in the statuses used in these two cultures, with the exception of the status of kinship. In the instance of kinship, Sensuron Dusun status differentiations are much more numerous than those used in the American city of Columbus.[1]

Hopi woman grinding corn (circa 1920). (Courtesy American Museum of Natural History.)

ciated with statuses presently stands as a barrier to generalizations concerning the nature of status-role behavior.

Ascribed and achieved status-role. One useful generalization has evolved from the many efforts to describe and analyze the numbers of statuses and their associated roles. This is the idea of grouping many different types of status-roles according to whether a cultural charter *ascribes* them, automatically assigns them, to individuals, or whether status-roles must be *achieved*, that is, learned through performance or

demonstration. Linton (1936) first suggested the usefulness of such general classifications of status-role forms. Linton's suggestions have been developed and discussed over the past three decades by sociologists and anthropologists. Table 8-3 notes the ways Banton, Nadel, and Southall, among others, have suggested that Linton's conception of ascribed and achieved statuses-roles may be modified in terms of recent studies.

Status-relationships and social identities. In considering some of the problems of analysis

Table 8-1. Some service status differentiations in the Northern Borneo, Tambunan Dusun village of Sensuron—1959, 1960

Bamboo wall maker	Fence maker	Midwife	Rubber gardener
Bark cloth maker	Gong trader	Money lender	Salt trader
Basket weaver	House builder	Musical instrument maker	Smith
Blow pipe maker	Hunter	Palm thatch maker	Spear maker
Blow pipe dart and case maker	Irrigation ditch builder	Plow and yoke maker	Tray maker
Bridge builder	Jar trader	Pottery maker	Tobacco gardener
Butcher	Kerabau (water buffalo) breeder	Rattan knot specialist	Tobacco shredder
Dam builder	Knife maker	Rattan rope maker	Weaver
Dry rice farmer	Male ritual specialist	Rice mill maker	Wet rice farmer
Female ritual specialist	Male ritual specialist apprentice	Rice and palm wine maker	Wood carver
Female ritual specialist apprentice	Mat maker	Ritual symbol maker	

Table 8-2. Some examples of service status differentiations in the Columbus, Ohio, telephone book—July, 1970 (A through C listings only)

Abstracters	Benefit plan consultants	Caterers
Accordion players	Beverage analysts	Cattle breeders
Accountants	Bicycle dealers	Cement contractors
Acoustical consultants	Biographers	Ceramic engineers
Actuaries	Blacksmiths	Certified public accountants
Advertising counselors	Boarding school consultants	Cesspool builders
Aerial crop dusters	Boat brokers	Chair dealers
Air ambulance services	Boiler dealers	Chaplains
Aircraft brokers	Bonding companies	Chauffeur services
Ambulance drivers	Bonesetters	Chemists
Animal dealers	Book dealers	Chemical engineers
Antique dealers	Booking agents	Child guidance counselors
Apothecaries	Bottle manufacturers	Chimney builders
Appraisers	Bowling instructors	Chiropodists
Arborists	Boxing and crating services	Chop suey manufacturers
Architects	Brake lining manufacturers	Church decorators
Asphalt paving contractors	Brass foundries	Cigar dealers
Attorneys	Brassiere manufacturers	Circular printers
Auctioneers	Brewers	Citizenship instructors
Auditors	Bricklayers	Claim adjusters
Automobile dealers	Bridge builders	Clipping services
Baby sitters	Building wreckers	Coal analysts
Bacteriologists	Butchers	Collection agencies
Bail bondsmen	Cabinet makers	Copy preparation services
Bakers	Cafeteria consultants	Correspondence schools
Bands	Caisson contractors	Cosmetic therapists
Bankers	Campaign managers	Coupon redemption centers
Barbecue builders	Candy brokers	Court reporters
Barbers	Carpenters	Crematory services
Baseball ticket agents	Carpet dyers	Criminologists
Baton twirling instructors	Carshakers	Custom house brokers
Bell manufacturers	Cartoonists	

of status-role, Goodenough (1965) has proposed a redefinition of the concept. He points out that, although Linton initially recognized polar social positions to consist of a cluster of social rights and duties and ideas concerning the ways these are put into effect in social situations, he then made the conceptual error of discussing status as referring only to kinds, or social categories, of persons (such as "teacher," "woman," and so on). Goodenough notes that most writers since Linton have followed this change without question, by treating a social category (such as

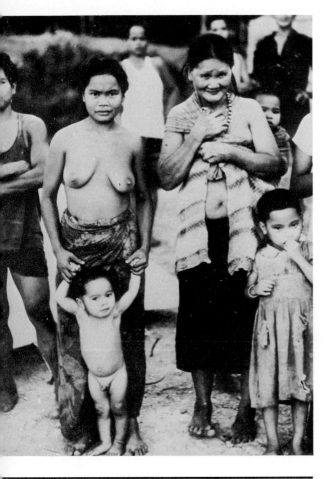

Left to right, a Dusun adolescent male, mother and son, and grandmother, grandson, and granddaughter (1959, Trus Madi). (T. R. Williams.)

"brother" or "chief"), together with all of its associated rights and duties, as one indivisible conceptual unit called a *status*.[2] For Goodenough, the "formal properties" of status involve only social rights, duties, privileges, powers, liabilities, and immunities and the ordered ways these are distributed in a society. Goodenough believes it would be much more useful to refer to social categories, or kinds or persons, as *social identities*, while reserving the term *status* for specific combinations of social rights, duties, and so on. Thus, Goodenough would describe and analyze ascribed and achieved *social identities*, and others, following Linton, would study ascribed and achieved statuses.

While adopting Linton's definitions of status-role as he considered new ways to analyze basic social interactions Goffman (1961) also noted that there was analytic efficiency to be gained in identifying the rights and duties usually associated with particular "social positions." Goodenough and Goffman agree that, in any social relationship, one individual's social *rights* over another are those things that one person, A, can demand of another, B, while social *duties* are those things the second person, B, owes to the first, A.

Goodenough also notes that social rights and duties between A and B serve to set the formal boundaries for interpersonal behavior. Thus, as

[2]See Merton, 1957a: 368–370.

Table 8-3. A classification of ascribed and achieved status-role*

Ascribed status-role				Achieved status-role				
Sex	**Age**	**Race**	**Kinship**	**Proprietary**	**Expressive**	**Service**	**Symmetrical**	**Asymmetrical**
Status-role based on sexual characters	Status-role based on chronological maturity	Status-role based on racial features	Status-role based on kin relations	Status-role based on special learning, knowledge, or skill	Status-role based on demonstration of special beliefs, creativity, or communicative abilities	Status-role based on occupational activities	Status-role based on social relationships of equality	Status-role based on social relationships of inequality
—	—	—	—	—	—	—	—	—
Male	Baby	Dusun	Son	Potter	Teacher	Partner	Leader,
Female	Boy	American	Mother	—	—	Accountant	Colleague	follower,
	Woman	Eskimo	Mother's	Potter	Artist	Biologist		Chairman,
	11 years		brother	Carver	Orator			member
				Shaman	Dancer			

*After Banton, M. 1965. *Roles.* London: Tavistock, p. 31; Nadel, S. F. 1957. *The Theory of Social Structure.* Glencoe, Ill.: Free Press; Southall, A. 1959. "An Operational Theory of Role," *Human Relations* 12:17–34.

hostess for a dinner party, an American woman may personally request that her guests wear "informal" clothing. It is her *social right* to make such a request. In turn, it is the *social duty* of guests to dress informally. But a hostess has no *social right* to dictate the color, style, or design of informal dress. It remains a guest's privilege to make such choices, providing they fully observe their duty toward a hostess exercising her social right in issuing an invitation to her home. Goodenough terms such a reciprocal and doubly contingent right-duty pair as a *status relationship.* He also notes that a status relationship often can be found widely repeated in a culture.[3] Thus, when entering new social situations, individuals must know the ways status relationships may be applied.

A TRUKESE STATUS RELATIONSHIP. In growing up on Truk, a Pacific island, children must learn all of the ways status relationships carry over into different social situations. For instance, the duties associated with one Trukese social right, that of claiming "social rank," involve at least six discrete activities.

1. To regularly use the special honorific greeting *fääjiro,* when encountering a person of higher social rank
2. To avoid being physically elevated over a person of higher social rank and therefore to engage in crouching or crawling motions if a higher ranked person is seated.
3. To avoid face-to-face social interactions with persons of higher social rank unless specifically requested by them to do so.
4. To honor all requests made by persons of higher social rank
5. To not speak harshly to or scold persons of higher social rank
6. To avoid striking persons of higher social rank.

Table 8-4 notes Goodenough's summary of the ways these social duties for Trukese individuals are carried from one situation to another when there are persons present who can claim

Sådåkån, a Tambunan (Sensuron) Dusun man (1959). (T. R. Williams.)

the right of higher social rank.[4] This particular Trukese status relationship (the *right* of claiming social rank; the *duty* of not setting oneself above a person with higher rank) is somewhat difficult for Americans and Europeans to conceive, since status relationships in these cultures involving the right of claiming social rank and the duty of social deference are often based on other social and cultural features.

Status-role number and complexity. It is important in considering the ways status relationships, or status-roles, are learned in the socialization process to recall that no culture provides children with analytic diagrams, such as Table 8-4, to study as they mature. For instance,

[3]Goffman (1961) uses the concept of "role set" in essentially the same way Goodenough (1965) has defined a status relationship. See also Merton, 1957a, and Gross, Mason, and McEachern, 1958.

[4]The Trukese pattern of social rank is manifest in the tabu of "setting oneself above another." For ease of discussion, this has been glossed, or interpreted, here as "claiming social rank." For further details see Goodenough, 1951: 111-119.

Table 8-4. Status duty of not setting oneself above another in Trukese society*

Social relationship in which status duty is owed	Must say *fääjiro*	Must crawl	Must avoid	Must obey	Must not scold	Must not fight
1. Non-kinsman to chief	Yes	Yes	Yes	Yes	Yes	Yes
Non-kinsman to *jitag*	Yes	Yes	Yes	Yes	Yes	Yes
2. Man to female *neji*	No	Yes	Yes	Yes	Yes	Yes
Man to Wi's *mwääni*	No	Yes	Yes	Yes	Yes	Yes
Woman to So of *mwääni*	No	Yes	No(?)	Yes	Yes	Yes
Woman to *mwääni*	No	Yes	Yes	Yes	Yes	Yes
Woman to So of Hu's older *pwiij*	No	Yes	Yes	Yes	Yes	Yes
Woman to Wi of *mwääni*	No	Yes	Yes	Yes	Yes	Yes
3. Man to older *pwiij*	No	No	Yes	Yes	Yes	Yes
Woman to older *pwiij*	No	No	Yes	Yes	Yes	Yes
4. Man to male *neji*	No	No	No	Yes	Yes	Yes
Man to Wi of older *pwiij*	No	No	No	Yes	Yes	Yes
Woman to Da of *mwääni*	No	No	No	Yes	Yes	Yes
Woman to Da of Hu's *pwiij*	No	No	No	Yes	Yes	Yes
Woman to So of Hu's younger *pwiij*	No	No	No	Yes	Yes	Yes
Woman to Da of Hu's *feefinej*	No	No	No	Yes	Yes	Yes
Woman to So of Hu's *feefinej*	No	No	No	Yes	Yes	Yes
Woman to Hu of older *pwiij*	No	No	No	Yes	Yes	Yes
Woman to Da's Hu	No	No	No	Yes	Yes	Yes
Woman to So's Wi	No	No	No	Yes	Yes	Yes
5. Man to younger *pwiij*	No	No	No	No	Yes	Yes
Man to Wi's older *pwiij*	No	No	No	No	Yes	Yes
Woman to younger *pwiij*	No	No	No	No	Yes	Yes
Woman to So of *pwiij*	No	No	No	No	Yes	Yes
Woman to Hu's older *pwiij*	No	No	No	No	Yes	Yes
6. Man to Wi of younger *pwiij*	No	No	No	No	No	Yes
Woman to own So	No	No	No	No	No	Yes
Woman to Hu's younger *pwiij*	No	No	No	No	No	Yes
7. Man to *semej*	No	No	No	No	No	No
Man to *jinej*	No	No	No	No	No	No
Man to *feefinej*	No	No	No	No	No	No
Man to Hu of *feefinej*	No	No	No	No	No	No
Man to Wi	No	No	No	No	No	No
Man to Wi's younger *pwiij*	No	No	No	No	No	No
Woman to *semej*	No	No	No	No	No	No
Woman to *jinej*	No	No	No	No	No	No
Woman to own Da	No	No	No	No	No	No
Woman to Da of *pwiij*	No	No	No	No	No	No
Woman to Hu	No	No	No	No	No	No
Woman to Hu of younger *pwiij*	No	No	No	No	No	No
Woman to Hu's *feefinej*	No	No	No	No	No	No

Translations of Trukese linguistic terms (from Goodenough, 1951: 94, 186-187).

jinej, "my mother," that is Mo, MoMo, MoSi, FaSi.

jitag, specialist in law, war, diplomacy, and rhetoric.

feefinej, "my sister."

mwääni, "my brother."

neji, "my child," that is, So, Da, SiCh, BrCh.

pwiij, "my siblings of the same sex," that is, Br, Si.

semej, "my father," that is, Fa, FaFa, FaBr, MoBr.

*After Goodenough, 1951: 113; 1965: 13.

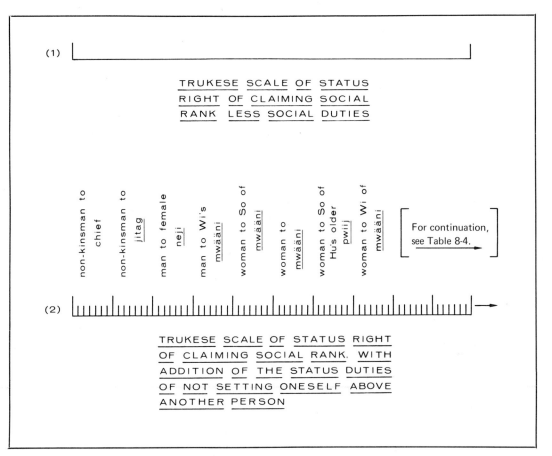

Fig. 19. Expansion of complexity in a status relationship scale in Trukese society. (After Goodenough, 1951, 1965.)

Trukese children, in common with children in all human societies, must master great complexity of social behavior (Table 8-4 includes 246 social duty actions) for each one of the status relationships or status-role classes used in their local societies.

In another theoretical context, Wallace (1961) has proposed that there is evidence in all human societies of a tendency toward individual effort in reducing all experience to some meaningful kind of order, as Goodenough suggests for status relationships, but at the same time also working toward greatly increasing the complexity within any classification of order that may be created.[5]

Thus, while there may be five, seven, or nine—or even thirteen—status-role or status relationship scales in any culture, it would be expected that there would be great complexity of behavior associated with each individual scale, without regard to the number of scales used. In fact, human status-roles (or status relationships) are characterized by enormous complexity and at the same time by systematic ordering of such complexity. This is reflected in the example of the one Trukese status relationship noted in Table 8-4; Trukese children must learn not only the right of claiming social rank in many different social situations, they must also learn the complex ways this right has been expanded by different definitions of social duty in each social

[5]See Wallace, 1961: 157.

situation. Fig. 19 illustrates the idea of role expansion of a status scale, following Goodenough's example of a Trukese status relationship.

In summary, there are at least two ways of thinking about the number and complexity status-roles. First, following the concepts of status-role advanced by Linton and refined recently by others, there are at least thirteen major status classes, each one possessing numerous internal differentiations and with a nearly infinite number of associated roles. These major classes seem to have order, when classified into "ascribed" or "achieved" status-roles. On the other hand, following the concepts formulated by Goodenough, the number of status relationships in a cultural charter will be limited to only seven (plus or minus two). Wallace's estimate of the tendency of humans to strive toward increasing the internal complexity of categories used to make order of their experience, when added to Goodenough's theoretical estimate, would seem to explain why so few status relationships can accommodate the very great complexity of human social relations.

All of these ideas are vital in considering the ways in which infants and children learn the details of the human cultural charter, since without a theory for making specific estimates of the numbers and types of tasks to be performed, the different ways these tasks will be carried out, and so on, which are specified in all cultural charters, it becomes a nearly impossible task to comprehend how infants and children can ever begin to grasp clearly, and in so brief a time, all of the many details and vast complexity apparently required in every society for successful social performances.

Added dimensions of status-role. A major problem in considering estimates of the number and complexity of status-roles or status relationships to be learned by children in the process of socialization is that there are a wide variety of other cultural features which also are involved in such behavior. For instance, human social interaction usually involves personal demeanor, including whole body orientations, movements, gestures, and physical distance or proximity of the persons involved. Thus, the demeanor of the hostess toward a guest at the time of the issuance of a dinner party invitation can carry specification of what is intended by her use of the term "informal." If an invitation is offered by a hostess to a male guest while she engages in sexually suggestive movements, it could indicate to a male guest a definition for informality quite different from the one to be noted by a hostess seated half a room distant while she issues her invitation for an "informal" dinner.

The use of features of costume to provide specific clues regarding status-role or status relationships is also common to all human societies. However, the forms of such features vary widely between societies, ranging from the full dress uniform of a United States Navy admiral to the wooden ear and lower lip plugs worn by adult Botocudo Indian women of the Amazon river basin. For an admiral or a Botocudo woman, incumbency in a particular status-role or status relationship may be symbolized through clues of costume, so that others of a society will know immediately, in a new situation, with whom they must be socially concerned. The responses of persons in a social situation are often to the clues manifested in features of costume which show status-role behavior potentials, that is, which indicate the possession of personal, political, or other kinds of power. Too, features of costume clearly may show the nature of status-role attachment, or the degree of involvement of a person in a particular status-role. The ear and lip plugs worn by Botocudo women, who ordinarily go about their affairs fully unclothed, symbolizes all of their feminine modesty, for without such plugs women are reported to feel "undressed" and hence as embarrassed as an American hostess might be if she appeared at her informal dinner party without wearing any clothing.

The styling of hair to indicate different sex, age, and service status-roles is also quite widespread in human society. Too, such styles have been used to denote specific clan or other kin group memberships, notably in some North American Indian and some African societies. In addition, cosmetic paints used as body and facial decorations, jewelry, tattoos, and regular practice of body deformations and mutilations, including foot and head binding, scarification, circumcision, subincision, and tooth filing, are used in human societies as indicators of status-roles. These clues to status-role may be combined with other clues of costume, hair styles, and demeanors.

Thus, it is usually necessary for children to learn multiple cultural clues for many different status-roles or status relationships, which can vary from time to time and in different social situations in complex combinations. In addition, children in most human societies must learn a very intricate and widely used status-role terminology. For instance, in the Trukese social relationship in Table 8-4, children must learn details of when and how to use the honorific greeting *fääjiro*. American children must learn to say "sir" and "m'am" at appropriate times and places and to avoid public rudeness in use of status-role terms noting less than ideal status-role conditions of age, sex, service, and so on ("funny old man," "old bag," and so on). Among the Swazi, a native people of Southeast Africa, status-role terminology is highly developed for distinguishing between commoners, nobles, and royalty. Swazi children are confronted very early in life with learning a quite complex vocabulary for successful social interaction.[6] Severe personal and economic penalties are imposed in Swazi society and many other societies for failure to regularly use precise status-role terminology. Such penalties range from the possibility of long-term imprisonment for an American Marine private showing open disrespect for his superior officers by use of "foul" language, to the complete social ostracism, and possible execution, which would have been imposed on an Hawaiian "commoner" violating the personal taboos of a king or queen through use of inappropriate status-role terminology.

Children in all human societies also must learn and correctly use a system of status-role *worth*. American Supreme Court Justices, physicians, nuclear physicists, "scientists," and "government scientists" have been ranked as the most influential and important of more than 100 well-known jobs specified in the American cultural charter. Table 8-5 lists the worth rankings given by Americans for some well-known status-roles. Nonliterate cultures also rank status-roles in a similar manner. For instance, 165 North Borneo Dusun adults (82 men, 83 women) living in Sensuron village in 1959 and 1960 verbally ranked the service statuses listed in Table 8-1 according to the "honor" and "personal power" accorded to persons who held such status-roles. The results of this verbal survey are noted in Table 8-6.[7]

In many cultures it is necessary for children to learn the subtle signs that distinguish such signs of *worth* from status-roles *esteem* signs. For instance, most adult Americans know that the two shoulder bars of a Marine captain, when compared to the two sleeve stripes of a Marine corporal, are signs of the worth placed upon the services of the two men to the Marine Corps. Many Americans also know that, if the corporal wears a pale blue ribbon with five white stars over his left blouse pocket and the captain has no such ribbon, the corporal is entitled to greater personal esteem, despite his lesser "worth," or rank, for he is a holder of the Congressional Medal of Honor, the highest symbol of wartime courage awarded by his country.

While learning the ways demeanor, costume, hair styles, cosmetics, jewelry, tattooing, body mutilations, status-role terminology, and worth and esteem signs may be features of status-role or status relationship behavior in a society, children must also be able to regularly distinguish between the *performance* of a role and a regular *performer* of a role. To use Goffman's (1961) example, children must know that, in an American funeral home, the three status-roles of the funeral director, the bereaved, and the deceased must be performed regularly, but that only the

---

[6]See Kuper, 1947, 1952, and 1963; Drucker, 1939.

[7]The methodology used in measurement of service status worth in a Dusun community follows Warner's (1960) ideas, as amended by Kornhauser (1953) and by Pfautz and Duncan (1950) and as developed in other forms in the work of Hollingshead (1949) and Kaufman (1944). For a discussion of the problems and methods in measurement of status-role worth, see Svalastoga (1965).

Table 8-5. Status-role prestige of occupations in the United States, 1925-1963*

Highest ranked twenty-five occupations	Lowest ranked twenty-five occupations
Supreme Court Justices	Garage mechanics
Physicians	Truck drivers
Nuclear physicists	Fishermen (who own boats)
Scientists	Clerks in stores
Government scientists	Milk route men
State governors	Streetcar motormen
Federal government cabinet officers	Lumberjacks
College professors	Restaurant cooks
Representatives (in Congress)	Singers (nightclub)
Chemists	Filling station attendants
Lawyers	Dock workers
Diplomats in foreign service	Railroad section hands
Dentists	Night watchmen
Architects	Coal miners
County judges	Restaurant waiters
Psychologists	Taxi drivers
Ministers	Farm hands
Corporate board members	Janitors
Mayors of large cities	Bartenders
Priests	Clothes pressers in a laundry
State government department heads	Soda fountain clerks
Civil engineers	Sharecroppers
Airline pilots	Garbage collectors
Bankers	Street sweepers
Biologists	Shoeshiner

*After Hodge, R. W., P. M. Siegel, and P. Rossi. "Occupational Prestige in the United States." 1964. *The American Journal of Sociology* **70**:286-301.

Table 8-6. Prestige rankings of 43 service statuses in the Northern Borneo Tambunan Dusun village of Sensuron, 1959-1960

Male ritual specialist	Smith	Plow and yoke maker	Rice and palm wine maker
Female ritual specialist	Spear maker	Palm thatch maker	Rubber gardener
Hunter	Knife maker	Butcher	Tobacco gardener
Midwife	Bark cloth maker	Ritual symbol maker	Gong trader
Dry rice farmer	Weaver	Female ritual specialist apprentice	Jar trader
Wet rice farmer	Bamboo wall maker	Male ritual specialist apprentice	Salt trader
Irrigation ditch builder	Basket weaver	Pottery maker	Kerabau (water buffalo)
Dam builder	Mat maker	Musical instrument maker	breeder
Blow pipe maker	Tray maker	Rattan knot specialist	Tobacco shredder
Blow pipe dart and case maker	Rice mill maker	Rattan rope maker	Fence maker
House builder	Wood carver	Bridge builder	Money lender

funeral director will be a continuing, or regular, performer in his status-role or status relationship. Children in every society must come to know or to be able to judge from evidences available to them in a specific social situation which persons will likely never again or only rarely will again engage in particular status-roles. A child's level of awareness of and success in learning the difference between performance of a status-role and a regular performer of a status-role may lend shape to his subsequent social interactions.

Too, children must learn details of the *commitment* of persons to certain of the status-roles they are assigned or fill regularly in a society.[8] For example, Dusun children must come to know and understand the clues that alert Dusun adults

[8]See Becker, 1960, and Goffman, 1961, for a discussion of the concept of status-role commitment.

to the fact that the old man who often sits and makes or repairs children's toys, tells children stories, or shows them the rudiments of carving a knife handle, weaving a rattan rope, or "old ways" to play a popular game, is also the leading male ritual specialist of the village and area. Dusun children must learn to perceive, from the clues given off in the old man's dress, hair style, tattoos, and particularly his demeanor, that he holds and exercises substantial authority over his fellows which is derived from a ritual specialist's ready access to the supernatural world. Dusun children younger than the age of 6 years usually have not learned to perceive the fact that, while the old man may hold other important status-roles in Dusun society, he has fully committed himself to the male ritual specialist status-role as a central fact of his personal existence.[9] Similarly, in each culture, children must learn, either from direct instruction by adults, or peers, or from their own observations, the significant clues of status-role commitment. Failure to learn such clues or to exercise social judgments based upon them can lead to repeated unsuccessful social performances.

At some point in the process of socialization children must also learn to understand the social functions of status-role, that is, to know and generally understand the part played by "proper" (or "eufunctional") status-role behavior in the continuing maintenance of the cultural patterns comprising the cultural charter. Children must also learn the ways "improper" (or "dysfunctional") status-role behavior can contribute to the dissolution or destruction of patterns in a cultural charter. Too, status-role behavior must generally be viewed by children in terms of its *manifest* and *latent* functions. Where the effects of "proper" status-role acts are openly acknowledged and acclaimed, such social behavior has a *manifest* function; in situations where the effect of eufunctional status-role behavior is not foreseen but tends to contribute to maintenance of a local cultural charter, such behavior has

a *latent* function.[10] At present, there is little descriptive data or analytic understanding of the exact ways most individuals come to generally perceive the necessity of eufunctional status-role acts.

Clubs, age-sets, and cultural transmission. Some cultures have chosen to make status-role behavior related to age and sex the basis of special social groupings. Such groups have been designated by the terms "club," "fraternity," "association," "sodality," and "age-grade" or "age-set." Recruitment to a kin group is based on birth. In contrast, the principle of recruitment to a club is based almost entirely on the attribute of sex, while recruitment to an age-set is based principally on chronological age.[11]

An understanding of clubs and age-sets is important for analysis of the socialization process because cultures with such social groups tend to use them regularly for the transmission of locally significant cultural forms.

Clubs are usually restricted to males.[12] Women's clubs, which are common in American culture, in fact are so rare in other cultures that Schurtz, in a turn of the century study, concluded that women must be fundamentally unsociable.[13] A modern interpretation of the predominance of male clubs in human social life would note that the tasks assigned to women in cultural charters usually leave little time for formation of and activities connected with voluntary, non-kinship groups.

In some human societies, cultural charters assign males the general responsibility for knowledge of action toward supernatural beings and forces.[14] In some societies, men are also given the primary responsibility for defense from external attack and for maintenance of internal order. Societies that assign men exclusively to these tasks also seem to provide them with

---

[9]For a brief description of Dusun conceptions of the supernatural and the activities of male ritual specialists, see Williams, 1965.

[10]See Merton, 1957a, for discussions of the social functions of status-role.

[11]For a comparative discussion of clubs, see Webster, 1908, and Hsu, 1963.

[12]Bohannan (1963: 154) says that "social groupings based on sex are rare" and notes that the criterion of marital state usually also applies in accepting members to such groups.

[13]See Schurtz, 1902.

[14]This statement is an estimate. For a discussion, see Simmons, 1945; Hickman, 1962; J. Brown, 1963; and Textor, 1967.

substantial freedom from routine tasks. Thus, men in such cultures actually spend only a small proportion of their time working, since the conduct of war or religious ritual does not occupy great amounts of time in everyday life in a majority of human cultures.[15]

When clubs occur in a culture they usually take one of two forms. A club may be wholly inclusive, that is, be composed of all of the men or all the women in a society, without regard to other status-roles. Clubs may also be highly exclusive, with only a select number of men or women.[16] Whether clubs are inclusive or exclusive, they are focused almost exclusively upon either sacred activities, that is, concerned with the supernatural, or secular activities, or are concerned with the nonmystical and nonmagical. Clubs focused upon sacred activities almost always conduct their affairs in secrecy, with nonmembers facing severe punishment, or even death, if they are caught observing ceremonies or sacred objects. Clubs focused upon secular activities usually make a point of public displays of their special concerns. On occasion, in some cultures, the clubs which ordinarily are secretive stage public activities, while secular clubs sometimes hold secret meetings.

Among Central Australian native cultures such as the Arunta all married men form an inclusive, sacred club. Similar inclusive, sacred clubs are found widely in West Africa, particularly among cultures now in the nations of Nigeria, Liberia, Sierra Leone, and the Republic of the Congo. In these areas, particularly in Sierra Leone and Liberia, women also have formed inclusive, sacred clubs that rival men's clubs in social prestige and political power. The Temne, Limba, and Mende of Sierra Leone and the Kpelle of Liberia have required both boys and girls, on completion of their puberty rituals (see below),

to become members of sacred, inclusive clubs for males or females.[17] In these cultures, a substantial amount of particular kinds of cultural information, especially information concerning magic, ritual, and the supernatural, is made available to children only through the inclusive, sacred clubs.

Inclusive, secular clubs were formed by many of the American Plains Indians, particularly the Cheyenne, Crow, Kiowa, and Wind River Shoshone societies. These clubs were open to all males, without regard to their age or marital status, so long as they expressed concern with fighting their best in time of war.[18]

Males in Northwest Coast American Indian societies, such as the Kwakiutl, and among the Pueblo Indians of the American Southwest, including the Hopi and Zuni, formed exclusive sacred clubs concerned essentially with magic, sacred ritual, and the supernatural.[19]

Among the Hopi and Zuni, children are led by adults to believe there are named supernatural beings, termed *katcina* (or *kachina*), who control rainfall and crop fertility and appear as masked ceremonial figures at certain times of the year. The *katcina* figures are adult males who are members of a *kiva*, or exclusive sacred club, generally concerned with maintaining the well-being of their community through magical and religious ceremonies. Boys between 8 and 10 years old are subjected by masked and elaborately costumed *katcina* figures to a public initiation ritual. Boys are sponsored by ceremonial "fathers" and are prepared for their ordeal by tales recounting the powers and deeds of the feared supernaturals and are reminded that *katcina* beings have carried rude and ignorant children off to the "other world." Then, the boys to be initiated into the *kiva* are taken to the entrance of the *kiva* structure and publicly beaten by *katcina* figures. Four days after their public whippings, boys are taken into the *kiva* structure with their ceremonial fathers, where

---

[15]Textor (1967: 160-161) reports from a 400-culture sample that only 41 cultures appear extremely bellicose and regularly seek warfare, while another 46 cultures exhibit only "moderate" or "negligible" bellicosity toward other societies. Data of the amount of bellicosity in the remaining 313 cultures of the sample could not be ascertained from the ethnographic literature.

[16]Clubs also have been classified as "voluntary" and "involuntary" in type (Hsu, 1963: 207).

[17]For discussions of Kpelle inclusive, secret clubs, see Gibbs, 1962, 1965; Welmers, 1949.

[18]For discussions of Cheyenne inclusive, secular clubs, see Grinnell, 1915, 1923; Hoebel, 1960.

[19]For a discussion of Kwakiutl exclusive, secret clubs, see Boas, 1895. For the Hopi, see Titiev, 1944.

the unmasked *katcina* figures dance and sing a ceremonial welcome to the new *kiva* members. Here the initiates learn that they have been severely beaten and thoroughly frightened by their own fathers and brothers.

Exclusive secular clubs are found widely distributed in the Melanesian culture region. For instance, the *Suai* of Bougainville Island, in the Solomon Islands, have male clubs concerned primarily with providing members with regular public feasts, at which great amounts of scarce foods are consumed.[20]

Clubs may also be *corporate groups*, that is, social groups that legally acquire and hold property in the form of land, ritual gear, and scarce economic goods transmitted from generation to generation in the name of the club. As corporate entities, depending on a local legal system, clubs may have a social position that entitles them to special protection, favored treatment, and privileges not accorded to other, non-kin groups.

All cultures use designations for social categories made up of persons at the same stage, or time, of their life cycles. There is great variation between cultures in designations used for life cycle stages. The term *age-grade* refers to the categories of people recognized by cultures as being at the same point ("baby," "old man," "adolescent") in their lives. Such collectivities of persons have no real social identity or corporate functions.

However, some cultures have formed *age-sets*, or social groups based on the principle of recruitment of persons of the same age, without regard to their kinship relations. The crucial distinction between an age-grade and an age-set lies in the fact that when they occur, age-sets are corporate social groups in which the major criterion of membership is chronological age. The use of age as a basis for status-role behavior is found in all cultures. But the forming of corporate, non-kin, exclusive social groups based solely on age is a practice found in less than 5 percent of all cultures. In one survey of cultural features (Murdock, 1957) only 23 of 547 cultures were

Model, Hopi mud head katcina (1969). (Courtesy Museum of Northern Arizona.)

noted as possessing age-sets.[21] Approximately three-quarters of the 23 cultures possessing age-sets are located in Africa, with the remainder in other world culture regions. In Africa, where only 15 percent of all cultures have age-sets,

---

[20]For a description of Suai exclusive, secular clubs, see Oliver, 1955.

[21]See Murdock, 1957, 1967; Coult and Habenstein, 1965.

Hopi katcina dance (date unknown). (Courtesy Museum of Northern Arizona, Neil Judd Collection.)

Kikuyu girls, Kenya (date unknown). (Courtesy American Museum of Natural History.)

such groups are most common among East African cultures, such as the *Nandi* and *Kikuyu*. Despite the low incidence of age-sets among all human cultures, such corporate, non-kin groups play a vital role in enculturation in the societies in which they occur.

For instance, among the Nandi of Kenya, males are grouped into a number of age-sets.[22] The first age-set is comprised of all boys under 12 years old. Boys advance to the second age-set after an initiation ritual. Such rituals are held once every 7 or 8 years. Newly initiated boys become "junior warriors" and for 4 years are subordinate to a third, or "senior warrior," age-set. At the end of 4 or more years, on the "retirement" of their seniors, the junior age-set advances

[22]For a description of Nandi age-sets, see Hollis, 1909. For a comparison of some other East African age-sets, see Prins, 1953.

Kikuyu boys, Kenya (date unknown). (Courtesy American Museum of Natural History.)

to become the senior warrior age-set. Retiring age-set warriors are permitted to marry and begin a routine of daily life and work, generally free of the demands of warfare and keeping internal order in their society.

After their marriages, Nandi males progress steadily through a series of additional age-sets, each with greater prestige, political and economic powers, and corporate functions; as members of an "old man" age-set, Nandi males can finally hold ultimate social authority.

Among the *Zulu* of South Africa age-sets are formed and function in ways similar to those of the Nandi, except that the organization of age-sets is very closely controlled by the Zulu king.[23] After their initiation, all the members of a junior warrior age-set from a local community report to the king's community, where with junior warrior age-sets from other communities they are organized into a special fighting unit, numbering several thousand men.

Zulu "armies" are formed of many such fighting age-sets. A Zulu age-set remains on duty as a fighting unit for approximately 10 years. Then all of the men of an age-set are released by the king to return to their local communities and are permitted to marry, have families, and assume the age-status of Zulu "elder," a term referring to all Zulu males from about 25 to 65 years of age. At 65 the men of the "elder" age-set become Zulu "ancestors," that is, are formally retired from active participation in the daily affairs of their communities.

Thus, Nandi and Zulu age-sets function as the basic units of military organization, aid in maintenance of internal order, and serve as units for large-scale labor. In addition, despite their somewhat different definitions of age for membership, age-sets in these societies become the basis of formal local government. In both societies, age-sets also function as a "law group," that is, as a means to protect the personal rights of members; a personal dispute in Nandi and Zulu society between members of different age-sets or with a kinsman becomes a dispute involving

---

[23]For a description of and references to Zulu age-sets, see Service, 1963.

whole age-sets. In addition to these functions, Nandi and Zulu age-sets are also charged with responsibility for conduct of certain special rituals concerned with warfare and safety. Thus, for Nandi and Zulu boys, direct access to most knowledge concerning defense, law, government, and political actions is confined to understanding gained as members of age-set groups.

Among the Nyakyusa of Tanzania, the organization of age-sets is considerably less concerned with warfare and internal peace-keeping activities.[24] At about 6 years of age boys join an age-set ranging in age up to 11 or 12 years. Until they become 12 years old, boys of an age-set spend most of each day together, tending herds of their fathers' cattle. At age 12 boys join another age-set, which lives together in a separate "boys' village." Boys return to parental households only for their meals. The remainder of their time is spent working in their fathers' gardens and in various social activities centered upon the "boys' village." Life in an age-set village is highly organized and centers upon individuals learning to work closely with others. When the members of an Nyakyusa age-set village are between 20 and 25 years old, they begin to marry and bring wives to the village, where permanent households are established. At the time a man marries, his father deeds him garden land. A married man no longer works for his father as a garden laborer and regularly takes meals in his new household.

When all or most members of an age-set village have married and in a period of 10 or so years from the time of the last marriage, the fathers of sons living in the age-set village hand over to the age-set all governmental powers and the final responsibility for internal village affairs. A few years after this time, the young sons of the members of the age-set village begin to set up their own age-set community near the age-set village of their fathers. Thus, in Nyakyusa society, the age-set takes on social functions often associated with kin groups in other cultures. Too, for older boys it supplants the nuclear

family in daily social life and becomes the central focus of the social organization, which is the dominant feature of adult life.

The Ngoni of Malawi separate all boys at the appearance of their "second teeth," that is, 6 or 7 years old, and place them in an age-set dormitory located within their community.[25] Boys live and eat in the dormitory until they marry or become seriously ill. Ngoni age-set dormitories function as residential "schools" for regular, formal instruction in war, economic, and ritual activities. Too, boys are instructed by their seniors in the age-set dormitory in the proper ways of social and personal deference and to comprehend that, in Ngoni society, age and physical strength are the principal criteria of public decision making and authority.

The transition to life in an age-set is generally an abrupt one, whether among the Nandi, Zulu, Nyakyusa, or the Ngoni. In each society, young boys are well fed and cared for and are described by trained observers as being socially confident to the point of being "impudent" (Read, 1968: 49). In the first months after joining the age-set, boys in each of the age-set cultures described here have to adjust quickly to being regularly hungry, since only their age-set seniors eat well and fully, to being punished regularly for talking out of turn, and to a nearly complete lack of adult protection and concern for their physical and emotional well-being. Ngoni men view age-set dormitory life as a primary way to ensure that boys learn traditional Ngoni culture without the "soft" and "unmanly" influence of Ngoni women. Similarly, Nandi, Zulu, and Nyakyusa males justify age-set life as the best preparation of boys for full knowledge of and participation in adult life.

In a comparative study of the forms and functions of age-sets, Eisenstadt (1965: 54) advanced the hypothesis that such groups occur in societies in which the regular allocation and distribution of status-roles is not based on membership in kinship groups. At first glance, such a hypothesis appears to be a useful one. It seems logical, in

---

[24]For a description of Nyakyusa age-sets, see Wilson, 1951.

[25]For a discussion of Ngoni age-sets, see Read, 1956, 1960, and 1968.

Western European and American terms, that when status-roles are not available in and through kinship groups, then a significant social alternative, such as age-sets, would be developed by a society. However, this logic does not tend to hold when a study is made of the available comparative data of status-role. Most societies allocate and distribute status-roles outside of kinship groups without forming or using age-sets. Hence, Eisenstadt's hypothesis is not sustained, perhaps because his work has not attended to the broader theoretical question of the ways *informal social groups* can also be involved in the allocation, distribution, and learning of status-roles in a society. Some examples of informal social groups in human societies would be children's play groups, neighborhoods, work teams, feasting societies, craft groups, "gangs," and "blood brotherhoods." Informal social groups are usually formed only for brief periods, for attainment of certain limited social aims.[26] Such groups usually function with the cultural values and norms of behavior widely employed in the culture in which the informal group exists. Individuals voluntarily become part of such informal social groups because they share the special interests or preferences manifested by the group. When children become part of informal social groups, they have a special and unofficial opportunity for learning important features of their local culture as these are employed by older members of the group in fulfillment and attainment of their special interests. Hence, informal social groups can occupy an important place in an enculturation process, since they make it possible for children to have repeated access to cultural content generally used by adults and without the special hazards of discipline, censure, and authority for misbehavior or failures to learn often imposed on children by kinship and other formal social groups such as churches and schools.

Thus, in not considering the ways that in-formal social groups can be involved in the allocation, distribution, and learning of status-roles in a society, Eisenstadt apparently missed the point that age-sets have other social counterparts that can provide individuals access to and knowledge concerning status-roles important in a society.

Ritual transitions in status-role. Between the ages of 11 and 15 years, children experience fundamental biological changes involving sexual maturation. The gradual changes, which are summed up by the term *puberty,* are taken in most cultures to mark a point between the status-roles of childhood and adulthood. However, the biological changes that occur in puberty may be socially recognized by a culture in varying degrees and forms. In some cultures, such as on the central Pacific Islands of the Samoa group, there are few formal social or ritual recognitions of sexual maturity. The Samoan transition from the status-roles of childhood to those of adulthood is marked by a gradual development of new activities and concerns and has no periods of induced social crises or personal stress.[27] A similar lack of concern for special social or ritual recognitions of puberty is also found in many other Pacific Island cultures, as well as in many native North American Indian cultures.[28]

However, cultures in other world areas, including some American Indian cultures such as the Hopi and Zuni, ritually observe puberty for one or for both sexes. These observances do not always occur at the onset or even during the actual time of puberty, since cultural definitions of the point in time when children take on the status-roles of adults may not at all coincide with the specific biological changes occurring in puberty.

The ritual acts used by cultures to symbolize the transition from childhood to adulthood status-roles vary in the degree of their complexity, public drama, and the amount and duration of

---

[26]In contrast, formal social groups exist over long periods of time and have four distinctive features: (1) a set of clearly stated group aims, (2) specific controls for behavior of members, (3) high valuation on "proper" intergroup relationships, and (4) expectation of inclusive personal knowledge by each member concerning all other members.

[27]See Mead, 1928.
[28]While many Pacific island cultures practice *superincision* (a limited form of circumcision) on boys sometime between infancy and marriage, this act does not appear to be associated with puberty or to be a ritual indication of the transition from childhood to adulthood. For a discussion of the ritual treatment of boys in a Pacific island culture, see Gifford, 1929.

personal pain imposed upon children subjected to these ceremonial and symbolic events. It is not uncommon for such ritual acts to involve a form of the symbolic "death" of infancy and childhood status-roles as a quite socially limited and culturally unproductive state and the symbolic "re-birth" of children in the status-roles of adults, able to fully enter into the affairs and engage in concerns of adult society. To illustrate some of the ways status-role transitions may be formally defined in a culture, a brief description will be given of the ritual acts used by the Arunta of Central Australia to mark the onset of adulthood.[29]

Arunta initiation rituals. Arunta boys usually undergo the first of a complex series of initiation rituals between 10 and 12 years of age. On occasion, when a boy has been regularly rude and disrespectful to the older men of his local group, he may be made to wait until he is between 14 and 16 years old before undergoing the first of the ritual acts marking a transition to adult status-roles.

The appearance of a boy's pubic or facial hair and other physical signs of sexual development are used by the Arunta as criteria for eligibility for initiation. Most Arunta boys have only vague general ideas concerning the rituals they face, since most of these events are conducted in secret and are rarely discussed by adults. As the time for initiation approaches, a boy may begin to boast to his friends that the "old men" will never catch him and that he is not afraid of whatever they will do to him. However, most boys are reported to look forward to the initiation rituals as an opportunity to gain adult freedoms and privileges.

Arunta initiation rituals follow very traditional forms, which vary only slightly from one generation to the next. The rules and practices governing these rituals are said by Arunta to have been handed down from mythical ancestors.

Among the Arunta the entire series of initi-

ation rituals follows the broad pattern of events that occur at the death of an aged and respected person. Thus, as a boy is led from the camp by the old men, women will wail for him as they do at death, while "bullroarers" (a flat board rapidly whirled at the end of a string) sound in the distance, to represent the voices of spirits waiting to "swallow" the novice and then vomit him up again to be reborn, as is believed to happen at the death of an individual.

Arunta boys tend to be passive subjects in the course of initiation rituals. They also are more nearly "pupils" and "learners" during their initiation than at any other time during their lives. The training and learning at the time of Arunta initiation centers upon boys learning the broad outline of secret knowledge of adult males, particularly ideas concerned with myth, magic, and special rituals for increase of sacred totems. Some details of secret knowledge are also transmitted over many years following completion of the initiation rituals.

The Arunta ritual transition in male status-roles involves four major events, occurring over a period of several years. First, a novice is taken away from his home camp by a group of old men, as women wail and the bullroarers sound. When the old men first enter a camp, a boy is told by a parent that a mythical python has come to swallow his foreskin and he is encouraged to take refuge with his mother, while his wailing adult female relations take up spears, form a protective ring about the boy and his mother, and threaten the old men. As the men approach the boy, the women flee in mock terror and then finally prostrate themselves, wailing as they do at the time of death.

The boy is led by the old men to a location used regularly to hide sacred totems. Here, fully initiated men draw blood from their arm veins, then paint the novice with the blood and ritually drink some of it. It is believed the "blood rite" gives an Arunta boy longevity, courage, and new strength. The ritual is also said to symbolically represent and therefore show the presence of mythical clan ancestors. Then, in rapid succession, a boy may have his nasal septum pierced, a middle upper front tooth knocked out, and be

---

[29]For some other descriptions of ritual observances of status-role transitions from childhood to adulthood, see Radcliffe-Brown, 1922; Gibbs, 1965: 197-240; Dozier, 1966: 57-65; Dozier, 1970: 140-142 and 155-162; Richards, 1956.

painted with a solution of red ochre. Arunta sometimes perform the septum-piercing operation before the first initiation ritual to save the great pain which comes with the tooth knocking blow following the piercing operation. The septum hole is said to be made to enhance a boy's manly looks. The practice of tooth evulsion is said to create a permanent look on the boy's face which resembles certain dark rain clouds and so to magically enhance his influence and control over the rainfall so vital in the desert life of the Arunta.

Patterns depicting clan totems are drawn in the red ochre smeared over the novice's body. The ochre is said to symbolically represent clan blood and strength. At the conclusion of these ritual acts a novice is given some general instructions in secret lore and knowledge, then sent with other novices to live in seclusion. During the 9 to 12 months of seclusion, novices must engage in certain ritual acts and avoid social contacts with their parents and female relatives.

The second stage of Arunta initiation rituals begins when novices are led back from seclusion by the old men to their home camp for a "tossing rite" and "presentation of gifts." The tossing rite involves male adults throwing the novice high into the air four times and then throwing burning coals and sticks over the head of a novice, as well as over the heads of the women dancing about the boy. Arunta believe that these acts symbolize the growing of a novice to the vigor and strength of manhood. Arunta also believe these acts express symbolically the conventional antagonism between the two generations (old and young) involved in the ritual.

Older men begin the second part of the initiation ritual by drawing blood from their arm veins and using it to secure down feathers on their bodies, which are placed in ways to denote sacred totem patterns. Then, novices are seated and covered to keep them from seeing the totemic acts conducted by the old men. However, novices are kept informed on the meanings of the songs they hear during the totemic rites. After this act, the covering is removed and the novice is permitted to see some of the ritual

Australian native male ritual specialist (date unknown). (Courtesy American Museum of Natural History.)

dancing by the old men and some of the major totemic emblems of their clan.

Then, just before a ritual circumcision is performed, all the other men make a path for the novice while holding smoking tree boughs and singing sacred songs. Several younger adult men kneel at the end of the path and form a "human table" on which the novice is circumcised. After his foreskin has been cut, the novice is led back to his seclusion camp, while the main Arunta camp picks up and moves some distance away, as is the custom at the death of an adult. Before the novice is led off to a second period of seclusion he is ceremonially presented two bullroarers and is allowed to sound them for the first time. A novice remains in seclusion until his penis heals. During this time, old men may again cut their arm veins and cover a novice's head and

Australian native totemic ritual dance (date unknown), Cundeelee, West Australia, Ngatajara. (Courtesy American Museum of Natural History.)

Australian native ritual bloodletting (date unknown), Laverton, Australia. (Courtesy American Museum of Natural History.)

chest with their blood to symbolize the boy's entrance into adult life.

When a circumcision scar is fully formed, a novice is permitted to return to his home camp, where he is ceremonially welcomed as an adult by his parents and close relatives. Immediately after his return home a novice is taken by close male relatives on a journey of the water holes and totemic locations in the countryside claimed by his local group and clan.

Before the third stage of ritual transition from childhood to adulthood, a boy is given from 12 to 24 months of regular, secret instruction in the magic, myths, and symbols of his local group and clan. These instructions are given in intensive sessions by old men especially knowledgeable in Arunta lore and belief providing examples of dances, showing objects, recounting folktales, and singing songs.

At the close of this period of instruction, a novice leaves his home camp, to the wailing sounds of women and low rumble of the distant bullroarers. Once again, the novice lives in seclusion, until completion of all of the third stage rituals. The third portion of the initiation process begins after a lengthy period of dancing by old men. Then, a novice is again led to a table formed by kneeling younger men, laid on

Australian native men form a "human table" for use in circumcision ritual (date unknown), Warburton Range, Australia. (Courtesy American Museum of Natural History.)

his back, and subjected to subincision, a surgical operation in which the urethra is slit open along most of the length of the penis. The novice is then placed face up on the ground, while the men cut open their own subincision scars and dance across the prostrate boy, dripping blood on him to symbolize his rebirth as an adult male. Arunta are said to believe that the penis represents the mythical python, while the incisure cut represents the uterus of the mythical "Fertility Mother." Thus, the subincised penis of a novice symbolically represents in the same body part the male and female sex organs. Arunta also are said to believe that the blood from a subincisure cut symbolizes both the blood of afterbirth and of menstruation; covering the prostrate initiate with reopened subincision wounds of initiated

men symbolizes his "birth" into adult life.[30]

On completion of the subincision ritual, a novice returns to his home camp. For the next 12 months he is given further special instructions in myth, magic, and ritual. During this time there may be other brief ritual acts, including a repetition of the "blood rite" used in the first stage of the initiation process, ritual feasting to properly introduce the novice to ancestor spirits, and a ritual during which the most sacred totem objects (djilbilba boards) are revealed and explained to the novice. It is common for a novice to reopen his subincisure wound during these

[30]For some recent discussions and reviews of other meanings of the subincision ritual, see Cawte, Djagamara, and Barrett, 1966; Singer and DeSole, 1967; Cawte, 1968. For a psychoanalytic interpretation of the subincision ritual, see Bettelheim, 1954.

rituals and to join in the dancing by the initiated men.

The fourth and final stage in the ritual transition from childhood to adulthood for Arunta boys involves a ritual of cicatrization, or scarring, of their bodies. The novice lies face down while older men make three to twelve broad cuts across his back. This ritual may be repeated a second and third time, with cicatrices being made on the novice's upper arms and thighs and across his lower abdomen. Healed and well-formed scars are signs that a novice has completed all four stages of initiation. Arunta boys are usually permitted to marry after the healing of the scars from the cicatrization ritual. However, there are other ceremonies at which he is permitted to be only an onlooker. Too, a novice is prohibited from attending other ritual acts until fully knowledgeable about sacred lore.

Arunta boys also may be subjected to a variety of other initiation ritual practices. It is not uncommon for a novice to have fingernails pulled off and to have his head severely cut or bitten bloody during the first and second stages of the ritual transition.

Arunta girls also undergo a series of formal ritual acts marking the transition from childhood to adulthood status-roles. This initiation process is less formal and dramatic and is not as prolonged as the one for boys. Too, girls receive no direct instruction in sacred knowledge and generally the entire community does not become involved in the rituals marking the initiation of a girl.

At the first signs of puberty, particularly the appearance of either pubic hair or at the time of first menstruation, a girl leaves to spend a week in seclusion at a shelter built some distance away from her home camp. During her seclusion a girl usually observes several taboos on food, listens to the stories and tales of an older woman who visits with her, and receives instructions concerning sexual and marriage behavior.

At the end of the period of seclusion, a girl bathes and is then ritually decorated by older women with body paint, shells, and ornaments and led back to her home camp with songs, shouts, and cries describing her new status-roles as a

woman. If a girl has not been given in marriage before the ritual seclusion period, arrangements are made immediately after her return home to secure her marriage. If she has been given in marriage before her seclusion, this social fact is formally confirmed by handing her over to her husband and his kin. This handing-over act can involve ritual sexual intercourse between the girl and a group of her husband's male kin. If arrangements for marriage have been made but not formally confirmed by public announcements, a girl may be "captured" by her future husband and several of the men he calls "brother" while she is out gathering food. Then these men may have sexual intercourse with the girl to confirm her adult status-roles.

On her return after a week of seclusion, a girl who has not been given in marriage, either formally or informally, may undergo a further series of ritual acts of initiation while waiting for marriage arrangements. Then, shortly after return from her seclusion, a girl is led back into the bush by a small group of older women and men. Here, after a series of brief rituals, she will be subjected to a ceremonial cutting of either her vulva, perineum, or hymen. After this act is completed a girl is decorated with red ochre, white clay, and string and shell necklaces. Before returning to the main camp she may have her nasal septum ritually pierced and be subjected to a ceremony of cicatrization to mark her new status-roles as a woman.[31]

Although other rituals take place in a woman's life, particularly at the time of childbirth, the rituals which occur at puberty emphasize a state of sexual maturity and ability to bear children and are seen by the Arunta to mark the formal transition from dependent daughter and child to generally independent wife and woman.

Studies of initiation rituals. Wherever ritual acts, particularly those involving formal public drama and severe personal pain, are found associated with the social recognition of puberty,

---

[31]It should be noted that initiation rituals for girls may vary between local groups of Arunta in the time sequence involved and rituals used. There is great variation in such rituals among Australian aboriginal societies.

a general cultural theme (see Chapter Nine) seems involved—a recognition of the transition from childhood to adulthood. However, since many cultures do not formally recognize this transition, there remains a substantial question of why there would be such a wide range of ritual practices involved in the way a common human biological fact is viewed by different cultures.

Cohen has considered this question by studying the social functions and meanings of the various forms of ritual acts that occur during the transition from child to adult.[32] Using a research sample of 65 societies, Cohen first classed each society in his sample as (1) concerned with enculturation of children for *social interdependence*, that is, where individuals are prepared emotionally and personally to be "anchored" in kin groups such as lineages and clans, and (2) concerned with enculturation of children for *social independence*, that is, where individuals are prepared to be "anchored" in the nuclear family. Cohen's contextual analysis of ethnographic data for each society in his sample led him to conclude that 28 societies enculturated children for social interdependence (or life anchored in kin groups), while 37 societies enculturated their children for social independence (or life anchored in the nuclear family).[33] Cohen's contextual analysis of ethnographic data also revealed that formal initiation rituals marking a status-role transition between childhood and adulthood were used by 18 (or approximately 65 percent) of the 28 societies which enculturate children for social interdependence. In contrast, Cohen found that 36 of 37 societies which enculturate children for social independence do not use rituals to mark the status-role transition from childhood to adulthood.

On the basis of Cohen's analysis it could be concluded that the wide scope of human concern over status-role transitions at puberty, ranging from an almost total lack of interest among Samoans to the elaborate ritual dramas and personal pain of the Arunta, may depend upon the

form of the patterns in the social relations subsystem of a culture. In other words, Cohen's data suggest that whether or not a culture socially marks a transition in status-roles from child to adult depends on a position (nuclear family or kin group) a child ordinarily will occupy during his adult social life.

In another comparative study of ritual transitions Brown has suggested, from her analysis of ethnographic descriptions of female initiation rituals in a sample of 75 societies, that formal and ritual observances of a status-roles transition occur when a young girl continues to reside at least half the time in her mother's household after her marriage, that is, when a society practices *uxorilocal* or *bilocal* residence after marriage.[34]

Brown also suggests that, when a society depends heavily upon the work of girls and young women to make a notable contribution to subsistence activities, there will be formal initiation rituals held to mark the transition from the status-roles of girl to woman.

Too, Brown suggests that those few (10 of 75) societies which subject a girl to great pain during status-role transition rituals do so because of a basic need to overcome severe conflicts of sexual identity fostered in female infants and young girls by their acute awareness that the scarce social and material resources on which they depend and therefore greatly desire are usually controlled by adult males.

In another study of ritual transitions in status-roles, Young has made a comparative analysis of the social functions of male initiation rituals which seem to broaden the conclusions offered by Cohen and Brown.[35] Young notes that male initiation rituals appear to be caused by the presence in a society of an exclusively male club or organization, which in turn is caused by a type of "middle level" economic system neither producing great surpluses of goods nor functioning

---

[32]See Cohen, 1964.
[33]Cohen's research sample includes 54 of the cultures listed in Appendix 1 of this text.

[34]See J. Brown, 1963. *Uxorilocal* (or "matrilocal") residence after marriage refers to the practice whereby a newly married couple lives in the household, or domicile, of the wife's family. *Bilocal* residence refers to the practice whereby a newly married couple may choose to live near the parents of either spouse. For a discussion of the problems in use of such classifications, see Bohannan, 1963: 86–99.
[35]See Young, 1962.

close to a survival level, which Young believes to be finally caused in its turn by the physical environment of a culture. Thus, for Young, the presence (or absence) of male initiation rituals, such as those found among the Arunta, depends upon a cause-effect sequence which he postulates as (1) *physical environment type* → (2) *"middle level" of economic production* → (3) *presence of exclusive male organizations* → (4) *use of male initiation rituals at puberty.*

Thus, Brown and Young have extended Cohen's conclusions concerning the social functions of initiation rituals to include other cultural practices including (1) certain marital residence patterns, (2) particular subsistence activities and types, (3) levels of economic organization and activity, (4) the presence of exclusive male organizations, (5) the presence of certain climatic types, and (6) degree of conflict in sexual identity common to a society. Brown's and Young's explanations seem to imply, as does Cohen's, that the reason some cultures do not formally observe a transition from childhood to adulthood is because of a distinct lack of concern with specific cultural patterns such as marital residence practices, subsistence practices, and sex identity conflicts.

Whiting, in his work on the causal effects of climate on ritual circumcision in the status-role transition from child to adult, has provided some indications that there may be further and alternative ways not only of viewing this particular transition but as well to more broadly defining and considering the origins and causal effects of all such ritual transitions.[36]

In a complexly structured argument involving a number of major assumptions concerning the ways certain patterns and climate are interrelated and the ways specific cultural practices, including (1) the practice of a mother and infant sleeping together for a long period during infancy while the father sleeps separately, (2) the practice of a postpartum taboo on sexual intercourse between parents for a year or more after a child's birth, and (3) virilocal residence after marriage, Whiting and his associates have noted statisti-

cally the effects of these factors on the status-role transitions from child to adult.[37]

Whiting (1964) has pointed out that there is a significantly biased geographical distribution of societies in which boys are circumcised during ritual observances of the status-role transition from child to adult; such a ritual practice commonly occurs in the tropical climate zones of Africa and a few Pacific Islands, while it is absent entirely in tropical South America, as well as in North America, and statistically is insignificant as a practice among Eurasian cultures. It is Whiting's belief that the three cultural practices just noted (exclusive MoCh sleeping arrangements, prolonged postpartum sex taboo, virilocal residence) occur together as a basic cultural solution to certain environmental problems which essentially are those found in hot, wet, humid, tropical areas.

In a tightly reasoned presentation based upon statistical analysis of the distribution of these three culture traits, Whiting demonstrates that the fact of the direct association between circumcision and tropical climate is comprehended best by understanding that exclusive MoCh sleeping arrangements seem strongly influenced by the average winter temperatures experienced by a culture, that a prolonged postpartum sex taboo is strongly influenced by protein deficiency in a nursing mother's diet, which in turn is a function of a rainy tropical climate, and that virilocal residence is directly associated with the practice of polygyny (see Chapter Seven), which in turn is directly associated with a prolonged postpartum sex taboo.

Whiting's fundamental theoretical contribution in this work is his basic concern for deriving a new method of understanding the difficult problem of causality in studies of the socialization process.[38] He notes correctly that the correlational method used in socialization studies cannot indicate the *direction* of causation. Whiting also points out that, in research on the social-

---

[36]See Whiting, 1964.

[37]*Virilocal* (or "patrilocal") residence refers to the practice whereby a newly married couple lives in the household, or domicile, of the husband's family.

[38]Whiting first formally expressed this concern in a work on the social functions of male initiation rituals. See Whiting, Kluckhohn, and Anthony, 1958.

ization process, the direction of causation of phenomena must for now rest upon estimates of the "relative plausibility" (Whiting, 1964: 524) of the observer's assumptions made about causal direction. Thus, in the study described, Whiting did not assume that temperature and climate are the *effect* of customs such as MoCh sleeping arrangements, a prolonged postpartum sex taboo, or the practice of virilocal residence at marriage. Any association, notes Whiting, between a climatic variable and a culture trait can only be plausibly interpreted either as an *effect* of climate on the culture trait or as an effect of climate on some other culture trait, or pattern, which in turn has a direct effect upon the trait in question. Thus, Whiting notes it is not reasonable to assume that exclusive MoCh sleeping arrangements cause a tropical climate, or that a postpartum sex taboo causes a rainy tropical climate. Whiting's basic contribution in this work is in the fact that he has proposed a systematic way to think about causation in studies of the socialization process in which some variables such as ecological factors determine or greatly influence the cultural patterns (or traits) associated with them. Whiting's innovative approach, which he has used in other studies, considerably broadens the suggestions for the causes of ritual observances of the transition from childhood to adulthood offered by Cohen, Brown, Young, and others, and may point the way to development of a genuine mathematical (rather than statistical) approach to studies of causation in the process of socialization.

▪ Class and socialization

Individuals behaving with respect to the same polar social positions, that is, status-roles, often develop awareness of their common interests, particularly in contrast to the interests of other individuals. When a large number of persons in a society act upon awareness of their common status-role positions, they may constitute a social class.

The personal interests and awareness that arise from holding similar polar social positions in one society may be quite different in other societies. In many societies such interests center upon the acquisition and use of scarce resources such as food, tools, land, and "money." But classes have also been formed on the basis of shared religious belief and action, or upon the conditions of personal freedom, that is, differentiations between "masters" and "slaves." Classes have been based upon exhibitions of courage in warfare, courtesy, and "handsomeness" of personal appearance.[39] Classes also may "cross-cut" kin groups in a society, as was the case among the Aztec of Mexico, where the "honorary lords" were recruited from all Aztec clans.

Subsistence type and class. On the basis of an analysis of Murdock's (1957; 1967) survey of world ethnographic data, it appears that there is a direct relationship between the major type of subsistence practiced by a culture and the presence of social classes. Among 101 cultures classified by Murdock as "hunting and gathering" in type, that is, cultures in which agriculture is entirely absent or only sporadically practiced, only one culture is noted as having a class system.[40] Among 189 cultures which practice intensive gardening as the major basis of their subsistence, approximately 99 cultures (52 percent of the total) are reported by Murdock to have social classes. Among 117 cultures which derive their major subsistence through plow agriculture, 68 cultures (58 percent of the total) are reported to have social classes; apart from slaves, most of these cultures have three or more social classes.

When data of differentiating individuals as "slaves" and "masters" among hunting-gathering, intensive gardening, and plow agriculture type cultures are included in consideration of a comparative analysis of human social classes, it can be said that two-thirds of hunting-gathering type cultures do not have classes, while social classes occur in more than nine of ten instances in gardening and plow agriculture type cultures. Thus, slavery as a form of human social class differentiation is found more commonly

---

[39]See Richardson, 1940, and Mishkin, 1940, for a description of the kinds of common interests used by the Kiowa, a North American Indian society, to define social classes.
[40]These figures are based on Murdock, 1957. They are changed slightly in Murdock, 1967.

than is the differentiation of freemen into social classes.[41]

Geographic distribution of classes. Another way to view social classes would be to note the geographic distribution of cultures reported by Murdock (1957; 1967) to have social classes among freemen. In the African culture region, 12 percent of all cultures are reported to have a social class system among freemen. Comparable figures for cultures with freemen classes for the Circum-Mediterranean region are 55 percent, for Eurasia 35 percent, for the Pacific Islands 5 percent, for North America 6 percent, and for the South American culture region 7 percent.[42]

There have been several explanations offered for the geographic distribution of social classes and for the direct relationship between cultural subsistence type and the presence of social differentiation by classes. Davis and Moore, following the ideas of Durkheim, have offered a "functional" theory of social class.[43] It is their view that all forms of stratification in a society, whether through classes or differentiation by age-sets, wealth distinctions, or religious or political distinctions, are essential to the basic existence of a society. Davis and Moore believe that the status-roles which are most important to the members of a society and which require the most intensive preparation or training are recognized unconsciously by the members of a society as the ones which must be held by the most qualified individuals. Therefore, Davis and Moore conclude that inequalities of status-roles must exist and that there will be a differential distribution of power, prestige, and income derived from particular status-roles, as a society selectively allots certain status-roles to qualified persons.

Thus, following a "functional" theory of social class, any awareness of common interests by persons in particular polar social positions would not matter in the initial formation of social classes. Rather, a recognition of common personal interests would follow the selection of individuals by the larger society to fill vital status-roles.[44]

This theoretical view by Davis and Moore and by others has produced vigorous debate in sociological journals, extending over a period of two decades.[45] The position most often articulated in contrast is a "conflict theory" of the formation and existence of social class.[46] Based upon and proceeding from modern analyses of the nineteenth century work of Marx and Engels, a conflict interpretation for the existence and distribution of social class in human society views all forms of human social differentiation, including classes, as the result of struggles between competing groups due to their opposing economic interests and aims, which in turn leads to the coercion and domination of one group by another group and hence to the presence of basic social differentiation in a society.

Thus, for conflict theorists, classes in human societies emerge not from recognition of common interests by individuals because they hold similar polar social positions, but because some social groups hold and use more economic power than some other social groups.

A major unresolved problem in a conflict theory for the explanation of the origin and existence of social classes is that the theory fails to adequately explain why, for instance, 20 of a sample of 101 cultures which depend primarily upon a hunting-gathering type subsistence have clear social differentiations based on wealth, but at the same time do not have and have not developed any type of classes. Similarly, a functional theory for the origin and existence of social classes cannot maintain, on the basis of comparative ethnographic data, that unequal rewards are necessary to the basic existence of

[41]Twenty-seven of the sample of 101 hunting-gathering cultures are reported to have differentiated between "freemen" and "slaves." In a total sample of 540 cultures, Murdock (1957) found that approximately 46 percent of the cultures in all geographical regions of the world make social differentiations between freemen and slaves (see Coult and Habenstein, 1965: 28, 522). In contrast, only 168, or approximately 41 percent, of a sample of 407 hunting-gathering, gardening, and plow agriculture cultures differentiate among freemen by social classes.

[42]These figures are based on data abstracted by Coult and Habenstein (1965: 27) from Murdock, 1957. Again, these figures exclude cultures which hold slaves.

[43]See Davis and Moore, 1945. See also Mayer, 1955; Reissman, 1959; Lipset and Bendix, 1959.

[44]K. Davis, 1949: 367.

[45]For a summary, see Wrong, 1959. See also Tumin, 1953; Pfautz, 1953; Lasswell, 1965.

[46]For a discussion of conflict theory of class, see Dahrendorf, 1959; Lenski, 1966.

any society. Analysis of Murdock's (1957; 1967) ethnographic data clearly indicates that there are 234 cultures of a world sample of 565 cultures, or 41 percent of the total number, which do not recognize or use social differentiations in the form of social classes (either among freemen or between freemen and slaves), age-sets, wealth distinctions, or distinctions between a nobility and commoners.

Lenski has attempted to incorporate comparative historical and modern ethnographic data in a synthesis of the "functional" and "conflict" theories concerning the origins and distribution of human social differentiations, including class.[47] On the basis of his comparative research, Lenski believes that both the functional and conflict ideas may be acceptable, since both theories present only partial views of a very complex situation. Lenski notes there is abundant observational evidence that individuals in all cultures will always choose their own or their group's interests over those of other persons or groups, particularly when faced with a scarcity of economic resources (food, land, tools, or money). This means, says Lenski, that individuals inevitably are in a continuing struggle with one another, with the struggle finally being mediated by common interest groups. Lenski also notes that individuals are really not equally endowed biologically and culturally for success in either attaining or defending their self-interest with respect to scarce economic goods. Because of these factors in human life, Lenski believes human societies have come to have the capacity to vary greatly in their forms of social differentiation. Lenski also believes that the basic forms of social differentiation become considerably elaborated upon, particularly in social classes, whenever there is an unequal amount of "power" accessible to or placed in the hands of some individuals to affect the distribution of economic surpluses created in a society. This is especially so, Lenski says, when individuals with great power join together in common self-interest groups. Hence, the essence of social stratification, in Lenski's synthesis of functional and

conflict ideas, is that personal power and privilege arising from a control of substantial economic surpluses leads to significant social differences.[48] Lenski's ideas have not been widely applied in research studies of class differentiations.

However, research evidences which have been derived in the past from measuring social class differences within cultures, through observations and tests of relative occupational and personal prestige, indicate that, in a contemporary urban, industrial society such as the United States, class differentiations are very important facts in social life and particularly in gaining access to learning the patterns of American culture.

Life chances and class. There are strong indications, regardless of how social class is measured or defined, that opportunities to stay alive, to be born alive, and to grow to adulthood, are directly related to relative social class position; there seems little question now that, at least in American and Western European societies, there is a marked decrease in the infant death rate with increasing family income and therefore with differential class position.[49] Both the frequency and duration of disabling and crippling infant and child illnesses are also demonstrably related, in the United States, to family income and therefore to social class position of the parents. And, the general state of American infant and child physical well-being, that is, the state of nourishment and therefore the potential for growth and development, are directly affected by the social classes of parents.

For a contemporary American child, the opportunity to learn the culture, particularly in formal educational settings such as schools and

---

[47]See Lenski, 1966; 1970.

[48]Thus, Lenski (1970: 496) defines class as "(1) An aggregation or group of people whose overall status is similar; (2) an aggregation or group of people who stand in a similar position with respect to some specific resource which affects their access to power, privilege or prestige."

[49]For details of data relating class and factors of social and cultural life, see Barber, 1957; Bendix and Lipset, 1953; K. Davis, 1949; Deutsch, Katz, and Jensen, 1968; Grey, 1969; Hollingshead and Redlich, 1958; Jackson, 1968; Kahl, 1957; Lipset and Bendix, 1959; K. Mayer, 1955; Myers and Bean, 1968; Reiss, Duncan, Hatt, and North, 1961; Reissman, 1959; Svalastoga, 1959, 1964, 1965; Tumin, 1967; Warner, 1953, 1960.

colleges, is directly affected by occupations of parents and hence by parents' social class. There is a clear relationship in the United States between amount of adult schooling, occupational achievement, and annual income. This relationship, which generally results in those persons with the least schooling being concentrated in the least desirable and lowest prestige manual labor and farm occupations, all with the lowest annual incomes, means that children of such parents have less opportunity for formal education, especially beyond the lower primary school grades. In American society, the highest annual incomes and lifetime earning expectations generally appear to be restricted to persons completing four or more years of college education. The relationship between parental education, occupation, and income also seems to significantly affect the development of a wide range of infants' and children's abilities and potentials (see Chapters Two and Four) and particularly those apparently vital in further learning of complex social and cultural information. In other words, whether American children develop some individual potentials and abilities to learn appears directly related to their relative social positions, which are generally dependent in turn upon the social class positions of parents. Too, as noted in Chapter Five, class position contributes directly to the kinds and degrees of social and cultural isolation experienced by children. When a social class position has produced long-term social or cultural isolation, persisting over several familial generations, consistently different forms of social and cultural behavior can arise, particularly with respect to cultural ideology, forms of kinship and kin groups, and differing judgments of the worth of some kinds of social behavior, such as sexual and "criminal" activities, as well as in "taste" for dress, personal adornment, and displays of personal power and prestige.[50] Statistics of arrests in the United States for deviant sexual and criminal behavior

clearly indicate that persons with the least education and annual income have a significantly greater chance of arrest and conviction than "middle-class" citizens. The research evidence of the relationships between social class and "life chances" were noted early in the present century by scholars concerned with studies of American and European societies.[51] Comments concerning differential life chances in particular social classes led to increasing attention being paid to research seeking to relate social class and the process of socialization. In most such research, the focus of concern has been upon the consequences for the individual of having matured in nuclear family and kin group settings in specific social classes. It has been assumed in much of this research that, since nuclear families and kin groups will have the economic resources, knowledge, and power typical of other families and kin groups in the same class, children will occupy essentially the same social class positions as their parents. Too, it has been assumed in such research that the enculturation of children by adult members of a nuclear family and kin group involves the transmission of particular cultural and social knowledge and styles of personal behavior usual for the social classes of adults.

Research on social class and socialization. Steere has noted that, in the United States, concern over relationships between social class and the socialization process extended over a period or more than 100 years before any systematic attempts were made by scholars to define and study such phenomena. A 1929 publication by Lynd and Lynd concerning life in an American community contained five chapters on enculturation in the "family" and schools, with particular reference to the ways social class affected a child's life chances. This research may be said to be the first to give specific attention to reporting and analyzing empirical data for specific evidence of relationships between social class and cultural transmission. This work was followed by more detailed empirical studies of social class and the socialization process made by

---

[50]Some descriptions of class differences in American society may be found in Davis, Gardner, and Gardner, 1941; Dollard, 1949; Gallaher, 1961; Hollingshead, 1949; Lynd and Lynd, 1929, 1937; Warner and Lunt, 1941; Warner and others, 1949; West, 1949.

[51]For instance, see Weber, 1946; Veblen, 1927.

Anderson (1936), Davis and Dollard (1940), Warner and Lunt (1941), Davis and others (1941), Davis and Havighurst (1946), Havighurst and Taba (1949), and Havighurst and Neugarten (1955).

A key research method in empirical studies of relations between class and socialization from 1929 through the late 1950's was to contrast the specific enculturation practices of different classes within one community. Thus, Davis and Havighurst (1946, 1947) and Ericson (1946), in a study based on a sample of 100 white and black lower and middle-class mothers in Chicago, noted that middle-class American families, whether white or black, were inflexible in following a rigid schedule of infant and child feeding, weaning, toilet training, and discipline, while lower class white and black families were flexible in regard to such enculturation practices. These data of class differences in enculturation were interpreted, in the context of psychological theories prevailing in the 1940's, as tending to produce children with markedly different personalities. Thus, middle-class children raised under inflexible schedules of enculturation were said to become very demanding, self-assertive, and rigid adults, particularly with respect to control of their sexual and aggressive impulses. In contrast, lower class children enculturated under a more flexible schedule of training than middle-class children were believed to become adults with a more spontaneous ability to cope successfully with their aggressive and sexual impulses.

A 1946 analysis by Green of the kinds and levels of children's anxiety resulting from a concern with securing love through successful performances according to parental expectations concluded that middle-class children, when compared to lower class children, were made more neurotic by middle-class enculturation practices. Green assumed that his conclusion was true because it seemed clear from the earlier empirical research concerning relations between social class and the socialization process, and particularly enculturation practices in American society, that middle-class parents focused upon maintaining very tight controls for sexual and aggressive impulses in order to aid their child in gain-

ing a more successful status-role achievement and greater mobility between social classes. Green also assumed that lower class children were free from most impulse control training because of a lack of any adult concern with success in status-role achievement. Hence, Green concluded that lower class children were much less anxious and neurotic because they were not made to conform to parental concerns about tightly controlled sexual and aggressive impulse controls. The conclusions drawn by Green were strongly supported by data of American social class and enculturation reported by Davis and Havighurst and by Ericson. Thus, by extension of this argument, a relationship between class and the socialization process seemed clearly defined.

However, a study by Sewell (1952), based on interviews with the mothers of 165 rural Wisconsin children, concerning relationships between reported early childhood enculturation practices and observations of later behavior by mothers and teachers, concluded that it was entirely unwarranted to make any inferential jump from supposedly class-determined enculturation practices to later childhood behavior and personality characteristics. In 1954, Maccoby, Gibbs, and their co-workers presented the results of a study of 198 "upper middle" and 174 "upper lower" mothers living in the Boston metropolitan area; the study was especially concerned with the relationship between social class position and enculturation practices. This work found that parents in the "upper middle" class were more "permissive and less severe" than parents of the "upper lower" class. These data, which were a full reversal of data offered by Davis and Havighurst and by Ericson in their Chicago study of social class and the socialization process, were interpreted by Maccoby, Gibbs, and colleagues as possibly reflecting either (1) basic changes through time in the child-rearing practices of the American "lower" and "middle" classes, or (2) different definitions of social class in the Chicago and Boston studies.

In a response to the Maccoby, Gibbs, and colleagues study, Havighurst and Davis (1955) offered a reanalysis of their earlier data, based on a subsample they believed to be more comparable to the ages of mothers interviewed in the Boston study of social class and socialization. On the basis of their second analysis, Davis and Havighurst concluded that there were in fact "substantial and large" disagreements between the Chicago and Boston studies, which they attributed to basic errors in research procedure and method in the different studies or to fundamental changes in child-rearing practices in the United States.

Noting the marked differences in the Chicago and Boston studies, Sewell and Haller (1956) designed a research project to test whether there really could be said to be any relationship between the social class of a family and a child's "personality adjustments," or behavior. On the basis of a study of 1,462 children in grades four through eight, in what was termed a "culturally homogeneous" small Wisconsin town, with a wide range of status-roles and distinct social classes, Sewell and Haller concluded that in fact there was a statistically "positive and significant" association between their measures of differential social status, or class, and a child's personality adjustment. This study indicated, as Davis and Havinghurst had concluded, that the contrasts and differences between the Chicago and Boston studies of social class and personality were the result either of methods used or of profound changes in class orientations with respect to enculturation.

Then, in a final report on the Boston study, Sears, Maccoby, and Levin (1957) noted that the evidence of their research clearly pointed to the fact that middle-class American mothers were generally more permissive and less punitive toward their children than working-class mothers. Too, the research conducted by Barker and Wright (1954) and by Miller and Swanson (1958) concerning social class and personality also appeared to lend substantial support to the conclusions of Sears, Maccoby, and Levin.

In 1957 Littman, Moore and Pierce-Jones published the results of research conducted in Eugene, Oregon. Using a sample of 206 pairs of white parents, each with identifiable social class differences and whose children were of preschool or school ages, these authors conducted detailed interviews on specific enculturation practices. On the basis of their statistical analyses of interview responses and measures of the parents' social class differences, they concluded there are in fact no profound differences in enculturation practices as a function or because of the social classes of parents.

This contradiction of both the Chicago and Boston studies concerning a relationship between social class and personality was followed by a study by Sewell and Haller (1959), which statistically demonstrated that Green's (1946) conclusions were essentially correct, that is, there is a specific relationship between a child's anxiety and neurosis and the social class of his parents. However, Sewell and Haller's data of class and anxiety were exactly the opposite of those noted by Davis and Havighurst (1946), by Ericson (1946), and by Green, since lower class children seemed to be more anxious than middle-class children. Sewell and Haller explained this reversal by noting that lower class children were acutely aware of their social class positions, in contrast to the positions of their middle-class schoolmates, which led them to "frustration" and "anxieties" resulting from their desire to change social class, but being unable to control any means to cause the desired change. Sewell and Haller (1959: 519) also supported this conclusion by noting that Davis had earlier (1944) demonstrated and documented the existence of the production of high levels of personal anxiety in children because of their concerns over their inability to change social classes.

At this point, because of the conflicting theoretical views and conclusions of these and other studies, Bronfenbrenner (1958) reviewed research concerning relationships between social class and the socialization process, particularly as this relationship affected personality development.[52] Bronfenbrenner pointed out that after World War I there had been a marked increase in the awareness of middle-class American parents concerning the fact that they were being portrayed in scientific literature, as well as in popular accounts, as rigid, demanding, and in-

---

[52]See also White, 1957.

flexible parents and as causing lasting harm to the personalities of their children. Hence, the new awareness by middle-class Americans of their parental acts had rapidly altered their whole orientation from rigid and inflexible to permissive and flexible enculturation practices. Bronfenbrenner concluded that middle-class American parents were in the process of becoming similar to working-class parents in their attitudes toward enculturation. Bronfenbrenner also proposed that the essential differences between the Chicago and Boston studies of social class and personality were not the result of methods of research, but reflected rapidly changing attitudes in different regions of the United States.[53]

In a 1961 review of research concerning the relationships between social class and the socialization process, Sewell noted Bronfenbrenner's conclusions regarding the influence of changing views of American parents in studies of class and socialization. Sewell pointed out that the confusion of theory from such studies represents conclusions that were founded upon such limited and biased research samples that no reliable scientific conclusions could possibly have been reached by investigators. Sewell also noted that no single study seeking to relate class and enculturation was representative of the whole of American society, or of any region of the United States, or even of any clearly definable social system. Too, Sewell observed that statistical techniques used in some studies were not at all appropriate for the problem studied and that there was an extreme lack of conceptual clarity in definitions of the terms "social class" and "personality." Sewell concluded that, because of such weaknesses in theory and method, more definite conclusions about the relationship between social class and the socialization process, including the consequences of social class position for children's personality, must await future studies carefully designed and systematically conducted by theoretically sophisticated scholars. In his closing remarks, Sewell also noted

some of the research procedures, techniques, and theoretical approaches that could be used in seeking to conduct future research relating social class and the socialization process.

In the decade of the 1960's research concerning relationships between class and the socialization process tended to follow some of the directions suggested by Sewell. For instance, after his earlier research seeking to relate social class position and parental authority, Kohn (1959a, 1959b, 1963) specified some patterns of cultural ideology, such as reliance upon self-direction as opposed to direction of activity imposed by the authority of social superiors, which seem to be involved in the lives of parents holding different status-role positions (Kohn, 1963). Kohn concluded that class differences in parent-child relationships are basically the product of differences in parental values reflecting differing conditions of social and cultural life, particularly those involving occupations.

Refining these ideas further, Kohn, in conjunction with Pearlin (1966), conducted a "cross-national" study comparing parental values and parent-child relations in Turin, Italy, and in Washington, D. C. Pearlin and Kohn concluded that three aspects of parental occupation—(1) degree of supervision experienced, (2) whether an individual works principally with things, people, or ideas, and (3) the degree of self-reliance required in a job—are directly related to parental expectations for their children in both an Italian and an American city, with middle-class parents in both cities greatly valuing children's self-reliance, while lower class parents valued their children's conformity to authority imposed by other persons. Pearlin and Kohn concluded their study by noting that a large part of the social class differences reported between the enculturation practices of middle-class and lower class parents in two different societies reflect the fact that differing patterns of cultural ideology influence parental occupations, which in turn influence the ways parents expect children to behave.

In later studies, Kohn, working in conjunction with Schooler (1969), refined the ideas of his earlier studies through a more precise specifica-

---

[53]For a study seeking to relate social class and enculturation practices used with adolescents, see Hollingshead, 1949. See also, Coleman, 1961, for research attempting to relate social class and peer group enculturation processes.

tion of the cumulative effects of the amount of education and of occupational position upon parental values and subsequently upon adult expectations for children.

However, despite such movement to more theoretically sophisticated and exacting definitions of the problem and use of new research procedures, it remains apparent that even though social class differences in a society may be established clearly, it still is not at all certain that such differences have any specific or lasting effects upon the enculturation process of a society. In a review of a series of articles edited by Grey (1969) concerning relationships between social class and personality, Lauer (1970) noted, as Sewell (1961) had nearly a decade earlier, that there still was no conclusive evidence from any research which indicates with clarity both the nature and operation of a relation between social class and the socialization process, and particularly where social mobility may be important.

Since the end of World War II, with some few exceptions, such as the study by Pearlin and Kohn (1966) and in some work similar to that conducted in Ceylon by Straus (1957), there has been a lack of attention to transcultural, holistic, and transtemporal variables in study of possible relationships between the phenomenon of social differentiation, whether in the form of class or age-grades, and the process of socialization. While this inattention is an understandable consequence of the primary professional concerns of the type of scholars conducting research on this question, it does shape any conclusions to be drawn from the existing body of research literature. Thus, it must be said that while data concerning the "life chances" of infants and children (neonatal death, infant mortality, and infant disease and malnutrition rates) seem indisputably related to the income, education, and occupations of parents in some urbanized and industrialized Western European societies and in American society, there is little empirical evidence of such a fact in the remainder of the world's nonliterate, nonurban and nonindustrial cultures. Furthermore, it is not at all certain at present that there is any type of transculturally and holistically valid relationship between class

position and the socialization process. The large amount of evidence, which is now transculturally and holistically certain, that human adults behave generally following their earlier social and cultural experiences, does not necessarily always mean that in every culture the social positions or occupations, education, or income in a society of a child's family or kin groups significantly and determinately shape and direct enculturation and an individual's personality and behavior. It seems to logically follow, in a Western cultural and social milieu, that if life chances are affected by parental occupation and income, and early experience does influence later behavior, then there should be a direct relationship between such social and cultural phenomena. However reasonable this logical analysis and these assumptions seem to a Western European or American scholar, they may not be at all valid in other and quite different cultural settings.

A considerable amount of well-defined research, based upon prior work, remains to be accomplished before it can be said with confidence that social class directly influences the socialization process in particular ways.

Caste and socialization. Some human societies have chosen to accentuate social differences by choosing to eliminate or severely restrict the possibility of access to or changes in achieved status-roles. This sometimes has been accomplished through linking specific occupations with the concept of descent, that is, through defining the essential tasks to be performed in a society as ascribed only through an individual's birth to parents with particular occupations. This practice may be reinforced by requiring children of parents holding specific occupations to practice group endogamy, that is, to marry only other children of parents holding the same occupations. A society which has social groups linked to specific occupations through descent and endogamy may be said to have *social castes.*

A society may have a number of social castes. When social castes become hierarchically organized and ranked for their worth, special qualities, and social attributes, a *caste system* may develop. Caste systems have been reported in societies of the Arabian Peninsula, Polynesia,

North Africa, East Africa, Guatemala, Japan, and native North America.

Perhaps the best known example of a caste system society was that of India prior to 1947. Many different occupations served as the basis for a large number of individual castes, while most castes were joined in a complex system in which some castes were believed to have greater social worth and esteem than other castes. The Indian caste system also had a complex religious basis and rationale, so that before being outlawed by the modern Indian Constitution, castes had come to have social rank and esteem not only on the basis of occupation but as well because of religious practices, such as the type of ritual sacrifice followed by the members of a caste.

In a society with castes or in one organized about a caste system, individuals tend to derive their personal esteem, rank, and prestige from their caste membership. Caste members find most personal choices closely defined and restricted by the attributes of their caste. In addition to narrowing their choices in marriage and occupation, individuals growing up in a caste or in a caste system may find their choices quite restricted in their style and color of dress, foods eaten, access to public places, political action, persons to be touched, education, and even the type of funeral permitted.

Individuals enculturated in a caste, or a society with a caste system, find the social group to which they belong provides the corporate and personal benefits of belonging to a trade union, a feasting society, a clan, a club, a health insurance company, a savings society, a political party, and a funeral association.

Descriptive accounts of the enculturation process in a society with castes or a caste system are fragmentary and incomplete, especially with reference to attention to the specific ways parents and other adults transmit cultural and social knowledge to infants and children and concerning the ways children behave as they learn the essential features of caste life.[54] It is clear,

[54]For some descriptions of enculturation features in castes or in caste systems, see Beals, 1962; Carstairs, 1958; Dube, 1955; Hutton, 1946; Lewis, 1958; Marriott, 1955; A. Mayer, 1960; Narain, 1964; Ryan, 1953; Tumin, 1952; Wiser and Wiser, 1963.

however, that children maturing in a caste or in a caste system have to learn a broad complex of definitions of status-roles. In fact, available ethnographic data appear to indicate that, while children growing up in a caste do have certain clearly defined limits on the ways they can act and upon the ideas to be learned, they also must learn the many ways they cannot act and the details of knowledge they are not supposed to acquire. In effect, enculturation in a caste or in a caste system tends to be quite complex due to "negative" culture which must be acquired, that is, because children also must learn well and quickly those aspects of culture they must not learn, yet still know, in order to act as though they do not know such things. Hence, it appears that the enculturation process is no less complex with regard to status-role learning in an Indian village, than it would be in noncaste societies in Truk, Samoa, the Central Australian desert, or the high plains of native North America.

▪ Conclusions

It is clear that children in every society must learn the many details of cultural patterns concerned with the assignment of tasks, the definitions of jobs to be performed, and the formal and informal practices of recruitment to such tasks. In all cultures, the process of learning a cultural charter involves children in the mastery of complex and highly detailed conceptions of the social statuses and roles. Children also must come to know and effectively use cultural conceptions of their own and of other persons' social rights and duties as these are associated with various tasks to be performed and the instructions for carrying them out. Children must also learn and understand the clues to different status-roles or status relationships implied in the demeanor, costumes, hair styles, cosmetic uses, jewelry, tattoos, body mutilations, special terminology, and prestige signs of other persons.

Little descriptive data is available at present for use in analysis of the ways infants and children actually learn and use status-roles, especially those associated with social class differences. It is clear, however, that such learning is a vital aspect of the socialization process. Goffman

(1961: 87) has concluded that the learning of social rights and duties comprises the "basic unit" of the entire socialization process, since he believes that it is through such learning that all tasks in a society are allocated and arrangements are devised to ensure a regular performance of social rights and duties. In contrast, Goodenough (1965) adapts a more cautious view of the overall importance of status-role learning in the socialization process. Goodenough believes that a large amount, but not all, of social learning in any society involves detailed knowledge of social duties to others and the specific situations in which such duties are owed.

However, there are no substantive evidences which demonstrate that status-role learning has a central role in the socialization process, or is critical to the existence and operation of that process. A useful theoretical approach to analysis of the socialization process would seem to be one which has no requirements that some categories, features, or parts of that process must be chosen over others as being fundamental or of primary importance. It is sufficient for the present to say that, if children are to become successful adults in a society, they obviously must learn the details of cultural patterns concerned with definitions of tasks to be performed in a society, the ways such tasks are performed, and the ways persons are recruited to such tasks. Children must also learn, in many societies, details of a cultural pattern concerned with social classes. However, successful adult performance in a society also involves knowing and following the details of many other cultural patterns, including kinship, kin groups, food quest, religious belief, grammar, and so on.

■ Summary

This chapter has been concerned with discussion of some of the possible relationships between the cultural patterns of status-role and class and the socialization process. The chapter began with a review of concepts and examples of status-role behavior and noted some of the kinds of signs, symbols, and ideas children must learn if they are to comprehend and success-

fully use status-roles. Then the discussion turned to a brief review of special social groups, clubs, and age-sets, which are based on selected aspects of status-role, such as sex and age, and which in some societies are regularly used in transmission of locally significant forms of culture.

In the next part of the discussion an account was given of ritual actions used in some societies to mark the transitions in status-roles culturally associated with the onset of puberty. A summary description was given of Arunta ritual observances marking puberty, to illustrate the complex ways some societies have chosen to dramatize a transition from status-roles of childhood to those of adulthood. This portion of the discussion also included a review of studies seeking to explain the existence and importance of ritual transitions in status-roles at puberty.

The second section of the chapter began with a review of the concept of social class and noted some relationships between the type of subsistence practiced in a society, its geographic location, and the presence or absence of social classes in that society. This discussion was followed by a brief review of major theories seeking to account for the existence of social classes in a society. Then, the discussion turned to an examination of the life chances and personal expectations of individuals born to parents in different social classes. This was followed by a review of studies seeking to demonstrate a relationship between social class and the socialization process. The chapter concluded with a summary of the ways castes, a special form of social class characterized by the linking of social groups to specific occupations through descent and endogamy, may be related to the process of socialization.

REFERENCES CITED AND SUGGESTED READINGS

Anderson, J. E. 1936. *The Young Child in the Home.* New York: Appleton-Century-Crofts.

Banton, M. (ed.) 1965a. *The Relevance of Models for Social Anthropology.* New York: Praeger.

_____. 1965b. *Roles; An Introduction to the Study of Social Relations.* London: Tavistock.

Barber, B. 1957. *Social Stratification.* New York: Harcourt, Brace.

Barker, R. G., and H. F. Wright. 1954. *Midwest and Its Children: The Psychological Ecology of an American Town.* Evanston, Ill.: Row, Peterson.

Bates, F. L. 1956. "Position, Role, and Status: Reformulation of Concepts," Social Forces 34:313-321.

Beals, A. R. 1962. Gopalpur; A South Indian Village. New York: Holt, Rinehart and Winston.

Becker, H. S. 1960. "Notes on the Concept of Commitment," American Journal of Sociology 66:32-40.

Bendix, R., and S. M. Lipset (eds.) 1953. Class, Status and Power; A Reader in Social Stratification. Glencoe, Ill.: The Free Press.

Benedict, R. 1938. "Continuities and Discontinuities in Cultural Conditioning," Psychiatry 1:161-167.

Bergel, E. E. 1962. Social Stratification. New York: McGraw-Hill.

Berreman, G. 1968. "Caste: The Concept of Caste." In D. A. Sills (ed.), International Encyclopedia of the Social Sciences. New York: Macmillan and The Free Press, pp. 333-339.

Bettelheim, B. 1954. Symbolic Wounds, Puberty Rites, and the Envious Male. New York: The Free Press.

Boas, F. 1895. The Social Organization and the Secret Societies of the Kwakiutl Indians. Washington, D. C.: U. S. National Museum, Reports.

Bohannan, P. 1963. Social Anthropology. New York: Holt, Rinehart and Winston.

Bronfenbrenner, U. 1958. "Socialization and Social Class Through Time and Space." In E. E. Maccoby, T. M. Newcomb, and E. L. Hartley (eds.), Readings in Social Psychology, ed. 3. New York: Holt, pp. 400-425.

_____. 1962. "The Role of Age, Sex, Class and Culture in Studies of Moral Development," Religious Education 53:5-17.

Broom, L. 1959. "Social Differentiation and Stratification." In R. K. Merton, L. Broom, and L. S. Cottrell, Jr. (eds.), Sociology Today. New York: Basic Books, pp. 429-441.

Brown, D. R. (ed.) 1968. The Role and Status of Women in the Soviet Union. New York: Teachers College Press.

Brown, J. K. 1963. "A Cross-Cultural Study of Female Initiation Rites," American Anthropologist 65:837-853.

Burton, R. V., and J. W. M. Whiting. 1961. "The Absent Father and Cross-Sex Identity," Merrill-Palmer Quarterly of Behavior and Development 7:85-95.

Carstairs, G. M. 1958. The Twice-Born; A Study of a Community of High-Caste Hindus. Bloomington, Ind.: Indiana University Press.

Cawte, J. E. 1968. "Further Comment on the Australian Subincision Ceremony," American Anthropologist 70:961-964.

Cawte, J. E., N. Djagamara, and M. Barrett. 1966. "The Meaning of Subincision of the Urethra to Aboriginal Australians," British Journal of Medical Psychology 39:245-253.

Centers, R. 1949. The Psychology of Social Classes. Princeton, N. J.: Princeton University Press.

Child, I. L. 1954. "Socialization." In G. Lindzey (ed.), Handbook of Social Psychology. Cambridge, Mass.; Addison-Wesley Press, pp. 655-692.

Cohen, Y. A. 1964. The Transition from Childhood to Adolescence. Chicago: Aldine.

Coleman, J. S. 1961. The Adolescent Society: The Social Life of the Teenager and Its Impact on Education. New York: The Free Press.

Coult, A. D., and R. W. Habenstein. 1965. Cross Tabulations of Murdock's World Ethnographic Sample. Columbia, Mo.: University of Missouri Press.

Cuber, J., and W. F. Kenkel. 1954. Social Stratification in the United States. New York: Appleton-Century-Crofts.

Dahrendorf, R. 1959. Class and Class Conflict in Industrial Society. Stanford: Stanford University Press.

Davis, A. 1944. "Socialization and Adolescent Personality." In Forty-Third Yearbook of the National Society for the Study of Education. Chicago: National Society for the Study of Education, Part I.

Davis, A., and J. Dollard. 1940. Children of Bondage. Washington, D. C.: American Council on Education.

Davis, A., B. B. Gardner, and M. R. Gardner. 1941. Deep South. Chicago: University of Chicago Press.

Davis, A., and R. J. Havighurst. 1946. "Social Class and Color Differences in Child Rearing," American Sociological Review 11:698-710.

_____. 1947. Father of the Man. Boston: Houghton-Mifflin.

Davis, K. 1949. Human Society. New York: Macmillan.

Davis, K., and W. Moore. 1945. "Some Principles of Stratification," American Sociological Review 10:242-249.

Deutsch, M., I. Katz, and A. R. Jensen (eds.) 1968. Social Class, Race and Psychological Development. New York: Holt, Rinehart and Winston.

Dobriner, W. 1963. Class in Suburbia. Englewood Cliffs, N. J.: Prentice-Hall.

Dollard, J. 1949. Caste and Class in a Southern Town. New York: Harper.

Douglas, J. W. B., and J. M. Blomfield. 1958. Children Under Five. London: Allen and Unwin.

Dozier, E. P. 1966. Hano; A Tewa Indian Community in Arizona. New York: Holt, Rinehart and Winston.

_____. 1970. The Pueblo Indians of North America. New York: Holt, Rinehart and Winston.

Drucker, P. 1939. "Rank, Wealth and Kinship in Northwest Coast Society," American Anthropologist 41:55-65.

Dube, S. C. 1955. Indian Village. Ithaca, N. Y.: Cornell University Press.

Dunham, H. W. 1961. "Social Structures and Mental Disorders: Competing Hypotheses of Explanation," Millbank Memorial Fund Quarterly 39:259.

Eisenstadt, S. N. 1956. *From Generation to Generation.* Glencoe, Ill.: The Free Press.

Ericson, M. C. 1946. "Child-Rearing and Social Status." *American Journal of Sociology* **52**:190-192.

Gallaher, A., Jr. 1961. *Plainville Fifteen Years Later.* New York: Columbia University Press.

Gans, H. J. 1962. *The Urban Villagers: Group and Class in the Life of Italian Americans.* New York: The Free Press.

_____. 1967. *The Levittowners; Ways of Life and Politics in a New Suburban Community.* New York: Pantheon.

Gerth, H., and C. W. Mills. 1953. *Character and Social Structure.* New York: Harcourt, Brace.

Gibbs, J. L. 1962. "Poro Values and Courtroom Procedures in a Kpelle Chiefdom," *Southwestern Journal of Anthropology* **19**:9-20.

_____. 1965. "The Kpelle of Liberia." In J. L. Gibbs (ed.), *Peoples of Africa.* New York: Holt, Rinehart and Winston, pp. 197-240.

Gifford, E. W. 1929. *Tongan Society.* Honolulu: Bernice P. Bishop Museum, Bulletin Number 61.

Goffman, E. 1956. "The Nature of Deference and Demeanor," *American Anthropologist* **58**:473-502.

_____. 1959. *The Presentation of Self in Everyday Life.* New York: Doubleday Anchor Books.

_____. 1961. *Encounters: Two Studies in the Sociology of Interaction.* Indianapolis: Bobbs-Merrill.

Goldschmidt, W. 1950. "Social Class in America—A Critical Review," *American Anthropologist* **52**:483-498.

Goodenough, W. H. 1951. *Property, Kin and Community on Truk.* New Haven: Yale University Publications in Anthropology, Number 46.

_____. 1965. "Rethinking 'Status' and 'Role;' Toward a General Model of the Cultural Organization of Social Relationships." In M. Banton (ed.), *The Relevance of Models for Social Anthropology.* New York: Praeger, pp. 1-24.

Gordon, M. M. 1958. *Social Class in American Sociology.* Durham, N. C.: Duke University Press.

Green, A. 1946. "The Middle Class Male Child and Neurosis," *American Sociological Review* **11**:31-41.

Grey, A. L. (ed.) 1969. *Class and Personality in Society.* New York: Atherton.

Grinnell, G. B. 1915. *The Fighting Cheyennes.* New York: Scribner.

_____. 1923. *The Cheyenne Indians: Their History and Ways of Life.* New Haven: Yale University Press.

Gross, N., W. S. Mason, and A. W. McEachern. 1958. *Explorations in Role Analysis: Studies of the School Superintendency Role.* New York: Wiley.

Havighurst, R. J., and A. Davis. 1955. "A Comparison of the Chicago and Harvard Studies of the Social Class Differences in Child Rearing," *American Sociological Review* **20**:438-442.

Havighurst, R. J., and H. Taba. 1949. *Adolescent Character and Personality.* New York: Wiley.

Havighurst, R. J., and B. L. Neugarten. 1955. *American Indian and White Children: A Socio-Psychological Investigation.* Chicago: University of Chicago Press.

Havighurst, R. J., and others. 1962. *Growing Up in River City.* New York: Wiley.

Hickman, J. M. 1962. "Dimensions of a Complex Concept: A Method Exemplified," *Human Organization* **21**:214-218.

Hiller, E. T. 1947. *Social Relations and Structures.* New York: Harper.

Hodge, R. W., and D. J. Treiman. 1968. "Social Participation and Social Status," *American Sociological Review* **33**:722-740.

Hodges, H. M., Jr. 1964. *Social Stratification: Class in America.* Cambridge, Mass.: Schenkman.

Hoebel, E. A. 1960. *The Cheyennes: Indians of the Great Plains.* New York: Holt, Rinehart and Winston.

Hollingshead, A. B. 1949. *Elmtown's Youth: The Impact of Social Classes on Adolescents.* New York: Wiley.

Hollingshead, A. B., and F. C. Redlich. 1958. *Social Class and Mental Illness: A Community Study.* New York: Wiley.

Hollis, A. C. 1909. *The Nandi.* London: Oxford University Press.

Homans, G. C. 1950. *The Human Group.* New York: Harcourt-Brace.

_____. 1961. *Social Behavior: Its Elementary Forms.* New York: Harcourt-Brace.

Hsu, F. L. K. 1963. *Clan, Caste and Club.* Princeton, N. J.: Van Nostrand.

Hughes, E. C. 1945. "Dilemmas and Contradictions of Status," *American Journal of Sociology* **50**:353-359.

Hutton, J. H. 1946. *Caste in India; Its Nature, Function and Origins.* Cambridge, England: The University Press.

Inkeles, A. 1960. "Industrial Man: The Relation of Status to Experience, Perception and Value," *American Journal of Sociology* **66**:1-31.

Jackson, J. A. (ed.) 1968. *Social Stratification.* London: Cambridge University Press.

Kahl, J. A. 1957. *The American Class Structure.* New York: Holt, Rinehart and Winston.

Kaufman, H. F. 1944. *Prestige Classes in a New York Rural Community.* Ithaca, N. Y.: Cornell University Agricultural Experiment Station, Memoir 260.

Kohn, M. L. 1959a. "Social Class and the Exercise of Parental Authority," *American Sociological Review* **24**:352-366.

_____. 1959b. "Social Class and Parental Values," *American Journal of Sociology* **64**:337-351.

_____. 1963. "Social Class and Parent-Child Relationships; An Interpretation," *American Journal of Sociology* **68**:471-480.

_____. 1969. *Class and Conformity: A Study in Values.* Homewood, Ill.: Dorsey.

Kohn, M. L., and E. E. Carroll. 1960. "Social Class and the Allocation of Parental Responsibilities," *Sociometry* **23**:372-392.

Kohn, M. L., and C. Schooler. 1969. "Class, Occupation and Orientation," American Sociological Review 34:659-678.

Kornhauser, R. R. 1953. "The Warner Approach to Social Stratification." In R. Bendix and S. M. Lipset (eds.), Class, Status and Power. Glencoe, Ill.: The Free Press.

Kuper, H. 1947. An African Aristocracy. London: Oxford University Press.

_____. 1952. The Swazi. London: International African Institute.

_____. 1963. The Swazi: A South African Kingdom. New York: Holt, Rinehart and Winston.

Lasswell, T. E. 1960. "Orientations Toward Social Classes," American Journal of Sociology 65:585.

_____. 1965. Class and Stratum; An Introduction to Concepts and Research. Boston: Houghton-Mifflin.

Lauer, R. H. 1970. "Review of Alan L. Grey (ed.) 1969. Class and Personality in Society." New York: Atherton, American Sociological Review 35:139.

Lenski, G. 1966. Power and Privilege: A Theory of Social Stratification. New York: McGraw-Hill.

_____. 1970. Human Societies. New York: McGraw-Hill.

Lewis, O. 1958. Village Life in Northern India. Champaign-Urbana, Ill.: University of Illinois Press.

Lindesmith, A. R., and A. L. Strauss. 1950. "A Critique of Culture—Personality Writings," American Sociological Review 15:587-600.

Linton, R. 1936. The Study of Man. New York: Appleton-Century-Crofts.

Lipset, S. M. 1959. "Democracy and Working-Class Authoritarianism," American Sociological Review 24:482-501.

Lipset, S. M., and R. Bendix. 1959. Social Mobility in an Industrial Society. Berkeley: University of California Press.

Little, K. 1960. "The Role of the Secret Society in Cultural Specialization." In S. Ottenberg and P. Ottenberg (eds.), Cultures and Societies of Africa. New York: Random House, pp. 199-213.

Littman, R. A., R. C. A. Moore, and J. Pierce-Jones. 1957. "Social Class Differences in Child Rearing: A Third Community for Comparison With Chicago and Newton," American Sociological Review 22:694-704.

Lowie, R. H. 1920. Primitive Society. New York: Boni and Liverwright.

Lynd, R., and H. Lynd. 1929. Middletown, New York: Harcourt-Brace.

_____. 1937. Middletown in Transition. New York: Harcourt-Brace.

Maccoby, E. E., P. K. Gibbs, and others. 1954. "Methods of Child Rearing in Two Social Classes." In W. E. Martin and C. B. Stendler (eds.), Readings in Child Development. New York: Harcourt-Brace, pp. 380-396.

MacRae, D. G. 1953. "Social Stratification," Current Sociology 2, Number 1, pp. 7-31.

Malinowski, B. 1944. A Scientific Theory of Culture and Other Essays. Chapel Hill: University of North Carolina Press.

_____. 1945. The Dynamics of Culture Change. New Haven: Yale University Press.

Marriott, M. (ed.) 1955. Village India. Chicago: University of Chicago Press.

Mayer, A. 1960. Caste and Kinship in Central India. Berkeley: University of California Press.

Mayer, K. B. 1955. Class and Society. New York: Random House.

McKinley, D. G. 1964. Social Class and Family Life. New York: The Free Press of Glencoe.

Mead, M. 1928. Coming of Age in Samoa. New York: Morrow.

Merton, R. K. 1957a. Social Theory and Social Structure. Glencoe, Ill.: The Free Press.

_____. 1957b. "The Role Set: Problems in Sociological Theory." British Journal of Sociology 8:106.

Metraux, A. 1946. "The Botocudo." In J. Steward (ed.), Handbook of South American Indians. Washington, D. C., Smithsonian Institution, Bureau of American Ethnology, Vol. I, p. 534.

Miller, D. R., and G. E. Swanson. 1958. The Changing American Parent. New York: Wiley.

_____. 1960. Inner Conflict and Defense. New York: Holt, Rinehart and Winston.

Miller, G. A. 1956. "The Magical Number Seven, Plus or Minus Two: Some Limits on Our Capacity for Processing Information," Psychological Review 63:81-97.

Mishkin, B. 1940. Rank and Warfare Among the Plains Indians. American Ethnological Society, Monograph Three. Seattle: University of Washington Press.

Murdock, G. P. 1957. "World Ethnographic Sample," American Anthropologist 59:664-687.

_____. 1967. Ethnographic Atlas. Pittsburgh: University of Pittsburgh Press.

Myers, J. K., and L. L. Bean. 1968. A Decade Later: A Follow-up of Social Class and Mental Illness. New York: Wiley.

Nadel, S. F. 1957. The Theory of Social Structure. Glencoe, Ill.: The Free Press.

Narain, B. 1964. "Growing Up in India," Family Process 3:127-154.

Oeser, O. A., and F. E. Emery. 1954. Social Structure and Personality in a Rural Community. New York: Macmillan.

Oeser, O. A., and S. B. Hammon (eds.) 1954. Social Structure and Personality in a City. New York: Macmillan.

Oliver, D. 1955. A Solomon Island Society. Cambridge, Mass.: Harvard University Press.

Orlansky, H. 1949. "Infant Care and Personality," Psychological Bulletin 46:1-48.

Ossowski, S. 1963. *Class Structure in the Social Consciousness.* New York: The Free Press (translated by Shelia Patterson).

Parsons, T. 1953. "A Revised Analytical Approach to the Theory of Social Stratification." In R. Bendix and S. M. Lipset (eds.), *Class Status and Power.* Glencoe, Ill.: The Free Press, pp. 92-128.

Parsons, T., and R. F. Bales. 1955. *Family, Socialization and Interaction Process.* Glencoe, Ill.: The Free Press.

Parsons, T., and K. B. Clark. 1966. *The Negro American.* New York: Houghton-Mifflin.

Paul, B. D. (ed.) 1955. *Health, Culture and Community.* New York: Russell Sage Foundation.

Pearlin, L. I., and M. L. Kohn. 1966. "Social Class, Occupation, and Parental Values; A Cross-National Study," American Sociological Review 31:466-479.

Pfautz, H. W. 1953. "The Current Literature on Social Stratification: Critique and Bibliography," American Journal of Sociology 58:391-418.

Pfautz, H. W., and O. D. Duncan. 1950. "A Critical Evaluation of Warner's Work in Community Stratification," American Sociological Review 15:205-215.

Prins, A. H. J. 1953. *East African Age-Class Systems: An Inquiry Into the Social Order of Galla, Kipsigis and Kikuyu.* Groningen and Djakarta: J. B. Wolters.

Radcliffe-Brown, A. R. 1922. *The Andaman Islanders.* Cambridge: Cambridge University Press.

Read, M. 1956. *The Ngoni of Nyasaland.* London: Oxford University Press.

_____. 1960. *Children of Their Fathers: Growing Up Among the Ngoni of Nysaland.* New Haven, Conn.: Yale University Press.

_____. 1968. *Children of Their Fathers: Growing Up Among The Ngoni of Malawi.* New York: Holt, Rinehart and Winston.

Reiss, A. J., O. D. Duncan, P. K. Hatt, and C. C. North. 1961. *Occupations and Social Status.* Glencoe, Ill.: The Free Press.

Reissman, L. 1959. *Class in American Society.* Glencoe, Ill.: The Free Press.

Richards, A. I. 1956. *Chisungu; A Girl's Initiation Ceremony Among the Bemba of Northern Rhodesia.* New York: Grove.

Richardson, J. 1940. *Law and Status Among the Kiowa Indians.* American Ethnological Society, Monograph One, Seattle: University of Washington Press.

Rose, A. M. (ed.) 1962. *Human Behavior and Social Processes.* Boston: Houghton-Mifflin.

Ryan, B. 1953. *Caste in Modern Ceylon.* New Brunswick, N. J.: Rutgers University Press.

Schapera, I. 1937. *The Bantu-Speaking Tribes of South Africa.* London: Routledge & Kegan Paul.

Schneider, D. M. 1968. *American Kinship: A Cultural Account.* Englewood Cliffs, N. J.: Prentice-Hall.

Schurtz, H. 1902. *Altersklassen und Mannerbunde.* Berlin: G. Reimer.

Sears, R. R., E. E. Maccoby, and H. Levin. 1957. *Patterns of Child Rearing.* Evanston, Ill.: Row, Peterson.

Service, E. R. 1963. *Profiles in Ethnology.* New York: Harper.

Sewell, W. H. 1952. "Infant Training and the Personality of the Child," American Journal of Sociology 58:150-159.

_____. 1961. "Social Class and Childhood Personality," Sociometry 24:340-356.

_____. 1963. "Some Recent Developments in Socialization Theory and Research," The Annals of the American Academy of Political and Social Science 349:163-181.

Sewell, W. H., and A. O. Haller. 1956. "Social Status and the Personality Adjustment of the Child," Sociometry 19:114-125.

_____. 1959. "Factors in the Relationship Between Social Status and the Personality Adjustment of the Child," American Sociological Review 24:511.

Sewell, W. H., P. H. Mussen, and C. W. Harris. 1955. "Relationships Among Child Training Practices," American Sociological Review 20:137-148.

Simmons, L. W. 1945. *The Role of the Aged in Primitive Society.* New Haven: Yale University Press.

Singer, M. B. 1961. "A Survey of Culture and Personality Theory and Research." In B. Kaplan (ed.), *Studying Personality Cross-Culturally.* New York: Harper and Row, pp. 9-90.

Singer, P., and D. DeSole. 1967. "The Australian Subincision Ceremony Reconsidered: Vaginal Envy or Kangaroo Bifid Penis Envy," American Anthropologist 69:355-358.

Southall, A. 1959. "An Operational Theory of Role," Human Relations 12:17-34.

Steere, G. H. 1964. "Changing Values in Childhood Socialization: A Study of United States Child Rearing Literature 1865-1929," Unpublished Doctoral Dissertation, University of Pennsylvania.

Straus, M. A. 1957. "Anal and Oral Frustration in Relation to Sinhalese Personality," Sociometry 20:21-31.

Svalastoga, K. 1959. *Prestige, Class and Mobility.* Copenhagen: Gyldendal.

_____. 1964. "Social Differentiation." In R. E. L. Faris (ed.), *Handbook of Modern Sociology.* Chicago: Rand McNally, pp. 530-575.

_____. 1965. *Social Differentiation.* New York: McKay.

Textor, R. B. 1967. *A Cross-Cultural Summary.* New Haven: Human Relations Area Files.

Titiev, M. 1944. *Old Oraibi.* Cambridge, Mass.: Harvard University, Papers of the Peabody Museum 22.

Tumin, M. M. 1952. *Caste in a Peasant Society; A Case Study in the Dynamics of Caste.* Princeton, N. J.: Princeton University Press.

_____. 1953. "Some Principles of Stratification: A Critical Analysis," American Sociological Review 18:387-394.

_____. 1967. *Social Stratification: The Forms and Functions of Inequality.* Englewood Cliffs, N. J.: Prentice-Hall.

Veblen, T. 1927. *The Theory of the Leisure Class.* New York: Heubsch.

Wallace, A. F. C. 1961. "The Psychic Unity of Human Groups." In B. Kaplan (ed.), *Studying Personality Cross-Culturally.* Evanston, Ill.: Row, Peterson, pp. 129-163.

Warner, W. L. 1953. *American Life: Dream and Reality.* Chicago: University of Chicago Press.

_____. 1960. *Social Class in America.* New York: Harper.

Warner, W. L., and P. S. Lunt. 1941. *The Social Life of a Modern Community.* New Haven: Yale University Press.

Warner, W. L., and others. 1949. *Democracy in Jonesville.* New York: Harper.

Weber, M. 1946. *From Max Weber: Essays in Sociology.* New York: Oxford University Press (edited and translated by H. H. Gerth and C. W. Mills).

Webster, H. 1908. *Primitive Secret Societies.* New York: Macmillan.

Welmers, W. E. 1949. "Secret Medicine: Magic and Rites of the Kpelle Tribe in Liberia," Southwestern Journal of Anthropology 5:208-243.

West, J. (C. Withers). 1945. *Plainville, U. S. A.* New York: Columbia University Press.

White, M. S. 1957. "Social Class, Child Rearing Practices and Child Behavior," American Sociological Review 22:704-712.

Whiting, J. W. M. 1961. "Socialization Process and Personality." In F. L. K. Hsu (ed.), *Psychological Anthropology.* Homewood, Ill.: Dorsey, pp. 355-380.

_____. 1964. "Effects of Climate on Certain Cultural Practices." In W. Goodenough (ed.), *Explorations in Cultural Anthropology.* New York: McGraw-Hill, pp. 511-544.

Whiting, J. W. M., R. Kluckhohn, and A. Anthony. 1958. "The Function of Male Initiation Ceremonies at Puberty." In E. E. Maccoby, T. Newcomb, and E. Hartley (eds.), *Readings in Social Psychology.* New York: Holt, Rinehart and Winston, pp. 359-370.

Williams, T. R. 1962. "Tambunan Dusun Social Structure," Sociologus 23:141-157.

_____. 1965. *The Dusun; A North Borneo Society.* New York: Holt, Rinehart and Winston.

_____. 1966. "Cultural Structuring of Tactile Experience in a Borneo Society," American Anthropologist 68:27-39.

Wilson, M. 1951. *Good Company.* London: Oxford University Press.

Wiser, W. H., and C. V. Wiser, 1963. *Behind Mud Walls.* Berkeley, Calif.: University of California Press.

Wrong, D. H. 1959. "The Functional Theory of Stratification: Some Neglected Considerations," American Sociological Review 24:772-782.

Young, F. W. 1962. "The Function of Male Initiation Ceremonies: A Cross-Cultural Test of an Alternative Hypothesis," American Journal of Sociology 67:379-396.

NINE TECHNOLOGY AND IDEOLOGY IN SOCIALIZATION

This chapter is concerned with a discussion of some examples of the relations between the socialization process and patterns in the cultural subsystems of technology and ideology. It begins with an account of the ways the technology subsystem pattern of shelter may be related to the process of socialization. Then the discussion turns to a consideration of the ways some patterns of the ideology subsystem, such as various cultural beliefs and values (including ideas about numbers, measures, nature, and society) and art, are possibly related to the socialization process. The chapter concludes with comment concerning study of the relations of interdependence between socialization and patterns in the cultural subsystems of technology and ideology.

■ Technology and socialization

In Chapter Seven it was noted that culture can be conceptualized as having four major subsystems: (1) social relations, (2) language, (3) technology, and (4) ideology. Each subsystem was said to be comprised of a large and varying number of whole categories, or patterns, of culture. The outline on pp. 125-126 lists nineteen patterns which seem to be part of the cultural subsystem of technology. The technology subsystem includes all those patterns of culture invented and used by man to transform his natural environment in ways that provide him with the materials needed for life in a particular physical setting. Specifically, technology is that part of human culture which enables man to produce from his physical environment those

manufactured goods and devices, or *artifacts,* which make it possible for humans to survive by culturally adapting to local conditions. Artifacts include tools and containers, processed foods, shelters, transport, items of clothing and adornment, and all other material objects produced and used by members of a society. Through invention and use of technology, humans are able to inhabit all of the earth's varied climate zones.

Complexity of technology. Contemporary human societies differ greatly in the complexity of their systems of technology. Some societies with a very limited technology have been restricted to one physical environment. However, some other human societies have been able to range widely across varied and sharply contrasting earth regions because of their invention and use of a more varied technology.

Because of the nature of their technology system, some societies also have been restricted to only one major use of their physical environment. The Plains Indians of North America hunted big game, principally the buffalo, but usually did not plant the rich earth of their area, for lack of the learned categories of behavior and belief, plans for action, and the artifacts needed to exploit this potential for a great food surplus. In contrast, the Iroquois Indians of the eastern woodlands of North America, with a more complex technology subsystem of culture, practiced hunting, fishing, food gathering, and horticulture to gain a living from their environment. Thus, the type and complexity of technology possessed by a society depends upon its past cultural history in gaining access to a physical setting. Changes in the technological type and complexity of a culture seem to be closely related to the nature of and changes in other patterns in the cultural subsystems of social relations, language, and ideology.

Sometimes individuals untrained in cultural analysis make the error of judging the nature of a whole culture only from its technology type and complexity. It is possible to make long lists of the different types of technology and of the complexity of artifacts used in gaining a living in many societies. On such a list, some societies could be ranked as "simple" or "less complex" than other societies in their system of technology. However simple or advanced a cultural subsystem of technology may appear, it is not necessarily true that an entire culture is also "simple" or "less advanced" or is not as "complex" as other cultures.

Research on technology. In the past century there has been a great amount of research on the nature of human technology. Much of the interest in the study of technology has stemmed from the fact that some early theories of human cultural evolution postulated that whole cultures were at various "stages" of social development, depending on the presumed state of their technological complexity. Studies of technology also were derived from the fact that artifacts remaining from human cultures are a principal source of evidence for study of early human history. Technology has been widely studied also because it is easier and often safer in an alien cultural setting to make detailed records of artifacts and ways of making a living from an environment, than to ask questions about topics such as magic, cannibalism, marriage, and so on.

There have been many notable studies of selected aspects of the technology subsystem in one society.[1] The ready availability of a great number of detailed publications concerned with technology has led to attempts to abstract general statements about both the subsystem of technology and the part played by that aspect of

culture in human cultural history and behavior. These discussions have ranged from an effort to theoretically relate artifacts to basic human needs, through attempts to undertake correlational analyses of features of technology and social relations, to use of the statistical technique of factor analysis to show that features of technology seem closely interrelated to aspects of the ideology subsystem of human culture.[2] Too, quite detailed and extensive studies have been made of the ways particular features of technology manifest themselves in human culture.[3] Considerable time and skill have been devoted to compiling detailed summaries of various features of human technology.[4]

Universal categories of technology. The result of intensive study of technology in specific cultures and of attempts to systematically compare these data has been a growing awareness among anthropologists that certain broad categories of technology are universal, or are found in all societies. The universal categories of technology are: (1) gathering or producing food, (2) shelter, (3) clothing, (4) tools and containers, and (5) transportation. As noted, these universal categories are not equally developed in all societies.

To illustrate the ways the process of socialization may be related to the patterns of technology, it is appropriate to select a pattern of this cultural subsystem which not only is universal in human society but is as well a pattern of technology which all children are subject to as they mature in all societies. A pattern of the technology subsystem which meets these requirements is the one concerned with shelter. Infants and children in most societies have little direct, initial contact or concern with the technology patterns involved in food gathering or production, manufacture of tools and containers, or transportation. In many societies, children are not required to wear clothing until they are 4 years of age or older. However, children in

---

[1]See Beals, 1935; Bogoras, 1904; Buck, 1930; Bunzel, 1929; Kroeber, 1901; Linton, 1923; Lowie, 1922; Osgood, 1940; Wissler, 1910.

[2]See Greenman, 1945; Hobhouse, Wheeler, and Ginsberg, 1915; Gouldner and Peterson, 1962.
[3]See Driver and Kroeber, 1932; Driver, 1956 and 1966; Driver and Massy, 1957; Ford, 1939; Freeman and Winch, 1957; Sawyer and LeVine, 1966.
[4]See Murdock, 1957 and 1967.

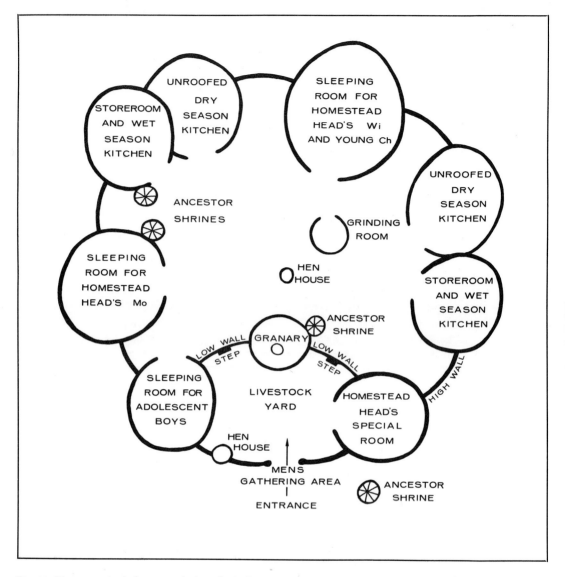

Fig. 20. Diagrammatic shelter ground plan of a Tallensi (Ghana) dwelling (not to scale). (After Fortes, M. 1949. *The Web of Kinship Among the Tallensi.* London: Oxford University Press, p. 53.)

all societies have direct and long-lasting experience with the technology subsystem pattern of shelter.

Explaining shelter variations. Contemporary human societies use shelters ranging from rock overhangs and caves through wind screens and tents to massive buildings. Shelters are constructed of nearly every available material. However, comparisons of human shelter data show

that, despite the seemingly endless diversity in type and materials used, humans actually make their shelters in a limited number of forms and with restricted kinds of materials. The ground plans of shelters in all human societies seem to be of only six types. The floor levels of all human shelters seem to comprise only four types. The construction of shelter walls involves only eleven types of material. The shape of all shelter roofs

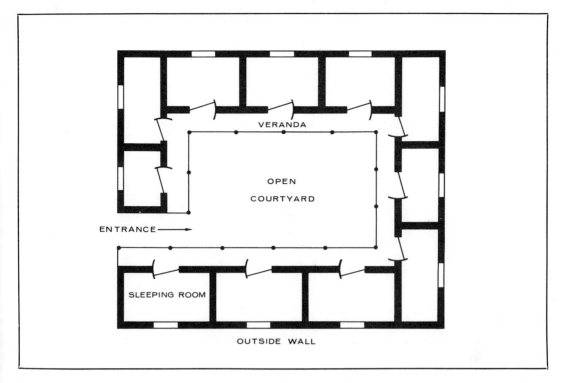

Fig. 21. Diagrammatic shelter ground plan of an Ashanti (Ghana) dwelling (not to scale). (After Fortes, M. 1959. "Primitive Kinship," Scientific American **200**:146.)

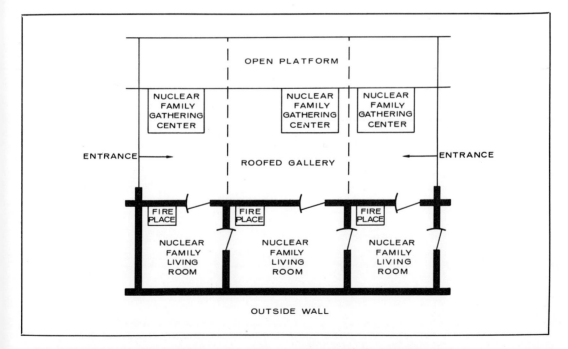

Fig. 22. Diagrammatic shelter ground plan of a section of an Iban (Sarawak, East Malaysia) dwelling (not to scale). (After Freeman, J. D. 1955. *Iban Agriculture.* London: Her Majesty's Stationery Office, pp. 1-5.)

Samoan house (circa 1930). (Courtesy American Museum of Natural History.)

involves only nine different types, while only eleven types of materials are regularly used for roof construction. The outline below lists these basic shelter forms, types, and materials. Figs. 20 to 22 illustrate some shelter ground plan types.

COMMON FEATURES OF SHELTER SHAPE, CONSTRUCTION, AND MATERIALS*

I. Ground plan of shelters
  A. Circular
  B. Elliptical or elongated with rounded ends
  C. Polygonal
  D. Quadrangular around (or partially around) an interior court
  E. Rectangular or square
  F. Semicircular

---

*See Murdock, G. P. 1967. *Ethnographic Atlas,* Pittsburgh: University of Pittsburgh Press, pp. 60-61.

II. Floor level of shelters
  A. Elevated slightly above the ground on a raised platform of earth, stone, or wood
  B. Floor formed by or level with the ground itself
  C. Raised substantially above the ground on piles, posts, or piers
  D. Subterranean or semi-subterranean, ignoring cellars beneath the living quarters

III. Wall materials of shelters
  A. Adobe, clay, or brick
  B. Bark
  C. Felt, cloth, or other fabric
  D. Grass, leaves, or other thatch
  E. Hides or skins
  F. Mats, latticework, or wattle
  G. Open walls
  H. Plaster, mud and dung, or wattle and daub
  I. Walls merging into roof materials
  J. Stone, stucco, concrete, or fired brick
  K. Wood, including logs, planks, poles, bamboo, or shingles

IV. Shape of roofs

- A. Beehive-shaped with pointed peak
- B. Conical
- C. Dome-shaped or hemispherical
- D. Semi-hemispherical
- E. Flat or horizontal
- F. Gabled; with two slopes
- G. Hipped or pyramidal; four slopes
- H. Rounded or semi-cylindrical
- I. Shed; with one slope

V. Roofing materials

- A. Bark
- B. Earth or turf
- C. Felt, cloth, or other fabric
- D. Grass, leaves, brush, or thatch
- E. Hides or skins
- F. Ice or snow
- G. Mats
- H. Plaster, clay, mud and dung, or wattle and daub
- I. Stone or slate
- J. Tile or fired brick
- K. Wood, including logs, planks, poles, bamboo, or shingles

There have been many attempts to explain variations in the types of human shelters and in the materials used to construct them. For the most part these explanations are "all-or-none" explanations, which select one physical, social, or cultural feature as a causative agent. A brief review of these different explanations follows, as an introduction to discussion of the possible relationships between the technology pattern of shelter and the process of socialization.

Shelter and climate. The simplest physical determination explanation for human shelter variation is the one which says man builds shelters primarily to protect himself from a specific climate. However, the record of shelter types developed within the climate areas of the earth makes it quite clear that shelters must be built for very many reasons other than protection from climate. Too, there has been no real building of shelters by some groups where there clearly is a very inhospitable climate. One example of such a society would be the Ona of Tierra del Fuego. The Ona lived in an almost arctic climate, where they developed a semicircular shaped, ground level floored, semihemispherical roofed structure covered on the sides and roof with animal hides. But this structure was used only for special ritual purposes. Ona nuclear families regularly lived alongside such structures in a simple brush windbreak.

On the other hand, very elaborate shelters are built in climates, such as the tropical Pacific, where in terms of the effects of climate alone the human need for protection would seem to be least critical. Too, in some societies the construction and use of shelters are the opposite of what would reasonably be expected under the climate explanation for shelter variations. The Hidatsa Indians of Missouri farmed in the period from April through November. As they worked their summer fields of corn and beans, small, extended families lived in circular, semi-subterranean, heavy log-walled shelters with dome-shaped wooden roofs covered over with a thick layer of turf. However, in the very cold period from December to March, while the Hidatsa hunted and moved their camps to follow the herds of game, they lived in "tepees," or circular, ground floored, conically shaped, hide-covered temporary frame structures. These two types of shelters were clearly adapted to the two styles of basic subsistence practiced by the Hidatsa (farming and hunting) although under a climatic explanation for shelter types the reverse would have been expected. In fact, similar "anti-climatic" solutions for shelter are not at all uncommon in human societies.[5]

Materials, construction techniques, site locations, and shelter. Three other physical determination explanations for variations in human shelters, put simply, say that the form of shelter in a society is determined solely by (1) the character of the materials used in building, (2) the kinds of construction techniques needed to work materials used, or (3) the site on which a shelter is constructed. No one of these explanations stands the test of comparison with the reported data of human shelters. There are many human shelters constructed of exactly the same materials but of quite different shapes. Shelters throughout the Polynesian and Melanesian Islands have been constructed through use of polished stone and shell adzes. Yet, despite the use of the same adze construction technique, shelters

---

[5] See Rapoport, 1969: 21-24, for other examples.

A Tungus (Siberia) shelter (date unknown). (Courtesy American Museum of Natural History.)

vary greatly in their form throughout these two culture areas.

Finally, there is no comparative evidence that the form of shelter in a society is determined by site location. If this particular physical determination argument were true, then shelters built on similar sites but in different societies would have the same form.

Social and cultural explanations. There are also at least four other ways the forms of human shelter have been explained. In contrast to the four physical deterministic explanations just noted, these explanations are based on selected social and cultural factors. However, in common with all of the physical deterministic explanations, each of the social and cultural explanations for variations in human shelter forms appear also to be a single causation ("all-or-none") explanation.

Need for defense. Perhaps the most typical social and cultural explanation is the one which says that humans build particular forms of shelter out of their need to defend themselves against attack. However, even where the defensive needs of a society are clearly high, the specific form of a living shelter may be very different from the shelter used in time of actual war. Thus, the Masai of East Africa use a different shelter type when at war and when at peace. In Venezuela, Indian groups chronically at war, such as the Piaroa, build circular shelters, while the nearby Motilon build rectangular shelters. Thus, the type of shelter used by a society does not seem generally related to an assumed need for defense.

Shelter and economics. Another common social and cultural explanation for human shelter form directly associates a specific economic system and a particular shelter type. However, such

A Toda (India) house and "dairy" (date unknown). (Courtesy American Museum of Natural History.)

economic explanations do not stand the test of comparison of data of known human shelter types. Thus, the economic systems of swidden, or "slash and burn," agriculturalists living in the same area may be identical, as is the case with the Murut and Dusun societies of Northern Borneo, but their house forms may vary widely. Nomadic peoples, who share a particular type of economic system based on the need for mobility to follow animals or seasonally maturing foods, vary widely in the types of shelters they use. The Mongol folding circular hut, or *yurt,* the Arab folding desert tents, the collapsible tepee of the Plains Indians of North America, the hexagonal portable tent of the Tibetans, and the transportable wooden houses of some American Indian societies of the Pacific Northwest are quite different forms of shelter in societies sharing an economic system based on nomadic life.

SHELTER AND RELIGION. A number of writers have advanced the view that human shelters basically are "religious structures" and that variations in types of structures reflect different religious systems.[6] Again, as in the preceding instances of choosing single social and cultural factors as causative reasons for shelter types, a review of the data of human shelter and of religious beliefs in a society shows no specific correspondence. Religious factors do enter into many features of shelter construction and use. But no causal relationship has been shown to exist between the type of a religious system in a society and the type of shelter it uses.

SHELTER AND KINSHIP. The relationship between the specific type of kinship and kin groups in a society and the typical form of its shelter

---

[6]See Eliade, 1961.

Pygmy house, Congo (1947). (Courtesy American Museum of Natural History.)

has long been a subject of interest to students of culture and society. The earliest attempt to study the possible relationships between shelter form and kinship and kin groups was Morgan's 1881 account of shelter type and social organization among North American Indians. Morgan assumed in his study that the "clan" was the universal and most ancient form of human social organization and was the fundamental unit of all "primitive" society. He also assumed that, since food and household hospitality seemed to be universal among American Indians, very early human social life was probably based on a simple form of communal economic organization. From these two assumptions, Morgan reasoned that the communal shelter types of the North American Iroquois, Pueblo, and Pacific Northwest Indian societies directly reflected the presence of their clans and their communal economic organization. However, Morgan was in error in his assumption concerning the basic and

ancient nature of the clan kin grouping. Too, Morgan did not know that food and house hospitality forms vary greatly among and even are missing in some American Indian societies. And the social form of sharing food and of living in common shelter are not generally related to the economic systems of either North American Indians or other peoples of the world.

Another nineteenth century attempt to directly relate types of shelter and social organization was made by Wundt, often called the "father of experimental psychology." Wundt noted that the use of a small cave by one early human nuclear family must have produced quite long-lasting social attitudes and behavior, some of which were later reflected in the building of single family shelters. Wundt also reasoned that the occupation of a large cave by several early human nuclear families would have later produced long-lasting attitudes and behaviors that would be reflected in an extended family type social organization and typical multiple family shelter types. Wundt's evolutionary psychological speculations were erroneous, since there are no evidences from comparative studies of shelter types and of social organization forms that any particular shelter form has been persistently associated in all of the human experience with any specific type of social organization.

A recent study by Whiting and Ayers (1968) of possible long-lasting correlations between the shape of shelter floor plans and certain social organizational features of culture has noted that in contemporary cultures some selected features of human social organization seem to be related to the *ground plan* of shelters typically built in a culture. After study of a world-wide sample of 136 societies, selected in a way which ensured that no two cultures were drawn from the same culture region or linguistic unit, Whiting and Ayers concluded that the shape of a culture's basic type of shelter is directly related to the two features of (1) the form of the family and (2) whether or not, within the family, there are some specific and clear distinctions made in social relations through use of different status terms and behavior. Whiting and Ayers believe the sequence of causation involved is from the social organization content of culture to the shape of shelter floor plan, that is, the shape of shelter is the "dependent variable," so that as the social organizational features of culture, such as family type, change, the shape of the basic shelter also changes. This hypothesis remains to be fully tested. What is very important about Whiting and Ayers' (1968) study is their belief in use of multiple causation explanations for the form of shelter. Their research is the first to really try to see more than one simple reason for a shelter type.

SHELTER AND CULTURAL STRUCTURING OF PERCEPTIONS. It can be concluded from the brief survey of various single causation explanations for the variations in human shelter types that shelters are built in every culture for a very complex set of reasons. Furthermore, these reasons appear to be related to and to derive from the ways a people perceive the world about them and from the cultural ideologies that shape their perceptions. Another way to state this would be to say that shelters are apparently not conceived in any human society simply as structures, but as integral and basic expressions of complexly interrelated cultural views and ideals. A hypothesis that states this in a more precise form is: given a particular climate, materials, and the limits of a specific system of technology, what finally decides the usual form of shelter in a society are the ways a people perceive the world and their places in it. Although this hypothesis has the appearance of another "single cause" explanation, in fact it is a multiple cause explanation, similar to that used by Whiting and Ayers.

It would be useful to cite some examples of the ways human perceptions are shaped by cultural experiences. A European electrical contractor working in Ghana, West Africa, noted that he constantly was confronted with the problem of his local laborers digging curved rather than straight trenches for laying conduits. The contractor would lay out a straight line between two points for his workers to follow in digging a conduit trench, but at the end of the job he invariably found the trench to have a curve in it. The laborers were recruited from the northern area of Ghana, where circular forms and styles predominate in construction and where straight lines play only a very minor role in everyday life. Thus, because of their prior cultural experiences, it was as difficult for the laborers to dig a straight trench as it would be for most Americans, who have grown up in a "carpentered" or straight-lined world, to draw a perfect freehanded circle.[7]

The Dusun of Northern Borneo have a very complex color designation system consisting of a set of basic hues, each of which is capable of qualification through use of specific cultural modifiers, such as "hot," "old," "strong," and so on. The basic hues can also be highly refined by Dusun through use of specific event or place designations. Thus, a color that has a particular hue, value, and chroma designation in the commonly used western European and American color nomenclature system will be noted by adult Dusun to be "yellow, the color of full-grown bamboo and like the light of the sun shining through an early morning rain." In the Dusun color system, the blue of a clear, tropical midday sky and the green of the underside of jungle

---

[7] See Herskovits, 1958: 267-268.

leaves are designated by the same color term. Dusun physically can "see" or differentiate between blue and green color yarns and color plates, but have only one word to designate these two colors, so obviously different to Europeans and Americans. One of several possible explanations for the failure of Dusun to have separate linguistic designations and to not readily attend to the physical distinctions between blue and green is that Dusun culture has evolved in a tropical rain forest environment, where green hues and their variations dominate the environment and where Dusun lived in small clearings, open only to the skies, with a heavy color border of tropical tree greens. Another explanation is that Dusun genetically lack certain kinds of macular eye pigments which make certain kinds of "blue-green" vision difficult or impossible.[8] Whatever the reason for the origins of the Dusun use of one basic color term for both blue and green hues, the fact remains that, to most Dusun adults, for all practical purposes, blue is green and green is blue.[9] In the same way, northern Ghananese can "see" a straight line, but live in a cultural world of curves and softened angles, and so tend to respond to events in terms of this world.

Another example of the way culture shapes the basic perceptions of a people would be the fundamental inability of two young Dusun girls to see the "litter" in the yard about a house. When we first moved into a Dusun house in the isolated Borneo mountain village of Sensuron, my wife became concerned about the danger of accidental fire in a deep carpeting of debris spread about under our house, which was built off the ground on hardwood piles; the litter stretched in all directions to neighboring houses. One morning my wife asked the two adolescent girls working with her in our household to go out under the house and to sweep the debris into a large pile and then carry it off to the nearby jungle.

Several hours later she discovered the girls sitting on the lower rung of our house ladder talking heatedly with several Dusun adults concerning the task they had been assigned. The Dusun girls could see no "litter" in the house yard and could not understand their task, since the area looked perfectly normal to them. The argument between the girls and the Dusun adults concerned the best way of helping my wife understand that there were no broken tools or other artifacts in the yard to pick up. The Tambunan Dusun word for "litter" or "trash" is most easily translated as "waste" and refers in general only to artifacts left about a house area in a disorderly fashion. But the problem of communication between the Dusun girls and my wife was not solely a linguistic one, since even after my wife's further careful explanations, the two young Dusun girls still could "see" no disorder or litter in the house area, although by this time a large crowd of our Dusun neighbors had gathered and were helping to try to figure out my wife's concerns. The event concluded when my wife decided that Dusun perceptions of order would not be changed through use of American logic, a product of another and very different cultural system. In the following days, our neighbors spent a great deal of time talking about the problem of our perceptions.

Shelter and socialization. Some anthropologists and social psychologists have made detailed studies of the ways culture and experience shape and direct the perception and cognition of a people.[10] These studies have generally concluded that the way humans see and understand themselves and the world about them is not only the consequence of genetically inherited factors and the product of their personal growth and development, but also is a result of the significant ways their cultural heritages prepare them to attend to or ignore selected aspects of their world. If a culture does not provide the definitions, associations, and terms for discussion and thought about particular features of the world, then indi-

[8]Stiles (1946) and Wald (1949) have suggested that genetic differences in macular pigmentation may cause certain populations to have less discrimination between blue and green colors. Ray (1952, 1953) has commented at length on "blue-green confusion" in human cultures.

[9]For some other discussions of the ways color perceptions are structured by cultural experiences, see Berlin and Kay, 1969; Ray, 1952 and 1953; Conklin, 1955; Monberg, 1971.

[10]See the discussions and references in Hallowell, 1951 and 1955. See also Kluckhohn, 1954: 931-940. A discussion by Segall, Campbell, and Herskovits (1966) is basic to current understanding of the cultural structuring of perceptions.

Tambunan Dusun (Sensuron) village scene (1959).
(T. R. Williams.)

viduals growing up in that culture will lack the basic ways necessary to cope in everyday affairs with some parts of their world. In other words, we usually do not see things as they really are, but as we are enculturated to see and understand them.

Research on this topic, which is very complex, has now proceeded to the point where it is possible to say that the socialization process generally involves the simultaneous development of an individual's sense of himself, of the objects about him, and of his conceptions of time and space. This means that, in discussing the ways a particular pattern in the technology subsystem of a culture, such as shelter, may be related to the socialization process, it is necessary to take specific account of the ways cultures define, discuss, and conceive objects, space, and time and the ways these are integrated by individuals in

their self-concepts and expressed in their personal actions.

Perhaps this point can be illustrated briefly by the ways a Dusun guide got himself, my eleven Dusun companions, and me lost in a mountainous, heavily forested area in the center of northern Borneo. I had selected the guide from among several candidates available in the remote village we had visited for 2 days. I had presumed that a Dusun would know his way about the area through which he hunted regularly. As it turned out, the guide had no real understanding of our direction of travel as we moved very slowly along the high, wet mountainsides. When the guide finally admitted to me that he had become completely lost from the path he had set out to follow, I asked my Dusun companions how it was possible for a local man, reportedly a skilled hunter, to become so lost in his home territory. The essence of their response was that the guide had been so busy talking and being an "important person" that he could not remember in proper sequence all of the object reference points (rocks, hill slopes, trees) which in conjunction with the passage of precisely defined spans of time of walking constituted his mental map of the path to be followed. In other words, the guide's usual ability to follow a track through the heavy mountain jungle had gotten distorted by his self-perception as a leader of "important people." This apparently interfered with his basic recall of vital object and space reference points and relationships. We spent that night camped high on a mountain slope, under the dark, massive overhang of a huge rock face. As I sat eating my evening meal I was bemused when the guide explained that he knew the rock shelter quite well, since he often camped there when hunting.

Most anthropologists have had similar experiences while immersed for long periods in other cultural settings. My days with the Dusun were filled with many contrasts between the ways my Dusun neighbors and I perceived the same events and objects and organized our thoughts about them. I learned that there were profound differences separating us which could be transcended only by my learning the basic cultural postulates guiding Dusun life and by suspending as best I could my use of those postulates on which my own culture rests.

When I investigated the specific ways the technology subsystem pattern of shelter is related to the Dusun enculturation process, I found it necessary to broaden my questions and observations to include the underlying cultural postulates which guide the ways Dusun view their world. In 1959 most of the houses in Sensuron, a Tambunan Dusun village in the interior of the Malaysian state of Sabah in northern Borneo, were constructed of split bamboo lashed to hardwood posts with rattan lines. The actual physical construction techniques in Dusun house-building appeared relatively simple. Ten to fifteen hardwood posts, between 20 and 30 feet in length and some 6 to 10 inches in diameter, are set upright into the ground in a pattern

enclosing a rectangular area about 15 by 25 feet. Then smaller diameter hardwood posts are tied horizontally along the outside distance between the main, upright house posts to form the edges of a floor frame. Floor frames are always built up about 3 to 4 feet from the ground. Next, smaller diameter posts are laid about 4 feet apart across the width of the house frame and tied into place with rattan lines. After this, a split, dried bamboo floor is laid out over the floor frame, trimmed at the edges of the floor, and tied down with rattan to the smaller house floor support poles. After the house floor is secured, small hardwood pole stringers are tied with rattan along the outside of the main house posts; a longitudinal pole is put in place about 3 feet and 6 feet up from the floor on all sides of the house. Three-foot wide split bamboo sections are secured vertically to these poles to form the outside house walls. After this, small hardwood poles are lashed with rattan vine from the top wall support up to the projecting tops of the main house posts, forming a peaked roof frame. A roof covering of either split bamboo half sections, or "tiles," or of sections of closely woven palm leaf (*atap*) material is then lashed across the roof frame poles to provide a water-tight covering. Most Sensuron houses built in this manner are constructed in less than 1 day. However, it usually takes a man months and sometimes several years to collect and prepare all of the materials used in construction.

I found as I talked with my Sensuron neighbors that building a house is one of the most meaningful social and religious acts in a man's entire lifetime. I learned that the collection of raw materials, their preliminary preparation, and house construction involved a broad range of Dusun beliefs about man's relationships to the supernatural, concepts of fortune, luck, illness, accident, and personal emotional well-being, magical practices, sacred numbers, kinship, and friendship relationships. I recorded the complex and lengthy ritual preparations which had to be used to properly select the best site for a house, to protect the builders from supernatural harm, and to ensure that occupants had lasting good fortune in their new home. I also learned that there were more than forty different rattan knots and lashing techniques used to secure house poles, frames, siding, and roof materials and that each of the rattan knots had specific names, very complex ritual meanings, and elaborate folktales concerning the consequences of its misuse.

I also learned from my Dusun friends that, for ritual and magical reasons, bamboo for house construction had to be cut at specific places and times of the year and that it had to be of a special diameter and length, and of the "right" color. I was told of the proper ways to dry bamboo not only to ensure its physical strength but so it would be "emotionally" strong as well. I soon became aware that Dusun regularly anthropomorphized (to attribute human properties to an object) and reified (to attribute human powers to an object) their houses. My Dusun friends perceived their homes as having bodies, with "arms" and "legs" and "muscles," a "head," a "belly," and so on. Dusun believe houses have to "stand" in a particular direction and not be "upside-down" on a hill slope. Dusun riddles, puns, and folktales contain many references or allusions to house parts and appearances which are cast in human terms. I learned that Dusun perceived a house as being "young and strong," "old and weak," "fat or skinny," or "worn out."

I also became aware that the interior arrangement of a Dusun house is based upon a series of very complexly interrelated ritual, magical, and social beliefs, so that each room or area and each major item of furnishing had a particular meaning and prohibitions associated with specific times of the day or week, month, and year, at times of social events, before and after childbirth and death, at times of marriage, harvest, warfare, and so on. Since my wife and I lived in a Dusun house rearranged somewhat to meet our needs, I became conscious also of the fact that my Dusun friends could be made quite uncomfortable in a house whose interior plan and furnishings were "out of order."

Thus, in the course of my inquiries about the act of building a typical Dusun house, I found that an apparently simple shelter construction technique involved many of the basic postulates used by Dusun to make their world coherent. I discovered that most Dusun adults in Sensuron have a very deep and enduring emotional investment in both the shape and the details of their houses. It was very difficult for Dusun to speak easily of houses and their associated meanings, unless they turned to strong condemnations of those very few village residents with some *tolun à purak* ("white man") house features, such as a tin roof or hand-sawn and nailed plank sides. Then the whole perceptual orientation of Dusun to their shelter form became readily apparent in the strong feelings of disgust, fear, and aggression displayed toward the few persons changing the traditional Dusun house style. I recorded one old Dusun woman saying, after spitting on the ground in great disgust, "You know that one [a man whose house had wooden sides and a tin roof] draws the attention of every evil spirit to this place; is it any wonder so many babies have died here this year with that man and his house in the middle of us!"

It is quite clear that many of an infant's earliest and continuing life experiences are set in the context of a particular type of shelter and its details. These experiences appear to contribute substantially to the structuring of perceptions of the self of the individual and to the ways individuals come to view objects, space, and time. This statement does not mean, nor is it meant to imply, that the early and continuing experiences of infants and children with a particular type of shelter are critical events (see Chapter Six) or are solely responsible for all of the ways they will perceive the world as adults. Such a claim would be in error, since other patterns in the cultural subsystems of technology, social relations, language, and ideology, as well as biological factors and unique life experience, all influence and are part of the ways people perceive themselves and their world. However, the statement does mean that, if the infants and children of a society are enculturated regularly in the context of a particular type of shelter, they probably will share as adults a perceptual set, preoccupation with, or "ready attention" to that special type of shelter. Furthermore, it means that as adults such persons would be much less

Interior of a Navaho house; sand painting for baby (circa 1935). (Courtesy American Museum of Natural History.)

receptive to drastic changes in their culture's pattern of shelter, since any marked change would mean altering a whole perceptual orientation toward the self and the world. As a consequence, the pattern of shelter in a culture tends to remain stable over a long period of time.

This means that, if we seek to understand the interrelations of the technology pattern of shelter and the enculturation process of a particular society, we must look both to the ways adults of that society perceive shelter and to the kinds of long-term life experiences and understandings infants and children gain in a particular type of shelter. Too, we must look to the consequences for children of having learned such perceptions from adults.

Dusun adults differ from Arunta, Ashanti,

American, or other human adults not only because they have been enculturated in different cultural systems but because those systems contain many different and uniquely interrelated patterns which contribute totally to local ways of viewing the world. In other words, it is not possible to make a Dusun into an Arunta, or an Arunta into an Ashanti, or an Ashanti into an American, etc., simply through changing shelter types. A Dusun looks at the world in Dusun terms and ways because he has been enculturated in the totality of Dusun culture, not solely because he has lived in a Dusun shelter.

As noted, the innovative effort by Whiting and Ayers (1968) in drawing some inferences from the shapes of shelters is one possible recent approach to study of the ways the human cultural pattern of shelter is related to the process of socialization. In using a carefully selected world-wide sample of ethnographic reports from 136 societies and following a statistical technique for cross-cultural study similar to the one discussed in Chapter Seven, Whiting and Ayers asked the specific question, "Given the shape of the floor plan of a dwelling, what can be said, and with what degree of confidence, concerning other features of the culture?" One of their principal conclusions, which is related to the specific concerns of this discussion, was that certain "aesthetic considerations" of culture are related to the type of shelter characteristically found in a society. Then, using a hypothesis derived from a number of studies concerning the relations between art styles and marriage practices in a society and the development of an individual's "cognitive style" in the socialization process, Whiting and Ayers concluded from their data that it is possible to predict from a "curvilinear" type floor plan that the chances are at least three to one that a society with such a shelter form practices a polygynous form of marriage.[11] Whiting and Ayers further concluded it is also possible to accurately predict that this relationship is the consequence of an "aesthetic" preference developed from a society's enculturation process, particularly when there is an intimate and exclusive relationship between mothers and infants during the first 2½ to 3 years after birth. In contrast, Whiting and Ayers believe it is possible to predict from a "rectilinear" type floor that a society practices a monogamous form of marriage and that this relationship is the consequence of an "aesthetic" preference developed from a society's enculturation process in which fathers and mothers are more equally important to a child during his early years of life.

Although they seem to restrict its use only to art styles, Whiting and Ayers (1968) also appear to indicate that the phrase *aesthetic considerations* can denote the broad variety of ways humans perceive the world about them. If this is so, then

[11]For studies suggesting causal relations between art styles, marriage forms, and socialization, see Whiting, Kluckhohn, and Anthony, 1958; Burton and Whiting, 1961; D'Andrade, 1962; Kuckenberg, 1963; Munroe, 1964.

Interior of a Tambunan Dusun (Sensuron) house (1960). (T. R. Williams.)

this study can be taken as a partial demonstration of some transculturally meaningful relationships between shelter and socialization. It must be noted, however, that the principal point of the Whiting and Ayers study was to assist archaeologists to interpret cultural data from their excavations of houses. Too, the statistical methods used in their study may not account for all of the contextual possibilities of data used.

The importance of such research and theory for understanding the relationships between the human pattern of shelter and the socialization process lies in the possibility of being able to specify precisely the ways shelter or other patterns in the cultural subsystems of technology, social relations, language, and ideology produce particular effects and consequences in learning culture. At present it can be said that it is believed that such a causal relationship (for shelter) exists yet we do not know the precise nature and details of that relationship.

In summary, the relationship between the socialization process and the technology subsystem pattern of shelter seems to involve much more than the ground plan, floor level, roof shape, or materials used in shelter walls and roofs. This relationship appears to involve a complex of attitudes, values, and beliefs derived from basic cultural postulates widely shared in a society and which shape, direct, and guide the perceptions of individuals toward themselves and the world about them.

■ Ideology and socialization

The ideology subsystem contains all those cultural patterns concerned with the basic style of thought, understanding, integrated assertations, and goals typical of a society. Specifically, the ideology subsystem contains all of the cultural beliefs, or ideas, which historically have been developed and are usual in a society. This subsystem also contains all of the cultural values, or ideals, widely shared in a society. The cultural ideas and ideals of a society are sometimes direct and actual reflections of the kinds of events which its members historically have experienced. Thus, American culture reflects, in concerns with "progress," an acute awareness of historic origin from a successful settlement of a continental wilderness. However, the cultural ideals and ideas of a society also may be factitious, that is, formed and adapted to artificial standards or after-the-fact interpretations of long past historical events.[12]

Research on ideology. Attempts to abstract and to compare valid statements about human cultural ideals and ideas have been a very important, although limited, part of past research and theory in anthropology and sociology. Some humanistic scholars, notably philosophers, have also been active in the comparative study of human cultural ideals and ideas.

Attempts to study and compare human ideologies have produced a great number of terms and concepts which have been used in conjunction with a variety of research methods. Some examples of these different terms and concepts are given in the outline below.

SOME EXAMPLES OF TERMS AND CONCEPTS
USED IN STUDIES OF CULTURAL IDEOLOGY

I.   **Ideational or cognitive terms and concepts**
   A. Master ideas
   B. Themes
   C. Premises
   D. Postulates
   E. Hypotheses
   F. Common denominators
   G. Enthymemes (unstated assumptions)

II. **Emotional or affective terms and concepts**
   A. Values
   B. Value attitudes
   C. Interests
   D. "Of courses"
   E. Value orientation

III. **Action or conative terms and concepts**
   A. Purposes
   B. Goals
   C. Life goals
   D. Ideas
   E. Sanctions
   F. Directives

IV. **Entire culture or holistic orientation terms and concepts**
   A. Ethos
   B. Eidos
   C. Total cultural pattern
   D. Interaction
   E. Focus
   F. Plot
   G. Style
   H. Set
   I. Climax
   J. Social cynosure
   K. Integrating factors
   L. Sociopsychological constellations
   M. Binary oppositions
   N. Systems of meanings
   O. Unconscious canons of choice
   P. Configurations

---

[12]In current American folk usage the term "ideology" has come to refer only to the theories and action programs making up a specific political and economic program, often foreign, which is viewed simply as factitious propagandizing. However, the term has much broader uses in discussion of the intellectual content and patterning of widely known ideas and values.

Themes and values in ideology. An excellent illustration of study of cultural ideology is to be found in Opler's discussion (1945) of themes in the culture of the Chiricahua Apache, a native North American Indian society. Opler defines a theme as, "a postulate or position, declared or implied, and usually controlling behavior or stimulating activity, which is tacitly approved or openly promoted in a society." Opler notes that there are many different themes in Chiricahua culture. For example, one theme notes that "men are physically, mentally, and morally superior to women." There are, says Opler, numerous "expressions" or translations of this theme in everyday Chiricahua conduct. Thus, if an unborn child has "lots of life," it is said to be a boy. Too, Chiricahua women are believed to be more unstable and excitable than men and so to do things that cause domestic or community troubles. Women also are believed to have much less will power than men and therefore to be easily tempted to sexual misconduct and harmful magic. Chiricahua political and social leaders are men, and males always are heads of families. Women are supposed to defer to men in all social activities. Men must precede women on paths and women must find special areas for eating away from the men. If male guests are present in a household, they must be served before any woman of the family. Women are prohibited from attending most important ceremonial and ritual activities. Menstruating women are considered a grave danger to the health of men and horses. Women are not permitted to sing dancing songs, or to play at most men's games.

Another Chiricahua theme is stated by Opler as a "quest for long life and an old age." Expressions of this theme are found in the fact that adults strive actively to achieve a long life through an incessant manipulation of supernatural powers and unflagging efforts in everyday life. Parents begin the quest for a long life for their children by placing the afterbirth and umbilical cord in a tree that ordinarily reaches great age, so the life and growth of the baby will parallel that of the tree. When a Chiricahua child wears his first moccasins, he is led carefully through four footprints outlined with pollen, a magical symbol of long life. The annual spring haircuts of children are accompanied by prayers for their longevity. Parents seek out the blessings of very old persons, so a child will live to be at least as old as the adult. Girls must undergo a detailed puberty ritual to live a long and healthy life. Adults of very old age command great deference and respect and are expected to speak first and take the lead in social greetings.

A third Chiricahua Apache theme is termed by Opler as "validation by participation." While the wisdom of age is highly valued by the Chiricahua, it is subordinate to and directly linked to personal performance. Chiricahua leaders in command during wars or in hunting parties are young men. When failing health or old age limits active participation, a leader yields readily to a younger man. Hence, as long as men are fit, age is an asset. When they cannot keep pace, age does not prevent retirement. Similarly, younger male ritual specialists actively and openly threaten various supernatural powers with the vigor of their magical acts. Chiricahua Apache believe that rituals for prevention and curing of disease are performed best by a vigorous and active man.

Opler has noted that Chiricahua themes are not always in a perfect balance with one another and that, on occasion, one theme plays a more predominant role than others in the culture, particularly during times of great change in culture.

Another illustration of research on cultural themes is to be found in the studies by Kluckhohn (1949) of the Navaho, a native North American Indian society. In a discussion of Navaho "ideological premises" (or themes), Kluckhohn presents an outline similar to the following.

NAVAHO THEMES

1. The Universe is orderly; all events are caused and interrelated.
   Corollary A. Knowledge is power.
   Corollary B. The basic quest is for harmony.
   Corollary C. Harmony can be restored only by orderly procedures.
   Corollary D. One price of disorder, in human terms, is illness.
2. The Universe tends to be personalized.
   Corollary A. Causation is identifiable in personalized terms.
3. The Universe is full of dangers.

4. Evil and Good are complementary and both are ever present.
5. Experience is conceived as a continuum differentiated only by sense data.
6. Morality is conceived in traditionalistic and situational terms rather than in terms of abstract absolutes.
7. Human relations are premised upon familistic ties.
8. Events, not actors or qualities, are primary.

Kluckhohn also presents a discussion of each of these Navaho ideological themes and corollaries in terms of their everyday expressions in Navaho life. For instance, with reference to the premise that the universe is orderly, Navaho believe no supernatural may capriciously grant the petitions of individuals, for even the gods are bound by irreversible natural laws. The universe is seen by Navaho to be composed of events bound together in specified ways that cannot be changed by gods or men. Every feature of daily life is believed to have one or more causes, arising from the ways the event is related in the cosmic scheme of things to other events; thus, if rain does not fall at the expected season, it is because "people are too mean," or proper ritual taboos have not been followed, or someone is using witchcraft. Navaho constantly test out the order between events. Before committing themselves to a very lengthy and expensive curing ritual, Navaho will try a portion to see if it works. If the small segment of ritual is seen to be effective, then this is taken as a sign that events are in fairly good order and that a full ritual may work. Navaho with knowledge of the ways the universe is ordered are believed to be successful and healthy because of their knowledge. Navaho strive to reduce friction in human relations in order to restore harmony and to maintain order in the universe. Navaho believe all ritual actions, art, folklore, and songs must have a balance or a harmony in their parts and a symmetry of form. Restoration of order in life is believed to be primarily a task of putting objects and human events back into their usual and symmetrical forms.

There also are a variety of specific everyday expressions of another Navaho premise, that the universe is full of dangers. Navaho life is set in the context of a difficult natural environment. Winters are long and cold, summers are arid and hot, and wild animals and human enemies have been present in the Navaho lands. However, Navaho accept these dangers in the terms of the first premise noted. These all are seen to be part of the natural order of the universe. It is because of their failure to know of the exact scheme of things which causes Navaho to see their world as a dangerous place. Navaho do not curse their destiny, for they accept the fact that, only by knowing the precise order of the universe, can they deal effectively with the lack of harmony affecting their lives. Since they also accept their general inability to ever really know more than a small part of the order of the universe, Navaho realize that their lives will be filled with the fears that follow the constant possibilities of causing error and disharmony through some personal action. When Navaho find themselves in a situation which they define as having the potential for causing great disorder, they will tend to do nothing since to act at all would contribute to further disorder.

There have been a number of other efforts to abstract the themes of different peoples, including American and European cultures. For instance, Hoebel's notable discussion (1954) of native law is organized about "basic postulates" or themes in Eskimo, Ifugao, Comanche, Kiowa, Cheyenne, Trobriand, and Ashanti cultures. The seventeen themes Hoebel has abstracted from Ashanti ethnographic data are listed below.

ASHANTI THEMES*

1. The gods and ancestral spirits control and direct the operation of all the forces of the universe.
2. All men must be allowed to participate, directly or indirectly, in the formulation of laws.
3. All major contraventions of the will of the ancestors or the gods are sins.
4. The ancestors will punish the group as a whole, if the group does not punish a sinner and atone for his misdeed.
5. The ancestors will try a man in the spirit world, if he takes advantage of a miscarriage of justice here.

---

*After Hoebel, E. A. *The Law of Primitive Man.* 1954. Cambridge, Mass.: Harvard University Press, pp. 252-254.

6. Past misfortunes are repugnant to the ancestral spirits.

7. Men are endowed with conscious wills, except when drunk or misdirected by an evil spirit in certain limited situations.

8. Blood is physical in nature and is inherited through the mother, thereby creating a physical bond of continuity in matrilineal descent.

9. The spirit is inherited through the father.

10. Basic property belongs to the ancestors.

11. A headman or chief is the representative of the ancestors of the group he governs, and a stool is symbolic of the collectivity of the ancestors.

12. Men are bound to their chiefs by personal fealty as well as by kinship.

13. A man, except when he dies in battle or of natural causes, must know why he dies.

14. Cursing with a forbidden oath is killing.

15. Incest destroys the universe.

16. Menstruation is spiritually unclean.

17. The sex rights of a husband in his wife are exclusive.

DuBois (1955) has presented an outline of themes in American culture. DuBois notes that this culture is organized about four "basic premises" (or themes).

1. The Universe is a Mechanism.

2. Man is Master of the Universe.

3. Men are Equal.

4. Men are Perfectible.

DuBois notes that on systematic analysis these premises yield the following three major "focal values."

1. A belief in material well-being which derives from the basic premise that man is master of the universe.

2. A belief in social conformity which derives from the basic premise that men are equal.

3. A belief in effort and optimism which derives from the basic premise that men are perfectible.

In turn, DuBois believes that analysis of each of these three "focal values" yields a series of "specific values" in American culture. She lists these specific values and some of their expressions in American life.

SPECIFIC VALUES IN AMERICAN LIFE

I. **Material well-being specific values**
   A. *A high standard of living*—Americans equate economic prosperity and social progress and expect that they have a right to demand a high level of living and consumption of goods. This right is supported by health insurance, social welfare plans and operations, and political hostility toward economic and professional interest groups, organizations and plans which threaten to limit a high standard of living.
   B. *Success in material goods carries a moral sanction*—Americans believe they have a right to be physically comfortable, after working hard, for virtue in daily labor carries the reward of attaining desired goods.
   C. *Manual labor is dignified*—Americans feel that hard work with one's hands and body is of superior worth and will "pay off" in material well-being.
   D. *Military logistics shape basic strategy*—Americans do not assume that unless all is lost personal heroism should come before providing proper supplies and equipment for fighting. American wars tend to be prepared for first by building bases and filling them with equipment, and then starting to fight. Usually there are three times or more "support" troops than "combat" troops.
   E. *Pain, brutality, and death are not to be tolerated*—Americans tend to be repelled by poverty, misery, cruelty, and physical suffering, since these all interfere with attainment of a material well-being.

II. **Conformity specific values**
   A. *Team work*—Americans believe that no single man can master the universe, so men must work together to meet their immediate tasks, to enable them to later cope with larger efforts.
   B. *Self-achievement has the goal of similarity*—Americans strive individually to achieve the end of being similar to others in the society.
   C. *Physical barriers are unwelcome*—Americans tend to believe fences, doors, walls, and other barriers separate the partners of the team in efforts to master life's problems.
   D. *Hostility toward authority figures*—Americans resist authority symbols for these accentuate status differences, rather than conformity and team work.

III. **Effort-optimism specific values**
   A. *Work is valuable*—Americans stress work activity as so necessary that even recreation and leisure must be work to be good.
   B. *Importance of education*—Formal education prepares children for their work careers and activities and so is to be strongly encouraged.
   C. *Vigor and impatience*—Americans stress specific action now, even at the expense of planning.
   D. *Emphasis on biologic youth*—American cultural heroes are young, strong, handsome, and healthy.

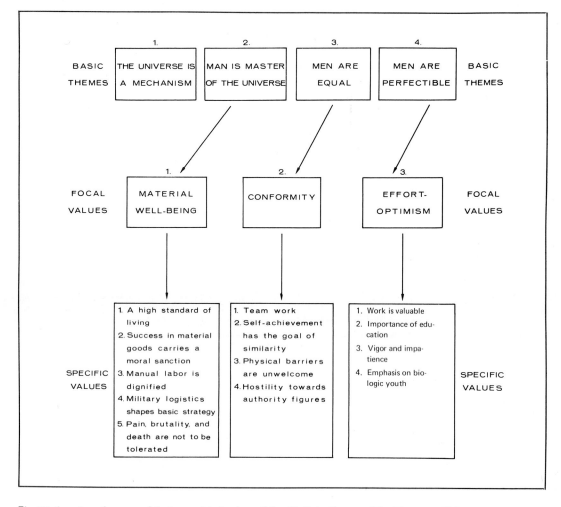

Fig. 23. American themes and their associated values. (After DuBois, C. 1955. "The Dominant Value Profile of American Culture," American Anthropologist **57**:1232-1239.)

A summary of the scheme used by DuBois is presented in Fig. 23.

A major problem in the analysis of themes is the fact that significant ideological variations in a culture have not been really accounted for in most discussions.

One major recent effort to understand ideological variations within and between cultures has been the research of Kluckhohn, Strodtbeck, and others (1961). These studies are based on the two assumptions that (1) there are a limited number of common human problems for which all peoples must find some solutions and (2) in all societies there will be some differentially preferred solutions to common problems at different times. Kluckhohn, Strodtbeck, and colleagues developed a five-section questionnaire concerned with the common problems of: (1) *human nature orientation* (what is the character of innate human nature?); (2) *man-to-nature orientation* (what is the relation of man to nature and supernature?); (3) *time orientation* (what is the temporal focus of human life?); (4) *activity orientation* (what is the usual style of human activity?); and (5) *relational orientation* (what is the usual style of a man's relationship to other men?). In order to encompass the range of value variations for these assumed common human problem areas, Kluckhohn and Strodtbeck defined the widest possible range of choices humans might have in each area.

I. **Human nature orientation**
   A. Evil
   B. Good and evil
   C. Good

II. **Man-to-nature orientation**
   A. Subjugation to nature
   B. Harmony with nature
   C. Mastery over nature

III. **Time orientation**
   A. Past
   B. Present
   C. Future

IV. **Activity orientation**
   A. Being
   B. Being-in-becoming
   C. Doing

V. **Relational orientation**
   A. Lineal
   B. Collateral
   C. Individualistic

Then, Kluckhohn, Strodtbeck, and co-workers presented their questionnaire to members of five different cultural communities located in the same general physical environment in the American Southwest. Two of the communities were American Indian (Navaho and Zuni), one was Spanish-American, another Mormon, and the fifth was a homestead village of American Texan and Oklahoman farmers. Before beginning actual field study, the authors made specific predictions, based on the literature of each of these five communities, regarding their principal orientation on four of the five common problem areas of their questionnaire (the human nature orientation was exempted from their predictions). These specific predictions are noted in Table 9-1. This table also notes the specific results obtained by these authors through application of their value orientations research questionnaire in each of the five communities studied.

These studies of cultural ideology have estab-

Table 9-1. Predicted and observed variations in dominant value orientations in five Southwestern American communities*

Orientation	Spanish Americans		Texans		Mormons		Zuni		Navaho	
	Predicted	Observed	Predicted	Observed	Predicted	Observed	Predicted	Observed	Predicted	Observed
Man-to-nature	Subjugation Over With	Subjugation Over With	Over Subjugation With	Over With Subjugation	With Over Subjugation	Over With Subjugation	No prediction	With Subjugation Over	With Subjugation Over	With Subjugation Over
Time	Present Future Past	Present Future Past	Future Present Past	Future Present Past	Future Present Past	Future Present Past	No prediction	Present Past Future	Present Past Future	Present Past Future
Activity	Being Doing	Being Doing	Doing Being	Doing Being	Doing Being	Doing Being	No prediction	Doing Being	Doing Being	Doing Being
Relational	Individualistic Lineal Collateral	Individualistic Lineal Collateral	Individualistic Collateral Lineal	Individualistic Collateral Lineal	Individualistic Collateral Lineal	Individualistic Collateral Lineal	No prediction	Collateral Lineal Individualistic	Collateral Lineal Individualistic	Collateral Lineal Individualistic

*After Kluckhohn, F., and F. Strodtbeck. 1961. *Variations in Value Orientations.* Evanston, Ill.: Row, Peterson, p. 351.

lished that there may be substantial differences between the styles of thought and understanding within different cultures. Some examples of other efforts to draw general conclusions about and establish some principles of patterns of human ideology are noted in the following section.

Studies of ideology and socialization. Few patterns of cultural belief and value have been studied with regard to their specific relationships to the socialization process. One pattern which has had some attention recently is art.

Much of art is decorative. Designs or marks are made by the users or manufacturers on the artifacts and objects employed in the everyday life of a culture. Sometimes decorative art is formal, that is, it directly shows cultural belief, value, or a theme expression. Decorative art also may be informal, that is, it may be used to show an aesthetic preference of individuals making or using artifacts. Individual artistic expressions also often reflect a consensus of generally pleasing appearances and standards of beauty widely shared in a society.

Human art may also be symbolic in nature. Some artifacts are deliberately made and decorated with forms and designs of very special cultural meanings. Symbolic art decoration usually conveys messages about the presence of supernatural and nonhuman forces revered and feared by human beings. Thus, a container with a sacred animal carved on the lid may not be a box, but represents the animal itself keeping watch over sacred objects stored within it. Objects used in religious and magical acts and rituals are usually infused with widely shared and deeply felt meanings expressed in symbolic form. The symbolic or decorative arts of a culture are not readily understood by persons unfamiliar with that tradition. For example, the "split representation" decorative and symbolic art style of the Kwakiutl, Haida, and Tsimshian Indians of the Northwestern coast of North America involves the dislocation of animal, human, and spirit forms into elements which are then recombined following traditional rules and aesthetic standards that have little to do with Western European conceptions of nature. Thus, it is necessary, when looking at a Haida painting of a bear, to imagine that the animal has been cut in two from head to tail, with a deep cleft between the eyes down to the level of the nose. The cleft head depicts two facial profiles that join at the mouth and nose. The remainder of the bear's body is similarly shown in two adjoining profiles.[13] This art form often uses the arbitrary dislocation of internal organs and other body parts, which are split off and then rejoined to the animal in some other place; a claw is made into a bird's beak, an eye becomes a leg or an arm joint, and so on.

Lévi-Strauss (1967) has noted that the split representation decorative and symbolic art style was also typical of the nineteenth century Maori of New Zealand, the Neolithic cultures of China (*Yangshao*), Japan (*Jomon*), and Siberia (Amur River Basin), and among the twentieth century Caduveo Indians of Paraguay and Southern Brazil. It is also found in the prehistoric Hopewell culture of Eastern North America. It is Lévi-Strauss' belief that this identity of art form and style among so many cultures separated by more than 2,000 years of time and with no known evidences of historic contact arises from the fact that all of these groups had social systems in which there were personal prestige struggles, intense rivalry between formal groups, and severe competitions for social and economic privileges as regular features of life. In other words, Lévi-Strauss feels that individual artists in these societies accidentally discovered, through their long-term experimentations with decorative and symbolic art, the same formal arrangement of themes of a cultural organized in terms of social hierarchies and hierarchical behavior.

Unlike Lévi-Strauss, anthropologists have tended until recently to be somewhat hesitant in making comparative studies attempting to relate art to patterns in other subsystems of human culture.

However, a number of studies of the possible relations between art and socialization have been published since 1957. For instance, Barry has published the results of his study of the relation-

---

[13]See Boas, 1927a, 1927b, and 1929.

ships between "child training" and the "pictorial arts" in thirty nonliterate cultures. Barry (1957) began his research on the relations between art and socialization with the assumption that an individual artist's personality is commonly expressed in his creations, so that individual differences in art styles in a culture are related directly to individual personality differences. Further, Barry assumed that, since the personality of an individual artist includes the consequences of the influential events which he has undergone in "socialization," the art styles of culture would directly reflect such events.

Barry then proceeded to apply these two assumptions to a whole culture. He reasoned that, if the assumptions were true for individuals, they would also be true for a "typical" individual in a small and relatively homogeneous population.

Then, using the measures of severity of socialization defined and discussed by Whiting and Child (1953) and some specific measures of art style developed by himself, Barry conducted a statistical test for the existence of a possible correlation between (1) the severity of "socialization" in a culture and (2) typical styles of art in a culture.

Barry's research procedures began with accepting the validity of the numerical scores and rankings for each of ten measures of severity of oral, anal, sexual, dependency, and aggression socialization used by Whiting and Child in their research. Then Barry sought in the ethnographic literature at least ten pictures of art works for each of thirty native societies. In all, he used a total of 549 pictures. He proceeded to judge each of the works of art on a seven-point scale for eighteen different criteria, such as shortness of lines, presence of a border, asymmetry of design, and so on. Barry then chose to consider eleven of his eighteen criteria as real measures of the complexity of the art style in a culture.

At this point Barry proceeded to employ statistical procedures to measure the possible correlations between his eleven variables of complexity of design and Whiting and Child's ten variables of severity of "socialization" in a culture. He concluded from his statistical analyses that, for each of the eleven art variables, the cultures above the median (the point in a series chosen so that half the cases are on one side and half on the other) in complexity of art design tended also to be above average in the severity of their "socialization" of oral, anal, sexual, dependency, and aggression systems of behavior. On the other hand, Barry noted that cultures below the median in complexity of art design tended to be below average in the severity of "socialization" of these same systems of behavior.

Barry drew the general conclusion from his data and analyses that the positive correlation between severity of socialization and complexity of design in art works indicated a specific "connecting link" between them which he notes to be the kind of typical personality produced in a society's enculturation process. In other words, Barry believes his study of relations between art and socialization demonstrates that cultures have simple or complex art styles because the typical personality types produced in a society by severe or relaxed child training practices lead to the kind of person capable of producing either a simple or a complex art design.

In another study of the relations between art and socialization, Fischer (1961) investigated the specific question of whether any features of culture may predispose an artist to regularly choose curvilinear (semicircular or circular) or rectilinear (rectangular) designs. Fischer began his research with the assumption that rectilinear designs represent the male body image, while curvilinear designs represent the female body image. He also made the assumption that "man projects his society into his art."

Fischer's specific research procedures began with his accepting the validity of the judgments of art styles for thirty cultures made by Barry in his study of the relations between complexity of design and severity of socialization. Then, using cultural and social data taken from the summaries listed in Murdock's *World Ethnographic Sample* (1957), Fischer proceeded to formulate six hypotheses concerning the relationships between the art style of a culture, its typical form of social relations, and the relative prestige or security of the sexes. Fischer's (1961: 81, 84) hypotheses were as follows.

1. Design repetitive of a number of rather simple elements should characterize the egalitarian societies; design integrating a number of unlike elements should be characteristic of hierarchical societies.
2. Design with a large amount of empty or irrelevant space should characterize the egalitarian societies; design with little irrelevant (empty) space should characterize the hierarchical societies.
3. Symmetrical design (a special case of repetition) should characterize the egalitarian societies; asymmetrical design should characterize the hierarchical societies.
4. Figures without enclosures should characterize the egalitarian societies; enclosed figures should characterize the hierarchical societies.
5. Straight lines, representing the male form, as opposed to curved, should be associated with societies which strongly favor male solidarity in residence.

Using Barry's criteria for design complexity, Fischer then employed statistical procedures to test these hypotheses against the ethnographic data summarized by Murdock. Fischer's statistical results tend to show a positive relationship between repetitive, open-spaced, symmetrical, and nonenclosed figure designs in the art of societies which regularly minimize individual differences in prestige and emphasize cooperation and mutual helpfulness. In contrast, Fischer's statistical data note that societies which emphasize differentiation of persons by social and economic rank and personal prestige and minimize personal cooperation will have art designs that integrate unlike elements, have little empty space, are asymmetrical, and contain enclosed figures. In addition, Fischer's statistical data concerning the relative prestige or security of the sexes (hypothesis number 5) were much less positive. To his surprise, Fischer found in testing the fifth hypothesis that, while he believed from psychological studies that rectilinear, or "male," art designs would be found regularly in cultures with patrilocal or avunculocal (see Chapter Seven) marriage residence patterns, which indicates possibly that men have high prestige, quite the opposite was true. In fact, Fischer discovered a statistical association in the opposite direction, that is, between curvilinear, or "female," design and a pattern of preference in a culture for patrilineal and avunculocal residence

after marriage. Fischer offered the *post hoc* explanation for this reversal of his hypothesis by pointing out that perhaps the reason for cultures with high male prestige having a dominant "female" (curvilinear) art style was that men in patrilineal and avunculocal type cultures, which accorded them high prestige, were more psychologically secure and extroverted and had more time to spend looking for pleasure in the opposite sex. Hence such psychological security, says Fischer, would explain the presence in high male prestige societies of curvilinear art designs.

However, in reviewing Fischer's *post hoc* reasoning concerning the reversal of the fifth hypothesis (see above), Whiting pointed out that psychological theory really suggests that psychological conflict and anxiety arising in enculturation rather than psychological security is the explanation for high male prestige in societies employing "female" art designs. This would be so, Whiting says, simply because more sexually frustrated and anxious males would tend to be more preoccupied with the female body and thus prefer use of curvilinear, or "female," art designs. Whiting reasoned further that, if his conflict and anxiety explanation for Fischer's statistical data were correct, then it could be predicted that in societies which emphasize patrilocal and avunculocal residence after marriage there would be a high degree of restriction on children's and adolescents' sex activities. Whiting (1968:128) reports that his test of this hypothesis (societies with patrilocal/avunculocal residence have severe restrictions on premarital sex activities) in 136 societies was statistically a positive one. Whiting concludes that patrilocal and avunculocal societies, with a preference for curvilinear art designs, tend to produce males who are more sexually inhibited because of restrictions on their sex activities in the enculturation process.

Following his theory of "psychological security" one step further, Fischer also reported, as part of his study, on the relationships between the form of marriage (monogamy, polygamy, and so on) in a culture and its dominant art style. He formulated two hypotheses concerning these possible relationships: (1) because of a higher degree of psychological security for men due to their sexual access to two or more women, polygamous cultures would use more curved designs in their art; and (2) because of a higher degree of psychological insecurity for men due to their sexual restriction to one woman, monogamous societies would use more straight line designs in their art. Fischer notes that a statistical testing of these two hypotheses showed them to be valid at "a statistically significant level." However, he made one important qualification of these results, with reference to the art designs of cultures which practice polygyny (see Chapter Seven). Sororal polygyny is different, notes Fischer, from ordinary polygyny, in that the co-wives are sisters and therefore because of their enculturation experiences tend more often to form a common front against the interests and wishes of an outsider, or husband. Cultures practicing soral polygyny were found by Fischer to be "intermediate" in their art design preference, between the two extremes of curvilinear and rectilinear design. Fischer also points out that the cultures with a hierarchical social structure tend to produce a severe competition between siblings, to the point where sororal polygyny hardly would work well. This, says Fischer, is why cultures with sororal polygyny nearly all tend to relatively simple art styles, in common with monogamous cultures.

Whiting, in reviewing these conclusions (that monogamous cultures were more likely to use a preponderance of straight lines in their art designs than cultures practicing nonsororal polygyny) pointed out that Fischer's use of a psychological security explanation was again contradicted by a number of recent, statistically based, transcultural studies of socialization.[14] Whiting points out that these studies, concerned generally with the specific effects of the "salience" or closeness of the mother and father to children during the first 2½ to 3 years of life on adult cognitive styles, all note that where a culture regularly established an intimate and exclusive relationship between mothers and children the form of the family usually is polygynous. In contrast,

cultures in which mothers and fathers are more equally important to children usually tend to be monogamous.

Whiting goes on to note that, in cultures with a close mother-child relationship, mothers are seen by children to control all the important resources and economic goods vital to children. Mothers in such cultures tend to occupy the position of highest prestige in the eyes of children. After weaning, says Whiting, in a polygynous family the preoccupation of a child with his mother's body should continue unabated. Such male children are presumed to be characterized by psychological conflict and anxiety.

In contrast, notes Whiting, in monogamous cultures, children learn that both men and women equally control the resources and goods important to children. And, after weaning, a child's preoccupation with his mother's body is much less intense. Such children tend to be characterized by psychological security.

Whiting conducted his own transcultural check of the relationship between curvilinear art designs and polygyny and between rectilinear art designs and monogamy, as reported by Fischer in his study. He confirmed Fisher's positive findings in his own survey of art design and social structure (1968: 130). However, in contrast to Fischer, and following the studies of salience in socialization, Whiting interprets this strong association as meaning that the presence of a curvilinear art design in a polygynous culture is the result of the usual enculturation practices of such groups, where during early childhood there is a high degree of mother-child salience. This is so, implies Whiting because high salience in enculturation produces psychological conflict and anxiety, hence adult male concerns with curvilinear art design, while low salience in enculturation produces psychological security, hence a greater adult male concern with rectilinear art designs.

The general theoretical view expressed in the studies by Barry, by Fischer, and by Whiting is that social conditions give rise to some psychological characteristics which are primary determinants of artistic creativity and that these characteristics are reflected directly in the typical

---

[14]See Whiting, Kluckhohn, and Anthony, 1958; Burton and Whiting, 1961; D'Andrade, 1962; Kuckenberg, 1963; Munroe, 1964.

style of a culture's decorative and symbolic art. Barry and Whiting tend to believe that the social conditions giving rise to important psychological characteristics involved in a typical art design are those found in the human socialization process. Fischer tends to look more to particular forms of human social life (hierarchical social relations, polygynous marriage preference, and so on) as being productive of those psychological characteristics which determine the typical designs of art in human culture. However, Fischer also gives reference to and makes note of the socialization processes in providing his *post hoc* explanations (for example, psychological security) for reversal of his one hypothesis and for the occurrence of particular art designs in association with specific marriage forms.

Without regard to whether the basic assumptions of these studies are correct, or their statistical and decontextualizing methods accurate in transcultural analysis (see Chapter Seven), or their logic in drawing conclusions is valid, the vital point of such innovative research is that it offers a clear demonstration that there are ways of discussing relationships between the socialization process and the ideology pattern of art.

Two other studies have been conducted of art design styles and their specific relationships to various social and cultural factors, including some features of the socialization process. Wolfe (1969) has studied the specific question of why some cultures produce a large amount of "high quality" art, while other cultures seem to produce little or no art of "less quality." Wolfe used statistical procedures to test his general hypothesis that "a high development of graphic and plastic art is associated with social structural features that set up barriers between males in local communities." Wolfe assumed that social barriers between males produce "emotions," which in turn would be directly reflected in the "emotions" involved in the art design and production of a culture. Wolfe then tested his hypothesis in 53 African cultures and concluded that it was generally true, at least in the case of African cultures. He notes that the statistically significant results of his research support his belief that art flourishes in those African cultures where males are

divided by important social barriers, as well as where settlements are fixed and nucleated (or compact). Wolfe feels that, if these African data are applicable to other world culture regions, then a transculturally valid relationship between social structure and art design may be established. Wolfe's discussion and conclusions imply that some features of the socialization process are directly involved in the art style of a culture through the "emotions" produced in particular social conditions, which are then reflected directly in the "emotions" displayed in art designs. Although he does not directly specify any enculturation practices among the 39 variables of social structure used in his study, there are in fact a number of features of the cultural transmission process discernible among the variables listed.

Another study indicating some possible relationships between art and the socialization process has been reported by Dennis (1966), who notes the differences in scores on the administration of the Goodenough "Draw-A-Man" test to 6- to 12-year-old children in 40 different groups located in some 13 cultures. The test scores reported by Dennis were collected in the period between 1928 and 1962. In the time from 1926 to about 1950 the Goodenough test was considered by many psychologists to be a "culture free" test, which measured inherent intelligence by drawings of human figures. However, by 1950 this assumption had been rejected by Goodenough herself. Dennis began the study reported here by noting that, while a Goodenough drawing test score obviously does not measure innate or biologically transmitted intelligence, it can be considered to show cultural and social differences in art design and drawing styles. Dennis proposed, following this assumption, the hypothesis that differences in the Goodenough test scores of children in different cultures would be reflected in their representational (or decorative) art. Dennis also advanced a second hypothesis that in many cultures Goodenough test scores are "indirect" measures of modernization and cultural change toward a European and American style of technology.

Dennis also began his study with the assumptions that in non-Western cultures, with little prior contact with European and American decorative art, but with a "high level of achievement" in respect to several art forms, such as wood carving, sculpture, pottery, masks, and sand-painting, children would earn high Goodenough test scores. In contrast, Dennis assumed that, in cultures with no prior contacts with European and American cultures and with a low level of artistic achievement, children would earn low Goodenough test scores. Therefore, Dennis reasoned, when children in a culture with a low level of artistic achievement begin to be exposed to a high level of artistic achievement through regular and increasing contacts with European and American decorative art, the increase in their Goodenough test scores would provide a rough index of local cultural change.

Dennis then presented data of test scores from the forty groups in thirteen cultures and a statistical analysis of their differences. He concludes that all of the significant differences between cultures on the Goodenough test scores seem attributable to the differences in exposure of children to representational art, either as it is native to a culture or as it has been introduced in the course of growing cultural change and modernization toward a European and American style of decorative art.

■ Conclusions

Studies of relationships between the socialization process and patterns in the cultural subsystems of technology and ideology presently are hampered by past inattention to reporting the details of these aspects of cultural transmission. A search of the literature of enculturation provides only fragmentary glimpses of the ways infants and children actually learn these aspects of culture.

For example, Opler (1946: 39-40) reports in a study of Jicarilla Apache Indian enculturation that when a boy is 4 or 5 years old his older brothers, father, or grandfather give him a toy bow and arrows to get him used to these essential adult tools. Opler notes that on occasion older men gather little boys together and teach them games which increase their skills in the use of these tools. Opler also reports that 6- and 7-year-old Jicarilla boys are encouraged to get up early in the morning to run after the horses, to chase them from their night pastures to a point near the encampment where they can be caught by adult males. Boys of this age are instructed not to mistreat horses when they run after them. They are told stories of horses abandoning masters during crucial times in the hunt or in war because of mistreatment by their owners. Opler also reports that at about 9 or 10 years of age Jicarilla boys are taught to ride rapidly with and without a saddle. Opler notes too that at 12 years of age, in preparation for warfare, boys are made to ride past and to practice shooting arrows at each other.

These few comments on the enculturation of Jicarilla boys to skill and awareness of the two technology trait complexes of the bow and arrow and the use of the horse in war and hunting are accompanied in Opler's report by a few other brief statements concerning the ways the bow and arrow and horse culture trait complexes are related to some other patterns in the technology and ideology subsystems of the Jicarilla Apache culture. But these brief comments do not at all provide a sense of the fullness, the great complexity of detail and of the vital importance in enculturation of these patterns of Jicarilla cultural subsystems of technology and ideology. A reading of the extensive literature on the Jicarilla and other closely related North American Plains Indian cultures makes it clear that the enculturation process for Jicarilla boys must have been very much more complex in the learning of some cultural patterns of technology and ideology than has been reported.[15]

Such reportorial limitations, due primarily to lack of space rather than an author's interests or abilities, have not been unusual in publications concerned with cultural transmission. A need now exists, however, for studies of the enculturation process in its relation to specific patterns of the technology and ideology subsystems, in order to provide the basis for meaningful transcultural generalizations concerning these aspects of cultural transmission.

Since in my study of Dusun enculturation I was aware that there were few detailed accounts

---

[15] See the comments of Wissler, 1914; Haines, 1938a and 1938b; Hoebel, 1954: 127-176; Ewers, 1955.

in the enculturation literature which described the ways children actually learn a particular pattern of technology or ideology, I concentrated on a recording of the details of a select number of patterns of the Dusun technology and ideology cultural subsystems. As my study proceeded, I tried to be alert to the ways these features of culture were transmitted by adults as they dealt directly or indirectly with infants and children. For instance, in my study I made a detailed record of the Dusun ideology pattern of measures, particularly those involving length, circumference, and height.

I found Dusun adults regularly used 24 measures of length, 2 main measures of circumference, and 11 measures of height. These measures are summarized in the following list. Whenever possible, I made detailed notes of the use of any of these measures by adults when children were present. I also recorded the details involved when I found a child using any one of these measures. At the close of more than 2 years of field study of the Dusun enculturation process, I had very detailed notes of specific instances of use of these measures in conjunction with many other Dusun patterns of culture. Although the Dusun system for measuring length, circumference, and height is simple, compared to those used in some other cultures, I discovered the Dusun to be incessant measurers in their everyday life. I found that many adult Dusun conversations involved some use of the measures noted in the list. For instance, such discussions centered upon the growth and health of the rice crop, the size of water buffalo, the nature of danger in crossing a flooded stream, estimates of male sexual powers, the judging of danger to domestic animal life from the length of a snake, the wasting of the body of a dying old man, the growth of the head of a baby girl, the proper ways to inscribe the boundaries of a hillside swidden rice field, the best division of inherited property, the placement of a new house in the "proper" relation to the houses nearby, and the crucial nature of evidence in a trial for theft. I recorded no single instance of a Dusun adult directly teaching a child any one of these measures. Yet I recorded many instances of children, some as young as

4 years old, using these measurement terms and definitions accurately and in a matter of fact way as they went about playing various games, settling their disputes, and engaging in conversations.

DUSUN MEASURES OF LENGTH, CIRCUMFERENCE, AND HEIGHT

MEASURES OF LENGTH

sėmbuku—"one bend of the first finger"
duonokė—"two bends of the first finger"
sėmȧpȧk—"one first finger full length"
sȧmpȧmulkul—"from the middle of the upturned knuckle of the thumb to the end of the first finger"
pėhėdokȧn—"from the end of the thumb across the knuckles to the edge of the palm"
sȧmpȧladun—"thumb against the hand; from the edge of the thumb to the edge of the palm"
sandȧŋau tudėduk—"tip of the outstretched thumb across to the tip of the outstretched first finger"
sandȧŋau berȧntȧt—"tip of the outstretched thumb across to the tip of the outstretched second finger"
tȧpȧnseko—"tip of the third finger to the elbow"
tȧpeŋlėnėn—"tip of the third finger to the armpit"
mėntȧtȧ—"tip of the third finger to the middle of the chest"
mėŋenȧn—"tip of the third finger across the chest to the opposite side of the body"
mėmėnbuŋ—"tip of the third finger across the chest to the middle of the opposite arm"
mėnuntėd—"tip of the third finger across the chest to the elbow of the opposite arm"
sȧndȧpė—"tip of the third finger across the chest to the tip of the third finger of the other hand or one span" (duodȧpė, two spans; taludȧpė, three spans; and so on for measures up to ten spans)

MEASURES OF CIRCUMFERENCE

ȧtubė—"first finger and thumb tips together to form a circle"
ȧgȧpėsnė—"to encircle with the arms" (e.g., a tree trunk, etc.)

MEASURES OF HEIGHT

gesȧem dė tȧhmpȧŋit—"up to the ankle"
gesȧem dė tȧtud—"up to the knee"
kȧpintȧŋė nė dėpė—"up to the thigh"
gesȧem id dȧuȧk—"up to the waist"
kȧnkȧb de tėan—"up to the chest"
gesȧem dė susu—"up to the nipples"
gesȧem dė pėkeluk—"up to the armpits"
gesȧem dė leuȧuȧ—"up to the shoulder tops"
gesȧem dė leo—"up to the throat"
gesȧem dė taliŋė—"up to the ears"
kalimbėn—"over the head"

I concluded that Dusun children learn this measurement system early and retain it well. I also concluded that this cultural pattern of the Dusun ideology subsystem was transmitted largely through a self-enculturation (or reflective and symbolic) process (see Chapter Four). As the Dusun children listened to and watched adults in their expressions of these measures of length, circumference, and height, they acquired a sense of the great importance to adults of knowing such information well and of being able to readily voice it. Children became aware that most Dusun adults know the measures of length, circumference, and height vital to their world, health, work, comfort, and so on.[16]

Although only a few examples of patterns of the technology and ideology subsystems of culture have been discussed here, it is clear that the present situation in research makes it difficult to offer many meaningful causal statements. It does seem quite clear that patterns of technology and ideology play an important part in the socialization process. However, since we are unsure of the specific ways technology and ideology patterns are related to cultural transmission in many different cultures, we can offer only very qualified statements. For instance, in the small sample of societies cited in Chapter Seven, there appears to be a tendency for at least half of the societies, without apparent regard to other cultural and social features (such as subsistence, kinship, kin groups, class, and so on) to place upon children the general burdens of properly learning technology and ideology patterns, in ways similar to those used by the Dusun of Borneo. In some societies, however, particularly those which are heavily urbanized and industrialized (such as the United States, England, France, Russia, and so on) some kinds of specific instruction in patterns of technology and ideology do occur regularly ("vocational education," "church schools," and so on); children

are not left entirely to themselves in learning these features of their culture. But even in these societies, children are apparently responsible for substantial portions of their own enculturation in the patterns of technology and ideology.

This particular statement, based on a reading of the literature of enculturation in a small sample of societies, is qualified by the fact that few of the studies of enculturation used in the sample really report the specific details of learning of most patterns of technology and ideology. Hopefully, this particular lack in socialization research should change rapidly, as detailed field research is conducted on the enculturation of children to patterns of technology and ideology in specific societies.

■ Summary

This chapter has been concerned with illustrating some of the ways the socialization process may be related to patterns in the technology and ideology subsystems of culture. The discussion began with an examination of possible relations between socialization and the technology pattern of shelter. Then consideration was given to the ways several ideology subsystem patterns, including ideas about numbers, measures, nature, society, and art, might be related to socialization. The chapter concluded with brief comment concerning studies of the interrelations between socialization and the technology and ideology subsystems of culture.

---

[16]These data of Dusun enculturation are noted here to illustrate the kinds of materials which may be necessary to conduct of transcultural research on the relations between the socialization process and patterns of the ideology subsystem. See Pettitt (1946) for a comparative study of North American Indian enculturation of patterns of technology and ideology.

REFERENCES CITED AND SUGGESTED READINGS

Albert, E. 1956. "The Classification of Values: A Method and Illustration," American Anthropologist 58:221-248.

Barry, H., III. 1957. "Relationships Between Child Training and the Pictorial Arts," Journal of Abnormal and Social Psychology 54:380-383.

Beals, R. 1935. Material Culture of the Pima, Papago and Western Apache. Berkeley: U.S. Department of the Interior, National Park Service.

Beals, R., and H. Hoijer. 1965. An Introduction to Anthropology, ed. 3. New York: Macmillan.

Belshaw, C. S. 1959. "The Identification of Values in Anthropology," American Journal of Sociology 64:555-562.

Berlin, B., and P. Kay. 1969. *Basic Color Terms; Their Universality and Evolution.* Berkeley: University of California Press.

Bidney, D. 1949. "The Concept of Meta-anthropology and Its Significance for Contemporary Anthropological Science." In F. S. C. Northrop (ed.), *Ideological Differences and World Order.* New Haven: Yale University Press, pp. 323-355.

_____. 1953a. *Theoretical Anthropology.* New York: Columbia University Press.

_____. 1953b. "The Concept of Value in Modern Anthropology." In A. L. Kroeber (ed.), *Anthropology Today.* Chicago: University of Chicago Press, pp. 682-699.

Boas, F. 1911. *The Mind of Primitive Man.* New York: Macmillan.

_____. 1927a. *Primitive Art.* Oslo: H. Aschehough.

_____. 1927b. "Primitive Art," Oslo: *Instituttet fur Sammenlingnende Kulturforskning* 8:223-224.

_____. 1929. *Primitive Art.* New York: Dover (New Edition; first published in 1929, republished by Dover in 1955).

_____. 1930. *The Religion of the Kwakiutl Indians.* New York: Columbia University Contributions to Anthropology, Number 10.

_____. 1932. *Anthropology and Modern Life.* New York: Norton.

_____. 1938. *General Anthropology.* New York: Heath.

_____. 1940. *Race Language and Culture.* New York: Macmillan.

Bogoras, W. 1904-1909. *The Chukchee. Material Culture.* New York: Memoirs of the American Museum of Natural History, Number 11.

Brandt, R. 1954. *Hopi Ethics; A Theoretical Analysis.* Chicago: University of Chicago Press.

Buck, P. 1930. *Samoan Material Culture.* Honolulu: Bishop Museum, Bulletin 75.

Bunzel, R. 1929. *The Pueblo Potter.* New York: Columbia University Contributions to Anthropology 8:1-124.

Burton, R. and J. W. M. Whiting. 1961. "The Absent Father and Cross-Sex Identity," *Merrill-Palmer Quarterly* 7:85-95.

Conklin, H. C. 1955. "Hanunóo Color Categories," *Southwestern Journal of Anthropology* 11:339-344.

D'Andrade, R. 1962. "Father Absence and Cross-Sex Identification," Unpublished Doctoral Dissertation, Harvard University.

Deffontaines, P. 1948. *Géographie et Religions,* ed. 9. Paris: Librairie Gallimard.

Dennis, W. 1966. "Goodenough Scores, Art Experience and Modernization," *The Journal of Social Psychology* 68:211-228.

Driver, H. 1956. "An Integration of Functional, Evolutionary and Historical Theory by Means of Correlations," *Indiana University Publications in Anthropology and Linguistics* 12:1-36.

_____. 1966. "Geographical-historical versus Psycho-functional Explanations of Kin Avoidances," *Current Anthropology* 7:131-160; 176-182.

Driver, H., and A. Kroeber. 1932. "Quantitative Expression of Cultural Relationships," *University of California Publications in American Archaeology and Ethnology* 31:211-256.

Driver, H., and W. Massey. 1957. "Comparative Studies of North American Indians," *Transactions of the American Philosophical Society* (n.s.) 47:165-460.

DuBois, C. 1955. "The Dominant Value Profile of American Culture." In M. Lantis (ed.), *The U.S.A. as Anthropologists See It,* *American Anthropologist* 57:1232-1239.

Edel, M., and A. Edel. 1959. *Anthropology and Ethics.* Springfield, Ill.: Charles C Thomas.

Eliade, M. 1961. *The Sacred and the Profane.* New York: Harper and Row.

Ewers, J. C. 1955. *The Horse in Blackfoot Indian Culture.* Washington, D. C.: Smithsonian Institution Press.

Fischer, J. L. 1961. "Art Styles as Cultural Cognitive Maps," *American Anthropologist* 63:79-93.

Fitch, J., and D. Branch. 1960. "Primitive Architecture and Climate," *Scientific American* 203:134-144.

Ford, C. 1939. "Society, Culture and the Human Organism," *Journal of General Psychology* 20:135-179.

Fortes, M. 1959. "Primitive Kinship," *Scientific American* 200:146-158.

Franck, K. 1946. "Preferences for Sex Symbols and Their Personality Correlates," *Genetic Psychology Monographs* 33:73-123.

Freeman, L., and R. Winch. 1957. "Societal Complexity: An Empirical Test of a Typology of Societies," *American Journal of Sociology* 62:461-466.

Goldenweiser, A. 1922. *Early Civilization.* New York: Knopf.

_____. 1933. *History, Psychology and Culture.* New York: Knopf.

_____. 1937. *Anthropology.* New York: Crofts.

Gouldner, A., and R. Peterson. 1962. *Notes on Technology and the Moral Order.* Indianapolis: Bobbs-Merrill.

Greenman, E. 1945. "Material Culture and the Organism," *American Anthropologist* 47:211-231.

Haines, F. 1938a. "Where Did the Plains Indians Get Their Horses?" *American Anthropologist* 40:112-117.

_____. 1938b. "The Northward Spread of Horses among the Plains Indians," *American Anthropologist* 40:429-437.

Hallowell, A. I. 1951. "Cultural Factors in the Structuralization of Perception." In J. H. Rohrer and M. Sherif (eds.), *Social Psychology at the Crossroads.* New York: Harper and Row, pp. 164-195.

_____. 1954. "The Self and Its Behavioral Environment," *Explorations* 2:108-165.

_____. 1955. *Culture and Experience.* Philadelphia: University of Pennsylvania Press. (Also republished in 1967. New York: Schocken.)

Hammond, P. 1966. *Yatenga; Technology in the Culture of a West African Kingdom.* New York: The Free Press.

Herskovits, M. 1958. "Some Further Comments on Cultural Relativism," *American Anthropologist* 60:266-273.

Hobhouse, L., G. Wheeler, and M. Ginsberg. 1915. *The Material Culture and Social Institutions of the Simpler Peoples: An Essay in Correlation.* London: Routledge and Kegan Paul.

Hoebel, E. A. 1954. *The Law of Primitive Man.* Cambridge, Mass.: Harvard University Press.

_____. 1966. *Anthropology; The Study of Man,* ed. 3. New York: McGraw-Hill.

Kavolis, V. 1968. *Artistic Expression: A Sociological Analysis.* Ithaca, N. Y.: Cornell University Press.

Keesing, F. 1958. *Cultural Anthropology.* New York: Holt, Rinehart and Winston.

Klimek, S., and W. Milke. 1935. "An Analysis of the Material Culture of the Tupi Peoples," *American Anthropologist* 37:71-91.

Kluckhohn, C. 1949. "The Philosophy of the Navaho Indians." In F. S. C. Northrop (ed.), *Ideological Differences and World Order.* New Haven: Yale University Press, pp. 356-384.

_____. 1951. "Values and Value Orientations in the Theory of Action." In T. Parsons and E. Shils (eds.), *Toward a General Theory of Action.* Cambridge, Mass.: Harvard University Press, pp. 388-433.

_____. 1954. "Culture and Behavior." In G. Lindzey (ed.), *Handbook of Social Psychology.* Cambridge, Mass.: Addison Wesley Press, pp. 921-976.

_____. 1955. "Ethical Relativity: sic et non," *Journal of Philosophy* 52:663-677.

_____. 1956. "Toward a Comparison of Value-Emphases in Different Cultures." In L. D. White (ed.), *The State of the Social Sciences.* Chicago: University of Chicago Press, pp. 116-132.

_____. 1959. "The Scientific Study of Values," *Proceedings of the American Philosophical Society* 102:469-476.

Kluckhohn, C., and F. Kluckhohn. 1947. "American Culture: Generalized Orientations and Class Patterns." In L. Bryson (ed.), *Conflicts of Power in Modern Culture.* New York: Harper and Row, pp. 106-128.

Kluckhohn, C., and D. Leighton. 1946. *The Navaho.* Cambridge, Mass.: Harvard University Press.

Kluckhohn, F., F. Strodtbeck, and others. 1961. *Variations in Value Orientations.* Evanston, Ill.: Row, Peterson.

Kroeber, A. 1901. "Decorative Symbolism of the Arapaho," *American Anthropologist* 3:308-336.

_____. 1920. "Masks and Moieties as a Culture Complex," *Journal of the Royal Anthropological Institute of Great Britain and Ireland* 50:452-460.

_____. 1941. "Salt, Dogs and Tobacco," *University of California Anthropological Records* 6:1-20.

Kroeber, A., and T. Parsons. 1958. "The Concepts of Culture and of Social System," *American Sociological Review* 23:582-583.

Kuckenberg, K. 1963. "Effect of Early Father Absence on Scholastic Aptitude," Unpublished Doctoral Dissertation, Harvard University.

Ladd, J. 1957. *The Structure of a Moral Code: A Philosophical Analysis of Ethical Discourse Applied to the Ethics of the Navaho Indians.* Cambridge, Mass.: Harvard University Press.

Leighton, D., and C. Kluckhohn. 1947. *Children of the People; The Navaho Individual and His Development.* Cambridge, Mass.: Harvard University Press.

Lévi-Strauss, C. 1967. *Structural Anthropology.* Garden City, N. Y.: Anchor.

Linton, R. 1923. *The Material Culture of the Marquesas Islands.* Honolulu: Memoirs of the B. P. Bishop Musem 8, Number 5.

_____. 1952. "Universal Ethical Principles: An Anthropological View." In R. N. Anshen (ed.), *Moral Principles of Action: Man's Ethical Imperatives.* New York: Harper and Row, Chapter 32.

_____. 1954. "The Problem of Universal Values." In R. F. Spencer (ed.), *Method and Perspective in Anthropology.* Minneapolis: University of Minnesota Press, pp. 145-168.

Lowie, R. 1922. *The Material Culture of the Crow Indians.* New York: Anthropological Papers of the American Museum of Natural History 21:201-270.

_____. 1940. *An Introduction to Cultural Anthropology.* New York: Farrar and Rinehart.

McElroy, W. A. 1954. "A Sex Preference for Shapes," *British Journal of Psychology* 45:209-216.

Mead, M. 1951a. "Anthropologist and Historian: Their Common Problems," *American Quarterly* 3:3-13.

_____. 1951b. *Soviet Attitudes toward Authority.* New York: McGraw-Hill.

Mead, M., and R. Métraux. 1953. *The Study of Culture at a Distance.* Chicago: University of Chicago Press.

Monberg, T. 1971. "Tikopia Color Classification, *Ethnology* 10:349-358.

Morgan, L. 1881. *Houses and House Life of the American Aborigines.* Washington, D. C.: Contributions to American Ethnology. Vol. 4. (Reprinted in 1965. Chicago: University of Chicago Press.)

Munroe, R. 1964. "Couvade Practices of the Black Caribbean: A Psychological Study," Unpublished Doctoral Dissertation, Harvard University.

Murdock, G. 1957. "World Ethnographic Sample," *American Anthropologist* 59:664-687.

_____. 1967. *Ethnographic Atlas.* Pittsburgh: University of Pittsburgh Press.

Northrop, F. 1953. "Cultural Values." In A. L. Kroeber (ed.), *Anthropology Today.* Chicago: University of Chicago Press, pp. 668-681.

Opler, M. E. 1941. *An Apache Life Way.* Chicago: University of Chicago Press.

_____. 1945. "Themes as Dynamic Forces in Culture," *American Journal of Sociology* 51:198-206.

_____. 1946. *Childhood and Youth in Jicarilla Apache Society.* Los Angeles: The Southwest Museum.

Osgood, C. 1940. *Ingalik Material Culture.* New Haven: Yale University Publications in Anthropology, 22.

Pettitt, G. 1946. *Primitive Education in North America.* Berkeley: University of California Press.

Rapoport, A. 1969. *House Form and Culture.* Englewood Cliffs, N. J.: Prentice-Hall.

Ray, V. 1952. "Techniques and Problems in the Study of Human Color Perception," Southwestern Journal of Anthropology 8:251-259.

_____. 1953. "Human Color Perception and Behavioral Response," Transactions, New York Academy of Sciences (Series 2) 16:98-104.

Robbins, M. 1966. "Material Culture and Cognition," American Anthropologist 68:745-748.

Sawyer, J., and R. LeVine. 1966. "Cultural Dimensions: a Factor Analysis of the World Ethnographic Sample," American Anthropologist 68:708-731.

Sayce, R. 1933. *Primitive Arts and Crafts; An Introduction to the Study of Material Culture.* Cambridge: Cambridge University Press.

Segall, M. H., D. T. Campbell, and M. J. Herskovits. 1966. *The Influence of Culture on Visual Perception.* Indianapolis: Bobbs-Merrill.

Steward, J. 1964. *Handbook of South American Indians,* Vol. I. Washington, D. C.: U. S. Government Printing Office.

Stiles, W. 1946. "Separation of the 'Blue' and 'Green' Mechanisms of Vision by Measurements of Increment Thresholds," Proceedings of the Royal Society 133:418-434.

Wald, G. 1949. "The Photochemistry of Vision," Documents in Ophthalmology 3:94-137.

Wallace, A. F. C. 1961. "The Psychic Unity of Human Groups." In B. Kaplan (ed.), *Studying Personality Cross-Culturally.* New York: Harper and Row, pp. 129-163.

Whiting, J., and B. Ayres. 1968. "Inferences from the Shape of Dwellings." In K. C. Chang (ed.), *Settlement Archaeology.* Palo Alto: National Press Books, pp. 117-133.

Whiting, J., and I. Child. 1953. *Child Training and Personality.* New Haven: Yale University Press.

Whiting, J., R. Kluckhohn, and A. Anthony. 1958. "The Function of Male Initiation Ceremonies at Puberty." In E. Maccoby, T. Newcomb, and E. Hartley (eds.), *Readings in Social Psychology.* New York: Holt, Rinehart and Winston, pp. 359-370.

Williams, T. R. 1965. *The Dusun; A North Borneo Society.* New York: Holt, Rinehart and Winston.

_____. 1967. *Field Methods in the Study of Culture.* New York: Holt, Rinehart and Winston.

_____. 1969. *A Borneo Childhood; Enculturation in Dusun Society.* New York: Holt, Rinehart and Winston.

Wissler, C. 1910. *The Material Culture of the Blackfoot Indians.* New York: Anthropological Papers of the American Museum of Natural History 5, Part One.

_____. 1914. "The Influence of the Horse in the Development of Plains Culture," American Anthropologist 16:1-25.

_____. 1922. *The American Indian.* New York: Oxford University Press.

_____. 1923. *Man and Culture.* New York: Crowell.

Wolfe, A. 1969. "Social Structural Bases of Art," Current Anthropology 10:3-44.

Wundt, W. 1928. "Ehe und Familie in der Primitiven Gesellschaft," Volkerpsychologie 7:190-246.

TEN LANGUAGE AND THE SOCIALIZATION PROCESS

This chapter is concerned with the ways language is related to the process of socialization. It begins with a brief summary of some ideas concerning the origins and evolution of language, then turns to a consideration of the inter-relations between language and thinking. Then, data are reviewed concerning the ways humans acquire language. Finally, the possible relations between language and the socialization process are discussed in terms of the importance of language for socialization.

■ Language origins and evolution

Among contemporary primates only *Homo sapiens* is born with a genetic capacity for learning and use of language.[1] It is biologically "normal" for modern humans to learn and use language. The basic anatomical structures involved in language use by *Homo sapiens* are not essentially different from those possessed by other primates. All primates have lungs, teeth, lips, vocal cords, palate, nasal passages, and tongue. All primates, including *Homo sapiens*, use these structures to produce a great variety of sounds. However, only *Homo sapiens* regularly uses these structures to make the sounds used in language behavior.

Fine control. An essential difference between *Homo sapiens* and other contemporary primates

in use of their similar structures for vocalizing (or "sound making") is the degree of *fine control* of pitch and of resonance of sounds, which are made possible by the fact that in modern man the larynx is positioned lower in the throat and much more distant from the palate area than in other primates. Among the nonhuman primates the larynx is very close to or in contact with the soft palate. The position of the modern human larynx has been said to be a consequence of the human bipedal adaptation; as the *foramen magnum* (the opening for the spinal cord on the underneath of the skull) moved forward with increasingly more erect posture and locomotion and as the jaw became smaller and less rugged, the larynx of evolving hominids appears to have descended into the mid-throat area. This created a long, uninterrupted area for sound resonation, making possible the unique low-pitched sound production which is typical of the speech of *Homo sapiens.*

Another evolutionary feature which seems to have occurred among evolving hominids, or populations ancestral to them, and which contributes directly to a delicate control of pitch and sound resonance in vocalization in *Homo sapiens* is the way in which the muscles of facial expression (see the following list), and especially the *obicularis oris*, which closes the lips in exact discrimination, provide for a very fine control of the front of the face area. It is likely that a fine contraction of facial muscles, and particularly the *obicularis oris*, which contributed to a broad variability and range in sound production in the buccal or mouth cavity would have been a nat-

---

[1] The classification of the phenomenon of language learning and use as a human *capacity*, rather than as a *species-characteristic behavior*, *reflex*, or *drive*, is based upon a belief that the great flexibility involved in language learning and use indicates the merit of considering such a label. Whether such a classification is finally valid remains to be judged on the basis of research yet to be conducted on the biological bases of human behavior.

urally selective advantage of some significance in animals newly developing a terrestrial social life.

MUSCLES OF FACIAL EXPRESSION IN HOMO SAPIENS*

buccinator—Compresses cheek
levator labii superioris—Elevates upper lip
risorius—Retracts angle of mouth
mentalis—Raises and protrudes lower lip, wrinkles chin
levator labii superioris alaeque nasi—Dilates nose aperatures
orbicularis oris—Closes lips
levator anguli oris—Makes facial furrows
depressor anguli oris—Depresses angle of mouth
depressor labii inferioris—Draws lower lip downward
zygomaticus major—Draws mouth upward
zygomaticus minor—Makes furrow between upper lip and nose

For instance, modern baboons can produce many quite humanoid "grunt" sounds. Andrew has suggested that this fact is related to baboons' need for a regular transfer of social information by a more explicit and much less ambiguous means than would be possible by use of only facial expressions or body motions. It might well be that similar selective evolutionary pressures also acted upon the bipedal hominids as they met requirements for survival in their social groups, by making such groups into a mobile refuge on the open grasslands over which they foraged for foodstuffs.

These changes in the course of human evolution, which are also related to the faculty of human hearing for a very close discrimination of pitch and especially in the pitch range used in *Homo sapiens* languages, mean that, while there are no significant gross anatomical differences between *Homo sapiens* and other primates in the structures involved in language learning and use, only modern man has evolved a facility for repeatedly making the kinds of exact sounds which seem vital to a language system.

Too, the ability or potential (see Chapter Four) of *Homo sapiens* to engage in imitation of sounds in his environment contributes to a greatly increased fine control over vocalization. Most of the primates continue to use the vocal sounds

*After Buettner-Janusch, J. 1966. *Origins of Man.* New York: Wiley, p. 77.

probably typical of their early nonprimate ancestors. Thus, high short calls, or "twitter" sounds, are common among the modern primates and in many members of the *Insectivora* order. Each group of modern primates also has some significant vocalizations which are typical, ranging from noisy expiration ("threat") sounds, a wailing and whooping call, to a rapid clicking sound. Of all the primates, however, only *Homo sapiens* seems to mimic or duplicate precisely many of the calls now typically used by other members of his order of animals. This broad ability for sound imitation seems to have no specific functional or anatomical basis in *Homo sapiens;* the duplications of vocalizations are made with the same general structures (lungs, lips, tongue, and so on) found in all the other primates. It may well be that the ability for human vocal duplication has arisen from an interaction between life experiences and human biological structure in each successive generation, with some naturally selective advantages accruing to those humans most able to use fine discriminations in their vocal communications.

Thus, fine control of vocalization in *Homo sapiens* involves a complex of biological features, including pitch production, facial muscle uses, hearing acuity, and vocal mimicry, each contributing significantly to man's production of the broad range of sounds used in human language. It is important not to confuse speech, or oral communication, with language. The human biological features involved in the production of speech provide a basis for language. But, as noted later in this chapter, language consists of a set of interrelated systems that can be studied and analyzed apart from the act of oral communication.

Brain and body size and language. But such features do not seem sufficient to account for the capacity for human language. In Chapter One it was noted that it seems reasonable to conclude that communication of ideas by vocalization probably occurred after a significant increase in the size of the brain in the evolutionary changes which occurred between the bipedal hominids of the Middle Pliocene and the *Homo* forms of the Middle Pleistocene.

This conclusion involves the basic assumption that at a certain "time threshold" or in a particular time period in hominid evolution the unspecialized nature of a certain sized brain (perhaps above 800 cc) made possible the invention and regular use of language. It has been suggested too that, not only an absolute increase in brain size, but also the increase of the *ratio* of brain weight to body size contributed significantly to the threshold appearance of human language. However, a comparison (see Table 10-1) of the ratio of brain size to body weight among primates calls this last statement into question and suggests that language learning and use is essentially a distinct capacity of *Homo sapiens* rather than a generalized feature of the primate order and which is dependent upon the development of a specific size of brain and its relation to a particular body size.

Lenneberg (1964, 1967) believes that language learning and use in *Homo sapiens* is a genetically based capacity which developed independently, although through the same time as the brain was increasing in size. Furthermore, he notes that this capacity in contemporary humans is inherited biologically and independently of a general intelligence or intellectual level. He points out that there are records of families in which the learning and use of language is lacking entirely in some but not other members. The appearance of this linguistic malfunction seems to follow usual human genetic patterns. There are records of persons clearly "subnormal" in intelligence but quite able to speak with effectiveness, dis-

tinction, and clarity, and sometimes in several different languages. Too, as noted in Chapter One, "mentally subnormal" persons (however this is demonstrated) very often have brain sizes at or exceeding the *Homo sapiens* average.

Thus, the origin of language learning and use may have been in the appearance of a genetic capacity which was developed quite independently of, but at the same time as, other body features and behavior forms, all of which contributed significantly to naturally selective advantages in the life of evolving hominid populations. If this was the situation, the survival edge gained by language learning and using hominids must have been immediate and of great significance, since creatures able to communicate the products of reflection and symboling discretely and efficiently would have made immense gains in their chances for survival and behavior. A genetic character which has naturally selective, or "dominant," advantage can spread very quickly throughout a species of animals (see Table 10-2). Hence, if language learning and use had its origins in a genetic change which occurred independently of but at the same time as other evolutionary changes, then the benefits which could have followed such a change as the coordinate use of the features of fine control of vocalizations (pitch, facial muscles, and so on) and reflection, symboling, bipedal locomotion, and so on, which were probably already in existence in more or less highly developed forms, would mean that when the gene change for language use and learning occurred, it took

Table 10-1. Brain size, body weight, and language learning and use*

Primate form	Body weight (in kilograms)	Brain weight (in kilograms)	Ratio of body-brain weight	Language facility
Male, *H. sapiens* (age 2.5)	13.5	1.100	12.3	Beginning
Male, *H. sapiens* (age 13.5)	45.0	1.350	35.0	Present
Male, *H. sapiens* (age 18)	64.0	1.350	47.0	Present
Male, *H. sapiens* (age 12; dwarf)	13.5	.400	34.0	Present
Male, chimpanzee (age 3)	13.5	.400	34.0	Absent
Female, chimpanzee (adult)	47.0	.450	104.0	Absent
Male, rhesus monkey (adult)	3.5	.090	40.0	Absent

*After Lenneberg, E. H. 1964. *New Directions in the Study of Language.* Cambridge, Mass.: M.I.T. Press.

place in a species which generally was biologically prepared for it and so spread quickly and very successfully to and in all the succeeding groups of hominids. The point is that, if human language learning and use is viewed as having its origins in a quite specific genetic change in evolving hominids of the Middle Pliocene to Middle Pleistocene, then man stands alone among the primates in this capacity. Repeated attempts to teach other primates to speak have generally failed, not only because other primates lack fine control of vocalizations, but probably because of an absence in other primates of the gene stuff—the DNA and RNA—requisite for language learning and use.

These comments are intended to suggest that only the capacity to learn and use a language is a genetic feature and not that language is itself formed or transmitted genetically. Human languages consist of basic units—termed *phonemes* and *morphemes*—of vocalization to which symbolic values are arbitrarily assigned in different human cultures. Human infants usually are born possessed of a capacity to mimic any of the phonemes used in any of the approximately 6,000 contemporary human languages.[2] But no human infant is born possessed of knowledge of the cultural values assigned to combinations of sounds, or morphemes, specially used by his biological parents and their social groups. Infants and children must learn to duplicate precisely all of the sound combinations to which adults have traditionally given quite arbitrary cultural meanings. As time passes, it becomes easier for an infant and child to mimic the many different combinations of sounds particularly used by the adults on whom he depends for life and health. However, it may be some time before a child really learns the full use of cultural values given to special sound

combinations in a society. For instance, the English word "love" can denote "desire," "courtesy," "affection," "favorite," and so on, and also is used in a great many significant combinations (such as love-lorn, love-making, love-sick, love-story). It is many years before English speaking children can learn all, or most, of the different cultural values assigned to even so common a combination of sounds as "love."

Human and animal communication. In discussion of the origins of human language, it is important to note that *Homo sapiens* is not the only life form on earth which carries on *communication* of some kind. In modern man, and among his primate contemporaries, communication involves both vocalizations and body movements. However, many different kinds of animals, including bees, fish (such as the three-spined stickleback), and herring gulls, use nonvocal means to communicate complex information among themselves concerning breeding, care of the young, social cooperation in food getting, and common defense against attacks from within or from outside of a species. This type of communication is generally kinesic, performed through use of body motions. Hence, it depends upon and has quite different properties than are implied in use of the term *language*. There is a "language of the bees" only insofar as vocalization is used to communicate between bees.

Linguistic scholars tend to define human language as principally involving a grammatical system, a phonological system, a morphophonemic system, a semantic system, and a phonetic system (see Hockett, 1958: 137-139).[3] The communicative acts of bees, three-spined sticklebacks, and of most animals using essentially a kinesic form of communication do not contain any of these vocally based systems. And no such systems have been discovered in the vocal com-

---

[2] There are some sounds, such as a "trilled r," which seem to be very difficult for persons to mimic in some populations that do not regularly use these kinds of vocalizations. It has been suggested that this means there is a genetic lack in all the humans in a population for mimicry of some sounds regularly used by all the members of other human populations. This is remotely possible, but it is more probable that any failure to be able to mimic vocalizations used in a language is a function of the individual's capacity for sound mimicry and that this is a function of fine vocal control or of hearing acuity rather than a function of the capacity for language learning and use.

[3] Hockett (1958: 137-138) defines these systems as: (1) *grammatical* system—a stock of morphemes, and the arrangements in which they occur; (2) *phonological* system—a stock of phonemes, and the arrangements in which they occur; (3) *morphophonemic* system—the code which ties together the grammatical and phonological systems; (4) *semantic* system—the ways in which various morphemes and combinations of morphemes can be arranged; (5) *phonetic* system—the ways in which sequences of phonemes are converted into sound waves by a speaker and are decoded from speech by a hearer.

Table 10-2. Time required for a given change in the percent frequency of a gene having a selective advantage of 1 percent*

Dominant gene		Recessive gene	
Change in percent frequency from	Number of generations	Change in percent frequency from	Number of generations
0.01-0.1	230	0.01-0.1	900,230
0.1-1.0	231	0.1-1.0	90,231
1.0-50.0	559	1.0-3.0	6,779
50.0-97.0	3,481	3.0-50.0	3,481
97.0-99.0	6,779	50.0-99.0	559
99.0-99.9	90,231	99.0-99.9	231
99.9-99.99	900,230	99.9-99.99	230

*After Boyd, W. C. 1953. *Genetics and the Races of Man.* Boston: Little, Brown, p. 146.

munications of other nonhuman animals, such as wolves and whales, despite intensive and systematic research efforts by many different scientifically competent individuals to recognize and to "decode" the vocalizations of such animals into one or all five of the systems characteristic of human language. These studies, which have also included many efforts to discover a "language" among the various species of nonhuman primates, have so far not been productive of evidences which can be used to say conclusively that, in fact, the vocalizations by man, which are ordered in the five systems of human language, have any real counterparts in the vocal uses or the kinesic uses of communication by other living forms. It appears, then, that human language, as specialized vocalization organized into a set of systems, is unique in the natural world.[4]

Time and language origins. In considering the origins of a naturally unique human language, Hockett has noted that the appearance in human vocal communication of vocal *productivity*, or the ways speakers may say something they have never heard or said before and be understood fully by those hearing them, may be regarded as "the one crucial development" linguistically setting man off from other primates. Hockett (1958: 581) believes this development, which he estimates occurred between 10 and 15 million years before the present, can be used to make the judgment of the point in evolutionary time when man developed a "genuine language." This conclusion may be regarded as premature, since the empirical evidences, that is, evidences gathered through use of the human senses or their extensions in the form of scientific instruments, which can relate the fossil evidences for the evolution of hominid structures and for hominid behavior are simply not that clear; this is especially so when consideration is given to the possible ways the specialized body structures of hominids of 10 million or more years before the present were involved in vocal communication. It is reasonable, however, on the face of the total of the empirical evidence now available, to make an informed guess that human language had its origins sometime, at the least, between 1 and 5 or more million years before the present. This does not mean at all that contemporary human languages should be regarded as similar to the "original" human language. In fact, studies of linguistic change indicate that, while it may be possible from contemporary language comparisons or use of written records to reconstruct the prototypes directly ancestral to one or several languages,

---

[4]Hockett (1958: 574-585) has considered this matter carefully and has concluded that there are seven "key properties" *(duality, productivity, arbitrariness, interchangeability, specialization, displacement,* and *cultural transmission)* characteristic of the five systems making up human language. Hockett notes that, while no system of vocal communication other than that used by man is organized into the systems typical of human language, some few of the nonhuman vocal communication types do contain one or even several of the key properties of human language. But, as he points out, all seven key properties are always present in any human language.

attempts to reconstruct the original human language forms of a million or more years ago are fruitless.

Language evolution. Conclusions derived from the study of human language evolution are uncertain since they depend heavily upon inferences which must be drawn from the limited empirical evidences presently available. Most estimates of the state of the genetic capacity for language learning and use in the hominid populations of the late Pliocene and early Pleistocene indicate a broad agreement among scholars that there probably were quite profound differences in the genetically transmitted language capacities of various hominid groups. It is probably in error to assume that a capacity for language learning and use appeared in only one Pliocene-Pleistocene hominid population and subsequently spread as a naturally selective advantage to all other such populations. There are adequate scientific reasons to assume that a language capacity could and probably did naturally appear in several hominid populations at the same evolutionary time threshold, in a genetic process termed *parallel evolution.*

Hence, it may be said that for a long period of time in the Pliocene and Pleistocene periods there probably were marked contrasts between evolving hominid populations with respect to the genetic capacity for language learning and use. However, these biological differences appear to have not persisted, for as a genetic capacity for language became common to hominid populations, inefficient modes and styles of vocalization and protolanguage would have been discarded, ignored, or eliminated, causing once quite dissimilar language learning and use styles to converge and become increasingly similar.

There is no evidence to show that as a convergence to similar language learning and use took place in evolving hominid populations that there were any changes in the capacity for such learning and use, that is, the changes which occurred were in language behavior and not in the capacity which made language behavior possible for evolving hominids.

The contemporary study of thousands of "living" human languages has demonstrated that all languages are equally efficient, despite being learned and used in very different ecological, social, and cultural settings. The languages of contemporary non-Western peoples, that is, groups living outside of the industrial, urban societies of Europe and the Americas, are not inferior in their structure, content, or meanings in comparison to any "modern" or "Western" languages. All contemporary human languages have a formal, recognizable grammatical structure which serves for the formulation of significant intellectual and aesthetic ideas and expressions by their speakers. There are no demonstrated features or characteristics which set off the languages of so-called "primitive" peoples from those of "civilized" peoples. Linguistic scholars now assume, on the basis of their long-term studies, that all of the world's languages are equal in their social adequacy and complexity. There is no relationship between the fact that a group possesses a written form of language and their specific level of sophistication, maturity, and complexity of a language or for the possibilities of its speakers to engage in specific and complex emotional, artistic, and social expressions. There are, in effect, no contemporary languages which are "natural" or "primitive" because they possess such a limited content their speakers are severely restricted in their ability to express complex ideas, feelings, and understandings. Too, there are no contemporary languages which are so simple that speakers depend more on gestures than on oral communication for exchanges of meaningful information. Where such "sign languages" exist, as among the Arunta, they are paralinguistic, that is, used to extend language rather than to supplant it.

Thus, while contemporary men learn and use more than 6,000 languages, which differ markedly in the ways vocal sounds are assigned arbitrary cultural meanings, contemporary languages are not themselves contrastive or different in their essential systems or with respect to the ways speakers can express complex ideas, emotions, and intentions to and concerns about behavior in a particular ecological setting.

If it can be assumed that the populations

of hominids of the Pliocene and Pleistocene eras had differential genetic capacities for language learning and use, then the question of whether this means that such languages then were different in their essential structures and the ways in which their speakers would express themselves becomes quite important in study of the process of socialization. It becomes important because there are distinct reasons to believe that the *convergence* of evolving hominid languages to the similar structure and use typical of the present took place in the generational acts of cultural transmission, that is, one specific mechanism for the elimination of inefficient modes and styles of different hominid languages and the changes in these many languages toward a common human language structure and use likely occurred in the process of socialization. Hence, while the specific adaptations which led to the evolution of a genetic capacity for language learning and use were naturally selective ones, and occurred primarily through the processes of gene change (mutation, natural selection, and so on), the convergence of the many hominid language structures and use styles to a common human language form could have occurred through a specific culturally selective means by which those hominid populations regularly transmitting culture in a socialization process were able to increasingly retain more of their experience and the sum of the products of reflections on experience in their local group, while other hominid populations could or did not do so. A marked retention of individual reflective products in the course of cultural transmission could have acted as a selective device in ways similar to those which operate in genetic transmission; biological changes which are notably useful to a population in its adaptations to a particular ecology tend to be retained in gene transmission. Similarly, changes in social and cultural behavior which favor and facilitate increased social cooperation, significant refinements of technology, explanations for hazardous events, or behavior likely to be destructive of life or a local ecology (for example, a campfire which burns out of control and destroys a forest will not only drive away all the game

animals and burn out all the plants used as food subsistence, but as well kills members of the society) would be retained more easily in a cultural transmission system or process operating through use of language. If such ideas and understandings had to be "rediscovered," "reinvented," or "rethought" in each successive generation because there were no ways to retain and easily transmit them, then a hominid population which was so limited would not compete well for the same ecological niche, or place, when faced with a population not only possessed of a genetic capacity for language learning and use but as well able to easily transmit, through language, the products of the experience and reflections of many preceding generations. It is an accepted axiom in ecology studies that two or more species which are closely related genetically cannot survive in the same ecological niche, since the food supplies necessary for survival in such locations ordinarily cannot support several species. In competitions for supremacy in an ecological setting, one species adapts more successfully than others of its kind and so in time becomes dominant.

In the long competition among the hominid populations for survival in their habitats, the genetic changes favoring a capacity for language learning and use would have been a significant edge. But the real advantage in competition between the hominid populations would have developed with the use of language as a means to readily and successfully transmit the cumulative products of experience and reflection, that is, culture, to each new generation.

The importance of the regular transmission of culture to each new generation was so significant as an adaptive advantage that no hominid population with a half or part way change to a cultural transmission process really had much of a chance to compete for survival. Man has often been termed the "killer ape" or the "hunter" when such competitions are discussed. It is not necessary for a species to physically eliminate its close relatives when competing with them for survival. The evolving hominid populations which underwent the genetic changes

Adults in communicative contact; Blackfoot Indian women in ceremonial dress (circa 1925). (Courtesy American Museum of Natural History.)

to language learning and use in a socialization process were not primarily predators upon others of their kind, or for that matter primarily or solely dependent on meat products for their survival. While it is true that the hominids of the late lower and middle Pleistocene eras hunted and trapped big game, it is also true that these populations had mixed subsistence of meat and plant products. One of the interesting facts of hominid evolution is that *Homo sapiens* has stood alone and as the dominant species of all the *Hominidae* species for at least the past 40,000 years. Modern man has had no close competitors for his ecological niches on earth for a very long period. It is doubtful that all such competitors were regularly sought out, killed, and then eaten; interbreeding of the hominid populations competing for survival would be much more likely.

It probably was most likely that the competitions for life were really won through accumulation of knowledge by language use and the selective advantage this provided to some populations. Thus, cultural transmission through use of language was a likely and very powerful mechanism for ecological supremacy for *Homo sapiens* populations and for their ancestors.

It is worthwhile to observe again that cultural transmission today is not entirely a process conducted through language; portions of human culture are transmitted without language being involved. In Chapter One it was noted that products of reflection and experience could be transmitted generationally through *inarticulate* means. The point which must be made in the context of a discussion of language evolution is that while culture, that is, behavior which is learned, patterned, shared, and transmitted from one generation to the next, was quite likely a phenomenon experienced by and known to the hominids of the Pliocene and perhaps an earlier (Miocene) period, it was characterized then by its transmission through nonlinguistic means. The appearance and development of language provided for the possibilities that culture, as a system of learned, shared, transmitted, and patterned behavior, based on the products of reflection and experience could become man's natural ecology; while it may be true that culture, as a phenomenon of hominid life, preceded the capacity for language learning and use, the process of transmitting culture through language seems the basis for the importance of culture in human life. Once the way was opened, through language, for articulate cultural transmission, the evolution of human culture and its vital place in human affairs was hardly avoidable or possible to escape. Language learning and use did not and does not make man "human," but it served and continues as a significant component of humanness.

It should also be pointed out once again that language is not the only cultural subsystem. However, language is, according to the judgment of Kroeber (1964: xvii), the most nearly autonomous, self-consistent, and self-contained cultural subsystem. Kroeber says he does not know why this should be so, but is willing to accept it as a fact, as most language scholars seem to do today. It could be speculated that the near autonomy of the language subsystem of culture derives from the ways other cultural subsystems (social relations, technology, ideology) have developed in and through the medium of language. While language does not seem to precede other human cultural subsystems, its present autonomy may be taken as evidence that it was a means for these subsystems developing to their present conditions. This point, language autonomy, is important in any consideration of the ways in which thought, language, and speech are interrelated and interdependent.

▪ Thought and language

A fundamental question in study of the interrelations between language and socialization is the degree to which human thought and behavior are actually influenced by language learning and use. Too, the basic questions of whether language learning and use affects the development of other capacities, such as cognition and learning, and whether people who speak different languages live in different realms of reality are also vital in the study of language and socialization.

Speech and thought. Speculation concerning the ways speech and thought are related has a long history in philosophical studies and more recently in academic psychology. Perhaps the extreme in answers to such speculations has been the one given in the period before 1920 by Watson, one of the founders of behaviorism in psychology. Watson asserted that human thought is simply silent speaking, with all thoughts having their origins as motor patterns in the larynx. The problems with Watson's statements concerning the relations between speech and thought are obvious ones, since followed to its logical conclusion, this idea would mean that in the time before hominids developed the capacity for language learning and use and in the time when language was developing to its contemporary form, no evolving primate would be, by Watson's definition, able to really "think," since they could not effectively speak, that is, had no motor patterns in the larynx to enable and facilitate thought. This conclusion would not be reasonable today, given the growing body of empirical evidences that tend to demonstrate that thinking and especially reflective thought among evolving hominids must have occurred well before the development of language and its key role in cultural transmission. Too, Watson's speculations on the link between language and thought would tend to rule out any cognitive processes in all contemporary animal forms other than *Homo sapiens*. This would be a patently untrue statement, if for no other reason than the fact that the laboratory study of learning clearly demonstrates that nonhuman animals acquire, store, retrieve, and decide upon and choose between alternate kinds of information gained through their life experiences. If thinking and cognition are broadly defined as active processes of conceptualization involving the integration of observed relationships between objects, or between events, or between objects and events, then thought and cognition occur among a great many different kinds of contemporary animals unable to use language or speech.

Another problem with Watson's statements concerning the relationship between speech and thought is that, if this hypothesis is followed, individuals who lose their larynx through surgery or accident should also lose their capacity to think. Experimental evidences from use of the drug curare to paralyze the larynx, while testing otherwise "normal" subjects for their thinking processes have demonstrated the unacceptability of Watson's ideas.

Piaget's studies. A more moderate position on the question of the relationships between speech and thought has been developed in the work of Piaget and his colleagues. Piaget has assumed throughout his research that thinking follows its own developmental style in children, with the development of language usually coming after the attainment of a certain level of thinking. Piaget has provided substantial experimental evidences, from his studies of young children, of some of the intricate ways that thinking and language are interrelated. His work makes it clear that in fact a human language capacity and a human cognitive capacity originally, that is, at birth and for some time, are independent entities. It seems from Piaget's studies that even though attempts are made to train younger children in special ways of language to talk about problem solving, such training is of very little use to children whose capacity for thinking has not developed to the state, point, or level at which they can meaningfully consider concepts represented in the special language. However, Piaget's work also demonstrates that the capacities for thought and language do begin to interpenetrate one another in very young children, after about 18 months to 2 years of age, and subsequently become so complexly related that by the age of 5 to 6 years it is exceedingly difficult to sort out the primary causal influences of the capacity for either thought or language.

Bruner's studies. Systematic efforts to trace the exact ways thought and language develop and become interrelated in younger children have been made by Jerome Bruner and his co-workers at the Harvard University Center for Cognitive Studies. Bruner's research has identified three main styles of children's thinking about their experiences: (1) *enactive* (action) *representation,* (2) *ikonic* (or image) *representation,* and (3) *symbolic representation.* He notes that very young children act out much of their everyday experience with their bodies and body parts, particularly their mouths and hands. He believes this style of representation is the earliest way all children think about themselves and their world; in the *enactive representation* stage of cognitive development, language plays a very small, although by no means an unimportant, part. Then, Bruner notes, as children mature, they develop a second thought style, of simultaneous comprehension of different experiences. An example of the *ikonic representation* mode of thought would be the way an adult can "read" or think about a map which shows visually the ways hundreds or even tens of thousands of objects are generally arranged. An *ikonic* style of thought provides humans with the means to move about through a complex landscape, through the products of human life, and deal effectively with the ways these are interconnected. Young children, under the age of 3 to 3½ years, have very great difficulty in simultaneous cognition, even though they have a normally developed language capacity which is being regularly used. Airlines, ship and bus lines, and other forms of public transportation which agree to carry younger children unaccompanied by their parents usually account for a child's lack of *ikonic* representations by attaching prominent name and destination tags to their clothing and providing adult employees as guides to help younger children overcome their inability to simultaneously relate their experiences one to the other.

Finally, Bruner believes that children develop a third style of thinking about their experiences, in which they use written and spoken symbols to represent objects, activities, and their interconnections. Bruner notes that adult thought tends to be predominantly symbolic, with lesser components of ikonic and enactive thought brought into play as needed to solve problems and deal with specific activities. He believes that the amount of adult style of thought developed through childhood depends upon learning to use and understand language and its written forms. Bruner's research seems to indicate, however, that the amount of adult thought finally developed is not related to a particular language, but more directly to the ways children learn and use linguistic symbols to substitute for experiences.

It is important to understand that both Piaget and Bruner share the view that the human cognition and language capacities are essentially *innate programs of action* which automatically unfold and develop in the course of growth and maturation. However, Piaget's writings concerning the ways the cognitive and language capacities develop indicate that he views these as being much more predetermined and prefixed than does Bruner. Bruner has noted that hominid evolution has provided a great range of possibilities for cognitive and language development. It is Bruner's belief that the unfolding of the two innately determined capacities depends primarily upon the kinds of tools and objects available to an infant and child as he reaches particular points of his physical growth. Bruner has recently advanced the hypothesis that the development of an infant's manual skills is quite vital in the later development of language and cognitive capacities, because such manual skills make possible the broad strategies, or procedures, for understanding and coping with the world which must be faced by an infant and young child. Bruner feels that, when a greater abundance of tools and objects is available to an infant, it will "tempt out," or draw forth, more self-initiated behavior, which when coupled with responsive parents, that is, parents encouraging such self-initiating acts, can serve as the specific precursor to the cognition and language capacities beginning their unfolding as innate programs of action. Thus, while Bruner sees the cognitive and language capacities as basic, innate human preadaptations, he also believes that only after their first ap-

pearances have been evoked by events, such as self-initiated behavior and responsive parents, will there be a significant unfolding of each capacity.

These ideas remain to be validated through studies in other cultural settings. Recent research by J. W. M. Whiting and his Harvard associates concerning cognitive development in African infants and children tends to indicate that the development of the language capacity and of other capacities is considerably more complex than has been proposed by either Piaget or Bruner or their associates. It seems, for instance, that the language capacity in different cultures interpenetrates and affects cognitive development in ways quite different from what appears to be true for American or European children. Too, Bruner's hypothesis concerning tool/object abundance, self-initiative activity, responsive parents, and unfolding of cognitive and language action, when followed to its logical end would mean that in those cultures where infants and children have very little access to tools/objects and parents are not overtly responsive to self-initiated acts, then children should show marked cognitive and language capacity differences when compared to children in cultures where the opposite is true. So far this logical product has been found to be unapplicable and unworkable; infants and children in those cultures which do or permit few of the things Bruner seems to believe are crucial for allowing the innate programs of cognitive and linguistic action to unfold seem to have children and adults as cognitively and as linguistically capable and competent, in the terms of the local culture, as persons in other cultures.

However, there seems little question that there are two distinct capacities, cognition and language learning and use, which are involved in the socialization process and that these capacities form in the adult an exceedingly complex reticulum, or net-like structure, which helps direct and guide human behavior.

Deaf children and thought. The research of Furth and his colleagues concerning cognitive development in congenitally deaf children provides added insight into the conclusions to be drawn from the studies of Piaget, Bruner, Whiting, and others. Deaf children, who have never heard language of any type, provide an important scientific "control group" as children unable to engage in usual and normal language learning and formal education. Furth and others have reasoned that it may be possible to observe in deaf children whether or not the learning and use of language makes possible all of the levels and modes of cognitive development noted by Piaget, Bruner, and other scholars, or whether language only enriches and enables such stages as they naturally unfold in children.

Furth (1966) reports on the basis of many different kinds of research studies conducted by himself and others that deaf children appear in fact to go through the same stages and modes of cognitive development as reported for normal children by Piaget, Bruner, and others. The major difference found by Furth between deaf and nondeaf children with respect to stages and modes of cognitive development was in regard to the rate of development. Some deaf children move through the various cognitive stages and modes much more slowly than do nondeaf children. Furth attributes this to the significantly lessened opportunities usually provided to deaf children for varied experiences, rather than due to their lack of language learning and use.

Furth has concluded that language learning and use has an *indirect* rather than a *causal* influence on cognitive development, that is, language learning and use is a means for speeding up and greatly enriching the development of thought since it is a vital means of efficient expressive communication about experience. But it seems that persons who are impaired or seriously lacking in their capacity for language learning and use also are not usually similarly deficient in their capacity to think about their experiences. Furth's studies thus tend to support the suggestions of Piaget, Bruner, and others that the cognitive and language capacities begin as clearly distinct, although interrelated by adulthood. If this is so, then the vital problem which remains for scholars concerned with human development and the socialization process is to determine the phases in human cognitive development in which language is specifically

important. A major current problem for linguistic scholars is to understand the influences of cognitive development upon language learning and use, that is, to determine whether certain language processes are possible of attainment before attainment of certain phrases of cognitive development.

A present central concern for students of both human development and language is to deal effectively with the problems raised by the demonstrated facts of the great lexical and grammatical diversity in different varieties of contemporary language.

Language diversity and human thought. Early in the nineteenth century, von Humboldt proposed the idea that individuals speaking different languages looked at and understood their social, cultural, and physical worlds in unique ways because of the particular grammatical structure of their languages. A grammar is the arrangement of the *morphemes* (words) used in a language and their relative position in speech (Hockett, 1958: 129). The idea that the form of the grammar of a language determines the thoughts of its speakers persisted through the nineteenth century, since it was easy for linguists and philosophers to note that a grammar was central to the structure of a language, was much more resistant to rapid change than other aspects of language, such as its vocabulary and phonology (or typical sound style), and was a prime means of expression of such metaphysically important categories in European and American thought as "time," "space," "action," "individual," and "object." By the close of the nineteenth century, Boas and others had developed this idea as part of their efforts to define ethnology, the comparative study of culture, as a science concerned with the causal links between human thought and the inner form of language. Boas believed that through study of the central aspects of language, such as grammatical structure, it would be possible to discover the original forms of human cognition and to avoid all the elaborate cultural facades which have been evolved by societies to protect and preserve the original contents of their thought.

Boas (1911) was the first person to demonstrate clearly that what appears as a single idea in one language may be grammatically expressed in other languages by a whole series of ideas. Boas did not distinguish between the two general ways that thought categories are known now to be expressed in language, that is, through *lexical* or word categories and through *grammatical* categories. Thus, to use one of Boas' well-known examples, Americans employ one lexical category, *snow,* to denote that category of experience that Greenland Eskimos know by the different lexical uses *aput* ("snow falling on the ground"), *qana* ("falling snow"), *piqsirpoq* ("drifting snow"), *qimuqsuq* ("a snowdrift"), and so on.

In contrast, Boas also noted that Americans use many different lexical categories to express ideas which other peoples express in one category. Thus, North American Dakota Indians express in only one lexical category *xtaka* ("to grip") the ideas of "to kick an object" *(naxtáka),* "to bind objects into bundles" *(paxtaka),* "to bite" *(yaxtaka),* "to be near to," *(išaxtaka),* and "to pound" *(boxtaka).*

Boas also first noted concisely the ways the grammatical categories of a language may structure expressions of complex ideas. He pointed out that to use the English expression, "The man is sick," is to express the idea that *"a definite single man at present sick."* However, as Boas points out, a speaker of *Kwakiutl,* a North American, Northwest coast Indian language would have to render this same expression through Kwakiutl grammar as *"definite man near him invisible sick near him invisible"* or as *"that invisible man lies sick on his back on the floor of the absent house,"* depending on whether the speaker chooses to talk in terms of human visibility and nearness in the first or second person, in terms of human invisibility and nearness in the third person, or in a definite and idiomatic sense. Boas pointed out that, in the Greenland Eskimo language, this same idea ("the man is sick") would be expressed grammatically as "(single) man sick," with no expression of time or place being involved. In Ponca, a dialect of another North American Indian language (Siouan), the concept in the same English expression would have to specify whether the person was at rest, or moving ("the moving

single man sick"). Boas concluded from his work on the links between lexical and grammatical categories and thought in different languages (Boas, 1920; 1938; 1942) that human thinking was causally related to and determined by grammatical structure. From this conclusion, Boas and others drew a corollary conclusion that if thought was determined by language structure, then all human thought was relative or specific to the language structure which determined it.

This conclusion later heavily influenced the studies and writings of a number of persons, including Sapir, Whorf, and Lee, each of whom followed leads suggested by Boas in trying to determine to what extent and in what ways the structure of language is causally related to the thought of its speakers. These scholars, at various times and in different ways, dealt with three general questions: (1) are language habits specifically related to other forms of culture? (2) do peoples with different language habits really differ profoundly in their thought habits? and (3) can linguistic habits really causally determine other forms of a culture?

In general, contemporary language scholars would give each of these questions a qualified affirmative answer, without going to the extent of portraying the influence of language structure on human thought in the quite absolute terms used by Sapir, Whorf, Lee, and some others. The demonstrated facts of the ways language changes, diffusion from one culture to another, and multilingualism, that is, the ways people think while regularly speaking two or more languages with very different structures, preclude acceptance of statements which propose an absolute causal relationship between language structure and thinking. There are now substantial evidences that people speaking only one language often make totally new conceptual distinctions and proceed to apply old and familiar linguistic terms to them, or sometimes after making new thought distinctions proceeding to a hybridizing or joining existing lexical and grammatical forms in their language, or at other times simply inventing or borrowing from another language new lexical or grammatical forms to find adequate expression for new ideas.

Communicative contact through a language; Dusun man responding to greeting by ethnographer (Trus Madi, 1960). (T. R. Williams.)

It now has been quite well documented that human individuals can learn the structure of other languages and adequately translate their new language back into understandable terms in the structure of their native language. It also is clear that the distribution through time and about the world of human ideas is not at all identical with specific languages. It has also been pointed out that the same system of metaphysics, or concepts about existence, the nature of the universe and of causation, has developed among peoples speaking languages with radically different lexical and grammatical structures, while widely diverse types of metaphysical systems have developed among peoples speaking the same language. If these statements are true, and they seem to be so, then it can be said that, while language structure is very important in human thought, there is not a critical or causal dependence of thought upon language structure.

These specific qualifications of what has come to be termed the *Sapir-Whorf-Lee hypothesis*, that

is, men speaking languages with different lexical and grammatical structures hear, see, and experience the world in profoundly different ways, can be illustrated briefly through reference to some examples of the modern studies of the relations between language structure and thought.[5]

Navaho and Papago language structure and culture. In a discussion of the ways the structure of Navaho, a North American Indian language, provides a broad framework for Navaho thought, concepts of reality, and understanding, Hoijer (1951) has pointed out that speakers of Navaho must use a system of verbs that are divided into two distinct classes, the *neuter* and the *active*. Neuter verbs in Navaho are used by speakers to report general states or conditions of life and contain no meanings of tense mode or aspect, but simply report a state of being, such as "being at rest," "standing," or "sitting." Some neuter Navaho verbs also report specific qualities—to be "blue," "white," "thin," "fat," or "tall." On the other hand, Navaho active verbs report specific events, movements, and actions. These are expressed mainly in regard to the aspect or mode of action and movement, rather than in a tense form. Thus, the active verb *nìǹdà:h* means "he moves to a sitting position." Here, a Navaho speaker's emphasis is on the incompleted action, and not on the present tense expression, which is a function of translating the Navaho verb *nìǹdà:h* into English, a language in which the present tense must be used to express the whole idea involved. If a Navaho speaker wishes to add a tense to the active verb form *nìǹdà:h,* he may add the form *dò* (technically called an "optional enclitic,") as in *nìǹdà:h-dò* "he will be moving to a sitting position," or as in *nìǹdá-dò* "he will have moved to a sitting position."

Hoijer notes that Navaho speakers must learn the details of five neuter and seven active verb categories in order to effectively use their language. More importantly, Navaho speakers must

[5]For some discussions of the nature and validity of the Sapir-Whorf-Lee hypothesis, see Bedau (1957), Black (1959), Brown (1958), Carroll (1958), Graves (1957), Hoijer (1953), Kluckhohn and Leighton (1961), Lenneberg (1953), and Lee (1938, 1959). See also the readings on this topic in Hymes (1964).

understand the basic cultural distinctions which underlie all the neuter and active categories of verbs. These distinctions can be learned by speakers of languages with different structures.

Hoijer points out that the conception which seems to be at the base of all five Navaho neuter verb categories is one which notes the existence of a state of events and of being, after all motion or movement has been withdrawn. In sharp contrast, Navaho active verbs report a state of being of motion, of events occurring. Thus, all twelve Navaho verb categories are primarily concerned with the reporting of events, or as Hoijer terms it, "eventing," one class having to do with "eventings solidified" (a withdrawal of motion) and one class concerned with "eventings in motion." But, Hoijer observes, even this basic Navaho conception of "eventings" seems in turn to rest upon and derive from a still more fundamental Navaho conception of reality, that of the relations between concrete, specific, corporeal bodies and their movement. As an illustration of this point, Hoijer notes in the Navaho way of speaking about an object moving, such as in the statements "he picks something up" or "he selects something," that there are twelve different verbs involved, all with the same prefix, *nâidì* ("the third person causes it to move upward"), but each with different enclitics, depending on the "it" being referred to in the prefix, *nâidì*. Thus, *nâidì-tì:h* ("the third person causes a long slender object to move upward"), *nâidì-ní:l* ("the third person causes a rigid container to move upward"), *nâidì-kà:h* ("the third person causes a fabric-like object to move upward"), and so on. This same complexity of specification of relations between bodies and their movement extends reciprocally to withdrawal of movement, such as *ʒil-siʔá* ("a round solid object lies at rest," that is, "a mountain lies at rest"), or *ʒil-ńʔá* ("round solid objects lie at rest in a row," that is, "a range of mountains lies extending from one point to another").

Hoijer summarizes these points by noting that the Navaho language emphasizes movement and specifies precisely the nature, direction, and status of all movement in great detail. Hoijer and others, particularly Kluckhohn (1946; 1960)

have observed that patterns of Navaho culture reflect these semantic themes of Navaho language, from kinship and kin groups through patterns of ideology and technology. Navaho myths and folktales most clearly reflect this semantic theme, for Navaho gods and folk-heroes move ceaselessly from one holy place to another, trying by their motion to repair and to reinstate the dynamic flux of the Navaho universe.

It is quite interesting to note that Hoijer concludes that his study of the relationships between Navaho language structure and thought, conducted by use of linguistic techniques, has very striking parallels in the conclusions about the Navaho cultural subsystem of ideology (see Chapter Nine) independently reached by Kluckhohn through use of nonlinguistic field research procedures. It could be concluded from this that the fact that two scholars working independently on studies of different aspects of Navaho culture and reaching similar conclusions reflects the broad ways in which language and thought are interrelated within a culture.

Another illustration of the broad relations between language categories and culture can be found in the ways Papago Indians (see Chapter Three) have constructed a taxonomy, or classification scheme, for their world through the classes of the nouns used in their language. The majority of nouns used in Papago are reported by Mathiot (1962) to be of a type termed technically as "quantifiable nouns," that is, nouns which specify the properties of *mass, aggregate,* and *individuality.* Papago regularly distinguish between features of mass on the one hand, and features of aggregate and individuality on the other. For instance, the term *ʔóʔohia* ("sand") is a mass noun. However, the term for "gravel" *(ʔóʔoḍ)* is an aggregate noun, as are the terms for "deer," "hair," "hailstones," or "servant." In contrast, the Papago individual noun class contains such terms as "coyote," "nose," "stone," and "wife." Both Papago aggregate and individual noun classes share the underlying characteristic of defining human experience as made up of definite bodies with specific outlines and features. In contrast the Papago noun class for mass rests upon an underlying assumption which defines experience in terms of the texture of bodies with definite outlines and features.

These two underlying assumptions (that experience has texture or definite shape and outline) are used by Papago to classify the vital features of their world into a broad two-part system of "living things" *(háʔicu dóakam)* and "growing things" *(háʔicu mo vúusañ).* The Papago class of "living things" includes all animated objects, such as people and animals, while the class of "growing things" refers to all inanimate objects, such as plants. An analysis by Mathiot (1962) of the Papago cultural taxonomy of experience notes that there is a strong tendency for "living things" to be named by use of individual nouns, while "growing things" are usually named as aggregate nouns. Most of the Papago taxonomy of experience consists of aggregate nouns, with only a few individual nouns. No instances of mass nouns are found throughout the Papago taxonomic system. Thus, it could be concluded that Papago tend to be concerned with definite outlines and features of their world rather than with its texture, or to state the conclusion in perceptual terms, Papago tend to see their experiences in terms of shapes and forms, rather than in terms of textures, or surface, qualities.

This structuring of the perception of reality through a particular use of noun classes, along with other linguistic features such as the number of nouns, that is, whether nouns are singular, plural, and so on, appears to contribute directly to the ways Papago have regularly dealt with their world. Most of the observers of Papago life have commented upon the style in which Papago tend to think about and to behave in social situations. This style has been termed as "personal plasticity" (Joseph, Spicer, and Chesky, 1949) and "personal adaptability" (Williams, 1958). Papago individuals regularly seem to observers from other cultures to be generally "unconcerned" or "uninterested" in the formal appearances of social and cultural actions and activities, so that when confronted with real or potential personal and social conflicts or very new and unexpected events, Papago remain placid and unruffled in their outlook, action, and demeanor. Papago life, as interpreted through the structure of the Papago language, is a continuing series of broad forms of experience. Hence, so long as the forms remain intact, most Papago do not respond to immediate shifts in the specific content of such forms. Another way to state this broad relationship between Papago language structure and culture would be to say in the contemporary vernacular of the American student that Papago do not get easily "turned on," "ticked off," or "hung up" by most events, so long as they perceive or assume that broad outlines and forms of their cultural experience remain unchanged. In comparison with Navaho culture, which is characterized by the flux, motion, and change in forms of reality, Papago culture tends to concentrate upon a view of reality which stresses the continuity and stability of forms of experience.

Thus, the conclusion which could be drawn from the modern studies of relationships between language structure and thought is that, while there are easily demonstrable broad relationships between language and thought, these relations are not so inflexible, determinate, and overpowering as they once were proposed or implied to be by Sapir, Whorf, Lee, and others. Men speaking languages with different structures can and often do approach reality and experience with very different categories arising from their languages. Men speaking different languages tend to react to and interpret events and situations in the terms made available in the structures of their languages. But men speaking different languages can transcend the lexical and grammatical structures of their languages to reach out to other ways of looking at their world and of facing old, as well as new, situations. In general, learning the lexical and grammatical structure of a language is a very good starting point for grasping the realities of life known widely in a culture. However, one does not come to "know" the Navaho, Papago, or any other culture through knowing only the structure of the language of that culture. The fact that categories of experience can be independently noted and interpreted by observers working in a culture with either solely linguistic or solely ethnographic methods indicates, that a language structure and other parts of a cultural structure (patterns of social relations, technology, and so on) have a great amount of independence and autonomy. A causal link from language structure to other patterns of culture does not exist except in a very general manner.

A broad range of different types of studies in the ethnography of communication (Gumperz and Hymes, 1964) and in the transcultural aspects of cognition (Romney and D'Andrade, 1964; Tyler, 1969) tend to provide further, substantial evidences demonstrating that, while language and other cultural patterns are inextricably linked together, language does not, except in very rare instances, directly control and dictate other cultural phenomena or events, even as these may be manifested in personal behavior. Language structures seem to be guides to the conduct of everyday affairs and to serve as ways of minimizing an extraordinary investment of personal attention in routine and repetitive activities, without precluding, or blocking off, the kinds of thought processes needed for general problem solving, for cultural and social change, and for significant revision of former routines of work and leisure activities.

▪ Learning language

There have been two different types of studies of the ways humans learn language. On the one hand, there are studies made in a "naturalistic" manner, that is, by observers (usually linguists) carefully noting the ways individual infants and children learn and use language in everyday contexts. A second type of study (usually conducted by psychologists) may be designated as "experimental," since observers have tended to work with infants and children in laboratories, under carefully controlled conditions. In both types of studies, a central interest has been in description and understanding of the specific knowledge and "abilities" persons must have in order to learn and use language. Both kinds of studies have been greatly handicapped by the fact that language learning can be described only by studying actual speech behavior and responses to speech behavior. This

means that early language learning and use must be inferred from events in human behavior, not all of which may correspond precisely to the "internal" events of language development in individuals.

This problem of research raises a variety of quite important questions, some of which have been referred to in the previous discussion of the relations between language and cognition. Thus, while the cognitive capacity of young children seems from the evidences of their behavior to be relatively limited for the first several years of life, there is, at the same time, a nearly complete mastery of the structure and rules of a native language in the first 4 to 5 years of life. In addition, children are exposed only to the selected aspects of the language spoken by their parents and those adults acting for their parents and are not given much overt language

Communicative contact through a language; Keningau Dusun woman teasing ethnographer (Baginda, 1963). (T. R. Williams.)

Blackfoot Indian child in the context of adult communication (circa 1910). (Courtesy American Museum of Natural History.)

instruction. Children usually master their native language equally well. Too, the language learning process seems to involve several stages which appear not to be directly related to other developmental sequences in human behavior. Solutions to these and similar questions must wait for further research which combines the techniques of the natural and laboratory settings and which transcend the now difficult barrier of what can be termed as the "outside-inside" relations between human behavior and language learning and use.

Cries, babbling, and language learning. Some linguists and psychologists have devoted a great amount of effort to studies of the pre-

cursors, or antecedents, of language in infants and very young children. These studies have finally laid to rest a number of once quite fashionable notions concerning language learning. One such notion was the idea that, if left entirely alone, human infants would begin speaking a "basic" or "ancient" human language.[6] However, systematic observation of both isolated and "normal" infants have produced clear evidences that children learn to speak only the languages spoken by the adult members of the culture

[6]For a recent hypothetical reconstruction of the origin of language by knowledgeable specialists, see Hockett and Ascher, 1964.

into which they are born, provided the other members of the culture expect them to do so. Thus, language learning in modern man depends upon regular communicative contact with adult speakers of a language or languages. Human infants do not possess a species-characteristic tendency, if they become isolated, to begin to speak some pristine, or aboriginal, human language. In fact, if left entirely alone, children will not speak at all, a fact well illustrated in the cases of Anna and Isabelle (see Chapter Five).

Another once fashionable notion is that it is "normal" for children to learn only one language, which then becomes the precise guide for all later language use and which automatically colors or influences profoundly the later learning of all other languages. There are, in fact, cultures where children simultaneously learn two or three quite different languages; in Tucson, Arizona, Pascua Yaqui infants and children regularly learn Yaqui and Spanish. There also are cultures where infants and children first learn a "baby language" and later learn the language used by the adults of their group. This process is discussed more fully in a later section of this chapter.

It is quite important to understand that today when linguists and psychologists observe language learning they use a fully developed conception of the nature of language. Language is not simply a set of specific calls, or distinct noises learned by an infant in a stimulus-response fashion. Infants and children must learn a complex set of rules, or a grammar, which controls the specific ways adult speakers put together minimally distinctive sounds, or *phonemes*, to make cognitively useful utterances. Thus, a language is not just a large collection of special sounds which infants practice and then make automatically. A language comprises a complex set of rules which determine for the speaker the particular sequences and patterns of speech sounds to be used in particular situations. Observers of language learning now tend to concentrate their attention upon the ways infants and young children acquire the rules and sounds of their languages, through watching very carefully the sequences of rule acquisition and sound production and trying to understand the ways these are interrelated with the physical growth and other behavioral maturation in the infant and child.

It once was believed that every child began learning his language or languages through an "instinctive" developing and shaping of infant cries and babblings toward the specific sounds of the local language. A great deal of attention was given in the eighteenth and nineteenth centuries, and in the early years of the present century, to descriptions of and discussions about the ways infant cries and babblings preceded learning and use of language.[7] Now that there is a general agreement among linguists and psychologists that languages—all languages—consist of grammars (rules) for organizing use of distinctive sounds, it has become quite easy to see that human infants and young children do not really develop out of their limited crying and babbling experiences the very complex rules and sounds found in all languages; such rules must be learned as a language is made available by adults in a culture. Isolated children (see Chapter Five) do not develop, from their crying and babbling, the phonemes and complex rules of grammar that are characteristic of languages.

This does not mean that an infant's cries or his first speech productions, such as babblings, may not be important for learning culture. It does mean that the learning of one subsystem of culture, language, now seems not specifically and directly related to these particular features of infant life and experience. However, it is possible that current and future research in linguistics and psychology may relate these special behavior forms of infants and young children to the process of language learning and use.

For instance, it has been suggested by Chomsky and some other linguists that every human infant is born possessed of a preadaptation to language learning and use, so that on the basis of a very few, even minimal, encounters with samples of the language forms of the adults who

---

[7] For some modern examples of the idea that infants begin to develop their language facility from different cries and babbling, see Miller and Dollard, 1941: 81; Mowrer, 1950: 699.

nurture them, infants would literally reinvent for themselves the rules of a local grammar system, and in fact most of all of the five (grammatical, phonological, morphophonemic, phonetic, and semantic) systems which characterize a language. Chomsky has indicated that this human preadaptation is of such an order that only a very few clues are needed to stimulate the competency each infant and child needs to function linguistically. In effect, such a human predisposition seems to be portrayed by some linguists as analogous to the programs fed into a high-speed computer which allows it, on the basis of a very few bits of electronically provided and quickly scanned information, to solve an entire problem, describe a whole situation, or calculate the most probable among a wide series of consequences. These innovative theoretical ideas have been evocative of recent wide-ranging searches for evidences to support such a hypothesis. For instance, they have stimulated even more wide-ranging theorizing. In Bruner's studies, referred to previously, concerns are expressed with the whole of all of the ways human infants possibly may be preadapted at birth to not only acquire language, but as well to discern for themselves the meaningful uses and logical rules of a broad scope of human activities, from technology through artistic and intellectual creativity. In fact, Bruner's work tends to suggest that there may well be one general species-characteristic predisposition for learning of all basic human skills, from language use, through intelligent and efficient uses of the eyes, hands, and tools, to the cognitive capacity, which is applied regularly to reinventing the rules for forms followed in local cultures. Bruner has in effect suggested that all men are born with a preexisting basic species-characteristic behavior form which is antecedent to all other such forms, which is used to test fragmentary clues from the many local environments and to reorder it, then to generate automatically hypotheses which make it possible to produce a general internal comprehension of the world of experience humans have yet to face. These highly innovative views are not yet supported by any body of strong scientific evidence, but they do suggest that cries and babbling, along with the gestures of infants, may in some broad way be related to the learning of language and other capacities. It must be said in conclusion that at present such infant actions and behavior forms do not seem to be required for language learning. It also must be said that this may well be an erroneous conclusion, if sound evidences can be provided for a general species-characteristic preadaptation for learning, which includes language.

Pivot and open class words. Intensive studies of the development of infant sound production by Irwin and his University of Iowa associates and by others provides substantial evidence that early sound patterns depend upon and are primarily a function of body growth and specific changes in the infant's anatomical and nervous systems.[8] In the first 10 days of life a few phones are clearly articulated, for instance, $i, e, a, u, h, w,$ and k. In the first year of life, infants significantly expand their range of phone productions; babies of 2 months have an average of seven phone uses, at 6 months the average is twelve phones, and at 12 months the average is eighteen phones. This still is well short of totals used in human languages; for instance, English contains thirty-four phones, while Navaho has forty-four phones. These phone utterance averages are significantly influenced by the position and posture of the growing infant. The shape of the oral cavity and the soft palate are considerably affected by the on-the-back, sitting, crawling, and walking positions of the growing infant. The phones developed and used at each age level seem to be regular in nature and not related to the languages used by the adults nurturing them; infants hearing only English also use the vowel and consonant sounds typical of German, French, and many so-called non-Western languages, while infants learning languages such as Dusun and Papago use phones typical of English.

Sometime after 9 months of age, infants begin to imitate directly the phonemic sound productions that emerge in their spontaneous play babblings. Most psychologists would now

---

[8]See Irwin, 1947a, 1947b, 1947c, 1948, and 1952.

agree that phonemes are not imitated from the speech of adults but are the results of self-stimulation to new sound productions which call the infant's attention to new types of sound production possibilities.[9]

Despite careful studies it is still difficult to determine the specific age when human infants use the first combinations of phonemes, which are put in a way having cultural and social meaning. Recurring sequences of phonemes which have meaning are called *morphemes*. When mothers' retrospective reports from different cultures are used, it appears that the average age for the first use of morphemes is about 11 months. Laboratory studies of "gifted" children indicate that some children use morphemes as early as 8 months. Most children in most cultures are using some morphemes by 13 to 14 months of age.

The first morphemes used tend to be employed as "total utterances," that is, a way of communicating a whole range of complex meanings. The morpheme *mama* may come to mean, to the baby and its parents, through the enculturation paradigm (see Chapter Four), "Mama feed me," or "Mama, I am tired and wet and irritated by all the noise about me," or "Mama, please bring me the toy over there and the one here by my side that I cannot reach easily." During this period of language learning babies do not use a grammatical system or rules for combining morphemes into sentence utterances.

The growth of morphemic competency in children accelerates markedly in the months and years following the onset of the first morphemic uses. Table 10-3 notes the average number of morphemes reported in one study to be recognized and used by American middle-class, midwestern children between 8 months and 6 years of age. At the same time children are learning increasingly greater numbers of morphemes, they also learn to articulate, or speak, them more clearly. Preschool American children are reported to pronounce approxi-

Table 10-3. Increase in morpheme use, American children, ages 1 to 6 years*

Age in years	Average number of single morphemes used
1	3
2	272
3	896
4	1,540
5	2,072
6	2,562

*After Smith, M. E. 1926. "An Investigation of the Development of the Sentence and the Extent of Vocabulary in Young Children," University of Iowa Studies in Child Welfare 3:(5).

mately 32 percent of their morphemes correctly at 2 years of age. By 3 years approximately 63 percent of morphemes are correctly formed, while at 6 years the figure of accurate morpheme use by preschool American children rises to 89 percent. Similarly, the comprehensibility of morpheme uses increases with age; 67 percent of American 2-year-old morpheme uses have been reported to be clearly comprehensible, with this figure rising to 89 percent for 2½-year-olds, 93 percent for 3-year-olds, and nearly 100 percent morpheme comprehensibility for 4-year-olds.[10] These data must be qualified by a notation that similar figures are generally not available from other cultures.[11] It can be assumed that morpheme knowledge, articulation, and comprehensibility increase at the same rates for all human children, but this assumption remains to be validated in actual transcultural research.

In general, linguists and psychologists agree that children do not really begin to use language until they put two or more morphemes together to form primitive sentences. This typically seems to occur first at about 18 to 20 months of age. The number of two-word utterances accelerates sharply between the time of their first use by a child and about 24 to 26 months of age.

---

[9]For a general discussion of language development, see McCarthy, 1954.

[10]For some examples of well-known studies of morpheme articulation and comprehensibility, see McCarthy, 1930 and 1954; Smith, 1935; Wellman and others, 1931.

[11]For some transcultural references to language learning, see Heinecke and Whiting, 1953; Hymes, 1961a, 1961b, and 1962.

The total number of different two-morpheme uses rises from between fourteen and twenty at 18 months, to 350 to 400 at 22 months, to over 2,500 at 26 months of age.

Studies of the ways American and European children learn to combine morphemes into sentence utterances indicate that there are, at least for these children, specific age-related stages of development involving hierarchical and regular constructions, or combinations of morphemes. Two-word sentences tend to include some uses of "pivot" or "operator" morphemes. These morphemes are limited in number and are added to very slowly. Some examples of pivot words in English would be "my," "this," "see," "on," "other," "more," "there," and "all gone." A pivot morpheme such as "on" is usually the second part of a two-morpheme sentence, although it also occurs as the first morpheme. An example of a second position pivot morpheme would be in an English speaking child's uses of "blanket on," "shoe on," "spoon on," and "hat on." Pivot morphemes can have many other morphemes, technically termed "open class" morphemes, attached to them in the first position of a two-morpheme sentence to make statements. Some examples of American children's open class morphemes in addition to those just given (blanket, shoe, spoon, hat) would be "toy," "hat," "milk," "car," "man," "woman," and "house." The open class of morphemes may contain a total of more than two hundred different uses for a 2-year-old American middle-class midwestern child.

It is important to understand that young children proceed to use language at first as if there were only the pivot and open classes of morphemes, although the morphemes contained in these two classes actually belong to many different classes in adult language uses (verbs, adjectives, nouns, prepositions, and so on). However, young children use them all as belonging only to the pivot or open classifications. This means that young children do not begin speaking by using or making an imitation of the language structures used by the adults who care for them. Rather, children start language learning and use by means of a system unique to children, which

is not a simply reduced or infantile imitation of adult language. Young children appear to have a grammar system quite different from the adult systems they have heard and are hearing as they begin to combine morphemes into primitive sentences. This fact is important because it eliminates the confusion which has been caused continually by the matter of "baby talk" in language learning.

It was assumed for a long time that infants and young children learned a greatly reduced or much simplified version of adult grammar because they also were forming and using the same morphemes used in adult language. This assumption, in a folk or common sense form, is widely held in many cultures. For instance, parents in cultures speaking languages as diverse as Arabic, Marathi, Comanche, Gilyak, English, and Spanish regularly speak to their children in "baby talk," to try to aid them in learning both the proper morpheme and grammatical uses of adult language.[12] Typically, however, "baby talk" is only a very limited subsystem of the adult language, containing between twenty-five and sixty morphemes which cover only a very restricted range of the whole of culturally important topics (some kinship terms, personal names, body functions, certain qualities of life—hot, cold, wet, dirty—and morphemes for describing some animals and a few nursery games—"patty cake," "whoops-a-daisy," "peek-a-boo," and so on). Baby talk morphemes are mostly open class morphemes and do not appear to provide the structure for the two-morpheme utterances of infants and young children. Thus, the two-word utterance system of grammar used by infants and young children is not learned through baby talk training by the adults of their culture.

Hierarchical constructions. At about 2 years of age, children begin to employ a few structured sentences in their play and interactions with adults and other children. This begins when a combination utterance of two open class morphemes (an *"open-open"* sentence) such as "woman"-"hat" is changed by adding a pivot word such as "other" to "woman" and "hat" to make

---

[12]For a discussion of baby talk in different languages, see Ferguson, 1964; Casagrande, 1948.

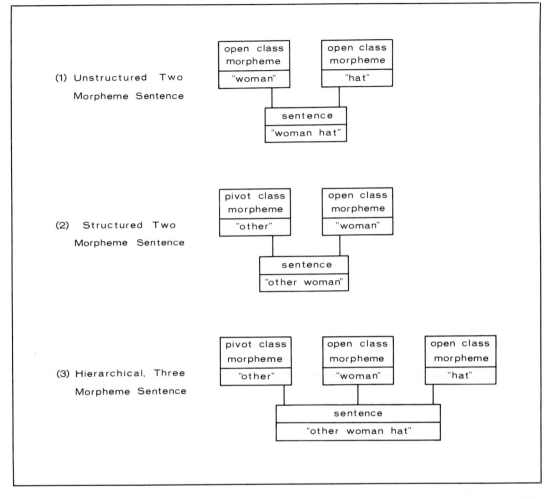

Fig. 24. The transition from unstructured two-morpheme sentences to hierarchical, three-morpheme sentences. The morphemes may also be reversed in this expression, as in "woman other hat" or "hat other woman" and still be examples of a hierarchical, three-morpheme sentence.

a three-unit utterance such as "other woman hat." This process is illustrated in Fig. 24. When children reach about 2½ years of age, the use of structured *pivot-open-open* (or *open-open-pivot*) type sentences is an increasingly regular part of their language. Too, at about this age, children begin to offer much more complex, multiple morpheme sentences. A number of laboratory studies indicate that by 3 years of age children tend to regularly use four-morpheme sentences, and at 4 years are speaking six to eight morpheme sentences. At the age of 5 years most children are using mostly multiple morpheme sentences, often including those with ten or more morphemes, which are increasingly structured according to the rules of grammar used by the adult speakers of the culture in which children are maturing.

In the time from the onset of three-word type sentences at about 2 years to some time close to 4 years of age, children tend to "overregulate" their uses of morphemes as they seek to employ their unique grammar system. Thus, children speaking English will typically use "strong verbs" inflected for the past tenses, in the same ways that adult speakers will inflect only "weak verbs."

Some examples of this kind of inflective over-regularization of morphemes in two- and three-morpheme sentences would be *goded* (for gone), *breaked* (for broken), *doed* (for did), *hitted* (for hit), and *runded* (for run). Another example of over-regularization is for English speaking 2- and 3-year-olds to use plurals similar to *mouses* (for mice), *dogses* (for dogs), *foots* (for feet), *cateses* (for cats), and *manses* (for men).

Psychological and linguistic studies of the overregularization process among 2- and 3-year-old European and American children tend to agree that these linguistic uses represent a consistent effort by young children to find and use consistent language patterns, so that they may go on, after a pattern is identified, to use it in speaking in new and more complex ways. To put this point in another way, 2- to 3-year-old children seem to strive in their language learning and use to seek out patterns and regularities for use in making more general statements which aid in ordering their everyday experiences.

When children reach the level of using four- and five-morpheme sentences, at 3 to 3½ years of age, they begin to drop the grammar forms initially developed in speaking and to more frequently use the grammars typical of the languages spoken by the adults caring for them. This transition, from the "child grammar" to the grammar of adult languages, has not been well studied outside of European and American cultures. The research efforts of Piaget, Bruner, and others on cognition have provided, through their uses of language learning and ability as evidences of cognitive development, most of the present suggestions concerning the steps in this complex transition. It is quite clear from such studies that European and American children all tend to go through the same steps in the transition from child grammar to adult grammar uses. However, there is substantive disagreement, at present, concerning the exact specification and nature of each of these steps.

Evidence from children's behavior seems to indicate that the grammar changeover process occurs with these kinds of steps. First, children show increasing efforts to systematize

their language use and employ the overregularizations noted above. Then, to break out from the limits imposed on their language use, children abandon the overregularizations for the regularities of grammatical form used by the adults about them. Next, children must detect the patterns of grammar form which adults use in regular ways of speaking a language. Then, children must learn to know and use well the variations from the adult grammar patterns, that is, they must comprehend and begin to use language normatively, or in a way which includes not only patterned form, but as well the common variations from patterns. Finally, children practice and regularly use the normative expressions of language common to and typical of the adults caring for them. These five or six or more steps in the transition from child grammar to adult grammar also seem to be present in other non-Western cultures. However, there have been only a few studies of this process outside Western cultures.

Perhaps the most important point to be made concerning this transition in language learning and use is that, although each child must face alone the almost overpowering complexities of the adult languages, most do so quite efficiently and successfully. It is clear from the literature of enculturation that adults in most cultures do not provide the kind of intensive training and experience which is necessary for a child to master adult grammar forms and to make a successful transition from typical child grammar uses. These facts of language learning seem to lend great weight to the conception that language learning and use is based upon and proceeds from a human biological preadaptation for such behavior. However, proponents of this conception of language learning and use tend to sometimes ignore some evidences which are to the contrary of their assumptions.

Variations in language learning and use. There are consistent indications that girls make greater progress than boys in language learning and use, particularly in the time of first uses of language, total numbers of morphemes mastered, the time of onset of three- and four-morpheme sentences, and morpheme and phoneme comprehensibility. There also appear to be consistent variations, at least in the United States and Europe, in language learning and use specifically linked not only to the sex of the child, but as well to the social, economic, and racial settings into which children are born and are enculturated. In general, children whose language efforts are positively and warmly approved by the adults about them tend to become more highly proficient in language use and to progress quickly through the child grammar period to acquisition and regular uses of adult grammar. In contrast, children whose language efforts are deprecated or punished by adults, in any of a variety of forms, tend to lag significantly behind their "rewarded" peers, often by a matter of many months or even years; children raised in institutional settings in America and Europe generally fall well behind their age mates enculturated in more "normal" settings. There also are research data which indicate that American and European twins and triplets may lag well behind only children in language learning and uses.

All of these data of variation in language learning and use seem to indicate that, if there is a biologically transmitted preadaptation for such behavior in human infants and young children, it is highly plastic, or differential, and markedly influenced and easily altered by non-biological cultural and social experiences and by biologically based sexual and fertility factors, which affect individuals as they are enculturated. The fact of Anna and Isabelle telescoping into a relatively brief time the language learning and uses said to ordinarily occupy children for all of the period of the first 5 or 6 years of their lives also raises a basic question about current assumptions concerning the biological human preadaptation to language learning and use. This does not deny that the process of language learning is not fundamentally biochemical and neuro-anatomical in its essence; on the contrary, it means that it may be too simplistic to try to reduce language learning and use to this level of conceptual abstraction and study. The variations of human language learning and uses are too complex and vital in human life to be explained away

by a biologically deterministic, although very aesthetically appealing, assumption. It is noteworthy that skilled and experienced scientists, when faced with a very complex problem (such as the fact that infants and children learn and use adult language without much instruction) will still turn to an *obscurum per obscurius* (explaining an unknown phenomenon by reference to a still more unknown phenomenon) type argument for explanation and reference.

■ Language and socialization

At present, many accounts of the interrelations of language and socialization tend to use statements of the form "For the sake of argument, A (language) will be considered prior to B (culture)." This form of statement is logically equivalent to saying regularly that "A (language) is basic to and of underlying significance to B (culture)." These kinds of statements and the logic form they imply make brief discussions of the interrelations between language and socialization very difficult.

There no longer is a real question of whether there are such interrelations, since it has been demonstrated clearly through the studies of isolated, deaf, and autistic children, of twins, and of the deculturation process that humans must be in regular communicative contact with other, linguistically competent persons if they are to become fully socialized. However, the specific questions of *how* and *why* language affects the socialization process, and *vice versa*, remain unsettled, since language is not reducible to or to be understood only by describing the cultural and social behavior of its speakers, or of the ways these persons have developed, arranged, and operate social, religious, economic, and other daily events. On the one hand, a language consists of whatever a person living in a culture has to know in order to vocally communicate with his fellows in a fashion which other persons will accept as corresponding to their own. On the other hand, as noted above, a language consists of a highly organized system of sounds and rules for making sounds, which can be studied, after an initial descriptive effort, quite apart from any of the behavior of individuals

Tambunan Dusun mother discussing enculturation with ethnographer while making a hen roost (Sensuron, 1959). (T. R. Williams.)

making the sounds and using rules of sound expression.

Today, many anthropologists and anthropological linguists would accept the statement that the relation of language to culture is that of one part to a larger whole, that is, language is but one part (or in the terms used in Chapter Seven, one subsystem) of an entire culture. This means that these scholars would reject the logical form and statements arising from that form, which imply that language is of primary significance for all of culture. These specialists tend

to see language as one of several ways of making accessible to its speakers historically created and derived concepts which individuals can employ in dealing with the events of the natural world and with each other. In this sense, language is seen as being used principally by individuals to get from the "outside" world of nature and social man into the substance of the "inside" of a culture, by acquiring the language spoken in and typical of a culture. In this way, individuals can gain some access to the "minds" and "selves" of their fellows, for language is both a way of expressing thought and feeling and of thinking and feeling about thought and emotion. Competent speakers of a language can take "into" themselves the thoughts of others in a culture and make these into their own, in the same or in some altered form. In this view, language is not a prime mover, or first cause, in human behavior, since as one subsystem of a larger cultural whole it does not dominate all of culture. In this view of the relation of language to culture, a culture consists of many different patterns which are not "translatable" or convertible to purely linguistic forms.

In this conception of the relations between language and culture, the part played by language in the socialization process tends to be emphasized in a *facilitative* sense; thus, it is *through* language infants and children come to know what others know and expect them to know. It is *through* language children and adults add to and change what is known and expected in a culture. It is *through* language that children can be reached by and respond to those persons, social agencies, and institutions (see Chapter Eight) involved in the socialization process. And it is *through* language that children learn of the enculturation conceptual system which is used in their local culture; this learning enables a child to become an active participant in the process of transmitting a culture.

However, a contrary view of the way language is related to culture tends to be reflected in the studies of some anthropologists and many psychologists, linguists, and biologists. In this view, language is a fully separate and easily distinguishable human system which is basic for all culture and human activity. In this view, language is generally *directive,* that is, language tends to cause and is believed responsible for human action. In one of its forms, the *directive* argument for language proposes that adults who do not "fit" readily or are not totally "competent" in their social and cultural behavior have become so because of their failure to adequately learn language. The directive assumption concerning the relations between language and culture is involved in many of the explanations which have been offered for why and how adults come to act in similar ways when they occupy the same status positions in a social structure. In this view, adults behave the same way when occupying the same status primarily because they share a language.

In the directive sense, infants and children are socialized because they are born into a culture which operates from the base of a language system. In this view of language, human personality, many abilities, and most individual social actions are seen as the result and consequence of having learned language. Too, following this view of language, individuals must struggle against the predetermined aspects of language, only rarely transcending, or rising above, the tyranny of words and sounds which dominate their lives.

Another approach to the interrelations between language and socialization involves a combination of both the *facilitative* and *directive* views just outlined briefly. While it is probably correct to note, as in the facilitative approach, that language does not dominate all human behavior and that all culture does not have linguistic components or aspects, it is equally correct, as in the directive approach, to say that many aspects of language are deeply involved and probably directly responsible for some specific kinds of human learning and action. Hallowell has demonstrated the advantages of combining the facilitative and directive approaches in his innovative and original discussions of the evolutionary growth of the interrelations of language and socialization. He has noted that today none of *Homo sapiens* culture, society, or personality can really be conceived as existing apart from language, but also notes it is still possible to analyze and subject to careful study these features (culture, society, and personality) of the human experience without assigning a high logical priority to language with respect to its relations to culture.

Hallowell has noted that it has been through language that uniquely human forms of the psychological processes of attention, perception, interest, memory, dreams, imagination, symbolic representations, ability to deal with the contrasts between the possible and the actual, the tangible and intangible, and differentiation between reality and fantasy have become operative and "alive," in man. Thus, in a theoretical approach which seeks to combine the *facilitative* and *directive* views, language is interrelated with both the formation and subsequent functioning of personality and the successes of humans in being able to comprehend and to deal with culture. Too, in this view, language is not only a vehicle for socialization; it is at one and the same time the means by which humans become both *more* and *less* like others in a culture, for through the time of the socialization process, by means of language, individuals take on from others those attributes of self and behavior which characterize most persons in their culture. And, while this is occurring, individuals also, through language, are becoming less and less psychologically like any other members of their culture, for language is not only one key to learning what others know, think, and feel, it is also a means for each individual to self-consciously reflect upon and then to shape his own unique self or personality. Thus, in this view of the role of language in socialization, new members of a culture are able simultaneously to join with and be apart from others, to be like and yet differentiate themselves from their fellows. Language is the medium, or the means, for persons to achieve "oneness" and "apartness" at the same time, and a way to handle both the social and cultural *centripedal* (proceeding toward the center) and *centrifugal* (proceeding away from the center) elements of the socialization process without great harm to themselves or their society and culture. Alone,

Tambunan Dusun girls discussing the abundance of lice in a friend's hair (Sensuron, 1959). (T. R. Williams.)

of California at Berkeley have made a number of studies of the acquisition of language in a variety of different cultures. Thus, K. Kernan has described and analyzed the interrelations of language and the enculturation process in Samoa, Blount has described and analyzed the acquisition of language by Luo (Kenya) children, Stross has reported the details of language acquisition and enculturation among Tenjapa (Mexico) children, Sanches has studied the relations between enculturation and the acquisition of grammar by Japanese children, and C. Kernan has reported some of the interrelations between language and enculturation in urban black American society.

These studies, and those similar to them by Howell, Mathiot, and others, hold promise of transcultural specification of interrelations between socialization and language. Thus, Blount has identified some developmental stages in the prelinguistic behavior of Luo children, which he relates to the language behavior of older children caretakers and adult nurses, while Stross has recorded both the verbal settings and Mexican children's participation in such settings, in an effort to demonstrate the relative importance of direct and overheard speech on first language learning and on subsequent cultural behavior. Such studies can provide for transcultural validation of theories of language, of cognition, and of the ways language and the socialization process may be specifically interrelated.

Language and socialization theory. In the theoretical paradigm developed in Chapter Four, it was proposed that socialization is a doubly contingent, or transactional, process. In this conceptual model, the cultural preoccupations of adults become the infant's and child's preoccupations. Language is one medium for gaining derived, or learned, preoccupations, as infants and children have their behavior culturally shaped through adult responses to them, by adult responses to their responses, the evaluations by adults of children's responses, and the growing ability of children to independently evaluate and to judge their own responses in terms of adult expectations.

The role of language in the transactional

the facilitative and the directive views of language do not adequately explain the ways humans become the kinds of adults they are when in Kluckhohn's words they have become, "like all men, some men, no other man."

In the last few years, a number of studies have combined the facilitative and directive approaches to language to provide evidences of some specific interrelations between language and the socialization process. For instance, Gumperz and his associates at the University interchange is an important one, for it is the one human communication medium with perhaps the most lasting impact. Other communication media involved in the long-term human transactional exchanges, such as inarticulate experience (see Chapter One), and tactile, kinesic, proxemic, and adumbrative (indications preceding formal communications necessary for mutual exchange of information) experiences all have roles in the doubly contingent process of informational exchange. But, language is an important way for adults finally and fully to convey their views to infants and children. The transactional theory of the socialization process is complete with the inclusion of language as a medium for exchanges of cultural information. In the absence of language learning and use, the theoretical paradigm of socialization is incomplete. It is possible to postulate and to demonstrate that individuals can become enculturated successfully to some degree to features of their local culture and society through nonverbal exchanges (use of the tactile or kinesic media of information). The dramatic ways in which Helen Keller and other persons afflicted with severely limiting physical handicaps have been reported to have acquired, shared, and used basic cultural information illustrates the fact that the socialization transactional process is not solely, or necessarily, dependent upon language. Yet, it is language which becomes and is the communication medium of importance as infants and children mature in a cultural milieu. Thus, it is through language that the socialization process becomes fully operative and takes on such a strategic role in human life.

■ Summary

This chapter has been concerned with discussion of the relations between language and the process of socialization. The topic of language origin and development was examined in the first section to provide a background of data and information for understanding of some of the ways language functions in the life of contemporary man. Then, some of the relations between speech and thought and between language structure and thought were examined briefly to note the complex and pervasive nature

of language. The third part of the chapter provided a brief summary of contemporary knowledge of infant and child language acquisition and use. The last section of the chapter noted some approaches to and discussed some results of studies of the interrelations between language and the socialization process.

REFERENCES CITED AND SUGGESTED READINGS

Allen, W. S. 1949. "Ancient Ideas on the Origin and Development of Language," Transactions of the Philological Society, London, 1948, pp. 35-60.

Andrew, R. 1962. "Evolution of Intelligence and Vocal Mimicking," Science 137:585-589.

_____. 1963a. "Evolution of Facial Expression," Science 142:1034-1041.

_____. 1963b. "The Origin and Evolution of the Calls and Facial Expressions of the Primates," Behaviour 20:1-109.

Altman, S. A. (ed.) 1967. Social Communication Among Primates. Chicago: University of Chicago Press.

Barker, G. C. 1945. "The Social Functions of Language," ETC.: A Review of General Semantics 2:228-234.

Beckey, R. E. 1942. "A Study of Certain Factors Related to Retardation of Speech," Journal of Speech Disorders 7:223-249.

Bedau, H. A. 1957. "Review of J. B. Carroll" (ed.), Language, Thought and Reality, Philosophy of Science 24:289-293.

Bernstein, B. 1960. "Language and Social Class: Research Note," British Journal of Sociology 11:271-276.

_____. 1961a. "Aspects of Language and Learning in the Genesis of the Social Process," Journal of Child Psychology and Psychiatry 1:313-324.

_____. 1961b. "Social Class and Linguistic Development." In A. H. Halsey, J. Floud, and A. Anderson (eds.) Education, Economy and Society. Glencoe, Ill.: The Free Press, pp. 288-314.

Birdwhistell, R. 1970. Kinesics and Context; Essays on Body Motion Communication. Philadelphia: University of Pennsylvania Press.

Black, M. 1959. "Linguistic Relativity: The Views of Benjamin Lee Whorf," Philosophical Review 68:228-238.

Bloch, B., and G. L. Trager. 1942. Outline of Linguistic Analysis. Baltimore: Linguistic Society of America.

Bloom, L. 1970. Language Development; Form and Function in Emerging Grammars. Cambridge, Mass.; M.I.T. Press.

Blount, B. G. 1969. "Acquisition of Language by Luo Children," Unpublished Doctoral Dissertation, University of California, Berkeley.

Boas, F. 1911. "Introduction." In F. Boas (ed.), *Handbook of American Indian Languages.* Washington, D. C.: Bureau of American Ethnology **40**:24-27; 42-43; 81.

_____. 1920. "The Methods of Ethnology," *American Anthropologist* **22**:311-321.

_____. 1934. *Geographical Names of the Kwakiutl Indians.* New York: Columbia University Contributions to Anthropology, Number 20, pp. 9-21.

_____. 1938. *General Anthropology.* New York: Heath.

_____. 1942. "Language and Culture." In *Studies in the History of Culture. The Disciplines of the Humanities.* Menasha, Wisconsin: Banta, pp. 178-184.

Bossard, J. H. S. 1945. "Family Modes of Expression," *American Sociological Review* **10**:226-237.

Bright, W. O. 1963. "Language." In B. J. Siegel (ed.), *Biennial Review of Anthropology, 1963.* Stanford: Stanford University Press, pp. 1-29.

_____. 1966. *Sociolinguistics.* The Hague: Mouton.

Brown, R. W. 1958. *Words and Things.* Glencoe, Ill.: Free Press.

Bruner, J. S., J. J. Goodnow, and G. A. Austin. 1956. *A Study of Thinking.* New York: Wiley.

Bruner, J. S., R. R. Olver, and P. M. Greenfield. 1966. *Studies in Cognitive Growth.* New York: Wiley.

Buettner-Janusch, J. 1966. *Origins of Man.* New York: Wiley.

Carpenter, E., and M. McLuhan. 1960. *Explorations in Communication: An Anthology.* Boston: Beacon.

Carroll, J. B. 1953. *The Study of Language.* Cambridge, Mass.: Harvard University Press.

_____. (ed.) 1956. *Language, Thought and Reality. Selected Writings of Benjamin Lee Whorf.* New York: Wiley.

_____. 1958. "Some Psychological Effects of Language Structure." In P. Hoch and J. Zubin (eds.), *Psychopathology of Communication.* New York: Grune and Stratton, pp. 28-36.

_____. 1964. *Language and Thought.* Englewood Cliffs, N. J.: Prentice-Hall.

Casagrande, J. B. 1948. "Comanche Baby Language," *International Journal of American Linguistics* **14**:11-14.

Chafe, W. (ed.) 1963. *Aspects of Language and Culture.* Seattle: University of Washington Press.

Chamberlain, A. F. 1896. *The Child and Childhood in Folk-Thought.* New York: Macmillan.

Chance, M., and C. Jolly. 1970. *Social Groups of Monkeys, Apes and Men.* New York: Dutton.

Cherry, C. 1957. *On Human Communication. A Review, A Survey, and a Criticism.* Cambridge, Mass.: M.I.T. Press.

Chomsky, C. 1969. *The Acquisition of Syntax in Children from 5 to 10.* Cambridge, Mass.: M.I.T. Press.

Chomsky, N. 1957. *Syntactic Structure..* The Hague: Mouton.

_____. 1965. *Aspects of the Theory of Syntax.* Cambridge, Mass.: M.I.T. Press.

_____. 1968. *Language and Mind.* New York: Harcourt, Brace.

Church, J. 1961. *Language and the Discovery of Reality. A Developmental Psychology of Cognition.* New York: Random House.

Dance, F. E. X. 1967. *Human Communication Theory.* New York: Holt, Rinehart and Winston.

De Laguna, F. (ed.) 1927. *Speech, Its Function and Development.* New Haven: Yale University Press. (Republished in 1963 by Indiana University Press.)

Dobzhansky, T. 1955. *Evolution, Genetics and Man.* New York: Wiley.

_____. 1960. "Individuality, Gene Recombination and Non-repeatability of Evolution," *Australian Journal of Science* **23**:71-78.

Du Brul, E. L. 1958. *Evolution of the Speech Apparatus.* Springfield, Ill.: Thomas.

Duncan, H. D. 1962. *Communication and the Social Order.* New York: Buckminster.

Elkind, D., and J. H. Flavell. 1969. *Studies in Cognitive Development.* London: Oxford.

Ferguson, C. A. 1964. "Baby Talk in Six Languages." In J. J. Gumperz and D. Hymes (eds.), *The Ethnography of Communication.* Special Publication, American Anthropologist **66**:103-114.

Furth, H. G. 1966. *Thinking Without Language: Psychological Implications of Deafness.* New York: Free Press.

Gardner, R. A., and B. T. Gardner. 1969. "Teaching Sign Language to a Chimpanzee," *Science* **169**: 664-672.

Gleason, H. A. 1961. *An Introduction to Descriptive Linguistics,* first rev. ed. New York: Holt, Rinehart and Winston.

Graven, J. 1967. *Non-Human Thought.* New York: Stein and Day.

Graves, R. 1957. "Comment on D. Lee, Lineal and Non-Lineal Codifications of Reality; Symbolization and Value," *Explorations* **7**:46-51; 67-73.

Greenberg, J. H. 1963. *Universals of Language.* Cambridge, Mass.: M.I.T. Press.

Gumperz, J. 1958. "Dialect Differences and Social Stratification in a North Indian Village," *American Anthropologist* **60**:668-682.

Gumperz, J., and D. Hymes (eds.) 1964. *The Ethnography of Communication,* Special Publication, American Anthropologist **66**: December, 1964.

Hall, E. T., and G. L. Trager. 1953. *The Analysis of Culture.* Washington, D. C.: American Council of Learned Societies.

Hallowell, A. I. 1950. "Personality Structure and the Evolution of Man," *American Anthropologist* **52**:159-173.

_____. 1953. "Culture, Personality and Society." In A. L. Kroeber (ed.), *Anthropology Today.* Chicago: University of Chicago Press, pp. 597-620.

_____. 1954. "Psychology and Anthropology." In J. Gillin (ed.), *For A Science of Social Man*. New York: Macmillan, pp. 160-226.

_____. 1955. *Culture and Experience*. Philadelphia: University of Pennsylvania Press.

Harris, Z. S. 1951. *Methods in Structural Linguistics*. Chicago: University of Chicago Press.

Heinecke, C. 1953. *Bibliography on Personality and Social Development of the Child*. (Bound with Whiting, B. B. 1953. *Selected Ethnographic Sources on Child Training*.) New York: Social Science Research Council, Pamphlet Number Ten.

Henle, P. (ed.) 1958. *Language, Thought and Culture*. Ann Arbor: University of Michigan Press.

Hockett, C. 1958. *A Course in Modern Linguistics*. New York: Macmillan.

_____. 1959. "Animal 'Languages' and Human Languages." In J. N. Spuhler (ed.), *The Evolution of Man's Capacity for Culture*. Detroit: Wayne State University Press, pp. 32-39.

_____. 1960. "The Origin of Speech," Scientific American, September, 1960, pp. 3-10.

Hockett, C., and R. Ascher. 1964. "The Human Revolution," Current Anthropology 5:135-168.

Hoijer, H. 1951. "Cultural Implications of Some Navaho Linguistic Categories," Language 27:111-120.

_____. 1953. "The Relation of Language to Culture." In A. L. Kroeber (ed.), *Anthropology Today*. Chicago: University of Chicago Press, pp. 554-573.

_____. 1954. *Language in Culture*. Comparative Studies of Cultures and Civilizations, Number 3, and Memoirs of the American Anthropological Association, Number 79. Chicago: University of Chicago Press.

Houston, S. H. 1969. "A Sociolinguistic Consideration of the Black English of Children in Northern Florida," Language 45:599-607.

Howell, R. W. 1967. "Linguistic Choice as an Index to Social Change," Unpublished Doctoral Dissertation, University of California, Berkeley.

Hymes, D. 1961a. "Linguistic Aspects of Cross-Cultural Personality Study." In B. Kaplan (ed.), *Studying Personality Cross-Culturally*. New York: Harper and Row, pp. 313-359.

_____. 1961b. "Functions of Speech: An Evolutionary Approach." In F. Gruber (ed.), *Anthropology and Education*. Philadelphia: University of Pennsylvania Press, pp. 55-83.

_____. 1962. "The Ethnography of Speaking." In T. Gladwin and W. C. Sturtevant (eds.), *Anthropology and Human Behavior*. Washington, D. C.: Anthropological Society of Washington, pp. 13-53.

_____. (ed.) 1964. *Language in Culture and Society*. New York: Harper and Row.

Irwin, O. C. 1947a. "Development of Speech During Infancy: Curve of Phonemic Frequencies," Journal of Experimental Psychology 37:187-193.

_____. 1947b. "Infant Speech: Consonantal Sounds According to Place of Articulation," Journal of Speech and Hearing Disorders 12:397-401.

_____. 1947c. "Infant Speech: Consonant Sounds According to Manner of Articulation," Journal of Speech and Hearing Disorders 12:402-404.

_____. 1948a. "Infant Speech: Development of Vowel Sounds," Journal of Speech and Hearing Disorders 13:31-34.

_____. 1948b. "Infant Speech: The Effect of Family Occupational Status and of Age on Use of Sound Types," Journal of Speech and Hearing Disorders 13:224-226.

_____. 1948c. "The Effect of Family Occupational Status and Age on Sound Frequency," Journal of Speech and Hearing Disorders 13:320-323.

_____. 1952. "Speech Development in the Young Child: 2. Some Factors Relating to the Speech Development of the Infant and Young Child," Journal of Speech and Hearing Disorders 17:269-279.

Irwin, O. C., and H. P. Chen. 1946a. "Infant Speech: Vowel and Consonant Frequency," Journal of Speech Disorders 11:123-125.

_____. 1946b. "Development of Speech in Infancy: Curve of Phonemic Types," Journal of Experimental Psychology 36:431-436.

Jacobs, R. A., and P. S. Rosenbaum. 1969. *English Transformational Grammar*. Waltham, Mass.: Blaisdell.

Jakobovits, L. A., and M. S. Miron. 1967. *Readings in the Psychology of Language*. Englewood Cliffs, N. J.: Prentice-Hall.

Jakobson, R., and M. Halle. 1966. *Fundamentals of Language*. The Hague: Mouton.

Joseph, A., R. B. Spicer, and J. Chesky. 1949. *The Desert People*. Chicago: University of Chicago Press.

Jerison, H. J. 1955. "Brain to Body Ratios and the Evolution of Intelligence," Science 121:447-449.

Kernan, C. M. 1969. "Language Behavior in a Black Urban Community," Unpublished Doctoral Dissertation, University of California, Berkeley.

Kernan, K. 1969. "The Acquisition of Language by Samoan Children." Unpublished Doctoral Dissertation, University of California, Berkeley.

Kluckhohn, C. 1960. "Navaho Categories," In S. A. Diamond (ed.), *Culture in History*. New York: Columbia University Press, pp. 65-98.

Kluckhohn, C., and D. Leighton. 1946. *The Navaho*. Cambridge, Mass.: Harvard University Press.

_____. 1961. "Notes on Some Anthropological Aspects of Communication," American Anthropologist 63:895-909.

Kohn, M. L. 1959a. "Social Class And Parental Authority," American Sociological Review 24:352-366.

_____. 1959b. "Social Class and Parental Values," American Journal of Sociology 64:337-351.

Kroeber, A. L. 1964. "Foreword." In D. Hymes (ed.),

Language in Culture and Society. New York: Harper and Row, pp. xvii-xix.

Lancaster, J. B. 1967. "Primate Communication Systems and the Emergence of Human Language," Unpublished Doctoral Dissertation, University of California, Berkeley.

Lee, D. C. 1938. "Conceptual Implications of an Indian Language," Philosophy of Science 5:89-102.

_____. 1959. *Freedom and Culture.* Englewood Cliffs, N. J.: Prentice-Hall.

Lehman, W. P. 1962. *Historical Linguistics.* New York: Holt, Rinehart and Winston.

Lenneberg, E. 1953. "Cognition in Ethnolinguistics," Language 29:463-471.

_____. 1964. *New Directions in the Study of Language.* Cambridge, Mass.: M.I.T. Press.

_____. 1967. *Biological Foundations of Language.* New York: Wiley.

Leopold, W. F. 1939-49. *Speech Development in a Bilingual Child: A Linguist's Record.* Evanston, Ill.: Northwestern University Press, 4 volumes.

_____. 1948. "The Study of Child Language and Infant Bilingualism," Word 1:249-259.

_____. 1952. *Bibliography of Child Language.* Evanston, Ill.: Northwestern University Press.

_____. 1953. "Patterning in Children's Language Learning," Language Learning 5:1-14.

Lotz, J. 1950. "Speech and Language," The Journal of the Acoustical Society of America 22:712-717.

_____. 1955. "On Language and Culture," International Journal of American Linguistics 21:187-189.

Lounsbury, F. 1960. "Language." In B. J. Siegel (ed.), *Biennial Review of Anthropology, 1961.* Stanford: Stanford University Press, pp. 185-209.

_____. 1962. "Language." In B. J. Siegel (ed.), *Biennial Review of Anthropology. 1959.* Stanford: Stanford University Press, pp. 279-322.

Luria, A. R. 1961. *The Role of Speech in the Regulation of Normal and Abnormal Behavior.* London: Pergamon.

Luria, A. R., and F. I. Yudovich. 1959. *Speech and the Development of Mental Processes in the Child.* London: Staples.

Lyons, J., and R. J. Wales (eds.) 1966. *Psycholinguistic Papers.* Edinburgh: Edinburgh University Press.

Mandelbaum, D. G. (ed.) 1949. *Selected Writings of Edward Sapir in Language, Culture, and Personality.* Berkeley: University of California Press.

Mathiot, M. 1962. "Noun Classes and Folk Taxonomy in Papago," American Anthropologist 64:340-350.

_____. 1966. "An Approach to the Study of Language and Culture Relations," Unpublished Doctoral Dissertation, Catholic University, Washington, D. C.

McCarthy, D. 1930. "The Language Development of the Pre-School Child," *Institute of Child Welfare Monograph Series,* Number 4, Minneapolis: University of Minnesota Press.

_____. 1954. "Language Development in Children." In L. Carmichael (ed.), *Manual of Child Psychology,* ed. 2. New York: Wiley, pp. 492-630.

Menyuk, P. 1969. *Sentences Children Use.* Cambridge, Mass.: M.I.T. Press.

Miller, G. A. 1951. *Language and Communiation.* New York: McGraw-Hill.

_____. 1954. "Psycholinguistics." In G. Lindzey (ed.), *Handbook of Social Psychology.* Cambridge, Mass.: Addison-Wesley, pp. 693-708.

Miller, N. E., and J. Dollard. 1941. *Social Learning and Imitation.* New Haven: Yale University Press.

Mowrer, O. H. 1950. "On the Psychology of 'Talking Birds'—A Contribution to Language and Personality Theory." In O. H. Mowrer (ed.), *Learning Theory and Personality Dynamics.* New York: Ronald, pp. 689-707.

Piaget, J. 1929. *The Child's Conception of the World.* New York: Humanities.

_____. 1947. *Judgement and Reasoning in the Child.* New York: Humanities.

_____. 1954. *Construction of Reality in the Child.* New York: Basic Books.

_____. 1955. *The Language and Thought of the Child.* Cleveland: World.

Piaget, J., and B. Inhelder. 1948. *The Child's Conception of Space.* New York: Humanities.

Romney, A. K., and R. G. D'Andrade. (eds.) 1964. "Transcultural Studies in Cognition," Special Publication, American Anthropologist 66: June, 1964.

Ruesch, J., and G. Bateson. 1951. *Communication. The Social Matrix of Psychiatry.* New York: Norton.

Sampson, O. C. 1956. "A Study of Speech Development in Children 18-30 Months," British Journal of Educational Psychology 26:194-202.

Sanches, M. 1969. "Features in the Acquisition of Japanese Grammar," Unpublished Doctoral Dissertation, Stanford University.

Sapir, E. 1949. "Selected Writings of Edward Sapir." In D. G. Mandelbaum (ed.), *Language, Culture, and Personality.* Berkeley and Los Angeles: University of California Press.

Schachtel, E. G. 1947. "On Memory and Childhood Amnesia," Psychiatry 10:1-26.

Sebeok, T. A. (ed.) 1968. *Animal Communication: Techniques of Study and Results of Research.* Bloomington, Indiana: University of Indiana Press.

Sebeok, T. A., and A. Ramsay (eds.) 1969. *Approaches to Animal Communication.* New York: Humanities Press.

Smith, F., and G. A. Miller. 1966. *The Genesis of Language; A Psycholinguistic Approach.* Cambridge, Mass.: M.I.T. Press.

Smith, M. E. 1935. "A Study of Some Factors Influencing the Development of the Sentence in

Preschool Children," Journal of Genetic Psychology **46**:182-212.

Strehlow, T. G. H. 1947. "On Aranda Traditions." In D. Hymes (ed.) 1964. *Language in Culture and Society.* New York: Harper and Row. (Reprinted from Strehlow, T. G. H. 1947. *Aranda Traditions.* Melbourne: Melbourne University Press, pp. xiv-xxi.)

Stross, B. M. 1969. "Language Acquisition by Tenjapa Tzeltal Children," Unpublished Doctoral Dissertation, University of California, Berkeley.

Tyler, S. A. (ed.) 1969. *Cognitive Anthropology.* New York: Holt, Rinehart and Winston.

Vygotsky, L. S. 1939. "Thought and Speech," Psychiatry **2**:29-54.

_____. 1962. *Thought and Language.* New York: M.I.T. Press and John Wiley. (Originally published in Russian in 1934.)

von Humboldt, W. 1836. "Über die Kawisprache." Part I. *Über die Verschiedenheit des Menschlichen Sprachbaues und Ihren Einfluss auf die geistige Entwickelung des Menschengeschlechts.* Bonn: Dümmlers Verlag (reprinted 1960).

Wallace, A. F. C. 1961. "The Psychic Unity of Human Groups." In B. Kaplan (ed.), *Studying Personality Cross-Culturally.* New York: Harper and Row, pp. 129-163.

_____. 1962. "Culture and Cognition," Science **135**:351-357.

Watson, J. B. 1924. *Behaviorism.* New York: Norton.

Wellman, B. L., I. M. Case, I. C. Mengert, and D. E. Bradbury. 1931. "Speech Sounds of Young Children," University of Iowa Studies in Child Welfare 5, Number Two.

Whorf, B. L. 1956. *Language, Thought and Reality.* New York: Wiley.

Witherspoon, G. 1971. "Navaho Categories of Objects at Rest," American Anthropologist **73**:110-127.

Williams, H. M. 1937. "An Analytical Study of Language Achievement in Preschool Children," University of Iowa Studies in Child Welfare **13**:35-46.

Williams, T. R. 1958. "The Structure of the Socialization Process in Papago Indian Society," Social Forces **36**:251-256.

EPILOGUE

After use of the first atomic bombs, some American scientists formed an association to promote peaceful uses of the knowledge they had helped to produce. Through the decade following World War II, this small group of scientists worked for laws and treaties placing limits on the uses and control of atomic devices. They also contributed to placing nuclear weapons production in the hands of a civilian government agency. Later, their efforts helped in securing an international treaty banning nuclear weapons tests in the atmosphere. These scientists were also an integral part of the movement to create a United States governmental agency concerned with arms control and with disarmament.

Such efforts were not without personal costs to those who participated in these activities. Some were denied access to documents or to the funds necessary to continue their complex and costly scientific studies. A few were vilified for their actions.

However, the example of individual scientists trying to be socially responsible for the products of their research did not go unnoticed by other scientists and students. Today, students expect that scientists will think seriously about the uses of their research. And scientists try to lead the way in raising fundamental questions concerning the use and control of the products of their research. Much of the current widespread concern about the quality of life in a world environment increasingly polluted by products of technology is the direct result of public activities by scientists concerned about the ways their basic inventions and understandings are being used.

At first glance, a fundamental comprehension of the nature of the socialization process hardly seems to be comparable to an understanding of the nuclear processes which led to awesome weapons. Yet, as time passes and our scientific understanding of cultural transmission becomes more precise and accurate, we face questions for use of such knowledge as complex as those in other areas of science.

I believe the time is not far distant when a scientific understanding of the process of socialization will be sufficient to be used to the great benefit or harm of man. We already know from studies of isolated and autistic individuals and from research on prisoners that it is possible to significantly alter the consequences of the human socialization process. From our preliminary studies of the ways culture and biology become interrelated in the socialization process, we now can see that it will be possible to literally "program" people to specific behavior and beliefs. We can discern now, if only faintly, the outlines of a scientific knowledge that will give men an understanding of themselves that can be as formidable as nuclear weapons, that is, the power to precisely shape other men's wills, values, thoughts, loyalties, and views, without use of drugs, degradation of their bodies, or forced routines of life.

It is true that a power of deciding the content, operation, and consequences of the cultural transmission process cannot lay waste to all life as can thermonuclear weapons, or upset the world's ecological balance as can massive engineering projects to redirect climate, river flow, or sea water circulation. The power from understanding the socialization process cannot kill fish in streams, mire sea birds in oil wastes, or sear human lungs with petrochemical by-products. But this power could be used by unscrupulous individuals to their own political and personal ends. If research on the socialization process continues to grow and accelerate at the rate of the past five decades, we will be faced soon with trying to decide what to do with the power derived from our knowledge.

We already face these problems in their formative states, as we are asked to accept public policies said to be based upon research on cultural transmission. Within the period of the writing of this work there have been many evidences of this fact in the heated arguments over the validity and effects of "remedial" childhood education programs sponsored by the federal government, concerning special television programs for preschool children, about the definition of an "equal" education, and whether some classes of children really are unable, due to their supposedly deficient genetic heritages, to learn cultural forms apparently easily acquired by other classes of children. American parents are asked in advertisements to read the latest books to understand ways they can prevent their babies from becoming "bedwetters" or "homosexuals" and to help them to be "better adjusted," to read more rapidly, or to achieve higher marks in school or college examinations. Television shows feature "experts" giving child rearing advice which is implied or actually said to be based on research, and sometimes is, on topics ranging from handling infant aggression to social alienation from parents in adolescence. Questions regarding which experts to believe and whether to believe them, which public policies are scientifically sound, and which actions one should take personally to prevent some undesirable later behavior by infants and children are already pressing upon us all.

A decade or so hence, such questions will be even more vexing, for whether we choose it or not, the trend in American society is to the forming of public policy and to the giving of advice on the basis of research on cultural transmission. In a free society, there is only one way to be certain that decisions concerning the content and operation of the enculturation process do not become the sole property of unprincipled individuals—to educate citizens to understanding the origins, nature, and consequences of that human process. Those who know American history will recognize this idea as Thomas Jefferson's solution to the problems created by the few in his time and society who sought to control the lives, the thoughts, and the destinies of their fellows. Jefferson believed the only certain way to protect individual freedom was to ensure that all men had access to the things everyone else knew, so knowledge could not be misapplied for private or political reasons.

Life in a free society near the close of the twentieth century has become more complex than Jefferson could have foreseen. Specialized knowledge has grown so vast and so technically complex that few men can master large amounts of it; very few persons reading these words will have full comprehension of quantum mechanics, population genetics, the literary tradition of Europe since Chaucer, linear programing of computers, the theory of viscoelasticity, and so on.

Perhaps it is not necessary for us to become especially informed on all the subjects that affect our daily lives. It can be argued, after all, that we rarely give thought to electromagnetic theory when we turn on a light, or to advanced principles in mechanics when we drive our automobiles. However, we do think occasionally about the consequences of climbing a high-voltage transmission tower and of a head-on auto collision at 70 miles per hour. Our problem is to judge, each for ourselves, the kinds of knowledge affecting our personal and social destinies.

I believe it is my responsibility to point out that we now face a time when it will be well for all of us to see to it that public policies based on socialization research are kept firmly in the hands of those persons publicly accountable by law to being fully responsible to all those affected by policy decisions. We must be concerned now that when public advice is given concerning the socialization process that it is done responsibly, with human as well as individual well-being as an uppermost concern.

It may be that this epilogue will be made unnecessary by our inability to come to a final scientific understanding of the socialization process. However, I do not believe that we should wait to begin thinking about the subject until, as in the case of the physicists, chemists, engineers, and others working under the pressures of national survival in war time, we find ourselves having produced knowledge capable of forever changing human life. The terrible choices ahead are not only extinction of human life through nuclear war or devastation of the environment by misuse of technology. I think the future also includes the possibility of the ultimate horror of a human life bereft of individual freedom, personal dignity, spontaneity, and choice. My hope is that, as we seem slowly to have come to some recognition of the grim consequences of nuclear weapons, or of pollution of our environment, we can begin also to understand the great responsibility each one of us has for our rapidly growing scientific knowledge of the socialization process and that together we will make all of the public decisions about the use of such understandings.

APPENDIX SELECTED READINGS ON ENCULTURATION

SUMMARY OF NAMES*

Abipon	Dusun	Malaitans	Siriono
Ainu	English	Malekula	Slave
Alor	Eskimo	Manus	Swazi
American	Fijians	Maori	Tallensi
Andamanese	Flathead	Marquesans	Tanala
Apache	French	Masai	Taos
Arab	German	Mexican	Tenetehara
Arapaho	Gusii	Murngin	Teton Dakota
Arapesh	Hopi	Nauru	Thonga
Arunta	Hupa	Navaho	Tikopia
Ashanti	Ifaulk	Ngoni	Tiv
Azande	Ifugao	Nuer	Tonga
Baganda	Ilocos	Nyakyusa	Trobriands
Baiga	Israeli	Okinawans	Trukese
Balahi	Japanese	Omaha	Tswana
Bali	Javanese	Ona	Turkana
Bapedi	Jivaro	Ontong-Javanese	Ulithians
Basuto	Kaingang	Paiute	Venda
Bemba	Kaska	Palaung	Wapisiana
Bena	Kikuyu	Papago	Warrau
Bushmen	Kiwai	Pondo	Wichita
Camayura	Klamath	Puerto Ricans	Winnebago
Chagga	Kongo	Pukapukans	Witoto
Chamorro	Koryak	Pygmies	Wogeo
Chenchu	Kutenai	Rājpūts	Yagua
Chewa	Kwakiutl	Riffians	Yakut
Cheyenne	Kwoma	Russian	Yoruba
Chinese	Lakher	R'wala	Yukaghir
Comanche	Lamba	Samoans	Yungar
Dahomean	Lapp	San Pedro	Zadruga
Deoli	Lepcha	Sanpoil	Zulu
Dobuans	Lesu	Sherente	Zuni

*For alternative names of cultures, see Textor, R. 1967. *A Cross Cultural Summary.* New Haven: Human Relations Area Files, Appendix One; Murdock, G. P. 1958. *Outline of World Cultures.* New Haven: Human Relations Area Files. Spellings are the most commonly used.

CULTURE REGION DISTRIBUTION OF SELECTED READINGS ON ENCULTURATION

New World cultures		Pacific cultures	Old World cultures		
North America	Central and South America	Australia, Borneo, Indonesia, New Guinea, and Pacific Islands	Eurasia	Europe and Circum-Mediterranean	Africa (Sub-Saharan)
American	Abipon	Alor	Ainu	Arab	Ashanti
Apache	Camayura	Arapesh	Andamanese	English	Azande
Arapaho	Jivaro	Arunta	Baiga	French	Baganda
Cheyenne	Kaingang	Bali	Balahi	German	Bapedi
Comanche	Ona	Chamorro	Chenchu	Israeli	Basuto
Eskimo	San Pedro	Dobuans	Chinese	Lapp	Bemba
Flathead	(Guatemala)	Dusun	Deoli	Riffians	Bena
Hopi	Sherente	Fijians	Japanese	Russian	Bushmen
Hupa	Siriono	Ifaulk	Koryak	R'wala	Chagga
Kaska	Tenetehara	Ifugao	Lakher	Zadruga	Chewa
Klamath	Wapisiana	Ilocos	Lepcha		Dahomean
Kutenai	Warrau	Javanese	Okinawans		Gusii
Kwakiutl	Witoto	Kiwai	Palaung		Kikuyu
Mexican	Yagua	Kwoma	Rājpūts		Kongo
Navaho		Lesu	Yakut		Lamba
Omaha		Malaitans	Yukaghir		Masai
Paiute		Malekula			Ngoni
Papago		Manus			Nuer
Puerto Ricans		Maori			Nyakyusa
Sanpoil		Marquesans			Pondo
Slave		Murngin			Pygmies
Taos		Nauru			Swazi
Teton Dakota		Ontong-Javanese			Tallensi
Wichita		Pukapukans			Tanala
Winnebago		Samoans			Thonga
Zuni		Tikopia			Tiv
		Trobriands			Tonga
		Trukese			Tswana
		Ulithians			Turkana
		Wogeo			Venda
		Yungar			Yoruba
					Zulu
Total New World cultures—39		Total Pacific cultures—31	Total Old World cultures—58		

SELECTED READINGS ON ENCULTURATION[1]

Abipon*
 Dobrizhoffer, M. 1822. *An Account of the Abipones, An Equestrian People of Paraguay.* 3 vols. London: J. Murray.

Ainu*
 Batchelor, J. 1895. *The Ainu of Japan: The Religions, Superstitions, and General History of the Hairy Aborigines of Japan.* New York: Revell.
 —————. 1901. *The Ainu and Their Folk-lore.* London: The Religious Tract Society.
 —————. 1927. *Ainu Life and Lore.* Tokyo: Kyobunkwan.

[1]Groups noted with an asterisk comprise the study sample referred to in Chapter Seven of the text. The readings suggested here are not "complete," that is, inclusive of all the possible and latest references. The references listed for each society will provide students with some sources on enculturation that can be used for preliminary comparisons. This is not a research bibliography. Hence, comparative statements drawn from the readings will be limited.

Howard, B. D. 1893. *Life with Trans-Siberian Savages.* London: Longmans, Green.

Alor*
 DuBois, C. 1944. *The People of Alor: A Socio-Psychological Study of an East Indian Island.* Minneapolis: University of Minnesota Press.

American*
 Barker, R. G., and H. F. Wright. 1954. *The Midwest and Its Children.* Evanston, Ill.: Row, Peterson.
 Bronfenbrenner, U. 1970. *Two Worlds of Childhood: U.S. and U.S.S.R.* New York: Russell Sage Foundation.
 Fischer, J. L., and A. Fischer. 1966. *The New Englanders of Orchard Town, U.S.A.* New York: Wiley, Vol. 5, Six Cultures Series, B. Whiting, ed.
 Gorer, G. 1948. *The American People.* New York: Norton.
 Havighurst, R., J. P. Bowman, G. Liddle, C. Matthews, and G. Pierce. 1962. *Growing Up in River City.* New York: Wiley.

Kluckhohn, C., and F. Kluckhohn. 1947. "American Culture: Generalized Orientations and Class Patterns." In L. Bryson (ed.), *Conflicts of Power in Modern Culture.* New York: Seventh Symposium, Conference on Science, Philosophy and Religion, pp. 106-128.

Lantis, M. (special ed.) 1955. "The U.S.A. as Anthropologists See It," American Anthropologist **57**:1113-1295.

McClelland, D. C. 1961. *The Achieving Society.* Princeton, N. J.: Van Nostrand.

Mead, M. 1942. *And Keep Your Powder Dry: An Anthropologist Looks at America.* New York: Morrow.

_____. 1948. "The Contemporary American Family as an Anthropologist Sees It," American Journal of Sociology **53**:453-459.

Riesman, D. 1950. *The Lonely Crowd.* New Haven, Conn.: Yale University Press.

Sears, R. R., E. Maccoby, and H. Levin. 1957. *Patterns of Child Rearing.* Evanston, Ill.: Row, Peterson.

Warner, W. L., and P. S. Lunt. 1941. *The Social Life of a Modern Community.* New Haven, Conn.: Yale University Press.

West, J. 1945. *Plainville, U.S.A.* New York: Columbia University Press. (See also Gallaher, A. 1961. *Plainville Fifteen Years Later.* New York: Columbia University Press.)

Wolfenstein, M. 1957. *Disaster: A Psychological Essay.* New York: The Free Press.

Andamanese*

Man, E. H. 1883. "On the Aboriginal Inhabitants of the Andaman Islands," Journal of the Royal Anthropological Institute of Great Britain and Ireland **12**:69-175, 327-434.

Radcliffe-Brown, A. R. 1922. *The Andaman Islanders.* Cambridge: Cambridge University Press.

Apache*[2]

Goodwin, G. 1942. *The Social Organization of the Western Apache.* Chicago: University of Chicago Press.

Opler, M. E. 1937. "An Outline of Chiricahua Apache Social Organization." In F. Eggan (ed.), *Social Anthropology of North American Tribes.* Chicago: University of Chicago Press.

_____. 1941. *An Apache Life Way.* Chicago: University of Chicago Press.

_____. 1946. *Childhood and Youth in Jicarilla Apache Society.* Los Angeles: The Southwest Museum.

Arab*

Ammar, H. 1954. *Growing Up in an Egyptian Village.* London: Routledge and Paul.

Granqvist, H. 1931. *Marriage Conditions in a Palestinian Village.* 2 vols. Helsingfors: Akademische Buchhandlung.

_____. 1947. *Birth and Childhood among the Arabs: Studies in a Muhammadan Village in Palestine.* Helsingfors: Söderström.

_____. 1950. *Child Problems Among the Arabs.* Helsingfors: Söderström.

Arapaho*

Hilger, Sister M. I. 1952. *Arapaho Child Life and Its Cultural Background.* Bureau of American Ethnology, Smithsonian Institute, Bulletin 148, Washington, D. C.: U.S. Government Printing Office.

Arapesh*

Mead, M. 1935. "The Mountain Dwelling Arapesh." In *Sex and Temperament in Three Primitive Societies.* New York: Morrow.

_____. 1937. "The Arapesh of New Guinea." In *Cooperation and Competition among Primitive Peoples.* New York: McGraw-Hill.

_____. 1938-1949. *The Mountain Arapesh.* I-V Anthropological Papers of the American Museum of Natural History **36**:145-349; **37**:317-451; **40**:163-419; **41**:289-390.

_____. 1949. *Male and Female: A Study of the Sexes in a Changing World.* New York: Morrow.

Arunta*

Spencer, B., and F. J. Gillen. 1899. *Native Tribes of Central Australia.* London: Macmillan.

_____. 1927. *The Arunta.* 2 vols. London: Macmillan.

Ashanti*

Rattray, R. S. 1927. *Religion and Art in Ashanti.* London: Clarendon Press.

_____. 1929. *Ashanti Law and Constitution.* London: Clarendon Press.

Azande*

Evans-Pritchard, E. E., 1937. *Witchcraft, Oracles, and Magic among the Azande.* London: Clarendon Press.

Baganda*

Ainsworth, M. D. S. 1967. *Infancy in Uganda.* Baltimore: Johns Hopkins Press.

Felkin, R. W. 1886. "Notes on the Waganda Tribe of Central Africa," Proceedings of the Royal Society of Edinburgh **13**:699-770.

Hattersley, C. W. 1908. *The Baganda at Home.* London: The Religious Tract Society.

Roscoe, J. 1902. "Further Notes on the Manners and Customs of the Baganda," Journal of the Anthropological Institute (n.s.) **5**:25-80.

Sempebwa, E. K. K. 1948. "Baganda Folk Songs: A Rough Classification," The Uganda Journal **12**:16-24.

---

[2]The term *Apache* refers to different societies such as the Chiricahua Apache and the Jicarilla Apache. The Chiricahua aboriginal range was in southeastern Arizona and southwestern New Mexico. The Jicarilla aboriginal range was in northern and eastern New Mexico. Both are "Eastern" Apache. The San Carlos and White Mountain Apache are "Western" Apache.

Wilson, C. T., and R. W. Felkin. 1882. *Uganda and the Egyptian Soudan*. 2 vols. London: Low, Marsten, Searle and Rivington.

Biaga*

Elwin, V. 1939. *The Baiga*. London: J. Murray.

Balahi*

Fuchs, S. 1950. *The Children of Hari: A Study of the Nimar Balahis in the Central Provinces of India*. Vienna: Verlag Herold.

Bali*

Bateson, G. 1949. "Bali: The Value System of a Steady State." In M. Fortes (ed.), *Social Structure: Essays Presented to A. R. Radcliffe-Brown*. London: Clarendon Press.

Bateson, G., and M. Mead. 1942. *Balinese Character: A Photographic Analysis*. W. G. Valentine (ed.), Vol. 2. New York: Special Publication of the New York Academy of Sciences (reprinted in 1962).

Belo, J. 1935. "The Balinese Temper," *Character and Personality* 4:120-146.

_____. 1936. "A Study of a Balinese Family," *American Anthropologist* 38:12-31.

_____. 1960. *Trance in Bali*. New York: Columbia University Press.

_____. (ed.) 1970. *Traditional Balinese Culture*. New York: Columbia University Press.

Covarrubias, M. 1937. "Birth to Marriage in Bali," *Asia* 37:414-419.

McPhee, C. 1946. *A House in Bali*. New York: John Day.

Mead, M. 1940. "Character Formation in Two South Sea Societies," *Transaction, American Neurological Association* 1940:99-103.

_____. 1941. "Back of Adolescence Lies Early Childhood," *Childhood Education* 18:58-61.

_____. 1946. "Research on Primitive Children." In L. Carmichael (ed.), *Manual of Child Psychology*. New York: Wiley, pp. 735-780.

_____. 1947. "Age Patterning in Personality Development," *American Journal of Orthopsychiatry* 17:231-240.

_____. 1949. *Male and Female: A Study of the Sexes in a Changing World*. New York: Morrow.

_____, and F. C. MacGregor. 1951. *Growth and Culture: A Photographic Study of Balinese Childhood*. New York: Putnam.

Bapedi*

Duggan-Cronin, A. M. 1928. "The Bapedi (Transvaal Basotho)." In A. M. Duggan-Cronin (ed.), *The Bantu Tribes of South Africa*. 2 vols. Cambridge: Deighton, Bell (see Vol. 2, Section 2).

Franz, G. H. 1931. "Some Customs of the Transvaal Basotho," *Bantu Studies* 5:241-246.

Harries, C. L. 1929. *The Laws and Customs of the Bapedi*. Johannesburg: Hortors.

Pitje, G. M. 1950. "Traditional Systems of Male Education Among Pedi and Cognate Tribes," *African Studies* 9:53-76; 105-124; 194-201.

Winter, J. A. 1914. "The Mental and Moral Capabilities of the Natives, Especially of Sekukuniland, Eastern Transvaal," *South African Journal of Science* 12:371-383.

Basuto*

Ashton, H. 1952. *The Basuto*. London: Oxford University Press.

Casalis, E. 1861. *The Basutos*. London: J. Nisbet.

Dutton, E. A. 1923. *The Basuto of Basutoland*. London: Jonathan Cape.

Mabille, H. E. 1906. "The Basuto of Basutoland," *Journal of the African Society* 5:233-251, 351-376.

Martin, M. 1903. *Basutoland: Its Legends and Customs*. London: Nichols.

Sheddick, V. G. J. 1953. "The Southern Sotho." In C. D. Forde (ed.), *Ethnographic Survey of Africa*. Part II. London: International African Institute.

Bemba*

Richards, A. I. 1939. *Land, Labour and Diet in Northern Rhodesia*. London: Oxford University Press.

_____. 1956. *Chisungu*. New York: Grove.

Bena*

Culwick, A. T., and G. M. Culwick. 1935. *Ubena of the Rivers*. London: Allen, Unwin.

Bushmen*

Thomas, E. M. 1959. *The Harmless People*. New York: Knopf.

Van der Post, L. 1958. *The Lost World of the Kalahari*. New York: Morrow.

_____. 1961. *The Heart of the Hunter*. New York: Morrow.

Camayura*

Oberg, K. 1953. *Indian Tribes of Northern Mato Grosso, Brazil*. Smithsonian Institution, Institute of Social Anthropology Publication 15. Washington, D. C.: U. S. Government Printing Office.

Chagga*

Dundas, C. 1924. *Kilimanjaro and Its People*. London: Witherby.

Raum, O. F. 1940. *Chaga Childhood*. London: Oxford University Press.

Chamorro*

Joseph, A., and V. F. Murray. 1951. *Chamorros and Carolinians of Saipan: Personality Studies*. Cambridge: Harvard University Press.

Thompson, L. M. 1947. *Guam and Its People*. Princeton, N.J.: Princeton University Press.

Chenchu*

Fürer-Haimendorf, C. von. 1943. *The Chenchus: Jungle Folk of the Deccan*. London: Macmillan.

_____. 1943. *Aboriginal Tribes of Hyderabad*. London: Macmillan.

Chewa*

Bruwer, J. 1949. "The Composition of a Cewa Village (Mudzi)," *African Studies* 8:191-198.

Ntara, S. Y. 1934. *Man of Africa*. London: The Religious Tract Society.

Richards, A. I. 1950. "Some Types of Family Structure Among the Central Bantu." In A. R. Radcliffe-Brown and C. D. Forde (eds.), *African Systems of Kinship and Marriage*. London: International African Institute, pp. 207-251.

Cheyenne*

Eggan, F. R. 1937. "The Cheyenne and Arapaho Kinship System." In F. R. Eggan, (ed.), *Social Anthropology of North American Tribes*. Chicago: University of Chicago Press, pp. 35-95.

Grinnell, G. B. 1915. *The Fighting Cheyennes*. New York: Scribner.

_____. 1923. *The Cheyenne Indians: Their History and Ways of Life*. 2 vols. New Haven, Conn.: Yale University Press.

Hilger, Sister M. I. 1946. "Notes on Cheyenne Child Life," *American Anthropologist* **48**:60-69.

Hoebel, E. A. 1960. *The Cheyennes: Indians of the Great Plains*. New York: Holt, Rinehart and Winston.

Llewellyn, K. N., and E. A. Hoebel. 1941. *The Cheyenne Way: Conflict and Case Law in Primitive Jurisprudence*. Norman: University of Oklahoma Press.

Chinese*

Chiang, Y. 1946. *A Chinese Childhood*. London: Methuen.

Feng, H. 1948. *The Chinese Kinship System*. Cambridge, Mass.: Harvard University Press.

Fitzgerald, C. P. 1941. *Tower of Five Glories*. London: Cresset.

Fried, M. H. 1953. *The Fabric of Chinese Society*. New York: Praeger.

Hsu, F. L. K. 1953. *Americans and Chinese: Two Ways of Life*. New York: Schuman.

Hu, H. C. 1948. *The Common Descent Group in China and Its Functions*. Viking Fund Publications in Anthropology 10. New York: Viking Fund.

Yang, M. C. 1945. *A Chinese Village*. New York: Columbia University Press.

Comanche*

Kardiner, A. 1945. "Analysis of Comanche Culture." In A. Kardiner and others (eds.), *The Psychological Frontiers of Society*. New York: Columbia University Press, pp. 81-100.

Linton, R. 1945. "The Comanche." In A. Kardiner and others (eds.), *The Psychological Frontiers of Society*. New York: Columbia University Press, pp. 47-80.

Dahomean*

Herskovits, M. J. 1938. *Dahomey: An Ancient West African Kingdom*. New York: Augustin.

Deoli*[3]

Carstairs, G. M. 1958. *The Twice Born: A Study of a Community of High Caste Hindus*. Bloomington, Ind.: Indiana University Press.

Dobuans*

Fortune, R. F. 1932. *Sorcerers of Dobu*. New York: Dutton.

Dusun*

Rutter, O. 1929. *The Pagans of North Borneo*. London: Hutchinson.

Staal, J. 1923-25. "The Dusuns of North Borneo," *Anthropos* **18-19**:958-977; **20**:120-138, 929-951.

Williams, T. R. 1969. *A Borneo Childhood: Enculturation in Dusun Society*. New York: Holt, Rinehart and Winston.

English*

Gorer, G. 1955. *Exploring English Character*. New York: Criterion.

Soddy, K. (ed.) 1956. *Mental Health and Infant Development*. 2 vols. New York: Basic Books.

Young, M. D., and P. Willmott. 1957. *Family and Kinship in East London*. London: Routledge and Paul.

Eskimo*[4]

Briggs, J. L. 1970. *Never in Anger; Portrait of an Eskimo Family*. Cambridge, Mass.: Harvard University Press.

Bugge, A. 1952. "The Native Greenlander—A Blending of Old and New," *Arctic* **5**:45-53.

Crantz, D. 1767. *The History of Greenland*. Vol. 1. London: Brethren's Society.

Egede, H. 1745. *A Description of Greenland*. London: Hitch.

Honigmann, I., and J. Honigmann. 1953. "Child Rearing Patterns Among the Great Whale River Eskimo," *University of Alaska Anthropology Papers* **2**:31-50.

Jenness, D. 1922. *The Life of the Copper Eskimo*. Report of the Canadian Arctic Expedition, 1913-1918. Ottawa: Acland.

Lantis, M. 1960. *Eskimo Childhood and Interpersonal Relationships*. Seattle: University of Washington Press.

Mirsky, J. 1937. "The Eskimos of Greenland." In M. Mead (ed.), *Cooperation and Competition Among Primitive Peoples*. New York: McGraw-Hill, pp. 51-86.

Nansen, F. 1893. *Eskimo Life*. London: Longmans, Green.

Ostermann, H. 1938. "Knud Rasmussen's Posthumous Notes on the Life and Doings of the East Greenlanders in Olden Times," *Meddelelser om Grønland* **109**:1-215.

Thalbitzer, W. 1923a. "The Ammassalik Eskimo II:

---

[3]"Deoli" is a pseudonym for a community of high caste Hindus in the Indian state of Rajasthan.

[4]The term "Eskimo" refers to a number of societies scattered through the Polar Arctic from North Alaska through Northern Canada to Greenland. These groups include the "North Alaska," "West Alaska," "Polar," "Caribou," and "Copper" Eskimo.

Language and Folklore," Meddelelser om Grønland **40**:113-564.

—————. 1923b. "The Ammassalik Eskimo. II. Social Customs and Mutual Aid," Meddelelser om Grønland **40**:575-739.

Fijians*

Quain, B. H. 1948. *Fijian Village*. Chicago: University of Chicago Press.

Flathead*

Turney-High, H. H. 1937. *The Flathead Indians of Montana*. Memoirs of the American Anthropological Association No. 47, Menasha, Wisc.: American Anthropological Association.

French*

Metraux, R., and M. Mead. 1954. *Themes in French Culture: A Preface to a Study of a French Community*. Stanford: Stanford University Press.

Soddy, K. (ed.) 1956. *Mental Health and Infant Development*. 2 vols. New York: Basic Books.

Wylie, L. W. 1957. *Village in the Vancluse*. Cambridge, Mass.: Harvard University Press.

German*

Bateson, G. 1943. "Cultural and Thematic Analysis of Fictional Films," Transactions, New York Academy of Sciences, Series 2, **5**:72-78.

Dicks, H. V. 1950. "Personality Traits and National Socialist Ideology," Human Relations **3**:111-154.

Erickson, E. H. 1950. *Childhood and Society*. New York: Norton.

Fromm, E. 1941. *Escape from Freedom*. New York: Holt, Rinehart and Winston.

Lowie, R. 1945. *The German People: A Social Portrait to 1914*. New York: Holt, Rinehart and Winston.

Metraux, R. 1955. "A Portrait of the Family in German Juvenile Fiction." In M. Mead and M. Wolfenstein (eds.) *Childhood in Contemporary Cultures*. Chicago: University of Chicago Press, pp. 253-276.

Rodnick, D. 1948. *Postwar Germans: An Anthropologist's Account*. New Haven, Conn.: Yale University Press.

Warren, R. A. 1967. *Education in Rebhausen; A German Village*. New York: Holt, Rinehart and Winston.

Gusii*

LeVine, R. A., and B. B. LeVine. 1966. *Nyansongo: A Gusii Community in Kenya*. New York: Wiley, Vol. 2, Six Cultures Series. B. Whiting, ed.

Mayer, P. 1949. *The Lineage Principle in Gusii Society*. London: International African Institute, Memoir 24.

Hopi*

Dennis, W. 1940. *The Hopi Child*. New York: Appleton-Century-Crofts.

Simmons, L. W. 1942. *Sunchief: The Autobiography of a Hopi Indian*. New Haven, Conn.: Yale University Press.

Stephen, A. M. 1936. *Hopi Journal of Alexander M. Stephen*. New York: Columbia University Press.

Parsons, E. C. 1921. "Hopi Mothers and Children," Man **21**:98-104.

Titiev, M. 1944. *Old Oraibi*. Cambridge, Mass.: Papers of the Peabody Museum 22.

Hupa*

Goddard, P. E. 1903. "Life and Culture of the Hupa," University of California Publications in American Archaeology and Ethnology **1**:1-88.

Taylor, E. S. 1947. "Hupa Birth Rites," Proceedings, Indiana Academy of Science **57**:24-28.

Wallace, W. J. 1947. "Hupa Child Training—A Study in Primitive Education," Educational Administration and Supervision **33**:13-25.

Ifaulk*

Burrows, E. G., and M. E. Spiro. 1953. *An Atoll Culture: Ethnology of Ifaulk in the Central Carolines*. New Haven, Conn.: Human Relations Area Files.

Ifugao*

Barton, R. F. 1930. *The Half-Way Sun: Life Among the Head-Hunters of the Philippines*. New York: Brewer and Warren.

—————. 1938. *Philippine Pagans: The Autobiographies of Three Ifugaos*. London: Routledge and Paul.

Ilocos*

Nydegger, W. F., and C. Nydegger. 1963. *Tarong: An Ilocos Barrio in the Philippines*. New York: Wiley, Vol. 6, Six Culture Series. B. Whiting, ed.

Israeli*

Bettelheim, B. 1969. *The Children of the Dream*. New York: Macmillan.

Rabin, A. I. 1965. *Growing Up in the Kibbutz*. New York: Springer.

Spiro, M. E. 1956. *Kibbutz: Venture in Utopia*. Cambridge, Mass.: Harvard University Press.

—————. 1958. *Children of the Kibbutz*. Cambridge, Mass.: Harvard University Press.

Japanese*

Benedict, R. 1946. *The Chrysanthemum and the Sword*. Boston: Houghton-Mifflin.

Dore, R. P. 1958. *City Life in Japan: A Study of a Tokyo Ward*. Berkeley: University of California Press.

Silberman, B. S. 1962. *Japanese Character and Culture: A Book of Selected Readings*. Tucson: University of Arizona Press.

Singleton, J. 1967. *Nichū; A Japanese School*. New York: Holt, Rinehart and Winston.

Javanese*

Geertz, H. 1961. *The Javanese Family: A Study of Kinship and Socialization*. New York: The Free Press.

Jivaro*

Karsten, R. 1935. *The Head-Hunters of Western Amazonas*. Helsingfors: Commentationes Humanum Litterarum, Societas Scientiarum Fennica 7, Number 1.

Stirling, M. W. 1938. "Historical and Ethnographical Material on the Jivaro Indians." Bulletin, Bureau

American Ethnology 117, Washington, D. C.: U. S. Government Printing Office.

Kaingang*

Henry, J. 1936. "The Personality of the Kaingang Indians," *Character and Personality* **5:**113-123.

_____. 1941. *Jungle People: A Kaingang Tribe of the Highlands of Brazil.* New York: Augustin.

Kaska*

Underwood, F. W., and I. Honigmann. 1947. "A Comparison of Socialization and Personality in Two Simple Societies," *American Anthropologist* **49:**557-577.

Kikuyu

Boyes, J. 1912. *John Boyes, King of the Wa-Kikuyu.* London: Methuen.

Kenyatta, J. 1938. *Facing Mount Kenya.* London: Seeker and Warburg.

Leakey, L. S. B. 1937. *White African.* London: Hodder and Stoughton.

Orde-Browne, G. 1925. *The Vanishing Tribes of Kenya.* London: Seeley, Service.

Kiwai*

Landtman, G. 1927. *The Kiwai Papuans of British New Guinea.* London: Macmillan.

Klamath*

Pearsall, M. 1950. "Klamath Childhood and Education," *Anthropological Records* **9:**339-351.

Spier, L. 1930. *Klamath Ethnography.* University of California Publications in American Archaeology and Ethnology 30. Berkeley: University of California Press.

Kongo*

Weeks, J. H. 1914. *Among the Prmitive Bakongo.* London: Seeley, Service.

Koryak*

Bergman, S. 1927. *Through Kamchatka by Dog-sled and Skis.* London: Seeley, Service.

Czaplička, M. A. 1914. *Aboriginal Siberia.* Oxford: Clarendon Press.

Kutenai*

Turney-High, H. H. 1941. *Ethnography of the Kutenai.* Memoirs of the American Anthropological Association 36. Menasha, Wisc.: American Anthropological Association.

Kwakiutl*

Benedict, R. F. 1934. *Patterns of Culture.* Boston: Houghton-Mifflin.

Boas, F. 1909. "The Kwakiutl of Vancouver Island," Memoirs, American Museum of Natural History **8:**307-515.

_____. 1921. "Ethnology of the Kwakiutl," Publications, U. S. Bureau of American Ethnology **35:**43-1481. (See also Codere, H. (ed.) 1960. *Kwakiutl Ethnography.* Chicago: University of Chicago Press.

_____. 1932. "Current Beliefs of the Kwakiutl Indians," *Journal of American Folklore* **45:**177-260.

Ford, C. S. 1941. *Smoke from their Fires: The Life of a Kwakiutl Chief.* New Haven, Conn.: Yale University Press.

Goldman, I. 1937. "The Kwakiutl Indians of Vancouver Island." In M. Mead (ed.), *Cooperation and Competition among Primitive Peoples.* New York: McGraw-Hill, pp. 180-209.

Wolcott, H. F. 1967. *A Kwakiutl Village and School.* New York: Holt, Rinehart and Winston.

Kwoma*

Whiting, J. W. M. 1941. *Becoming a Kwoma.* New Haven, Conn.: Yale University Press.

Lakher*

Parry, N. E. 1932. *The Lakhers.* London: Macmillan.

Lamba*

Doke, C. M. 1931. *The Lambas of Northern Rhodesia.* London: Harrap.

Lapp*

Turi, J. 1931. *Turi's Book of Lappland.* London: Cape.

Whitaker, I. 1955. *Social Relations in a Nomadic Lappish Community.* Vol. 2. Oslo: Utgitt av Norsk Folkmuseum.

Lepcha*

Gorer, G. 1938. *Himalayan Village.* London: Michael Joseph.

Morris, J. 1938. *Living with Lepchas.* London: Heinemann.

Lesu*

Powdermaker, H. 1933. *Life in Lesu.* New York: Norton.

Malaitans

Hogbin, H. I. 1939. *Experiments in Civilization: The Effects of European Culture on a Native Community of the Solomon Islands.* London: Routledge and Paul.

Malekula*

Deacon, A. B. 1934. *Malekula: A Vanishing People in the New Herbrides.* London: Routledge and Paul.

Leggatt, T. W. 1893. "Malekula, New Herbrides," Reports of the Australian Association for the Advancement of Science **4:**697-708.

Manus*

Fortune, R. F. 1935. *Manus Religion.* Philadelphia: American Philosophical Society.

Mead, M. 1930. *Growing Up in New Guinea.* New York: Morrow.

_____. 1932. "An Investigation of the Thought of Primitive Children, with Special Reference to Animism," *Journal of the Royal Anthropological Institute* **62:**173-190.

_____. 1949. *Male and Female: A Study of the Sexes in a Changing World.* New York: Morrow.

_____. 1956. *New Lives for Old: Cultural Transformation—Manus, 1928-1953.* New York: Morrow.

Maori*

Ausubel, D. P. 1961. *Maori Youth.* New York: Holt, Rinehart and Winston.

Beaglehole, E., and P. Beaglehole. 1946. *Some Modern*

Maoris. Wellington, N. Z.: New Zealand Council for Educational Research.

Best, E. 1924a. *The Maori.* Polynesian Society Memoir 5, 2 vols. Wellington, N. Z.: Polynesian Society.

_____. 1924b. *The Maori as He Was: A Brief Account of Maori Life as It was in Pre-European Days.* Wellington, N. Z.: Dominion Museum.

Buck, P. H. 1949. *The Coming of the Maori.* Wellington, N. Z.: Whitcombe, Tombs.

Kessing, F. M. 1928. *The Changing Maori.* Maori Board of Ethnological Research Memoir 4, New Plymouth, N. Z.: Maori Board of Ethnological Research.

Ritchie, J. E. 1963. *The Making of a Maori.* Wellington, N. Z.: Reed and Reed.

Marquesans*

Handy, E. S. C. 1923. *The Native Culture in the Marquesas.* Bernice P. Bishop Museum Bulletin 9, Honolulu, Hawaii: Bernice P. Bishop Museum.

Linton, R. 1939. "Marquesan Culture." In A. Kardiner (ed.), *The Individual and His Society.* New York: Columbia University Press, pp. 137-196.

Masai*

Hollis, A. C. 1905. *The Masai: Their Language and Folklore.* Oxford: Clarendon Press.

MacQueen, P. 1909. *In Wildest Africa.* Boston: L. C. Page.

Mexican*

Lewis, O. 1951. *Life in a Mexican Village: Tepoztlan Restudied.* Urbana: University of Illinois Press.

_____. 1959. *Five Families: Mexican Case Studies in the Culture of Poverty.* New York: Basic Books.

_____. 1961. *The Children of Sanchez: Autobiography of a Mexican Family.* New York: Random House.

Redfield, R. 1930. *Tepoztlan: A Mexican Village.* Chicago: University of Chicago Press.

Romney, K., and R. Romney. 1966. *The Mixtecans of Juxtlahuca, Mexico.* New York: Wiley, Vol. 4, Six Cultures Series. B. Whiting, ed.

Murngin*

Warner, W. L. 1937. *A Black Civilization.* New York: Harper and Row.

Webb, T. T. 1933. "Aboriginal Medical Practice in East Arnhem Land," *Oceania* 4:91-98.

Nauru*

Stephen, E. 1936. "Notes on Nauru," *Oceania* 7:34-63.

Navaho*

Kluckhohn, C. 1944. *Navaho Witchcraft.* Papers of the Peabody Museum of American Archaeology and Ethnology, Vol. 22, No. 2, Cambridge, Mass.: The Peabody Museum.

_____. 1947. "Some Aspects of Navaho Infancy and Early Childhood." In G. Roheim (ed.), *Psychoanalysis and the Social Sciences.* Vol. 1. New York: International Universities Press, pp. 37-86.

_____. 1960. "A Navaho Politician," In J. B. Casagrande (ed.), *In the Company of Man.* New York: Harper and Row, pp. 439-465.

_____, and D. Leighton. 1946. *The Navaho.* Cambridge, Mass.: Harvard University Press.

Kluckhohn, F., and F. L. Strodtbeck. 1961. *Variations in Value Orientations.* Evanston, Ill.: Row, Peterson.

Leighton, D., and C. Kluckhohn. 1947. *Children of the People.* Cambridge, Mass.: Harvard University Press.

Reichard, G. A. 1928. *Social Life of the Navaho.* New York: Columbia University Contributions to Anthropology 7.

Ngoni*

Read, M. 1956. *The Ngoni of Nyasaland.* New York: Oxford University Press.

_____. 1960. *Children of Their Fathers: Growing Up Among the Ngoni of Nyasaland.* New Haven, Conn.: Yale University Press.

_____. 1968. *Children of Their Fathers: Growing Up Among the Ngoni of Malawi.* New York: Holt, Rinehart and Winston.

Nuer*

Evans-Pritchard, E. E. 1936. "Daily Life of the Nuer in Dry-Season Camps." In L. H. Dudley-Buxton (ed.), *Custom is King.* London: Hutchinson, pp. 289-299.

_____. 1940. *The Nuer: A Description of the Modes of Livelihood and Political Institutions of a Nilotic People.* Oxford: Clarendon Press.

_____. 1950. "The Nuer Family." *Sudan Notes and Records* 31:21-42.

Howell, P. P. 1954. *A Manual of Nuer Law.* London: Oxford University Press.

Jackson, H. C. 1923. "The Nuer of the Upper Nile Province," *Sudan Notes and Records* 6:59-107.

Seligman, C. G., and B. Z. Seligman. 1932. *Pagan Tribes of the Nilotic Sudan.* London: Routledge and Paul.

Tucker, A. N. 1933. "Children's Games and Songs in the Southern Sudan," *Journal of the Royal Anthropological Institute* 63:165-187.

Nyakyusa*

Wilson, M. H. 1950. "Nyakyusa Kinship," In A. R. Radcliffe-Brown, and C. D. Forde (eds.), *African Systems of Kinship and Marriage.* London: International African Institute, pp. 111-139.

_____. 1951. *Good Company: A Study of Nyakyusa Age-Villages.* London: Oxford University Press.

Okinawans*

Haring, D. G. 1969. *Okinawan Customs.* Rutland, Vermont: Tuttle.

Maretzki, T. W., and H. Maretzki. 1966. *Taira: An Okinawan Village.* New York: Wiley, Vol. 7, Six Culture Series. B. Whiting (ed.)

Omaha*

Fletcher, A. C., and F. LaFlesche. 1911. "The Omaha

Tribe," Annual Reports of the Bureau of American Ethnology **27**:17-654.

Fortune, R. F. 1932. *Omaha Secret Societies*. New York: Columbia University Press.

LaFlesche, F. 1963. *The Middle Five: Indian Schoolboys of the Omaha Tribe*. Madison, Wisc.: University of Wisconsin Press.

Ona*

Bridges, E. L. 1949. *Uttermost Part of the Earth*, New York: Dutton.

Lothrop, S. K. 1928. "The Indians of Tierra del Fuego," Contributions From the Museum of the American Indians **10**:48-105.

Ontong-Javanese*

Hogbin, H. I. 1930. "Spirits and the Healing of the Sick in Ontong Java," Oceania **1**:146-166.

————. 1931a. "Education at Ontong Java," American Anthropologist **33**:601-614.

————. 1931b. "The Social Organization of Ontong Java," Oceania **1**:399-425.

Paiute*

Whiting, B. B. 1950. *Paiute Sorcery*. Viking Fund Publications in Anthropology 15, New York: Viking Fund.

Palaung*

Milne, L. 1924. *The Home of an Eastern Clan*. Oxford: Clarendon Press.

Papago*

Densmore, F. 1929. *Papago Music*. Bulletin of the Bureau of American Ethnology 90. Washington, D. C.: U. S. Government Printing Office.

Joseph, A., R. B. Spicer, and J. Chesky. 1949. *The Desert People*. Chicago: University of Chicago Press.

Underhill, R. M. 1939. *Social Organization of the Papago Indians*. Columbia University Contributions to Anthropology 30, New York: Columbia University Press.

————. 1942. "Child Training in an Indian Tribe," Marriage and Family Living **4**:80-81.

Williams, T. R. 1958. "The Structure of the Socialization Process in Papago Indian Society," Social Forces **36**:251-256.

Pondo*

Hunter, M. 1936. *Reaction to Conquest*. London: International African Institute.

Puerto Ricans*

Landy, D. 1959. *Tropical Childhood: Cultural Transmission and Learning in a Rural Puerto Rican Village*. Chapel Hill, N. C.: University of North Carolina Press.

Pukapukans*

Beaglehole, E., and P. Beaglehole. 1938. *Ethnology of Pukapuka*. Bernice P. Bishop Museum Bulletin 150, Honolulu: The Museum.

————. 1941. "Personality Development in Pukapukan Children." In L. Spier, A. I. Hallowell, and S. S. Newman (eds.), *Language, Culture and Personality*. Menasha, Wisc.: Sapir Memorial Fund, pp. 282-298.

Pygmies*

Turnbull, C. 1962. *The Lonely African*. New York: Simon and Schuster.

Rājpūts*

Minturn, L., and J. T. Hitchcock. 1966. *The Rājpūts of Khalapur, India*. New York: Wiley, Vol. 3, Six Cultures Series. B. Whiting, ed.

Riffians*

Coon, C. S. 1931. *Tribes of the Rif*. Harvard African Studies, Vol. 9, Cambridge, Mass.: Peabody Museum of Harvard University.

Westermarck, E. A. 1926. *Ritual and Belief in Morocco*. London: Macmillan.

Russian*

Bauer, R., A. Inkeles, and C. Kluckhohn. 1956. *How the Soviet System Works: Cultural, Psychological and Social Themes*. Cambridge, Mass.: Harvard University Press.

Gorer, G., and J. Rickman. 1949. *The People of Great Russia*. London: Cresset.

Mead, M. 1951. *Soviet Attitudes Toward Authority*. New York: McGraw-Hill.

————. 1951. "What Makes the Soviet Character?" Natural History **60**:296-303, 336.

————. 1954. "The Swaddling Hypothesis: Its Reception," American Anthropologist **56**:395-409.

Miller, W. W. 1960. *The Russians as People*. New York: Dutton.

R'wala*

Musil, A. 1928. *The Manners and Customs of the R'wala Bedouins*. New York: Czech Academy of Sciences and Arts and Charles R. Crane.

Samoans*

Hiroa, Te Rangi (Peter H. Buck). 1930. *Samoan Material Culture*. Bernice P. Bishop Museum Bulletin 75, Honolulu: Bernice P. Bishop Museum.

Mead, M. 1928. *Coming of Age in Samoa*. New York: Morrow.

————. 1928. "A Lapse of Animism among a Primitive People," Psyche **9**:72-77.

————. 1928. "The Role of the Individual in Samoan Culture," Journal of the Royal Anthropological Institute **58**:481-495.

————. 1930. *Social Organization of Manua*. Bernice P. Bishop Museum Bulletin 76. Honolulu, Hawaii: Bernice P. Bishop Museum.

————. 1937. *Cooperation and Competition among Primitive Peoples*. New York: McGraw-Hill.

————. 1949. *Male and Female: A Study of the Sexes in a Changing World*. New York: Morrow.

Su'apa'ia, K. 1962. *Samoa: The Polynesian Paradise*. New York: Exposition Press.

San Pedro*

Paul, B. D. 1950. "Symbolic Sibling Rivalry in a Guatemalan Indian Village," American Anthropologist **52**:205-218.

_____. 1950. *Life in a Guatemalan Indian Village.* Chicago: Delphian Society.

_____, and L. Paul. 1952. "The Life Cycle." In S. Tax (ed.), *Heritage of Conquest.* Glencoe, Ill.: The Free Press, pp. 174-192.

Sanpoil*

Ray, V. F. 1933. *The Sanpoil and Nespelem.* Seattle: University of Washington Press.

Sherente*

Nimuendajú, C. 1942. *The Serente.* Publication of the Frederick Webb Hodge Anniversary Fund 4, Los Angeles: The Southwest Museum.

Siriono*

Holmberg, A. R. 1950. *Nomads of the Long Bow.* Institute of Social Anthropology, Smithsonian Institution Publication 10, Washington, D. C.: U. S. Government Printing Office.

Slave*

Honigmann, J. J. 1946. *Ethnography and Acculturation of the Fort Nelson Slave.* Yale University Publications in Anthropology 33, New Haven, Conn.: Yale University Press.

Swazi*

Kuper, H. 1947. *An African Aristocracy.* London: Oxford University Press.

_____. 1950. "Kinship among the Swazi." In A. R. Radcliffe-Brown and C. D. Forde (eds.), *African Systems of Kinship and Marriage.* London: International African Institute, pp. 86-110.

Marwick, B. A. 1940. *The Swazi.* Cambridge: Cambridge University Press.

Tallensi*

Fortes, M. 1938. *Social and Psychological Aspects of Education in Taleland.* London: Oxford University Press.

_____. 1949. *The Web of Kinship Among the Tallensi.* London: Oxford University Press.

Tanala*

Linton, R. 1933. *The Tanala.* Publication of the Field Museum of Natural History, Anthropological Series 22. Chicago: Field Museum of Natural History.

_____. 1939. "The Tanala of Madagascar." In A. Kardiner (ed.), *The Individual and His Society.* New York: Columbia University Press, pp. 251-290.

Taos*

Parsons, E. 1936. *Taos Pueblo.* General Series in Anthropology 2, Menasha, Wisc.: Banta.

Tenetehara*

Wagley, C., and E. Galvão. 1949. *The Tenetehara Indians of Brazil.* New York: Columbia University Press.

Teton Dakota*

Erikson, E. 1939. "Observations on Sioux Education," Journal of Psychology 7:101-156.

_____. 1950. *Childhood and Society.* New York: Norton.

MacGregor, G. 1946. *Warriors Without Weapons.* Chicago: University of Chicago Press.

Mekeel, H. S. 1936. "An Anthropologist's Observations on Indian Education," Progressive Education 13:151-159.

Mirsky, J. 1937. "The Dakota." In M. Mead (ed.), *Cooperation and Competition among Primitive Peoples.* New York: McGraw-Hill, pp. 382-427.

Thonga*

Junod, H. A. 1927. *The Life of a South African Tribe.* 2 vols. London: Macmillan.

Tikopia*

Firth, R. W. 1936. *We, the Tikopia.* New York: American Book.

Tiv*

Akiga (B. Akiga Sai). 1939. *Akiga's Story: The Tiv Tribe as Seen by One of Its Members.* London: Oxford University Press (trans. Rupert East).

Bohannan, P. 1954. *Tiv Farm and Settlement.* London: Her Majesty's Stationery Office.

_____. 1957. *Justice and Judgment among the Tiv.* London: Oxford University Press.

Bohannan, P., and L. Bohannan. 1953. *The Tiv of Central Nigeria.* London: International African Institute.

Tonga*

Colson, E. 1958. *Marriage and the Family Among the Plateau Tonga of Northern Rhodesia.* Manchester: Manchester University Press.

Trobriands*

Lee, D. 1940. "A Primitive System of Values," Philosophy of Science 7:355-378.

Malinowski, B. 1922. *Argonauts of the Western Pacific.* London: Routledge.

_____. 1926. *Crime and Custom in Savage Society.* New York: Harcourt.

_____. 1927. *Sex and Repression in Savage Society.* New York: Harcourt.

_____. 1929. *The Sexual Life of Savages in North-West Melanesia: An Ethnographic Account of Courtship, Marriage and Family Life Among the Natives of the Trobriand Islands, British New Guinea.* 2 vols. New York: Liveright.

_____. 1935. *Coral Gardens and Their Magic: A Study of the Method of Tilling of the Soil and Agricultural Rites in the Trobriand Islands.* 2 vols. London: Allen and Unwin.

Trukese*

Fischer, A. M. 1950. *The Role of the Trukese Mother and Its effect on Child Training.* Final S. I. M. Report, Pacific Science Board. Washington: National Research Council.

Goodenough, W. 1951. *Property, Kin and Community on Truk.* New Haven, Conn.: Yale University Publications in Anthropology, 46.

Tswana*

Brown, J. T. 1926. *Among the Bantu Nomads.* Philadelphia: Lippincott.

Dornan, S. S. 1925. *Pygmies and Bushmen of the Kalahari*. London: Seeley.

Duggan-Cronin, A. M. 1928. "The Bechuana." In A. M. Duggan-Cronin (ed.), *The Bantu Tribes of South Africa*. 2 vols. Cambridge: Deighton, Bell.

Livingstone, D. 1857. *Missionary Travels and Researches in South Africa*. New York: Murray.

Schapera, I. 1938. *A Handbook of Tswana Law and Custom*. London: Oxford University Press.

————. 1940. *Married Life in an African Tribe*. London: Faber and Faber.

Turkana*

Gulliver, P. H. 1951. *A Preliminary Survey of the Turkana*. Communications from the School of African Studies 26. Capetown: University of Capetown Press.

————. 1955. *The Family Herds*. London: Routledge.

Rayne, H. 1919. "Turkana," Journal of the African Society **18**:183-189, 254-265.

White, R. F. 1920. "Notes on the Turkana Tribe," Sudan Notes and Records **3**:217-222.

Ulithians*

Lessa, W. A. 1950. *The Ethnography of Ulithi Atoll*. C. I. M. A. Final Report 28, Los Angeles: University of California Press. (Mimeographed.)

————. 1966. *Ulithi; A Micronesian Design for Living*. New York: Holt, Rinehart and Winston.

Venda*

Gottschling, E. 1905. "The Bawenda: A Sketch of Their History and Customs," Journal of the Anthropological Institute **35**:365-386.

Stayt, H. A. 1931. *The BaVenda*. London: International Institute of African Languages and Cultures, Oxford University Press.

Wessmann, R. 1908. *The Bawenda of the Spelonken*. London: African World.

Wapisiana*

Farabee, W. C. 1918. *The Central Arawaks*. Anthropological Publication of the University of Pennsylvania Museum 9, Philadelphia: University of Pennsylvania Press.

Warrau*

Schomburgk, R. 1922. *Travels in British Guiana, 1840-44*. Vol. 1. Georgetown, British Guiana: Daily Chronicle Office.

Wichita*

Schmitt, K., and I. O. Schmitt. *Wichita Kinship, Past and Present*. Norman, Okla.: University Book Exchange.

Winnebago*

Ostreich, N. 1948. "Trends of Change in Patterns of Child Care and Training Among the Wisconsin Winnebago," Wisconsin Archaeologist **29**:39-140.

Radin, P. 1916. *The Winnebago Tribe*. Annual Reports, Bureau of American Ethnology, Smithsonian Institution **37**:33-550.

Witoto*

Whiffen, T. 1915. *The North-West Amazons*. New York: Duffield.

Wogeo*

Hogbin, H. I. 1943. "A New Guinea Infancy: From Conception to Weaning in Wogeo," Oceania **13**:285-309.

————. 1946. "A New Guinea Childhood: From Weaning Till the Eighth Year in Wogeo," Oceania **16**:275-296.

————. 1970. *The Island of Menstruating Men*. Scranton: Chandler.

Yagua*

Fejos, P. 1943. *Ethnography of the Yagua*. Viking Fund Publication in Anthropology 1, New York: The Wenner-Gren Foundation.

Yakut*

Iokhel'son, V. I. 1933. "The Yakut," Anthropological Papers of the American Museum of Natural History **33**:33-225.

Yoruba*

Bascom, W. 1969. *The Yoruba of Southwestern Nigeria*. New York: Holt, Rinehart and Winston.

Delano, I. U. 1937. *The Soul of Nigeria*. London: Werner Laurie.

Ward, E. 1936. "The Parent-Child Relationship Among the Yoruba," Primitive Man **9**:56-63.

————. 1937. *Marriage Among the Yoruba*. Catholic University of America Anthropological Series 4, Washington, D. C.: Catholic University of America.

————. 1938. *The Yoruba Husband-Wife Code*. Catholic University of America Anthropological Series 6, Washington, D. C.: Catholic University of America.

Yukaghir*

Iokel'son, V. I. 1926. *The Yukaghir and the Yukaghirized Tungus*. New York: Stechert.

Yungar*

Grey, G. 1841. *Journals of Two Expeditions of Discovery in Northwest and Western Australia*. London: Boone.

Nind, S. 1832. "Description of the Natives of King George's Sound (Swan River Colony) and Adjoining Country," Journal of the Royal Geographic Society **1**:21-57.

Zadruga*[5]

Tomašic, D. A. 1948. *Personality and Culture in Eastern European Politics*. New York: G. W. Stewart.

Zulu*

Bryant, A. T. 1949. *The Zulu People*. Pietermaritzburgh: Shuter and Shuter.

Krige, E. J. 1936. *The Social System of the Zulus*. London: Longmans, Green.

Mahlobo, G. W. K., and E. J. Krige. 1934. "Transi-

[5] The term *Zadruga* refers to a peasant cooperative association in South Slav culture and not to a specific society.

tion from Childhood to Adulthood amongst the Zulus," Bantu Studies 8:157-191.

Schapera, I. (ed.) 1937. *The Bantu-Speaking Tribes of South Africa: An Ethnographic Survey.* London: Routledge and Paul.

Zuni*

Benedict, R. F. 1934. "The Pueblos of New Mexico." In *Patterns of Culture.* Boston: Houghton-Mifflin, pp. 57-129.

————. 1935. *Zuni Mythology.* Columbia University Contributions to Anthropology 21, 2 vols., New York: Columbia University Press.

Bunzel, R. L. 1929. *The Pueblo Potter: A Study of the Creative Imagination in Primitive Art.* New York: Columbia University Press.

————. 1933. *Zuni Texts.* Publication of the American Ethnological Society 15, New York: G. E. Stechert.

Goldfrank, E. S. 1945. "Socialization, Personality, and the Structure of Pueblo Society (with particular reference to Hopi and Zuni)," American Anthropologist 47:516-539.

Parsons, E. 1917. "Notes on Zuni, Parts I and II," Memoirs of the American Anthropological Association 4:151-327.

Stevenson, M. C. 1901-1902. "The Zuni Indians: Their Mythology, Esoteric Fraternities, and Ceremonies," Annual Report, Bureau of American Ethnology 23:13-608.

GLOSSARY

ability the skilled performance of particular kinds of learned behavior, especially those involved in specific ways of shaping, altering, or directing events, both internal and external, which affect an organism (see **capacities** and **skill**)

Abosom a native language term used by the Ashanti to refer to the Gods protecting patrilineal kin groups, or *ntoro*

absolute nutritional dependence refers to the fact that the *Homo sapiens* infant is completely dependent upon others for its care and feeding

abusa a native term for the Ashanti matrilineal kin group

achieved status a status earned or learned through performance and demonstration

acquired drive instrumental behavior that develops from positive reinforcements of stimuli arising in the social and cultural environments of an organism (see **secondary drive**)

action language punishment use of culturally standardized body postures to indicate disapproval of behavior.

action language reward use of culturally standardized body postures to indicate approval of behavior

adapt to be possessed of a genetic heritage that allows survival in a given environment

adaptation a biological character or cluster of characters possessed by a population of animals, selected by the natural environment, that increases the chances of survival for a population

affinal refers to patterns of kinship behavior based on a social recognition of relationships established through marriage

age-grade categories of people recognized in a culture as being at the same point in the life cycle

age-set a social group based on the principle of recruitment of persons of the same age, without regard to their kinship relations

alchera a native language term used by the Arunta of Central Australia to designate the mythical past and its events

alimentary canal a tube or passage that functions in the digestion and the absorption of food and that begins in most animals at the mouth and ends at the anus.

anaclitic characterized by an extreme dependence, in which all psychological functions are suppressed or are secondary to drives

anal sphincters the circular band of muscles that encircle the opening at the lower end of the colon, through which wastes are excreted

anatomy the morphology or body structure of an organism

anthropology a science concerned with the comparative study and of human physical and cultural characteristics

antibody a specific substance produced by an organism in response to the introduction of a particular antigen and capable of uniting with that antigen

antigen any protein substance which, when introduced into the body, will stimulate the formation of specific antibodies

ape a common name for the members of the *Pongidae* family

apocryphal a false or spurious account

arboreal tree-living

archaeological refers to the remains, usually artifacts and often bones, left by humans at their living and working sites

Archeozoic a geologic era that began some 1,500,000,000 years ago and ended approximately 925,000,000 years before the present

artifact objects purposely shaped by animals, especially man, to alter or deal with a natural environment

Arunta a native society of Central Australia

ascribed status automatic assignment of a status in a society

Ashanti a native society of West Africa

Australopithecine a genus of fossil hominids containing two species, *A. africanus* and *A. robustus*, which existed from the middle Pliocene to the middle Pleistocene epoch

autism   a psychological state characterized by extreme emotional and social withdrawal and absorption in fantasies

avoidance conditioning   a form of operant conditioning in which introduction of a harmful stimulus is avoided by a correct response by the subject (see **escape conditioning**)

avunculocal family kin group   a type of extended family kin group in which unmarried males leave their households to reside with a mother's brother and then after marriage bring their wives to reside in their mother's brother's household

baboon   a common name for a large, ground dwelling monkey of the genus *Papio*

bayi   the native language term used by the Ashanti to denote a special form of witchcraft that a mother can use to discipline unruly children

behavior   the total movement activity of an animal

behavior kind   a concept that refers to ethnographic records of well-identified adults behaving repeatedly in ways that can be counted and classified

Bemba   a native society of East Africa

bilateral kin group   a type of consanguineal kin group in which children are said to be equally related to and descended from their father and mother and the ancestors of their father and mother

biology   the nature, that is, the structure and functioning, of living organisms

bipedalism   locomotion using two feet

Botocudo   a native society of the Amazon river basin

brachiation   locomotion using the arms

brainstem reticular system   a network of intercellular fibers forming the core of the brainstem which reach the brain cortex and which appear to be involved in the transmission of visceral, auditory, visual, and other nerve impulses

brono   a native language term used by the Ashanti to refer to a subdivision or "ward" of an established village, occupied by members of the same matrilineage

capacities   genetically based patterns of behavior brought into operation at particular stages of growth and development only when elicited through specific combinations of physical, cultural, and social circumstances

carnivores   and order of flesh eating animals that includes dogs and cats

caste   an endogamous social group linked to a specific occupation

catarrhini   the group of primates which includes men, apes, and Old World monkeys

Cheyenne   a native North American Indian society

chimpanzee   a common name for a member of the ape family which is smaller and more arboreal than the gorilla

chordata   the phylum of animals which at some time in their lives have a notochord, or rod-like cord of cells, that forms the chief supporting structure of the body; in man the notochord appears during embryonic development

churinga   a personal totem symbol used by the Arunta of Central Australia at the time of a boy's initation into his father's patrilineal descent group

ciliary muscles   the muscle in a portion of the eyeball which affects adjustment of the thickness of the lens

clan   a type of unilineal kinship group which is based on a working compromise that some affines, or relatives by marriage, are to be included, while some consanguineal relatives are to be excluded; a clan may be a greatly enlarged lineage or a grouping of a number of lineages which trace their descent from the same known or often mythical ancestor

class   a group of persons acting on the basis of their awareness of common or shared status-roles

classic conditioning   the type of conditioning in which a conditioned stimulus and an unconditioned stimulus are used, or paired, together (see **respondent conditioning** and **operant conditioning**)

cognition   an idea or a thought

cognitive   refers to the process of thinking

colon   the part of the large intestine extending from its beginning at the cecum to the rectum

concept   an idea of something, formed by mentally combining all of its features

configuration of culture   a concept used in cultural anthropology studies to denote a grouping of patterns of culture with similar forms, functions, or meanings; a whole category of culture

consanguineal   refers to patterns of kinship behavior based on social recognition of common biological descent; all those relatives whose connecting links are one of common ancestry

contagion   the spread of disease by direct or indirect contact

contextual analysis   a methodological procedure and a theoretical assumption used in anthropology which notes that each aspect of culture must be viewed and studied in terms of its interdependence with other aspects of culture

cranial capacity   a measurement of the volume or space filled by the contents of the skull

Cretaceous   a geologic epoch that began approximately 120,000,000 years before the present and lasted until some 60,000,000 years ago

critical events   a hypothesis that there are specific events which occur during the development of human infants and children which influence similar events during adult life

critical periods   a hypothesis that there are times in the development of animals during which the individual is most receptive to learning from particular kinds of experience

cross-cousin   a cousin whose related parents are siblings of different sex, that is, the children of *Ego's* mother's brother or father's sister (see **parallel cousin**)

cultural charter patterns of culture which detail the work to be undertaken in a society, the ways tasks are to be performed, and the recruitment of persons to such tasks

cultural ecology the mutual relationships between man and his surrounding environments which are shaped and directed by the products of learned, shared, patterned, and transmitted behavior (see **ecology**)

cultural environment the surroundings of man, including the products of learned, shared, patterned and transmitted behavior (see **natural environment**)

cultural transmission the process of socialization

culture explicit and implicit patterns of learned behavior which make up the distinctive achievements of human groups; culture consists of traditional ideas and their related values, which are the products of action and also are conditioning elements for further action; culture is seen in both artifacts and patterned behavior which is widely shared in a society and is transmitted from one generation to the next

culture-bound studies and conclusions limited because research has been conducted within only one culture, or a few closely related cultures (see **transcultural**)

culture-fair a term used to refer to a psychological test that is free of culturally specific or limiting items

cumulative evolutionary adaptations the biological inheritance of genetic modifications which have occurred in a population through long periods of time

curare a substance derived from tropical plants of the genus *Strychnos*, used in medicine and research for arresting the action of motor nerves; also used by some South American Indians as a hunting poison

Dahomean a native society of West Africa

deoxyribonucleic acid (DNA) any of the class of nucleic acids that contains deoxyribose, found mainly in the nuclei of cells; with ribonucleic acid (RNA), a vehicle for the transmission of genetic information

diachronic having reference to changes in the facts of a system through time (see **synchronic**)

Dobu a native society of Melanesia

drive an aroused state in an organism in which behavior tends to be oriented toward reducing stimuli that are noxious or to remove a condition of deprivation

duolocal family kin group a type of extended family kin group in which the husband and father and wife and mother do not regularly reside with one another, but remain as members of their own nuclear families, with children usually residing with their mother

Dusun a native society of northern Borneo

ecology the mutual relationships of different organisms and the environments in which they live

eight class system among the Arunta of the northern part of the Central Australian desert an individual must learn that there are eight groups of important persons, consisting of all the members of the two Arunta moieties, two generational groups and all first and all second cross cousins in each of the two moieties, which define the locations of possible marriage partners and set rules for proper social behavior outside of the nuclear family, local group, patrilineal descent.group, and clan (see **four class system**)

electroencephalogram a graphic record made by a special machine that shows the electrical activity of the brain

emotion visceral changes that result from an animal's response to an experience; emotion is the physiological form in which an animal experiences the consequences of reflection

enculturation the process of transmitting a particular culture (see **socialization**)

endogamy a rule of marriage that requires an individual to take a husband or wife from inside of the local or kin groups to which they belong (see **exogamy**)

environment the total surroundings of an organism (see **natural environment** and **cultural environment**)

Eocene a geologic epoch that began about 55,000,000 years before the present and ended approximately 35,000,000 years ago

escape conditioning a form of operant conditioning in which a harmful stimulus is removed after a "correct" response by the subject (see **avoidance conditioning**)

ethnocentrism a tendency to regard the ways of one's own culture and society as inherently superior and to judge all of the ways of other cultures in terms of a local culture

ethnographic a written record setting forth the details and interrelations of the parts of a culture

ethnographic present a descriptive account of a culture written as though the people being described all live today as they once did in the past; a literary device

ethology the scientific study of animal learning and behavior

evolution biological descent with cumulative adaptive changes in the genetic and behavioral features of whole populations of animals

exogamy a rule of marriage that requires an individual to take a wife or husband from outside of the local or kin groups to which they belong (see **endogamy**)

extended family kin group a type of kin group created when two or more nuclear family kin groups are linked together through either a special form of parent-child or brother-sister kin relationship

extrapolate   to infer an unknown entity or quantity from something already known

feral   existing in a natural state; having reverted to a natural condition

fie   the native language term for the Ashanti dwelling group

focal value   a concept abstracted through relating statements made by persons in a culture concerning the worthwhileness of conduct and cultural goals and the kinds of behavior such persons regularly use

four class system   among the Arunta of the southern part of the Central Australian desert an individual must learn that there are four groups of important persons, consisting of all the members of the two Arunta moieties and two generational groups, which define the locations of possible marriage partners and set rules for proper social behavior outside of the nuclear family, local group, patrilineal descent group, and clan (see **eight class system**)

fraternal polyandry   the marriage of two or more brothers to one woman at the same time

free soiling   a *Homo sapiens* species-characteristic behavior form in which the infant freely releases accumulated bowel and bladder wastes

Galton's question   a methodological caution to ensure that in making transcultural comparisons the cultures chosen for study have no known history of cultural contact, borrowing, or common language and physical origins.

glycogen   a polysaccharide ($C_6H_{10}O_5$) that makes up the principal carbohydrate storage material in animals

gorilla   a common name for the largest member of the ape family

gracile   light, slender, or thin in appearance

grammatical system of language   a stock of morphemes and the arrangements in which they occur

holistic   an approach to the study of culture based on the assumption that every part of culture is interrelated with every other part

hominid   the family which includes all species of *Homo* as well as all of the Australopithecines

hominoid   the superfamily which includes men and apes

Homo   the genus to which modern man, *Homo sapiens*, belongs

Homo sapiens   the only living species of the genus *Homo*

hormone   any one of a number of internally secreted compounds, such as insulin or thyroxine, formed in the endocrine glands, that affect the functions of specific organs or tissues

hyperkeratosis   a thickening of the horny layer of the skin

ideology   all of the cultural beliefs or values which have been developed and used in a society

imprinting   a process of strong, often irreversible, social attachment to stimuli learned early in life in a specified period of limited duration

inarticulate experience   experience involving the generational transmission of learned behavior without the use of sounds, particularly sounds formed into language

incest tabu   a social rule prohibiting close relatives from having sexual intercourse; the kinds of relatives included or excluded as sexual partners vary from culture to culture

infantilization   the biological process through which adult *Homo sapiens* exhibit specific body characteristics typical of the infant ape (see **neoteny**)

inkata   a native language term used by the Arunta of Central Australia to designate the senior male in a patrilineal descent group

innervate   to communicate or transport nervous energy or impulses

instinct   a term and concept used in the social sciences until the 1940's; the concept of *species-characteristic behavior* now has largely replaced *instinct* in studies of human behavior

instrumental   movements by an organism directed at attaining a specific goal, or reinforcement

intrauterine   within the uterus

intrinsic reward   approval for behavior arising in the context of specific situations

intrinsic situational punishment   social situations which confront an individual with implied disapproval of behavior

iris   a part of the anatomy of the eye which is the contracting, circular diaphragm forming the colored part of the eye and with a circular opening, or pupil, at its center.

Jurassic   a geologic epoch that began about 180,000,000 years before the present and ended approximately 120,000,000 years ago

kinaesthesia   the style of movement imparted through the stresses in muscles, tendons and joints of the body

kindred   a local group that is comprised of bilateral relatives, that is, all persons related to a specific individual

kin group   any social grouping based on recognition of kinship ties and regular use of kinship terms

kinship   ways of defining the social, rather than biological, relationships which lead to a continuity between generations and maintenance of particular features of social living

kra   a native language term used by the Ashanti to refer to an aspect of the self inherited directly from the father

language   a complex set of verbal habits that is organized into three central subsystems (grammatical, phonological, morphophonemic) and two peripheral subsystems (semantic, phonetic); all human languages possess all five subsystems

larynx   the air passage and vocal organ between the tongue and trachea

law of effect   the principle that asserts that the response of an organism to a stimulus is automatically strengthened if it is followed by a reward or automatically extinguished if followed by a punishment (also termed the "principle of reinforcement")

learning any permanent modification of behavior by an animal based on reinforced or rewarded experience

lexical refers to the words or vocabulary used in a language

local group a collection of nuclear families

lineage a type of unilineal, consanguineal kin group that traces descent from a known, common ancestor, who lived about five or six generations before *Ego's* generation

locomotion the power to move from place to place

locus a place or locality

mammal a class of vertebrates

material reward a tangible remuneration as an incentive for repetition of approved forms of behavior

matrilateral family kin group a type of extended family kin group based on close, nonsexual relationships between a brother and sister, in which the wife, her husband, and their children reside together but do not interact socially as a nuclear family

matrilineage a type of unilineal, consanguineal kin group that traces its descent from a known, common female ancestor who lived about five or six generations before *Ego's* generation

matrilineal kin group a type of unilineal, consanguineal kin group in which *Ego's* descent is traced exclusively through the mother and mother's female ancestors

mbanbiuma a native language term used by the Arunta of Central Australia to designate a special ritual concerned with increases in the numbers of totem animals and plants

Mesozoic a geologic era that began approximately 220,000,000 years ago and ended about 60,000,000 years before the present

metabolic the sum of the physical and chemical processes in an organism by which protoplasm is produced and maintained and by means of which energy is made available for behavior

Miocene a geologic epoch that began some 25,000,000 years before the present and ended approximately 12,000,000 years ago.

mmusuaban a native language term used by the Ashanti to refer to a matrilineal clan

mogya a native language term used by the Ashanti to denote the essence of their biological heritage from their mother and their mother's female ancestors

moiety when a society is divided into two unilineal kin groups, so that each individual is a member of one or the other of the groups, it possesses moieties; moieties also are based on residence and choice

monkey a common name for a grade of *Anthropoidea* whose members all possess tails

morpheme a minimal unit of language, comprised of one or more phonemes, that carries a unitary cultural and social meaning for both speakers and hearers (see **phoneme**)

morphophonemic system of language a code which ties together the grammatical and phonological subsystems of language

motor pattern an activity skill, such as walking, that requires fine coordination of body parts

Nana a native language term used by the Asanti as a designation for "grandparent" and as well for senior political and religious leaders

natural environment the surroundings of an organism which are unshaped or altered by forms of cultural behavior

natural selection genetic selection which occurs without direction or plan by anyone

Neanderthals a generic name used for a group, or taxon, of fossil men; the earliest forms of the species *Homo sapiens*

neoteny in *Homo sapiens,* the phenomenon of being a fully mature animal while exhibiting many of the body characteristics of the infant ape (see **infantilization**)

neurophysiological the normal functioning of the nervous system

non-seasonal sexuality the regular and continuous sexual interest of the *Homo sapiens* male in the *Homo sapiens* female

ntoro a native language term used by the Ashanti to denote the essence of spirituality believed inherited from the father and father's male ancestors

nuclear family a family kin grouping comprised of a married man and woman and their children and characterized by eight special social relationships based on sex and descent

nucleic acid a chemical compound vital for all life, comprised of oxygen, hydrogen, nitrogen, carbon, and phosphorus

Nuer a native society of the Nilotic Sudan

Numbakulla a native language term used by the Arunta of Central Australia to refer to a founding hero ancestor of Arunta society

Oligocene a geologic epoch that began approximately 35,000,000 years ago and ended about 25,000,000 years before the present

Onyankopon a native language term used by the Ashanti to refer to the creator God

operant conditioning the type of conditioning in which the subject's responses are instrumental in obtaining reinforcements

optic nerve either one of the second pair of cranial nerves that consist of sensory tracts that conduct impulses from the retina to the brain

Ordovician a geologic epoch that began approximately 500,000,000 years before the present and lasted until approximately 450,000,000 years ago

organic bridgeheads a term used in this text to refer to specific links between human biology and culture in the process of socialization

organic emphasis of hearing an accentuation of the

sense of hearing in *Homo sapiens* as the consequence of primate evolutionary adaptations

organic emphasis of sight   an accentuation of the sense of sight in *Homo sapiens* as the consequence of primate evolutionary adaptations

organic repression of smell   a limitation of the sense of smell in *Homo sapiens* as the consequence of primate evolutionary adaptations

organism   a form of life made up of interdependent parts that together maintain life processes

ostracoderm   any one of numerous living and fossil, small salt and fresh water crustaceans having bodies covered by a hinged bivalve shell

palate   the roof of the mouth; often termed as either the *hard* (the forward portion) or the *soft* (the back portion) palate

Paleocene   a geologic epoch that began some 60,000,000 years ago and ended approximately 55,000,000 years before the present

Papago   a native North American Indian society

parallel cousin   a cousin whose related parents are siblings of the same sex, that is, the children of *Ego's* mother's sister or father's brother (see **cross-cousin**)

patrilineage   a type of unilineal, consanguineal kin group that traces its descent from a known, common male ancestor who lived about five or six generations before *Ego's* generation

patrilineal kin group   a type of unilineal, consanguinal kin group in which *Ego's* descent is traced exclusively through the father and father's male ancestors

pellagra   a disease caused by a deficiency of niacin in the diet

pepsinogen   a *zymogen* from gastric cells that changes into an enzyme because of some internal change in an organism

pharynx   the tube or cavity that connects the mouth and nasal passages with the esophagus

phone   a speech sound

phoneme   the smallest unit of sound recognized and used by speakers of a language (see **morpheme**)

phonetic system of language   the ways in which sequences of phonemes are converted into sound waves by the articulation of a speaker and are decoded from speech by a hearer

phonological system of language   a stock of phonemes and the arrangements in which they occur

phratries   unilineal kin groups consisting of two or more clans which recognize a special bond of concern as clans, particularly with reference to other phratries in a society

phylogenetic reductionism   the assumption that the behavior of all individuals in a species and that of all species occurs according to the same set of biological laws

physical punishment   the use of blows and social isolation to elicit desired forms of behavior

physiology   the normal organic functioning of an animal

Pithecanthropian   a term used for a group of hominids, now usually considered to be a single species termed *Homo erectus,* that was directly ancestral to *Homo sapiens*

placoid   plate-like scales or skin surface

platyrrhine   broad-nosed; a term used to describe all of the New World monkeys

pleasure principle   the tendency to satisfy basic id impulses

Pleistocene   a geologic epoch that began approximately 2,000,000 years before the present and ended approximately 15,000 years ago

Pliocene   a geologic epoch that began approximately 12,000,000 years ago and ended about 2,000,000 years before the present

polyandrous family kin group   a type of extension of the nuclear family kin group in which a woman is wife and mother in two or more nuclear families, that is, a woman is married to two or more men at the same time

polygamous family kin group   a type of extension of the nuclear family kin group in which two or more nuclear families are joined through sharing one husband and father or one wife and mother

polygynous family kin group   a type of extension of the nuclear family kin group in which a man is husband and father in two or more nuclear families, that is, a man is married to two or more women at the same time

pongidae   the family of primates that includes the gibbon, gorilla, orang-utan, and chimpanzee and many fossil forms

postulate   a proposition assumed to be true and used in the proof of other propositions

primate   the order of mammals to which *Homo sapiens* belongs

process of socialization   abstract statements of empirical reference concerning the transmission of human culture (see **socialization** and **socialization process**)

propensity   a natural inclination or tendency

psychoanalysis   a method of treating illness, developed by Sigmund Freud, which stresses insight on the part of the patients into their unconscious conflicts

psychology   a science concerned with study of human behavior and mental phenomena

puberty   a series of gradual biological changes involving sexual maturation

pyloric valve   the valve between the opening from the stomach to the duodenum

ramage   a bilaterally extended kinship group which centers upon a particular *Ego*

reality principle   the action of the ego in attempts to identify and to eliminate potentially painful stimuli

reason   the capacity to form conclusions, make judgements, or draw inferences

reflection   the capacity to go beyond observed properties of particular objects or events, to draw on the basis of past or present experiences inferences about unobserved properties of such objects or events

reflexes relatively fixed or sterotyped responses to stimuli, usually involving only a specific body part, that can be modified through experiences (see **taxes**)

remuneration to give, bestow, or compensate

repetition-compulsion behavior forms that are unusually resistant to elimination by adverse stimuli

respondent conditioning an unlearned response to a specific stimulus; the conceptual opposite of operant conditioning (see **classic conditioning**)

retina the innermost coat of cells on the back part of the eyeball that receives visual images

reward and punishment elements such as food, water, or electrical shock experienced by an organism which affects its behavior

ribonucleic acid (RNA) any of the class of nucleic acids that contain ribose, found mainly in the cytoplasm of cells; with deoxyribonucleic acid (DNA) a vehicle for transmission of genetic information

rickets a childhood disease characterized by softening and deformities of the bones as the consequence of malnutrition

role the precise ways rights and duties associated with a polar social position, or status, are put into operation (see **status**)

secondary drive a drive which develops as a consequence of positive reinforcement of stimuli arising from an organism's environments (see **acquired drive**)

semantic system of language the association of various morphemes, combinations of morphemes, and the arrangements in which morphemes can be put, with things and situations, or kinds of things and situations

shaman an individual who specializes in dealing with the supernatural as a healer and an intermediary

shaping modification of behavior through reinforcement of successive and larger steps that lead to the behavior desired by the experimenter

skill competent performance of a task (see **ability** and **capacities**)

social identity social categories or kinds of persons recognized in a society

socialization the process of transmission of human culture

socialization process abstract statements of empirical reference concerning the transmission of human culture (see **socialization** and **process of socialization**)

sociology a science concerned with study of the structure and functioning of human social groups

soft palate the part of the palate near the uvula (see **palate**)

somatic pertaining to body cells

sororal polygyny the marriage of two or more sisters to one man at the same time

space of recognition an awareness by an animal of its environment which is limited, or extended, by its sensory and brain structures and their capacities

spear thrower a device used to propel or add extra thrust to a spear

species-characteristic behavior all the forms of behavior by an animal having a physical-chemical basis, that are exhibited widely in a species and generally subject to a minimum of modification through experience

sphincter a circular band of "voluntary" or "involuntary" muscle that encircles a body opening or one of the body's hollow organs

status a polar position in a pattern of reciprocal social behavior (see **role**)

status relationship a reciprocal and doubly contingent right-duty pair or set widely known and used in a society

stereoscopic vision sight in which each eye sees an object from slightly different points of view, to produce a single image of the object with the appearance of depth or relief

stimulus any form of environmental energy capable of affecting an organism

stimulus-response reinforcement learning the association and reinforcement of any number of stimulus-response connections stemming from reduction of body needs

sunsum a native language term used by the Ashanti to refer to an aspect of the self inherited directly from the father

susu a native language term used to refer to the matrilateral family kin group among the Dobu of Melanesia

symbolic something which is used for or regarded as representing something else, such as an object representing an idea

symbolic interaction a mutual exchange of information between animals through the use of signs which stand for or represent experience

synchronic having reference to the facts of a system at one point in time and without regard to the history of such facts (see **diachronic**)

tactile pad a fleshy portion of the anatomy very sensitive to touch; in *Homo sapiens* each fingertip has a tactile pad

taro either one of two varieties of stemless plants cultivated in tropic regions of the world

taxes continuous sterotyped movements of an organism, usually involving the whole body toward a particular direction, as a response to an external stimulus; taxes generally are not modifiable through experience

taxis the singular form of **taxes**

taxon (plural, **taxa**) a group of animals related by descent from a common ancestor

taxonomy the classification of plants or animals in a way that places them in groups according to their structural relationships and the ordering of such groups into a ranked set; the ranked set used in this text, which is a conventional one in evolutionary studies, is:

kingdom
  subphylum
    phylum
      class
        subclass
          order
            suborder
              superfamily
                family
                  subfamily
                    genus
                      species

technology   the subsystem of culture that enables man to produce from the natural environment the artifacts that make it possible to survive through culturally adapting to a local setting

teleological   a kind of reasoning that explains events in terms of their contributions to the achievement of the goals of a larger plan or design

theme   a postulate or position, declared or implied, and usually controlling behavior or stimulating activity, which is tacitly approved or openly promoted in a society

tool   an object used to perform or to make easy a mechanical operation, which is directed toward changing the natural environment to facilitate survival

transcultural   statements derived from research concerned with the universally human, or general statements true of all human cultures, rather than one or a few cultures (see **culture-bound**)

transtemporal   a concern in research with the nature of events or processes as they have existed through the long span of historic and prehistoric time

tree shrew   an order of squirrel-like, generally arboreal animals, classified either as a separate primate suborder *(Tupaiodea)* or as members of the lemur suborder of the primates

trial and error   the elimination of "wrong moves" and the consolidation of "right moves" as an organism modifies its behavior through experience

Triassic   a geologic epoch that began approximately 220,000,000 years before the present and ended approximately 180,000,000 years ago

urethral sphincters   the circular band of muscles that encircle the membranous tube that extends from the urinary bladder to the outside of the body

uxorilocal family kin group   a type of extended family kin group in which the groom is required to leave his paternal household and reside with his bride, either in or close by the household of the bride's parents (also may be termed a *matrilocal family kin group*)

verbal punishment   uses of speech to convey disapproval of behavior

verbal reward   uses of speech to elicit desired behavior or to approve and encourage repetition of approved behavior

vertebrate   the subphylum which contains all animals with backbones, such as birds, fish, reptiles, and mammals

vibrissa   hair with nerve endings at the base that can serve as a sense detector in touching objects

virilocal family kin group   a type of extended family kin group in which the bride is required to reside with the groom either in or close by the household of the groom's parents (also may be called a *patrilocal family kin group*)

visceral   the organs in the cavities of the body, particularly those in the abdominal cavity

xenophobia   a morbid and unreasonable fear of strangers, particulary strangers from other cultures

yafunu   a native language term used by the Ashanti to refer to the segment or part of the matrilineage residing together as a *fie,* or dwelling group

yoga   any one of the methods or exercises through which freedom of the self is sought from its non-eternal and impermanent states

Zinjanthropus   an *Australopithecine* fossil form discovered in Tanzania, East Africa, in 1959

Zuni   a native North American Indian society

 # INDEX

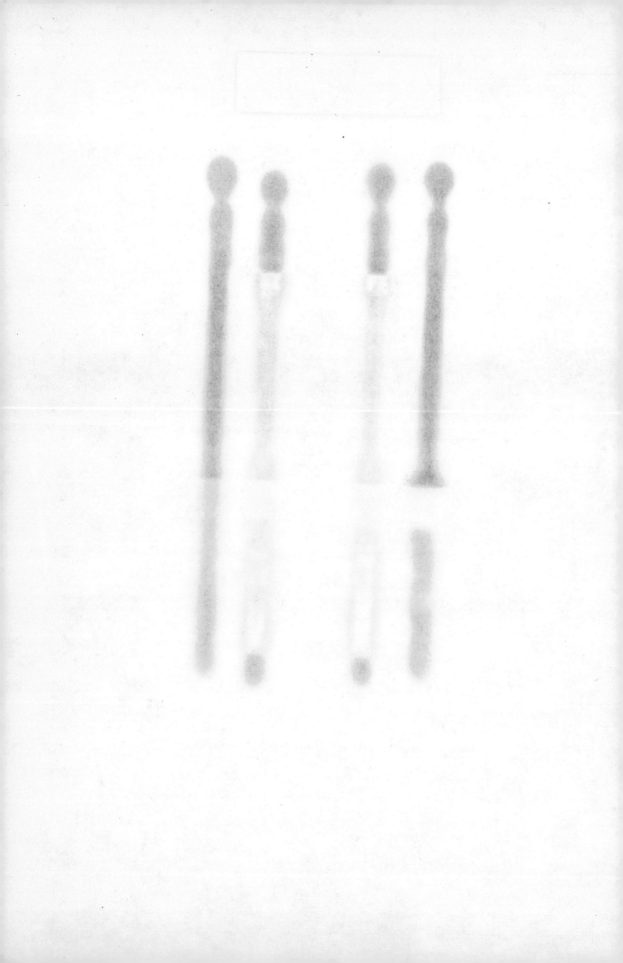